One-Stop Internet Resources

Log on to ca.hss.glencoe.com

ONLINE STUDY TOOLS

- Study Central
- Chapter Overviews
- ePuzzles and Games
- Self-Check Quizzes
- Vocabulary e-Flashcards
- Multi-Language Glossaries

ONLINE RESEARCH

- Student Web Activities
- Web Resources
- Current Events
- State Resources
- Beyond the Textbook Features

FOR TEACHERS

- Teacher Forum
- Web Activity Lesson Plans

Also Featuring a Complete Interactive Student Edition

GLENCOE
CALIFORNIA SERIES

DISCOVERING OUR PAST

Medieval and Early Modern Times

JACKSON J. SPIELVOGEL, PH.D.

NATIONAL
GEOGRAPHIC

Mc Graw Hill **Glencoe**

New York, New York   Columbus, Ohio   Chicago, Illinois   Peoria, Illinois   Woodland Hills, California

Authors

Jackson J. Spielvogel is associate professor emeritus of history at the Pennsylvania State University. He received his Ph.D. from The Ohio State University, where he specialized in Reformation history under Harold J. Grimm. His articles and reviews have been published in several scholarly publications. He is coauthor (with William Duiker) of *World History,* published in 1994 (3rd edition, 2001). Professor Spielvogel has won five major university-wide awards, and in 1997, he became the first winner of the Schreyer Institute's Student Choice Award for innovative and inspiring teaching.

The National Geographic Society, founded in 1888 for the increase and diffusion of geographic knowledge, is the world's largest nonprofit scientific and educational organization. Since its earliest days, the Society has used sophisticated communication technologies, from color photography to holography, to convey geographic knowledge to a worldwide membership. The Education Products Division supports the Society's mission by developing innovative educational programs—ranging from traditional print materials to multimedia programs including CD-ROMs, videodiscs, and software.

About the Cover: The medieval and early modern era was a time of great conflict and change. Top: The first Alcazar fortress in Segovia, Spain, was built by Muslim rulers about A.D. 1000. Towers and buildings were added by King John of Castile in the 1100s and by Spanish rulers in the 1400s and 1500s. Left: Armor made of plate-mail became popular in Western Europe in the 1200s and 1300s as protection against the crossbow. Right: The Hakurojo Castle in Hemeji, Japan, is also known as the White Heron Castle because its towers and white walls resemble a heron in flight. The castle was begun in 1601 by Ikeda Terumasa, the son-in-law of the Shogun Tokugawa Ieyasu, and took nine years to build.

 **Glencoe**

The McGraw·Hill Companies

Send all inquiries to:
Glencoe/McGraw-Hill
8787 Orion Place
Columbus, OH 43240-4027

ISBN: 0-07-868876-0

Printed in the United States of America.

7 8 9 10 071/055 15 14 13 12

Contributing Authors, Consultants, and Reviewers

Contributing Authors

Stephen F. Cunha, Ph.D.
Professor of Geography
Director, California Geographic Alliance
Humboldt State University
Arcata, California

Douglas Fisher, Ph.D.
Professor
San Diego State University
San Diego, California

Nancy Frey, Ph.D.
Assistant Professor
San Diego State University
San Diego, California

Robin C. Scarcella, Ph.D.
Professor and Director
Academic English/ESL
University of California, Irvine
Irvine, California

Emily M. Schell, Ed.D.
Visiting Professor, San Diego State University
Social Studies Education Director
SDSU City Heights Educational Collaborative
San Diego, California

David Vigilante
Associate Director
National Center for History in the Schools
San Diego, California

Ruben Zepeda II, Ed.D.
Adviser, Instructional Support Services
Los Angeles Unified School District
Los Angeles, California

Academic Consultants

Winthrop Lindsay Adams
Associate Professor of History
University of Utah
Salt Lake City, Utah

Sari J. Bennett
Director, Center for Geographic Education
University of Maryland Baltimore County
Baltimore, Maryland

Richard G. Boehm
Jesse H. Jones Distinguished Chair in
    Geographic Education
Texas State University
San Marcos, Texas

Stephen F. Dale, Ph.D.
Department of History
The Ohio State University
Columbus, Ohio

Sheilah Clarke-Ekong
Associate Professor of Anthropology and
    Interim Dean
Evening College
University of Missouri, St. Louis
St. Louis, Missouri

Timothy E. Gregory
Professor of History
The Ohio State University
Columbus, Ohio

Robert E. Herzstein
Department of History
University of South Carolina
Columbia, South Carolina

Kenji Oshiro
Professor of Geography
Wright State University
Dayton, Ohio

Joseph R. Rosenbloom
Adjunct Professor, Jewish and Near
    Eastern Studies
Washington University
St. Louis, Missouri

Guy Welbon, Ph.D.
Department of History
University of Pennsylvania
Philadelphia, Pennsylvania

FOLDABLES **Dinah Zike**
Educational Consultant
Dinah-Might Activities, Inc.
San Antonio, Texas

Reading Consultants

Maureen D. Danner
Project CRISS
National Training Consultant
Kalispell, Montana

ReLeah Cossett Lent
Florida Literacy and Reading Excellence
    Project Coordinator
University of Central Florida
Orlando, Florida

Steve Qunell
Social Studies Instructor
Montana Academy
Kalispell, Montana

Carol M. Santa, Ph.D.
CRISS: Project Developer
Director of Education
Montana Academy
Kalispell, Montana

Bonnie Valdes
Master CRISS Trainer
Project CRISS
Largo, Florida

Teacher Reviewers

Jane Dickey
Don Julio Junior High School
North Highlands, California

Elaina Greenberg
John Adams Middle School
Los Angeles, California

Rhonda Rumrey
C.A. Jacobs Intermediate
Dixon, California

Grant Schuster
Dale Junior High
Anaheim, California

Kelly VanAllen
Pine Grove Elementary School
Santa Maria, California

California Advisory Board

Eric E. Anderson
American Government Instructor
Pomona Unified School District
Pomona, CA

John Charles Burdick
Social Studies Adviser
Local District H/Los Angeles Unified
School District
Los Angeles, CA

Jan Coleman-Knight
History Department Chair
Thornton Junior High School
Fremont Unified School District
Fremont, CA

Stephen F. Cunha, Ph.D.
Professor of Geography
Director, California Geographic Alliance
Humboldt State University
Arcata, CA

Gail Desler
Social Studies Teacher/Technology
Integration Specialist
Elk Grove Unified School District
Elk Grove, CA

Matt Duffy
Social Science Teacher
C.A. Jacobs Intermediate
Dixon Unified School District
Dixon, CA

Douglas Fisher, Ph.D.
Professor
San Diego State University
San Diego, CA

Susan Fisher
Social Studies, English, and Drama Teacher
Los Angeles Unified School District
Los Angeles, CA

Nancy Frey, Ph.D.
Assistant Professor
San Diego State University
San Diego, CA

Brent E. Heath, Ph.D.
Social Studies Chair/GATE Facilitator
De Anza Middle School
Ontario-Montclair School District
Ontario, CA

L. Martha Infante
History and Geography Teacher
Bethune Middle School
Los Angeles Unified School District
Los Angeles, CA

Donna J. Leary
Educational Consultant
University of California, Berkeley
Berkeley, CA

Helen Ligh
Social Studies and Language Arts Teacher
Macy Intermediate
Montebello Unified School District
Monterey Park, CA

Barbara S. Lindemann, Ph.D.
Professor of History and Ethnic Studies
History Department Chair
Santa Barbara City College
Santa Barbara, CA

Reynaldo Antonio Macías
World History Teacher
Mark Twain Middle School
Los Angeles Unified School District
Los Angeles, CA

Jennifer Metherd
Program Coordinator
Tehama County Department of Education
Red Bluff, CA

Derrick K. Neal
Social Studies Department Chair
Patrick Henry Middle School
Los Angeles Unified School District
Los Angeles, CA

Robin C. Scarcella, Ph.D.
Professor and Director
Academic English/ESL
University of California, Irvine
Irvine, CA

Emily M. Schell, Ed.D.
Visiting Professor, San Diego State University
Social Studies Education Director
SDSU City Heights Educational Collaborative
San Diego, CA

Dale Steiner, Ph.D.
Professor of History
California State University, Chico
Chico, CA

Roy Sunada
Social Studies Teacher/AP Coordinator
Marshall Fundamental Secondary School
Pasadena Unified School District
Pasadena, CA

David Vigilante
Associate Director
National Center for History in the Schools
San Diego, CA

Ruben Zepeda II, Ed.D.
Adviser, Instructional Support Services
Los Angeles Unified School District
Los Angeles, CA

Contents

Mansa Musa ▶

◀ Pilgrimage to Makkah

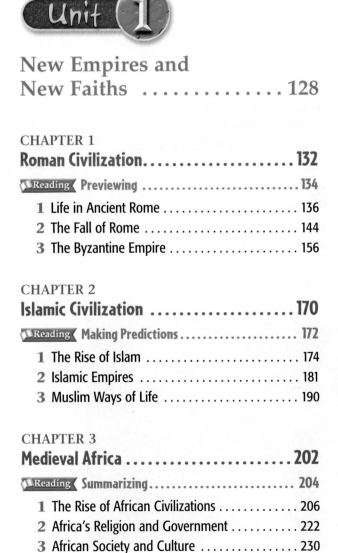

Contents

▼ Delegates at 1787 Constitutional Convention

Features

Primary Source

Analyzing Primary Sources

WORLD LITERATURE

Features

◀ Genghis Khan

▲ Catherine de' Medici

Biography

SkillBuilder Handbook

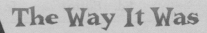
You Decide . . .

Linking Past & Present

The Way It Was

▼ **Modern-day musicians**

African Music

▲ **Traditional African musicians**

Primary Source Quotes

Ed. = Editor   Tr. = Translator   V = Volume

▲ Zheng He

Primary Source Quotes

▼ from "The Flood"

Maps, Charts, Graphs, and Diagrams

National Geographic Maps

NATIONAL GEOGRAPHIC The Middle East c. A.D. 600

Maps, Charts, Graphs, and Diagrams

Charts and Graphs

Diagrams

▼ The *Santa María*

A Guide to the California Standards

For Students and Their Families

What are the California History–Social Science Content Standards?

The California Department of Education has developed content standards for every course at every grade level. These standards can be found on the California Department of Education website. The History–Social Science Content Standards for grade 7 are designed to measure a student's knowledge of world history between the years from the fall of Rome to the Age of Enlightenment. The content of *Discovering Our Past* matches these standards.

Why should students be aware of these standards?

In grade 8, students will be tested on what they learn in grades 6 and 7 world history courses and in their United States history course in grade 8.

▼ California state capitol, Sacramento

Historical and Social Sciences Analysis Skills

To help you learn and understand content standards for any course you take, it is important to master the following skills. These skills focus on critical thinking, analysis, and research and will be represented like this: **CA HR1.**

Chronological and Spatial Thinking

CS1. Students explain how major events are related to one another in time.

CS2. Students construct various time lines of key events, people, and periods of the historical era they are studying.

CS3. Students use a variety of maps and documents to identify physical and cultural features of neighborhoods, cities, states, and countries and to explain the historical migration of people, expansion and disintegration of empires, and the growth of economic systems.

Research, Evidence, and Point of View

HR1. Students frame questions that can be answered by historical study and research.

HR2. Students distinguish fact from opinion in historical narratives and stories.

HR3. Students distinguish relevant from irrelevant information, essential from incidental information, and verifiable from unverifiable information in historical narratives and stories.

HR4. Students assess the credibility of primary and secondary sources and draw sound conclusions from them.

HR5. Students detect the different historical points of view on historical events and determine the context in which the historical statements were made (the questions asked, sources used, author's perspectives).

Historical Interpretation

HI1. Students explain the central issues and problems from the past, placing people and events in a matrix of time and place.

HI2. Students understand and distinguish cause, effect, sequence, and correlation in historical events, including the long- and short-term causal relations.

HI3. Students explain the sources of historical continuity and how the combination of ideas and events explains the emergence of new patterns.

HI4. Students recognize the role of chance, oversight, and error in history.

HI5. Students recognize that interpretations of history are subject to change as new information is uncovered.

HI6. Students interpret basic indicators of economic performance and conduct cost-benefit analyses of economic and political issues.

History –Social Science Standards

World History and Geography: Medieval and Early Modern Times

Main Standard WH7.1 Students analyze the causes and effects of the vast expansion and ultimate disintegration of the Roman Empire.

Supporting Standard WH7.1.1 Study the early strengths and lasting contributions of Rome (e.g., significance of Roman citizenship; rights under Roman law; Roman art, architecture, engineering, and philosophy; preservation and transmission of Christianity) and its ultimate internal weaknesses (e.g., rise of autonomous military powers within the empire, undermining of citizenship by the growth of corruption and slavery, lack of education, and distribution of news).

Supporting Standard WH7.1.2 Discuss the geographic borders of the empire at its height and the factors that threatened its territorial cohesion.

Supporting Standard WH7.1.3 Describe the establishment by Constantine of the new capital in Constantinople and the development of the Byzantine Empire, with an emphasis on the consequences of the development of two distinct European civilizations, Eastern Orthodox and Roman Catholic, and their two distinct views on church-state relations.

▼ Golden Gate Bridge, San Francisco

Main Standard WH7.2 **Students analyze the geographic, political, economic, religious, and social structures of the civilizations of Islam in the Middle Ages.**

Supporting Standard WH7.2.1 Identify the physical features and describe the climate of the Arabian peninsula, its relationship to surrounding bodies of land and water, and nomadic and sedentary ways of life.

Supporting Standard WH7.2.2 Trace the origins of Islam and the life and teachings of Muhammad, including Islamic teachings on the connection with Judaism and Christianity.

Supporting Standard WH7.2.3 Explain the significance of the Qur'an and the Sunnah as the primary sources of Islamic beliefs, practice, and law, and their influence in Muslims' daily life.

Supporting Standard WH7.2.4 Discuss the expansion of Muslim rule through military conquests and treaties, emphasizing the cultural blending within Muslim civilization and the spread and acceptance of Islam and the Arabic language.

Supporting Standard WH7.2.5 Describe the growth of cities and the establishment of trade routes among Asia, Africa, and Europe, the products and inventions that traveled along these routes (e.g., spices, textiles, paper, steel, new crops), and the role of merchants in Arab society.

Supporting Standard WH7.2.6 Understand the intellectual exchanges among Muslim scholars of Eurasia and Africa and the contributions Muslim scholars made to later civilizations in the areas of science, geography, mathematics, philosophy, medicine, art, and literature.

Main Standard WH7.3 Students analyze the geographic, political, economic, religious, and social structures of the civilizations of China in the Middle Ages.

Supporting Standard WH7.3.1 Describe the reunification of China under the Tang Dynasty and reasons for the spread of Buddhism in Tang China, Korea, and Japan.

Supporting Standard WH7.3.2 Describe agricultural, technological, and commercial developments during the Tang and Song periods.

Supporting Standard WH7.3.3 Analyze the influences of Confucianism and changes in Confucian thought during the Song and Mongol periods.

Supporting Standard WH7.3.4 Understand the importance of both overland trade and maritime expeditions between China and other civilizations in the Mongol Ascendancy and Ming Dynasty.

Supporting Standard WH7.3.5 Trace the historic influence of such discoveries as tea, the manufacture of paper, wood-block printing, the compass, and gunpowder.

Supporting Standard WH7.3.6 Describe the development of the imperial state and the scholar-official class.

▼ San Francisco row houses

Main Standard WH7.4 Students analyze the geographic, political, economic, religious, and social structures of the sub-Saharan civilizations of Ghana and Mali in Medieval Africa.

Supporting Standard WH7.4.1 Study the Niger River and the relationship of vegetation zones of forest, savannah, and desert to trade in gold, salt, food, and slaves; and the growth of the Ghana and Mali empires.

Supporting Standard WH7.4.2 Analyze the importance of family, labor specialization, and regional commerce in the development of states and cities in West Africa.

Supporting Standard WH7.4.3 Describe the role of the trans-Saharan caravan trade in the changing religious and cultural characteristics of West Africa and the influence of Islamic beliefs, ethics, and law.

Supporting Standard WH7.4.4 Trace the growth of the Arabic language in government, trade, and Islamic scholarship in West Africa.

Supporting Standard WH7.4.5 Describe the importance of written and oral traditions in the transmission of African history and culture.

Main Standard WH7.5 Students analyze the geographic, political, economic, religious, and social structures of the civilizations of Medieval Japan.

Supporting Standard WH7.5.1 Describe the significance of Japan's proximity to China and Korea and the intellectual, linguistic, religious, and philosophical influence of those countries on Japan.

Supporting Standard WH7.5.2 Discuss the reign of Prince Shotoku of Japan and the characteristics of Japanese society and family life during his reign.

Supporting Standard WH7.5.3 Describe the values, social customs, and traditions prescribed by the lord-vassal system consisting of *shogun*, *daimyo*, and *samurai* and the lasting influence of the warrior code throughout the twentieth century.

Supporting Standard WH7.5.4 Trace the development of distinctive forms of Japanese Buddhism.

Supporting Standard WH7.5.5 Study the ninth and tenth centuries' golden age of literature, art, and drama and its lasting effects on culture today, including Murasaki Shikibu's *Tale of Genji*.

Supporting Standard WH7.5.6 Analyze the rise of a military society in the late twelfth century and the role of the samurai in that society.

▼ Windmills

Main Standard WH7.6 Students analyze the geographic, political, economic, religious, and social structures of the civilizations of Medieval Europe.

Supporting Standard WH7.6.1 Study the geography of Europe and the Eurasian land mass, including their location, topography, waterways, vegetation, and climate and their relationship to ways of life in Medieval Europe.

Supporting Standard WH7.6.2 Describe the spread of Christianity north of the Alps and the roles played by the early church and by monasteries in its diffusion after the fall of the western half of the Roman Empire.

Supporting Standard WH7.6.3 Understand the development of feudalism, its role in the medieval European economy, the way in which it was influenced by physical geography (the role of the manor and the growth of towns), and how feudal relationships provided the foundation of political order.

Supporting Standard WH7.6.4 Demonstrate an understanding of the conflict and cooperation between the Papacy and European monarchs (e.g., Charlemagne, Gregory VII, Emperor Henry IV).

Supporting Standard WH7.6.5 Know the significance of developments in medieval English legal and constitutional practices and their importance in the rise of modern democratic thought and representative institutions (e.g., Magna Carta, parliament, development of habeas corpus, an independent judiciary in England).

Supporting Standard WH7.6.6 Discuss the causes and course of the religious Crusades and their effects on the Christian, Muslim, and Jewish populations in Europe, with emphasis on the increasing contact by Europeans with cultures of the Eastern Mediterranean world.

Supporting Standard WH7.6.7 Map the spread of the bubonic plague from Central Asia to China, the Middle East, and Europe and describe its impact on global population.

Supporting Standard WH7.6.8 Understand the importance of the Catholic church as a political, intellectual, and aesthetic institution (e.g., founding of universities, political and spiritual roles of the clergy, creation of monastic and mendicant religious orders, preservation of the Latin language and religious texts, St. Thomas Aquinas's synthesis of classical philosophy with Christian theology, and the concept of "natural law").

Supporting Standard WH7.6.9 Know the history of the decline of Muslim rule in the Iberian Peninsula that culminated in the Reconquista and the rise of Spanish and Portuguese kingdoms.

Main Standard WH7.7 Students compare and contrast the geographic, political, economic, religious, and social structures of the Meso-American and Andean civilizations.

Supporting Standard WH7.7.1 Study the locations, landforms, and climates of Mexico, Central America, and South America and their effects on Mayan, Aztec, and Incan economies, trade, and development of urban societies.

Supporting Standard WH7.7.2 Study the roles of people in each society, including class structures, family life, warfare, religious beliefs and practices, and slavery.

Supporting Standard WH7.7.3 Explain how and where each empire arose and how the Aztec and Incan empires were defeated by the Spanish.

Supporting Standard WH7.7.4 Describe the artistic and oral traditions and architecture in the three civilizations.

Supporting Standard WH7.7.5 Describe the Meso-American achievements in astronomy and mathematics, including the development of the calendar and the Meso-American knowledge of seasonal changes to the civilizations' agricultural systems.

Main Standard WH7.8 Students analyze the origins, accomplishments, and geographic diffusion of the Renaissance.

Supporting Standard WH7.8.1 Describe the way in which the revival of classical learning and the arts fostered a new interest in humanism (i.e., a balance between intellect and religious faith).

Supporting Standard WH7.8.2 Explain the importance of Florence in the early stages of the Renaissance and the growth of independent trading cities (e.g., Venice), with emphasis on the cities' importance in the spread of Renaissance ideas.

Supporting Standard WH7.8.3 Understand the effects of the reopening of the ancient "Silk Road" between Europe and China, including Marco Polo's travels and the location of his routes.

Supporting Standard WH7.8.4 Describe the growth and effects of new ways of disseminating information (e.g., the ability to manufacture paper, translation of the Bible into the vernacular, printing).

Supporting Standard WH7.8.5 Detail advances made in literature, the arts, science, mathematics, cartography, engineering, and the understanding of human anatomy and astronomy (e.g., by Dante Alighieri, Leonardo da Vinci, Michelangelo di Buonarroti Simoni, Johann Gutenberg, William Shakespeare).

Main Standard WH7.9 Students analyze the historical developments of the Reformation.

Supporting Standard WH7.9.1 List the causes for the internal turmoil in and weakening of the Catholic church (e.g., tax policies, selling of indulgences).

Supporting Standard WH7.9.2 Describe the theological, political, and economic ideas of the major figures during the Reformation (e.g., Desiderius Erasmus, Martin Luther, John Calvin, William Tyndale).

Supporting Standard WH7.9.3 Explain Protestants' new practices of church self-government and the influence of those practices on the development of democratic practices and ideas of federalism.

Supporting Standard WH7.9.4 Identify and locate the European regions that remained Catholic and those that became Protestant and explain how the division affected the distribution of religions in the New World.

Supporting Standard WH7.9.5 Analyze how the Counter Reformation revitalized the Catholic church and the forces that fostered the movement (e.g., St. Ignatius of Loyola and the Jesuits, the Council of Trent).

Supporting Standard WH7.9.6 Understand the institution and impact of missionaries on Christianity and the diffusion of Christianity from Europe to other parts of the world in the medieval and early modern periods; locate missions on a world map.

Supporting Standard WH7.9.7 Describe the Golden Age of cooperation between Jews and Muslims in medieval Spain that promoted creativity in art, literature, and science, including how that cooperation was terminated by the religious persecution of individuals and groups (e.g., the Spanish Inquisition and the expulsion of Jews and Muslims from Spain in 1492).

▼ California farmland

Main Standard WH7.10 Students analyze the historical developments of the Scientific Revolution and its lasting effect on religious, political, and cultural institutions.

Supporting Standard WH7.10.1 Discuss the roots of the Scientific Revolution (e.g., Greek rationalism; Jewish, Christian, and Muslim science; Renaissance humanism; new knowledge from global exploration).

Supporting Standard WH7.10.2 Understand the significance of the new scientific theories (e.g., those of Copernicus, Galileo, Kepler, Newton) and

the significance of new inventions (e.g., the telescope, microscope, thermometer, barometer).

Supporting Standard WH7.10.3 Understand the scientific method advanced by Bacon and Descartes, the influence of new scientific rationalism on the growth of democratic ideas, and the coexistence of science with traditional religious beliefs.

Main Standard WH7.11 Students analyze political and economic change in the sixteenth, seventeenth, and eighteenth centuries (the Age of Exploration, the Enlightenment, and the Age of Reason).

Supporting Standard WH7.11.1 Know the great voyages of discovery, the locations of the routes, and the influence of cartography in the development of a new European worldview.

Supporting Standard WH7.11.2 Discuss the exchanges of plants, animals, technology, culture, and ideas among Europe, Africa, Asia, and the Americas in the fifteenth and sixteenth centuries and the major economic and social effects on each continent.

Supporting Standard WH7.11.3 Examine the origins of modern capitalism; the influence of mercantilism and cottage industry; the elements and importance of a market economy in seventeenth-century Europe; the changing international trading and marketing patterns, including their

locations on a world map; and the influence of explorers and map makers.

Supporting Standard WH7.11.4 Explain how the main ideas of the Enlightenment can be traced back to such movements as the Renaissance, the Reformation, and the Scientific Revolution and to the Greeks, Romans, and Christianity.

Supporting Standard WH7.11.5 Describe how democratic thought and institutions were influenced by Enlightenment thinkers (e.g., John Locke, Charles-Louis Montesquieu, American founders).

Supporting Standard WH7.11.6 Discuss how the principles in the Magna Carta were embodied in such documents as the English Bill of Rights and the American Declaration of Independence.

▼ California's Pacific Coast

English–Language Arts Standards

Items that relate to an English–Language Arts Standard will be represented like this: **CA 7RW1.3**

Reading

7RW1.0 Word Analysis, Fluency, and Systematic Vocabulary Development

Vocabulary and Concept Development

7RW1.1 Identify idioms, analogies, metaphors, and similes in prose and poetry.

7RW1.2 Use knowledge of Greek, Latin, and Anglo-Saxon roots and affixes to understand content-area vocabulary.

7RW1.3 Clarify word meanings through the use of definition, example, restatement, or contrast.

7RC2.0 Reading Comprehension (Focus on Informational Materials)

Structural Features of Informational Materials

7RC2.1 Understand and analyze the differences in structure and purpose between various categories of informational materials (e.g., textbooks, news-papers, instructional manuals, signs).

7RC2.2 Locate information by using a variety of consumer, workplace, and public documents.

7RC2.3 Analyze text that uses the cause-and-effect organizational pattern.

Comprehension and Analysis of Grade-Level-Appropriate Text

7RC2.4 Identify and trace the development of an author's argument, point of view, or perspective in text.

7RC2.5 Understand and explain the use of a simple mechanical device by following technical directions.

Expository Critique

7RC2.6 Assess the adequacy, accuracy, and appro-priateness of the author's evidence to support claims and assertions, noting instances of bias and stereotyping.

7RL3.0 Literary Response and Analysis

Structural Features of Literature

7RL3.1 Articulate the expressed purposes and char-acteristics of different forms of prose (e.g., short story, novel, novella, essay).

Narrative Analysis of Grade-Level-Appropriate Text

7RL3.2 Identify events that advance the plot and determine how each event explains past or present action(s) or foreshadows future action(s).

7RL3.3 Analyze characterization as delineated through a character's thoughts, words, speech patterns, and actions; the narrator's description; and the thoughts, words, and actions of other characters.

7RL3.4 Identify and analyze recurring themes across works (e.g., the value of bravery, loyalty, and friendship; the effects of loneliness).

7RL3.5 Contrast points of view (e.g., first and third person, limited and omniscient, subjective and objective) in narrative text and explain how they affect the overall theme of the work.

Literary Criticism

7RL3.6 Analyze a range of responses to a literary work and determine the extent to which the literary elements in the work shaped those responses.

Writing

7WS1.0 Writing Strategies

Organization and Focus

7WS1.1 Create an organizational structure that balances all aspects of the composition and uses effective transitions between sentences to unify important ideas.

7WS1.2 Support all statements and claims with anecdotes, descriptions, facts and statistics, and specific examples.

7WS1.3 Use strategies of note taking, outlining, and summarizing to impose structure on composition drafts.

Research and Technology

7WS1.4 Identify topics; ask and evaluate questions; and develop ideas leading to inquiry, investigation, and research.

7WS1.5 Give credit for both quoted and paraphrased information in a bibliography by using a consistent and sanctioned format and methodology for citations.

7WS1.6 Create documents by using word-processing skills and publishing programs; develop simple databases and spreadsheets to manage information and prepare reports.

Evaluation and Revision

7WS1.7 Revise writing to improve organization and word choice after checking the logic of the ideas and the precision of the vocabulary.

▼ California's Pacific Coast

7WA2.0 Writing Applications (Genres and Their Characteristics)

7WA2.1 Write fictional or autobiographical narratives:

   a. Develop a standard plot line (having a beginning, conflict, rising action, climax, and denouement) and point of view.

   b. Develop complex major and minor characters and a definite setting.

   c. Use a range of appropriate strategies (e.g., dialogue; suspense; naming of specific narrative action, including movement, gestures, and expressions).

7WA2.2 Write responses to literature:

   a. Develop interpretations exhibiting careful reading, understanding, and insight.

   b. Organize interpretations around several clear ideas, premises, or images from the literary work.

   c. Justify interpretations through sustained use of examples and textual evidence.

7WA2.3 Write research reports:

   a. Pose relevant and tightly drawn questions about the topic.

   b. Convey clear and accurate perspectives on the subject.

   c. Include evidence compiled through the formal research process (e.g., use of a card catalog, *Reader's Guide to Periodical Literature,* a computer catalog, magazines, newspapers, dictionaries).

   d. Document reference sources by means of footnotes and a bibliography.

7WA2.4 Write persuasive compositions:

   a. State a clear position or perspective in support of a proposition or proposal.

   b. Describe the points in support of the proposition, employing well-articulated evidence.

   c. Anticipate and address reader concerns and counterarguments.

7WA2.5 Write summaries of reading materials:

   a. Include the main ideas and most significant details.

   b. Use the student's own words, except for quotations.

   c. Reflect underlying meaning, not just the superficial details.

Written and Oral English Language Conventions

7WC1.0 Written and Oral English Language Conventions

Sentence Structure

7WC1.1 Place modifiers properly and use the active voice.

Grammar

7WC1.2 Identify and use infinitives and participles and make clear references between pronouns and antecedents.

7WC1.3 Identify all parts of speech and types and structure of sentences.

7WC1.4 Demonstrate the mechanics of writing (e.g., quotation marks, commas at end of dependent clauses) and appropriate English usage (e.g., pronoun reference).

Punctuation

7WC1.5 Identify hyphens, dashes, brackets, and semicolons and use them correctly.

Capitalization

7WC1.6 Use correct capitalization.

Spelling

7WC1.7 Spell derivatives correctly by applying the spellings of bases and affixes.

Listening and Speaking Strategies

7LS1.0 Listening and Speaking Strategies Comprehension

7LS1.1 Ask probing questions to elicit information, including evidence to support the speaker's claims and conclusions.

7LS1.2 Determine the speaker's attitude toward the subject.

7LS1.3 Respond to persuasive messages with questions, challenges, or affirmations.

Organization and Delivery of Oral Communication

7LS1.4 Organize information to achieve particular purposes and to appeal to the background and interests of the audience.

7LS1.5 Arrange supporting details, reasons, descriptions, and examples effectively and persuasively in relation to the audience.

7LS1.6 Use speaking techniques, including voice modulation, inflection, tempo, enunciation, and eye contact, for effective presentations.

Analysis and Evaluation of Oral and Media Communications

7LS1.7 Provide constructive feedback to speakers concerning the coherence and logic of a speech's content and delivery and its overall impact upon the listener.

7LS1.8 Analyze the effect on the viewer of images, text, and sound in electronic journalism; identify the techniques used to achieve the effects in each instance studied.

7SA2.0 Speaking Applications (Genres and Their Characteristics)
Using the speaking strategies of grade seven outlined in Listening and Speaking Standard 1.0, students:

7SA2.1 Deliver narrative presentations:

a. Establish a context, standard plot line (having a beginning, conflict, rising action, climax, and denouement), and point of view.

b. Describe complex major and minor characters and a definite setting.

c. Use a range of appropriate strategies, including dialogue, suspense, and naming of specific narrative action (e.g., movement, gestures, expressions).

7SA2.2 Deliver oral summaries of articles and books:

a. Include the main ideas of the event or article and the most significant details.

b. Use the student's own words, except for material quoted from sources.

c. Convey a comprehensive understanding of sources, not just superficial details.

7SA2.3 Deliver research presentations:

a. Pose relevant and concise questions about the topic.

b. Convey clear and accurate perspectives on the subject.

c. Include evidence generated through the formal research process (e.g., use of a card catalog, *Reader's Guide to Periodical Literature*, computer databases, magazines, newspapers, dictionaries).

d. Cite reference sources appropriately.

7SA2.4 Deliver persuasive presentations:

a. State a clear position or perspective in support of an argument or proposal.

b. Describe the points in support of the argument and employ well-articulated evidence.

▼ California's state flower

Correlation to the California Standards

Historical and Social Sciences Analysis Skills	Student Edition Pages
Chronological and Spatial Thinking	
CS1. Students explain how major events are related to one another in time.	108–09, 110–11, 126–27, 201, 371, 434
CS2. Students construct various time lines of key events, people, and periods of the historical era they are studying.	108–09, 110–11, 201, 241, 273, 301, 434, 477, 499
CS3. Students use a variety of maps and documents to identify physical and cultural features of neighborhoods, cities, states, and countries and to explain the historical migration of people, expansion, and disintegration of empires, and the growth of economic systems.	112–15, 116–17, 165, 168, 180, 189, 197, 200, 201, 214, 240, 241, 290, 301, 318, 372, 413, 416, 444, 455, 480, 481, 508
Research, Evidence, and Point of View	
HR1. Students frame questions that can be answered by historical study and research.	118–19, 239, 290, 333, 391, 417, 445, 492, 509
HR2. Students distinguish fact from opinion in historical narratives and stories.	118–19, 197, 445
HR3. Students distinguish relevant from irrelevant information, essential from incidental information, and verifiable from unverifiable information in historical narratives and stories.	118–19, 464
HR4. Students assess the credibility of primary and secondary sources and draw sound conclusions from them.	120–21, 167, 315, 319, 391, 415, 443, 501, 507
HR5. Students detect the different historical points of view on historical events and determine the context in which the historical statements were made (the questions asked, sources used, author's perspectives).	120–21, 180, 199, 241, 291, 317, 319, 345, 444, 479, 501, 541, 543
Historical Interpretation	
HI1. Students explain the central issues and problems from the past, placing people and events in a matrix of time and place.	122–23, 169, 291, 509
HI2. Students understand and distinguish cause, effect, sequence, and correlation in historical events, including the long- and short-term causal relations.	122–23, 153, 165, 168, 169, 197, 200, 201, 240, 259, 266, 287, 289, 308, 315, 318, 333, 343, 354, 363, 369, 372, 373, 393, 400, 413, 416, 417, 429, 434, 441, 445, 464, 477, 480, 492, 499, 508, 530, 541, 544
HI3. Students explain the sources of historical continuity and how the combination of ideas and events explains the emergence of new patterns.	122–23, 273, 290, 354, 373, 393, 545
HI4. Students recognize the role of chance, oversight, and error in history.	124–25, 481
HI5. Students recognize that interpretations of history are subject to change as new information is uncovered.	124–25, 290, 417, 464, 481
HI6. Students interpret basic indicators of economic performance and conduct cost-benefit analyses of economic and political issues.	124–25, 153, 214, 343, 391, 416, 481, 499

History–Social Science Content Standards for Grade 7	Student Edition Pages
WH7.1 Students analyze the causes and effects of the vast expansion and ultimate disintegration of the Roman Empire.	136–43, 144–53, 154–55, 156–65, 166–67
WH7.1.1 Study the early strengths and lasting contributions of Rome (e.g., significance of Roman citizenship; rights under Roman law; Roman art, architecture, engineering, and philosophy; preservation and transmission of Christianity) and its ultimate internal weaknesses (e.g., rise of autonomous military powers within the empire, undermining of citizenship by the growth of corruption and slavery, lack of education, and distribution of news).	137–43, 145–47, 148, 149–53, 154–55
WH7.1.2 Discuss the geographic borders of the empire at its height and the factors that threatened its territorial cohesion.	137–38, 149–51
WH7.1.3 Describe the establishment by Constantine of the new capital in Constantinople and the development of the Byzantine Empire, with an emphasis on the consequences of the development of two distinct European civilizations, Eastern Orthodox and Roman Catholic, and their two distinct views on church-state relations.	147, 157–59, 160, 161–65
WH7.2 Students analyze the geographic, political, economic, religious, and social structures of the civilizations of Islam in the Middle Ages.	174–80, 181–89, 190–97
WH7.2.1 Identify the physical features and describe the climate of the Arabian peninsula, its relationship to surrounding bodies of land and water, and nomadic and sedentary ways of life.	175–76, 185–86
WH7.2.2 Trace the origins of Islam and the life and teachings of Muhammad, including Islamic teachings on the connection with Judaism and Christianity.	176–77, 178, 179–80
WH7.2.3 Explain the significance of the Qur'an and the Sunnah as the primary sources of Islamic beliefs, practice, and law, and their influence in Muslims' daily life.	179–80
WH7.2.4 Discuss the expansion of Muslim rule through military conquests and treaties, emphasizing the cultural blending within Muslim civilization and the spread and acceptance of Islam and the Arabic language.	176–77, 182–89
WH7.2.5 Describe the growth of cities and the establishment of trade routes among Asia, Africa, and Europe, the products and inventions that traveled along these routes (e.g., spices, textiles, paper, steel, new crops), and the role of merchants in Arab society.	175–76, 182–89, 191–92
WH7.2.6 Understand the intellectual exchanges among Muslim scholars of Eurasia and Africa and the contributions Muslim scholars made to later civilizations in the areas of science, geography, mathematics, philosophy, medicine, art, and literature.	184, 193–94, 195, 196–97, 198–99, 225
WH7.3 Students analyze the geographic, political, economic, religious, and social structures of the civilizations of China in the Middle Ages.	252–59, 260–66, 267–70, 271, 272–73, 281–87
WH7.3.1 Describe the reunification of China under the Tang Dynasty and reasons for the spread of Buddhism in Tang China, Korea, and Japan.	253–57
WH7.3.2 Describe agricultural, technological, and commercial developments during the Tang and Song periods.	261–66, 288–89

History–Social Science Content Standards for Grade 7	Student Edition Pages
WH7.3.3 Analyze the influences of Confucianism and changes in Confucian thought during the Song and Mongol periods.	258–59, 272–73
WH7.3.4 Understand the importance of both overland trade and maritime expeditions between China and other civilizations in the Mongol Ascendancy and Ming Dynasty.	272–73, 284, 285, 286–87, 288–89
WH7.3.5 Trace the historic influence of such discoveries as tea, the manufacture of paper, wood-block printing, the compass, and gunpowder.	261–64, 268–70
WH7.3.6 Describe the development of the imperial state and the scholar-official class.	258–59, 282–83
WH7.4 Students analyze the geographic, political, economic, religious, and social structures of the sub-Saharan civilizations of Ghana and Mali in Medieval Africa.	206–14, 222–29, 230–37, 238–39
WH7.4.1 Study the Niger River and the relationship of vegetation zones of forest, savannah, and desert to trade in gold, salt, food, and slaves; and the growth of the Ghana and Mali empires.	207–14, 232, 233–34
WH7.4.2 Analyze the importance of family, labor specialization, and regional commerce in the development of states and cities in West Africa.	209–14, 231
WH7.4.3 Describe the role of the trans-Saharan caravan trade in the changing religious and cultural characteristics of West Africa and the influence of Islamic beliefs, ethics, and law.	223–24, 226, 227–29, 232, 233–37
WH7.4.4 Trace the growth of the Arabic language in government, trade, and Islamic scholarship in West Africa.	224–225, 226, 227–29
WH7.4.5 Describe the importance of written and oral traditions in the transmission of African history and culture.	209–14, 227, 231, 235–37
WH7.5 Students analyze the geographic, political, economic, religious, and social structures of the civilizations of Medieval Japan.	296–301, 302–08, 309–15
WH7.5.1 Describe the significance of Japan's proximity to China and Korea and the intellectual, linguistic, religious, and philosophical influence of those countries on Japan.	299, 300, 301, 303, 310–12
WH7.5.2 Discuss the reign of Prince Shotoku of Japan and the characteristics of Japanese society and family life during his reign.	299, 300, 314–15
WH7.5.3 Describe the values, social customs, and traditions prescribed by the lord-vassal system consisting of *shogun, daimyo,* and *samurai* and the lasting influence of the warrior code throughout the twentieth century.	304–08
WH7.5.4 Trace the development of distinctive forms of Japanese Buddhism.	301, 303, 310–12
WH7.5.5 Study the ninth and tenth centuries' golden age of literature, art, and drama and its lasting effects on culture today, including Murasaki Shikibu's *Tale of Genji.*	310–12, 313, 316–17
WH7.5.6 Analyze the rise of a military society in the late twelfth century and the role of the samurai in that society.	304–06

History–Social Science Content Standards for Grade 7	Student Edition Pages
WH7.6 Students analyze the geographic, political, economic, religious, and social structures of the civilizations of Medieval Europe.	324–33, 334–43, 346–54, 355–63, 364–69
WH7.6.1 Study the geography of Europe and the Eurasian land mass, including their location, topography, waterways, vegetation, and climate and their relationship to ways of life in Medieval Europe.	325–26, 340–43
WH7.6.2 Describe the spread of Christianity north of the Alps and the roles played by the early church and by monasteries in its diffusion after the fall of the western half of the Roman Empire.	331–33
WH7.6.3 Understand the development of feudalism, its role in the medieval European economy, the way in which it was influenced by physical geography (the role of the manor and the growth of towns), and how feudal relationships provided the foundation of political order.	335–43, 344–45
WH7.6.4 Demonstrate an understanding of the conflict and cooperation between the Papacy and European monarchs (e.g., Charlemagne, Gregory VII, Emperor Henry IV).	326–28, 329, 330–33
WH7.6.5 Know the significance of developments in medieval English legal and constitutional practices and their importance in the rise of modern democratic thought and representative institutions (e.g., Magna Carta, parliament, development of habeas corpus, an independent judiciary in England).	347–49, 370–71
WH7.6.6 Discuss the causes and course of the religious Crusades and their effects on the Christian, Muslim, and Jewish populations in Europe, with emphasis on the increasing contact by Europeans with cultures of the Eastern Mediterranean world.	352–54, 356–59
WH7.6.7 Map the spread of the bubonic plague from Central Asia to China, the Middle East, and Europe and describe its impact on global population.	365–66, 370–71
WH7.6.8 Understand the importance of the Catholic church as a political, intellectual, and aesthetic institution (e.g., founding of universities, political and spiritual roles of the clergy, creation of monastic and mendicant religious orders, preservation of the Latin language and religious texts, St. Thomas Aquinas's synthesis of classical philosophy with Christian theology, and the concept of "natural law").	331–33, 356–61, 362, 363
WH7.6.9 Know the history of the decline of Muslim rule in the Iberian Peninsula that culminated in the Reconquista and the rise of Spanish and Portuguese kingdoms.	367, 369
WH7.7 Students compare and contrast the geographic, political, economic, religious, and social structures of the Meso-American and Andean civilizations.	450–55, 456–64, 470–77
WH7.7.1 Study the locations, landforms, and climates of Mexico, Central America, and South America and their effects on Mayan, Aztec, and Incan economies, trade, and development of urban societies.	453–55, 457, 460–62, 464
WH7.7.2 Study the roles of people in each society, including class structures, family life, warfare, religious beliefs and practices, and slavery.	458, 459, 460–62, 463, 464
WH7.7.3 Explain how and where each empire arose and how the Aztec and Incan empires were defeated by the Spanish.	460–62, 463, 464, 471–74, 475, 476–77, 478–79

History–Social Science Content Standards for Grade 7	Student Edition Pages
WH7.7.4 Describe the artistic and oral traditions and architecture in the three civilizations.	458, 459, 460–62, 464
WH7.7.5 Describe the Meso-American achievements in astronomy and mathematics, including the development of the calendar and the Meso-American knowledge of seasonal changes to the civilizations' agricultural systems.	458, 460–64
WH7.8 Students analyze the origins, accomplishments, and geographic diffusion of the Renaissance.	384–91, 394–400, 408–13
WH7.8.1 Describe the way in which the revival of classical learning and the arts fostered a new interest in humanism (i.e., a balance between intellect and religious faith).	395
WH7.8.2 Explain the importance of Florence in the early stages of the Renaissance and the growth of independent trading cities (e.g., Venice), with emphasis on the cities' importance in the spread of Renaissance ideas.	385–91, 392–93
WH7.8.3 Understand the effects of the reopening of the ancient "Silk Road" between Europe and China, including Marco Polo's travels and the location of his routes.	387–89
WH7.8.4 Describe the growth and effects of new ways of disseminating information (e.g., the ability to manufacture paper, translation of the Bible into the vernacular, printing).	397–400, 423–24
WH7.8.5 Detail advances made in literature, the arts, science, mathematics, cartography, engineering, and the understanding of human anatomy and astronomy (e.g., by Dante Alighieri, Leonardo da Vinci, Michelangelo di Buonarroti Simoni, Johann Gutenberg, William Shakespeare).	395, 396, 397–400, 409–13, 414–15
WH7.9 Students analyze the historical developments of the Reformation.	422–29, 430–34, 435–41
WH7.9.1 List the causes for the internal turmoil in and weakening of the Catholic church (e.g., tax policies, selling of indulgences).	423–26, 427, 428–29, 442
WH7.9.2 Describe the theological, political, and economic ideas of the major figures during the Reformation (e.g., Desiderius Erasmus, Martin Luther, John Calvin, William Tyndale).	423–26, 427, 428–29, 431–34, 442–43
WH7.9.3 Explain Protestants' new practices of church self-government and the influence of those practices on the development of democratic practices and ideas of federalism.	431–34
WH7.9.4 Identify and locate the European regions that remained Catholic and those that became Protestant and explain how the division affected the distribution of religions in the New World.	428–29, 432–34, 436–37, 438, 439–41
WH7.9.5 Analyze how the Counter Reformation revitalized the Catholic church and the forces that fostered the movement (e.g., St. Ignatius of Loyola and the Jesuits, the Council of Trent).	436–37, 438, 439, 440–41
WH7.9.6 Understand the institution and impact of missionaries on Christianity and the diffusion of Christianity from Europe to other parts of the world in the medieval and early modern periods; locate missions on a world map.	286–87, 440–41

History–Social Science Content Standards for Grade 7	Student Edition Pages
WH7.9.7 Describe the Golden Age of cooperation between Jews and Muslims in medieval Spain that promoted creativity in art, literature, and science, including how that cooperation was terminated by the religious persecution of individuals and groups (e.g., the Spanish Inquisition and the expulsion of Jews and Muslims from Spain in 1492).	439–40
WH7.10 Students analyze the historical developments of the Scientific Revolution and its lasting effect on religious, political, and cultural institutions.	514–23, 524–30
WH7.10.1 Discuss the roots of the Scientific Revolution (e.g., Greek rationalism; Jewish, Christian, and Muslim science; Renaissance humanism; new knowledge from global exploration).	515–18
WH7.10.2 Understand the significance of the new scientific theories (e.g., those of Copernicus, Galileo, Kepler, Newton) and the significance of new inventions (e.g., the telescope, microscope, thermometer, barometer).	517–20, 521
WH7.10.3 Understand the scientific method advanced by Bacon and Descartes, the influence of new scientific rationalism on the growth of democratic ideas, and the coexistence of science with traditional religious beliefs.	522–23, 525–26, 528
WH7.11 Students analyze political and economic change in the sixteenth, seventeenth, and eighteenth centuries (the Age of Exploration, the Enlightenment, and the Age of Reason).	486–92, 493–95, 496, 497–99, 502–05, 524–30, 531–41
WH7.11.1 Know the great voyages of discovery, the locations of the routes, and the influence of cartography in the development of a new European worldview.	487–92, 506–07
WH7.11.2 Discuss the exchanges of plants, animals, technology, culture, and ideas among Europe, Africa, Asia, and the Americas in the fifteenth and sixteenth centuries and the major economic and social effects on each continent.	487–88, 497–99, 500–01, 503–05
WH7.11.3 Examine the origins of modern capitalism; the influence of mercantilism and cottage industry; the elements and importance of a market economy in seventeenth-century Europe; the changing international trading and marketing patterns, including their locations on a world map; and the influence of explorers and map makers.	494–95, 497–99
WH7.11.4 Explain how the main ideas of the Enlightenment can be traced back to such movements as the Renaissance, the Reformation, and the Scientific Revolution and to the Greeks, Romans, and Christianity.	525–26, 528
WH7.11.5 Describe how democratic thought and institutions were influenced by Enlightenment thinkers (e.g., John Locke, Charles-Louis Montesquieu, American founders).	525–26, 527, 528–30, 534–43
WH7.11.6 Discuss how the principles in the Magna Carta were embodied in such documents as the English Bill of Rights and the American Declaration of Independence.	525–26, 528

English–Language Arts Standards for Grade 7	Student Edition Pages
Reading **7RW1.0 Word Analysis, Fluency, and Systematic Vocabulary Development**	
7RW1.2	143, 169
7RC2.0 Reading Comprehension (Focus on Informational Materials)	143, 153, 165, 169, 180, 189, 197, 214, 229, 237, 240, 259, 266, 273, 287, 301, 308, 315, 318, 333, 343, 345, 354, 363, 369, 372, 391, 400, 413, 429, 434, 441, 444, 464, 480, 492, 505, 508, 509, 523, 530
7RC2.1	319
7RC2.2	189, 197, 241, 259, 287, 308, 315, 343, 354, 363, 372, 400, 416, 441, 444, 455, 481, 505, 523
7RC2.3	143, 153, 168, 180, 229, 240, 266, 287, 301, 308, 343, 369, 429, 434, 455, 464, 477, 480, 501, 508, 523, 530, 544
7RC2.4	189
7RL3.0 Literary Response and Analysis	468
7RL3.1	279, 406
7RL3.2	220, 406
7RL3.3	220, 279, 468
Writing **7WS1.0 Writing Strategies**	
7WS1.2	153
7WS1.3	214, 241, 545
7WA2.0 Writing Applications (Genres and Their Characteristics)	199, 266, 291, 301, 413, 545
7WA2.1	169, 201, 239, 241, 259, 273, 279, 319, 345, 393, 417, 468, 477, 501
7WA2.2	220, 279, 317, 406
7WA2.3	201, 229, 291, 319, 354, 369, 373, 400, 444, 468, 505, 509, 545
7WA2.4	189, 241, 308, 363, 391, 445, 455, 481, 492, 499, 505
7WA2.5	143, 153, 169, 180, 237, 287, 291, 301, 333, 373, 391, 441, 455, 480, 509, 541

At-Home Standards Review

To Students and Their Families

Welcome to seventh-grade world history. As you begin your journey through medieval and early modern times, take a few moments each day to review what you learned in sixth grade about ancient civilizations.

By reviewing and building on what you already know, you will gain a better understanding of what you are about to learn. A sample review question is provided for each day of the school week. Try to answer one question each day. **If you need to look back at what you learned last year, visit the Online California Standards Review and Practice at ca.hss.glencoe.com.**

WEEK 1

Content Standard WH6.1 Students describe what is known through archaeological studies of the early physical and cultural development of humankind from the Paleolithic era to the agricultural revolution.

Directions: Select the best answer for each of the following questions.

MONDAY — WH6.1.1

1 Which tools found by archaeologists indicate that Paleolithic societies hunted animals?

A spear, bow and arrow

B sharp-edged tools

C scraping tools

D all of the above

TUESDAY — WH6.1.1

2 In the Paleolithic Age, women

A herded, farmed, and hunted.

B made spears, traps, and bows and arrows.

C looked after children and searched for berries, nuts, and grains.

D looked after children and farmed.

WEDNESDAY — WH6.1.2

3 Farming as an economic activity developed

A in different areas of the world at the same time.

B in the Pacific islands and spread westward.

C in China and then spread to Europe.

D in Asia and then in Africa.

THURSDAY — WH6.1.3

4 Which of the following developments began during the Neolithic Age?

A hunting and gathering

B domestication of animals and plants

C use of fire for cooking

D toolmaking

FRIDAY — WH6.1.3

5 What development of the Neolithic Age is called a revolution?

A the making of tools

B the overthrow of harsh rulers

C the development of an alphabet

D the rise of farming

Answers on page 31

WEEK 2

Content Standard WH6.2 Students analyze the geographic, political, economic, religious, and social structures of the early civilizations of Mesopotamia, Egypt, and Kush.

Directions: Select the best answer for each of the following questions.

MONDAY — WH6.2.2

1 Which of these is a Sumerian invention?

A paper

B plow

C concrete

D gunpowder

TUESDAY — WH6.2.4

2 The Code of Hammurabi marked an important step toward

A the growth of absolute monarchy.

B creating a monotheistic religion.

C bringing all of the Middle East under Babylonian rule.

D a fair system of justice.

WEDNESDAY — WH6.2.5

3 The chief purpose of the pyramids was to serve as

A tombs for Egyptian rulers.

B temples in honor of the sun god.

C treasuries to store Egypt's wealth.

D warehouses to store grain.

THURSDAY — WH6.2.8

4 Both Kushites and Egyptians believed that their rulers

A were powerful but ordinary people.

B were related to the gods.

C had to be willing to accept criticism.

D should stay out of religious affairs.

FRIDAY — WH6.2.1

Use the passage below and your own knowledge to answer the question.

This passage is part of a hymn written in ancient Egypt about 2100 B.C. It shows the importance of the Nile River to the Egyptian people.

You create the grain, you forth the barley, assuring perpetuity [survival] to the temples. If you cease your toil and your work, then all that exists is in anguish."

—author unknown, "Hymn to the Nile"

5 Why was the Nile River important to ancient Egypt?

A The Nile's massive floods kept invaders from attacking Egypt.

B The Nile served as a border that separated Egypt from Kush.

C Nile floods and soil deposits helped in growing crops.

D The Nile linked Egypt to resources in the Sahara.

Answers on page 31

WEEK 3

Content Standard WH6.3 Students analyze the geographic, political, economic, religious, and social structures of the Ancient Hebrews.

Directions: Select the best answer for each of the following questions.

MONDAY — WH6.3.2

1 The Torah, or the laws of the Israelites, became the first part of
A the Code of Hammurabi.
B the Sermon on the Mount.
C the Hebrew Bible.
D the Twelve Tables.

TUESDAY — WH6.3.3

2 King David was successful at
A building the temple in Jerusalem.
B writing many of the Psalms.
C proclaiming Yahweh as the only god of Israel.
D leading the Israelites into Canaan.

WEDNESDAY — WH6.3.4

3 Moses helped the Israelites escape from slavery in
A Mesopotamia.
B Egypt.
C Canaan.
D Syria.

THURSDAY — WH6.3.5

4 Johanan ben Zakkai helped Judaism survive after the destruction of the temple by
A creating a new order of priests.
B setting up a new Jewish government.
C founding a school that became a center of Torah studies.
D leading the Jews to Egypt.

FRIDAY — WH6.3.1

Use the passage below and your own knowledge to answer the question.

It is told, Moses received the Ten Commandments and other laws from God.

1. *Do not worship any god except me.*
2. *Do not . . . bow down and worship idols.*
3. *Do not misuse my name.*
4. *Remember that the Sabbath Day belongs to me.*
5. *Respect your father and mother.*
6. *Do not murder.*
7. *Be faithful in marriage.*
8. *Do not steal.*
9. *Do not tell lies about others.*
10. *Do not want anything that belongs to someone else.*

— Exodus 20:3-17

5 Which of the following commands are found in the Ten Commandments?
A be loyal only to God
B pray to God five times a day
C renounce war against one's enemies
D abstain from eating meat on holy days

Answers on page 31

WEEK 4

Content Standard WH6.4 Students analyze the geographic, political, economic, religious, and social structures of the early civilization of Ancient Greece.

Directions: Select the best answer for each of the following questions.

MONDAY — WH6.4.4

1 The *Iliad* and the *Odyssey* describe
- **A** the heroic deeds of warriors
- **B** the struggle between nobles and farmers.
- **C** the romances of nobles.
- **D** the thoughts of priests who seek refuge in nature.

TUESDAY — WH6.4.5

2 Which Persian ruler began building a large empire in the Middle East?
- **A** Alexander
- **B** Darius
- **C** Cyrus
- **D** Zoroaster

WEDNESDAY — WH6.4.6

3 Athens was a democracy, while Sparta was
- **A** ruled by a powerful king
- **B** an oligarchy, ruled by a small group of people
- **C** a theocracy, ruled by religious leaders
- **D** ruled by an elected president

THURSDAY — WH6.4.7

4 Which of the following was a result of Alexander the Great's conquests?
- **A** the building of Alexandria as a center of business and trade
- **B** the spread of Greek culture to Europe
- **C** the rebuilding of Sparta
- **D** the founding of a new religion

FRIDAY — WH6.4.2

Use the passage below and your own knowledge to answer the question.

Pericles is believed to have said about the government of Athens:

Our constitution does not copy the laws of neighboring states; we are rather a pattern to others than imitators ourselves. Its administration favours the many instead of the few; that is why it is called a democracy. . . . The freedom which we enjoy in our government extends also to our ordinary life.

— Pericles, as recorded by Thucydides, *History of the Peloponnesian War*

5 According to Pericles, why is Athens considered a democracy?
- **A** Athenian men and women both have the right to vote.
- **B** Athens looks after the interests of many citizens instead of only a small group.
- **C** Athens' government is run by workers and farmers.
- **D** Athens' government has banned slavery.

WEEK 5

Content Standard WH6.5 Students analyze the geographic, political, economic, religious, and social structures of the early civilizations of India.

Directions: Select the best answer for each of the following questions.

MONDAY WH6.5.1

1 Which of the following climatic factors influenced early Indian civilization?

A fierce desert winds

B volcanic eruptions

C monsoons

D destructive ice flows

TUESDAY WH6.5.3

2 The ancient writings known as the Upanishads primarily describe

A the forms of government in early India.

B the relations between masters and servants.

C the life of the common people.

D the search for a universal spirit.

WEDNESDAY WH6.5.5

3 Buddhism became popular in part because it rejected

A dharma.

B the Hindu gods.

C the caste system.

D life after death.

THURSDAY WH6.5.6

4 The founder of India's first great empire was

A Chandragupta Maurya.

B Siddhartha Gautama.

C Krishna.

D Asoka.

FRIDAY WH6.5.7 Read the passage below and answer the following question.

Indian author Kalidasa's poem *The Cloud Messenger* is one of the most popular poems in the Sanskrit language.

*I see your body in the sinuous creeper [plant],
   your gaze
in the started eyes of deer,
your cheek in the moon, your hair in the
plumage of peacocks,
and in the ripples of river I see your
sidelong glances,
but alas, my dearest, nowhere do I find your
   whole likeness"*

— Kalidasa, *The Cloud Messenger*

5 What type of story is told in Kalidasa's *The Cloud Messenger?*

A a tale in which talking animal characters present lessons about life

B a love story where he sees his loved one in nature

C an epic about the king Rama who misses his kidnapped wife Sita

D a war story about brave warriors and their heroic deeds

Answers on page 31

WEEK 6

Content Standard WH6.6 Students analyze the geographic, political, economic, religious, and social structures of the early civilizations of China.

Directions: Select the best answer for each of the following questions.

MONDAY WH6.6.5

1 What was a major achievement of the emperor Shi Huang Di?

A the conquest of Southeast Asia

B the acceptance of Buddhism as a state religion

C the creation of a Chinese navy

D the beginnings of the Great Wall of China

TUESDAY WH6.6.2

2 The civil service exams during the Han dynasty were based on

A the thoughts of Daoism

B law, history, and the teachings of Confucius

C Buddhist philosophy

D Han Gaozu's political beliefs

WEDNESDAY WH6.6.7

3 Most of China's trade in expensive goods went

A by sea to various Pacific islands.

B overland on the Silk Road to western places.

C by camel caravan to Russia.

D through the Grand Canal to the South China Sea.

THURSDAY WH6.6.8

4 What religion became popular in China after the fall of the Han dynasty?

A Buddhism

B Christianity

C Islam

D Shintoism

FRIDAY WH6.6.3 Read the passage below and answer the following question.

In *Analects*, the Chinese thinker and teacher Confucius gave his view on how the problems of Chinese society could be solved:

There are those who act without knowing; I will have none of this. To hear a lot, choose the good, and follow it, to see a lot and learn to recognize it: this is next to knowledge.

— Confucius, *Analects*

5 This excerpt shows that Confucius's major concern was

A political reform.

B separation of religion and government.

C good behavior.

D economic development.

Answers on page 31

WEEK 7

Content Standard WH6.7 Students analyze the geographic, political, economic, religious, and social structures during the development of Rome.

Directions: Select the best answer for each of the following questions.

MONDAY — WH6.7.1

1 According to a traditional legend, who founded the city of Rome?

A Helen of Troy

B Romulus and Remus

C Aristotle and Plato

D Julius Caesar

TUESDAY — WH6.7.2

2 Who could hold political office in early Rome?

A any citizen

B women

C only plebeians

D only patricians

WEDNESDAY — WH6.7.4

3 The reign of Augustus began a period of 200 years that was known for

A peace.

B tax reform.

C religious tolerance.

D civil war.

THURSDAY — WH6.7.6

4 Which apostles were important founders of early Christian churches?

A James and Augustus

B Julius and Andrew

C Peter and Paul

D Saul and Livy

FRIDAY — WH6.7.8 Read the passage below and answer the following question.

In this excerpt, the author Virgil calls Rome to greatness.

Yours be the care, O Rome, to subdue the whole World for your empire!
These be the arts for you—the order of peace to Establish,
Them that are vanquished to spare, and them that are haughty to humble!

— Virgil, *Aeneid*

5 What does Virgil say Romans should do?

A conclude peace treaties with other empires

B conquer and subdue other peoples

C write more poetry and plays

D create a republican form of government

Answers on page 31

Answer Key

The answers for the At-Home Standards Review presented on the previous pages are listed below. Use this answer key to check your understanding of the grade 6 social studies course.

WEEK 1
page 24

1 A
2 C
3 A
4 B
5 D

WEEK 2
page 25

1 B
2 D
3 A
4 B
5 C

WEEK 3
page 26

1 C
2 B
3 B
4 C
5 A

WEEK 4
page 27

1 A
2 C
3 B
4 A
5 B

WEEK 5
page 28

1 C
2 D
3 C
4 A
5 B

WEEK 6
page 29

1 D
2 B
3 B
4 A
5 C

WEEK 7
page 30

1 B
2 D
3 A
4 C
5 B

Previewing Your Textbook

Follow the reading road map through the next few pages to learn about using your textbook, *Discovering Our Past: Medieval and Early Modern Times*. Knowing how your text is organized will help you discover interesting events, fascinating people, and faraway places.

Unit Preview

Your textbook is divided into units. Each unit begins with four pages of information to help you begin your study of the topics.

WHY IT'S IMPORTANT

Each unit begins with a **preview** of important events and *Why It's Important* to read about them.

TIME LINE

A time line shows you **when** the events in this unit happened. It also compares events and people from different places.

MAP

This map shows you **where** the events in this unit happened.

PLACES TO LOCATE

You can look for these important places to locate as you read this unit.

PEOPLE TO MEET

People who have made an impact on world history are highlighted throughout your text.

Unit Review

A **Unit Review** falls at the end of the unit and **compares** the contents.

COMPARISON CHART

All of the different civilizations talked about in this unit are **compared** in a chart.

WORLD MAP

A **map** shows you where each civilization existed.

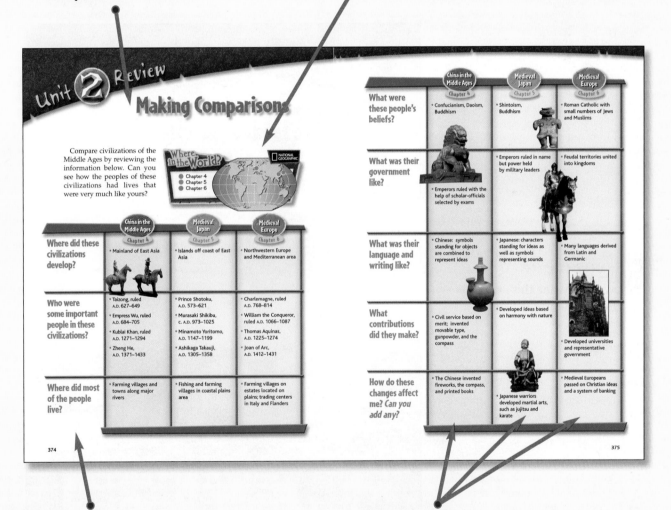

QUESTIONS

The chart answers the **same questions** about each group of people making it easier to compare them.

CHAPTERS

The most **important ideas** in each chapter are listed in the columns.

Chapters

Each unit of your textbook is divided into chapters. Each chapter starts by giving you some background information about what you will be reading.

CHAPTER TITLE
The chapter title tells you the main topic you will be reading about.

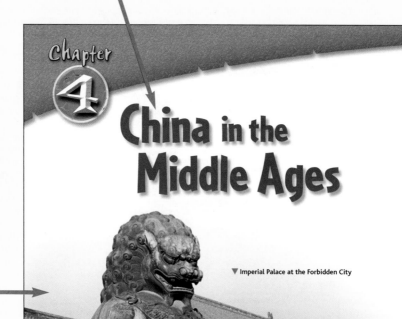

Chapter 4
China in the Middle Ages

▼ Imperial Palace at the Forbidden City

NATIONAL GEOGRAPHIC Where & When?

A.D. 600	A.D. 900	1200	1500
A.D. 581 Wendi founds Sui dynasty	A.D. 868 Chinese print world's first book	1206 Genghis Khan unites the Mongols	1405 Zheng He begins overseas voyage

COLORFUL PHOTO
Shows you what this part of the world is like.

WHERE AND WHEN?
Here you can see where and when events in this chapter happened.

Big Ideas

Throughout your text important ideas are given at the beginning of each chapter. These ideas alert you to the big themes of history that occur over and over again.

BIG IDEAS
The important ideas of each section are explained for you.

HISTORY ONLINE
This tells you where you can go online for more information.

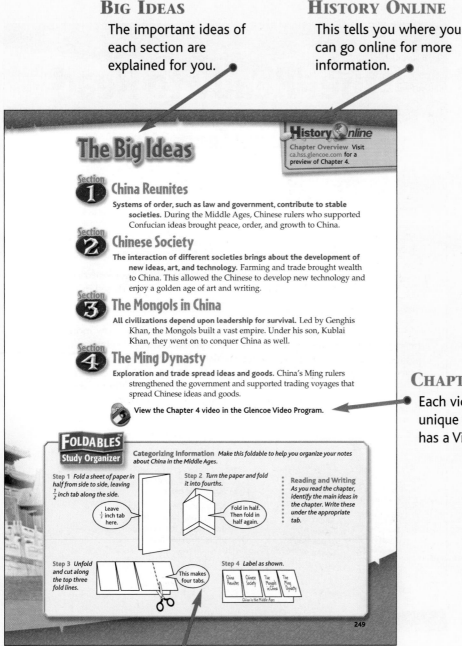

CHAPTER VIDEO
Each video program highlights a unique topic in the chapter and has a Viewer's Guide.

FOLDABLES™
Use the Foldables™ Study Organizer to take notes as you read the chapter.

Chapter Reading Skill

Because reading about Social Studies is different than reading a novel or magazine, every chapter of your text offers help with reading skills.

READING SKILL

This shows you what reading skill you will be learning about—**Making Connections.**

LEARN IT!

This explains how the skill applies to the **reading** you do every day.

READING TIP

The Reading Tip tells you more about making **connections** in your reading.

Chapter 4 Get Ready to Read

Making Connections

Reading Skill

1 Learn It!

Making connections means relating what you read to what you already know. Read the excerpts below.

Text-to-self: personal experiences

Have you ever eaten at a Chinese restaurant? How important do you think rice is to the Chinese diet? What kind of foods do you eat every day?

Text-to-world: events in other places

How popular is tea in China today? What is the most popular drink in the United States?

Farmers also developed new kinds of rice, which grew well in poor soil, produced more per acre, grew faster, and were resistant to disease.

These changes helped farmers grow more and more rice. China's farmers also began to grow tea, which became a popular drink. They made improvements in other crops as well. With more food available, the number of people in China greatly increased.

— *from page 261*

Reading Tip

The better the connection is, the easier it is to remember. Be sure to make connections with memorable ideas or experiences from your life.

Text-to-text: what you have read before

Have you ever read about China's population? How important is the food supply to them today?

250

PRACTICE IT!

Next comes an easy-to-follow **practice** activity.

APPLY IT!

Here is an opportunity to **apply** what you have learned.

WRITING

Writing about what you read will help you remember the events.

2 Practice It!

With a partner, read the following paragraphs. Make a list of the connections you made and compare them to your partner's list. Discuss what things in your lives relate to the story of Marco Polo.

One of the most famous European travelers to reach China was Marco Polo (MAHR • koh POH • loh). He came from the city of Venice in Italy. Kublai Khan was fascinated by Marco Polo's stories about his travels. For about 16 years, Polo enjoyed a special status in the country. Kublai sent him on many fact-finding and business trips. For three of those years, Polo ruled the Chinese city of Yangchow. When Polo finally returned to Europe, he wrote a book about his adventures. His accounts of the wonders of China amazed Europeans.

—from page 273

Read to Write
Choose one of the three types of connections that you make most often. Write a brief paragraph explaining why.

Kublai Khan presents ▶ gift to Marco Polo.

3 Apply It!

Choose five words or phrases from this chapter that make a connection to something you already know.

251

Reading Skills Handbook

Using Types of Reference Materials
Dictionaries and other reference sources can help you learn new words and how to use them. Check out these reference sources. You can find these in your local public or school library as well as on the Internet.

- A **dictionary** gives the pronunciation, the meaning or multiple meanings, and often examples of how to use the words. Some dictionaries also provide illustrations or diagrams to help define words, other forms of words, their parts of speech, and synonyms. You might also find the historical background of a word, such as its Greek, Latin, or Anglo-Saxon origins.
- A **glossary** is a word list that appears at the end—or Appendix—of a book or other written work and includes only words that are in that work. Like dictionaries, glossaries include the pronunciation and definitions of words.
- A **thesaurus** lists groups of words that have the same, or almost the same, meaning. Words with similar meanings are called synonyms. Seeing the synonyms of words can help you build your vocabulary.

Recognizing Word Meanings Across Subjects

Have you ever learned a new word in one class and then noticed it in your reading for other subjects? The word probably will not mean exactly the same thing in each class. But you can use what you know about the word's meaning to help you understand what it means in a different subject area. Look at the following example from three different subjects:

- **Social studies:** One *product* manufactured in the southern part of the United States is cotton cloth.
- **Math:** After multiplying the numbers five and five, explain how you arrived at the *product*.
- **Science:** One *product* of photosynthesis is oxygen.

CHECKING YOUR UNDERSTANDING

The following sentence does not include real English words, but you can use what you have learned about English syntax to decode the sentence. First read the sentence. Then answer the questions that follow.

The shabs smatously graled the mul-bulowed rotfabs.
1. What is the verb in the sentence?
2. What is the subject?
3. What is the object?

52 Reading Skills Handbook

READING SKILLS HANDBOOK

Located on pages 50–59 is a handbook that is full of reading strategies to help you read your text. You can look back at this handbook as you read.

CHECK UNDERSTANDING

Did you understand the reading lesson?

Previewing Your Textbook

Sections

A section is a division, or part, of a chapter. The first page of the section, the Section Opener, helps you set a purpose for reading.

GUIDE TO READING
Read the **connection** between what you already know and what you are about to read.

CONTENT VOCABULARY
Points out important social studies **terms** and how to say them.

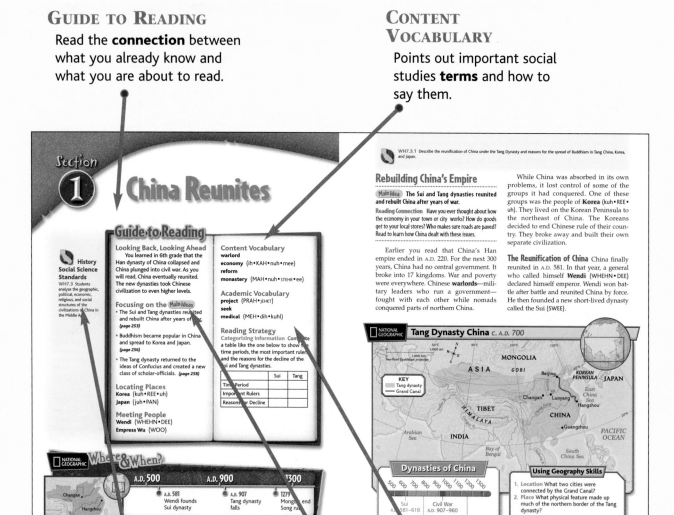

CALIFORNIA HISTORY–SOCIAL SCIENCE STANDARDS
Content Standards covered in this section.

MAIN IDEAS
Preview the **main ideas** of each section which are repeated in the reading.

ACADEMIC VOCABULARY
Tells you other **new words** you might not know that will come up in your reading.

CALIFORNIA STATE STANDARDS

The California History–Social Science standard that is covered on the pages you are about to read is listed here.

READING CHECK

This is a **self check** question to see if you understand the main ideas.

WH7.3.3 Analyze the influences of Confucianism and changes in Confucian thought during the Song and Mongol periods.
WH7.3.6 Describe the development of the imperial state and the scholar-official class.

New Confucian Ideas

Main Idea The Tang dynasty returned to the ideas of Confucius and created a new class of scholar-officials.

Reading Connection Have you ever seen someone get a reward that he or she did not earn? Read to learn how China's rulers tried to avoid this problem when hiring government officials.

You have already learned about Confucius and his teachings. Confucius and his followers believed that a good government depended on having wise leaders who ruled to benefit the people. The civil service examinations introduced by Han rulers were a product of Confucian ideas. These examinations were supposed to recruit talented government officials.

After the fall of the Han dynasty, no national government existed to give civil service examinations. Confucianism lost much support, and Buddhism with its spiritual message won many followers. Tang and Song rulers, however, brought Confucianism back into favor.

What Is Neo-Confucianism? The Tang dynasty gave its support to a new kind of Confucianism called neo-Confucianism. This new Confucianism was created, in part, to reduce Buddhism's popularity. It taught that life in this world was just as important as the afterlife. Followers were expected to take part in life and help others.

Although it criticized Buddhist ideas, this new form of Confucianism also picked up some Buddhist and Daoist beliefs. For many Chinese, Confucianism became more than a system of rules for being good. It became a religion with beliefs about the spiritual world. Confucian thinkers taught that if people followed Confucius's teachings, they would find peace of mind and live in harmony with nature.

The Song dynasty, which followed the Tang, also supported neo-Confucianism. The Song even adopted it as their official philosophy, or belief system.

Scholar-Officials Neo-Confucianism also became a way to strengthen the government. Both Tang and Song rulers used civil service examinations to hire officials. In doing so, they based the bureaucracy on a merit system. Under a merit system, people are accepted for what they can do and not on their riches or personal contacts.

The examinations tested job seekers on their knowledge of Confucian writings. To pass, it was necessary to write with style as well as understanding. The tests were supposed to be fair, but only men could take them. Also, only rich people had the money to help their sons study for the tests.

Passing the tests was very difficult. However, parents did all they could to prepare their sons. At the age of four, boys started learning to write the characters of the Chinese language. Later, students had to memorize all of Confucius's writings. If a student recited the passages poorly, he could expect to be hit by his teacher.

After many years of study, the boys took their examinations. Despite all the preparation, only one in five passed. Those who failed usually found jobs helping officials or teaching others. However, they would never be given a government job.

▲ Chinese scholar-officials on horseback

Over the years, the examination system created a new wealthy class in China. This group was made up of scholar-officials. Strict rules set the scholar-officials apart from society. At the same time, these scholar-officials began to influence Chinese thought and government well into modern times.

Reading Check Describe How did Confucianism change in China?

History Online Study Central Need help understanding the impact of New Confucian ideas? Visit ca.hss.glencoe.com and click on Study Central.

Primary Source — Defending Confucianism

Han Yü (A.D. 768 to A.D. 824) encouraged the Chinese people to remain faithful to Confucianism.

"What were the teachings of our ancient kings? Universal love is called humanity. To practice this in the proper manner is called righteousness. To proceed according to these is called the Way.... They offered sacrifices to Heaven and the gods came to receive them.... What Way is this? I say: This is what I call the Way, and not what the Taoists [Daoists] and the Buddhists called the Way...."

—Han Yü, "An Inquiry on The Way" (Tao)

▲ Han Yü

DBQ Document-Based Question

Why does Han Yü think Confucianism should be followed?

Section 1 Review

Reading Summary
Review the **Main Ideas**
- While the Sui dynasty was short-lived, the Tang and Song dynasties lasted for hundreds of years and returned power and prosperity to China.
- Buddhism became popular in China and also spread to Korea and Japan.
- A new kind of Confucianism developed in China during the Tang and Song dynasties, and the government used civil service tests to improve itself.

What Did You Learn?
1. What made Buddhism so popular in China?
2. How was neo-Confucianism a response to Buddhism's popularity and what did it teach?

Critical Thinking
3. Compare and Contrast Create a diagram to show how the reigns of Wendi and Yangdi were similar and how they were different. CA 7RC2.0

Wendi   Yangdi

4. **The Big Ideas** Which policies of the Tang government helped stabilize China? CA HI2.
5. Cause and Effect What events led to the fall of the Tang dynasty? CA HI2.
6. Analyze Why had Confucianism fallen out of favor in China before the Tang and Song dynasties? CA 7RC2.3
7. **Reading** Making Connections Civil service exams were stressful events. Write a paragraph about a test you had to take. How does your experience compare to China's exams? CA 7RC2.1

258 CHAPTER 4 • China in the Middle Ages
CHAPTER 4 • China in the Middle Ages 259

SECTION REVIEW

Here you can review the main topics and answer questions about what you have read.

STUDY CENTRAL

Here you can receive help with homework.

CALIFORNIA STATE STANDARDS

The oval shows the California Historical and Social Sciences Analysis Skills and English–Language Arts content standards covered by this question.

Previewing Your Textbook

Chapter Assessment

These pages offer you a chance to check how much you remember after reading the chapter.

VOCABULARY REVIEW

Content and **academic** vocabulary are reviewed here.

MAIN IDEAS

Revisit the **Main Ideas** found in your reading.

HISTORICAL AND SOCIAL SCIENCES ANALYSIS SKILLS

English–Language Arts standards covered are listed in ovals.

Chapter 4 Assessment
Standard WH7.3

Review Content Vocabulary

Match the word in the first column with its definition in the second column.

____ 1. treason   a. groups of related families loosely joined together

____ 2. warlord   b. change that brings improvement

____ 3. terror   c. disloyalty to the government

____ 4. economy   d. military leader who also runs a government

____ 5. reform   e. a count of the number of people

____ 6. steppe   f. violent actions meant to scare others

____ 7. tribe   g. organized way to buy, sell, and produce

____ 8. census   h. wide grassy plain

Review the Main Ideas

Section 1 • China Reunites
9. What did the Sui and Tang dynasties do to improve China?
10. How did the Tang rulers change China?

Section 2 • Chinese Society
11. How did Tang rulers strengthen China's economy?
12. What kind of technologies did the Chinese develop?

Section 3 • The Mongols in China
13. Why were the Mongols able to build a huge empire?
14. How did the Mongols rule China?

Section 4 • The Ming Dynasty
15. How did the Ming rulers affect China?
16. Why did the Portuguese want to explore Africa and Asia?

Critical Thinking

17. **Analyze** How did the return of Confucianism affect Chinese society and government? **CA HI3.**
18. **Predict** How would China be different today if Tang rulers had not tried to stop Buddhism in A.D. 845? **CA HI4.**
19. **Hypothesize** The Mongols built a vast empire, but the Yuan dynasty lasted only about 100 years. Create a hypothesis that might explain this situation. **CA HR1.**

Geography Skills

Study the map below and answer the following questions.

20. **Location** What was the length of the Grand Canal? **CA CS3.**
21. **Human/Environment Interaction** What part of Asia did the Tang control that helped China's trade? **CA CS3.**
22. **Region** What geographic features helped the Tang dynasty expand? **CA CS3.**

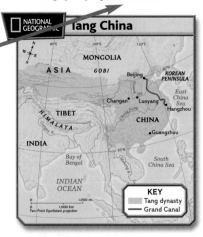

Tang China

290   CHAPTER 4 • China in the Middle Ages

40

Previewing Your Textbook

WRITING ABOUT BIG IDEAS

You are reminded about the chapter **Big Ideas** here.

HISTORY ONLINE

Go to the web for a quick **self-check** quiz.

REVIEW ARROWS

Look for the *Review* arrows that tell you are **reviewing** material you have learned before.

Read to Write

23. The Big Ideas **Persuasive Writing** Imagine you are a Portuguese merchant. You have just traveled to China to persuade the Chinese people to trade with your country. Create a script detailing the dialogue that would take place between you and a representative of the Chinese government. **CA 7WA2.5**

24. Using Your FOLDABLES On your foldable, add details to the main headings in Section 2. Think about how the changes and arts described there might have had an impact on people's lives. Write a story about a family whose life is affected by these changes. Illustrate your story. **CA HI1.**

Using Academic Vocabulary

25. All the words in the chart below are verbs. Complete the chart by changing them into past tense verbs.

Term	Past Tense
encounter	
contact	
seek	
erode	
compile	

Linking Past and Present

26. Expository Writing Write a short essay that describes similarities and differences between the Imperial City of the Ming dynasty and the United States capital, Washington, D.C. **CA 7WA2.0**

Understanding Change

27. When the Portuguese traders first went to China, they were not quickly accepted. Write an essay that describes why they were not accepted and how that eventually changed. Be sure to discuss the role of trade and its benefits in China. **CA HI2.**

Building Citizenship

28. Writing Research Reports How did neo-Confucianism strengthen government in China? How does the use of a merit system reflect the way that jobs in the U.S. government are given? How is it different? **CA 7WA2.3**

History Online

Self-Check Quiz To help you prepare for the Chapter Test, visit ca.hss.glencoe.com

Reviewing Skills

29. Reading Skill **Making Connections** The voyages of Zheng He introduced China to many other cultures. His journeys took him to parts of Asia, Africa, and the Middle East. Use your local library and the Internet to identify other important explorers who have helped cultures learn about one another. Explain your findings in a short essay. **CA 7WA2.3**

30. Analysis Skill **Understanding Perspective** Major exploration and trade was stopped by Chinese leaders in 1433. Write a letter to the emperor explaining why you think this is a good or bad decision. What are the benefits to exploration and trade with the outside world? What possible harm can come from opening a country's borders to foreigners? **CA HR5.**

Standards Practice

Select the best answer for each of the following questions.

31 **What helped the Chinese economy to improve during the Tang dynasty?**

A wars and lower taxes
B farming and trade
C wars and farming
D exploration and education

32 **The Tang and Song dynasties encouraged the Chinese people to practice**

A neo-Confucianism.
B Buddhism.
C Confucianism.
D Daoism.

STANDARDS PRACTICE AND REVIEW

Answer practice questions to help you master the **California standards.**

CHAPTER 4 • China in the Middle Ages **291**

41

Previewing Your Textbook

California History–Social Science Standards

In your textbook, on pages 1–22—in the **Guide to California Standards**—you will find a listing of all of the California History–Social Science standards. All of these are covered in *Discovering Our Past: Medieval and Early Modern Times*.

TO PARENTS AND STUDENTS

Here is an explanation of what is contained in the **Guide to California Standards**.

ANALYSIS SKILLS

Here is a list of standards that relate to **thinking and research skills** you can use in all of your classroom subjects.

SUPPORTING STANDARD

Each main standard has **more specific** sub-standards.

MAIN STANDARD

This is the **main idea** of the standard.

Previewing Your Textbook

CALIFORNIA STATE SYMBOL

Look for the California state symbol and the standard at the top or the side of the page.

CALIFORNIA STANDARDS [SIDE]

Sometimes you will find standards covered listed in the side column of the page.

CALIFORNIA STANDARDS [TOP]

Most often the standards covered on the page will be listed at the top.

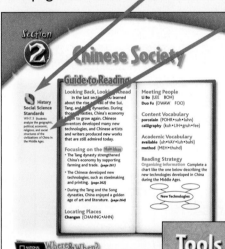

ARTIFACT

Many interesting **artifacts** are shown throughout the text.

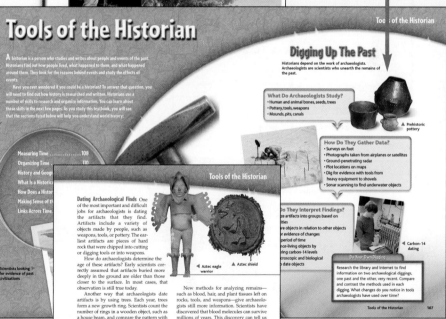

TOOLS OF THE HISTORIAN ANALYSIS SKILLS

This section gives you an overview of how historical detectives find out about the history of the world. These detectives use the Historical and Social Sciences Analyses. The Historical Analysis Skills are noted for you.

THINKING LIKE A HISTORIAN

Questions help you pick out the **important information** from the reading.

Previewing Your Textbook

California Standards Handbook

This handbook found on pages 568–589 gives you another chance to practice your understanding of the **7th grade History–Social Science content standards** you are required to know.

MAIN STANDARD

The chart shows the **main standards** you need to know.

WHERE CAN I FIND IT?

Tells you where in your text you can read more about this standard.

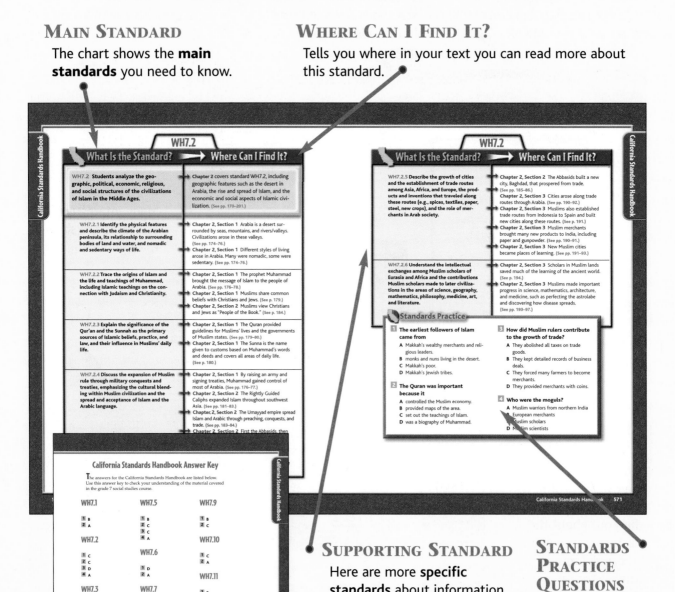

SUPPORTING STANDARD

Here are more **specific standards** about information you should know.

ANSWER KEY

Answers to the Practice Questions are given for you to **check yourself.**

STANDARDS PRACTICE QUESTIONS

Practice questions are written in the same way you will see them on the standards test.

Special Features

Special Features supply more information about topics in the chapter or unit. They help history come alive. Here is a sample of the *World Literature* feature.

WORLD LITERATURE

CHINA'S BRAVEST GIRL
THE LEGEND OF HUA MU LAN

by Charlie Chin

Before You Read

The Scene: This story takes place in China around A.D. 400.
The Characters: Hua Mu Lan is a brave young woman who disguises herself as a soldier.
The Plot: Hua Mu Lan volunteers to fight in a war in order to protect her father.

Vocabulary Preview

darts: moves quickly
weaves: laces together strands of material
perfumed: scented

yield: to give wa...
banquet: large fe...

Have you eve... tried to help or protec... a family member or ... riend? How did that m...ake you feel? In th... story, a daughter ... rue ... o help her

Red and gold banners adorn the house.
A banquet is prepared for all.
She wears the finest jade[4] and silk
for the wedding in her husband's hall.

The Pipa player sang the last verse
His rewards had been foretold:
for his skill a seat of honor;
for his song a ring of gold.

The legend of young Hua Mu Lan
whose bravery saved her nation
is loved by the Chinese people
and retold each generation.

[4]**jade:** a green gemstone

Responding to the Literature

1. Why did Hua Mu Lan's father have to go into battle?
2. How long did Mu Lan stay away from home?
3. **Drawing Conclusions** After reading her story, what do think of the character of Hua Mu Lan? What does the author do to make Mu Lan a sympathetic and heroic character? **CA 7RL3.3**
4. **Understanding Poetry** This story is written in poetry form. How does the presentation of this tale as a poem change the story for the reader? How does the author use poetry to move the story along? After answering these questions, write a short story version of Hua Mu Lan's tale. How does your version differ from the one you have just read? How are they the same? **CA 7RL3.1 CA 7WA2.1**
5. **Read to Write** Imagine that you are one of Hua Mu Lan's fellow soldiers. How might you have reacted if you found out that she was a woman? Would this change how you viewed her? Write an essay that explains how you would react to the situation. **CA 7WA2.2**

279

Reading on Your Own...

From the California Reading List

Are you interested in amazing events in China, the exciting life of a samurai, or life in medieval Europe? If so, check out these other great books.

Nonfiction

The Great Wall of China by Leonard Everett Fisher recounts the story and construction of this amazing wall. Learn the political and social reasons for its creation and meet several interesting characters in Chinese history. *The content of this book is related to* History–Social Science Standard WH7.3.

Fiction

Mysterious Tales of Japan by Rafe Martin is a collection of scary stories in a Japanese setting. These edge-of-your-seat Japanese tales are filled with mystery and offer a look at the Shinto and Buddhist belief systems. *The content of this book is related to* History–Social Science Standard WH7.5.

Biography

Images Across the Ages: Japanese Portraits by Dorothy and Thomas Hoobler recounts the lives of important Japanese people. This book includes firsthand accounts from the people who lived during that time. *The content of this book is related to* History–Social Science Standard WH7.5.

Fiction

Catherine, Called Birdy by Karen Cushman, a Newbery Award winner, tells the story of a teenage girl in the thirteenth century. Catherine is determined to marry for love even though her father wants to marry her to the first rich man he can find. This story lets you see into the daily life and family customs of medieval times. *The content of this book is related to* History–Social Science Standard WH7.6.

280

BEFORE YOU READ
Get an idea of what the literature selection is about before you read.

DOCUMENT-BASED QUESTIONS
Respond to questions based on the reading.

VOCABULARY PREVIEW
Alerts you to new words and terms.

READING ON YOUR OWN
Read more about this time in world history. These titles are just suggestions.

Previewing Your Textbook

ANALYZING PRIMARY SOURCES

You will be given an opportunity to judge the value and truthfulness of a variety of **primary and secondary sources.**

READER'S DICTIONARY

Reader's Dictionary helps you with **unfamiliar words.**

CALIFORNIA STANDARD

The **History–Social Science standard** covered here is noted.

Analyzing Primary Sources

WH7.3.2 Describe agricultural, technological, and commercial developments during the Tang and Song periods. WH7.3.4 Understand the importance of both overland trade and maritime expeditions between China and other civilizations in the Mongol Ascendancy and Ming Dynasty.

A Growing China

In the Middle Ages, China changed dramatically. Improvements in farming techniques helped increase food production and boost the economy. As China's food supply increased, so did its population. For example, from A.D. 750 to A.D. 1100, China's population doubled from about 50 million to 100 million people. Chinese technology, agriculture, and economic activity continued to advance through the Ming dynasty.

Read the following passages and study the photo. Then answer the questions that follow.

▲ Painting of Chinese landscape

Reader's Dictionary

palanquin (PA•luhn•KEEN): a covered vehicle made up of a couch, usually enclosed by curtains, and carried by people on their shoulders

profusion (pruh•FYOO•zhuhn): large amount; abundance

barbarian: foreigner

buffeted (BUH•fuht•uhd): fought against

crags: steep, rugged rocks or cliffs

Planting Rice

The image to the right depicts Chinese farmers planting rice. Rice is an excellent food crop—it stores well, offers good nutrition, and is easy to cook. During the Middle Ages, the production of rice expanded steadily. Improvements in water pumps and the making of dams allowed farmers to make the land suitable for growing rice.

Chinese Ships

During the Middle Ages, the Chinese developed merchant ships that were the most advanced in the world. The following is a description of Chinese ships during the 1100s.

The ships which sail the Southern Sea and south of it are like houses. When their sails are spread they are like great clouds in the sky. Their rudders are several tens of feet long. A single ship carries several hundred men. It has stored on board a year's supply of grain.

—Zhou Qufei as quoted in Chronicle of the Chinese Emperors

▲ This image of Chinese farmers was made from a woodcut design. Images like this one were very popular in China during the Middle Ages, but often they were too expensive for people like these farmers to afford.

DBQ Document-Based Questions

The Cities of the Song
1. What kinds of people have come to the medicine fair?
2. How did some of the people who traveled to the medicine fair get there? Why do you think they made such a trip?

Planting Rice
3. Do you think rice farming was easy? Explain. Use the picture to support your answer.

Chinese Ships
4. What do you suppose was the purpose of such ships?
5. What comparisons does the writer make about the ships?

Read to Write
6. Using the primary sources you have just examined, write an essay describing how economic prosperity and the rise of trade during the Middle Ages affected Chinese society.

CHAPTER 4 • China in the Middle Ages   289

WH7.3.3 Analyze the influences of Confucianism and changes in Confucian thought during the Song and Mongol periods. WH7.3.6 Describe the development of the imperial state and the scholar-official class.

New Confucian Ideas

Main Idea The Tang dynasty returned to the ideas of Confucius and created a new class of scholar-officials.

Reading Connection Have you ever seen someone get a reward that he or she did not earn? Read to learn how China's rulers tried to avoid this problem when hiring government officials.

You have already learned about Confucius and his teachings. Confucius and his followers believed that a good government depended on having wise leaders who ruled to benefit the people. The civil service examinations introduced by Han rulers were a product of Confucian ideas. These examinations were supposed to recruit talented government officials.

After the fall of the Han dynasty, no national government existed to give civil service examinations. Confucianism lost much support, and Buddhism with its spiritual message won many followers. Tang and Song rulers, however, brought Confucianism back into favor.

What Is Neo-Confucianism? The Tang dynasty gave its support to a new kind of Confucianism called neo-Confucianism. This new Confucianism was created, in part, to reduce Buddhism's popularity. It taught that life in this world was just as important as the afterlife. Followers were expected to take part in life and help others.

Although it criticized Buddhist ideas, this new form of Confucianism also picked up some Buddhist and Daoist beliefs. For many Chinese, Confucianism became more than a system of rules for being good. It became a religion with beliefs about the spiritual world. Confucian thinkers taught that if people followed Confucius's teachings, they would find peace of mind and live in harmony with nature.

The Song dynasty, which followed the Tang, also supported neo-Confucianism. The Song even adopted it as their official philosophy, or belief system.

Scholar-Officials Neo-Confucianism also became a way to strengthen the government. Both Tang and Song rulers used civil service examinations to hire officials. In doing so, they based the bureaucracy on a merit system. Under a merit system, people are accepted for what they can do and not on their riches or personal contacts.

Primary Source Defending Confucianism

Han Yü (A.D. 768 to A.D. 824) encouraged the Chinese people to remain faithful to Confucianism.

"What were the teachings of our ancient kings? Universal love is called humanity. To practice this in the proper manner is called righteousness. To proceed according to these is called the Way.... They offered sacrifices to Heaven and the gods came to receive them.... What Way is this? I say: This is what I call the Way, and not what the Taoists [Daoists] and the Buddhists called the Way...."

—Han Yü, "An Inquiry on The Way" (Tao)

▲ Han Yü

DBQ Document-Based Question

Why does Han Yü think Confucianism should be followed?

258   CHAPTER 4 • China in the Middle Ages

DOCUMENT-BASED QUESTIONS

Following the reading, you will be asked to answer some questions based on the document—or reading—you have just completed.

MORE PRIMARY SOURCES

Shorter Primary Source selections are also included in the text.

YOU DECIDE

Two sides of an issue are presented. Imagine you were there and could give your opinion.

You Decide . . .

WH7.6.3 Understand the development of feudalism, its role in the medieval European economy, the way in which it was influenced by physical geography (the role of the manor and the growth of towns), and how feudal relationships provided the foundation of political order.

Feudalism: Good or Bad?

Feudalism was the major social and political order in medieval Europe. It developed as power passed from kings to local lords.

Good?

Feudalism brought together two powerful groups: lords and vassals. The lords gave vassals land in return for military and other services. Feudalism was a help to Western Europeans for the following reasons:

- Feudalism helped protect communities from the violence and warfare that broke out after the fall of Rome and the collapse of strong central government in Western Europe. Feudalism secured Western Europe's society and kept out powerful invaders.

- Feudalism helped restore trade. Lords repaired bridges and roads. Knights arrested bandits, enforced laws, and made it safe to travel.
- Feudalism benefited lords, vassals, and peasants. Lords gained a dependable fighting force in their vassals. Vassals received land for their military service. Peasants were protected by their lords. The lord built mills, blacksmith shops, and wood-working shops.
- Feudal ceremonies, oaths, and contracts required lords and vassals to be faithful and to carry out their duties. These agreements later helped shape the development of European governments.
- Feudalism did not allow one person or organization to become too powerful. Power was shared. This led to European ideas about limited government, constitutions, and civil rights.

◀ Serfs working the land

344

◀ Landowning nobles often served as knights.

Bad?

Feudalism did not always work as well in real life as it did in theory, and it caused many problems for society.

- Feudalism provided some unity and security in local areas, but it often did not have the strength to unite larger regions or countries. Small feudal governments could not afford big projects, such as building aqueducts, sewers, or fleets of ships, that might benefit society.
- Because there was no strong central government to enforce laws fairly, people often turned to force, violence, and warfare. This led

to many wars among lords. Feudalism protected Western Europe from outside invaders, but it did not bring peace to a region.

- Lords or vassals often placed their personal interests over the interests of the areas they ruled. Feudal lords had complete power in their local areas and could make harsh demands on their vassals and peasants.
- Feudalism did not treat people equally or let them move up in society. A person born a serf was supposed to remain a serf, just as a person born a lord received special treatment without earning it.
- Most peasants were serfs. They were not allowed to leave their lord's lands. Serfs had to work three days each week as a payment to the lords or vassals for allowing them to farm for themselves on other days. The serfs were restricted in movement and even daily activities because they could not leave the land without permission.

You Be the Historian

Checking for Understanding
1. Do you think feudalism helped or hurt Western Europe's development? CA HI5.
2. Is there any way feudal lords could have worked their lands without using serfs? CA 7RC2.0
3. Imagine you live in a feudal society. Write an autobiographical story about your life as a lord, vassal, or serf and your relationship with the other two groups. Your entries should show feudalism as a good or bad order.

345

Biography

GENGHIS KHAN
c. A.D. 1167–1227
Mongol Leader

WH7.3 Students analyze the geographic, political, economic, religious, and social structures of the civilizations of China in the Middle Ages.

Was Genghis Khan a ruthless warrior who enjoyed causing death and destruction, a skilled leader who improved the lives of those in his empire, or both? Genghis Khan built a huge empire across Asia using loyal, strong, and well-trained warriors. Although the wars he and his sons fought were brutal and bloody, they eventually brought peace and prosperity to most of Asia.

Genghis Khan was named Temujin by his father, the Mongol chief Yisugei. Folklore says Temujin had a large blood clot in his right hand, which meant he was destined to become a great warrior. Temujin grew up in his father's camp along the Onon River in Mongolia.

Temujin's father arranged a marriage for his nine-year-old son. His wife came from another tribe, and the marriage helped bring wealth to his family. Borte, his wife at age ten, was beautiful. Temujin and Borte had four sons when they both became older.

Years later, when his father was killed by the Tartars and his loyal warriors left the tribe, Temujin lost his wealth. His poverty and the disloyalty of his father's soldiers angered him so much that he decided to become a great warrior. Over time, Temujin became Ghengis Khan.

◀ Genghis Khan's camp

"Life is short, I could not conquer the world."
—attributed to Genghis Khan

◀ Genghis Khan

Then and Now
In Mongolia today, Genghis Khan is considered a national hero. What do you think? Was Genghis Khan a villain or a hero?

271

BIOGRAPHIES

Read more about important people and what they achieved.

DOCUMENT-BASED QUESTIONS

Here you answer questions about what you have read.

Previewing Your Textbook

CONNECTING PAST AND PRESENT

See the connections between what it was like then and what it is like today.

---

supported the building of Buddhist temples. Many Chinese Buddhists became monks and nuns. They lived in places called **monasteries** (MAH•nuh•STEHR•eez), where they meditated and worshiped.

Buddhist temples and monasteries provided services for people. They ran schools and provided rooms and food for travelers. Buddhist monks served as bankers and provided **medical** care.

Not all Chinese people liked Buddhism, however. Many thought that it was wrong for the Buddhist temples and monasteries to accept donations. Others believed that monks and nuns weakened respect for family life because they were not allowed to marry.

In the early A.D. 800s, Tang officials feared Buddhism's growing power. They saw Buddhism as an enemy of China's traditions. In A.D. 845 the Tang had many Buddhist monasteries and temples destroyed. Buddhism in China never fully recovered.

Chinese Buddhism Spreads East As you read earlier, Korea broke free of China when the Han dynasty fell in A.D. 220. For several hundred years after, Korea was divided into three distinct kingdoms.

In the A.D. 300s, Chinese Buddhists brought their religion to Korea. About A.D. 660, the Koreans united to form one country. After that, with government support, Buddhism grew even stronger in Korea.

Buddhism later spread to the nearby islands of **Japan** (juh•PAN). According to legend, one of Korea's kings wrote to Japan's emperor. The letter contained a statue of the Buddha and Buddhist writings. "This religion is the most excellent of all teach...passed, Japan as...

✓ Reading...

Chinese p...

The Way It Was

Focus on Everyday Life

Civil Service Exams Proficiency tests and final exams today take a lot of preparation, but they are not as difficult as China's civil service examinations given during the Tang dynasty. Men of almost all ranks tried to pass the exams so they could hold government jobs and become wealthy. Thousands attempted the tests, but only a few hundred people qualified for the important positions.

Chinese boys began preparing for the exams in primary school. After many years of learning to read and write more than 400,000 words and sayings, the boys—now men in their twenties or early thirties—would take the first of three levels of exams. Students traveled to huge testing sites to take the tests. Food and beds were not provided, so they had to bring their own. Many men became sick or insane because of the stress of the tests and the poor conditions under which they were tested.

▶ Students taking civil service exams

After Wendi died, his son Yangdi (YAHNG•DEE) took the Chinese throne. Yangdi wanted to expand China's territory. He sent an army to fight the neighboring Koreans, but the Chinese were badly defeated. At home, Yangdi took on many ambitious building **projects**. For example, the Great Wall had fallen into ruins, and Yangdi had it rebuilt.

Yangdi's greatest effort went into building the Grand Canal. This system of waterways linked the Chang Jiang (Yangtze River) and Huang He (Yellow River). The Grand

Canal became an important route for shipping products between northern and southern China. It helped unite China's economy. An **economy** (ih•KAH•nuh•mee) is an organized way in which people produce, sell, and purchase things.

History Online
Web Activity Visit ca.hss.glencoe.com and click on *Chapter 4—Student Web Activity* to learn more about China.

Linking Past & Present

Grand Canal and Three Gorges Dam

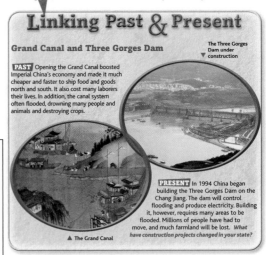

The Three Gorges Dam under ▼ construction

PAST Opening the Grand Canal boosted Imperial China's economy and made it much cheaper and faster to ship food and goods north and south. It also cost many laborers their lives. In addition, the canal system often flooded, drowning many people and animals and destroying crops.

PRESENT In 1994 China began building the Three Gorges Dam on the Chang Jiang. The dam will control flooding and produce electricity. Building it, however, requires many areas to be flooded. Millions of people have had to move, and much farmland will be lost. *What have construction projects changed in your state?*

▲ The Grand Canal

---

he wanted to write poems to the woman he loved, he wrote in the **vernacular** (vuhr•NA•kyuh•luhr). The vernacular is the everyday language people speak in a region—Italian, French, or German, for example. When authors began writing in the vernacular, many more people could read their work.

HISTORY MAKERS

Movable Type c. 1450

Johannes Gutenberg, a German goldsmith, built a printing press modeled after a winepress. Once the press was completed, Gutenberg spent two years printing his first book. For each page, he set metal letters in a frame, rolled ink over the frame, and pressed the frame against paper. Around 1455, he completed printing what is now known as the Gutenberg Bible, or the 42 Line Bible. This was the first book printed using movable metal type, sparking a revolution in publishing and reading.

▼ Gutenberg Bible

In the early 1300s, **Dante Alighieri** (DAHN•tay A•luh•GYEHR•ee), a poet of Florence, wrote one of the world's greatest poems in the vernacular. It is called *The Divine Comedy.* As a young man, Dante was involved in politics, but when noble families began fighting over power, he had to leave Florence. That was when he wrote his long poem—more than 14,000 lines. *The Divine Comedy* tells the gripping tale of the main character's journey from hell to heaven.

Another important writer who used the vernacular was Chaucer. Chaucer wrote in English. In his famous book, *The Canterbury Tales,* he describes 29 pilgrims traveling to the city of **Canterbury** (KAN•tuhr•BEHR•ee). The book describes the levels of English society, from the nobles at the top to the poor at the bottom. The English Chaucer used in his writing is the ancestor of the English we speak today.

The Printing Press Spreads Ideas The printing press was a key to the spread of... early 1450s, **Johannes Gutenberg** (yoh•HAHN•uhs GOO•tuhn•BUHRG) developed a printing press that used movable metal type. This type of printing press made it possible to print many books much more quickly. With more books available, more people learned to read. Scholars could read one another's works and **debate** their ideas in letters. Ideas grew and spread more quickly than ever before in Europe.

The Chinese had already invented movable type, but it did not work well with their large alphabet of characters. For Europeans, the printing press was a big improvement. It was easy to use with linen paper, another Chinese invention.

Gutenberg's Bible, printed in the 1450s, was the first European book produced on the new press. Soon books flooded Europe.

HISTORY MAKERS

Read about history makers who changed history forever!

Scavenger Hunt

Discovering Our Past: Medieval and Early Modern Times contains a wealth of information. The trick is to know where to look to access all the information in the book.

If you run through this scavenger hunt exercise with your teacher or parents, you will see how the textbook is organized, and how to get the most out of your reading and study time. Let's get started!

1 What civilizations are discussed in Unit 2?

2 What is the topic of Chapter 10?

3 Who is the topic of the *Biography* on page 396?

4 What *Reading Skill* will you be learning about on pages 134–135?

5 What does the *Foldables*™ *Study Organizer* on page 483 ask you to do?

6 Two of the key terms in Chapter 5, Section 2, *vassal* and *feudalism*, are found on page 308. What makes it easy to find them?

7 There are several *History Online* boxes in Chapter 11. One box offers a preview of the chapter and others provide help with homework. What does the last box provide help with?

8 What standards are listed on page 3?

9 What is the topic of *The Way It Was* feature on page 142?

10 What is the first Big Idea introduced on page 381?

READING TO LEARN

This handbook focuses on skills and strategies that can help you understand the words you read. The strategies you use to understand whole texts depend on the kind of text you are reading. In other words, you do not read a textbook the way you read a novel. You read a textbook mainly for information; you read a novel for the story and the characters. To get the most out of your reading, you need to choose the right strategy to fit the reason you are reading. This handbook can help you learn about the following reading strategies:

- how to identify new words and build your vocabulary;
- how to adjust the way you read to fit your reason for reading;
- how to use specific reading strategies to better understand what you read;
- how to use critical thinking strategies to think more deeply about what you read; and
- how to understand text structures to identify an author's ideas.

TABLE OF CONTENTS

Identifying Words and Building Vocabulary

What do you do when you come across a word you do not know as you read? Do you skip over the word? If you are reading a novel, you use the context to understand the meaning of the word. But if you are reading for information, an unfamiliar word may get in the way of your understanding. When that happens, follow the strategies below to learn how to say the word and what it means.

Reading Unfamiliar Words

Sounding Out the Word One way to figure out how to say a new word is to sound it out, syllable by syllable. Look carefully at the word's beginning, middle, and ending. For example, in the word *coagulate,* what letters make up the beginning sound or beginning syllable of the word? *Co* rhymes with *so.* Inside *coagulate,* do you see a word you already know how to pronounce? The syllable *ag* has the same sound as the *ag* in *bag,* and the syllable *u* is pronounced like the letter *u.* What letters make up the ending sound or syllable? *Late* is a familiar word you already know how to pronounce. Now try pronouncing the whole word: **co ag u late.**

Determining a Word's Meaning

Using Syntax Like all languages, the English language has rules and patterns for the way words are arranged in sentences. The way a sentence is organized is called the syntax. If English is your first language, you have known this pattern since you started using sentences. If you are learning English now, you may find that the syntax is different from the patterns you know in your first language.

In a simple sentence in English, someone or something (the subject) does something (the predicate or verb) to or with another person or thing (the object): *The soldiers attacked the enemy.* Sometimes adjectives, adverbs, and phrases are added to add details to the sentence: *The courageous young soldiers fearlessly attacked the well-entrenched enemy shortly after dawn.*

Knowing about syntax can help you figure out the meaning of an unfamiliar word. Just look at how syntax can help you figure out the following nonsense sentence: *The blizzy kwarkles sminched the flerky fleans.* Your experience with English syntax tells you that the action word, or verb, in this sentence is *sminched.* Who did the *sminching?* The *kwarkles.* What kind of *kwarkles* were they? *Blizzy.* Whom did they *sminch?* The *fleans.* What kind of *fleans* were they? *Flerky.* Even though you don't know the meaning of the words in the nonsense sentence, you can make some sense of the entire sentence by studying its syntax.

Using Context Clues You can often figure out the meaning of an unfamiliar word by looking at its context, the words and sentences that surround it. To learn new words as you read, follow these steps for using context clues.

- Look before and after the unfamiliar word for a definition or a synonym, a general topic associated with the word, a clue to what the word is similar to or different from, or an action or a description that has something to do with the word.
- Connect what you already know with what the author has written.
- Predict a possible meaning.
- Use the meaning in the sentence.
- Try again if your guess does not make sense.

Using Types of Reference Materials

Dictionaries and other reference sources can help you learn new words and how to use them. Check out these reference sources. You can find these in your local public or school library as well as on the Internet.

- A **dictionary** gives the pronunciation, the meaning or multiple meanings, and often examples of how to use the words. Some dictionaries also provide illustrations or diagrams to help define words, other forms of words, their parts of speech, and synonyms. You might also find the historical background of a word, such as its Greek, Latin, or Anglo-Saxon origins.
- A **glossary** is a word list that appears at the end—or Appendix—of a book or other written work and includes only words that are in that work. Like dictionaries, glossaries include the pronunciation and definitions of words.
- A **thesaurus** lists groups of words that have the same, or almost the same, meaning. Words with similar meanings are called synonyms. Seeing the synonyms of words can help you build your vocabulary.

Recognizing Word Meanings Across Subjects

Have you ever learned a new word in one class and then noticed it in your reading for other subjects? The word probably will not mean exactly the same thing in each class. But you can use what you know about the word's meaning to help you understand what it means in a different subject area. Look at the following example from three different subjects:

- **Social studies:** One *product* manufactured in the southern part of the United States is cotton cloth.
- **Math:** After multiplying the numbers five and five, explain how you arrived at the *product*.
- **Science:** One *product* of photosynthesis is oxygen.

CHECKING YOUR UNDERSTANDING

The following sentence does not include real English words, but you can use what you have learned about English syntax to decode the sentence. First read the sentence. Then answer the questions that follow.

The shabs smatously graled the mul-bulowed rotfabs.

1. What is the verb in the sentence?
2. What is the subject?
3. What is the object?

Reading for a Reason

Why are you reading that paperback mystery? What do you hope to get from your history textbook? And are you going to read either of these books in the same way that you read a restaurant menu? The point is, you read for different reasons. The reason you are reading something helps you decide on the reading strategies you use with a text. In other words, how you read will depend on why you are reading.

Knowing Your Reason for Reading

In school and in life, you will have many reasons for reading, and those reasons will lead you to a wide range of materials:

- **To learn and understand new information,** you might read news magazines, textbooks, news on the Internet, books about your favorite pastime, encyclopedia articles, primary and secondary sources for a school report, instructions on how to use a calling card, or directions for a standardized test.
- **To find specific information,** you might look at the sports section for the score of last night's game, a notice on where to register for a field trip, weather reports, bank statements, or television listings.
- **To be entertained,** you might read your favorite magazine, e-mails or letters from friends, the Sunday comics, or even novels, short stories, plays, or poems!

Adjusting How Fast You Read

How quickly or how carefully you should read a text depends on your purpose for reading it. Because there are many reasons and ways to read, think about your purpose and choose the strategy that works best. Try out these strategies:

- **Scanning** means quickly running your eyes over the material, looking for key words or phrases that point to the information you are looking for. Scan when you need to find a particular piece or type of information. For example, you might scan a newspaper for movie show times.
- **Skimming** means quickly reading a piece of writing to find its main idea or to get a general overview of it. For example, you might skim the sports section of the daily newspaper to find out how your favorite teams are doing. Or you might skim a chapter in your textbook to prepare for a test.
- **Careful reading** involves reading very slowly and paying close attention with a purpose in mind. Read carefully when you are learning new concepts, following complicated directions, or preparing to explain information to someone else.

CHECKING YOUR UNDERSTANDING

If you were working on a research paper on the American Revolution, how would you adjust the speed at which you were reading for each of the following cases?

1. You have just found a 1,200-page work that covers the entire colonial and revolutionary era of the British colonies in North America.

2. You have discovered an article in a leading history magazine that supports every point that you are trying to make.

Understanding What You Read

Reading without understanding is like trying to drive a car on an empty gas tank. Fortunately, there are techniques you can use to help you concentrate on and understand what you read. Skilled readers adopt a number of strategies before, during, and after reading to make sure they understand what they read.

Preparing to Read

It is important to set the stage before you read. Following these steps will make the reading process more rewarding.

Previewing If you were making a preview for a movie, you would want to let your audience know what the movie is like. When you preview a piece of writing, you are trying to get an idea about the piece. Follow these steps to preview your reading assignments.

- Look at the title and any illustrations that are included.
- Read the headings, subheadings, and anything in bold letters.
- Skim the passage to see how it is organized.
- Set a purpose for your reading.

Using What You Know You already know quite a bit about what you are going to read. You bring knowledge and personal experience to a selection. Drawing on what you learned in a previous class is called *activating prior knowledge,* and it can help you create meaning in what you read. Ask yourself, *What do I already know about this topic?*

Predicting *Predicting* requires using background and prior knowledge, as well as the ability to make educated guesses. Make educated guesses before you read and while you read to figure out what might happen in the story or article you are reading.

Reading the Text

Following these suggestions while you read will help ensure that you get the most out of your reading.

Visualizing Creating pictures in your mind as you read—called *visualizing*—is a powerful aid to understanding. As you read, set up a movie theater in your imagination. Picture the setting—city streets, the desert, or the moon. If you can visualize, selections will be more vivid, and you will recall them better later on.

Identifying Sequence When you discover the logical order of events or ideas, you are identifying *sequence*. Do you need to understand step-by-step directions? Are you reading a persuasive speech with the reasons listed in order of importance? Look for clues and signal words that will help you find the way information is organized.

Determining the Main Idea When you look for the *main idea* of a selection, you look for the most important idea. The examples, reasons, and details that further explain the main idea are called *supporting details.* Some main ideas are clearly stated within a passage—often in the first sentence of a paragraph, or sometimes in the last sentence of a passage. Other times, however, an author does not directly state the main idea. Instead, he or she provides details that help readers figure out what the main idea is.

Questioning By learning how to analyze questions, you will quickly learn where to look for information as you read. Questions vary in many ways. One of the ways that questions vary is by how explicit or implied the question is compared with the text. These types of questions fall into four categories:

- **Right there** questions can be answered based on a line from the text.
- **Think and search** questions can be answered by looking in a few different places in the text.
- **Author and you** questions can be answered by thinking about the text but that also require your prior knowledge.
- **On your own** questions cannot be answered by the text and rely on the reader.

Clarifying Clear up, or clarify, confusing or difficult passages as you read. When you realize you do not understand something, try these techniques to help you clarify the ideas. *Reread* the confusing parts slowly and carefully. *Look up* unfamiliar words. Simply *talk out* the part to yourself.

Monitoring Your Comprehension As you read, check your understanding by using the following strategies.

- **Summarize** what you read by pausing from time to time and telling yourself the main ideas of what you have just read. Answer the questions *Who? What? Where? When? Why?* and *How?* Summarizing tests your comprehension by encouraging you to clarify key points in your own words.
- **Paraphrase** what you have just read to see whether you really got the point. Paraphrasing is retelling something in your own words. If you cannot explain it clearly, you should probably reread the text.

CHECKING YOUR UNDERSTANDING

1. How does visualizing help you understand what you read in your textbook or when you read for pleasure?

2. How can you determine the main idea of a selection if the author never explicitly explains what it is?

3. Why is clarifying an important skill for you to develop?

Thinking About Your Reading

Sometimes it is important to think more deeply about what you have read so you can get the most out of what the author says. These critical thinking skills will help you go beyond what the words say and get at the important messages of your reading.

Interpreting

When you listen to your best friend talk, you do not just hear the words he or she says. You also watch your friend, listen to the tone of voice, and use what you already know about that person to put meaning to the words. In doing so, you are interpreting what your friend says. Readers do the same thing when they interpret as they read. *Interpreting* is asking yourself *What is the writer really saying here?* and then using what you know about the world to help answer that question.

Inferring

You may not realize it, but you make inferences every day. Here is an example: You run to the bus stop a little later than usual. No one is there. "I have missed the bus," you say to yourself. You might be wrong, but that is the way our minds work. You look at the evidence (you are late; no one is there) and come to a conclusion (you have missed the bus).

When you read, you go through exactly the same process because writers do not always directly state what they want you to understand. They suggest certain information by providing clues and interesting details. Whenever you combine those clues with your own background and knowledge, you are making an inference.

Drawing Conclusions

Skillful readers are always *drawing conclusions,* or figuring out much more than an author says directly. The process is like a detective solving a mystery. You combine information and evidence that the author provides to come up with a statement about the topic. Drawing conclusions helps you find connections between ideas and events and gives you a better understanding of what you are reading.

Making Connections

One way that you can remember what you have read is by making connections with the text. Your teacher often expresses these connections aloud so that you and your classmates have a model. Your teacher may also ask you to make connections with the text and share them with the class. The most common connections include:

- **Text-to-self** connections, in which you remember something from your own life that serves as a connection with what is being read. *(While reading about the Civil War, you think about a fight you had with a relative.)*
- **Text-to-world** connections, in which you remember something that is happening or has happened in the world that serves as a connection with what is being read. *(While reading about the Civil War, you remember reading a newspaper article about the civil war in Somalia.)*
- **Text-to-text** connections, in which you remember something you have read elsewhere that serves as a connection with what is being read. *(While reading about the Civil War, you recall the novel* Red Badge of Courage.)*

Analyzing

Analyzing, or looking at separate parts of something to understand the entire piece, is a way to think critically about written work. In analyzing persuasive *nonfiction,* you might look at the writer's reasons to see if they actually support the main point of the argument. In analyzing *informational text,* you might look at how the ideas are organized to see what is most important.

Distinguishing Fact From Opinion

Distinguishing between fact and opinion is an important reading skill. A *fact* is a statement that can be proved. An *opinion,* on the other hand, is what a writer believes on the basis of his or her personal viewpoint. Writers can support their opinions with facts, but an opinion is something that cannot be proved.

Evaluating

When you form an opinion or make a judgment about something you are reading, you are *evaluating*. If you are reading informational texts or something on the Internet, it is important to evaluate how qualified the author is to be writing about the topic and how reliable the information is that is presented. Ask yourself whether the author seems biased, whether the information is one-sided, and whether the argument presented is logical.

Synthesizing

When you *synthesize,* you combine ideas (maybe even from different sources) to come up with something new. It may be a new understanding of an important idea or a new way of combining and presenting information. For example, you might read a manual on coaching soccer, combine that information with your own experiences playing soccer, and come up with a winning plan for coaching your sister's team this spring.

CHECKING YOUR UNDERSTANDING

1. How does making connections with what you have read help you remember more?

2. How do analyzing and synthesizing differ?

3. How do facts and opinions differ? Why is it important to differentiate between the two as you study history?

Understanding Text Structure

Good writers do not just put together sentences and paragraphs in any order. They structure each piece of their writing in a specific way for a specific purpose. That pattern of organization is called text structure. When you know the text structure of a selection, you will find it easier to locate and recall an author's ideas. Here are four ways that writers organize text.

Comparison and Contrast

Comparison-and-contrast structure shows the *similarities* and *differences* among people, things, and ideas. Maybe you have overheard someone at school say something like "He is better at throwing the football, but I can run faster than he can." This student is using comparison-and-contrast structure. When writers use comparison-and-contrast structure, they often want to show you how things that seem alike are different or how things that seem different are alike.

Signal words and phrases: *similarly, on the one hand, on the other hand, in contrast to, but, however*

Cause and Effect

Just about everything that happens in life is the cause or the effect of some other event or action. Sometimes what happens is pretty minor: You do not look when you are pouring milk *(cause)*; you spill milk on the table *(effect)*. Sometimes it is a little more serious: You do not look at your math book before the big test *(cause);* you mess up on the test *(effect).*

Writers use cause-and-effect structure to explore the reasons for something happening and to examine the results of previous events. This structure helps answer the question that everybody is always asking: *Why?* A historian might tell us why an empire rose and fell. Cause-and-effect structure is all about explaining why things are as they are.

Signal words and phrases: *so, because, as a result, therefore, for the following reasons*

Problem and Solution

How did scientists overcome the difficulty of getting a person to the moon? How will I brush my teeth when I have forgotten my toothpaste? These questions may be very different in importance, but they have one thing in common: Each identifies a problem and asks how to solve it. *Problems and solutions* are part of what makes life interesting. Problems and solutions also occur in fiction and nonfiction writing.

Signal words and phrases: *how, help, problem, obstruction, difficulty, need, attempt, have to, must*

Sequence

Take a look at three common forms of sequencing, the order in which thoughts are arranged.

- **Chronological order** refers to the order in which events take place. First, you wake up; next, you have breakfast; then, you go to school. Those events do not make much sense in any other order.
  Signal words: *first, next, then, later, finally*

- **Spatial order** tells you the order in which to look at objects. For example, consider this description of an ice-cream sundae: *At the bottom of the dish are two scoops of vanilla. The scoops are covered with fudge and topped with whipped cream and a cherry.* Your eyes follow the sundae from the bottom to the top. Spatial order is important in descriptive writing because it helps you as a reader to see an image the way the author does.
  Signal words: *above, below, behind, next to*

- **Order of importance** is going from most important to least important or the other way around. For example, a typical news article has a most important to least important structure.
  Signal words: *principal, central, important, fundamental*

CHECKING YOUR UNDERSTANDING

Read the following paragraph and answer the questions about the selection's text structure below.

The Huntington City Council recently approved an increase in the city sales tax. Recognizing the need to balance the city's budget, the council president Matt Smith noted that the council had no choice. The vote ended more than a year of preparing voters for the bad news. First, the council notified citizens that there would be a public discussion last April. Then, the council issued public statements that the vote would take place in November. Finally, the council approved the increase last week even though many residents opposed it. On one hand, the increase will increase revenues. On the other hand, more taxes could lead to fewer shoppers in the city's struggling retail stores.

1. How does the writer use comparison and contrast text structure?

2. How does the writer use problem and solution text structure?

3. What signal words show that the writer is setting the chronological order of events?

REFERENCE ATLAS

NATIONAL GEOGRAPHIC

ATLAS KEY

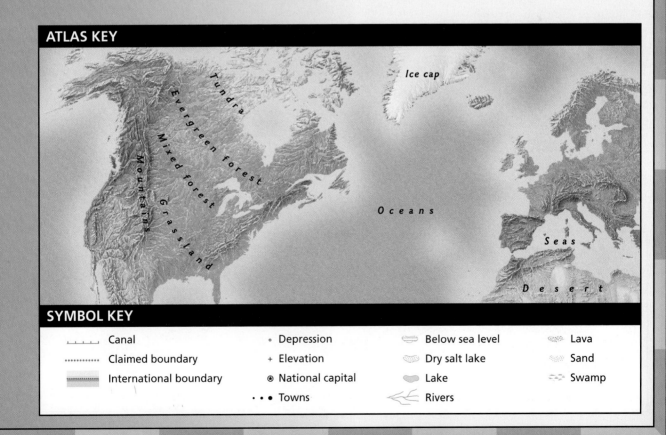

Ice cap

Tundra

Evergreen forest

Mixed forest

Mountains

Grassland

Oceans

Seas

Desert

SYMBOL KEY

⊥⊥⊥⊥ Canal	∘ Depression	Below sea level	Lava
············· Claimed boundary	+ Elevation	Dry salt lake	Sand
International boundary	⊛ National capital	Lake	Swamp
	• • Towns	Rivers	

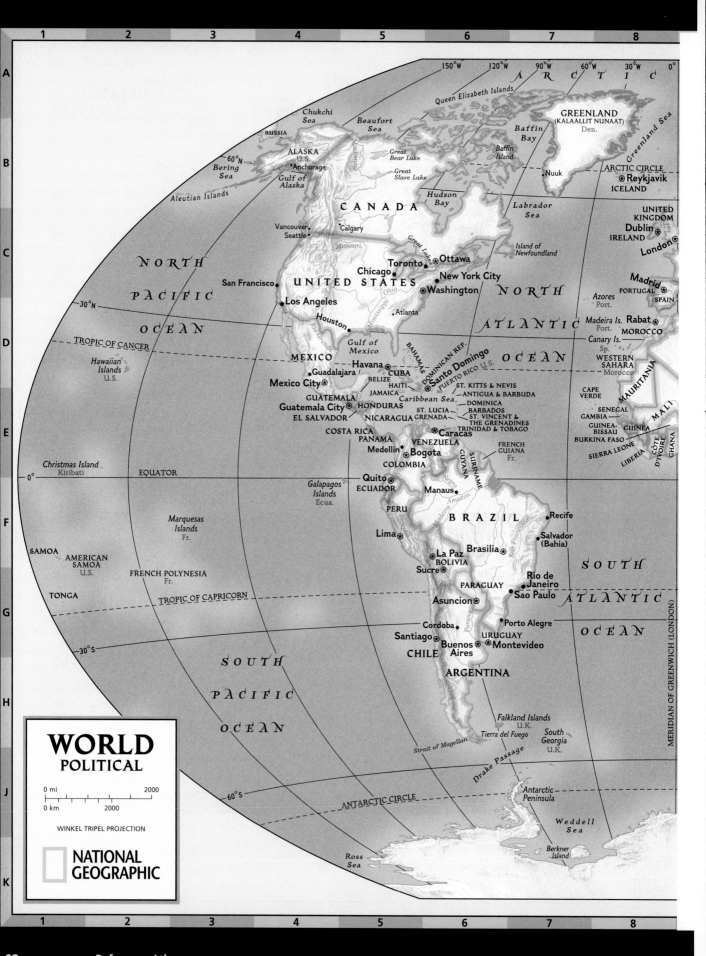

WORLD
POLITICAL

0 mi   2000

0 km   2000

WINKEL TRIPEL PROJECTION

NATIONAL GEOGRAPHIC

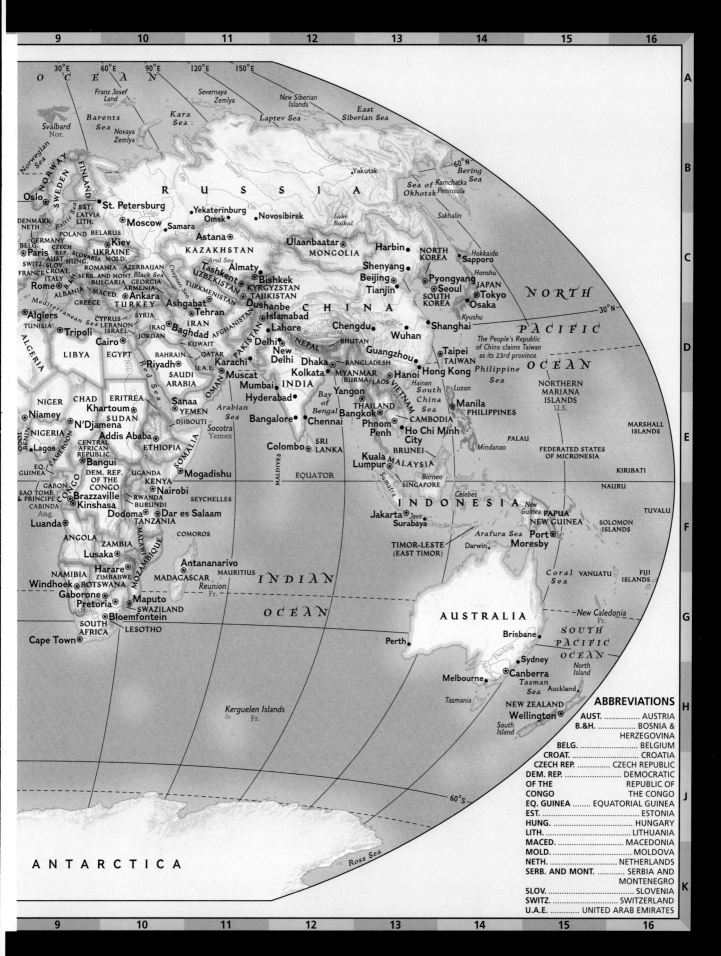

ABBREVIATIONS

AUST.	AUSTRIA
B.&H.	BOSNIA & HERZEGOVINA
BELG.	BELGIUM
CROAT.	CROATIA
CZECH REP.	CZECH REPUBLIC
DEM. REP. OF THE CONGO	DEMOCRATIC REPUBLIC OF THE CONGO
EQ. GUINEA	EQUATORIAL GUINEA
EST.	ESTONIA
HUNG.	HUNGARY
LITH.	LITHUANIA
MACED.	MACEDONIA
MOLD.	MOLDOVA
NETH.	NETHERLANDS
SERB. AND MONT.	SERBIA AND MONTENEGRO
SLOV.	SLOVENIA
SWITZ.	SWITZERLAND
U.A.E.	UNITED ARAB EMIRATES

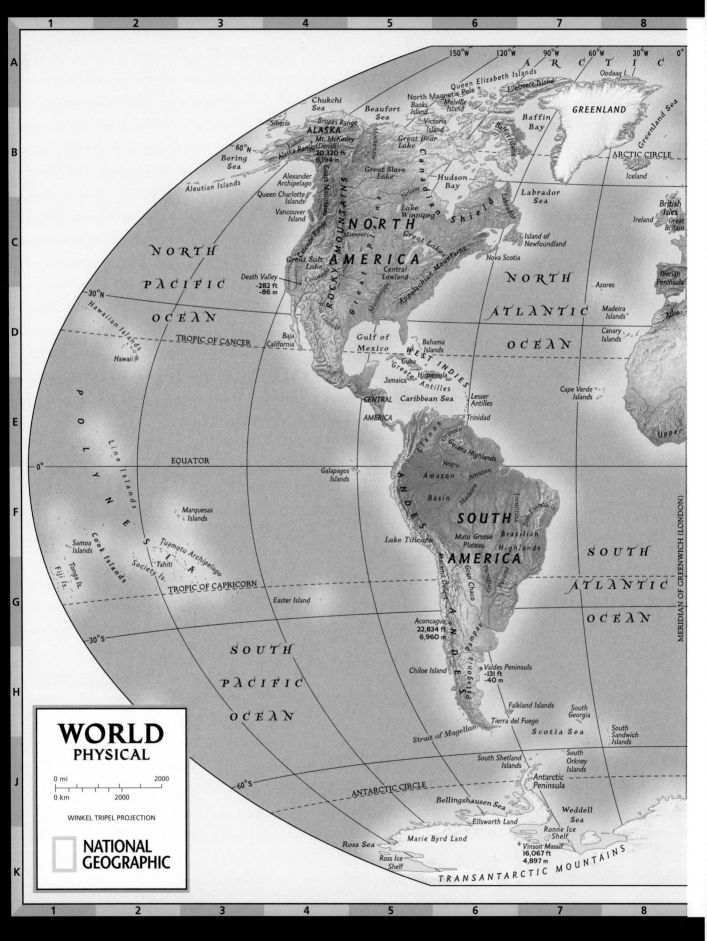

WORLD
PHYSICAL

0 mi   2000
0 km   2000

WINKEL TRIPEL PROJECTION

NATIONAL
GEOGRAPHIC

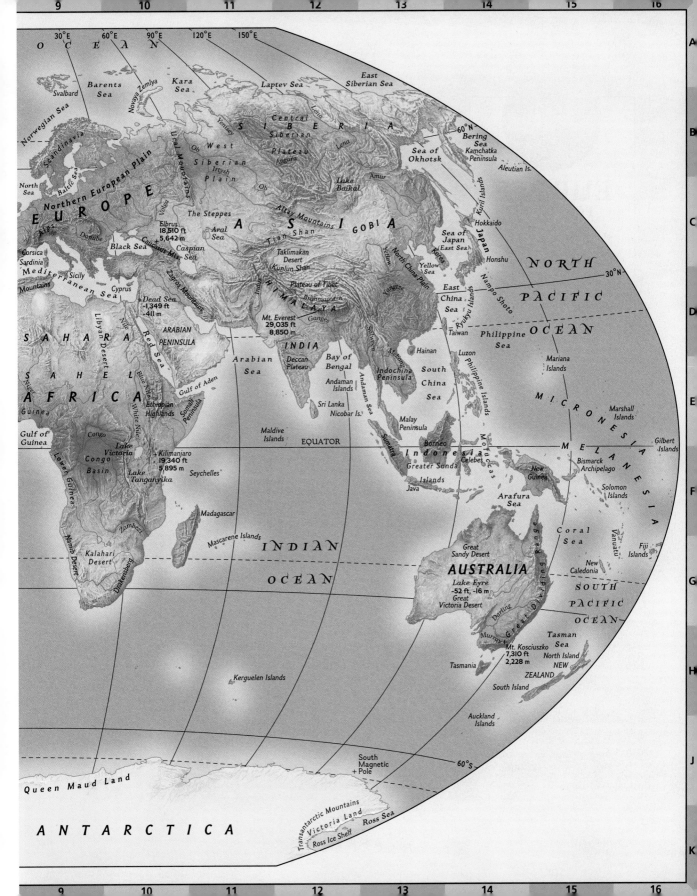

EUROPE
POLITICAL

0 mi ———— 400
0 km ———— 400

AZIMUTHAL EQUIDISTANT PROJECTION

NATIONAL GEOGRAPHIC

ATLANTIC
OCEAN

Akureyri
⊛ Reykjavik
ICELAND

ARCTIC CIRCLE

Norwegian Sea

Tromso

N O R W A Y

Trondheim
Are
Alesund
Sundsvall
Bergen

Faroe Islands
Den.
Torshavn

Shetland
Islands
Lerwick

Orkney Islands

Rockall
U.K.

Isle of Lewis

Inverness

UNITED •Aberdeen
SCOTLAND
Glasgow ⊛ Edinburgh
NORTHERN
IRELAND ⊛ Belfast
IRELAND Irish
Dublin⊛ Sea Liverpool
•Cork   •Manchester
KINGDOM
WALES •Birmingham
Cardiff• ENGLAND
London ⊛
Southampton•

Stavanger

Oslo ⊛

S W E D E N

Uppsala •
Stockholm ⊛
⊛ Goteborg
Gotland

Skagerrak
DENMARK
Copenhagen •
Arhus
• Malmo
• Kiel
• Hamburg

Gulf of

Baltic

Gdansk •

North
Sea

Celtic
Sea
Land's End

The
Hague•
Brussels ⊛
BELGIUM
LUX.

NETH.
•Amsterdam

GERMANY

Berlin ⊛

POLAND
Bydgoszcz

Lodz •

English Channel
Brest•
Le Havre•
Rennes•
•Paris

•Bonn
•Frankfurt
Rhine

Wroclaw ⊛
⊛ Prague
CZECH REP.

Oder

Nantes•

La Rochelle•
Bay of
Biscay
Bordeaux•

FRANCE
Strasbourg•

Limoges•

Lyon•

Munich•
Zurich•
Bern ⊛
SWITZERLAND
Geneva•
A L P S

LIECH.

Bratislava ⊛
Vienna ⊛
SLOVAKIA

AUSTRIA

SLOVENIA HUNGARY
Ljubljana ⊛
Milan•
Turin•
Venice•
Genoa•

Budapest ⊛

⊛ Zagreb
CROATIA

A Coruna•
Vigo•
Porto•
Coimbra•

Lisbon ⊛
Cape
St. Vincent

Cadiz•
GIBRALTAR
U.K.

Bilbao•
Valladolid•

Donostia-
San Sebastian•
Pyrenees

ANDORRA
• Zaragoza

Madrid ⊛

S P A I N

Valencia•

Cordoba•
Seville•
•Malaga

Murcia•
•Cartagena

Toulouse•

MONACO
•Nice
Marseille•

SAN
MARINO

Adriatic Sea

BOSNIA &
HERZEGOVINA
Sarajevo ⊛

Barcelona•

Palma•

Balearic
Islands
Sp.

Corsica
Fr.

Sardinia
It.

Cagliari•

ITALY

VATICAN
CITY ⊛Rome

Naples•

Tyrrhenian
Sea

Tirana ⊛
ALBANIA

Ionian
Sea

M e d i t e r r a n e a n

AFRICA

Strait of Gibraltar

Palermo•
Sicily
•Messina
•Catania

Valletta •
MALTA

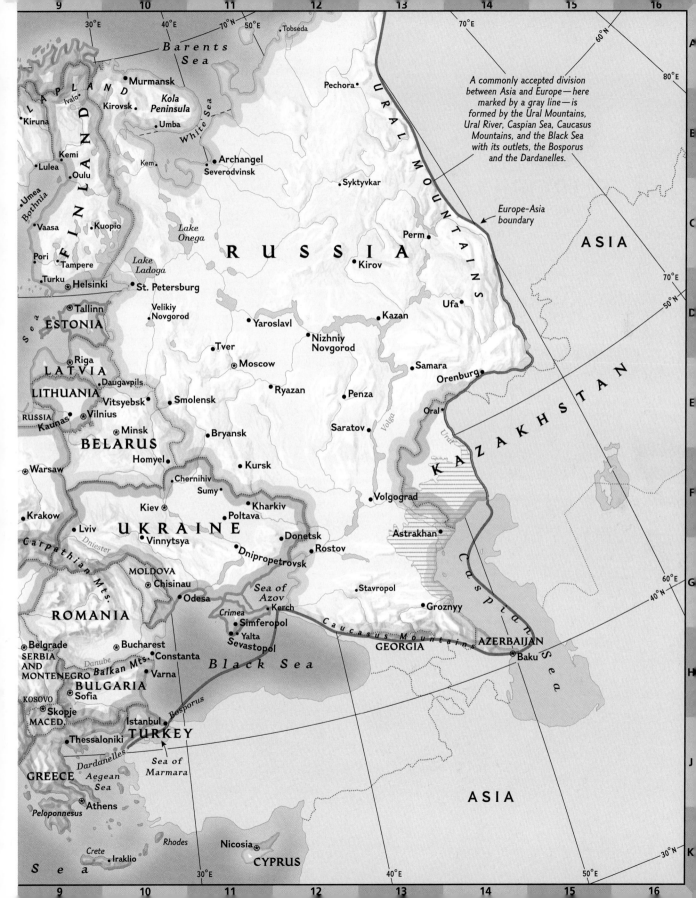

Barents Sea

30°E 40°E 70°N 50°E •Tobseda

•Murmansk
Kirovsk•
Kola Peninsula
Kiruna• Ivalo• Kirovsk•
Kemi• •Umba *White Sea* •Pechora
Lulea• Oulu•
•Archangel
•Severodvinsk

A commonly accepted division between Asia and Europe—here marked by a gray line—is formed by the Ural Mountains, Ural River, Caspian Sea, Caucasus Mountains, and the Black Sea with its outlets, the Bosporus and the Dardanelles.

80°N 60°N 70°E

•Syktyvkar

60°N

Umea• •Vaasa
Bothnia *Lake Onega*

R U S S I A

ASIA

Pori• *Lake Ladoga* •Perm Europe-Asia boundary
Tampere• •Kirov
Turku• •Helsinki •St. Petersburg
•Ufa

70°E

Sea ⊛Tallinn Velikiy• •Novgorod
E S T O N I A •Yaroslavl •Kazan
•Riga •Tver •Nizhniy Novgorod
L A T V I A ⊛Moscow •Samara
L I T H U A N I A •Smolensk •Ryazan •Orenburg
Vitsyebsk• •Penza •Oral
RUSSIA •Vilnius •Bryansk •Saratov
Kaunas ⊛Minsk •Kursk *Volga*
⊛Warsaw B E L A R U S Homyel•
•Chernihiv
Krakow• Sumy• •Kharkiv
•Lviv Kiev⊛ •Poltava •Volgograd
U K R A I N E •Donetsk
Vinnytsya• •Dnipropetrovsk •Rostov •Astrakhan
Dniester MOLDOVA ⊛Chisinau *Sea of Azov* •Stavropol
R O M A N I A •Odesa *Crimea* •Kerch •Groznyy
⊛Belgrade •Simferopol GEORGIA AZERBAIJAN
SERBIA AND *Danube* •Bucharest •Yalta *Caucasus Mountains* •Baku⊛
MONTENEGRO *Balkan Mts.* •Constanta •Sevastopol
KOSOVO B U L G A R I A •Varna *Black Sea*
⊛Skopje Sofia• *Bosporus*
MACED. Istanbul• T U R K E Y
•Thessaloniki *Dardanelles*
G R E E C E *Aegean Sea* *Sea of Marmara* A S I A
Peloponnesus •Athens
Crete *Rhodes* Nicosia⊛
Sea •Iraklio C Y P R U S

50°N 60°E
40°N
K A Z A K H S T A N
Caspian Sea
50°E
30°N
40°E

EUROPE
PHYSICAL

0 mi   400
0 km   400

AZIMUTHAL EQUIDISTANT PROJECTION

NATIONAL GEOGRAPHIC

60°N

40°W

30°W

30°W
50°N

20°W
40°N

ICELAND
Reykjavik

ARCTIC CIRCLE

Faroe Islands

Shetland Islands

Orkney Islands

Outer Hebrides

Highlands

British Isles

Edinburgh

Belfast
UNITED
IRELAND
Dublin
Irish Sea

Great Britain

KINGDOM

Cardiff

London

North Sea

Norwegian Sea

N

SCANDINAVIA

SWEDEN

NORWAY

Gulf of

Oslo

Stockholm

Jutland
DENMARK
Copenhagen
Zealand

Baltic

Amsterdam
NETH.

Berlin

N
O
R
POLAND

Oder

ATLANTIC OCEAN

English Channel

Seine

Paris

BELGIUM
Brussels
LUX.

GERMANY

Rhine

Elbe

Prague
CZECH REP.

Brittany

Loire

FRANCE

Danube

Bratislava
Vienna
SLOVAKIA

LIECH.

AUSTRIA

Budapest
HUNGARY

Bay of Biscay

Mont Blanc
15,771 ft
4,807 m

Bern
SWITZ.

A
L
P
S

SLOVENIA
Ljubljana
Zagreb
CROATIA

Drava

Danube

Sava

Massif Central

Rhone

MONACO

Riviera

Po

SAN MARINO

Adriatic Sea

BOSNIA &
Sarajevo
HERZEGOVINA

Cantabrian Mountains

Pyrenees

ANDORRA

Corsica

VATICAN CITY
ITALY
Rome

Apennines

PORTUGAL
Douro
IBERIAN
Madrid
Ebro
SPAIN
PENINSULA

Lisbon
Tagus

Tirana
ALBANIA

GIBRALTAR
Baetic Mountains
Strait of Gibraltar

Balearic Islands

Sardinia

Tyrrhenian Sea

Ionian Sea

M e d i t e r r a n e a n

AFRICA

30°N
10°W

0°

Sicily
Etna
10,902 ft
3,323 m

Valletta
MALTA

10°E

MERIDIAN OF GREENWICH (LONDON)

70°N

0°

10°E

20°W

10°W

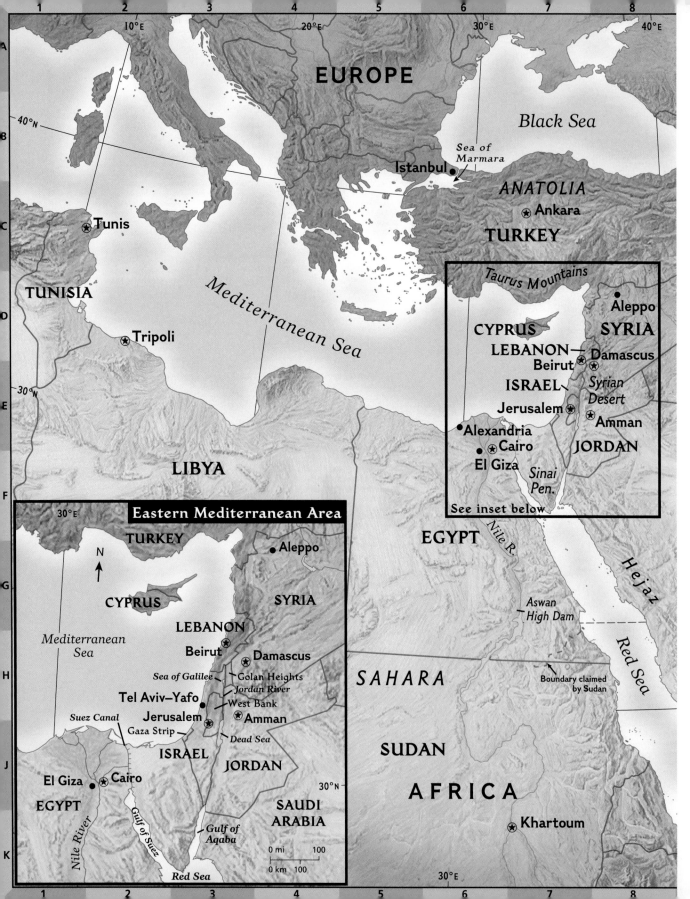

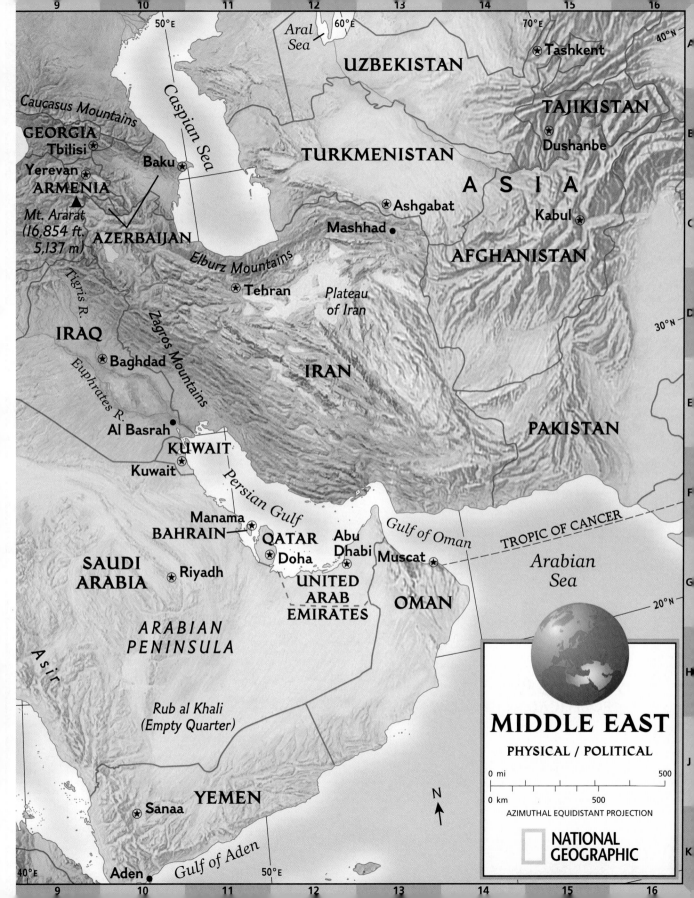

MIDDLE EAST

PHYSICAL / POLITICAL

0 mi · · · · · 500

0 km · · · · · 500

AZIMUTHAL EQUIDISTANT PROJECTION

NATIONAL GEOGRAPHIC

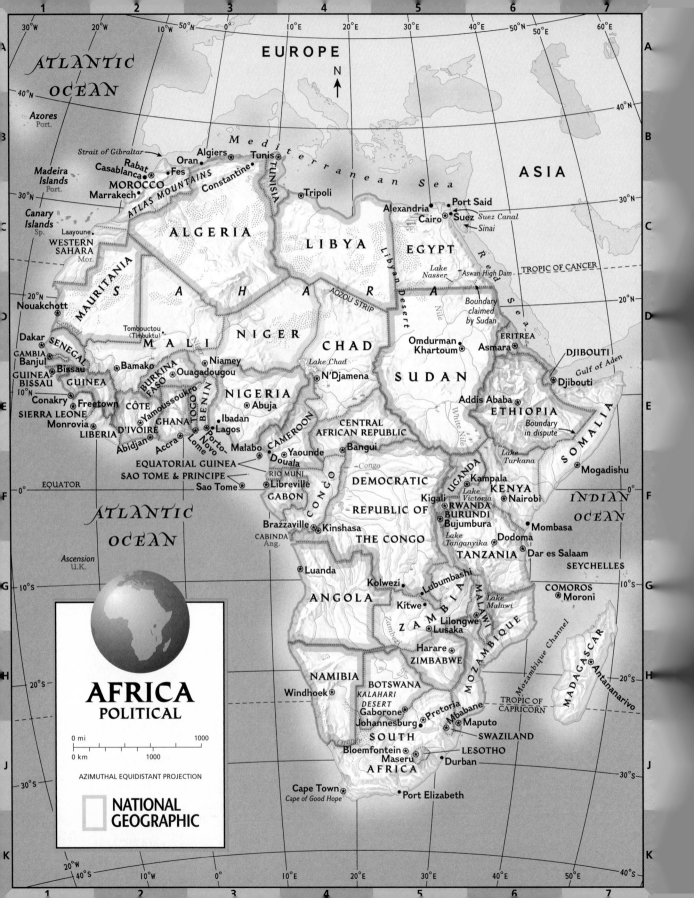

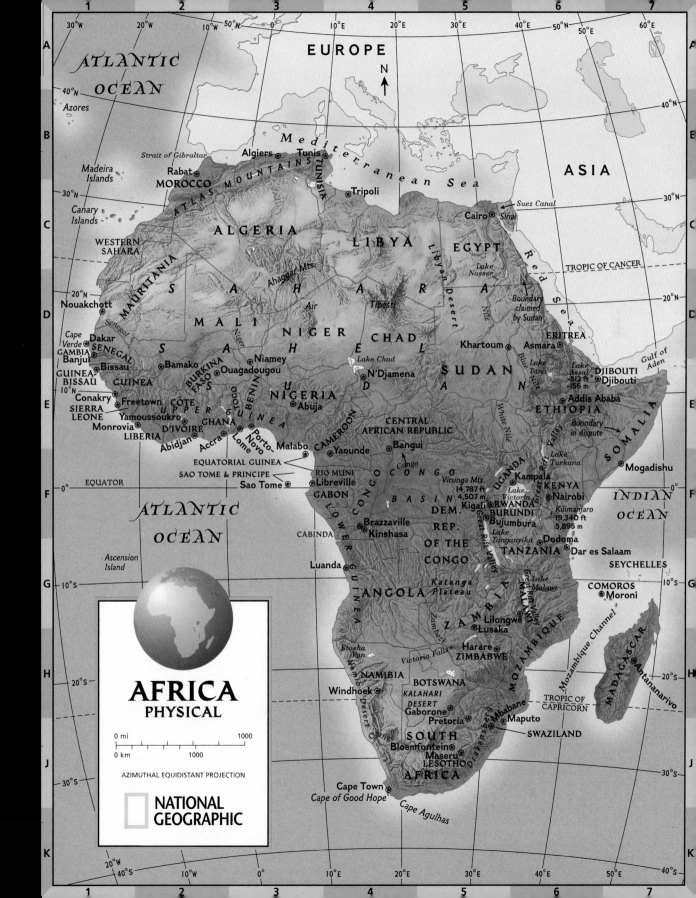

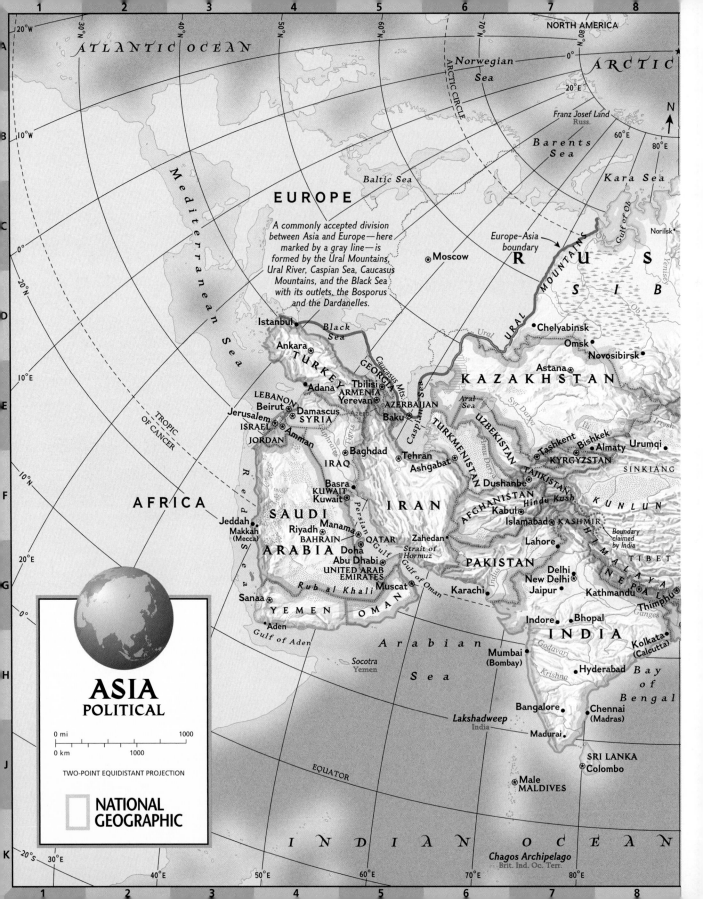

ASIA
POLITICAL

A commonly accepted division between Asia and Europe—here marked by a gray line—is formed by the Ural Mountains, Ural River, Caspian Sea, Caucasus Mountains, and the Black Sea with its outlets, the Bosporus and the Dardanelles.

Europe-Asia boundary

0 mi — 1000
0 km — 1000

TWO-POINT EQUIDISTANT PROJECTION

NATIONAL GEOGRAPHIC

ATLANTIC OCEAN

ARCTIC

Norwegian Sea

ARCTIC CIRCLE

Franz Josef Land
Russ.

Barents Sea

Kara Sea

Baltic Sea

EUROPE

⊕ Moscow

R U S S I B

Europe-Asia boundary

U R A L   M O U N T A I N S

Gulf of Ob

Ob

Norilsk •

Ob

Yenisey

Mediterranean Sea

Istanbul
Black Sea
Ankara ⊛
TURKEY
Adana •
GEORGIA
Tbilisi ⊛
ARMENIA
Yerevan ⊛
AZERBAIJAN
Azerb.
Baku ⊛
Caucasus Mts.
Caspian Sea

Chelyabinsk •
Ural
Omsk •
Novosibirsk •
Astana •
KAZAKHSTAN

Aral Sea
Syr Darya
UZBEKISTAN
Tashkent ⊛
Bishkek ⊛
Almaty •
Urumqi •
KYRGYZSTAN
SINKIANG

LEBANON
Beirut ⊛
Damascus ⊛
Jerusalem ⊛
ISRAEL
JORDAN
Amman ⊛
SYRIA
Euphrates
Tigris
Baghdad ⊛
IRAQ
Basra •
KUWAIT
Kuwait ⊛
SAUDI
Manama ⊛
BAHRAIN
Riyadh ⊛
QATAR
Doha ⊛
ARABIA
Abu Dhabi ⊛
UNITED ARAB
EMIRATES
Rub al Khali
Muscat ⊛
Sanaa ⊛
YEMEN
OMAN

TROPIC OF CANCER

Red Sea

AFRICA

Jeddah •
Makkah (Mecca)

Aden •
Gulf of Aden

Socotra
Yemen

Persian Gulf
Gulf of Oman
Strait of Hormuz

IRAN
Tehran ⊛
Ashgabat ⊛
TURKMENISTAN
Amu Darya
Zahedan •
Dushanbe ⊛
TAJIKISTAN
AFGHANISTAN
Kabul ⊛
Hindu Kush
KUNLUN
Islamabad ⊛
KASHMIR
Boundary claimed by India
Lahore •
TIBET
PAKISTAN
HIMALAYA
Delhi •
New Delhi ⊛
Jaipur •
Kathmandu ⊛
NEPAL
Thimphu ⊛
Karachi •
Indus
Indore •
Bhopal •
Ganges
INDIA
Godavari
Krishna
Mumbai (Bombay) •
Hyderabad •
Bangalore •
Chennai (Madras) •
Bay of Bengal
Madurai •
SRI LANKA
Colombo ⊛
Lakshadweep India
Male
MALDIVES

Arabian Sea

NORTH AMERICA

N

20°E
60°E
80°E

0°
20°N
10°N
0°
20°S

20°W
10°W
0°
10°E
20°E
30°E
40°E
50°E
60°E
70°E
80°E

30°N
40°N
50°N
60°N
70°N
80°N

EQUATOR

INDIAN OCEAN

Chagos Archipelago
Brit. Ind. Oc. Terr.

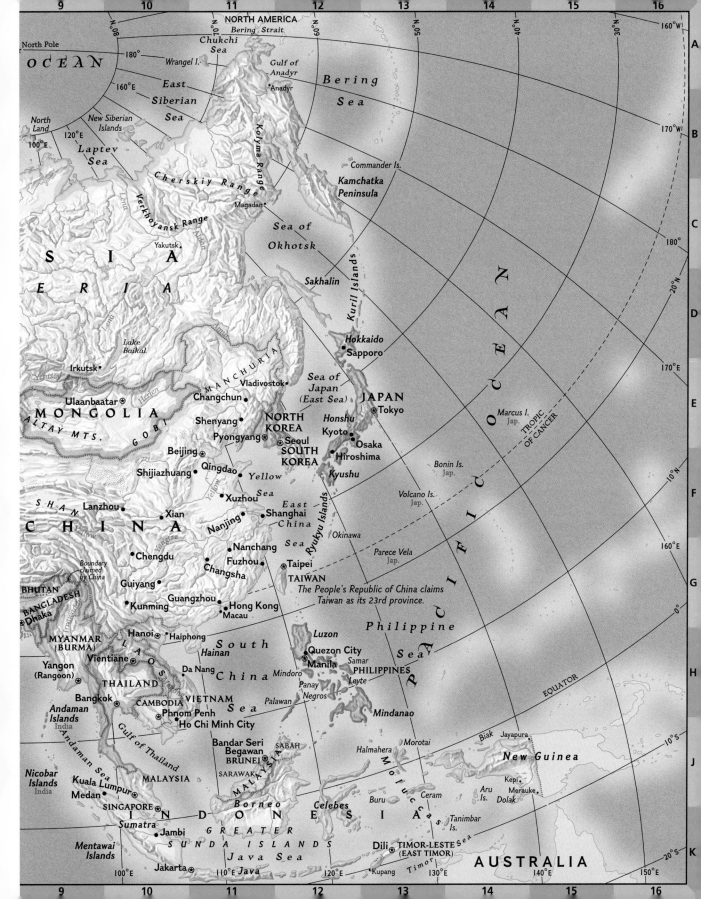

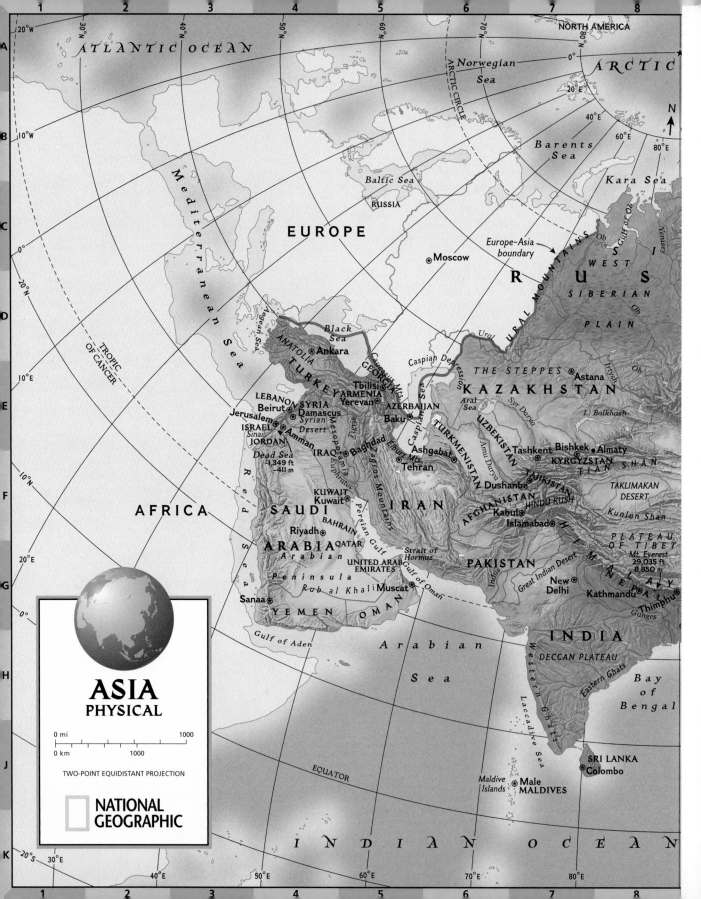

ATLANTIC OCEAN

NORTH AMERICA

ARCTIC

Norwegian
Sea

Barents
Sea

Kara Sea

Baltic Sea

RUSSIA

EUROPE

⊕ Moscow

Europe-Asia
boundary

R U S S I A

WEST
SIBERIAN
PLAIN

Gulf of Ob

Yenisey

Ob

Irtysh

Ob

Mediterranean Sea

Aegean Sea

Black
Sea

ANATOLIA

⊕ Ankara

TURKEY

GEORGIA

Tbilisi

ARMENIA

Yerevan

Caucasus Mts.

Caspian Depression

Ural

URAL MOUNTAINS

THE STEPPES

⊕ Astana

KAZAKHSTAN

Aral
Sea

L. Balkhash

Syr Darya

AZERBAIJAN

Baku

Caspian Sea

TURKMENISTAN

UZBEKISTAN

Tashkent

Bishkek ● Almaty

KYRGYZSTAN

TIAN SHAN

Ashgabat ⊕

Amu Darya

Dushanbe

TAJIKISTAN

TAKLIMAKAN
DESERT

LEBANON

Beirut

SYRIA

Damascus

Jerusalem

ISRAEL

Amman

JORDAN

Dead Sea
-1,349 ft
-411 m

Syrian
Desert

Mesopotamia

Euphrates

Tigris

IRAQ

Baghdad

Zagros Mountains

Elburz Mts.

Tehran

⊕

Kunlun Shan

IRAN

AFGHANISTAN

HINDU KUSH

Kabul⊕

Islamabad⊕

PLATEAU
OF TIBET

Mt. Everest
29,035 ft
8,850 m

KUWAIT

Kuwait

BAHRAIN

Persian Gulf

SAUDI

Riyadh ⊕

QATAR

ARABIA

Arabian

UNITED ARAB
EMIRATES

Strait of
Hormuz

Gulf of Oman

PAKISTAN

Indus

Great Indian Desert

HIMALAYA

New ⊕
Delhi

NEPAL

Kathmandu ⊕

Thimphu ⊕

BHUTAN

Red Sea

AFRICA

Peninsula

Rub al Khali

Muscat

OMAN

Gulf of Oman

Sanaa ⊕

YEMEN

Gulf of Aden

Arabian

Sea

INDIA

DECCAN PLATEAU

Western Ghats

Eastern Ghats

Bay
of
Bengal

Ganges

ARCTIC CIRCLE

TROPIC
OF CANCER

ASIA
PHYSICAL

0 mi   1000

0 km   1000

TWO-POINT EQUIDISTANT PROJECTION

NATIONAL
GEOGRAPHIC

Laccadive
Sea

SRI LANKA

⊕ Colombo

Maldive
Islands

● Male

MALDIVES

EQUATOR

INDIAN OCEAN

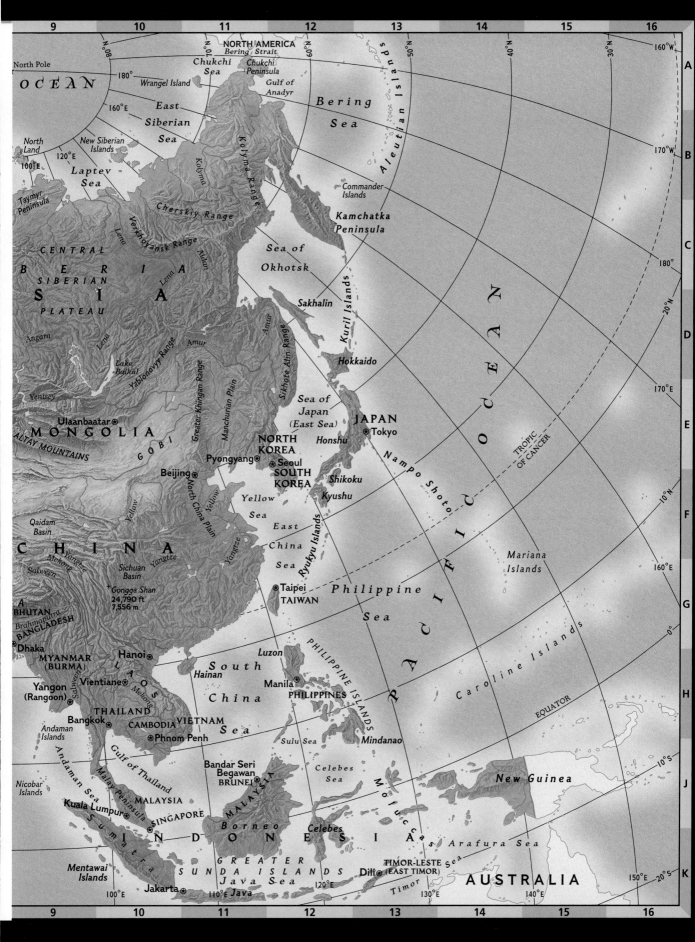

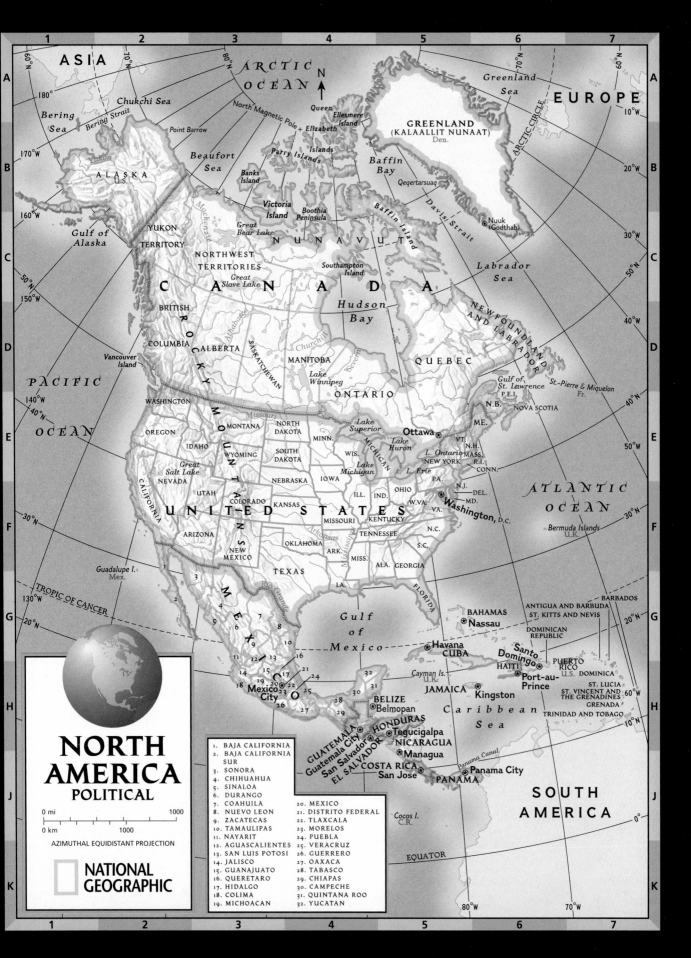

NORTH AMERICA
POLITICAL

0 mi · · · · · 1000
0 km · · · · · 1000

AZIMUTHAL EQUIDISTANT PROJECTION

NATIONAL GEOGRAPHIC

1. BAJA CALIFORNIA
2. BAJA CALIFORNIA SUR
3. SONORA
4. CHIHUAHUA
5. SINALOA
6. DURANGO
7. COAHUILA
8. NUEVO LEON
9. ZACATECAS
10. TAMAULIPAS
11. NAYARIT
12. AGUASCALIENTES
13. SAN LUIS POTOSI
14. JALISCO
15. GUANAJUATO
16. QUERETARO
17. HIDALGO
18. COLIMA
19. MICHOACAN
20. MEXICO
21. DISTRITO FEDERAL
22. TLAXCALA
23. MORELOS
24. PUEBLA
25. VERACRUZ
26. GUERRERO
27. OAXACA
28. TABASCO
29. CHIAPAS
30. CAMPECHE
31. QUINTANA ROO
32. YUCATAN

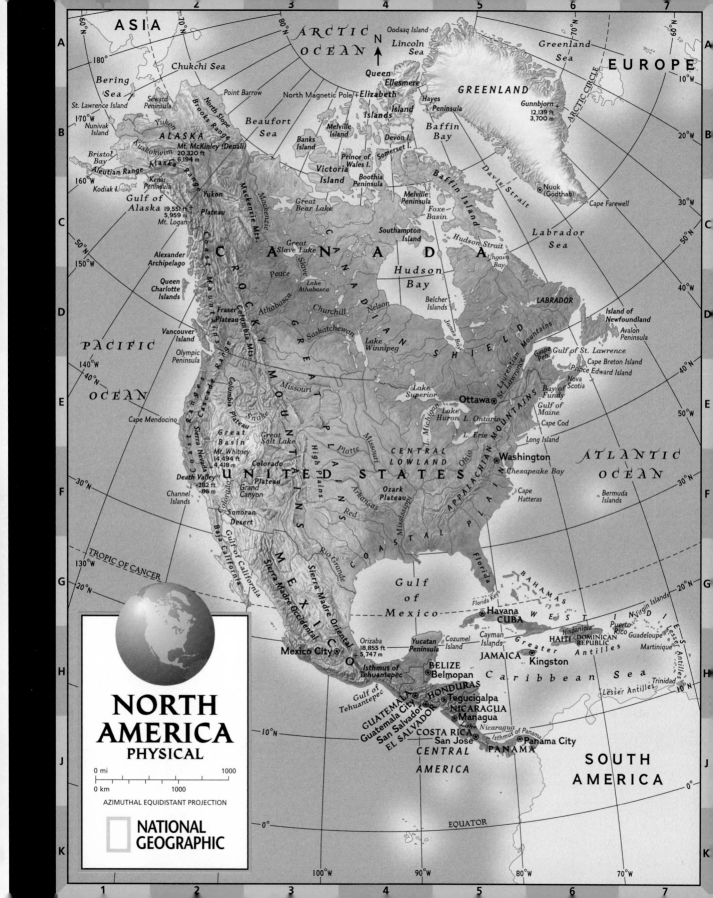

NORTH AMERICA
PHYSICAL

0 mi   1000

0 km   1000

AZIMUTHAL EQUIDISTANT PROJECTION

NATIONAL GEOGRAPHIC

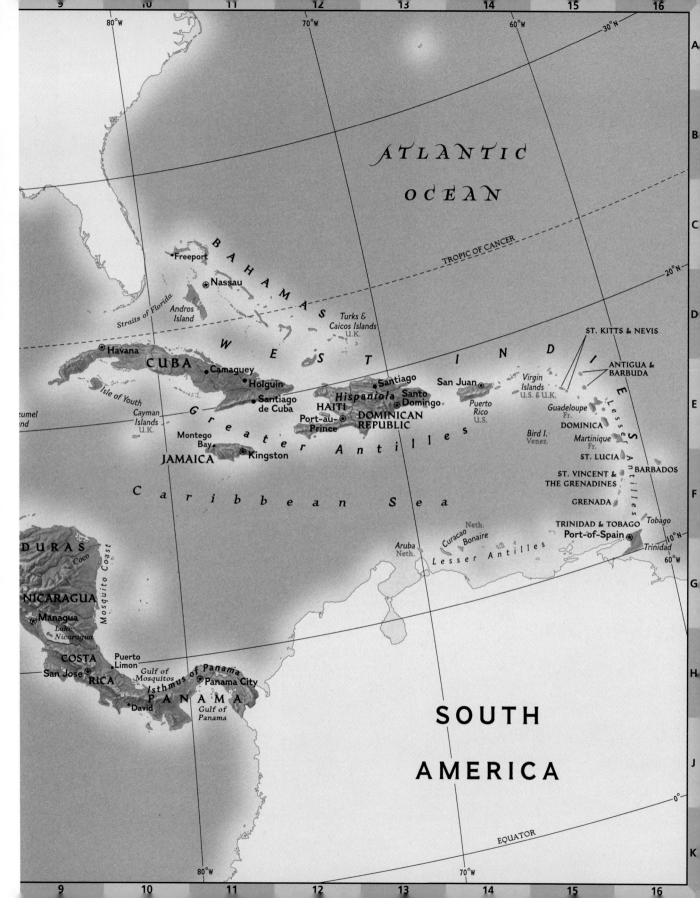

ATLANTIC

OCEAN

TROPIC OF CANCER

20°N

BAHAMAS

•Freeport

⊛Nassau

Straits of Florida

Andros
Island

Turks &
Caicos Islands
U.K.

ST. KITTS & NEVIS

W   E   S   T

I   N   D   I   E   S

ANTIGUA &
BARBUDA

⊛Havana

CUBA

•Camaguey

•Holguin

•Santiago

San Juan ⊛

Virgin
Islands
U.S. & U.K.

Isle of Youth

•Santiago
de Cuba

HAITI

Santo
Domingo

Puerto
Rico
U.S.

Guadeloupe
Fr.

zumel
and

Cayman
Islands
U.K.

G   r   e   a   t   e   r

Hispaniola

Port-au-⊛
Prince

DOMINICAN
REPUBLIC

DOMINICA

Bird I.
Venez.

Martinique
Fr.

Montego
Bay

•

A   n   t   i   l   l   e   s

ST. LUCIA

JAMAICA

⊛Kingston

BARBADOS

ST. VINCENT &
THE GRENADINES

C   a   r   i   b   b   e   a   n   S   e   a

GRENADA

Neth.

Curacao
Bonaire

TRINIDAD & TOBAGO
Port-of-Spain ⊛

Tobago

10°N

Aruba
Neth.

Lesser Antilles

Trinidad

60°W

DURAS

Coco

Mosquito Coast

NICARAGUA

⊛Managua

Lake
Nicaragua

COSTA

Puerto
Limon

Gulf of
Mosquitos

Isthmus of Panama

Panama City ⊛

SOUTH

San Jose ⊛

RICA

PANAMA

•David

Gulf of
Panama

AMERICA

EQUATOR

0°

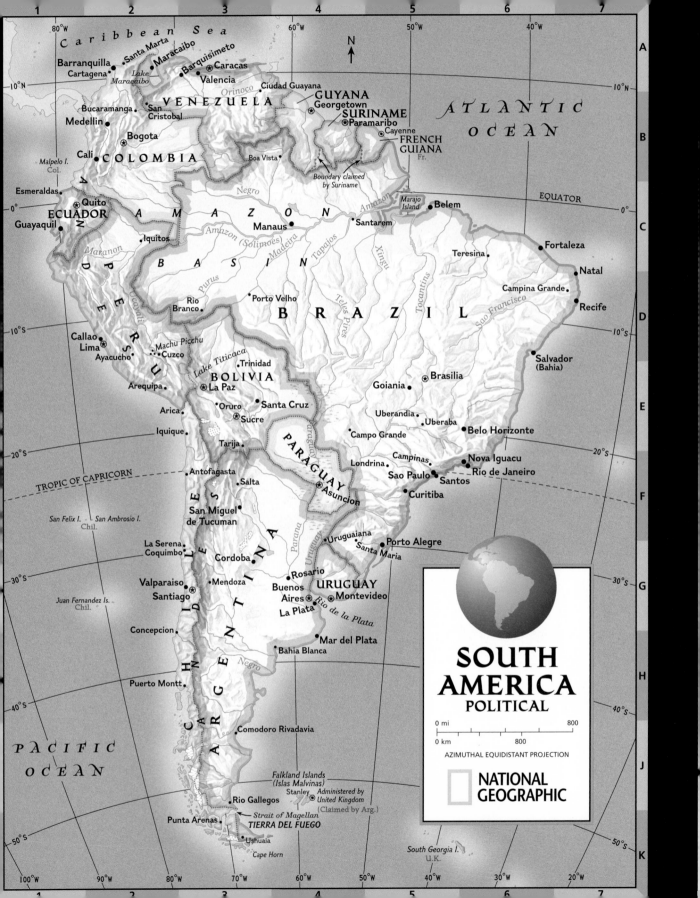

SOUTH AMERICA POLITICAL

0 mi 800
0 km 800

AZIMUTHAL EQUIDISTANT PROJECTION

NATIONAL GEOGRAPHIC

Map labels:

Caribbean Sea

A T L A N T I C O C E A N

1 2 3 4 5 6 7

80°W 70°W 60°W 50°W 40°W

N

10°N

Lake Maracaibo

⊛ Caracas

Orinoco

VENEZUELA

GUYANA
⊛ Georgetown
SURINAME
⊛ Paramaribo
Cayenne
FRENCH GUIANA

⊛ Bogota
COLOMBIA

GUIANA HIGHLANDS

Angel Falls
Total drop=
3,212 ft 979 m

Boundary claimed
by Suriname

Negro

Amazon

Marajo
Island

EQUATOR 0°

⊛ Quito
ECUADOR

A M A Z O N

Amazon

Ucayali *Purus* *Madeira* *Tapajos* *Xingu*

S e l v a s

B A S I N

B R A Z I L

Teles Pires

Tocantins

São Francisco

10°S

Lima ⊛

Machu Picchu

Lake Titicaca

BOLIVIA
⊛ La Paz

MATO GROSSO

PLATEAU

B R A Z I L I A N

⊛ Brasilia

H I G H L A N D S

Altiplano

⊛ Sucre

Salar
de Uyuni

20°S

P A R A G U A Y

Paraguay

GRAN CHACO

⊛ Asuncion

Iguazu
Falls

TROPIC OF CAPRICORN

San Felix I. San Ambrosio I.

30°S

Parana *Uruguay*

A R G E N T I N A

P A M P A S

Aconcagua 22,834 ft
6,960 m

Santiago ⊛

Buenos
Aires ⊛

URUGUAY
⊛ Montevideo

Rio de la Plata

Juan Fernandez Is.

Negro

40°S

Chiloe Island

-131 ft
-40 m Valdes Peninsula

P A C I F I C

O C E A N

Taitao
Peninsula

Gulf of
San Jorge

Wellington I.

Falkland Islands
(Islas Malvinas)
Stanley

Strait of Magellan
Tierra del Fuego

Cape Horn

South Georgia I.

50°S

P A T A G O N I A

A N D E S

P E R U

1 2 3 4 5 6 7

100°W 90°W 80°W 70°W 60°W 50°W 40°W 30°W 20°W

A B C D E F G H J K

**SOUTH
AMERICA**
PHYSICAL

0 mi ———— 800
0 km ———— 800

AZIMUTHAL EQUIDISTANT PROJECTION

**NATIONAL
GEOGRAPHIC**

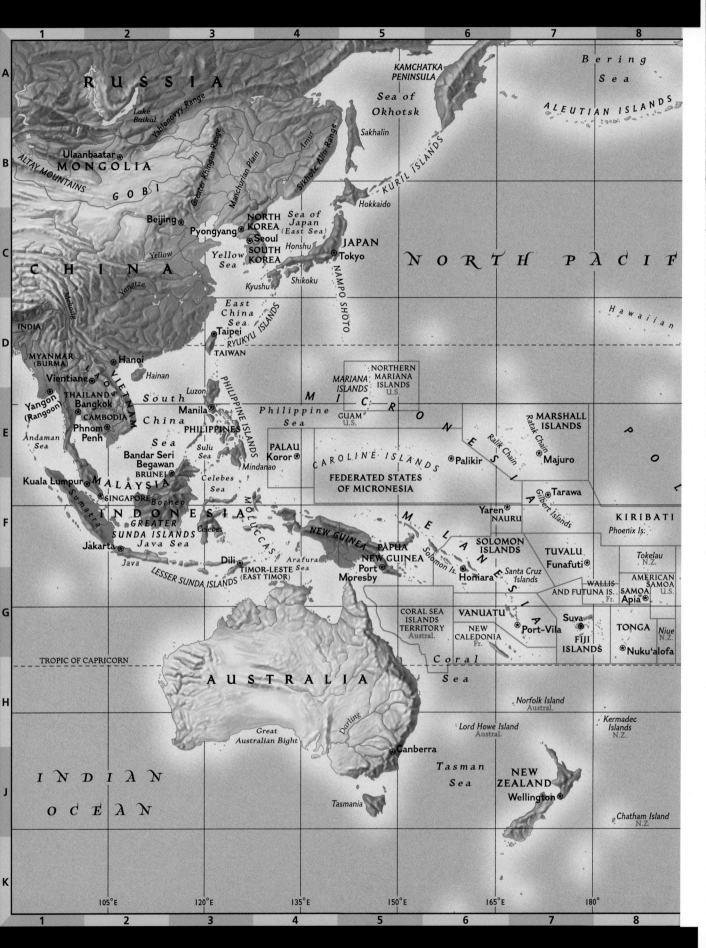

Reference Atlas

PACIFIC
RIM
PHYSICAL/POLITICAL

0 mi   1500
0 km   1500

MILLER CYLINDRICAL PROJECTION

NATIONAL
GEOGRAPHIC

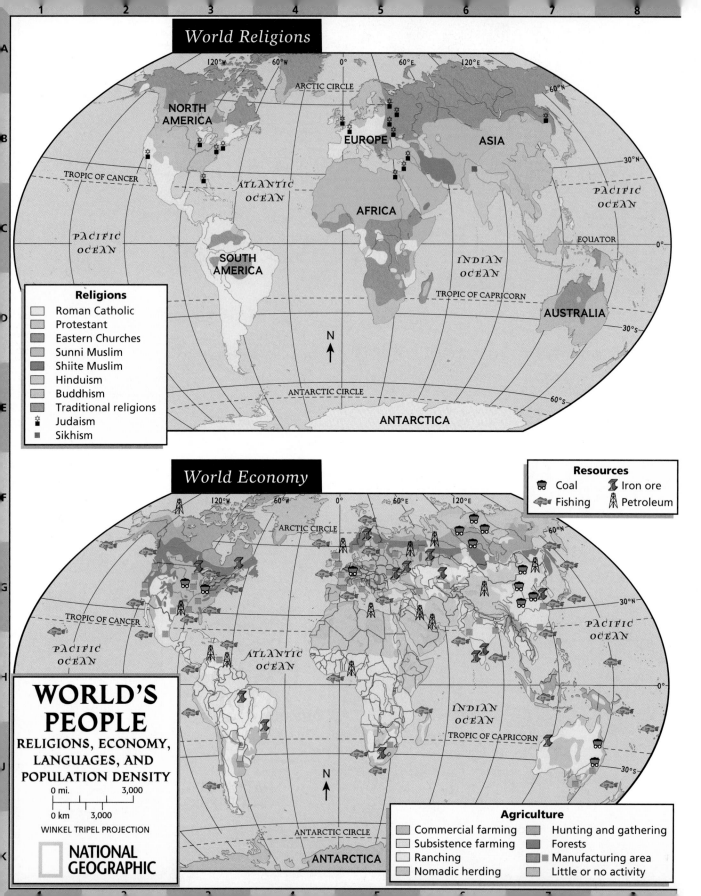

World Religions

Religions
- ☐ Roman Catholic
- ☐ Protestant
- ☐ Eastern Churches
- ☐ Sunni Muslim
- ☐ Shiite Muslim
- ☐ Hinduism
- ☐ Buddhism
- ☐ Traditional religions
- ✡ Judaism
- ■ Sikhism

NORTH AMERICA

SOUTH AMERICA

EUROPE

ASIA

AFRICA

AUSTRALIA

ANTARCTICA

ATLANTIC OCEAN

PACIFIC OCEAN

PACIFIC OCEAN

INDIAN OCEAN

ARCTIC CIRCLE
TROPIC OF CANCER
EQUATOR
TROPIC OF CAPRICORN
ANTARCTIC CIRCLE

120°W   60°W   0°   60°E   120°E
60°N   30°N   0°   30°S   60°S

N

World Economy

Resources
- Coal
- Fishing
- Iron ore
- Petroleum

WORLD'S PEOPLE
RELIGIONS, ECONOMY, LANGUAGES, AND POPULATION DENSITY

0 mi. ———— 3,000
0 km ———— 3,000
WINKEL TRIPEL PROJECTION

NATIONAL GEOGRAPHIC

ATLANTIC OCEAN

PACIFIC OCEAN

PACIFIC OCEAN

INDIAN OCEAN

ANTARCTICA

ARCTIC CIRCLE
TROPIC OF CANCER
TROPIC OF CAPRICORN
ANTARCTIC CIRCLE

120°W   60°W   0°   60°E   120°E
60°N   30°N   0°   30°S

N

Agriculture
- ☐ Commercial farming
- ☐ Subsistence farming
- ☐ Ranching
- ☐ Nomadic herding
- ☐ Hunting and gathering
- ☐ Forests
- ■ Manufacturing area
- ☐ Little or no activity

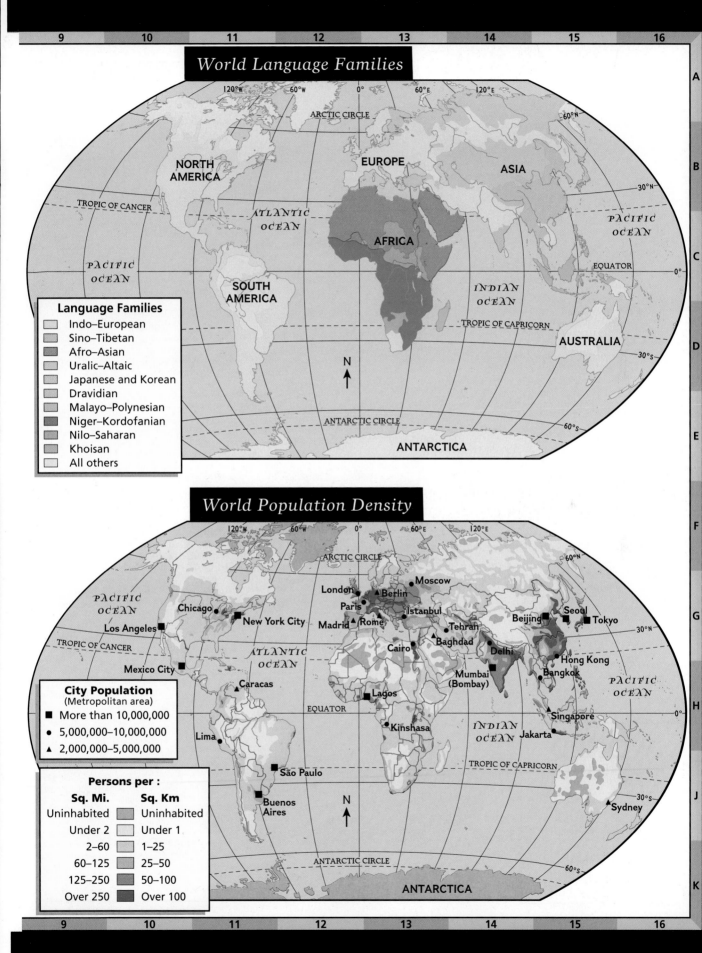

World Language Families

Language Families
- Indo–European
- Sino–Tibetan
- Afro–Asian
- Uralic–Altaic
- Japanese and Korean
- Dravidian
- Malayo–Polynesian
- Niger–Kordofanian
- Nilo–Saharan
- Khoisan
- All others

World Population Density

City Population
(Metropolitan area)
- ■ More than 10,000,000
- ● 5,000,000–10,000,000
- ▲ 2,000,000–5,000,000

Persons per :	
Sq. Mi.	**Sq. Km**
Uninhabited	Uninhabited
Under 2	Under 1
2–60	1–25
60–125	25–50
125–250	50–100
Over 250	Over 100

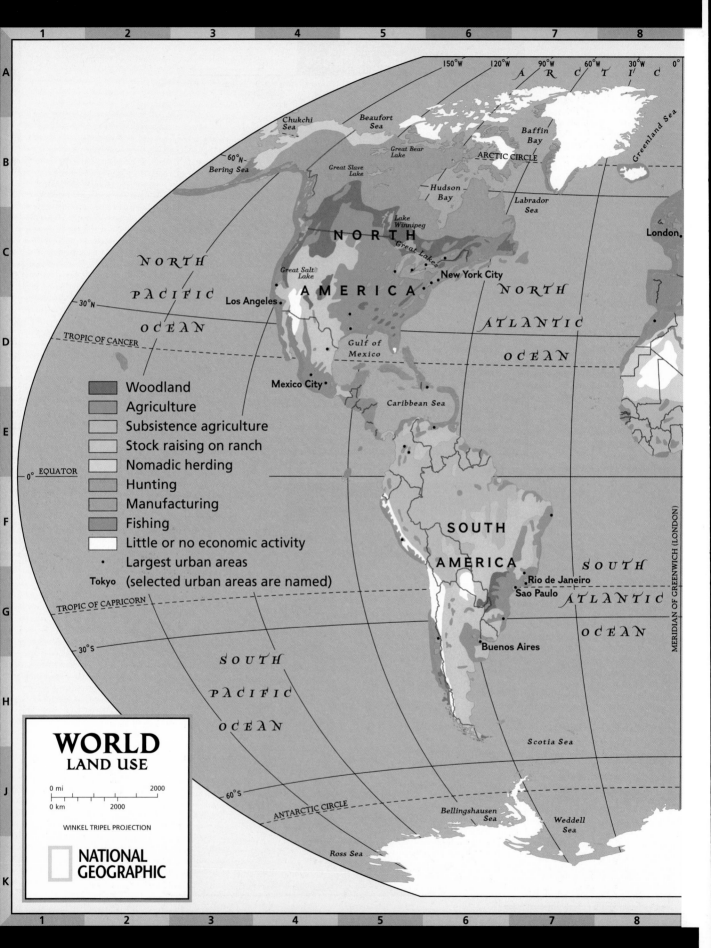

150°W   120°W   90°W   60°W   30°W   0°

A R C T I C

Chukchi
Sea

Beaufort
Sea

Baffin
Bay

Greenland Sea

60°N
Bering Sea

Great Bear
Lake

ARCTIC CIRCLE

Great Slave
Lake

Hudson
Bay

Labrador
Sea

Lake
Winnipeg

N O R T H

London

Great Lakes

N O R T H

C

Great Salt
Lake

A M E R I C A

New York City

N O R T H

30°N

PACIFIC

Los Angeles

A T L A N T I C

TROPIC OF CANCER

OCEAN

OCEAN

Gulf of
Mexico

Mexico City

Caribbean Sea

Woodland

Agriculture

Subsistence agriculture

Stock raising on ranch

Nomadic herding

0° EQUATOR

Hunting

Manufacturing

Fishing

S O U T H

Little or no economic activity

A M E R I C A

S O U T H

• **Largest urban areas**

Rio de Janeiro

Tokyo **(selected urban areas are named)**

Sao Paulo

A T L A N T I C

TROPIC OF CAPRICORN

G

OCEAN

30°S

Buenos Aires

S O U T H

PACIFIC

MERIDIAN OF GREENWICH (LONDON)

H

OCEAN

J

60°S

ANTARCTIC CIRCLE

Bellingshausen
Sea

Weddell
Sea

Scotia Sea

Ross Sea

K

WORLD
LAND USE

0 mi   2000

0 km   2000

WINKEL TRIPEL PROJECTION

**NATIONAL
GEOGRAPHIC**

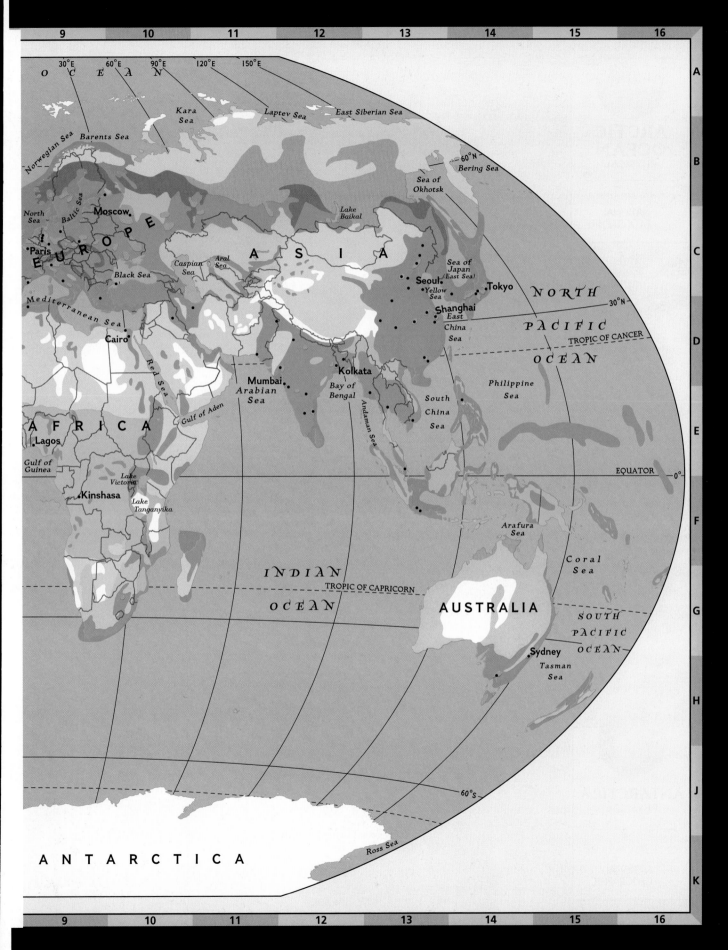

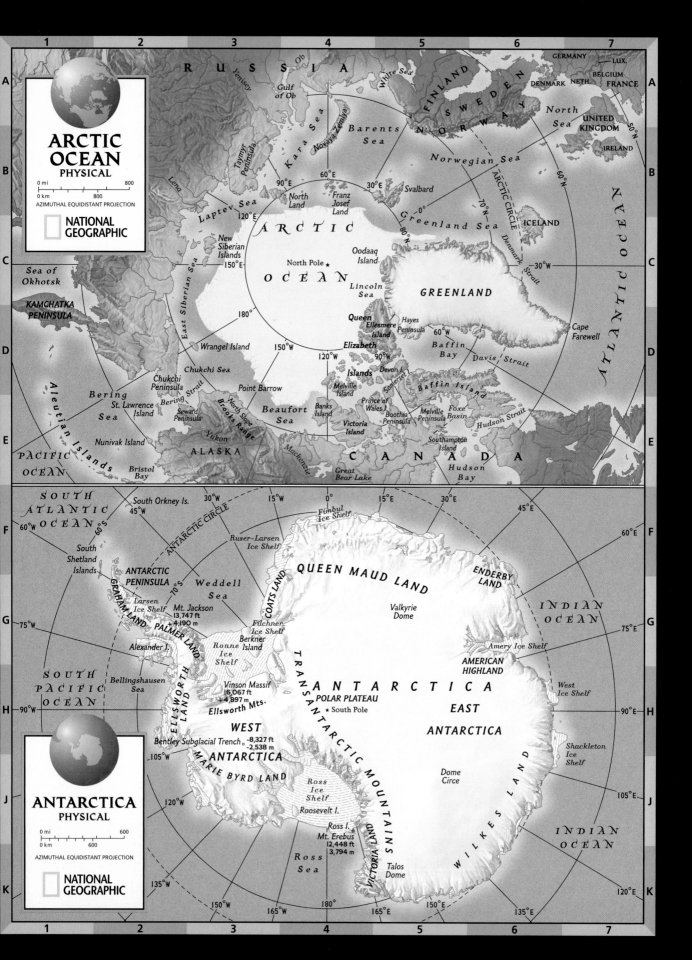

ARCTIC OCEAN PHYSICAL

0 mi 800
0 km 800
AZIMUTHAL EQUIDISTANT PROJECTION

NATIONAL GEOGRAPHIC

GERMANY
LUX.
BELGIUM
FRANCE
DENMARK NETH.
UNITED KINGDOM
IRELAND
ICELAND
ATLANTIC OCEAN

RUSSIA
Ob
Gulf of Ob
Yenisey
White Sea
FINLAND
SWEDEN
NORWAY
North Sea
Norwegian Sea
ARCTIC CIRCLE
Taymyr Peninsula
Kara Sea
Novaya Zemlya
Barents Sea
Svalbard
Greenland Sea
Denmark Strait
Lena
90°E
60°E
30°E
0°
70°N
60°N
Laptev Sea
120°E
North Land
Franz Josef Land
ARCTIC
New Siberian Islands
150°E
OCEAN
North Pole ★
Oodaaq Island
GREENLAND
Cape Farewell
East Siberian Sea
180°
Lincoln Sea
Queen
Baffin Bay
Davis Strait
Sea of Okhotsk
Wrangel Island
150°W
120°W
Elizabeth
Ellesmere Island
Hayes Peninsula
60°W
KAMCHATKA PENINSULA
Chukchi Sea
Islands
Devon I.
90°W
Baffin Island
Chukchi Peninsula
Point Barrow
Melville Island
Somerset I.
Foxe Basin
Bering St. Lawrence Island
Bering Strait
North Slope Brooks Range
Beaufort Sea
Banks Island
Prince of Wales I.
Boothia Peninsula
Melville Peninsula
Hudson Strait
Aleutian Islands
Seward Peninsula
Victoria Island
Southampton Island
PACIFIC OCEAN
Nunivak Island
Yukon
ALASKA
Mackenzie
CANADA
Hudson Bay
Bristol Bay
Great Bear Lake

ANTARCTICA PHYSICAL

0 mi 600
0 km 600
AZIMUTHAL EQUIDISTANT PROJECTION

NATIONAL GEOGRAPHIC

SOUTH ATLANTIC OCEAN
60°W
South Orkney Is.
45°W
30°W
15°W
ANTARCTIC CIRCLE
0°
15°E
30°E
45°E
60°E
60°S
Finbul Ice Shelf
South Shetland Islands
Ruser-Larsen Ice Shelf
ANTARCTIC PENINSULA
GRAHAM LAND
70°S
Weddell Sea
COATS LAND
QUEEN MAUD LAND
ENDERBY LAND
INDIAN OCEAN
75°W
Larsen Ice Shelf
Mt. Jackson 13,747 ft +4,190 m
PALMER LAND
Filchner Ice Shelf
Berkner Island
Valkyrie Dome
Amery Ice Shelf
75°E
Alexander I.
Ronne Ice Shelf
AMERICAN HIGHLAND
SOUTH PACIFIC OCEAN
Bellingshausen Sea
ELLSWORTH LAND
Vinson Massif 16,067 ft +4,897 m
Ellsworth Mts.
ANTARCTICA
TRANSANTARCTIC MOUNTAINS
EAST ANTARCTICA
West Ice Shelf
90°W
90°E
Bentley Subglacial Trench -8,327 ft -2,538 m
POLAR PLATEAU
★ South Pole
Shackleton Ice Shelf
105°W
WEST
ANTARCTICA
MARIE BYRD LAND
Ross Ice Shelf
Roosevelt I.
Dome Circe
105°E
120°W
WILKES LAND
INDIAN OCEAN
135°W
Ross I.
Mt. Erebus 12,448 ft 3,794 m
VICTORIA LAND
Ross Sea
Talos Dome
120°E
150°W
165°W
180°
165°E
150°E
135°E

90   Reference Atlas

NATIONAL GEOGRAPHIC

Geography Handbook

The story of the world begins with geography—the study of the earth in all of its variety. Geography describes the earth's land, water, and plant and animal life. It is the study of places and the complex relationships between people and their environment.

The resources in this handbook will help you get the most out of your textbook—and provide you with skills you will use for the rest of your life.

▼ The Gui River, Guilin, China

▲ Saharan sand dunes, Morocco

The Amazon, Brazil ▶

I Study Geography?

Six Essential Elements

Recently, geographers have begun to look at geography in a different way. They do this to understand how our large world is connected. They break down the study of geography into Six Essential Elements. You should think of these elements as categories into which to sort information you learn about the world's geography.

Being aware of these elements will help you sort out what you are learning. Examples of each of the Essential Elements detailed in maps throughout *Discovering Our Past* are explained here.

Element 1

The World in Spatial Terms
Geographers first take a look at where a place is located. **Location** serves as a starting point by asking "Where is it?" Knowing the location of places helps you develop an awareness of the world around you.

Element 2

Places and Regions
Place has a special meaning in geography. It means more than where a place is. It also describes what a place is like. It might describe physical characteristics such as landforms, climate, and plant or animal life. Or it might describe human characteristics, including language and way of life.

To help organize their study, geographers often group places into regions. **Regions** are united by one or more common characteristics.

Element 3

Physical Systems
When studying places and regions, geographers analyze how **physical systems**—such as hurricanes, volcanoes, and glaciers—shape the earth's surface. They also look at communities of plants and animals that depend upon one another and their surroundings for survival.

Human Systems

Geographers also examine **human systems,** or how people have shaped our world. They look at political boundary lines and why people settle in certain places. A key theme is the continual **movement** of people, ideas, and goods.

Environment and Society

What is the relationship between people and their natural surroundings? This is what the theme of **human/environment interaction** investigates. It also shows how people affect the environment.

The Uses of Geography

Knowledge of geography helps us understand people, places, and environments over time. Knowing how to use the tools of geography prepares you for our modern society.

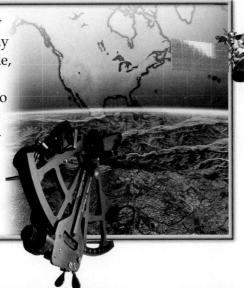

Five Themes

Some geographers study geography through five themes. The **Five Themes of Geography** are (1) location, (2) place, (3) human/environment interaction, (4) movement, and (5) regions. You will see these highlighted throughout *Discovering Our Past.*

How Do I Use Maps and Globes?

Hemispheres

To locate a place on the earth, geographers use a system of imaginary lines that crisscross the globe. One of these lines, the **Equator,** circles the middle of the earth like a belt. It divides the earth into "half spheres," or **hemispheres.** Everything north of the Equator is in the Northern Hemisphere. Everything south of the Equator is in the Southern Hemisphere.

Another imaginary line runs from north to south. It helps divide the earth into half spheres in the other direction. Find this line—called the **Prime Meridian**—on a globe. Everything east of the Prime Meridian for 180 degrees is in the Eastern Hemisphere. Everything west of the Prime Meridian is in the Western Hemisphere.

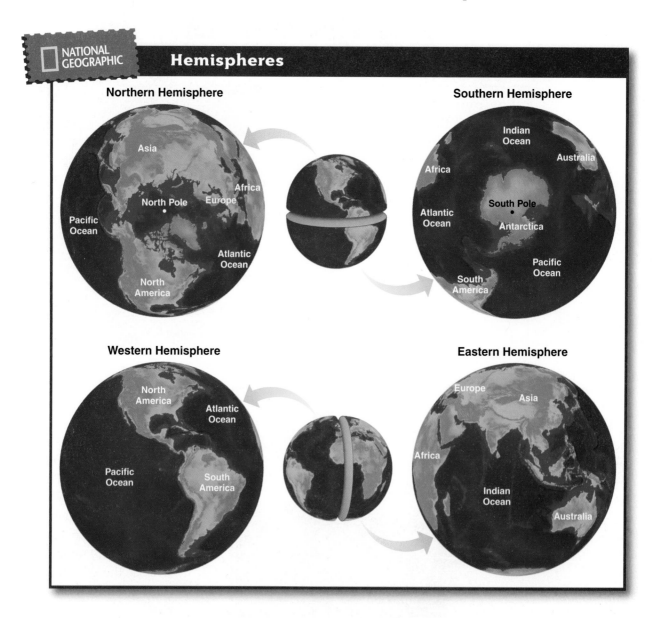

NATIONAL GEOGRAPHIC

Hemispheres

Northern Hemisphere
Asia
Africa
Europe
North Pole
Pacific Ocean
Atlantic Ocean
North America

Southern Hemisphere
Indian Ocean
Australia
Africa
Atlantic Ocean
South Pole
Antarctica
Pacific Ocean
South America

Western Hemisphere
North America
Atlantic Ocean
Pacific Ocean
South America

Eastern Hemisphere
Europe
Asia
Africa
Indian Ocean
Australia

Understanding Latitude and Longitude

Lines on globes and maps provide information that can help you easily locate places on the earth. These lines—called **latitude** and **longitude**—cross one another, forming a pattern called a grid system.

Latitude

Lines of latitude, or **parallels,** circle the earth parallel to the **Equator** and measure the distance north or south of the Equator in degrees. The Equator is at 0° latitude, while the North Pole lies at latitude 90°N (north).

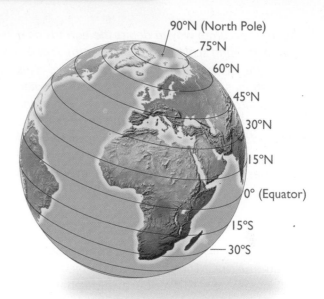

Longitude

Lines of longitude, or **meridians,** circle the earth from Pole to Pole. These lines measure distances east or west of the starting line, which is at 0° longitude and is called the **Prime Meridian** by geographers. The Prime Meridian runs through the Royal Observatory in Greenwich, England.

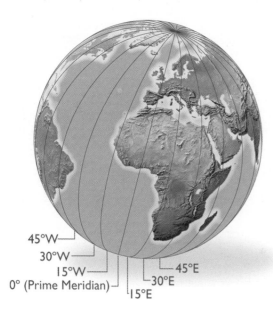

Absolute Location

The grid system formed by lines of latitude and longitude makes it possible to find the absolute location of a place. Only one place can be found at the point where a specific line of latitude crosses a specific line of longitude. By using degrees (°) and minutes (′) (points between degrees), people can pinpoint the precise spot where one line of latitude crosses one line of longitude—an **absolute location.**

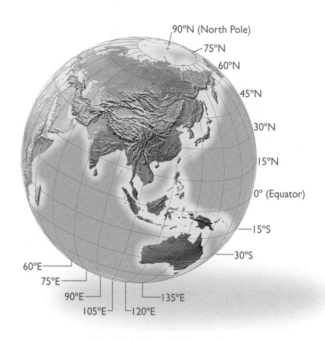

to Maps

The most accurate way to depict the earth is as a *globe*, a round scale model of the earth. A globe gives a true picture of the continents' relative sizes and the shapes of landmasses and bodies of water. Globes accurately represent distance and direction.

A *map* is a flat drawing of all or part of the earth's surface. Unlike globes, maps can show small areas in great detail. Maps can also display political boundaries, population densities, or even voting returns.

From Globes to Maps

Maps, however, do have their limitations. As you can imagine, drawing a round object on a flat surface is very difficult. **Cartographers,** or mapmakers, use mathematical formulas to transfer information from the round globe to a flat map. However, when the curves of a globe become straight lines on a map, the size, shape, distance, or area can change or be distorted.

Great Circle Routes

Mapmakers have solved some problems of going from a globe to a map. A **great circle** is an imaginary line that follows the curve of the earth. Traveling along a great circle is called following a **great circle route.** Airplane pilots use great circle routes because they are the shortest routes.

The idea of a great circle shows one important difference between a globe and a map. Because a globe is round, it accurately shows great circles. On a flat map, however, the great circle route between two points may not appear to be the shortest distance. Compare Maps A and B on the right.

Mapmaking With Technology

Technology has changed the way maps are made. Most cartographers use software programs called **geographic information systems (GIS).** This software layers map data from satellite images, printed text, and statistics. A **Global Positioning System (GPS)** helps consumers and mapmakers locate places based on coordinates broadcast by satellites.

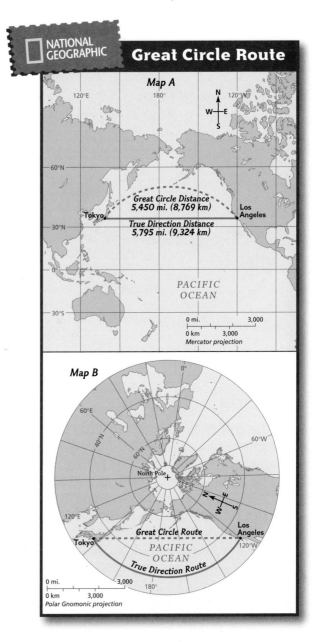

NATIONAL GEOGRAPHIC

Great Circle Route

Map A

Great Circle Distance
5,450 mi. (8,769 km)

True Direction Distance
5,795 mi. (9,324 km)

Tokyo

Los Angeles

PACIFIC OCEAN

0 mi. 3,000
0 km 3,000
Mercator projection

Map B

North Pole

Los Angeles

Great Circle Route

Tokyo

PACIFIC OCEAN

True Direction Route

0 mi. 3,000
0 km 3,000
Polar Gnomonic projection

Common Map Projections

Imagine taking the whole peel from an orange and trying to flatten it on a table. You would either have to cut it or stretch parts of it. Mapmakers face a similar problem in showing the surface of the round earth on a flat map. When the earth's surface is flattened, big gaps open up. To fill in the gaps, mapmakers stretch parts of the earth. They choose to show either the correct shapes of places or their correct sizes. It is impossible to show both. As a result, mapmakers have developed different **projections,** or ways of showing the earth on a flat piece of paper.

Goode's Interrupted Equal-Area Projection

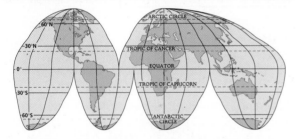

▲ Take a second look at your peeled, flattened orange. You might have something that looks like a map based on **Goode's Interrupted Equal-Area** projection. A map with this projection shows continents close to their true shapes and sizes. This projection is helpful to compare land areas among continents.

Robinson Projection

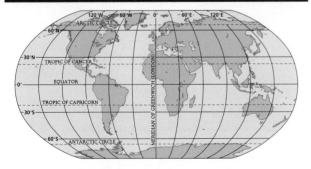

▲ A map using the **Robinson** projection has minor distortions. Land on the western and eastern sides of the Robinson map appears much as it does on a globe. The areas most distorted on this projection are near the North and South Poles.

Winkel Tripel Projection

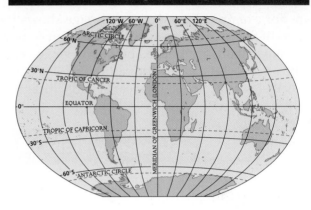

▲ The **Winkel Tripel** projection gives a good overall view of the continents' shapes and sizes. Land areas in a Winkel Tripel projection are not as distorted near the Poles as they are in the Robinson projection.

Mercator Projection

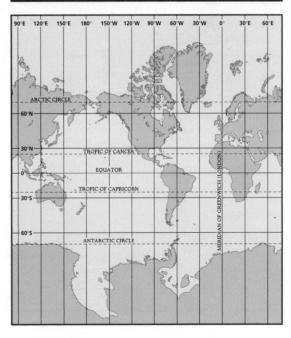

▲ The **Mercator** projection shows true direction and land shapes fairly accurately, but not size or distance. Areas that are located far from the Equator are quite distorted on this projection. Alaska, for example, appears much larger on a Mercator map than it does on a globe.

Parts of Maps

Map Key An important first step in reading a map is to note the map key. The **map key** explains the lines, symbols, and colors used on a map. For example, the map on this page shows the various climate regions of the United States and the different colors representing them. Cities are usually symbolized by a solid circle (•) and capitals by a (✪). On this map, you can see the capital of Texas and the cities of Los Angeles, Seattle, New Orleans, and Chicago.

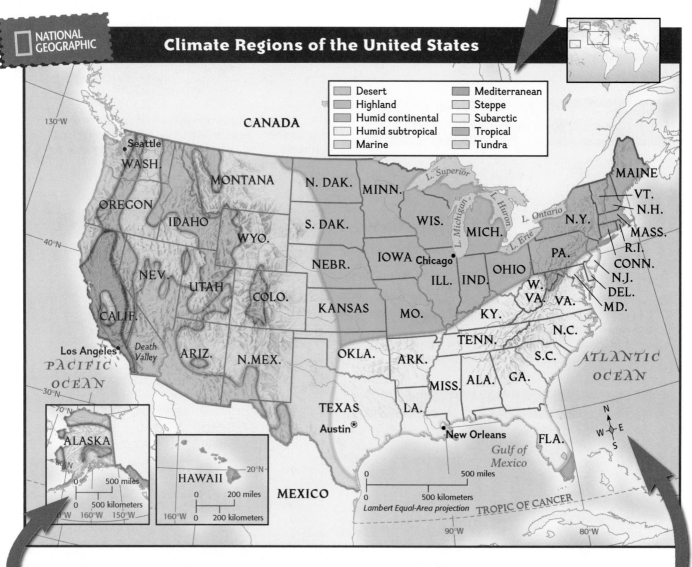

NATIONAL GEOGRAPHIC

Climate Regions of the United States

Desert
Highland
Humid continental
Humid subtropical
Marine
Mediterranean
Steppe
Subarctic
Tropical
Tundra

130°W
CANADA
Seattle
WASH.
OREGON
40°N
IDAHO
MONTANA
N. DAK.
MINN.
S. DAK.
WIS.
L. Superior
L. Michigan
L. Huron
MICH.
L. Ontario
L. Erie
MAINE
VT.
N.H.
N.Y.
MASS.
R.I.
PA.
CONN.
N.J.
DEL.
MD.
NEV.
UTAH
WYO.
COLO.
NEBR.
IOWA
Chicago
ILL.
IND.
OHIO
W. VA.
VA.
CALIF.
Death Valley
ARIZ.
N.MEX.
KANSAS
MO.
KY.
TENN.
N.C.
Los Angeles
PACIFIC OCEAN
30°N
OKLA.
ARK.
S.C.
ATLANTIC OCEAN
MISS.
ALA.
GA.
70°N
TEXAS
LA.
ALASKA
60°N
Austin
New Orleans
FLA.
Gulf of Mexico
HAWAII
20°N
0 500 miles
0 500 kilometers
0 200 miles
0 200 kilometers
160°W
160°W 150°W
MEXICO
N
W E
S
0 500 miles
0 500 kilometers
Lambert Equal-Area projection
TROPIC OF CANCER
90°W
80°W

Scale A measuring line, often called a **scale bar,** helps you figure distance on the map. The map scale tells you what distance on the earth is represented by the measurement on the scale bar.

Compass Rose A map has a symbol that tells you where the **cardinal directions**—north, south, east, and west—are positioned.

Types of Maps

General Purpose Maps

Maps are amazingly useful tools. Geographers use many different types of maps. Maps that show a wide range of general information about an area are called **general purpose maps.** Two of the most common general purpose maps are physical and political maps.

Physical Maps

Physical maps call out landforms and water features. The physical map of Sri Lanka (below) shows rivers and mountains. The colors used on physical maps include brown or green for land and blue for water. In addition, physical maps may use colors to show **elevation**—the height of an area above sea level. A key explains what each color and symbol stands for.

Spain: Political

Political Maps

Political maps show the names and boundaries of countries, the location of cities and other human-made features of a place, and often identify major physical features. The political map of Spain (above), for example, shows the boundaries between Spain and other countries. It also shows cities and rivers within Spain and bodies of water surrounding Spain.

Sri Lanka: Physical

Elevations

Feet		Meters
3,280		1,000
1,640		500
650		200
380		100
0		0

▲ Mountain peak
⊛ National capital
• Major city

Special Purpose Maps

Some maps are made to present specific kinds of information. These are called **thematic** or **special purpose maps.** They usually show themes or patterns, often emphasizing one subject or theme. Special purpose maps may present climate, natural resources, and population density. They may also display historical information, such as battles or territorial changes. The map's title tells what kind of special information it shows. Colors and symbols in the map key are especially important on these types of maps. Special purpose maps are often found in books of maps called atlases.

One type of special purpose map uses colors to show population density, or the average number of people living in a square mile or square kilometer. As with other maps, it is important to first read the title and the key. The population density map of Egypt shows that the Nile River valley and delta are very densely populated.

Some other special purpose maps such as the one of China's Defenses are not presented in color. They are printed in black and white. This is an example of a map you might find on a standardized test or in a newspaper.

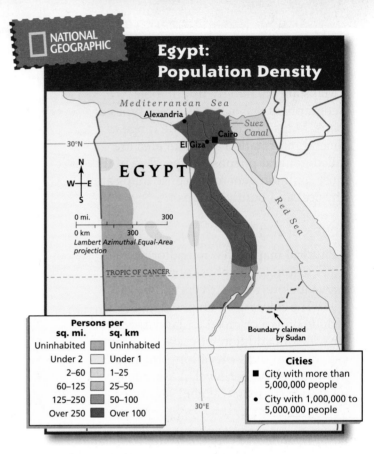

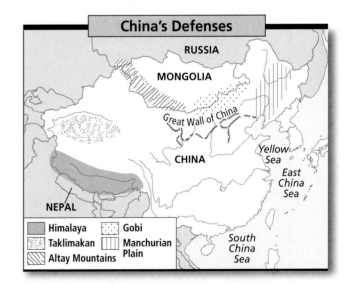

Using Graphs, Charts, and Diagrams

Bar, Line, and Circle Graphs

A graph is a way of summarizing and presenting information visually. Each part of a graph gives useful information. First read the graph's title to find out its subject. Then read the labels along the graph's **axes**—the vertical line along the left side of the graph and the horizontal line along the bottom. One axis will tell you what is being measured. The other axis tells what units of measurement are being used.

Graphs that use bars or wide lines to compare data visually are called **bar graphs.** Look carefully at the bar graph (right) that compares world languages. The vertical axis lists the languages. The horizontal axis gives speakers of the language in millions. By comparing the lengths of the bars, you can quickly tell which language is spoken by the most people. Bar graphs are especially useful for comparing quantities.

NATIONAL GEOGRAPHIC

Comparing World Languages

Chinese (Mandarin) 874
Hindi 366
English 341
Spanish 322
Bengali 207
Portuguese 176
Russian 167
Japanese 125
German 100
Korean 78

Languages (vertical axis)

Number of Native Speakers (in millions)

Source: *The World Almanac*, 2003.

Bar graph

A **line graph** is a useful tool for showing changes over a period of time. The amounts being measured are plotted on the grid above each year and then are connected by a line. Line graphs sometimes have two or more lines plotted on them. The line graph (below) shows that the number of farms in the United States has decreased since 1940.

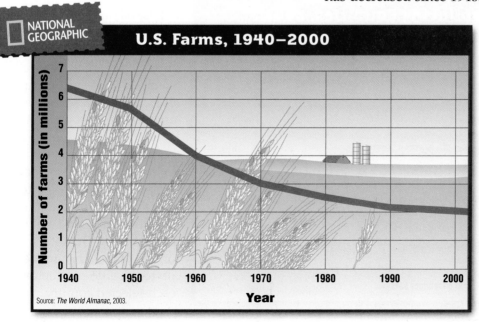

NATIONAL GEOGRAPHIC

U.S. Farms, 1940–2000

Number of farms (in millions)
7
6
5
4
3
2
1
0

1940 1950 1960 1970 1980 1990 2000

Year

Source: *The World Almanac*, 2003.

Line graph

You can use **circle graphs** when you want to show how the whole of something is divided into its parts. Because of their shape, circle graphs are often called pie graphs. Each "slice" represents a part or percentage of the whole "pie." On the circle graph at right, the whole circle (100 percent) represents the world's population in 2002. The slices show how this population is divided among some of the most heavily populated areas of the world.

Charts

Charts present facts and numbers in an organized way. They arrange data, especially numbers, in rows and columns for easy reference. To interpret the chart, first read the title. Look at the chart on page 183. It tells you what information the chart contains. Next, read the labels at the top of each column and on the left side of the chart. They explain what the numbers or data on the chart are measuring.

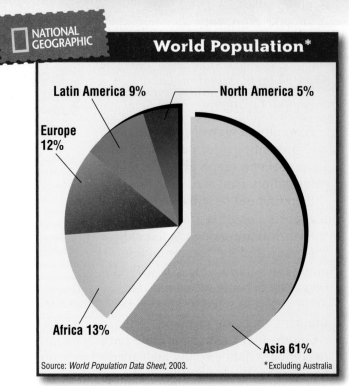

NATIONAL GEOGRAPHIC

World Population*

Latin America 9%

North America 5%

Europe 12%

Africa 13%

Asia 61%

Source: *World Population Data Sheet*, 2003. *Excluding Australia

Circle graph

Pictographs

Like bar and circle graphs, pictographs are good for making comparisons. **Pictographs** use rows of small pictures or symbols, with each picture or symbol representing an amount. Look at the pictograph (left) showing the number of automobiles produced in the world's five major automobile-producing countries. The key tells you that one car symbol stands for 1 million automobiles. The total number of car symbols in a row adds up to the auto production in each selected country.

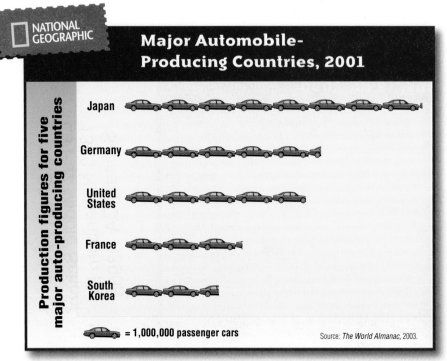

NATIONAL GEOGRAPHIC

Major Automobile-Producing Countries, 2001

Production figures for five major auto-producing countries

Japan

Germany

United States

France

South Korea

🚗 = 1,000,000 passenger cars

Source: *The World Almanac*, 2003.

Pictograph

Climographs

A **climograph,** or climate graph, combines a line graph and a bar graph. It gives an overall picture of the long-term weather patterns in a specific place. Climographs include several kinds of information. The green vertical bars on the climograph of Moscow (right) show average monthly amounts of precipitation (rain, snow, and sleet). These bars are measured against the axis on the right side of the graph. The red line plotted above the bars represents changes in the average monthly temperature. You measure this line against the axis on the left side.

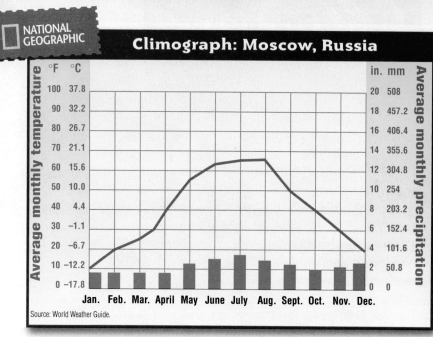

NATIONAL GEOGRAPHIC

Climograph: Moscow, Russia

Source: World Weather Guide.

Climograph

Diagrams

Diagrams are drawings that show steps in a process, point out the parts of an object, or explain how something works. An **elevation profile** is a type of diagram that can be helpful when comparing the elevations—or height—of an area. It shows an exaggerated side view of the land as if it were sliced and you were viewing it from the side. The elevation profile of Africa (below) clearly shows sea level, low areas, and mountains.

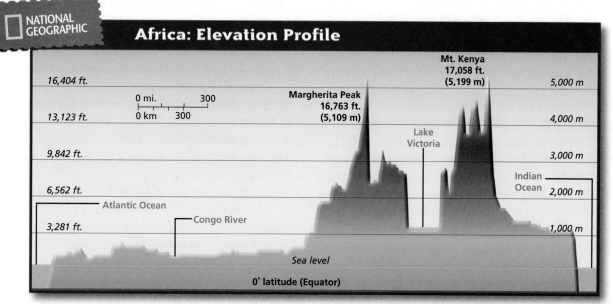

NATIONAL GEOGRAPHIC

Africa: Elevation Profile

Diagram

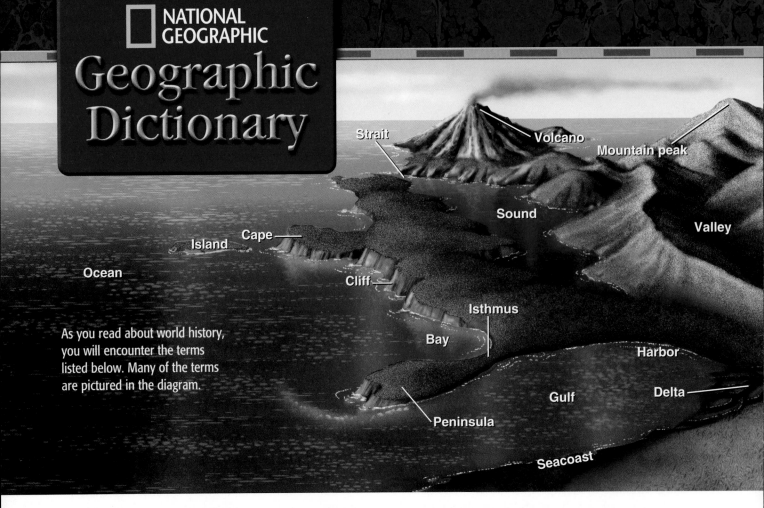

NATIONAL GEOGRAPHIC
Geographic Dictionary

Strait · **Volcano** · **Mountain peak** · **Sound** · **Valley** · **Island** · **Cape** · **Ocean** · **Cliff** · **Isthmus** · **Bay** · **Harbor** · **Gulf** · **Delta** · **Peninsula** · **Seacoast**

As you read about world history, you will encounter the terms listed below. Many of the terms are pictured in the diagram.

absolute location exact location of a place on the earth described by global coordinates

basin area of land drained by a given river and its branches; area of land surrounded by lands of higher elevation

bay part of a large body of water that extends into a shoreline, generally smaller than a gulf

canyon deep and narrow valley with steep walls

cape point of land that extends into a river, lake, or ocean

channel wide strait or waterway between two landmasses that lie close to each other; deep part of a river or other waterway

cliff steep, high wall of rock, earth, or ice

continent one of the seven large landmasses on the earth

cultural feature characteristic that humans have created in a place, such as language, religion, housing, and settlement pattern

delta flat, low-lying land built up from soil carried downstream by a river and deposited at its mouth

divide stretch of high land that separates river systems

downstream direction in which a river or stream flows from its source to its mouth

elevation height of land above sea level

Equator imaginary line that runs around the earth halfway between the North and South Poles; used as the starting point to measure degrees of north and south latitude

glacier large, thick body of slowly moving ice

gulf part of a large body of water that extends into a shoreline, generally larger and more deeply indented than a bay

harbor a sheltered place along a shoreline where ships can anchor safely

highland elevated land area such as a hill, mountain, or plateau

hill elevated land with sloping sides and rounded summit; generally smaller than a mountain

island land area, smaller than a continent, completely surrounded by water

isthmus narrow stretch of land connecting two larger land areas

lake a sizable inland body of water

latitude distance north or south of the Equator, measured in degrees

longitude distance east or west of the Prime Meridian, measured in degrees

lowland land, usually level, at a low elevation

map drawing of the earth shown on a flat surface

meridian one of many lines on the global grid running from the North Pole to the South Pole; used to measure degrees of longitude

mesa broad, flat-topped landform with steep sides; smaller than a plateau

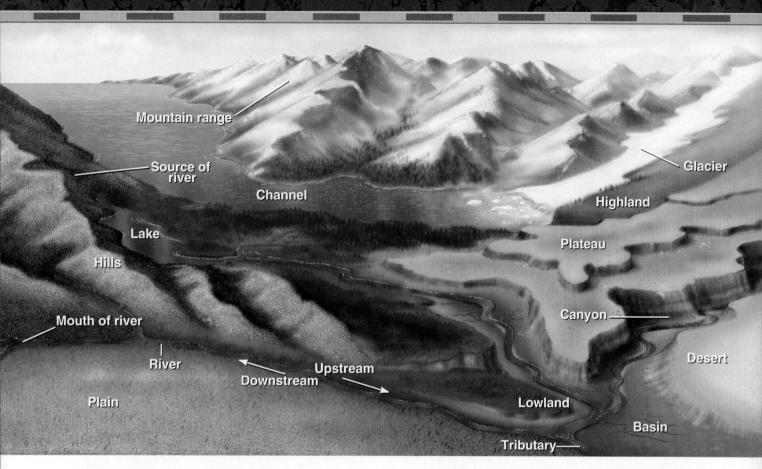

Mountain range

Source of river

Channel

Glacier

Highland

Lake

Plateau

Hills

Canyon

Mouth of river

Desert

River

Upstream

Downstream

Plain

Lowland

Basin

Tributary

mountain land with steep sides that rises sharply (1,000 feet [305 m] or more) from surrounding land; generally larger and more rugged than a hill

mountain peak pointed top of a mountain

mountain range a series of connected mountains

mouth (of a river) place where a stream or river flows into a larger body of water

ocean one of the four major bodies of salt water that surround the continents

ocean current stream of either cold or warm water that moves in a definite direction through an ocean

parallel one of many lines on the global grid that circle the earth north or south of the Equator; used to measure degrees of latitude

peninsula body of land jutting into a lake or ocean, surrounded on three sides by water

physical feature characteristic of a place occurring naturally, such as a landform, body of water, climate pattern, or resource

plain area of level land, usually at a low elevation and often covered with grasses

plateau area of flat or rolling land at a high elevation, about 300–3,000 feet (91–914 m) high

Prime Meridian line of the global grid running from the North Pole to the South Pole through Greenwich, England; starting point for measuring degrees of east and west longitude

relief changes in elevation over a given area of land

river large natural stream of water that runs through the land

sea large body of water completely or partly surrounded by land

seacoast land lying next to a sea or ocean

sea level position on land level with surface of nearby ocean or sea

sound body of water between a coastline and one or more islands off the coast

source (of a river) place where a river or stream begins, often in highlands

strait narrow stretch of water joining two larger bodies of water

tributary small river or stream that flows into a larger river or stream; a branch of the river

upstream direction opposite the flow of a river; toward the source of a river or stream

valley area of low land between hills or mountains

volcano mountain created as liquid rock or ash erupts from inside the earth

Tools of the Historian

A historian is a person who studies and writes about people and events of the past. Historians find out how people lived, what happened to them, and what happened around them. They look for the reasons behind events and study the effects of events.

Have you ever wondered if you could be a historian? To answer that question, you will need to find out how history is researched and written. Historians use a number of skills to research and organize information. You can learn about these skills in the next few pages. As you study this textbook, you will see that the sections listed below will help you understand world history:

Scientists looking ▶ for evidence of past civilizations

Digging Up The Past

Historians depend on the work of archaeologists. Archaeologists are scientists who unearth the remains of the past.

What Do Archaeologists Study?
- Human and animal bones, seeds, trees
- Pottery, tools, weapons
- Mounds, pits, canals

▲ Prehistoric pottery

How Do They Gather Data?
- Surveys on foot
- Photographs taken from airplanes or satellites
- Ground-penetrating radar
- Plot locations on maps
- Dig for evidence with tools from heavy equipment to shovels
- Sonar scanning to find underwater objects

How Do They Interpret Findings?
- Organize artifacts into groups based on similarities
- Compare objects in relation to other objects
- Look for evidence of changes over a period of time
- Date once-living objects by measuring carbon-14 levels
- Use microscopic and biological tests to date objects

◀ Carbon-14 dating

Do Your Own Digging

Research the library and Internet to find information on two archaeological diggings, one past and the other, very recent. Compare and contrast the methods used in each digging. What changes do you notice in tools archaeologists have used over time?

Organizing Time

 Historical and Social Sciences Analysis Skills

Chronological and Spatial Thinking

CS1. Students explain how major events are related to one another in time.

CS2. Students construct various time lines of key events, people, and periods of the historical era they are studying.

Periods of History Historians divide history into blocks of time known as *periods,* or *eras.* For example, a period of 10 years is called a *decade.* A period of 100 years is known as a *century.* Centuries are grouped into even longer time periods, which are given names.

The first of these long periods is called *Prehistory.* Prehistory refers to the time before people developed writing, about 5,500 years ago. This is followed by the period known as *Ancient History,* ending c. A.D. 500. (c., or circa, means "about"). Historians call the next thousand years the *Middle Ages,* or the medieval

◀ Tools made by prehistoric people

▲ A young couple of ancient Rome

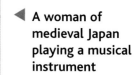

◀ A woman of medieval Japan playing a musical instrument

◀ Educated Europeans of the early modern period discussing new ideas

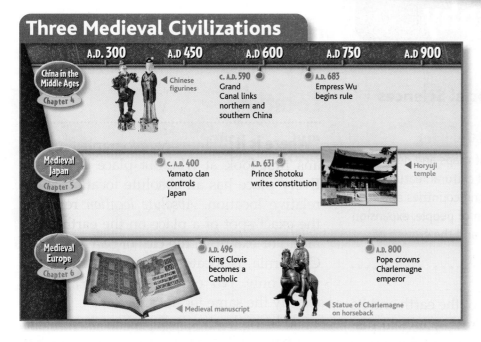

Three Medieval Civilizations

| | A.D. 300 | A.D. 450 | A.D. 600 | A.D. 750 | A.D. 900 |

China in the Middle Ages — Chapter 4
Chinese figurines
c. A.D. 590 Grand Canal links northern and southern China
A.D. 683 Empress Wu begins rule

Medieval Japan — Chapter 5
c. A.D. 400 Yamato clan controls Japan
A.D. 631 Prince Shotoku writes constitution
Horyuji temple

Medieval Europe — Chapter 6
A.D. 496 King Clovis becomes a Catholic
A.D. 800 Pope crowns Charlemagne emperor
Medieval manuscript
Statue of Charlemagne on horseback

A time line also labels historical events. Each event on the time line appears beside the date when the event took place. Sometimes events and their dates are shown on a single time line. In other cases, two or more time lines are stacked one on top of the other. These are called multilevel time lines. They help you to compare events in different places at certain periods of time. For example, the multilevel time line on this page shows events in three medieval civilizations from A.D. 300 to A.D. 900. The skill lesson "Reading a Time Line" on page 553 will help you learn to work with time lines.

period. After that, from c.1500, *Modern History* begins and continues to the present day. In this book, you will study history from prehistory to the end of the ancient period.

What Is a Time Line?

Which came first: the American Civil War or World War II? Did the train come before or after the invention of the airplane? In studying the past, historians focus on *chronology,* or the order of dates in which events happened.

You might be wondering how to make sense of the flow of dates and events. An easy way is to use or make a time line. A *time line* is a diagram that shows the order of events within a period of time.

Most time lines are divided into sections in which the years are evenly spaced. In some cases, however, a spread of time may be too long to show all of the years. To save space, a period of time may be omitted from the time line. A slanted or jagged line appears on the time line to show this break in time. For example, time lines of prehistory use breaks because of their large spreads of time.

Thinking Like a Historian

1. **Reading a Time Line** Look over the time line above to get an idea of what a time line shows. What is the title? When does it begin and end? What two features make this time line different from many other time lines? Why are they used?

2. **Understanding a Time Line** Why do you think some dates on the time line might be marked with a "c."?

3. **Making a Time Line** Create a time line using the terms B.M.B. (before my birth) and A.M.B. (after my birth). Fill in the time line with five key events that happened before and after you were born. Illustrate the time line with copies of photos from your family album.

Movement

"How do people in one area affect people in other areas?" Historians answer this question with the theme of *movement*. Throughout history, people, ideas, goods, and information have moved from place to place. Transportation—the movement of people and goods—has allowed people to use products made in places far away. This has increased the exchange of ideas and cultures. Communication—the movement of ideas and information—has allowed people to find out about other parts of the world. Today people receive almost instant communication by radio, television, and computer.

The movement of people to different places is called migration. Why have people migrated throughout history? Some have been forced to move because of wars, famine, or enslavement. Others have chosen to move to seek a better life. During the A.D. 400s, various groups of Germanic peoples invaded the Roman Empire. They were pushed out of their lands by other groups. At the same time, they were drawn to Rome's fertile fields, milder climate, and advanced civilization. The Germanic invasions led to the fall of the Roman Empire. The invaders set up kingdoms in Roman territory.

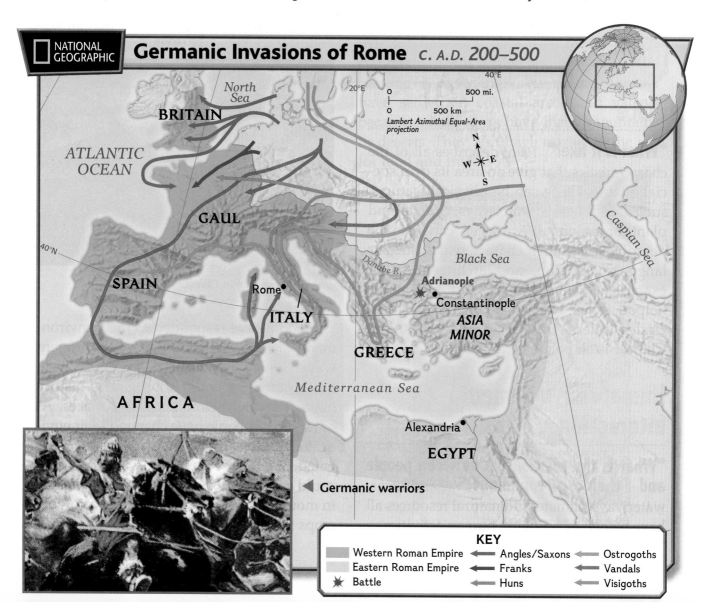

NATIONAL GEOGRAPHIC

Germanic Invasions of Rome C. A.D. 200–500

Germanic warriors

KEY

Western Roman Empire	Angles/Saxons — Ostrogoths
Eastern Roman Empire	Franks
Battle	Huns — Vandals — Visigoths

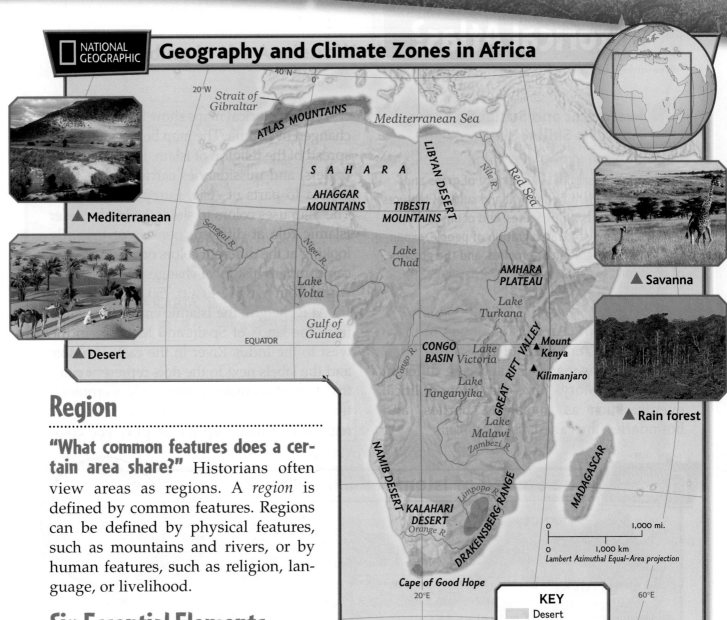

Geography and Climate Zones in Africa

▲ Mediterranean

▲ Desert

▲ Savanna

▲ Rain forest

KEY
Desert
Mediterranean
Rain forest
Savanna

Region

"What common features does a certain area share?" Historians often view areas as regions. A *region* is defined by common features. Regions can be defined by physical features, such as mountains and rivers, or by human features, such as religion, language, or livelihood.

Six Essential Elements

Recently geographers have broken down the study of geography into *Six Essential Elements.* These elements are:

- The World in Spatial Terms
- Places and Regions
- Physical Systems
- Human Systems
- Environment and Society
- The Uses of Geography

You will learn about these elements in the Geography Handbook on pages 92–93. Knowing them will help you in your study of history.

Thinking Like a Historian

1. **Identifying** How are absolute location and relative location different?

2. **Analyzing Themes** What characteristics do geographers use to describe a place?

3. **Linking History and Geography** Make a list of the Five Themes of Geography. Under each theme, explain how you think geography has shaped the history of your community.

Links Across Time

Historical and Social Sciences Analysis Skills

Chronological and Spatial Thinking

CS1. Students explain how major events are related to one another in time.

Unit 1 New Empires and New Faiths

After 500 B.C., strong governments and new religions arose in many parts of the world. The Romans, who lived in present-day Italy, created a form of government called a republic. Their ideas— that laws apply equally to all citizens, and that rulers must obey the law— shaped later Western nations. Today, the United States is a republic under the rule of law. The U.S. Congress is the part of our national government that makes laws. Its upper body—the United States Senate—is partly modeled on the Senate of the ancient Roman Republic.

▲ U.S. Congress

▼ Roman Senate

Unit 2 The Middle Ages

The period from about A.D. 500 to A.D. 1500 is known as the Middle Ages. During this time, trade routes expanded, and ideas and goods spread from one people to another. In both medieval Europe and Japan, central government weakened, and warriors played an important role in daily life. Today armored vehicles play an important role on the battlefield, just as armored horsemen did in medieval times.

Battle tank in the desert ▲

Armor of ▶
medieval knight

Unit 3 A Changing World

Beginning about A.D. 1500, people in many parts of the world lived through a time of far-reaching change. Empires, or vast territories under one ruler, rose and fell. Thinkers developed new ideas about government and began to use scientific ideas to explore nature and the human body. They also invented new instruments to help them in their work. One discovery or invention led to another, creating an explosion of knowledge. Advances in science begun at that time are still going on today as scientists explore outer space.

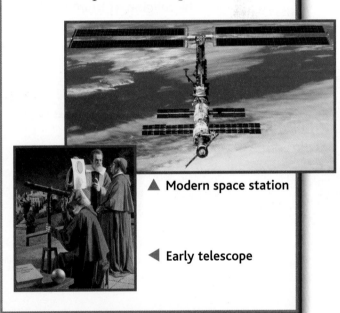

▲ **Modern space station**

◀ **Early telescope**

Thinking Like a Historian

As you read *Discovering Our Past: Medieval and Early Modern Times*, notice how the past affects the present. When you begin each unit, collect newspaper or magazine articles about a current event from the area you are studying. Then, after completing each unit, write down how you think a past event in that region is related to the current event.

Unit 1

New Empires and New Faiths

Why It's Important

Each civilization that you will study in this unit made important contributions to history.

- Roman ideas about law shaped our ideas of law today.
- The religion of Islam has hundreds of millions of followers around the world today.
- African civilization supplied salt and gold to Europe and the Middle East, and developed musical styles that are still popular today.

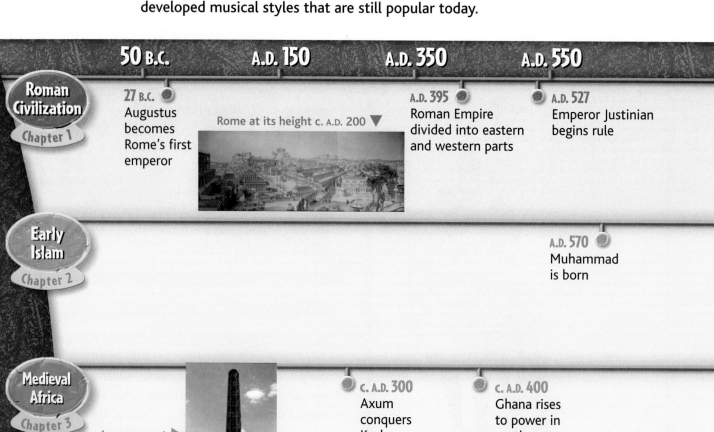

	50 B.C.	A.D. 150	A.D. 350	A.D. 550

Roman Civilization
Chapter 1

27 B.C.
Augustus becomes Rome's first emperor

Rome at its height c. A.D. 200 ▼

A.D. 395
Roman Empire divided into eastern and western parts

A.D. 527
Emperor Justinian begins rule

Early Islam
Chapter 2

A.D. 570
Muhammad is born

Medieval Africa
Chapter 3

A monument ▶ from Axum

C. A.D. 300
Axum conquers Kush

C. A.D. 400
Ghana rises to power in northwest Africa

NATIONAL GEOGRAPHIC Where in the World?

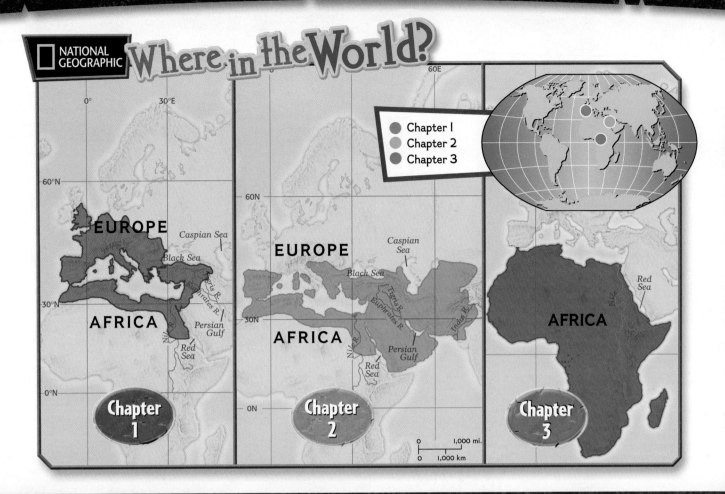

- Chapter 1
- Chapter 2
- Chapter 3

Chapter 1

EUROPE

AFRICA

Caspian Sea
Black Sea
Tigris R.
Euphrates R.
Persian Gulf
Red Sea

Chapter 2

EUROPE

AFRICA

Caspian Sea
Black Sea
Tigris R.
Euphrates R.
India R.
Persian Gulf
Red Sea
Nile R.

Chapter 3

AFRICA

Red Sea
Nile

1,000 mi.
1,000 km

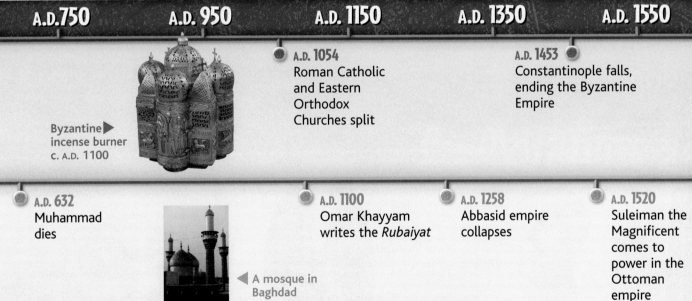

A.D. 750   A.D. 950   A.D. 1150   A.D. 1350   A.D. 1550

A.D. 1054
Roman Catholic and Eastern Orthodox Churches split

A.D. 1453
Constantinople falls, ending the Byzantine Empire

◀ Byzantine incense burner
C. A.D. 1100

A.D. 632
Muhammad dies

◀ A mosque in Baghdad

A.D. 1100
Omar Khayyam writes the *Rubaiyat*

A.D. 1258
Abbasid empire collapses

A.D. 1520
Suleiman the Magnificent comes to power in the Ottoman empire

C. A.D. 700
Arab Muslims settle in Africa

C. A.D. 1000
Empire of Songhai is established

A.D. 1312
Mansa Musa begins rule of Mali Empire

A.D. 1492
Sunni Ali dies

Places to Locate

EUROPE

①

NORTH
AMERICA

Roman Pantheon

**See Roman Civilization
Chapter 1**

①

*Atlantic
Ocean*

④

AFRICA

⑤

Hagia Sophia

**See Roman Civilization
Chapter 1**

②

SOUTH
AMERICA

Pacific Ocean

People to Meet

Constantine

C. A.D. 280–337
Roman emperor
Chapter 1, page 148

Theodora

C. A.D. 500–548
Byzantine empress
Chapter 1, page 160

Muhammad

C. A.D. 570–632
**Muslims believe Allah
dictated the Quran to
Muhammad**
Chapter 2, page 178

ASIA

Indian Ocean

3 Kaaba

See Islamic Civilization Chapter 2

4 Djenne Mosque

See Africa's Civilizations Chapter 3

5 African savanna

See Africa's Civilizations Chapter 3

Omar Khayyam

A.D. 1048–1131
Islamic poet and philosopher
Chapter 2, page 195

Mansa Musa

Ruled A.D. 1312–1337
King of Mali
Chapter 3, page 226

Ibn Khaldun

A.D. 1332–1406
Islamic scholar
Chapter 2, page 195

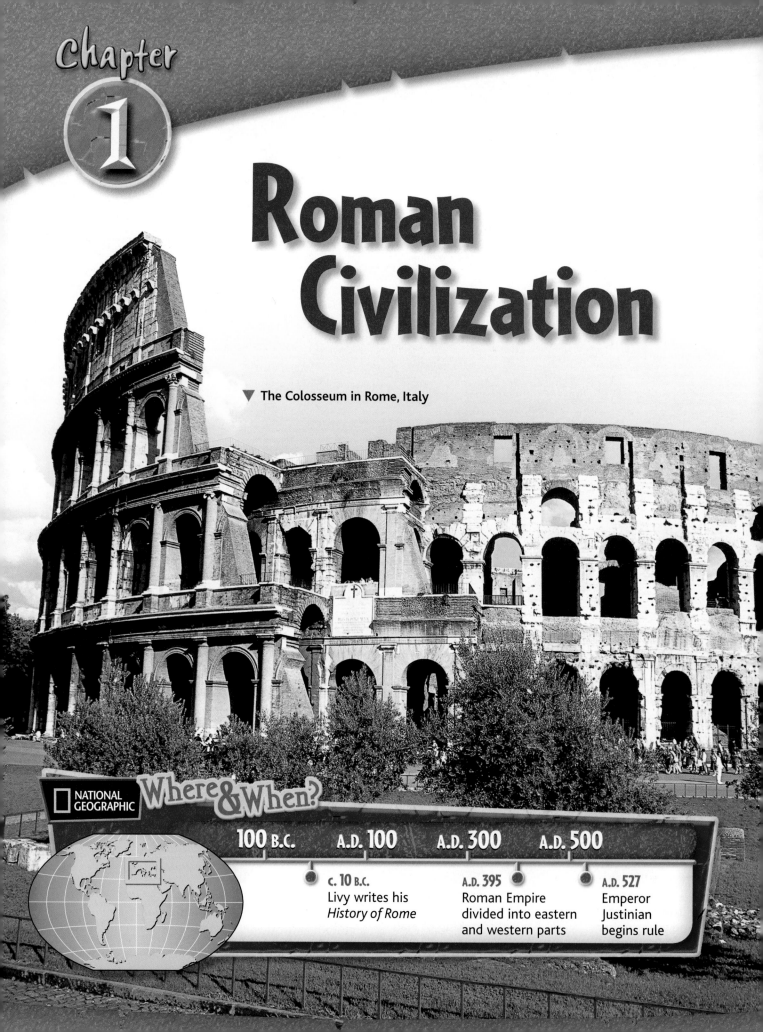

Roman Civilization

▼ The Colosseum in Rome, Italy

NATIONAL GEOGRAPHIC *Where & When?*

100 B.C.	A.D. 100	A.D. 300	A.D. 500

c. 10 B.C.
Livy writes his *History of Rome*

A.D. 395
Roman Empire divided into eastern and western parts

A.D. 527
Emperor Justinian begins rule

The Big Ideas

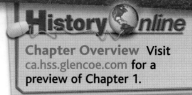

Section 1 Life in Ancient Rome

The interaction of different societies brings about the development of new ideas, art, and technology. The Romans learned from the Greeks, especially in areas of art, architecture, and mythology. However, the Romans changed what they borrowed to suit their own needs.

Section 2 The Fall of Rome

Studying the past helps us to understand the present. Rome finally fell when Germanic invaders swept through the empire in the A.D. 400s. Despite this, Roman achievements in government, law, language, and the arts are still important today.

Section 3 The Byzantine Empire

Physical geography plays a role in how civilizations develop and decline. Because it was centered at Constantinople, the Byzantine Empire developed a culture based on Roman, Greek, and Christian ideas. It also established a powerful trading economy.

 View the Chapter 1 video in the Glencoe Video Program.

FOLDABLES™ Study Organizer

Organizing Information *Make this foldable to help you organize and analyze information by asking yourself questions about Roman civilization.*

Step 1 *Fold a sheet of paper into thirds from top to bottom.*

Step 2 *Turn the paper horizontally, unfold it, and label the three columns as shown.*

Life in Ancient Rome | The Fall of Rome | The Byzantine Empire

Reading and Writing *As you read the chapter, write the main ideas for each section in the appropriate columns of your foldable. Then write one statement that summarizes the main ideas in each column.*

Get Ready to Read

Previewing

1 Learn It!

Before you read, take time to preview the chapter. This will give you a head start on what you are about to learn. Follow the steps below to help you quickly read, or skim, Section 1.

2–The (Main Idea) under each main head tells you the main point of what you are about to read.

3–The **Reading Connection** helps you to link what you might already know to what you are about to read.

A Prosperous Empire

(Main Idea) **By expanding the empire and reorganizing the military and government, Augustus created a new era of prosperity.**

Reading Connection What makes a good or bad leader? Think about this question as you read about Augustus and other Roman emperors.

Rome's first emperor, Augustus . . .

What Did Augustus Achieve?

1–Read the main headings in large red type. They show the main topics covered in the section or chapter.

4–Under each main head, read the subheads in blue type. Subheads break down each main topic into smaller topics.

Reading Tip

As you skim, also look at pictures, maps, and charts.

2 Practice It!

Section 3
The Byzantine Empire

Read to Write
Use each main head, the main ideas, and the subheads in Section 2 of this chapter to create a study outline.

Skim all of the main heads and main ideas in Section 3 starting on page 156. Then, in small groups, discuss the answers to these questions.

- Which part of this section do you think will be most interesting to you?
- What do you think will be covered in Section 3 that was not covered in Section 2?
- Are there any words in the Main Ideas that you do not know how to pronounce?
- Choose one of the Reading Connection questions to discuss in your group.

Ancient Constantinople ▶

3 Apply It!

Skim Section 2 on your own. Write one thing in your notebook that you want to learn by reading this chapter.

Life in Ancient Rome

Guide to Reading

History Social Science Standards

WH7.1 Students analyze the causes and effects of the vast expansion and ultimate disintegration of the Roman Empire.

Looking Back, Looking Ahead

You learned in 6th grade about Rome's rise to power. Life in Rome was not easy, but as the empire grew, its people accomplished many things in art, science, and engineering.

Focusing on the Main Ideas

• By expanding the empire and reorganizing the military and government, Augustus created a new era of prosperity. *(page 137)*

• In addition to their own developments in science and engineering, Roman artists and writers borrowed many ideas from the Greeks. *(page 139)*

Meeting People

Augustus (aw•GUHS•tuhs)
Virgil (VUHR•juhl)
Horace (HAWR•uhs)
Galen (GAY•luhn)
Ptolemy (TAH•luh•mee)

Content Vocabulary

Pax Romana (pahks roh•MAH•nah)
vault (VAWLT)
satire (SA•TYR)
ode (OHD)
anatomy (uh•NA•tuh•mee)
aqueduct (A•kwuh•DUHKT)
Stoicism (STOH•uh•SIH•zuhm)

Academic Vocabulary

distinct (dih•STIHNGKT)
emphasis (EHM•fuh•suhs)

Reading Strategy

Compare and Contrast Use a Venn diagram like the one below to show similarities and differences between Roman culture and Greek culture.

Roman Culture Greek Culture

NATIONAL GEOGRAPHIC Where & When?

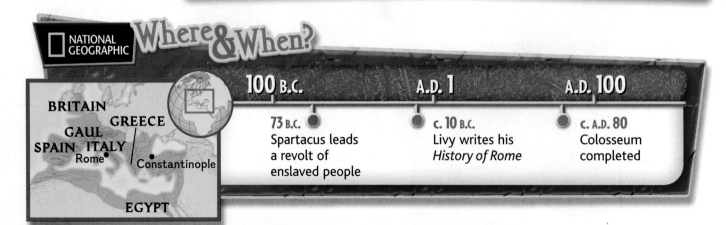

BRITAIN
GAUL GREECE
SPAIN ITALY
Rome •
• Constantinople
EGYPT

100 B.C.

73 B.C.
Spartacus leads a revolt of enslaved people

A.D. 1

c. 10 B.C.
Livy writes his *History of Rome*

A.D. 100

c. A.D. 80
Colosseum completed

WH7.1.1 Study the early strengths and lasting contributions of Rome (e.g., significance of Roman citizenship; rights under Roman law; Roman art, architecture, engineering, and philosophy; preservation and transmission of Christianity) and its ultimate internal weaknesses (e.g., rise of autonomous military powers within the empire, undermining of citizenship by the growth of corruption and slavery, lack of education, and distribution of news). **WH7.1.2** Discuss the geographic borders of the empire at its height and the factors that threatened its territorial cohesion.

A Prosperous Empire

Main Idea By expanding the empire and reorganizing the military and government, Augustus created a new era of prosperity.

Reading Connection What makes a good or bad leader? Think about this question as you read about Augustus and other Roman emperors.

Rome's first emperor, **Augustus** (aw•GUHS•tuhs), ruled from 27 B.C. to A.D. 14. He paved the way for 200 years of peace and prosperity in Rome. The emperors who followed him were not all good rulers, but they helped the Roman Empire reach its peak. For centuries, the Mediterranean region had been filled with conflict. Under Augustus and his successors, the region was controlled by one empire. A long era of peace began with Augustus and lasted until A.D. 180. It was called the *Pax Romana* (pahks roh•MAH•nah), or "Roman Peace."

What Did Augustus Achieve?

Upon becoming emperor in 27 B.C., Augustus set out to make the empire strong and safe. To provide security, he built a permanent, professional army of about 150,000 men—all Roman citizens. Augustus also created a special unit called the Praetorian Guard. This force consisted of about 9,000 men in charge of guarding the emperor. The Praetorian Guard later became very influential in Roman politics.

Augustus's legions conquered new territories and added vast stretches of northern Europe to the empire. All of Spain and Gaul came under Roman rule, as did land in what is today Austria, Hungary, Romania, and Bulgaria.

Meanwhile, Augustus rebuilt Rome. "I found Rome a city of brick," he boasted, "and left it a city of marble." The arts flourished as never before, and Augustus also imported grain from Africa to feed the poor. He knew that a well-fed population would be less likely to cause trouble.

Augustus devoted much of his energy to improving Rome's government. During his reign, more than 50 million people lived in the Roman Empire. To rule this huge population, Augustus appointed a proconsul, or governor, for each of Rome's provinces. Augustus often traveled to the provinces to see how the governors were doing.

Augustus reformed the Roman tax system to make it fairer. He also reformed the legal system to create a set of laws for people in the provinces who were not citizens.

Who Came After Augustus?

After ruling for almost 40 years, Augustus died in A.D. 14. No law stated how the next emperor was to be chosen. Augustus, however, had trained a relative, Tiberius, to follow him. The next three emperors—Caligula (kuh•LIH•gyuh•luh), Claudius, and Nero (NEE•roh)—also came from Augustus's family. They are called the Julio-Claudian emperors. Unfortunately, they were not all fit to lead. Tiberius and Claudius ruled well. Caligula and Nero, however, proved to be cruel leaders.

After Nero, Rome passed through a period of disorder until Vespasian, a general and one of Nero's proconsuls, took the throne. Vespasian restored peace and order. He put down several rebellions in the empire, including the Jewish rebellion in Palestine. Troops commanded by his son Titus defeated the Jews and destroyed the Jewish temple in Jerusalem in A.D. 70.

During his reign, Vespasian began construction of the Colosseum—a huge amphitheater. His sons oversaw an era of growth and prosperity in Rome.

The Roman Empire at Its Height

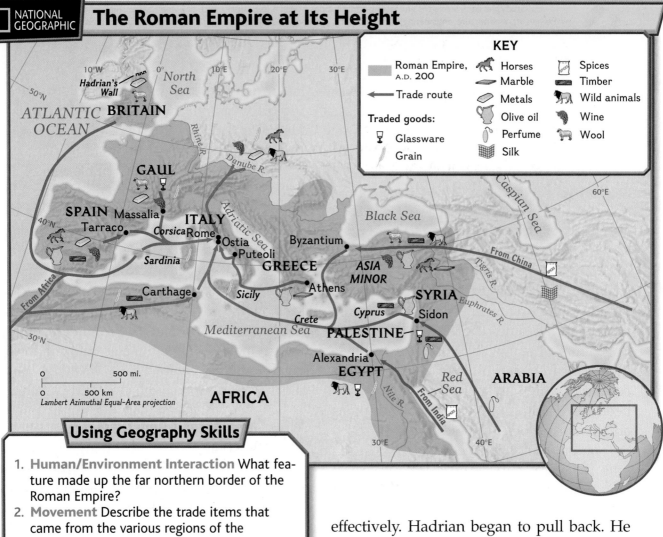

KEY

Roman Empire, A.D. 200

← Trade route

Traded goods:

Glassware

Grain

🐎 Horses

Marble

Metals

Olive oil

Perfume

Silk

Spices

Timber

🦁 Wild animals

Wine

Wool

Using Geography Skills

1. **Human/Environment Interaction** What feature made up the far northern border of the Roman Empire?
2. **Movement** Describe the trade items that came from the various regions of the empire.

Find NGS online map resources @ www.nationalgeographic.com/maps

A Unified Empire At the beginning of the A.D. 100s, a series of rulers who were not related to Augustus or Vespasian came to power. These five emperors—Nerva, Trajan, Hadrian (HAY•dree•uhn), Antoninus Pius, and Marcus Aurelius—are known as the "good emperors." They presided over nearly a century of prosperity, from A.D. 96 to A.D. 180. Agriculture flourished, trade increased, and the standard of living rose.

The empire reached its largest size under Trajan. It spread beyond the Mediterranean and included Britain and part of western Mesopotamia.

Trajan's successors, however, realized that the empire had grown too big to rule

effectively. Hadrian began to pull back. He removed troops from most of Mesopotamia. In Europe, he set the empire's northern boundaries at the Rhine River (RYN) and Danube River (DAN•YOOB). He also built Hadrian's Wall across northern Britain to keep out the Picts and Scots—two warlike people who lived in northern Britain. Rome focused on protecting borders rather than expanding.

In the A.D. 100s, the Roman Empire was one of the greatest empires in history. It included about 3.5 million square miles (9.1 million square km). Its people spoke different languages—mostly Latin in the west and Greek in the east. They also practiced different local customs. What unified the empire, though, were Roman law, Roman rule, and a shared identity as Romans.

✓ **Reading Check** **Explain** What did Augustus do to make the empire safer and stronger?

WH7.1.1 Study the early strengths and lasting contributions of Rome (e.g., significance of Roman citizenship; rights under Roman law; Roman art, architecture, engineering, and philosophy; preservation and transmission of Christianity) and its ultimate internal weaknesses (e.g., rise of autonomous military powers within the empire, undermining of citizenship by the growth of corruption and slavery, lack of education, and distribution of news).

Roman Culture

Main Idea In addition to their own developments in science and engineering, Roman artists and writers borrowed many ideas from the Greeks.

Reading Connection Are there people in your life that you admire? What have you learned from them? Read to find out what the Romans learned from the Greeks.

The Romans admired and studied Greek statues, buildings, and ideas. They copied the Greeks in many ways. However, they changed what they borrowed to suit their own needs.

What Was Roman Art Like? The Romans admired Greek art and architecture. They placed Greek-style statues in their homes and public buildings. Roman artists, however, carved statues that looked **distinctly** different from those of the Greeks. Greek statues were made to look perfect. People were shown young, healthy, and with beautiful bodies. Roman statues were more realistic and included wrinkles, warts, and other less attractive features.

In building, the Romans also turned to the Greeks for ideas. They used Greek-style porches and rows of columns called colonnades. But they also designed their own features, such as arches and domes. Roman builders were the first to make full use of the arch. Arches supported bridges, aqueducts, and buildings. Rows of arches were often built against one another to form a **vault** (VAWLT), or curved ceiling. Using this technique, the Romans were able to build domes.

The Romans were the first people to invent and use concrete, a mixture of volcanic ash, lime, and water. When it dried, this mix was as hard as rock. Concrete made buildings sturdier and allowed them to be built taller.

Rome's concrete buildings were so well built that many still stand today. One of the most famous is the Colosseum, completed about A.D. 80. It was a huge arena that could seat about 60,000 people. Another famous building is the Pantheon, a temple built to honor Rome's gods. The Pantheon's domed roof was the largest of its time.

▼ **This Roman bridge still stands in Spain.** *In what other structures were arches used?*

The Book of Epodes

In this poem excerpt, Horace praises the lifestyle of those who farm their family's land.

▲ Horace

"Happy the man who, far from business and affairs

Like mortals of the early times,

May work his father's fields with oxen of his own,

Exempt [free] from profit, loss, and fee,

Not like the soldier roused by savage trumpet's blare,

Not terrified by seas in rage,

Avoiding busy forums and the haughty doors Of influencial [influential] citizens."

—Horace, *The Book of Epodes*

DBQ Document-Based Question

According to Horace, what kinds of things does the farmer avoid?

Roman Literature

Roman authors based much of their writing on Greek works. For example, the Roman writer **Virgil** (VUHR•juhl) drew some of his ideas from Homer's *Odyssey*. Virgil's epic poem, the *Aeneid* (uh•NEE•uhd), describes the adventures of the Trojan prince Aeneas and how he came to Italy. Virgil presents Aeneas as the ideal Roman—brave, self-controlled, and loyal to the gods.

Rome's other famous writers also looked to the Greeks for inspiration. Using Greek models, the poet **Horace** (HAWR•uhs) wrote **satires** (SA•TYRZ). These works poked fun at human weaknesses. Horace also composed **odes** (OHDZ), or poems that express strong emotions about life. The Roman writer Ovid wrote works that were based on the Greek myths. The poet Catullus also admired Greek writings. He wrote short poems about love, sadness, and envy.

Like the Greeks, Rome's historians recorded the events of their civilization. One of Rome's most famous historians was Livy. He wrote his *History of Rome* about 10 B.C. In this book, Livy describes Rome's rise to power. Livy greatly admired the deeds of the early Romans, and he believed that history had important moral lessons to teach people.

Livy celebrated Rome's greatness, but the Roman historian Tacitus took a darker view. He believed that Rome's emperors had taken people's freedom. Tacitus also thought Romans were losing the values that made them strong. He accused them of wasting time on sports and other pleasures.

Also like the Greeks, the Romans enjoyed plays. Roman plays were often based on Greek tragedies and comedies. Playwrights, such as the tragedy writer Seneca and the comedy writers Plautus and Terence, wrote plays for religious festivals. Romans especially liked plays with humor.

Roman authors influenced later writers in Europe and America, but the language of the Romans had an even bigger impact on future generations. Latin became Europe's language for government, trade, and learning until about A.D. 1500. Latin became the basis of many modern European languages, such as Italian, French, and Spanish, and shaped many others. Many of the English words we use today come from Latin.

Roman Science and Engineering

The Romans also learned from Greek science. A Greek doctor named **Galen** (GAY•luhn) brought many medical ideas to Rome. For example, he **emphasized** the importance of anatomy (uh•NA•tuh•mee), the study of body structure. To learn about inner organs, Galen cut open dead animals and recorded his findings. Doctors in Europe studied Galen's books for more than 1,500 years.

Another important scientist of the Roman Empire was **Ptolemy** (TAH•luh•mee). Ptolemy lived in Alexandria, in Egypt. He studied the sky and carefully mapped over 1,000 different stars. He also studied the motion of planets and stars and created rules explaining their movements.

Even though Ptolemy incorrectly placed Earth at the center of the universe, educated people in Europe accepted his ideas for centuries. Ptolemy also produced detailed maps of the world as he knew it. As you will learn in Chapter 10, Europeans, including Christopher Columbus, relied on Ptolemy's maps when they began exploring the world in the 1400s.

While Roman scientists tried to understand how the world worked, Roman engineers built an astonishing system of roads and bridges to connect the empire. Roman engineers built roads from Rome to every part of the empire. These roads were well built, and some have survived to this day.

The Romans also used advanced engineering to supply their cities with freshwater. Engineers built **aqueducts** (A•kwuh•DUHKTS) to bring water from the hills into the cities. Aqueducts were long troughs supported by rows of arches. They carried water over long distances. At one time, 11 great aqueducts fed Rome's homes, bathhouses, fountains, and public bathrooms. Roman cities also had sewers to remove waste.

The Roman Colosseum

The Colosseum in Rome could hold some 60,000 people. It was made of concrete and had a removable canvas awning to protect spectators from the hot sun.
What was concrete made from?

A system of cages, ropes, and pulleys brought wild animals up to the Colosseum floor from rooms underground. ▼

The Way It Was

Sports & Contests

Ancient Roman Sports Sports were important to the Romans. Paintings on vases, frescoes [moist plaster], and stone show Romans playing ball, including a version of soccer. Roman girls are shown exercising with handheld weights and throwing an egg-shaped ball.

Some Roman sporting events took place in the Colosseum. Wild beast fights, battles between ships, and gladiator contests attracted Roman spectators by the thousands. Chariot racing was held in the Circus Maximus, and the drivers wore team colors of red, white, green, and blue.

▲ Scene showing gladiators in battle

Connecting to the Past
1. How do we know sports were important to the Romans?
2. How are today's sports different from Roman sports? How are they similar?

Roman Religion and Philosophy The ancient Romans worshiped many gods and goddesses. They also believed that spirits lived in natural things, such as trees and rivers. Greek gods and goddesses were popular in Rome, although they were given Roman names. For example, Zeus became Jupiter, the sky god, and Aphrodite became Venus, the goddess of love and beauty. Roman emperors also were worshiped as gods. This practice strengthened support for the government.

Romans honored their gods and goddesses by praying and offering food. Every Roman home had an altar for its household gods. At these altars, the head of the family carried out rituals. Government officials made offerings in temples. There the important gods and goddesses of Rome were honored. Some Roman priests looked for messages from the gods. They studied the insides of dead animals or watched the flight of birds, looking for meaning.

As the empire grew larger, Romans came into contact with other religions. These religions were allowed, as long as they did not threaten the government. Those that did faced severe hardships. Believers in one of these religions, Christianity, were persecuted for many years by Roman officials. Eventually, however, their faith was adopted by a Roman emperor and became the official state religion of Rome.

The Romans also borrowed ideas from Greek philosophy. For example, they borrowed and modified, or changed slightly, the Greek philosophy of **Stoicism** (STOH•uh•SIH•zuhm). For Romans, Stoicism was not about finding happiness through reason as it was for the Greeks. Instead, Stoicism encouraged Romans to live in a practical way.

Stoic philosophers urged people to participate in public affairs, to do their civic duty, and to treat conquered peoples well.

They also urged people to hold back their emotions, and to accept life's problems and deal with them as they came.

Perhaps the best-known Stoic philosophers of ancient Rome were Epictetus (EH•pihk•TEE•tuhs) and Seneca. Epictetus taught his ideas to two emperors, Trajan and Marcus Aurelius. Marcus Aurelius adopted Stoic ideas and wrote a book on Stoicism called *Meditations*.

Seneca was the Emperor Nero's tutor and helped Nero rule the Roman Empire when Nero was a young man. Seneca wrote several essays on ethics and Stoic philosophy, and he stressed that a good ruler should be merciful.

Seneca also wrote nine plays. All of his plays were tragedies, and they were very influential during the Renaissance in Europe. Many playwrights of that era, including William Shakespeare, wrote tragedies with themes similar to Seneca's plays.

Greek and Roman Gods

Greek God	Roman God	Role
Ares	Mars	god of war
Zeus	Jupiter	chief god
Hera	Juno	wife of chief god
Aphrodite	Venus	goddess of love
Artemis	Diana	goddess of the hunt
Athena	Minerva	goddess of wisdom
Hermes	Mercury	messenger god
Hades	Pluto	god of underworld
Poseidon	Neptune	god of the sea
Hephaestus	Vulcan	god of fire

Reading Check **Explain** How did the Romans improve on Greek ideas in architecture?

Study Central Need help understanding how the Romans lived? Visit ca.hss.glencoe.com and click on Study Central.

Section 1 Review

Reading Summary

Review the Main Ideas

- Under Augustus and later emperors, Rome entered an era of prosperity.

- Roman art, literature, and science borrowed much from the Greeks. Roman engineers made advances, including the development of cement, the arch, aqueducts, and domes. Romans also developed religion and philosophy.

What Did You Learn?

1. What were some of Ptolemy's scientific achievements?

2. How were the Roman and Greek religions similar?

Critical Thinking

3. **Compare and Contrast** Draw a chart like the one below. Fill in details comparing Roman and Greek art and architecture. **CA 7RC2.0**

Greek Art	Roman Art

Greek Architecture	Roman Architecture

4. **Analyze** Why is the Roman language important? **CA 7RW1.2**

5. **Summarize** In a short essay summarize Roman art and architecture. **CA 7WA2.5**

6. **The Big Ideas** The Romans borrowed ideas from other peoples. Do you think our culture today borrows ideas from other peoples? Explain **CA 7RC2.3**

7. **Reading** **Previewing** Look ahead to Section 2. Write down all of the Main Ideas in that section. Use these main ideas to create a preview of the material. **CA 7RC2.0**

The Fall of Rome

Guide to Reading

History Social Science Standards

WH7.1 Students analyze the causes and effects of the vast expansion and ultimate disintegration of the Roman Empire.

Looking Back, Looking Ahead

In Section 1, you learned about Roman life and achievements when the empire was at its height. Over time, however, the Roman Empire began to have problems, and it gradually grew weaker. Eventually, Rome fell to outside invaders.

Focusing on the Main Ideas

• Poor leadership, a declining economy, and attacks by Germanic tribes weakened the Roman Empire. *(page 145)*

• Rome finally fell when invaders swept through the empire during the A.D. 400s. *(page 149)*

• Rome passed on many achievements in government, law, language, and the arts. *(page 152)*

Locating Places
Constantinople
(KAHN•STAN•tuhn•OH•puhl)

Meeting People
Diocletian (DY•uh•KLEE•shuhn)
Constantine (KAHN•stuhn•TEEN)
Theodosius
(THEE•uh•DOH•shuhs)
Alaric (A•luh•rihk)
Odoacer (OH•duh•WAY•suhr)

Content Vocabulary
inflation (ihn•FLAY•shuhn)
barter (BAHR•tuhr)
reform (rih•FAWRM)

Academic Vocabulary
stable (STAY•buhl)
purchase (PUHR•chuhs)
consider (kuhn•SIH•duhr)

Reading Strategy
Sequencing Information Create a diagram showing the causes of the fall of the Roman Empire.

		Fall of the Roman Empire

NATIONAL GEOGRAPHIC Where & When?

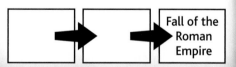

BRITAIN
GAUL
SPAIN   ITALY
Rome •
Constantinople
GREECE
EGYPT

A.D. 250	A.D. 350	A.D. 450
A.D. 284 Diocletian tries to reform empire	**A.D. 395** Roman Empire divided into eastern and western parts	**A.D. 476** Rome's last emperor overthrown

WH7.1.1 Study the early strengths and lasting contributions of Rome (e.g., significance of Roman citizenship; rights under Roman law; Roman art, architecture, engineering, and philosophy; preservation and transmission of Christianity) and its ultimate internal weaknesses (e.g., rise of autonomous military powers within the empire, undermining of citizenship by the growth of corruption and slavery, lack of education, and distribution of news).

The Decline of Rome

Main Idea Poor leadership, a declining economy, and attacks by Germanic tribes weakened the Roman Empire.

Reading Connection What do you do when you face a difficult problem? Do you try to solve it yourself? Do you ask other people for help? Read to learn about the problems the Roman Empire faced and how its leaders responded.

In A.D. 180 Marcus Aurelius died. His son, Commodus (KAH•muh•duhs), became emperor. Commodus was cruel and wasted money. Instead of ruling Rome, Commodus spent much of his time fighting as a gladiator. In A.D. 192 the emperor's bodyguard killed him. Nearly a century of confusion and fighting followed.

After Commodus, emperors called the Severans ruled Rome. Much of their time was spent putting down revolts and protecting Rome's borders. The Severans stayed in power by paying the army well, but they ignored the growing problems of crime and poverty.

Political and Social Problems When the last Severan ruler died in A.D. 235, Rome's government became very **unstable.** For almost 50 years, army leaders fought each other for the throne. During this time, Rome had 22 different emperors.

Poor leadership was not Rome's only difficulty. Fewer Romans honored the old ideals of duty, courage, and honesty. Many government officials took bribes. As problems

The Decline of Rome

Weak Roman Government
• Dishonest government officials provide poor leadership.

Social Problems
• Famine and disease spread throughout the empire.

Declining Economy
• Income and wages fall.
• Wealthy fail to pay taxes.

Reform Fails and Rome Divides in Two
• Government fails to keep order.
• Violence and tension increase.
• Diocletian divides the empire.

Eastern Roman Empire
• Constantinople becomes the new capital.
• The empire survives attacks and prospers.

Western Roman Empire
• Numerous attacks threaten the empire.
• Territory is slowly lost to invaders.

Byzantine Empire
• This empire is created from the Eastern Roman Empire and lasts nearly 1,000 years.

Rome Falls
• The city of Rome falls in A.D. 476.
• The Western Roman Empire is divided into Germanic kingdoms by A.D. 550.

Understanding Charts

Many issues, including a weak government, lack of food, and fewer jobs, led to Rome's decline.
1. According to the flow chart, what occurred after reform failed?
2. **Cause and Effect** What were the final effects of the Roman Empire being split in two?

increased, talented people often refused to serve in government. Many wealthy citizens even stopped paying taxes. Fewer people attended schools, and a large number of the empire's people were now enslaved. Wealthy Romans supported slavery because it was a cheap way to get work done.

Economic and Military Problems During the A.D. 200s, Rome's economy began to erode. As government weakened, law and order broke down. Roads and bridges were destroyed, and trade routes became unsafe. Information could not be sent quickly across the empire, and Rome's army could no longer organize quickly enough to drive out invaders. Roman soldiers and invaders seized crops and destroyed fields. Farmers grew less food, and hunger began to spread.

As the economy worsened, people **purchased** fewer goods. Artisans produced less, and shopkeepers lost money. Many businesses closed, and the number of workers dropped sharply. Many workers had to leave jobs and serve in the army.

Rome also began to suffer from **inflation** (ihn•FLAY•shuhn), or rapidly increasing prices. Inflation happens when money loses its value. How did this happen? The weak economy meant fewer taxes were paid. With less money coming in, the Roman government could not afford to defend its territories and had to find a way to pay its soldiers and officials. One way for the government to get the money it needed was to put less gold in its coins.

By putting less gold in each coin, the government could make extra coins and pay for more things. People soon learned that the coins did not have as much gold in them, and the coins began losing value. Prices went up, and many people stopped using money altogether. They began to **barter** (BAHR•tuhr), or exchange goods without using money.

Meanwhile, invaders swept into the empire. In the west, Germanic tribes raided Roman farms and towns. In the east, armies from Persia pushed into the empire's territory. As fighting increased, the government could no longer enlist and pay Romans as soldiers. It began using Germanic warriors in the army. However, these Germanic soldiers were not loyal to Rome.

Primary Source — Distrust of Money

As the Roman Empire declined, people stopped trusting the value of money.

"Whereas [because] the public officials have assembled and have accused the bankers of the exchange banks of having closed them because of their unwillingness to accept the divine coin of the emperors, it has become necessary to issue an order to all owners of the banks to open them and to accept and exchange all coin except the absolutely spurious [false] and counterfeit—and not alone to them but to those who engage in business transactions of any kind."

▲ Roman coins

—"Distrust of Imperial Coinage," *Oxyrhynchus Papyrus*, no. 1411, Vol. 2, A.S. Hunt, trans.

DBQ Document-Based Question

What do you think was happening to the economy of the empire as people stopped using the official money?

What Were Diocletian's Reforms?

In A.D. 284 a general named **Diocletian** (DY•uh•KLEE•shuhn) became emperor. To stop the empire's decline, he introduced **reforms** (rih•FAWRMZ), or political changes to make things better. Because the empire was too large for one person to rule, Diocletian divided it into four parts. He named officials to rule these areas but kept authority over all.

Diocletian also worked to boost the economy. To slow inflation, he issued rules that set the prices of goods and the wages to be paid to workers. To make sure more goods were generated, he ordered workers to remain at the same jobs until they died. Diocletian's reforms failed. The people ignored the new rules, and Diocletian did not have enough power to make them obey.

Who Was Constantine?

In A.D. 305 Diocletian retired from office. After a period of conflict, another general named **Constantine** (KAHN•stuhn•TEEN) became emperor in A.D. 312. To aid the economy, Constantine issued several orders. The sons of workers had to follow their fathers' trades, the sons of farmers had to work the land their fathers worked, and the sons of soldiers had to serve in the army.

Constantine's changes did not halt the empire's decline in the west. As a result, Constantine moved the capital from Rome to a new city in the east. He chose the site of the Greek city of Byzantium (buh•ZAN•tee•uhm). There he built a forum, an amphitheater called the Hippodrome, and many palaces. The city became known as **Constantinople** (KAHN•STAN•tuhn•OH•puhl). Today, Constantinople is called Istanbul.

✓ Reading Check **Explain** How did Diocletian try to reverse the decline of Rome?

The Way It Was

Focus on Everyday Life

Slavery in the Roman Empire Public and private slavery were common in Roman society. Public slaves were held by the state. They took care of important buildings and served government officials. Educated public slaves were used to help organize the governments of conquered areas.

Private slaves were held by individuals. They were often forced to work long hours and could be sold at any time. Wealthy Romans had hundreds or even thousands of enslaved people. Most enslaved people worked on farms.

Most enslaved people were men. This was probably because their work required great strength. Some enslaved men also became gladiators. Enslaved women made clothing and cooked for their owner's family.

▼ Roman slaves at work

Connecting to the Past
1. What was the main difference between public and private enslavement?
2. Which jobs were probably considered the most desirable by enslaved people?

Biography

WH7.1.1 Study the early strengths and lasting contributions of Rome (e.g., significance of Roman citizenship; rights under Roman law; Roman art, architecture, engineering, and philosophy; preservation and transmission of Christianity) and its ultimate internal weaknesses (e.g., rise of autonomous military powers within the empire, undermining of citizenship by the growth of corruption and slavery, lack of eduction, and distribution of news).

CONSTANTINE THE GREAT
c. A.D. 280–337

First Christian Roman Emperor

Constantine was the first Roman Emperor to become a Christian, although he was not baptized until near his death in A.D. 337. He first came to believe in Christianity many years earlier, when he was a military leader. Constantine believed he had seen a flaming cross in the sky that said, "By this sign thou shall conquer." The next day his army was victorious in an important battle. He believed that the cross was a call to the Christian God.

During his reign, Constantine granted new opportunities to Christians and helped advance the power of the early Catholic Church. At the Council of Nicea in A.D. 325, he encouraged discussion about the acceptance of the Trinity (Father, Son, and Holy Spirit). He also boosted the political positions and power of bishops within the Roman government.

Even though Constantine had many political and religious successes, his life was filled with controversy and tragedy. Constantine married a woman named Fausta. His eldest son from a previous marriage was named Crispus. Fausta accused Crispus of crimes and claimed that he was planning to seize the throne. Constantine was so shocked that he had his son killed. Constantine later discovered that Fausta had lied because she wanted her own son to be in line for the throne. He then had Fausta killed.

▲ Constantine

▲ **Modern-day Constantinople**

Then and Now

Constantine believed freedom of religion was important for the success of his empire and made sure that Christians could no longer be persecuted. What part of the U.S. Constitution protects freedom of religion?

WH7.1.1 Study the early strengths and lasting contributions of Rome (e.g., significance of Roman citizenship; rights under Roman law; Roman art, architecture, engineering, and philosophy; preservation and transmission of Christianity) and its ultimate internal weaknesses (e.g., rise of autonomous military powers within the empire, undermining of citizenship by the growth of corruption and slavery, lack of education, and distribution of news). WH7.1.2 Discuss the geographic borders of the empire at its height and the factors that threatened its territorial cohesion.

Rome Falls

Main Idea Rome finally fell when invaders swept through the empire during the A.D. 400s.

Reading Connection How would you feel if a favorite place—a shop, park, or recreation center—was closed after being open for many years? Read to learn how the Romans had to face an even greater loss when their city and empire fell.

Both Diocletian and Constantine failed to save the Roman Empire. When Constantine died in A.D. 337, fighting broke out again. A new emperor called **Theodosius** (THEE•uh•DOH•shuhs) finally gained control and ended the fighting.

Ruling the empire proved to be difficult. Theodosius decided to divide the empire after his death. In A.D. 395, the Roman Empire split into two separate empires. One was the Western Roman Empire, with its capital at Rome. The other was the Eastern Roman Empire, with its capital at Constantinople.

Rome Is Invaded As Rome declined, it was no longer able to hold back the Germanic tribes on its borders. Many different Germanic groups existed—Ostrogoths, Visigoths, Franks, Vandals, Angles, and Saxons. They came from the forests and marshes of northern Europe.

These Germanic groups were in search of warmer climates and better grazing land for their cattle. They also were drawn by Rome's wealth and culture. In addition, many were fleeing the Huns, fierce warriors from Mongolia in Asia.

In the late A.D. 300s, the Huns entered Eastern Europe and defeated the Ostrogoths (AHS•truh•GAHTHS). The Visigoths, fearing they would be next, asked the Eastern Roman emperor for protection. He let them settle just inside the empire's border. In return, they promised to be loyal to Rome.

Before long, trouble broke out between the Visigoths and Romans. The empire forced the Visigoths to buy food at very high prices. The Romans also kidnapped and enslaved many Visigoths.

Finally, the Visigoths rebelled against the Romans. In A.D. 378 they defeated Roman legions at the Battle of Adrianople (AY•dree•uh•NOH•puhl). After that defeat, Rome was forced to surrender land to the Visigoths inside Roman territory.

 **Rome Is Attacked**

In this excerpt from one of his letters, the Christian leader Jerome describes attacks on the Roman provinces.

▲ Saint Jerome

"Who would believe that Rome, victor over all the world, would fall, that she would be to her people both the womb and the tomb.... Where we cannot help we mourn and mingle with theirs our tears.... There is not an hour, not even a moment, when we are not occupied with crowds of refugees, when the peace of the monastery is not invaded by a horde of guests so that we shall either have to shut the gates or neglect the Scriptures for which the gates were opened."

—Jerome, "News of the Attacks"

DBQ **Document-Based Question**

Does Jerome think the gates of the monastery should be shut? Explain.

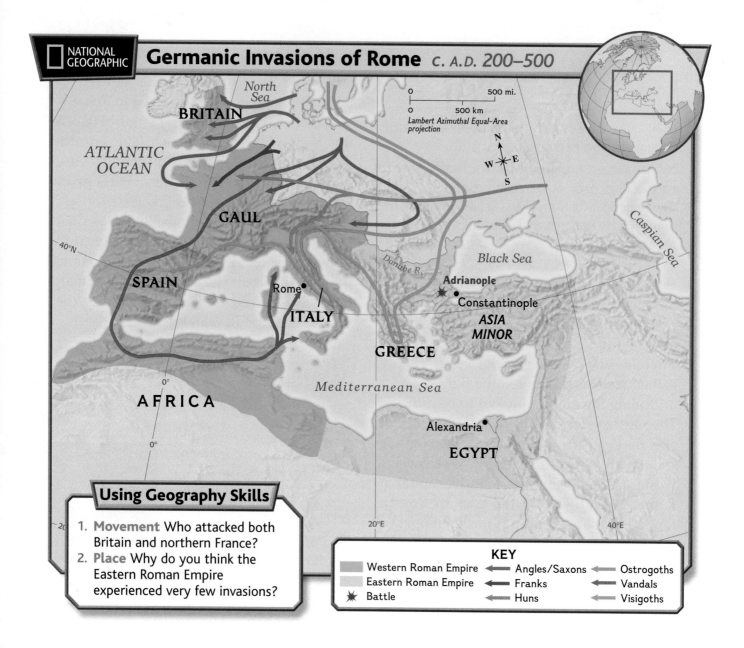

Germanic Invasions of Rome C. A.D. 200–500

NATIONAL GEOGRAPHIC

North Sea

BRITAIN

ATLANTIC OCEAN

GAUL

SPAIN

Rome

ITALY

AFRICA

Mediterranean Sea

GREECE

Danube R.

Black Sea

Adrianople

Constantinople

ASIA MINOR

Caspian Sea

Alexandria

EGYPT

40°N

0°

0°

20°E

40°E

500 mi.

500 km

Lambert Azimuthal Equal-Area projection

Using Geography Skills

1. **Movement** Who attacked both Britain and northern France?
2. **Place** Why do you think the Eastern Roman Empire experienced very few invasions?

KEY

Western Roman Empire	Angles/Saxons	Ostrogoths
Eastern Roman Empire	Franks	Vandals
Battle	Huns	Visigoths

The Germanic tribes now knew that Rome could no longer defend itself. More and more Germanic warriors crossed the borders in search of land. In the winter of A.D. 406, the Rhine River in Western Europe froze. Germanic groups crossed the frozen river and entered Gaul, which is today France. The Romans were too weak to force them back across the border.

In A.D. 410 the Visigoth leader **Alaric** (A•luh•rihk) and his soldiers captured the city of Rome. They burned records and looted the treasury. Rome's capture shocked the empire's people. It was the first time Rome had been conquered in 800 years.

Another Germanic group known as the Vandals overran Spain and northern Africa. They enslaved some Roman landowners and drove others away. Then the Vandals sailed to Italy. In A.D. 455 they entered Rome. They spent 12 days stripping buildings of everything valuable and burning them. From these attacks came the English word *vandalism*, which means "the willful destruction of property."

▲ An image showing the Visigoths invading Rome. *What leader did the Visigoths overthrow to take control of Rome?*

Rome Falls By the mid-A.D. 400s, several Germanic leaders held high posts in Rome's government and army. In A.D. 476 a Germanic general named **Odoacer** (OH•duh•WAY•suhr) took control, overthrowing the western emperor, a 14-year-old boy named Romulus Augustulus (RAHM•yuh•luhs aw•GUHS•chah•luhs). After Romulus Augustulus, no emperor ever again ruled from Rome. Historians often use this event to mark the end of the Western Roman Empire.

Odoacer controlled Rome for almost 15 years. Then a group of Visigoths seized the city and killed Odoacer. They set up a kingdom in Italy under their leader, Theodoric (thee•AH•duh•rihk). Elsewhere in Europe, other Germanic kingdoms arose. For example, in the Roman province of Gaul, where France is today, a Germanic people called the Franks took power in A.D. 486. Ten years later, Clovis, the Frankish king, became a Catholic. Before long, nearly all of the Franks became Catholic, helping to spread Christianity in Europe.

By A.D. 550, the Western Roman Empire had faded away. Many Roman beliefs and practices remained in use, however. For example, Europe's new Germanic rulers adopted the Latin language, Roman laws, and Christianity. Although the Western Roman Empire fell to Germanic invaders, the Eastern Roman Empire prospered. It became known as the Byzantine Empire and lasted nearly 1,000 more years.

✔ **Reading Check** **Identify** Which event usually marks the fall of the Western Roman Empire?

WH7.1.1 Study the early strengths and lasting contributions of Rome (e.g., significance of Roman citizenship; rights under Roman law; Roman art, architecture, engineering, and philosophy; preservation and transmission of Christianity) and its ultimate internal weaknesses (e.g., rise of autonomous military powers within the empire, undermining of citizenship by the growth of corruption and slavery, lack of education, and distribution of news).

The Legacy of Rome

Main Idea Rome passed on many achievements in government, law, language, and the arts.

Reading Connection Did you know that the words "doctor," "animal," "circus," and "family" come from Latin, the Roman language? Read to discover other things we have borrowed from the Romans.

A legacy is something that someone leaves to future generations of people. The Romans left a large legacy. Our world would be very different if the Romans had never existed. Many words in the English language and many of our ideas about government come from the Romans. The same is true for our system of laws and our knowledge about building. Roman rule also allowed Christianity to spread.

Roman Ideas and Government Today

Roman ideas about law, as first written in the Twelve Tables, still exist. Like the Romans, we believe that all people are equal under the law. We expect our judges to decide cases fairly, and we **consider** a person innocent until proven guilty.

Linking Past & Present

Roman and Modern Architecture

PAST Early Romans borrowed architectural ideas from the Greeks, but they also developed their own style. Roman designs often included vaults, columns, domes, and arches. New architectural ideas meant that buildings could be constructed in new ways. Because of concrete and a new design, Roman theaters did not have to be built on natural slopes to have tiered seating.

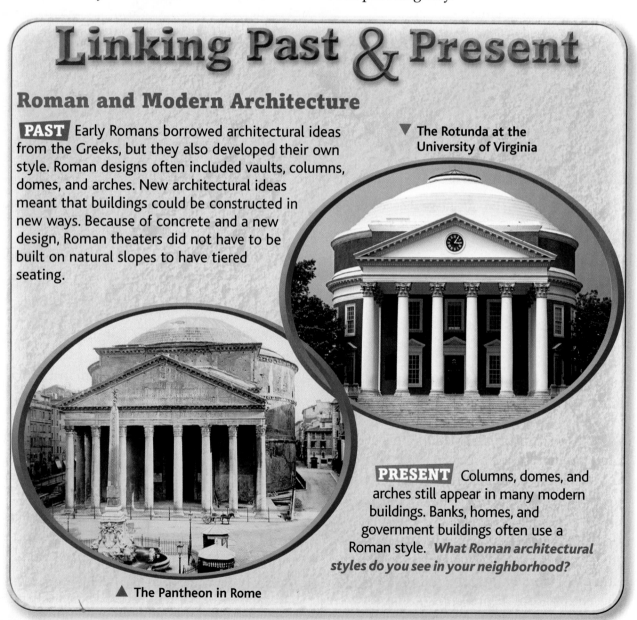

▼ The Rotunda at the University of Virginia

▲ The Pantheon in Rome

PRESENT Columns, domes, and arches still appear in many modern buildings. Banks, homes, and government buildings often use a Roman style. *What Roman architectural styles do you see in your neighborhood?*

Roman ideas about government and citizenship are also important today. Like the early Romans, Americans believe that a republic made up of equal citizens is the best form of government. We also believe that a republic works best if citizens do their duty, participate in government, and work to make their society better.

Roman Influence on Culture Today the alphabet of the Latin language, which expanded from 22 to 26 letters, is used throughout the Western world. Latin shaped the languages of Italy, France, Spain, Portugal, and Romania.

Many English words also come from Latin. Scientists, doctors, and lawyers still use Latin phrases. Every known species of plant and animal has a Latin name. Today, many people still read the works of Romans such as Virgil, Horace, Livy, and Tacitus.

Ancient Rome also left a lasting impact on architecture. We still use concrete for construction, and Roman architectural styles are still used in public buildings today. When you visit Washington, D.C., or the capital city of any state, you will most likely see buildings with domes and arches inspired by Roman architecture.

Christianity As you probably know, Christianity is one of the major religions in the world today. Christianity began in the Roman Empire. When Rome's government adopted Christianity in the A.D. 300s, it helped the new religion to grow and spread.

 **Reading Check** **Compare** Which aspects of the Roman Empire are reflected in present-day cultures?

History Online

Study Central Need help with the fall of Rome? Visit ca.hss.glencoe.com and click on Study Central.

Section 2 Review

Reading Summary
Review the Main Ideas

- A series of weak emperors, invasions by outsiders, and a number of other factors led to a greatly weakened Roman Empire.

- Numerous invasions by Germanic peoples led to the fall of Rome in A.D. 476.

- Roman ideas about government and Roman architecture are just some of the legacies of ancient Rome.

What Did You Learn?

1. What social problems helped cause the empire's decline?

2. Why did the Roman government use Germanic warriors in its army?

Critical Thinking

3. **Summarizing Information** Draw a diagram like the one below. Fill in details about Rome's legacy in government, law, and citizenship. **CA 7RC2.0**

Roman Legacies

4. **Cause and Effect** What caused Rome's economy to weaken? How did inflation affect Rome? **CA HI6.**

5. **Describe** Who were the Visigoths, and why are they important? **CA HI2.**

6. **The Big Ideas** What is the influence of Rome's language and architecture today? **CA 7RC2.3**

7. **Persuasive Writing** Write an essay explaining what you think is the main reason for the decline and fall of the Roman Empire and what might have been done to prevent it. **CA 7WS1.2; 7WA2.5**

You Decide . . .

Was the Fall of Rome Inevitable?

Yes

Many historians believe that the decline and fall of Rome could not have been avoided. The problems the empire faced were too great. One famous historian of ancient Rome, Englishman Edward Gibbon, wrote

" . . . the decline of Rome was the natural and inevitable effect of immoderate greatness. Prosperity ripened the principle of decay; the causes of destruction multiplied with the extent of conquest; and, as soon as time or accident had removed the artificial supports, the stupendous fabric yielded to the pressure of its own weight."

—Edward Gibbon, *The Decline and Fall of the Roman Empire*

Some historians think many factors made the fall of Rome inevitable, including the following:

- Rulers were weak, ineffective, and corrupt.
- There was no system for choosing a new emperor.
- The empire was too big to govern well.
- The army relied on permanent paid soldiers, not temporary citizen volunteers.
- Plague and famine weakened the population.

- The empire relied too much on slavery.
- People refused to pay taxes, and the government could not raise enough money.
- Without enough money the government put less gold in its coins, money lost its value, and prices began to rise.
- The cost of the army was too high, and it declined in size over time.
- Attacks by outside invaders and lack of money for roads and bridges caused trade to decline.
- The division of the empire into East and West caused a lack of unity.

▲ **Visigoths entering Rome**

▲ Roman general and his soldiers

- strengthen the army by increasing pay
- reinforce the empire's borders against invasion
- rebuild roads and bridges and build new ships to increase trade
- develop a better communication system to help the government control the empire
- force people to leave Rome and other cities and return to the countryside where more food and clean water were available
- reduce the number of slaves or abolish slavery
- break up large estates and give the land to former slaves, poor people in the cities, and members of the army as a reward for their loyalty
- develop a new system of currency with money that held its value

No

Other historians believe the Romans could have solved the problems facing their empire. Some possible solutions to Rome's problems include the following:

- develop a system for choosing a new emperor
- restore power to the Senate and other parts of the government so more people would support the government
- end corruption by enforcing the law and punishing corrupt officials
- increase the size of the army, possibly by asking all citizens to serve in times of emergency

You Be the Historian

Checking for Understanding

1. Define *immoderate*. Identify some ways in which being too great would weaken a country. `CA 7RW1.3; 7RC2.3`

2. Do you think a country or empire can become too large to rule effectively? Explain your reasons. `CA 7RC2.3` `CA CS3.`

3. Which of the causes of Rome's fall do you think would be the easiest to correct? The most difficult? Write a short essay explaining how you would solve this problem. `CA 7WA2.4`

Section 3

The Byzantine Empire

Guide to Reading

History Social Science Standards

WH7.1 Students analyze the causes and effects of the vast expansion and ultimate disintegration of the Roman Empire.

Looking Back, Looking Ahead

In the last section, you learned that even though the Roman Empire in the West fell, the Eastern Roman Empire survived and prospered. It became known as the Byzantine Empire. The Byzantines developed a new civilization based on Greek, Roman, and Christian ideas.

Focusing on the Main Ideas

- The Eastern Roman Empire grew rich and powerful as the Western Roman Empire fell. *(page 157)*

- The policies and reforms of Emperor Justinian and Empress Theodora helped make the Byzantine Empire strong. *(page 158)*

- Church and government worked closely together in the Byzantine Empire. *(page 161)*

- The Byzantines developed a rich culture based on Roman, Greek, and Christian ideas. *(page 163)*

Locating Places

Black Sea
Aegean Sea (ih•JEE•uhn)

Meeting People

Justinian (juh•STIH•nee•uhn)
Theodora (THEE•uh•DOHR•uh)
Belisarius (BEH•luh•SAR•ee•uhs)
Tribonian (truh•BOH•nee•uhn)

Content Vocabulary

mosaic (moh•ZAY•ihk)
saint (SAYNT)
regent (REE•juhnt)

Academic Vocabulary

utilize (YOO•tuhl•EYEZ)
image (IH•mihj)
stress (STREHS)

Reading Strategy

Cause and Effect Complete a chart to show the causes and effects of Justinian's new law code.

| Causes | → | New Code of Laws | → | Effects |

NATIONAL GEOGRAPHIC **Where & When?**

BALKAN PENINSULA
SPAIN ITALY
Rome
Constantinople
ASIA MINOR
EGYPT

A.D. 525

A.D. 550

A.D. 575

A.D. 527 Emperor Justinian begins rule

A.D. 537 Hagia Sophia completed

A.D. 565 Justinian dies

The Rise of the Byzantines

Main Idea The Eastern Roman Empire grew rich and powerful as the Western Roman Empire fell.

Reading Connection Think of your own community. How have groups of people from different backgrounds contributed to its character? What would your town or city be like without these contributions from all the different groups? Read to learn about the different groups that made up the Byzantine Empire.

The Eastern Roman, or Byzantine, Empire reached a high point in the A.D. 500s. At this time, the empire stretched west to Italy, south to Egypt, and east to the border with Arabia. Greeks made up the empire's largest group, but many other peoples were found within the empire. They included Egyptians, Syrians, Arabs, Armenians, Jews, Persians, Slavs, and Turks.

Why Is Constantinople Important?

In the last section, you learned that Emperor Constantine moved the capital of the Roman Empire from Rome to a new city called Constantinople. Constantine's city became the capital of the Byzantine Empire. By the A.D. 500s, Constantinople had become one of the world's great cities.

One reason for Constantinople's success was its location. It lay on the waterways between the **Black Sea** and the **Aegean Sea** (ih•JEE•uhn). Its harbors offered a safe shelter for fishing boats, trading ships, and warships. Constantinople also sat at the crossroads of trade routes between Europe and Asia. Trade made the city extremely wealthy.

Constantinople had a secure land location. Lying on a peninsula, Constantinople was easily defended. Seas protected it on three sides, and on the fourth side, a huge wall guarded the city. Invaders could not easily take Constantinople.

▲ The ancient walled city of Constantinople

Influence of Greek Culture

The Byzantines at first followed Roman ways. Constantinople was known as the "New Rome." Its public buildings and palaces were built in the Roman style. The city even had an oval arena called the Hippodrome, where chariot races and other events were held.

Byzantine political and social life also were based on that of Rome. Emperors spoke Latin and enforced Roman laws. The empire's poor people received free bread and shows. Wealthy people lived in town or on large farming estates. In fact, many of them had once lived in Rome.

History Online

Web Activity Visit ca.hss.glencoe.com and click on *Chapter 1—Student Web Activity* to learn more about Roman civilization.

WH7.1.3 Describe the establishment by Constantine of the new capital in Constantinople and the development of the Byzantine Empire, with an emphasis on the consequences of the development of two distinct European civilizations, Eastern Orthodox and Roman Catholic, and their two distinct views on church-state relations.

As time passed, the Byzantine Empire became less Roman and more Greek. Most Byzantines spoke Greek and honored their Greek past. Byzantine emperors and officials began to speak Greek too. The ideas of non-Greek peoples, like the Egyptians and the Slavs, also shaped Byzantine life. Still other customs came from Persia to the east. All of these cultures blended together to form the Byzantine civilization. Between A.D. 500 and A.D. 1200, the Byzantines had one of the world's richest and most advanced empires.

✓ **Reading Check** **Explain** Why did the Byzantine Empire have such a blending of cultures?

Emperor Justinian

Main Idea The policies and reforms of Emperor Justinian and Empress Theodora helped make the Byzantine Empire strong.

Reading Connection Do you sometimes rewrite reports to make them easier to understand? Read to learn how Justinian rewrote and reorganized the Byzantine law code.

Justinian (juh•STIH•nee•uhn) became emperor of the Byzantine Empire in A.D. 527 and ruled until A.D. 565. Justinian was a strong leader. He controlled the military, made laws, and was supreme judge. His orders could not be questioned.

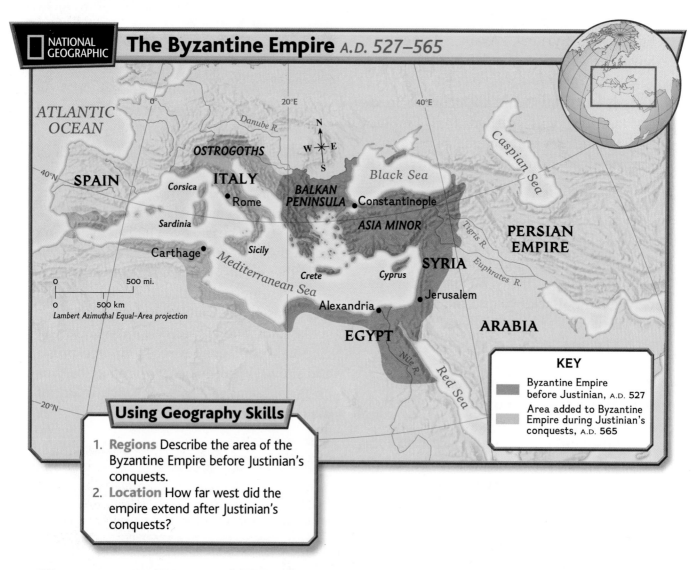

NATIONAL GEOGRAPHIC

The Byzantine Empire A.D. 527–565

KEY

- Byzantine Empire before Justinian, A.D. 527
- Area added to Byzantine Empire during Justinian's conquests, A.D. 565

Using Geography Skills

1. **Regions** Describe the area of the Byzantine Empire before Justinian's conquests.
2. **Location** How far west did the empire extend after Justinian's conquests?

Justinian's wife, the empress **Theodora** (THEE•uh•DOHR•uh), helped him run the empire. Theodora, a former actress, was intelligent and strong-willed, and she helped Justinian choose government officials. Theodora also convinced him to give women more rights. For the first time, a Byzantine wife could own land. If she became a widow, income from the land would help her take care of her children.

In A.D. 532 Theodora helped save Justinian's throne. Angry taxpayers threatened to overthrow Justinian and stormed the palace. Justinian's advisers urged him to leave Constantinople. Theodora, however, told him to stay and fight. Justinian took Theodora's advice. He stayed in the city and crushed the uprising. By doing this, Justinian not only restored order but also strengthened his power to rule.

Justinian's Conquests
Justinian wanted to reunite the Roman Empire and bring back Rome's glory. To do this, he had to conquer Western Europe and northern Africa. He ordered a general named **Belisarius** (BEH•luh•SAR•ee•uhs) to strengthen and lead the Byzantine army.

When Belisarius took command, he reorganized the Byzantine army. Instead of foot soldiers, the Byzantine army **utilized** cavalry—soldiers mounted on horses. Byzantine cavalry wore armor and carried bows and lances, which were long spears.

During Justinian's reign, the Byzantine military conquered most of Italy and northern Africa and defeated the Persians in the east. However, Justinian conquered too much too quickly. After he died, the empire did not have the money to finance an army large enough to hold all of the territory in the west. About three years after he died, much of Northern Italy was lost to an invading tribe of Germans.

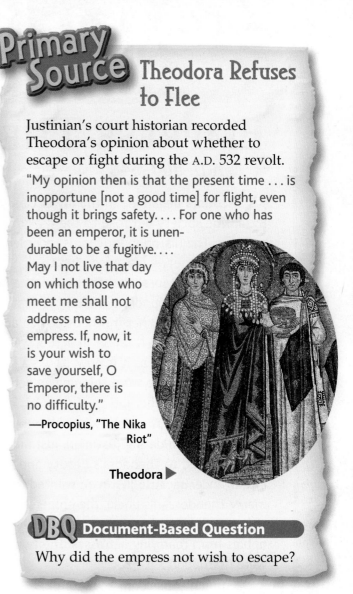

Primary Source
Theodora Refuses to Flee

Justinian's court historian recorded Theodora's opinion about whether to escape or fight during the A.D. 532 revolt.

"My opinion then is that the present time . . . is inopportune [not a good time] for flight, even though it brings safety. . . . For one who has been an emperor, it is unendurable to be a fugitive. . . . May I not live that day on which those who meet me shall not address me as empress. If, now, it is your wish to save yourself, O Emperor, there is no difficulty."

—Procopius, "The Nika Riot"

Theodora ▶

DBQ Document-Based Question

Why did the empress not wish to escape?

Justinian's Law Code
Justinian decided that the empire's laws were disorganized and too difficult to understand. He ordered a group of legal scholars headed by **Tribonian** (truh•BOH•nee•uhn) to reform the law code.

The group's new simplified code became known as the Justinian Code. Officials, businesspeople, and individuals could now more easily understand the empire's laws. Over the years, the Justinian Code has had a great influence on the laws of almost every country in Europe.

✓ **Reading Check** **Explain** What did Justinian accomplish during his reign?

Biography

WH7.1.3 Describe the establishment by Constantine of the new capital in Constantinople and the development of the Byzantine Empire, with an emphasis on the consequences of the development of two distinct European civilizations, Eastern Orthodox and Roman Catholic, and their two distinct views on church-state relations.

EMPRESS THEODORA

c. A.D. 500–548

Theodora began life in the lower class of Byzantine society but rose to the rank of empress. The historian Procopius recorded the events of her early life. According to Procopius, Theodora's father worked as a bear keeper at the Hippodrome. After his death, Theodora followed her mother's advice and became an actress. A career in acting was not as glamorous then as it is now. It was a job of the lower class, like wool spinning, which was Theodora's other job.

Even though Theodora was of the lower class, she began dating Justinian. Justinian was attracted to Theodora's beauty and intelligence. Because Justinian wanted to marry Theodora, his uncle, the emperor, changed the law that prevented upper-class nobles from marrying actresses. The two were married in A.D. 525.

Justinian considered Theodora his intellectual equal. In his writings, Justinian said he asked for Theodora's advice on laws and policies. At Theodora's urging, he granted more rights to women. Some historians believe Theodora had great power within the royal court, perhaps more than Justinian. For example, nearly all the laws passed during Theodora's reign as empress mention her name. Theodora and Justinian had no children together. When Theodora died from cancer in A.D. 548, Justinian was overcome with grief. He had her portrait incorporated into many works of art, including numerous Byzantine mosaics.

▲ **Empress Theodora advises Emperor Justinian.**

> **"She was extremely clever and had a biting wit."**
> —Procopius, *The Secret History*

Then and Now

Name a modern-day female political leader that you think has great influence in making and changing laws. Explain your choice.

The Byzantine Church

Main Idea Church and government worked closely together in the Byzantine Empire.

Reading Connection In our country, religion and government are separated. Read to learn about the relationship between religion and government in the Byzantine Empire.

As you learned earlier, the church of Rome survived the fall of the Western Roman Empire. Its head, the pope, became the strongest leader in Western Europe. Under the pope, the Latin churches of the region became known as the Roman Catholic Church. In the East, however, the Roman Empire continued. It developed into the Byzantine Empire (BIH•zuhn•TEEN EHM•PYR). Like Roman Catholics in the West, the Byzantines developed their own form of Christianity. It was based on their Greek heritage and was known as the Eastern Orthodox Church.

Church and State Church and government worked closely together in the Byzantine Empire. The Byzantines believed their emperor represented Jesus Christ on Earth. The emperor was crowned in a religious ceremony.

The emperor also chose the patriarch of Constantinople, the leading Church official in the Byzantine Empire. In this way, the emperor controlled the Church as well as the government. Byzantines believed that God wanted them to preserve and spread Christianity. All Church and government officials were united in this goal.

Religious Arguments Byzantines, from the emperor down to the poorest farmer, were very interested in religious matters. In homes and shops, they argued about religious questions. For example, Byzantines loved to discuss the exact relationship between Jesus and God.

In the A.D. 700s, a major dispute divided the Church in the Byzantine Empire. The argument was over the use of icons (EYE•kahnz). Icons are pictures or **images** of Jesus, Mary (the mother of Jesus), and the saints, or Christian holy people. Many Byzantines honored icons. They covered the walls of their churches with them. A few important icons were even believed to work miracles.

Some Byzantines, however, wanted an end to the use of icons. They thought that honoring them was a form of idol worship forbidden by God. Supporters of icons, however, claimed that icons were symbols of God's presence in daily life. These images, they said, helped explain Christianity to people.

Emperor Leo III did not approve of icons. In A.D. 726 he ordered all icons removed from the churches. Government

▲ This gold Byzantine incense burner is in the shape of a church. *What was the Christian church that developed in the Byzantine Empire called?*

officials who carried out his orders were known as iconoclasts (eye•KAH•nuh•KLASTS), or image breakers. We use this word today to mean someone who attacks traditional beliefs or institutions.

Most Byzantines, many church leaders, and even the pope in Rome opposed the emperor's order. In fact, the dispute over icons damaged ties between the churches of Rome and Constantinople. Over the next 100 years, the argument cooled, and the use of icons became accepted once again. They are still an important part of Eastern Orthodox religious practice.

Conflicts Between Churches
Icons were not the only issue that caused bitterness between the churches of Constantinople and Rome.

▲ This icon on wood shows the archangel Gabriel, who served as a messenger for God according to the Bible. *What reasons were given to support the use of icons?*

The most serious argument was about how churches were to be run. The pope claimed that he was the head of all Christian churches. The Byzantines did not accept the pope's claim. They believed the patriarch of Constantinople and other bishops were equal to the pope.

Making matters worse was the fact that each church sometimes refused to help the other when outsiders attacked. In the late A.D. 700s, the Byzantine emperor refused to help the pope when Italy was invaded. The pope turned instead to a Germanic people called the Franks for help. The Franks were Roman Catholics and loyal to the pope.

The pope was grateful to the Franks for stopping the invasion. In A.D. 800 he gave the Frankish king, Charlemagne (SHAHR•luh•MAYN), the title of emperor. This angered the Byzantines. They believed the leader of the Byzantines was the only true emperor.

This conflict pointed out the differences in how each church felt about relations with the government. In the Byzantine Empire, the emperor was in control, with church leaders respecting his wishes. In the West, however, the pope claimed both spiritual and political power. He often quarreled with kings over church and government affairs.

Finally, after centuries of tension, the pope and the patriarch of Constantinople took a drastic step in their ongoing feud. In A.D. 1054 they excommunicated (EHK•skuh•MYOO•nuh•KAY•tuhd) each other. Excommunication means to declare that a person or group no longer belongs to the church. This began a schism (SKIH•zuhm), or separation, of the two most important branches of Christianity. The split between the Roman Catholic and Eastern Orthodox Churches has lasted to this day.

✓ **Reading Check** **Describe** How did church and government work together in the Byzantine Empire?

WH7.1.3 Describe the establishment by Constantine of the new capital in Constantinople and the development of the Byzantine Empire, with an emphasis on the consequences of the development of two distinct European civilizations, Eastern Orthodox and Roman Catholic, and their two distinct views on church-state relations.

Byzantine Civilization

Main Idea **The Byzantines developed a rich culture based on Roman, Greek, and Christian ideas.**

Reading Connection Do you think a multicultural population adds to a country's interest and success? Read to learn how the diverse groups of the Byzantine Empire contributed to its culture.

From the A.D. 500s to the A.D. 1100s, the Byzantine Empire was the center of trade between Europe and Asia. Trade goods from present-day Russia in the north, Mediterranean lands in the south, Latin Europe in the west, and Persia and China in the east passed through the empire. From Asia, ships and caravans brought luxury goods to Constantinople. These included spices, gems, metals, and cloth. For these items, Byzantine merchants traded farm goods as well as furs, honey, and enslaved people from northern Europe.

This enormous trade made the Byzantine Empire very rich. However, most Byzantines were not merchants. Instead they were farmers, herders, laborers, and artisans. One of the major Byzantine industries was weaving silk. It developed around A.D. 550. According to legend, at that time Byzantine travelers smuggled silkworm eggs out of China in hollow bamboo sticks. Brought to Constantinople, the silkworms fed on mulberry leaves and produced silk threads. Weavers then used the threads to make the silk cloth that brought wealth to the empire.

▲ Sculpture showing chariot racing at the Hippodrome

▲ Byzantine jewelry

▲ The style of the Hagia Sophia, shown here, and other Byzantine churches influenced the architecture of churches throughout Russia and Eastern Europe.
What does the name "Hagia Sophia" mean?

The Way It Was

Focus on Everyday Life

Byzantine Mosaics Imagine taking bits of glass and turning them into beautiful masterpieces. Byzantine artists did just that starting around A.D. 330. Roman mosaics were made of natural-colored marble pieces and decorated villas and buildings. Byzantine mosaics were different. They were made of richly colored, irregular pieces of glass and decorated the ceilings, domes, and floors of Byzantine churches.

Byzantine mosaics were created to honor religious or political leaders. The centers of domes—because they were the highest points of the churches—were commonly reserved for images of Jesus.

Mosaics were expensive. They were ordered and paid for by emperors, state officials, or church leaders. Many mosaics are still intact and can be seen today inside churches, monasteries, and museums.

Mosaic from the Byzantine Empire ▶

Connecting to the Past

1. Why do you think the name of the person who paid for the mosaic—rather than the name of the person who made the mosaic—was often recorded in the inscription?

2. What types of art do present-day artists make with glass?

Byzantine Art and Architecture The Byzantine Empire lasted approximately 1,000 years. For much of that time, Constantinople was the largest and richest city in Europe. The Byzantines were highly educated and creative. They preserved and passed on Greek culture and Roman law to other peoples. They gave the world new methods in the arts.

Justinian and other Byzantine emperors supported artists and architects. They ordered the building of churches, forts, and public buildings throughout the empire. Constantinople was known for its hundreds of churches and palaces. One of Justinian's greatest achievements was building the huge church called Hagia Sophia (HAH•jee•uh soh•FEE•uh), or "Holy Wisdom." It was completed in A.D. 537 and became the religious center of the Byzantine Empire. It still stands today in Istanbul.

Inside Hagia Sophia, worshipers could see walls of beautiful marble and mosaics. **Mosaics** (moh•ZAY•ihks) are pictures made from many bits of colored glass or stone. They were an important type of art in the Byzantine Empire. Mosaics mainly showed figures of **saints** (SAYNTS), or Christian holy people.

Byzantine Women The family was the center of social life for most Byzantines. Religion and the government **stressed** the importance of marriage and family life. Divorces were rare and difficult to get.

Byzantine women were not encouraged to lead independent lives. They were expected to stay home and take care of their families. However, women did gain some important rights, thanks to Empress Theodora. Like Theodora, some Byzantine women became well educated and involved in politics. Several royal women served as regents. A **regent** (REE•juhnt) is a person who stands in for a ruler who is too young or too ill to govern. A few ruled the empire in their own right.

Byzantine Education Learning was highly respected in Byzantine culture. The government supported the training of scholars and government officials. In Byzantine schools, boys studied religion, medicine, law, arithmetic, grammar, and other subjects. Wealthy Byzantines sometimes hired tutors to teach their children. Girls usually did not attend schools and were taught at home.

Most Byzantine authors wrote about religion. They stressed the need to obey God and save one's soul. To strengthen faith, they wrote about the lives of saints. Byzantine writers gave an important gift to the world. They copied and passed on the

▲ This Byzantine religious text is beautifully illustrated. *What did Byzantine boys study at school?*

writings of the ancient Greeks and Romans. Without Byzantine copies, many important works from the ancient world would have disappeared forever.

Reading Check **Identify** What church is one of Justinian's greatest achievements?

History Online

Study Central Need help understanding the rise of the Byzantine Empire? Visit ca.hss.glencoe.com and click on Study Central.

Section 3 Review

Reading Summary
Review the Main Ideas

- With its capital at Constantinople and strong Greek influences, the Byzantine Empire grew powerful and wealthy.

- The Byzantine emperor, Justinian, reconquered much of the land of the old Roman Empire. He also issued a new law code known as the Justinian Code.

- The Eastern Orthodox Church worked closely with the empire.

- As the Byzantine Empire grew wealthy from trade, art, architecture, and education flourished.

What Did You Learn?

1. What is a mosaic, and where were mosaics found in the Byzantine Empire?

2. How did silk weaving develop in the Byzantine Empire?

Critical Thinking

3. **Organizing Information** Draw a diagram like the one below. Fill in details about Constantinople's location. **CA** 7RC2.0

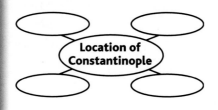

Location of Constantinople

4. **Describe** What were the consequences of Justinian's wars in Italy, North Africa, and Persia? **CA** HI2.

5. **The Big Ideas** How did geography influence Byzantine trade? **CA** CS3.

6. **Analyze** What important service did Byzantine writers provide to the rest of the world? Explain its significance. **CA** HI2.

7. **Analysis** **Understanding Geography** Study the map on page 158. Explain why geography made it hard for the Byzantine Empire to expand north or west. **CA** CS3.

Analyzing Primary Sources

WH7.1 Students analyze the causes and effects of the vast expansion and ultimate disintegration of the Roman Empire.

Problems in Rome

You have read about many of the problems of the Roman Empire. These included poor leadership, a declining economy, and attacks by Germanic tribes. Other problems also faced Rome, including the unemployed poor in Rome who did not have enough to eat and emperors who did not have a plan for choosing the next ruler of Rome. Roman rulers tried to address these problems, but they were not always successful.

Read the passages on pages 166 and 167, and answer the questions that follow.

▲ Roman coin

Reader's Dictionary

entail: to be involved in something
detriment (DEH•truh•muhnt): damage
largess (lahr•JEHS): gifts
dole: a government gift

plebs (PLEHBS): the common people
vied: competed
sesterce (SEHS•TUHRS): a Roman coin roughly equivalent to one U.S. dollar

"Bread and Circuses"

The city of Rome may have had over one million people at its height. Many people were unemployed and could not buy food. They were also bored and restless. Unhappy hungry people might rebel. The following passage by the Roman writer Fronto explains how emperors tried to solve these problems.

It was the height of political wisdom for the emperor not to neglect even actors and the other performers of the stage, the circus, and the arena, since he knew that the Roman people is held fast by two things above all, the grain supply and the shows, that the success of the government depends

▲ Gladiators in battle

on amusements as much as on serious things. Neglect of serious matters **entails** the greater **detriment,** of amusements the greater unpopularity. The money **largesses** are less eagerly desired than the shows; the largesses appease only the grain-**doled plebs** singly and individually, while the shows keep the whole population happy.

—Fronto, "Bread and Circuses"

"Empire for Sale"

One of the main problems that faced Rome was how to choose a new emperor. The following passage by Dio Cassius describes the imperial crisis of A.D. 193.

Didius Julianus . . . when he heard of the death of [Emperor] Pertinax, hastily made his way to the [Praetorian] camp and, standing at the gates of the enclosure, made bids to the soldiers for the rule over the Romans. . . . For, just as if it had been in some market or auction room, both the city and its entire Empire were auctioned off. The sellers were the ones who had slain their emperor, and the would-be buyers were Sulpicianus and Julianus, who **vied** to outbid each other. . . . They gradually raised their bids up to 20,000 **sesterces** per soldier. Some of the soldiers would carry word to Julianus, "Sulpicianus offers so much; how much more do you bid?" And to Sulpicianus in turn, "Julianus promises so much; how much do you raise him?" Sulpicianus would have won the day. . . . had not Julianus raised his bid no longer by a small amount but by 5,000 at one time. . . . So the soldiers, captivated by this extravagant bid . . . received Julianus inside and declared him emperor.

—Dio Cassius, "Empire for Sale"

Justinian's Laws

Slavery was common in both the Roman empire and the Byzantine empire. The use of enslaved workers during a time of high unemployment helped weaken the Roman Empire. When the Byzantine emperor Justinian created his law codes, he included regulations about slavery based on the old Roman slave laws. The following laws come from the Institutes, a collection of some of Justinian's laws.

Book I, Chapter III

4. Slaves either are born or become so. They are born so when their mother is a slave; they become so either by the law of nations, that is, by captivity, or by the civil law, as when a free person, above the age of twenty, suffers himself to be sold, that he may share the price given for him.

Book I, Chapter VIII

1. Slaves are in the power of masters, a power derived from the law of nations: for among all nations it may be remarked that masters have the power of life and death over their slaves, and that everything acquired by the slave is acquired for the master.

2. But at the present day none of our subjects may use unrestrained violence towards their slaves, except for a reason recognized by law. . . .

—The Institutes

DBQ Document-Based Questions

"Bread and Circuses"

1. How did the grain doles help keep order?

2. Why was it important for emperors not to neglect actors? Why was this more important than the grain dole?

"Empire for Sale"

3. How did Julianus become emperor?

4. What does this process of choosing an emperor say about the loyalty and power of the soldiers?

Justinian's Laws

5. Besides being born enslaved, what other ways could a person become enslaved?

6. Based on the laws shown, how do you think enslaved people were treated? Explain.

Read to Write

7. Write a short essay using these primary sources to answer this question: What problems do these sources reveal that may have helped cause the Roman Empire to fall?
   CA HR4.

Review Content Vocabulary

Match the definitions in the second column to the terms in the first column.

____ 1. anatomy
____ 2. inflation
____ 3. regent
____ 4. mosaic
____ 5. ode

a. pictures made of many bits of colored glass or stone
b. increasing prices
c. emotional poem about life's ups and downs
d. study of the body's structure
e. a person who stands in for a ruler who cannot govern

Review the Main Ideas

Section 1 • Life in Ancient Rome

6. How did Augustus strengthen the Roman Empire?

7. What did the Romans borrow from the Greeks? What did they develop on their own?

Section 2 • The Fall of Rome

8. What weakened the Roman Empire?

9. What caused the fall of Rome?

10. In what areas of today's society can we see Roman influence?

Section 3 • The Byzantine Empire

11. What role did trade play in the success of the Byzantine Empire?

12. What policies and reforms helped make the Byzantine Empire strong?

13. How did the Byzantine emperor maintain control over the church?

14. What different groups of people contributed to the Byzantine culture?

Critical Thinking

15. **Explain** What advances took place while the "five good emperors" ruled Rome? **CA 7RC2.3**

16. **Cause and Effect** Why did Alaric's capture of Rome shock the Roman people? **CA HI2.**

17. **Predict** What do you think would have happened if Theodosius had not divided the Roman Empire? **CA HI2.**

Geography Skills

Study the map below and answer the following questions.

18. **Place** Which areas were conquered by Justinian's military? **CA CS3.**

19. **Human/Environment Interaction** Why do you think Justinian decided to conquer lands to the west of his empire? **CA CS3.**

20. **Movement** What made it difficult for the Byzantine Empire to hold on to Justinian's conquests? **CA CS3.**

NATIONAL GEOGRAPHIC

Byzantine Empire

ATLANTIC OCEAN
SPAIN
Corsica
Sardinia
ITALY
Rome
Carthage
Sicily
Constantinople
Crete
Mediterranean Sea
Danube R.

500 mi.
500 km
Lambert Azimuthal Equal-Area projection

KEY
Byzantine Empire before Justinian, A.D. 527
Byzantine Empire after Justinian's conquests, A.D. 565

N W E S

Read to Write

21. **The Big Ideas** **Making Connections** In this chapter you learned that the culture of the Byzantine Empire was greatly influenced by the Romans and Greeks, as well as the Egyptian, Slavic, and Persian cultures. Think about the culture of the United States. Work with a classmate to prepare a report identifying parts of U.S. culture that were influenced by other cultures. **CA HI2.**

22. **Using Your** **FOLDABLES** Use the information in your foldable to create a study guide. Your study guide should include five questions that focus on the main ideas of each section. **CA 7RC2.0**

Using Academic Vocabulary

23. Change each of the words in the list below into a verb or an adjective. Check in a dictionary to see if your answers are correct.

> distinct   consider
> emphasis   stress
> stable

Building Citizenship

24. **Analyzing** Growing political and social problems helped set the stage for Rome's final fall. Traditional Roman ideas of duty, courage, and honesty lost their importance before Rome fell. Why do you think duty, courage, and honesty are important in keeping a society strong? **CA 7WA2.5**

Linking Past and Present

25. **Language Connections** Do research to find 10 words that we still use today that come from Latin. Create a chart to show these words as well as the Latin words from which they come. Be sure to include a definition with each entry. **CA 7RW1.2**

26. **Using Maps** Look at the map of the Roman Empire on page 138. Using a map of modern-day Europe, create a list of countries today that were once part of the Roman Empire. **CA CS3.**

Reviewing Skills

27. **Reading Skill** **Previewing** Imagine that a friend has to read Section 3 The Byzantine Empire and he or she asks you what the section is about. How would you go about previewing the section to give him or her a basic idea of the events that occur within the section? Write a few paragraphs explaining how to preview the section. **CA 7RC2.0**

28. **Analysis Skill** **Making Choices** What were some of the methods Rome's leaders used to strengthen the empire? How well did these methods work? What choices would you have made if you had been emperor? Write a short essay describing what you would do to make Rome strong if you were a Roman leader. **CA HI1.** **CA 7WA2.1**

Standards Practice

Read the passage below and answer the following question.

> "Who would believe that Rome, victor over all the world, would fall, that she would be to her people both the womb and the tomb. . . ."

29 The passage above, by St. Jerome, was most likely written during the reign of which emperor?

   A Julius Ceasar

   B Augustus

   C Theodosius

   D Constantine

Chapter 2

Islamic Civilization

Muslims gather around the Kaaba ▼
at the Great Mosque in Makkah.

A.D. 600   A.D. 900   1200   1500

c. A.D. 610
Muhammad
receives
prophetic call

A.D. 750
Abbasids
overthrow
Umayyads

c. 1100
Omar Khayyam
writes the
Rubaiyat

c. 1375
Ibn Khaldun
writes
histories

The Big Ideas

History Online

Chapter Overview Visit ca.hss.glencoe.com for a preview of Chapter 2.

Section 1 The Rise of Islam

Religion influences how civilization develops and how culture spreads. The religion of Islam originated in Arabia. It was based on the teachings of Muhammad.

Section 2 Islamic Empires

Exploration and trade spreads ideas and goods. Followers of Islam, called Muslims, built large empires and spread their faith through trade and conquest throughout the Middle East and the Mediterranean.

Section 3 Muslim Ways of Life

The Interaction of different societies brings about the development of new ideas, art, and technology. Muslims were skilled traders and builders. They established large cities and made many advances in mathematics, science, and the arts.

 View the Chapter 2 video in the Glencoe Video Program.

FOLDABLES™ Study Organizer

Categorizing Information *Make the following foldable to organize information about the people and places of Islamic civilization.*

Step 1 *Collect two sheets of paper and place them about 1 inch apart.*

Keep the edges straight.

Step 2 *Fold down the top edges of the paper to form four tabs.*

This makes all the tabs the same size.

Step 3 *When all the tabs are the same size, crease the paper to hold the tabs in place and staple the sheets together. Turn the paper and label each tab as shown.*

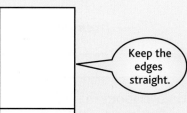

Islamic Civilization
The Rise of Islam
Islamic Empires
Muslim Ways of Life

Staple along the fold.

Reading and Writing *As you read, use your foldable to write down what you learn about Islamic civilization. Write facts on each appropriate tab.*

Making Predictions

Reading Skill

1 Learn It!

A prediction is a guess, based on what you already know. Making predictions before you read can help you understand and remember what you read. One way to predict while reading is to guess what the author will tell you next. Read the paragraph below from Section 1. Make predictions about what you will read in the rest of the section.

> Can you predict how people will react to these ideas?

> Think about what you may already know about Islam. Predict how popular it will become.

Muhammad also preached that all people were equal and that the rich should share their goods. In Makkah, where most people lived humbly, this vision of a just society was very powerful. Muhammad was saying that wealth was not as important as leading a good life. When the Day of Judgment arrived, he said God would reward the good people and punish the evildoers.

— from page 176

> What do you know about the beliefs of other religions compared to Islam? Predict how followers of other religions will react.

Reading Tip

Read titles and headings to help you predict what details are covered in each section.

After you read the rest of the chapter, go back to see if your predictions were correct.

2 Practice It!

Read the paragraph below from Section 3 of this chapter.

What Were Muslim Cities Like? Trade helped the leading Muslim cities grow. Baghdad, Cairo, and Damascus were located on trade routes that ran from the Mediterranean Sea to central Asia. However, Muslim cities were not only places of trade. They also became important centers of government, learning, and the arts.

—from page 192

Read to Write ·····

Select one photograph in this chapter. Without reading the caption, write a prediction of what you think the caption might say. Check the caption to see if your prediction is correct.

Predict what information will be discussed throughout this section, and write down your predictions. Then as you read this section, discuss your guesses with a partner, and decide if they were correct.

▲ **Arab bazaar**

3 Apply It!

Before you read the chapter, skim the questions on pages 200–201 in the Chapter Assessment. Choose three questions and predict what the answers will be.

Section 1

The Rise of Islam

History Social Science Standards

WH7.2 Students analyze the geographic, political, economic, religious, and social structures of the civilizations of Islam in the Middle Ages.

Guide to Reading

Looking Back, Looking Ahead

Previously, you learned about early empires in southwest Asia. During the A.D. 600s, people called Arabs began a new empire in the region. The driving force behind their empire building was the religion of Islam.

Focusing on the Main Ideas

- The deserts, coastline, and oases of Arabia helped shape the Arab way of life. *(page 175)*

- The prophet Muhammad brought the message of Islam to the people of Arabia. *(page 176)*

- The Quran provided guidelines for Muslims' lives and the governments of Muslim states. *(page 179)*

Locating Places

Makkah (MAH•kuh)
Kaaba (KAH•buh)
Madinah (mah•DEE•nah)

Meeting People

Bedouin (BEH•duh•wuhn)
Muhammad (moh•HAH•muhd)

Content Vocabulary

oasis (oh•AY•suhs)
sheikh (SHAYK)
caravan (KAR•uh•VAN)
Quran (koh•RAHN)

Academic Vocabulary

intense (ihn•TEHNS)
transport (trans•POHRT)

Reading Strategy

Organizing Information Use a diagram like the one below to identify the Five Pillars of faith.

Five Pillars of Faith				

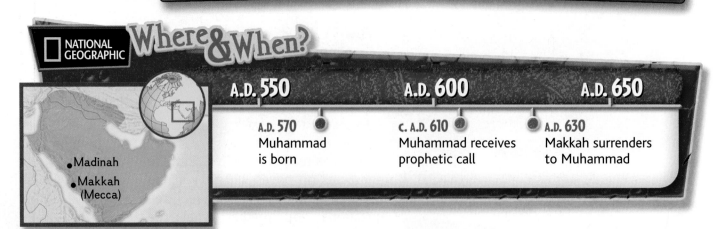

NATIONAL GEOGRAPHIC Where & When?

•Madinah
•Makkah (Mecca)

A.D. 550

A.D. 570
Muhammad is born

A.D. 600

c. A.D. 610
Muhammad receives prophetic call

A.D. 650

A.D. 630
Makkah surrenders to Muhammad

WH7.2.1 Identify the physical features and describe the climate of the Arabian peninsula, its relationship to surrounding bodies of land and water, and nomadic and sedentary ways of life. WH7.2.5 Describe the growth of cities and the establishment of trade routes among Asia, Africa, and Europe, the products and inventions that traveled along these routes (e.g., spices, textiles, paper, steel, new crops), and the role of merchants in Arab society.

Daily Life in Early Arabia

Main Idea The deserts, coastline, and oases of Arabia helped shape the Arab way of life.

Reading Connection Do you ever think about how rainfall shapes your life? Read on to find out how lack of rain helped shape the Arabs' way of life.

Surrounded by the Red Sea on the west, the Persian Gulf on the east, and the Arabian Sea to the south, the Arabian Peninsula is mostly a desert. The heat is **intense,** and a sandstorm can blind any traveler. Water is found only at **oases** (oh•AY•seez), green areas fed by underground water. Not all of Arabia is dry, however. In the mountains of the southwest, enough rain falls to support plants such as juniper and olive trees.

In ancient times, the peninsula was bounded by many different civilizations. For example, Egypt and Kush were to the west, Mesopotamia and Persia were to the north and east, and the Israelites, the Greeks, and Romans were to the north and west. Records from these civilizations indicate that many people visited or crossed the Arabian Peninsula, but few stayed.

To survive the Arabian climate, early Arabs organized into tribes whose members were very loyal to one another. The head of the tribe was called a **sheikh** (SHAYK). Some tribes lived a settled lifestyle in villages near oases or wells, or in mountain valleys.

Who Are the Bedouins?
Some Arabs were desert herders. To water and graze their camels, goats, and sheep, they went from oasis to oasis. They were called **Bedouins** (BEH•duh•wuhnz). Bedouins lived in tents and ate dried fruits and nuts. They drank the milk of their animals. Only rarely would they eat meat. Their animals were much too valuable to be used as food.

Trade and Towns
Many Arabs lived in villages where they farmed or raised animals. These villages were near oases or in the mountain valleys. Some villagers were merchants who **transported** goods across the desert. To fend off attacks by Bedouins, many traveled in a **caravan** (KAR•uh•VAN), or group of traveling merchants and animals.

By about A.D. 500, Arabian merchants handled most trade between India and the Mediterranean Sea. As their trade grew, Arab merchants founded towns along the trade routes in Arabia. **Makkah** (MAH•kuh), also known as Mecca, became the largest and richest of them all. It was a crossroads for merchants, and it was also an important religious site.

▼ Today, many Bedouins still roam the desert and live in tents. *Where did Bedouins graze their animals in the desert?*

▲ Bedouin woman making bread

175

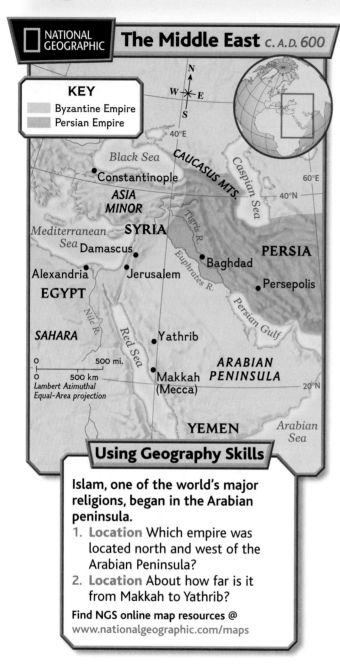

NATIONAL GEOGRAPHIC

The Middle East c. A.D. 600

KEY
- Byzantine Empire
- Persian Empire

Using Geography Skills

Islam, one of the world's major religions, began in the Arabian peninsula.

1. **Location** Which empire was located north and west of the Arabian Peninsula?
2. **Location** About how far is it from Makkah to Yathrib?

Find NGS online map resources @ www.nationalgeographic.com/maps

In the middle of Makkah was the **Kaaba** (KAH•buh), a low square building surrounded by statues of gods and goddesses. Arabs believed that the great stone inside the Kaaba was from heaven. Pilgrims, people who travel to a holy place, flocked to Makkah. Arabians worshiped many gods, but the most important was Allah. Allah was considered to be the creator.

✓ **Reading Check** **Analyze** How did geography shape life in Arabia?

Muhammad: Islam's Prophet

Main Idea The prophet Muhammad brought the message of Islam to the people of Arabia.

Reading Connection Have you ever heard someone speak and been moved to tears? The following paragraphs tell about a prophet who moved the Arab people with his words.

Muhammad's Message In A.D. 570 a man named **Muhammad** (moh•HAH•muhd) was born in Makkah. An orphan, he was raised by an uncle. As a teenager, he worked in the trusted job of caravan leader and eventually became a successful merchant. He married and had children.

Despite his success, Muhammad was dissatisfied. He felt that the wealthy town leaders should return to the old ways. He thought they should honor their families, be fair in business, and help the poor.

Muhammad went into the hills to pray. In about A.D. 610, he said he was visited by an angel and told to preach Islam. *Islam* means "surrendering to the will of Allah." *Allah* is the Arabic word for "God."

Inspired, Muhammad returned to Makkah. Everywhere he went, he told people to destroy statues of false gods and to worship only Allah, the one true God.

Muhammad also preached that all people were equal and that the rich should share their goods. In Makkah, where most people lived humbly, this vision of a just society was very powerful. Muhammad was saying that wealth was not as important as leading a good life. When the Day of Judgment arrived, he said God would reward the good people and punish the evildoers.

Opposition to Islam Slowly Muhammad convinced people that his message was true. At first, only his family became

Muslims, or followers of Islam. Soon, however, many of the poor were attracted to his message that goods should be shared.

Wealthy merchants and religious leaders did not like Muhammad's message. They thought he was trying to take away their power. They made his life difficult and beat and tortured his followers.

In A.D. 622 Muhammad and his followers left Makkah. They moved north to a town called Yathrib (YA•thruhb). The journey of Muhammad and his followers to Yathrib became known as the Hijrah (HIH•jruh). The word comes from Arabic and means "breaking off relationships." Later Muslims made the year A.D. 622 the first year of a new Muslim calendar. Yathrib welcomed Muhammad and his followers. Their city was renamed **Madinah** (mah•DEE•nah), which means "the city of the prophet."

Muhammad's Government

The people of Madinah accepted Muhammad as God's prophet and their ruler. Muhammad proved to be an able leader. He applied the laws he believed God had given him to all areas of life. Muhammad created an Islamic state—a government that uses its political power to uphold Islam. He required all Muslims to place loyalty to the Islamic state above loyalty to their tribe.

To defend his new government, Muhammad built an army. The leaders of Makkah feared he would attack. In A.D. 630 they agreed to a treaty to give control of the city to Muhammad. He then made it a holy city of Islam. Two years later, Muhammad died. By this time, Islam had begun to spread to all of Arabia.

Reading Check **Explain** Why did Muhammad's message appeal to the poor?

A pilgrimage to Makkah ▶

Journey to Makkah

A pilgrimage to the holy city of Makkah often involved a long, difficult journey across deserts and other rough country. Muslim travelers carried palm leaves to show that they were on a pilgrimage. *Where was Muhammad born?*

WH7.2.2 Trace the origins of Islam and the life and teachings of Muhammad, including Islamic teachings on the connection with Judaism and Christianity.

Biography

MUHAMMAD

A.D. 570–632

Muhammad experienced great poverty and many hardships early in his life. His father, Abd Allah, died before he was born. His grandfather, Abd al-Muttalib, took care of Muhammad in Makkah for a short time. Abd al-Muttalib felt that Makkah was an unhealthy place to raise a baby, but he could not leave because he was a political leader in the city. So he entrusted Muhammad to a tribe of nomads. They took the baby Muhammad to their home, the desert.

When Muhammad was six years old, his mother died. Two years later, when Muhammad was eight, his grandfather also died. Arab custom did not allow minors to inherit anything, so the property and money from Muhammad's father and grandfather could not be passed down to him. To survive, Muhammad needed the protection of Abu Talib, his uncle who now headed the family.

Under the care of Abu Talib, Muhammad traveled by camel on trading journeys to Syria. On one of these trips, when he was about twenty-five years old, Muhammad met a wealthy woman named Khadijah. She and Muhammad married and had four daughters. They also had at least two sons who did not live past childhood.

Muhammad's marriage to Khadijah made him a wealthy man and a member of Makkah's prosperous merchant class. However, Muhammad could not forget his early experiences. His childhood had deeply influenced Muhammad and made him a thoughtful person. He often would go up into the hills near Makkah and spend nights in a cave. Alone there, he would reflect on the problems he saw in Makkah. It was in these hills that Muhammad claimed an angel told him, "You are the Messenger of God."

▲ The Mosque of the Prophet in Madinah contains Muhammad's tomb.

Then and Now

Are any of the problems Muhammad saw in Makkah similar to problems in society we see today? Explain.

WH7.2.2 Trace the origins of Islam and the life and teachings of Muhammad, including Islamic teachings on the connection with Judaism and Christianity. **WH7.2.3** Explain the significance of the Qur'an and the Sunnah as the primary sources of Islamic beliefs, practice, and law, and their influence in Muslims' daily life.

Islam's Teachings

Main Idea The Quran provided guidelines for Muslims' lives and the governments of Muslim states.

Reading Connection Do you ever wonder how you should act in certain situations? In the following paragraphs, you will learn where Muslims looked for guidance.

Islam, Judaism, and Christianity have some beliefs in common. Like Jews and Christians, Muslims believe in one God. Muslims believe this one God holds all power and created the universe. They also believe that God determines right and wrong. People are expected to obey God's laws if they want to be blessed in the afterlife.

Jews, Christians, and Muslims also believe that God spoke to people through prophets. For Muslims, early prophets were Abraham, Moses, Jesus, and finally Muhammad. For Christians, Jesus was more than a prophet. He was the son of God and therefore divine. In Islam, Muhammad is seen as a prophet and a very good person but not as divine.

What Is the Quran? Muslims wrote down the messages that Muhammad said he received from Allah. These writings became the **Quran** (koh•RAHN), or holy book of Islam. For Muslims, the Quran is God's written word. For this reason, Muslims strive to follow the Quran.

The Quran instructs Muslims about how they should live. Many of its moral teachings are like those of the Bible. For example, Muslims are told to be honest and to treat others fairly. They are to honor their parents, show kindness to their neighbors, and give generously to the poor. Murder, lying, and stealing are forbidden.

▲ A child studies the Quran

▲ **Muslim pilgrims surround the Kaaba in Makkah.** *When did Muhammad's soldiers take control of Makkah?*

Many rules in the Quran apply to Muslims' daily life. According to these rules, Muslims should not eat pork, drink liquor, or gamble. The Quran also has rules about marriage, divorce, family life, property rights, and business practices.

Muslims are expected to fulfill the Five Pillars of Islam, or acts of worship. These are shown in the chart at the right.

Scholars of Islam also created a law code that explains how society should be run. This code is taken from the Quran and the Sunna (SUH•nuh). The Sunna is the name given to customs based on Muhammad's words and deeds. Islam's law code covers all areas of daily life. It applies the Quran to family life, business, and government.

Reading Check **Evaluate** What role do the Quran and Sunna play in Muslim daily life?

The Five Pillars of Islam

Belief	Muslims must declare that there is no god but Allah and that Muhammad is his prophet.
Prayer	Muslims must pray five times per day facing toward Makkah.
Charity	Muslims must give to the poor.
Fasting	Muslims must not eat from dawn to dusk during the sacred holiday of Ramadan.
Pilgrimage	Muslims should visit Makkah once in their life.

▲ The Five Pillars are acts of worship that all Muslims must carry out. *How many times should Muslims pray each day?*

History Online

Study Central Need help with the beginnings of Islam? Visit ca.hss.glencoe.com and click on Study Central.

Section 1 Review

Reading Summary

Review the Main Ideas

- In the desert of the Arabian Peninsula, the Arab people were mostly herders and traders.

- In the town of Makkah, Muhammad began to preach a new religion, Islam, which soon spread to all of Arabia.

- Muslims believe that Muhammad was Allah's final prophet and that their holy book, the Quran, is Allah's written word.

What Did You Learn?

1. What are oases, and why were they important to Arabs?

2. Name some activities the Quran prohibits.

Critical Thinking

3. **Compare and Contrast** Draw a Venn diagram to compare and contrast Islam, Judaism, and Christianity. **CA 7RC2.0**

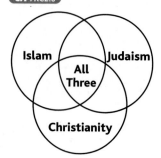

4. **Conclude** Why do you think Muhammad's teachings were popular with poorer people? **CA HR5.**

5. **The Big Ideas** How did Muhammad link religion and government? **CA 7RC2.3**

6. **Writing Summaries** Prepare a summary of the basic beliefs of Islam. **CA 7WA2.5**

7. **Reading** **Making Predictions** Before reading Section 2, write a short essay predicting where and why Islam would spread from Arabia. Refer to the region's geography as well as Islam's beliefs. **CA CS3.**

Section 2 Islamic Empires

Guide to Reading

Looking Back, Looking Ahead

In Section 1, you learned how Islam spread from Madinah to Makkah. In time, Islam's followers brought their beliefs to all of Southwest Asia and parts of Southeast Asia, Africa, and Europe.

Focusing on the Main Ideas

• Arabs spread Islam through teaching, conquest, and trade. (page 182)

• While Muslims split into two groups, the Arab Empire reached new heights. (page 185)

• Turks and Moguls built Muslim empires in Asia, Africa, and Europe. (page 187)

Meeting People

Umayyad (oo•MY•uhd)
Sufi (SOO•fee)
Abbasid (uh•BA•suhd)
Suleiman I (SOO•lay•MAHN)
Mogul (MOH•guhl)
Akbar (AK•buhr)

Locating Places

Damascus (duh•MAS•kuhs)
Indonesia (IHN•duh•NEE•zhuh)
Timbuktu (TIHM•BUHK•TOO)
Baghdad (BAG•dad)
Delhi (DEH•lee)

Content Vocabulary

caliph (KAY•luhf)
Shiite (SHEE•EYET)
Sunni (SU•nee)
sultan (SUHL•tuhn)

Academic Vocabulary

policy (PAH•luh•see)
devote (dih•VOHT)
style
impose (ihm•POHZ)

Reading Strategy

Cause and Effect Create a diagram to show why the Arabs were successful conquerors.

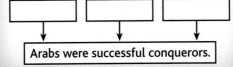

Arabs were successful conquerors.

History Social Science Standards

WH7.2 Students analyze the geographic, political, economic, religious, and social structures of the civilizations of Islam in the Middle Ages.

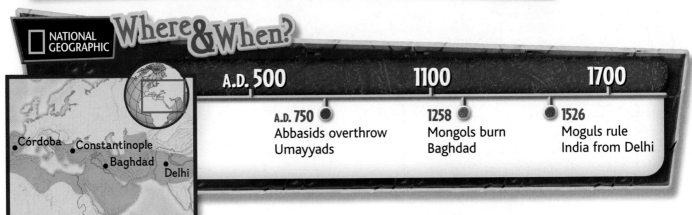

NATIONAL GEOGRAPHIC Where&When?

A.D. 500 — 1100 — 1700

A.D. 750 Abbasids overthrow Umayyads

1258 Mongols burn Baghdad

1526 Moguls rule India from Delhi

Córdoba · Constantinople · Baghdad · Delhi

WH7.2.4 Discuss the expansion of Muslim rule through military conquests and treaties, emphasizing the cultural blending within Muslim civilization and the spread and acceptance of Islam and the Arabic language. **WH7.2.5** Describe the growth of cities and the establishment of trade routes among Asia, Africa, and Europe, the products and inventions that traveled along these routes (e.g., spices, textiles, paper, steel, new crops), and the role of merchants in Arab society.

The Spread of Islam

Main Idea Arabs spread Islam through teaching, conquest, and trade.

Reading Connection When you come up with a new idea, how do you let others know about it? Read on to find out how Arabs spread Islam.

Muhammad died in A.D. 632, and conflicts began in the Muslim community over who should be the **caliph** (KAY•luhf), or successor to the Messenger of God. A powerful group of Muslim leaders chose the new leader, but disagreements continued.

The first four caliphs were Abu Bakr, Umar, Uthman, and Ali. They ruled from Madinah. Each of the four had a personal connection to Muhammad. For example, the first caliph was Muhammad's father-in-law,

Abu Bakr. The fourth caliph was Ali, his first cousin and son-in-law. Each of the four caliphs wanted to spread Allah's message to everyone.

These four caliphs lived simply, treated others fairly, and also fought hard for Islam. They wanted to make sure that Islam flourished. However, Abu Bakr had to put down a rebellion by many Arabs who were not certain whom to follow after Muhammad's death. He also began the conquest of Syria but died in A.D. 634.

His successors continued the conquest of the region by following the land routes north, east, and west. In A.D. 636 Muslim armies began the conquest of Persia. They soundly defeated the Persian armies and soon captured the Persian capital. In A.D. 642 they destroyed another Persian army in

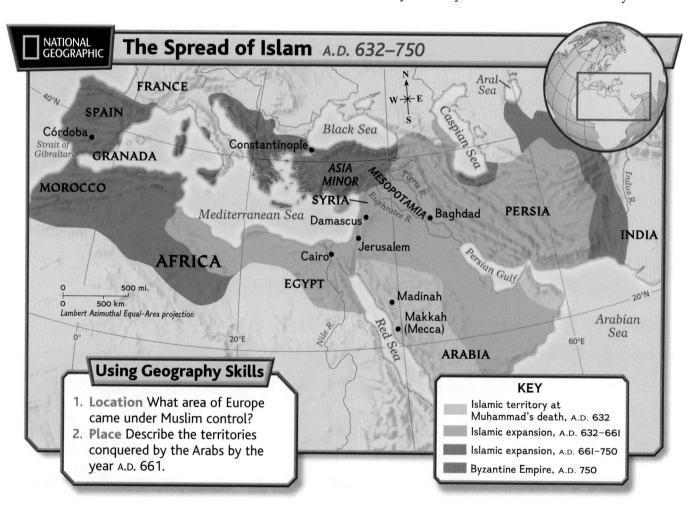

NATIONAL GEOGRAPHIC

The Spread of Islam A.D. 632–750

Using Geography Skills

1. **Location** What area of Europe came under Muslim control?
2. **Place** Describe the territories conquered by the Arabs by the year A.D. 661.

KEY
- Islamic territory at Muhammad's death, A.D. 632
- Islamic expansion, A.D. 632–661
- Islamic expansion, A.D. 661–750
- Byzantine Empire, A.D. 750

The First Four Caliphs

	Abu Bakr	Umar	Uthman	Ali
Relationship to Muhammad	father-in-law	friend	son-in-law, member of the Umayyad family	first cousin, son-in-law
Career	merchant	merchant	merchant	soldier, writer
Caliphate	A.D. 632–634	A.D. 634–644	A.D. 644–656	A.D. 656–661
Achievements as Caliph	spread Islam to all of Arabia; restored peace after death of Muhammad; created code of conduct in war; compiled Quran verses	spread Islam to Syria, Egypt, and Persia; redesigned government; paid soldiers; held a census; made taxes more fair; built roads and canals; aided poor	spread Islam into Afghanistan and eastern Mediterranean; organized a navy; improved the government; built more roads, bridges, and canals; distributed text of the Quran	reformed tax collection and other government systems; spent most of caliphate battling Muawiya, the governor of Syria

◀ Islamic glass horse

Understanding Charts

Under the caliphs, Islam spread through the Middle East and into North Africa.
1. Which caliph organized a navy?
2. **Compare** What achievements did Umar and Ali have in common?

central Persia. In A.D. 651 the last Persian ruler was killed, and the former kingdom of Persia came under the rule of the caliph.

Meanwhile, Muslim armies conquered Syria and the lands along the east coast of the Mediterranean. By A.D. 637, both Damascus and Jerusalem had surrendered. Later, the Muslims defeated a Byzantine army that was defending Egypt, and in A.D. 642 Egypt surrendered. By the year A.D. 661, when the fourth caliph died, the Arab Empire had expanded to include all of southwest Asia.

Expansion continued under the **Umayyad** (oo•MY•uhd) caliphs, who ruled from A.D. 661 to A.D. 750. They chose the city of **Damascus** (duh•MAS•kuhs) in Syria to be their capital. Muslims then spread eastward into the lands beyond Persia. They entered India and traveled northwest to the mountains of Afghanistan.

They also explored the North African coast of the Mediterranean. The sea made travel westward easy, but the mountains and deserts made it difficult to travel south into central Africa.

The Muslims Build an Empire Just 100 years after Muhammad's death, the Islamic state became a great empire. Why were the Arabs so successful?

Arabs had always been good on horseback and good with the sword, but as Muslims, they also were inspired by their religion. They were fighting to spread Islam. Muslims believed anyone who died in battle for Islam would go to paradise.

▲ The Umayyad Mosque, also known as the Great Mosque of Damascus, took about 10 years to build.

The Arabs were also successful because they usually let conquered peoples practice their own religion. They called Christians and Jews "People of the Book," meaning that these people, too, believed in one God and had holy writings. Muslims did not treat everyone equally, though. Non-Muslims had to pay a special tax.

When a people are conquered, they tend to adopt the religion and customs of their new rulers. In the Arab Empire, many conquered people converted to Islam and learned Arabic. The customs of the conquered countries also influenced the Arabic rulers. Eventually, the term *Arab* meant only that a person spoke Arabic, not that he or she was from Arabia.

Preaching and Trading
Muslims also spread Islam by preaching. A group called **Sufis** (SOO•feez) spent their time praying and teaching Islam. They won many followers throughout the Arab Empire.

Arab merchants also helped to spread Islam. They set up trading posts throughout southeast Asia and taught Islam to the people there. Today, the country of **Indonesia** (IHN•duh•NEE•zhuh) includes more Muslims than any other nation in the world.

Some Arab merchants crossed the Sahara to trade with kingdoms in West Africa. In the 1300s, the west African city of **Timbuktu** (TIHM•BUHK•TOO) became a leading center of Muslim learning.

The Muslims in Spain
As the Muslims crossed from North Africa into Spain, they carried their religion, customs, and traditions with them. They made the city of Córdoba the center of politics and culture in Spain. Muslim scholars and philosophers studied the works of the ancient Greeks and wrote commentaries on them. In fact, Muslims in Spain helped to preserve many ancient texts.

Many of Islam's great philosophers came from Spain. For example, Averroës, also known as Ibn Rushd, was a lawyer and doctor in Córdoba. He is best known, however, for his writings about Aristotle. His works later influenced the thinking of Christian and Jewish philosophers during the Middle Ages.

The Islamic culture in Spain was friendly toward other cultures. In particular, the Jewish population in Córdoba thrived. One Jewish scholar known as Maimonides organized a collection of Jewish oral law. He also wrote other legal and philosophical works, including one in Arabic.

Another Spanish Jew of the period, Solomon ben Gabirol, wrote poetry and philosophy. One of his pieces dealt with a Greek philosophy called Neoplatonism. Ben Gabirol could also write in Arabic. After one of his pieces called *The Well of Life* was translated into Latin, it influenced the thinking of many philosophers in Europe.

Reading Check **Explain** How did Arabs spread the religion of Islam through trade?

WH7.2.1 Identify the physical features and describe the climate of the Arabian peninsula, its relationship to surrounding bodies of land and water, and nomadic and sedentary ways of life. WH7.2.4 Discuss the expansion of Muslim rule through military conquests and treaties, emphasizing the cultural blending within Muslim civilization and the spread and acceptance of Islam and the Arabic language. WH7.2.5 Describe the growth of cities and the establishment of trade routes among Asia, Africa, and Europe, the products and inventions that traveled along these routes (e.g., spices, textiles, paper, steel, new crops), and the role of merchants in Arab society.

Struggles Within Islam

Main Idea While Muslims split into two groups, the Arab Empire reached new heights.

Reading Connection Have you ever belonged to a club whose members could not agree on a leader? Read to find out what happened when Muslims disagreed about who should lead them.

From the moment Muhammad died, Muslims began arguing about who had the right to be caliph. The quarrel over who should succeed Muhammad eventually split the Muslim world into two groups, the Sunnis and the Shiites. This division has remained to the present day. Today most Muslims are Sunnis. Iran and Iraq have the largest populations of Shiites.

How Did Islam Split? **Shiites** (SHEE•EYETS) believed that Ali, Muhammad's son-in-law, should succeed him and that all future caliphs should be Ali's descendants. According to the Shiites, the Umayyad caliphs in Damascus had no right to rule.

Sunnis (SU•nees), who outnumbered Shiites, accepted the Umayyad dynasty as rightful caliphs, though they did not always agree with their **policies.** Over time, the Shiites and Sunnis developed different religious practices and customs.

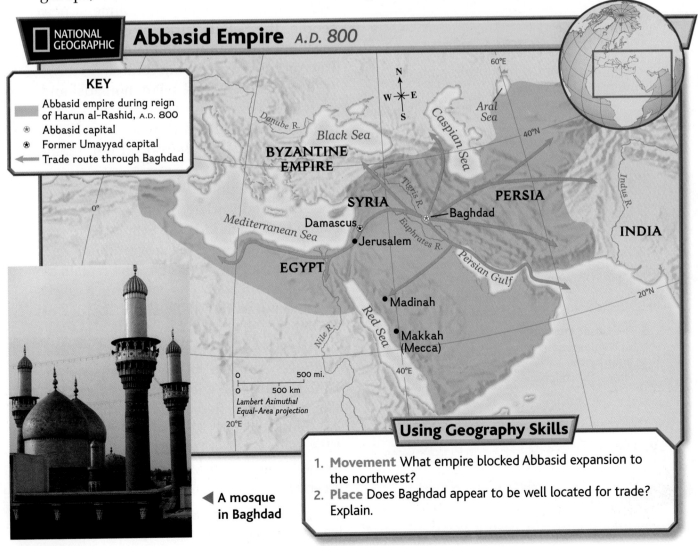

NATIONAL GEOGRAPHIC

Abbasid Empire A.D. 800

KEY
- Abbasid empire during reign of Harun al-Rashid, A.D. 800
- ✸ Abbasid capital
- ✸ Former Umayyad capital
- ← Trade route through Baghdad

Danube R.

Black Sea

BYZANTINE EMPIRE

Mediterranean Sea

SYRIA
Damascus ✸
• Jerusalem

EGYPT

Aral Sea

Caspian Sea

Tigris R.

✸ — Baghdad

Euphrates R.

Persian Gulf

PERSIA

Indus R.

INDIA

Red Sea

Nile R.

• Madinah

• Makkah (Mecca)

0   500 mi.
0   500 km
Lambert Azimuthal
Equal–Area projection

◄ A mosque in Baghdad

Using Geography Skills

1. **Movement** What empire blocked Abbasid expansion to the northwest?
2. **Place** Does Baghdad appear to be well located for trade? Explain.

CHAPTER 2 • Islamic Civilization   **185**

Who Were the Abbasids? The **Abbasids** (uh•BA•suhds) were the dynasty that came after the Umayyads. The Umayyads lost power in A.D. 750 because they angered many Muslims, especially in Persia. Persian Muslims felt that Arab Muslims got special consideration. They got the best jobs and paid fewer taxes.

When these Muslims rebelled, people all over the empire joined them. They overthrew the Umayyads, and a new dynasty began. The new caliph was a descendant of Muhammad's uncle. His name was Abu al-Abbas. The new Abbasid dynasty lasted until 1258.

Primary Source

Royal Caliphs

Ibn Khaldun recorded historical events and his interpretation of them.

▲ The Great Mosque of Damascus built by the Umayyad caliphs

"When one considers what God meant the caliphate to be, nothing more needs [to be said] about it. God made the caliph his substitute to handle the affairs of His servants. He is to make them do the things that are good for them and forbid them to do those that are harmful. He has been directly told so. A person who lacks the power to do a thing is never told to do it."

—Ibn Khaldun, *"The Muqaddimah"*

DBQ Document-Based Question

According to Khaldun, what is the relationship between God and the caliph?

The Abbasids **devoted** their energies to trade, scholarship, and the arts. They also built a new capital, **Baghdad** (BAG•dad). Baghdad prospered because it was beside the Tigris River and near the Euphrates River. It was a good location to trade since many people used the rivers to ship goods north and south.

The Abbasid dynasty is also known for bringing Persian influence into the empire. Baghdad was very close to Persia, and the Abbasid rulers came to know and love the art and literature of Persia.

The Seljuk Turks Time brought many changes in the 500 years of Abbasid rule. In Egypt and Spain, the Muslims wanted their own caliphs. About the same time, a new people, the Seljuk Turks of central Asia, began moving south into the Arab Empire. The Abbasids were losing control.

The Seljuk Turks were nomads and great warriors. At first, the Abbasids hired them as soldiers. Soon, however, the Seljuk Turks decided to take power for themselves.

The Seljuks took over much of what is now Iran and Turkey. Then, in 1055, they boldly took Baghdad. The Seljuks were satisfied to rule only the government and army. They let the Abbasid caliph remain as the religious leader. The Seljuk ruler called himself **sultan** (SUHL•tuhn), or "holder of power."

For 200 more years, the Seljuks ruled with the Abbasid caliphs. Then, in the 1200s, another people attacked the empire. These were the fierce Mongols of central Asia you will read about in Chapter 4. In 1258 they captured Baghdad and burned it to the ground. The Mongol attack brought an end to the Arab Empire.

✓ **Reading Check** **Contrast** What is the difference between Shiite and Sunni Muslims?

WH7.2.4 Discuss the expansion of Muslim rule through military conquests and treaties, emphasizing the cultural blending within Muslim civilization and the spread and acceptance of Islam and the Arabic language.

WH7.2.5 Describe the growth of cities and the establishment of trade routes among Asia, Africa, and Europe, the products and inventions that traveled along these routes (e.g., spices, textiles, paper, steel, new crops), and the role of merchants in Arab society.

Later Muslim Empires

Main Idea Turks and Moguls built Muslim empires in Asia, Africa, and Europe.

Reading Connection How do you react when someone treats you unfairly? Read on to find out how Muslims in Turkey and India treated the people they conquered.

The Arabs built—and lost—the first Muslim empire. Later on, other Muslim groups created empires in Asia, Africa, and Europe. One of the largest and most powerful of these empires was the Ottoman empire that began in Turkey. Another was the Mogul empire in India.

Who Were the Ottomans?
In the late 1200s, a group of Turks in the northwest corner of Asia Minor began to build a new empire. The ruler of these Turks was named Osman, and as a result, these Turks became known as the Ottoman Turks.

The Ottomans quickly conquered most of the land that today makes up the country of Turkey. They attacked the Byzantine Empire and pushed north into Europe. In 1453 they seized Constantinople, the Byzantine capital. They changed the city's name to Istanbul and made it the center of their empire.

Ottoman armies also marched south, conquering Syria, Palestine, Egypt, Mesopotamia, and parts of Arabia and North Africa. They used guns and cannons to fight their battles and built a large navy to control the Mediterranean Sea.

Like the Seljuks, the Ottomans called their leader a sultan. The most famous of the sultans was **Suleiman I** (SOO•lay•MAHN), who ruled in the 1500s. Suleiman was a man of many talents. He was enthusiastic about architecture and built many schools and mosques.

Suleiman was also a brilliant general, who brought Ottoman armies north into Europe. He even threatened the great European capital of Vienna. For all these reasons, Ottomans called him Suleiman the Magnificent.

After his rule, the Ottoman empire began to weaken. Little by little, they lost territory. The empire finally collapsed at the end of World War I.

Muslims pray beneath the large decorated dome of Selimiye Mosque in Edirne, Turkey. Suleiman built this beautiful mosque for his son Selim II. *What were some of the reasons that Suleiman was called "the Magnificent"?*

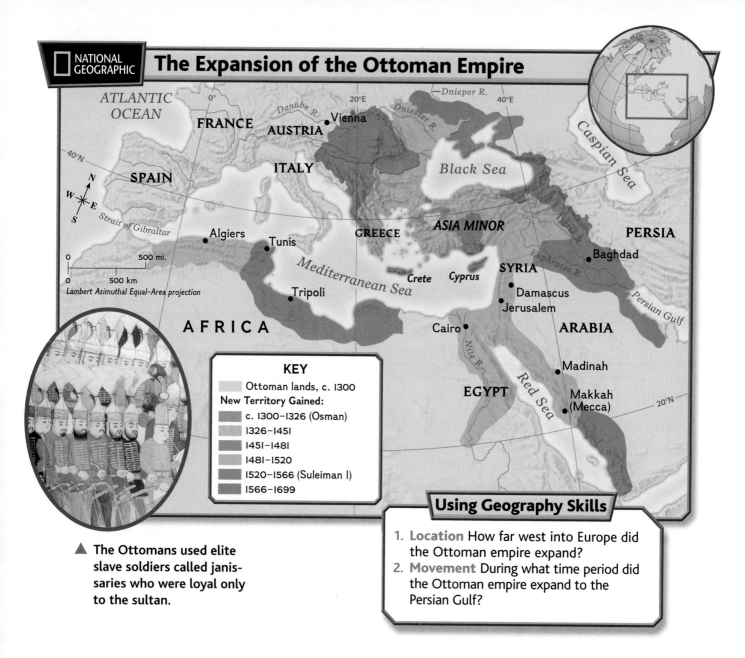

The Expansion of the Ottoman Empire

KEY

Ottoman lands, c. 1300
New Territory Gained:
- c. 1300-1326 (Osman)
- 1326-1451
- 1451-1481
- 1481-1520
- 1520-1566 (Suleiman I)
- 1566-1699

▲ The Ottomans used elite slave soldiers called janissaries who were loyal only to the sultan.

Using Geography Skills

1. **Location** How far west into Europe did the Ottoman empire expand?
2. **Movement** During what time period did the Ottoman empire expand to the Persian Gulf?

The Ottoman Government The Ottoman empire ruled many different people, including Turks, Arabs, Greeks, Albanians, Armenians, and Slavs. These groups practiced several religions. While many were Muslims, others were Christians or Jews.

The government made different laws for non-Muslims. They had to pay a special tax, and in return, they were allowed to practice their religion. They also could make their own laws to run their own communities. These groups chose leaders to present their views to the sultan. Many of them, serving as slaves, helped the sultan run the government.

As the empire grew, the sultans began giving more responsibility for running the government to officials called viziers. Over time, the viziers gained great political power, and some were even more powerful than the sultan.

The sultans also created a new army of soldiers called the janissaries. The janissaries were slaves, usually Christians or other conquered peoples from European lands. These soldiers became Muslims, were trained in warfare, and were loyal only to the sultan. This new army helped the sultan maintain power over the nobles and other conquered people who might rebel.

Who Were the Moguls? During the 1500s, the **Moguls** (MOH•guhlz) created another Muslim empire in India. These Muslim warriors came from the mountains north of India through the Khyber Pass. The Moguls used guns, cannons, elephants, and horses to conquer territory. In 1526 they made the city of **Delhi** (DEH•lee) the center of their empire.

The greatest Mogul ruler was **Akbar** (AK•buhr). He brought peace and stability to the part of India he ruled by treating all his subjects fairly. Most of India's people were Hindu. He allowed them to practice their religion. Both Hindus and Muslims served in Akbar's government.

Times were good in India under Akbar. Farmers and artisans produced more food and goods than the Indians needed. As a result, trade increased. Muslim merchants brought paper, gunpowder, and fine porcelain from China to India. In addition, Muslim architects introduced new building **styles,** such as the arch and dome, to India.

After Akbar, the Mogul empire began to decline. Later rulers spent too much money trying to expand the empire and **imposed** heavy taxes on the people. Others tried to force the Hindus to convert to Islam and banned the building of Hindu temples. These policies led to many rebellions, and parts of the empire broke away.

At the same time the Moguls began losing power over their subjects, they had to deal with European merchants who wanted to take over their land. The merchants came to India to trade but used their military power to take over Mogul territory. Eventually, the Mogul empire collapsed, and Great Britain took control of most of India.

✓ **Reading Check** **Describe** How did Constantinople change in 1453?

History Online

Study Central Need help understanding the spread of Islam? Visit ca.hss.glencoe.com and click on Study Central.

Section 2 Review

Reading Summary

Review the Main Ideas

- Arab armies spread Islam as far west as Spain and as far east as India. Muslim traders helped spread the religion to southeast Asia and west Africa.

- Despite splitting into two groups, the Sunni and the Shiite, Muslim power reached its greatest height under the Abbasids.

- In the 1400s and 1500s, two great Muslim empires, the Ottoman and the Mogul, arose.

What Did You Learn?

1. How did the Muslims treat conquered peoples?

2. How far did the Arab Empire spread under the Umayyads?

Critical Thinking

3. **Organizing Information** Draw a chart to organize information about the Ottoman and Mogul empires. **CA 7RC2.2**

Ottoman Empire	Mogul Empire

4. **Contrast** Describe the differences between the Shiite and Sunni Muslims. **CA 7RC2.0**

5. **The Big Ideas** Besides conquests by Arab armies, how was Islam spread? **CA CS3.**

6. **Evaluate** What evidence in the text suggests that Akbar was a great ruler? **CA 7RC2.4**

7. **Persuasive Writing** Which Muslim empire—the Umayyads, the Ottomans, or the Moguls—treated its non-Muslim subjects the most fairly? Write a paragraph to defend your answer. **CA 7WA2.4**

Muslim Ways of Life

Guide to Reading

Looking Back, Looking Ahead

In Section 2, you learned that many Muslim rulers brought peace and order to their empires. Peace and order helped trade to increase. Trade, in turn, brought great wealth to the Muslim empires.

Focusing on the Main Ideas

- Although Muslim traders enjoyed great success and cities grew, most Muslims lived in villages in the country. *(page 191)*

- Muslims made valuable contributions in math, science, and the arts. *(page 193)*

Locating Places
Granada (gruh•NAH•duh)
Agra (AH•gruh)

Meeting People
Mamun (mah•MOON)
al-Razi (ahl•RAH•zee)
Ibn Sina (IH•buhn   SEE•nuh)
Omar Khayyam (OH•MAHR   KY•YAHM)
Ibn Khaldun (IH•buhn   KAL•DOON)

Content Vocabulary
mosque (MAHSK)
bazaar (buh•ZAHR)
minaret (MIH•nuh•REHT]
crier (KRY•uhr)

Academic Vocabulary
widespread (WYD•SPREHD)
innovate (IH•nuh•VAYT)

Reading Strategy
Organizing Information Create a pyramid to show the social classes in the early Muslim world.

History Social Science Standards

WH7.2 Students analyze the geographic, political, economic, religious, and social structures of the civilizations of Islam in the Middle Ages.

NATIONAL GEOGRAPHIC Who & When?

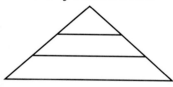

A.D. **800**   **1100**   **1400**

c. A.D. **900**
Al-Razi writes medical texts

c. **1100**
Omar Khayyam writes the *Rubaiyat*

c. **1375**
Ibn Khaldun writes histories

WH7.2.5 Describe the growth of cities and the establishment of trade routes among Asia, Africa, and Europe, the products and inventions that traveled along these routes (e.g., spices, textiles, paper, steel, new crops), and the role of merchants in Arab society.

Trade and Everyday Life

Main Idea Although Muslim traders enjoyed great success and cities grew, most Muslims lived in villages in the country.

Reading Connection Have you ever visited a mall or a farm market? These are both places where people gather to sell goods. Read to learn about Muslim traders and their marketplaces.

Muslims were the leading merchants in the Middle East and northern Africa until the 1400s. Their caravans traveled overland from Baghdad to China. Their ships crossed the Indian Ocean to India and Southeast Asia. They carried a variety of goods, including spices, cloth, glass, steel and carpets. On their return, they brought rubies, silk, ivory, gold, and slaves. Islamic traders also traded a number of crops, including sugar, rice, lemon, spinach, oranges, saffron, plums, and cotton.

History Online

Web Activity Visit ca.hss.glencoe.com and click on *Chapter 2—Student Web Activities* to learn more about Islamic civilization.

The Success of Muslim Traders Several things explain the success of Muslim trade. When Muslim empires expanded, they spread the Arabic language. As a result, Arabic became the language of trade and government. Muslim rulers also made trade easier by providing merchants with coins for buying and selling goods.

Muslim merchants kept detailed records of their business deals and the money they made. In time, these practices developed into a new business—banking. Muslims respected traders for their skills and the wealth they created.

▼ **Muslims shop at a textile market.**
What was a bazaar in a Muslim city?

CHAPTER 2 • Islamic Civilization   **191**

Focus on Everyday Life

Muslim Carpets and Weavings

Carpets were woven in the Middle East long before the coming of Islam. They became popular in the Islamic world because Muslims used them in their daily worship.

Carpets were often made of sheep's wool or goat hair. Shepherds might knot them by hand, or the carpets might be made on portable looms. Flowers and geometric shapes were popular designs.

The carpets used for the Muslims' daily prayers are called prayer rugs. No matter where Muslims live, they pray five times daily. They kneel down on their prayer rugs and pray facing toward Makkah. Prayer rugs are small and can be folded and carried from place to place.

Fine carpets of silk and wool are often hung on the walls of mosques and public buildings. They are considered fine art.

▲ A Muslim woman weaving a rug

Connecting to the Past

1. What animals were needed to make carpets?
2. What is the main reason Muslim carpets have continually been in demand?

What Were Muslim Cities Like? Trade helped the leading Muslim cities grow. Baghdad, Cairo, and Damascus were located on trade routes that ran from the Mediterranean Sea to central Asia. However, Muslim cities were not only places of trade. They also became important centers of government, learning, and the arts.

Muslim cities looked very similar. The major buildings were palaces and mosques. **Mosques** (MAHSKS) are Muslim houses of worship. They also serve as schools, courts, and centers of learning.

Another important part of every Muslim city was the **bazaar** (buh•ZAHR), or marketplace. Stalls and shops made up the bazaars. Sellers in the stalls and shops sold goods from Asia. Buyers from all over, including Europe, searched for goods to purchase, take home, and sell.

Although cities were important, most Muslims lived in villages and farmed the land. Because water was scarce, Muslim farmers used irrigation to bring water to their crops. They grew wheat, rice, beans, and melons in the fields. They raised almonds, blackberries, apricots, figs, and olives in their orchards. Some farmers also raised flowers for use in perfume.

At first, Muslim villagers owned small farms. Later, wealthy landowners took over some of these farms and formed large estates. Farmers and enslaved people worked for the landowners.

Muslim Society Muslim people were divided into social groups based on power and wealth. At the top were government leaders, landowners, and traders. Below them were artisans, farmers, and workers. The lowest group were enslaved people.

As in other civilizations, slavery was **widespread.** Because Muslims could not be enslaved, traders brought enslaved people

WH7.2.6 Understand the intellectual exchanges among Muslim scholars of Eurasia and Africa and the contributions Muslim scholars made to later civilizations in the areas of science, geography, mathematics, philosophy, medicine, art, and literature.

from non-Muslim areas. Many of these people were prisoners of war. They often served as servants or soldiers and could buy back their freedom.

Men and women had distinct roles in the Muslim world. As in other parts of the world, men ran government, society, and business. Women, on the other hand, helped run Muslim families. They also could inherit wealth and own property. Many places had laws requiring women to cover their faces and to wear long robes in public.

Reading Check **Explain** How did Muslim rulers give their merchants an advantage?

Muslim Achievements

Main Idea **Muslims made valuable contributions in math, science, and the arts.**

Reading Connection Did you know that the numbers you use are called Arabic numerals? Read on to find out what other contributions Muslims made.

Arabic was the common language of the Muslim empires. You have already read how Arabic language encouraged trade. It also helped different people in the empires to share knowledge. For example, in A.D. 830 the Abbasid caliph **Mamun** (mah•MOON)

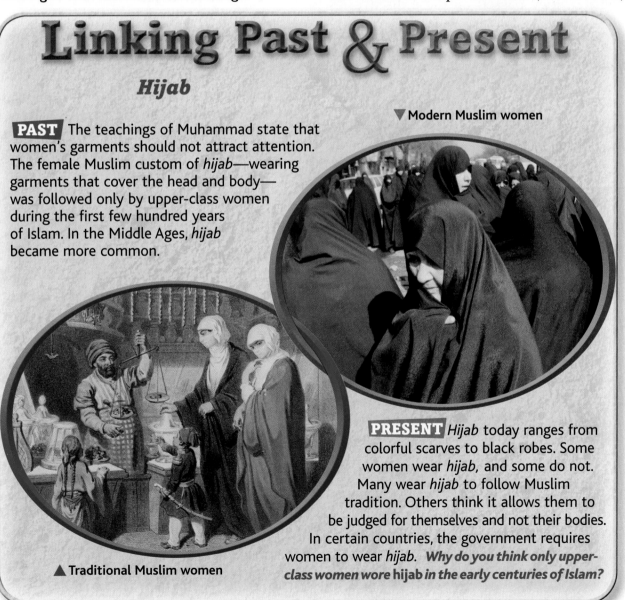

Linking Past & Present

Hijab

▼ **Modern Muslim women**

PAST The teachings of Muhammad state that women's garments should not attract attention. The female Muslim custom of *hijab*—wearing garments that cover the head and body— was followed only by upper-class women during the first few hundred years of Islam. In the Middle Ages, *hijab* became more common.

PRESENT *Hijab* today ranges from colorful scarves to black robes. Some women wear *hijab*, and some do not. Many wear *hijab* to follow Muslim tradition. Others think it allows them to be judged for themselves and not their bodies. In certain countries, the government requires women to wear *hijab*. *Why do you think only upper-class women wore* hijab *in the early centuries of Islam?*

▲ **Traditional Muslim women**

founded the House of Wisdom in Baghdad. Mamun staffed his center with Christian, Jewish, and Muslim scholars. These scholars exchanged ideas and rewrote Greek, Persian, and Indian works in Arabic.

Scholars in Muslim lands saved much of the learning of the ancient world. Europeans in the West had lost this knowledge after the Western Roman Empire fell. Through Muslim scholars, western Europeans found out about Aristotle and other ancient Greek thinkers.

Mathematics and Science Muslims made important **innovations** in mathematics. Later, they passed on these discoveries to Europeans. For example, Muslims invented algebra, a type of mathematics still taught in schools today. The Arabs also borrowed the symbols 0 through 9 from Hindu scholars in India. These numbers were later used by Europeans. Today, they are known as "Arabic numerals."

Muslims also made progress in science. Muslim scientists who studied the heavens perfected the Greek astrolabe. Sailors utilized this tool to study the stars and then determine their location at sea. Muslim scientists used the astrolabe to measure the size and distance around the earth. Based on their measurements, they realized that the earth is round.

Other Muslim scientists experimented with metals and kept records of their work. As a result, the Arabs are considered the founders of chemistry. One of the best-known Muslim chemists was **al-Razi** (ahl•RAH•zee), who lived from A.D. 865 to A.D. 925. Al-Razi developed a system for categorizing substances as animal, mineral, or vegetable. He also wrote books for doctors that helped them to identify diseases.

Arab doctors were the first to discover that blood circulates, or moves to and from the heart. The Persian doctor **Ibn Sina** (IH•buhn SEE•nuh) showed how diseases spread from person to person. As they worked, Muslim doctors published their findings.

Primary Source — The Mystery of Smallpox

The Muslim scientist al-Razi urged scientists and doctors to search for the causes of disease, rather than just treatments.

"Although [scholars] have certainly made some mention of the treatment of the Small-Pox . . . there is not one of them who has mentioned the cause of the existence of the disease, and how it comes to pass that hardly any one escapes it . . ."

—Al-Razi, "On the Causes of Small-Pox"

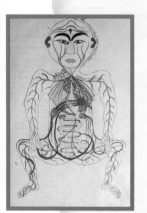

▲ Muslim medical drawing

Al-Razi's own theory about the cause of smallpox was incorrect. His efforts to find the cause, however, helped change how doctors and scientists investigated diseases.

DBQ Document-Based Question

Why was al-Razi concerned about previous scholars' studies of smallpox?

◄ Muslim scientists took the Greek astrolabe and made it better. It helped sailors determine their longitude and latitude and even tell the time of day. *What were Muslim scientists able to tell about the world when they used an astrolabe?*

Biography

WH7.2.6 Understand the intellectual exchanges among Muslim scholars of Eurasia and Africa and the contributions Muslim scholars made to later civilizations in the areas of science, geography, mathematics, philosophy, medicine, art, and literature.

OMAR KHAYYAM
1048–1131
and IBN KHALDUN
1332–1406

Omar Khayyam—who was born in Persia—was a mathematician, astronomer, and philosopher, but he is best known as a poet. Scholars believe that Khayyam wrote only parts of his most famous poem, the *Rubaiyat,* but they are certain that at least 120 verses and the main concepts are his. Stanza XII reads:

> "A Book of Verses underneath the Bough,
> A Jug of Wine, a Loaf of Bread—and Thou
> Beside me singing the Wilderness—
> Oh, Wilderness were Paradise enow [enough]!"
>
> —Omar Khayyam, *Rubaiyat*

▲ Omar Khayyam

Khayyam wrote books on algebra and music before he was 25 years old. He led an observatory for 18 years and developed a more accurate calendar.

Ibn Khaldun is one of the most famous Arab scholars. He was a historian, geographer, sociologist, and politician. He was born in Tunisia and worked for the rulers of Tunis and Morocco. He also served as ambassador to one of the Spanish kingdoms and as a judge in Cairo, Egypt. He wrote much about social and political change. His best-known work is *Muqaddimah* (Introduction), written in 1375. It is the first volume of his book *Kitab al-Ibar* (universal history). In this book, he tried to develop a scientific way to analyze events. He is one of the first historians to study how geography, economics, and culture affect history.

▲ Ibn Khaldun

Then and Now

The *Rubaiyat* is a collection of 4-line verses called quatrains. Find a modern poem that is made up of quatrains.

Muslim Writing The Quran is probably the most famous collection of writings in the Muslim world, but Muslims produced other famous works, as well. One of the most well known is *The Thousand and One Nights,* also called *The Arabian Nights.* It includes tales from India, Persia, and Arabia.

Another Muslim, the Persian poet **Omar Khayyam** (OH•MAHR KY•YAHM), wrote parts of the *Rubaiyat* (ROO•bee•AHT) around 1100. Many consider it one of the finest poems ever written.

In addition to stories and poems, Muslims wrote history. The great Muslim historian **Ibn Khaldun** (IH•buhn KAL•DOON) wrote in 1375 that all civilizations rise, grow, and then fall. He also was one of the first historians to study the effect of geography and climate on people.

Art and Buildings Muslims developed a distinct form of art based on Islam. Muslims are not allowed to show images of Muhammad or the events of his life in art. They believe that such images might cause people to worship Muhammad instead of Allah. Instead, designs entwined with flowers, leaves, and stars make up most Muslim art. Muslims use these designs to decorate walls, books, rugs, and buildings.

Muslims were known for their beautiful buildings. Mosques filled Muslim cities like Baghdad, Damascus, Cairo, and Istanbul.

Islamic Mosque

In Islamic cities and towns, mosques were centers of religious and daily life. Besides being places of worship, mosques also served as meeting places, schools, and courts. *What was the most striking architectural feature of a mosque?*

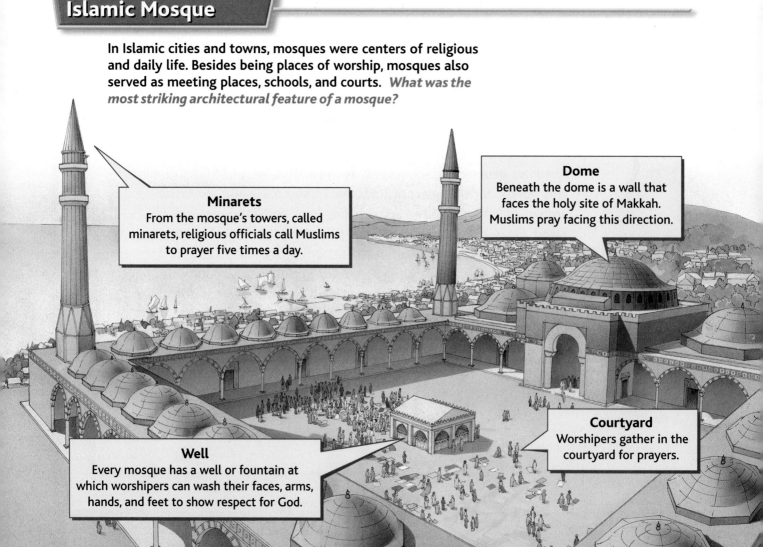

Minarets
From the mosque's towers, called minarets, religious officials call Muslims to prayer five times a day.

Dome
Beneath the dome is a wall that faces the holy site of Makkah. Muslims pray facing this direction.

Well
Every mosque has a well or fountain at which worshipers can wash their faces, arms, hands, and feet to show respect for God.

Courtyard
Worshipers gather in the courtyard for prayers.

Domes top many of the mosques, but a mosque's most striking feature is its **minarets** (MIH•nuh•REHTS). These are towers from which a **crier** (KRY•uhr), or announcer, calls believers to prayer five times a day.

Islamic rulers lived in large brick palaces. These palaces often had courtyards at their center. To cool the courtyards, palace builders added porches, fountains, and pools. To provide protection, they surrounded the palaces with walls. The most famous example of a Muslim palace is the Alhambra (al•HAM•bruh) in **Granada** (gruh•NAH•duh), Spain. It was built in the 1300s.

Another famous Muslim building is the Taj Mahal in **Agra** (AH•gruh), India. The Mogul ruler Shah Jahan built it as a tomb for his wife after she died in 1629. Made of marble and precious stones, the Taj Mahal is one of the world's most beautiful buildings.

▲ The Taj Mahal took more than 20 years to build. *Where is the Taj Mahal located?*

Today, the Muslim empires are gone. However, Islam is still a major world religion. About one out of every six persons in the world is a Muslim.

Reading Check **Identify** What contributions did Muslims make in math and science?

History Online

Study Central Need help understanding Islamic culture? Visit ca.hss.glencoe.com and click on Study Central.

Section 3 Review

Reading Summary
Review the Main Ideas

- There were many Muslim cities such as Baghdad, Cairo, and Damascus, but most Muslims remained farmers in small villages.

- Muslim scholars made important discoveries in fields such as algebra and chemistry, and Muslim writers, artists, and architects also produced important works.

What Did You Learn?

1. Describe the three Muslim social groups.

2. What contributions did Muslims make in the field of medicine?

Critical Thinking

3. **Organizing Information** Draw a chart like the one below. Fill in details about Muslim contributions in the areas of math, science, and the arts. **CA 7RC2.0**

Math	Science	Arts

4. **The Big Ideas** Which Muslim contribution do you think had the greatest effect on later civilizations? **CA HI2.**

5. **Summarize** Describe several factors that made Muslim trade strong. **CA CS3.**

6. **Analyze** How did the Arabic language and Muslim leaders help preserve and advance the world's knowledge? **CA 7RC2.2**

7. **Analysis** **Distinguishing Fact From Opinion** Use the Internet or your local library to learn more about Ibn Khaldun. Were his writings based on opinion or fact? Explain. **CA HR2.**

Analyzing Primary Sources

WH7.2.6 Understand the intellectual exchanges among Muslim scholars of Eurasia and Africa and the contributions Muslim scholars made to later civilizations in the areas of science, geography, mathematics, philosophy, medicine, art, and literature.

A Glimpse Into the World of Islam

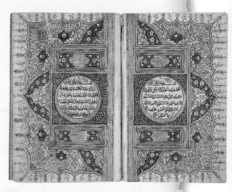

▲ The Quran

The most important book in the Islamic world is the Quran. However, poetry and literature were also widely read in the Middle Ages and were often used to discuss important ideas and morals.

Read the passages on pages 198 and 199, and then answer the questions that follow.

Reader's Dictionary

piety (PY•uh•tee): religious faith

wit: intelligence

maharaja (MAH•huh•RAH•juh): Hindu prince

incurred (ihn•KUHRD): brought upon onself

The *Rubaiyat* of Omar Khayyam

◀ The Muslim poet Omar Khayyam

Many of the stanzas of Omar Khayyam's famous poem include ideas about our short time on Earth. They also ask questions about what happens when we die.

27

Myself when young did eagerly frequent
Doctor and Saint, and heard great Argument
About it and about: but evermore
Came out by the same Door as in I went.

28

With them the Seed of Wisdom did I sow,
And with my own hand labour'd it to grow:
And this was all the Harvest that I reap'd—
"I came like Water, and like Wind I go."

51

The Moving Finger writes; and, having writ,
Moves on: nor all thy **Piety** nor **Wit**
Shall lure it back to cancel half a Line,
Nor all thy Tears wash out a Word of it.

—Edward Fitzgerald,
The Rubáiyát of Omar Khayyám

The Thousand and One Nights

The Thousand and One Nights is one of the world's greatest storybooks. Also known as The Arabian Nights, *these stories originally were handed down orally for centuries in the Arab world. A European editor added some tales that have become well-known, but were not in the medieval Arabic collection, such as "The Story of Aladdin," "The Voyages of Sindbad the Sailor," and "Ali Baba and the Forty Thieves." In the following excerpt from "The First Voyage of Sindbad the Sailor," Sindbad arrives on an island after being forced overboard by a sea monster.*

The ship arrived in which I had embarked at Bussorah. I at once knew the captain, and I went and asked him for my bales. "I am Sindbad," said I, "and those bales marked with his name are mine."

When the captain heard me speak thus, "Heavens!" he exclaimed, "whom can we trust in these times! I saw Sindbad perish with my own eyes. . . . [W]hat a false tale to tell, in order to possess yourself of what does not belong to you!" . . . The captain was at length persuaded that I was no cheat; for there came people from his ship who knew me. . . .

I took out what was most valuable in my bales, and presented them to the **maharaja**. . . . He was pleased at my good luck, accepted my present, and in return gave me one much more considerable. Upon this I took leave of him, and went aboard the same ship after I had exchanged my goods for the commodities of that country. I carried with me wood of aloes, sandals, camphire, nutmegs, cloves, pepper, and ginger.

—From *Arabian Nights' Entertainments*

The Quran

The Quran is the holy book of Islam. The verses below come from Chapter 1, verses 2-7.

Praise be to Allah, the Lord of the Worlds,
The Compassionate, the Merciful,
Master of the Day of Judgement,
Only You do we worship, and only You do we
    implore for help.
Lead us to the right path,
The path of those You have favoured
Not those who have **incurred** Your wrath or
    have gone astray.

—Quran

DBQ Document-Based Questions

The Rubaiyat *of Omar Khayyam*

1. In the first two stanzas, what does Khayyam explain about science and religion?

2. In the last stanza, what is Khayyam saying about life?

The Thousand and One Nights

3. Why do you think Sindbad gave the maharaja his most expensive items?

4. What is different about the Sindbad story compared to the quotes from Khayyam and from the Quran?

The Quran

5. What qualities does Allah have, according to this quote?

6. What do you think the speaker means by "the right path"?

Read to Write

7. Compare the three primary sources you have just read. Each presents a different view of life. Write a short essay describing these different views. CA HR5. CA 7WA2.0

Review Content Vocabulary

Write the key term that completes each sentence.

a. caravan   e. sheikh
b. caliph   f. bazaar
c. sultan   g. Sunnis
d. minaret   h. Shiites

1. A crier called Muslims to prayer from the ___ of a mosque.
2. After Muhammad died, his followers chose a ___ to lead them.
3. The most famous ___ was Suleiman I.
4. In each Muslim city, a ___ sold goods to local and out-of-town merchants.
5. Arab merchants traveling in a ___ used camels to carry goods across the desert.
6. Each tribe of early Arabs was led by a ___.
7. The ___ believed that Muhammad's son-in-law should succeed him.
8. According to the ___, the Umayyad dynasty were the rightful caliphs.

Review the Main Ideas

Section 1 • The Rise of Islam
9. How did geography affect Arab life?
10. What guidelines did the Quran provide for the governments of Muslim states?

Section 2 • Islamic Empires
11. How did the Arabs spread Islam?
12. Why did Muslims split into two groups?
13. What two empires continued to spread Islam after the Arab Empire collapsed?

Section 3 • Muslim Ways of Life
14. What three major Muslim cities were on trade routes from the Mediterranean?
15. What scientific advances were made by early Muslims?
16. What is significant about Ibn Khaldun's recording of history?

Critical Thinking

17. **Compare** How are Islam, Judaism, and Christianity similar? **CA HI2.**
18. **Evaluate** Do you think a government that allows people to practice any religion they choose will be stronger than one that does not? Explain. **CA CS3.**

Geography Skills

Study the map below and answer the following questions.

19. **Movement** Why was the Abbasid empire unable to expand to the Black Sea? **CA CS3.**
20. **Region** What bodies of water could Abbasid merchants use to trade with the outside world? **CA CS3.**
21. **Place** Look at the locations of Damascus and Baghdad. Which do you think would have been the best location for a capital city? Why? **CA CS3.**

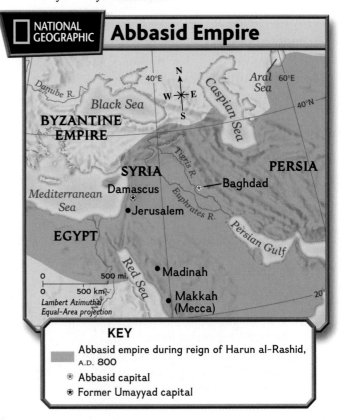

NATIONAL GEOGRAPHIC

Abbasid Empire

KEY
- Abbasid empire during reign of Harun al-Rashid, A.D. 800
- ✳ Abbasid capital
- ✳ Former Umayyad capital

Read to Write

22. **The Big Ideas** **Creating Maps** Use information from the text and a world atlas to create a map that shows major trade routes in Muslim areas. What kinds of goods were traded? How did these trade routes affect the spread of Islam? **CA CS3.**

23. **Using Your** **FOLDABLES** Write a poem or short story using the facts from your completed foldable. **CA 7WA2.1**

Using Academic Vocabulary

24. Complete the chart below to fill in the missing adjectives and verbs.

Adjective	Verb
	impose
devoted	
intense	
	innovate
	style

Linking Past and Present

25. **Evaluating Impact** Which Islamic invention or development do you think has the greatest effect on the world today? Explain your choice. **CA HI2.**

Building Citizenship

26. **Analyzing Documents** Do research to find out how the United States Constitution protects religious freedoms. Do you think the religious policies of the Muslim empires would be allowed under the U.S. Constitution? Explain. **CA 7WA2.3**

Economics Connection

27. **Researching** Routes throughout Arabia brought traders to and from the Muslim world. Arab traders were able to buy and sell goods from all over the world. Use your local library and the Internet to find out what kinds of items were traded by the Arabs. Write a research report describing these items and the different values that they had. Include details about the lives and times of Arab traders and the impact that trade had on the economies of Arab peoples and empires. **CA 7WA2.3** **CA HI6.**

Reviewing Skills

28. **Reading Skill** **Making Predictions** Use the maps that appear throughout this chapter to help you predict which countries practice the Islamic faith today. Keep track of all the countries that you think have a majority of Muslims. Use your local library to find out if you are correct. **CA CS3.**

29. **Analysis Skill** **Creating Time Lines** Use information from the chapter to create a time line that follows the rise of Islam in the world. For each time line entry, give a brief summary of the person or event and the impact that followed. **CA CS1.; CS2.**

 Standards Practice

Select the best answer for each of the following questions.

30 The religion of Islam is based on the teachings of

A Abraham.

B Omar Khayyam.

C Muhammad.

D Bedouin herders.

31 How did Islam spread throughout Europe, Africa, and Asia?

A followers made pilgrimages to Makkah (Mecca)

B European kings converted to Islam

C the Quran was printed in China

D through Arab merchants and traders

Medieval Africa

Islamic mosque and marketplace in Djenne, Mali ▼

NATIONAL GEOGRAPHIC Where&When?

A.D. 300	A.D. 700	1100	1500
c. A.D. 300 Axum conquers Kush	c. A.D. 750 Arab Muslim traders settle in East Africa	1324 Mansa Musa travels to Makkah	c. 1441 First enslaved Africans arrive in Europe

The Big Ideas

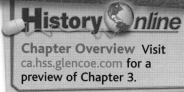

Chapter Overview Visit ca.hss.glencoe.com for a preview of Chapter 3.

Section 1 The Rise of African Civilizations

Physical geography plays a role in how civilizations develop. Africa's geography influenced the rise of its civilizations. The growth of trade led to the exchange of goods and ideas.

Section 2 Africa's Religion and Government

Religion influences how civilization develops and how culture spreads. Traditional religions, Christianity, and Islam shaped early African culture. African rulers developed different forms of government.

Section 3 African Society and Culture

Different social, economic, and political classes can exist in a society. The family was the foundation of African society. A growing slave trade, however, disrupted African society.

 View the Chapter 3 video in the Glencoe Video Program.

Categorizing Information *Make this foldable to help you organize your notes about medieval Africa.*

Step 1 *Draw a map of Africa on one side of a sheet of paper.*

Step 2 *Fold the sheet of paper into thirds from top to bottom.*

Step 3 *Unfold, turn the paper over (to the clean side), and label as shown.*

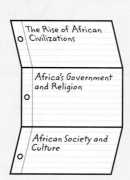

The Rise of African Civilizations

Africa's Government and Religion

African Society and Culture

Reading and Writing *As you read about the civilizations of Africa, write down three main questions under each heading. Then write an answer to each question.*

3 Get Ready to Read

Summarizing

Reading Skill

1 Learn It!

Summarizing helps you organize information, focus on main ideas, and reduce the amount of information to remember. To summarize, restate the important facts in a short sentence or paragraph. Be brief and do not include too many details. Read the text on page 223 labeled **Traditional African Religions.** Then read the summary below, and look at the important facts from that passage.

Important Facts

Summary

Traditional African religions shared certain beliefs and provided a guide for living together.

For centuries, Europeans believed Africans did not have a religion.

Most African groups shared the Igbo belief in one supreme god.

Even though Africans practiced their religion differently in different places, their beliefs served similar purposes.

Many Africans honored their ancestors.

Reading Tip

As you summarize, be careful not to change the author's original meanings or ideas.

2 Practice It!

With a partner, read about **African Culture** on pages 235–237. Each of you should then summarize the important facts. Compare your summaries to see which details you and your partner chose to include or exclude.

Read to Write ·····
Read Section 1. Then write a one-paragraph summary that includes what you remember about Africa's geography and the rise of African civilizations.

When you are finished with your summary, look at the following list to see if you included all the important ideas.

- Enslaved Africans developed rich cultures that influenced many other cultures, including our own.

- Early African art was often religious in nature, told stories, and also served practical purposes.

- Music and dance played important roles in almost all aspects of African life.

- Africans preserved their storytelling tradition.

▲ African women wearing *kente* cloth

3 Apply It!

Practice summarizing as you read this chapter. Stop after each section and write a brief summary.

The Rise of African Civilizations

Guide to Reading

History Social Science Standards

WH7.4 Students analyze the geographic, political, economic, religious, and social structures of the sub-Saharan civilizations of Ghana and Mali in Medieval Africa.

Looking Back, Looking Ahead

Egypt and Kush were Africa's first great civilizations. In this section, you will learn about African civilizations that developed later.

Focusing on the Main Ideas

- Africa has a vast and varied landscape made up of shifting sand dunes, rain forests, sweeping savannas, large deserts, and coastal plains. *(page 207)*

- African empires grew rich from trading gold and salt. *(page 209)*

Locating Places

Benue River (BAYN•way)
Ghana (GAH•nuh)
Mali (MAH•lee)
Timbuktu (TIHM•BUHK•TOO)
Songhai (SAWNG•HY)
Axum (AHK•SOOM)

Meeting People

Sundiata Keita (sun•dee•AH•tuh KY•tuh)
Mansa Musa (MAHN•sah moo•SAH)
Sunni Ali (sun•EE ah•LEE)

Content Vocabulary

plateau (pla•TOH)
griot (GREE•OH)
dhow (DOW)

Academic Vocabulary

fee
diminish (duh•MIH•nihsh)
prime

Reading Strategy

Summarizing Information Create diagrams showing the accomplishments of medieval African civilizations.

Accomplishments

NATIONAL GEOGRAPHIC Where & When?

A.D. 300	A.D. 900	A.D. 1500
c. A.D. 450 Kingdom of Ghana begins	c. A.D. 750 Arab Muslim traders settle in East Africa	1468 Sunni Ali captures Timbuktu

Timbuktu
Kilwa
Great Zimbabwe

WH7.4.1 Study the Niger River and the relationship of vegetation zones of forest, savannah, and desert to trade in gold, salt, food, and slaves; and the growth of the Ghana and Mali empires.

Africa's Geography

Main Idea Africa has a vast and varied landscape made up of shifting sand dunes, rain forests, sweeping savannas, large deserts, and coastal plains.

Reading Connection How can geography discourage people from exploring another place? Read to learn about the geographic features that made it difficult for people to travel across parts of Africa.

In 1906 a teacher named Hans Vischer explored what he called the "death road," a trade route connecting western Africa to the coast of the Mediterranean Sea. The "death road" crossed more than 1,500 miles (2,414 km) of the Sahara, the world's largest desert. To get lost meant certain death.

Only nomads living in the region knew the way, but Vischer hoped to map the route. Like the desert nomads, his life depended upon finding oases. Upon his return, Vischer amazed people with stories of the Sahara. He told of swirling winds and shifting sand dunes.

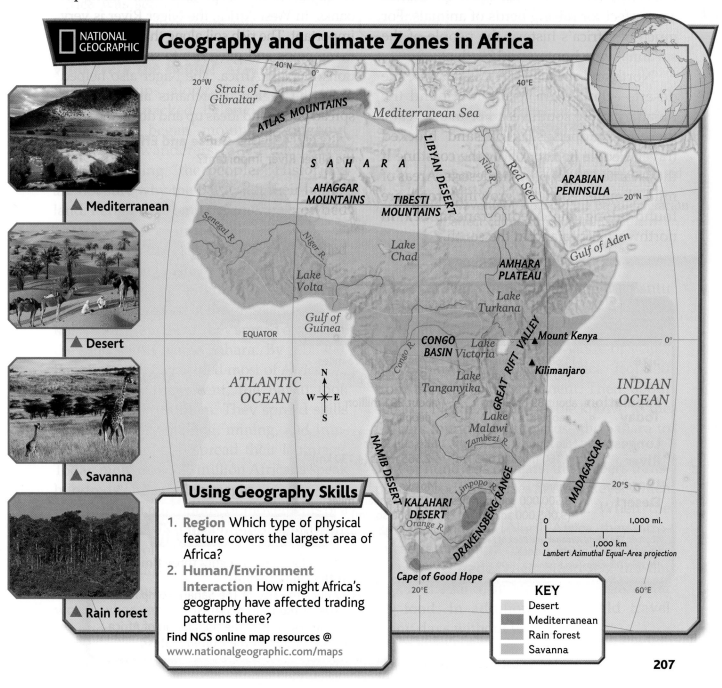

NATIONAL GEOGRAPHIC

Geography and Climate Zones in Africa

▲ Mediterranean

▲ Desert

▲ Savanna

▲ Rain forest

Using Geography Skills

1. **Region** Which type of physical feature covers the largest area of Africa?
2. **Human/Environment Interaction** How might Africa's geography have affected trading patterns there?

Find NGS online map resources @ www.nationalgeographic.com/maps

KEY
- Desert
- Mediterranean
- Rain forest
- Savanna

0   1,000 mi.

0   1,000 km

Lambert Azimuthal Equal-Area projection

▲ While many of the caravans that crossed the desert going to and from West Africa included about 1,000 camels, some caravans may have had as many as 12,000 camels. *What were some of the items traded by caravans?*

Rise of Ghana

Traders grouped hundreds, maybe even thousands, of camels together to form caravans. They traded salt and cloth from North Africa and the Sahara for gold and ivory from western Africa. The trade led to the growth of cities in western Africa. Eventually, rulers of these cities began to build empires. In the Middle Ages, these African empires were bigger than most European kingdoms in wealth and size. The first empire to develop was **Ghana** (GAH•nuh).

Ghana rose to power in the A.D. 400s. It was located where several trade routes came together. Trade routes reached across the Sahara into North Africa and down the Niger River (NY•juhr) to kingdoms in the rain forest. Some extended all the way to Africa's east coast. For traders to meet, they had to pass through Ghana. Passage required a **fee**—a tax paid to Ghana's rulers. These taxes made Ghana rich.

Why did traders pay the taxes? First, Ghana knew how to make iron weapons. Like ancient Kush, it used these weapons to conquer its neighbors. Although Ghana owned no gold mines, it controlled the people who did. Second, Ghana built a huge army. Third, people wanted the trade items, especially salt and gold, at almost any price. West Africans needed salt to flavor and preserve food, and Berber merchants wanted gold so they could buy goods from Europe and the Arabs.

How Did Mali Begin?

Ghana's power eventually declined. The discovery of new gold mines outside Ghana's control reduced the taxes it collected. In addition, heavy farming robbed the soil of minerals and made it harder to grow enough crops. Constant warfare also hurt Ghana. Ghana's rulers had accepted the religion of Islam. However, they fought with North African Muslims, who captured the capital of

Ghana in 1076 and briefly controlled the empire.

In the 1200s, the kingdom of **Mali** (MAH•lee) conquered what was left of the rapidly **diminishing** empire of Ghana. West African **griots** (gree•ohz), or storytellers, give credit to a great warrior-king named **Sundiata Keita** (sun•dee•AH•tuh KY•tuh)—the "Lion Prince." Sundiata, who ruled from 1230 to 1255, seized the capital of Ghana in 1240. He then won control of lands from the Atlantic coast to the trading city of **Timbuktu** (TIHM•BUHK•TOO). His conquests put Mali in control of the gold-mining areas, allowing him to rebuild the gold and salt trade.

Rise of Songhai

Mali began a slow decline after the death of its last strong king, **Mansa Musa** (MAHN•sah moo•SAH), in 1337. The kings who followed failed to stop Berber invaders who soon conquered Timbuktu.

In 1468 **Sunni Ali** (sun•EE ah•LEE), the leader of **Songhai** (SAWNG•hy), stormed into Timbuktu and drove out the Berbers. He then began a campaign of conquest. Sunni Ali utilized Songhai's location along the Niger River. He ordered a fleet of war canoes to seize control of the river trade. His armies then swept into the Sahara and seized the Berber salt mines. By the time of his death in 1492, Sunni Ali had built the largest empire in West Africa.

The empire lasted almost 100 more years. In 1591, however, a small army from the Arab kingdom of Morocco crossed the Sahara. Soldiers with cannons and guns easily cut down Songhai soldiers armed with swords, spears, and bows. Within months, Songhai's empire was gone.

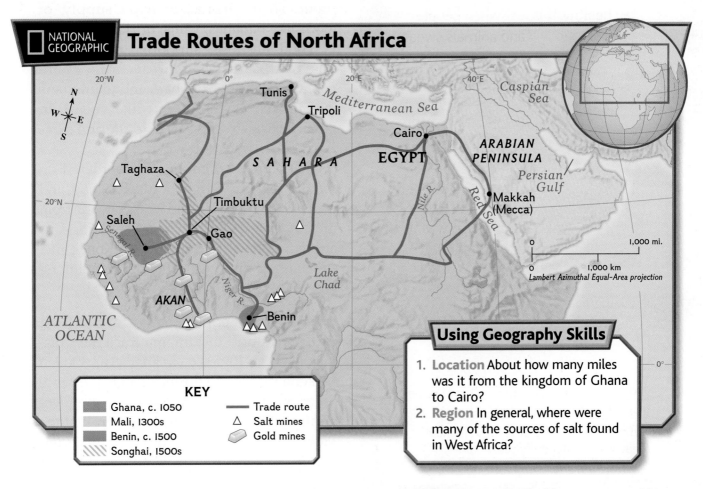

NATIONAL GEOGRAPHIC

Trade Routes of North Africa

Using Geography Skills

1. **Location** About how many miles was it from the kingdom of Ghana to Cairo?
2. **Region** In general, where were many of the sources of salt found in West Africa?

KEY

- Ghana, c. 1050
- Mali, 1300s
- Benin, c. 1500
- Songhai, 1500s
- Trade route
- △ Salt mines
- Gold mines

Focus on Everyday Life

Africa's Salt Mines Salt mining began in the Sahara in the Middle Ages. Ancient miners worked underground and in sand dunes to extract solid blocks of salt. The salt trade became a successful business for the African people. In ancient times, salt was so desirable that it was traded ounce for ounce for gold.

There are many salt deposits in western Africa because part of the desert was once a shallow sea made up of salt water. When the sea dried up, salt was left behind.

People need a small amount of salt to stay healthy. It is lost when people and animals sweat, so people need some in their food. In ancient times, before refrigerators or canned foods were invented, salt was used to keep foods from going bad. It also was used to add flavor to food.

◀ African salt mine today

Kingdoms of the Rain Forest Ghana, Mali, and Songhai ruled the wide-open savannas. However, the dense rain forests along the Equator kept them from expanding to the southern coast. People living in the rain forests built their own kingdoms and empires. They included Benin, which arose in the Niger delta, and Kongo, which formed in the Congo River basin.

Griots who live in the Niger delta still tell stories about King Ewuare (eh•WOO•ah•ray), who founded the empire of Benin around 1440. In describing his ancestor's accomplishments, one storyteller boasted that the king had captured 201 towns and villages and made them pay tribute.

Farmers in the rain forest kingdoms enjoyed many natural advantages, including farmable soil and a warm, wet climate. In cleared-out areas of the forest, they often produced a surplus, or extra supply, of foods like bananas, yams, or rice.

Food surpluses supported rulers and a class of artisans. Kongo weavers, for example, wove fabrics from bark and plant fibers that looked to Europeans like velvet. In Benin, artists excelled at sculpting and carving metal, wood, and ivory.

Rain forest kingdoms that bordered on the dry savannas traded surplus food and crafts for copper, salt, and leather goods from the savannas. Later, when the Europeans arrived, traders from Benin and Kongo met ships along the coast. They traded, among other things, captives taken in war.

East Africa People today in the East African country of Ethiopia trace their history back to 1005 B.C. In that year, Queen Makeda rose to the throne of a great empire called Saba or Sheba. According to the *Glory of Kings*, Ethiopia's oldest written history, Makeda traveled to meet with King Solomon, ruler of the Israelites. On her return, Makeda introduced ancient Israel's religion to her empire. Over time, eastern Africa would feel the impact of two other religions—Christianity and Islam.

What Was Axum? Like other empires, Saba declined. However, Ethiopia, known in ancient times as Abyssinia, did not. Its power was centered in a city-state called **Axum** (AHK•SOOM). Axum owed its strength to its location on the Red Sea. Goods from Africa flowed into Axum, which served as a **prime** trading center for the ancient Mediterranean and East Asian worlds.

Axum fought neighboring Kush for control of trade routes to inland Africa.

Around A.D. 300, King Ezana of Axum sent his armies against Kush and defeated it. A few years later, Ezana helped to bring a new religion to Africa when he converted to Christianity. In A.D. 334 he made it the official religion of Axum. Within a few hundred years, another religion—Islam—brought many changes to Axum and other trading states along Africa's eastern coast.

Coastal City-States Arab traders from the Arabian Peninsula had been coming to eastern Africa long before the rise of Islam in the early A.D. 600s. They invented a wind-catching, triangular sail that let them sail to

African Trading Empires A.D. 100–1600

	Axum	Ghana	Mali	Songhai	Zimbabwe
Location	East Africa	West Africa	West Africa	West Africa	SE Africa
	AXUM Adulis	GHANA Saleh	MALI Timbuktu	SONGHAI Gao	ZIMBABWE Great Zimbabwe
Time Period	c. 100–1400	c. 400–1200	c. 1200–1450	c. 1000–1600	c. 700–1450
Goods Traded	ivory, frankincense, myrrh, slaves	iron products, animal products, salt, gold	salt, gold	salt, gold	gold, copper, ivory
Key Facts	King Ezana converted to Christianity; made it the official religion.	Taxes from traders passing through made Ghana rich.	King Mansa Musa built mosques and libraries.	Songhai gained control of West African trade by conquering Timbuktu and mastering trade by river.	Kings Mutota and Matope built the region's biggest empire.

Understanding Charts

Large trading kingdoms developed in several areas of Africa.
1. Which kingdom developed earliest?
2. Generalize What were some of the common trade items of the West African empires?

Africa. The sails powered sailboats called **dhows** (DOWZ).

In the A.D. 700s, many Arab Muslim traders settled in East African city-states. Here Africans and Arab Muslims shared goods and ideas. By the 1300s, a string of trading ports extended down the East African coast. They included Mogadishu (MAH•guh•DIH•shoo), Kilwa, Mombasa, and Zanzibar. These ports became major links in an Indian Ocean trading network. They traded with places as far away as East Asia, including establishing trade with China.

What Was the Great Zimbabwe?
Another great trading center known as Zimbabwe (zihm•BAH•BWAY) arose inland in southeast-ern Africa. Founded around A.D. 700 by the Shona people, Zimbabwe supplied gold, copper, and ivory to the East African coast. From there, African goods were shipped to Arabia, Persia, India, and China.

During the 1400s, two kings—Mutota and his son Matope—made Zimbabwe into a large empire. It stretched from south of the Zambezi River to the Indian Ocean. Evidence of Zimbabwe's power can still be seen at the ruins of the Great Zimbabwe, the empire's capital where more than 300 huge stone buildings still stand—silent reminders of Zimbabwe's past greatness.

✓ **Reading Check** **Analyze** Why did West Africa become the center of three large trade empires?

History Online

Study Central Need help understanding Africa's trading empires? Visit ca.hss.glencoe.com and click on Study Central.

Section 1 Review

Reading Summary
Review the Main Ideas

- The continent of Africa has varied landscapes, including rain forests, grasslands, and deserts. Most Africans draw on a common ancestry through the Bantu.

- Beginning in about A.D. 300, a succession of kingdoms, including Ghana, Mali, and Songhai, arose in West Africa. In addition, rain forest kingdoms, including Benin and Kongo, traded with the surrounding savanna kingdoms.

What Did You Learn?

1. Describe Africa's grasslands.

2. What items were traded in the kingdoms of West Africa?

Critical Thinking

3. **Organize Information** Draw a chart like the one below. For each region, describe the role of trade that developed there. **CA 7RC2.2**

West Africa	Rain Forest Kingdoms	East Africa

4. **Economics Connection** How did the kingdom of Ghana use taxation to strengthen and increase the wealth of its empire? **CA HI6.**

5. **The Big Ideas** How do you think the history of Africa and its kingdoms might have been different if Africa's geography had been different? **CA CS3.**

6. **Compare and Contrast** Which of the kingdoms discussed in this section developed away from the coast? How did the economies of these kingdoms compare to other African kingdoms? **CA 7RC2.0**

7. **Reading** **Summarizing** Create an outline of Section 1 that summarizes the rise and fall of empires in West Africa. **CA 7WS1.3**

SUNDIATA
THE HUNGERING LION

Retold by Kenny Mann

Before You Read

The Scene: This story takes place in Mali on the continent of Africa in the 1100s.

The Characters: Balla Fasseke is the griot who tells the story of Sundiata. Sundiata is the Lion King of Mali. Sogolon and Maghan Kon Fatta are Sundiata's parents. Sassouma is the first wife of Maghan Kon Fatta. Sumanguru is a rival king.

The Plot: The Lion King of Mali, Sundiata, is denied the throne. Sundiata has to prove that he is the rightful king.

Vocabulary Preview

guardian: one who takes care of another person

infirmity: weakness

brewed: prepared by boiling

smiths: metalworkers

multitude: a great number of people

exile: period of time away from one's country

lance: a steel-tipped spear

Have you ever known someone who overcame obstacles to achieve great things? In this story, a young leader must learn to speak and walk in order to take control of his kingdom.

As You Read

Keep in mind that this story is a mixture of fact and legend. However, a king named Sundiata did conquer new lands and expand trade while he ruled the kingdom of Mali.

O people, hear my story! I am Balla Fasseke (bah•lah fah•SEE•kay) of Mali. I am a *griot.*[1] I am the guardian of the word. In my mind rest the stories of my people and the history of our land. O hear me and remember, for I speak the truth.

Long, long ago, the last king of Ghana fell to the sword of Sumanguru, the Sosso king; Sumanguru, the cruel warrior and mighty sorcerer; Sumanguru, who was to meet his fate at the hands of Sundiata, the Lion King of Mali.

I am Sundiata's *griot.* O hear me, for I speak the truth!

Sundiata was born of Sogolon, who married Maghan Kon Fatta, the ruler of Mali, whose totem[2] was the lion. Sogolon was brought to the king as a maiden, disfigured by a hunchback and ill looks. But she was said to possess the mighty spirit of a buffalo, strong and courageous. Her coming had been foretold to the king, and he took Sogolon as his wife and came to love her.

When Sundiata was born, the king rejoiced. The great royal drums carried the news all over the kingdom. But his first wife, Sassouma, was jealous. Her son should inherit the throne! What need had her husband of another son? She vowed that Sundiata would never become king.

---

[1] **griot:** storyteller
[2] **totem:** animal or plant serving as the symbol of a family or clan

In time, Sassouma saw that she had nothing to fear, for Sundiata was stricken by a strange infirmity. He could neither speak nor walk! How great was Sogolon's sorrow! For seven long years, she tried to cure her son. She consulted with all the wise men of the kingdom and brewed herbs and potions, but to no avail.[3] And Sundiata's father, King Maghan Kon Fatta, despaired. But his *griot,* who was my father, advised the king. "The young seed must endure the storm," he said. "And from this small seed shall spring a great tree."

One day, when the king felt death approach, he called the child to him. "I shall give you the gift each king gives to his heir," he said. And on that day, my people, the king gave me—Balla Fasseke—to Sundiata to be his *griot,* as my father had been the king's *griot,* and his father before that. And on that day, for the first time in his life, Sundiata spoke. "Balla, you shall be my *griot,*" he said. And the king knew that his son—the son of the lion and the buffalo—was worthy to be king.

But when Maghan Kon Fatta died, the councilors ignored his wishes. It was the son of Sassouma who ascended the throne, and not Sundiata, the rightful heir. And Sassouma persecuted Sogolon and her son with evil hatred and banished them to a dark corner of the palace. Oh, how Sogolon's tears flowed in her unhappiness! When Sundiata saw his mother's despair, he looked at her calmly and said, "Today I will walk." Then he sent me, Balla Fasseke, to the royal forges.[4] "Tell the smiths to make me the sturdiest iron rod possible," he ordered.

---

[3] **avail:** benefit
[4] **forges:** furnaces where metal is heated and shaped

Six men were needed to carry the iron rod to Sogolon's house. They threw it on the ground before Sundiata. A huge multitude of people had gathered to see if Sundiata would walk. "Arise, young lion!" I commanded. "Roar, and may the land know that from henceforth, it has a master!"

Sundiata gripped the rod with his two hands and held it upright in the ground. Beads of sweat poured from his face. A deathly silence gripped the people. All at once, with a mighty thrust, Sundiata stood upright. The crowd gasped. The iron rod was bent like a bow. And Sogolon, who had been dumb with amazement, suddenly burst into song:

> *Oh day, oh beautiful day,*
> *Oh day, day of joy,*
> *Allah Almighty, this is the finest*
> *day you have created,*
> *My son is going to walk!*
> *Hear me, people, for I speak the truth!*

Sundiata threw away the rod, and his first steps were those of a giant.

From that day on, Sundiata grew in strength. He became a fine hunter and was much loved by all the people. But Sassouma, whose son was now king, feared Sundiata's growing power. Her plots to kill him failed. And she knew that I would perform any deed to bring Sundiata to the throne. So, to separate us, Sassouma sent me far away to the court of the demon king, Sumanguru. And there I remained for several years. I pretended allegiance to Sumanguru, but always I waited for the day when I would sing the praises of Sundiata once more.

Sogolon fled the palace and took Sundiata far from Sassouma's hatred. For seven years they lived in exile, finding food and shelter wherever they could. At last, they came to the city of Mema. Here they met with good luck, for the king of Mema took a liking to Sundiata and treated him like a son. He admired Sundiata's courage and leadership. This king decided to make the young boy his heir and teach him the arts of government and war. And thus, Sundiata grew to manhood.

One day, messengers came running to Sundiata. "Sumanguru has invaded Mali!" they cried. "The king and his mother, Sassouma, have fled. Only you can save our people. Return, young lion, and reclaim your throne!"

This, O people, was the moment of Sundiata's destiny. The king of Mema gave him half his forces. And as Sundiata rode at their head, more and more men joined him until a great army thundered across the plains. And from far-distant Mali, Sumanguru, too, raced to meet his destiny. And I, O my people, I followed, for I knew that soon I would be reunited with Sundiata, my Lion King.

And so it was. Sundiata led his army from Mema, and Sumanguru came from Mali. The two great armies met in battle on the plains of Kirina. I took my chance and escaped at last from Sumanguru. Through the thick clouds of dust and the battle cries of the warriors, I galloped to Sundiata's side. Oh, how great was our joy!

My years with Sumanguru had not been in vain, O my people, for I had learned that Sumanguru feared the magic power of a white rooster. He believed that one touch of the rooster's spur[5] would defeat him

---

[5]**spur:** a sharp spine on the leg of some birds

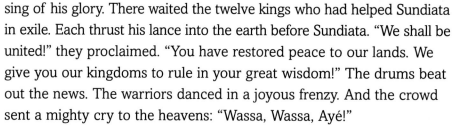

forever. And this very spur I had fastened to an arrow, which I gave to my lord, Sundiata.

With deadly aim, Sundiata sent the arrow speeding across the battlefield toward Sumanguru. True as a hawk in flight, it met its mark, grazing the sorcerer's shoulder. With a great scream of fear, Sumanguru turned on his horse and fled.

Far away he rode, to the caves of Mount Koulikoro. There we saw Sumanguru, the demon king, fall to his knees and turn to stone. His soldiers, discouraged by his flight, ceased to fight and were defeated.

And so Sundiata returned to Mali to reclaim his throne, and I, Balla Fasseke, went with him to sing of his glory. There waited the twelve kings who had helped Sundiata in exile. Each thrust his lance into the earth before Sundiata. "We shall be united!" they proclaimed. "You have restored peace to our lands. We give you our kingdoms to rule in your great wisdom!" The drums beat out the news. The warriors danced in a joyous frenzy. And the crowd sent a mighty cry to the heavens: "Wassa, Wassa, Ayé!"

And thus did I bear witness to the birth of the great kingdom of Mali. And thus did I see Sundiata become its first emperor.

So listen, O my people, and remember, for I speak the truth. May you live to tell this story to your children, that the name of Sundiata— the Lion King—shall live forever.

Responding to the Literature

1. Why did the king give Sundiata a griot?

2. Who did Sundiata defeat to gain control of Mali?

3. **Identify** Foreshadowing is when a storyteller gives you hints of something to come later. This story contains many suggestions that foreshadow Sundiata's successful reign as king. Identify three such hints in the first six paragraphs. `CA 7RL3.2`

4. **Analyze** Why do you think Sundiata did not walk after receiving his mother's treatments but *did* walk when his half-brother was made king? `CA 7RL3.3`

5. **Read to Write** Suppose you are Sundiata's father. Write a brief speech stating your reasons for choosing Sundiata to be the next king. `CA 7WA2.2`

Reading on Your Own...

If you would like to read more about ancient Rome, Islam,
or Africa, check out these other great books.

Nonfiction

Gladiator by Richard Watkins describes the life of gladiators. Read about the games, the weapons and equipment used, and various opponents from humans to exotic animals. *The content of this book is related to* History–Social Science Standard WH7.1.

Fiction

Detectives in Togas by Henry Winterfeld is a story of a group of boys who stumble across a mystery at their school. One of their classmates is accused of a terrible crime, and they must find the truth before he goes to prison. *The content of this book is related to* History–Social Science Standard WH7.1.

Nonfiction

Science in Medieval Islam: An illustrated Introduction by Howard R. Turner details many scientific achievements of medieval Islam from astronomy to medicine and much more. Learn how this knowledge helped the rest of the world. *The content of this book is related to* History–Social Science Standard WH7.2.

Biography

Mansa Musa: The Lion of Mali by Khephra Burns recounts the story of one of Mali's most legendary kings named Mansa Musa. Kidnapped by slave traders when he was a boy, he grew up to become a triumphant and famous king. *The content of this book is related to* History–Social Science Standard WH7.4.

Africa's Religion and Government

Guide to Reading

History Social Science Standards

WH7.4 Students analyze the geographic, political, economic, religious, and social structures of the sub-Saharan civilizations of Ghana and Mali in Medieval Africa.

Looking Back, Looking Ahead

In Section 1, you read about some of the kingdoms and empires that developed in Africa. To hold their kingdoms and empires together, Africans had to create their own governments. One unifying force was the religion of Islam, but many Africans continued to practice their traditional religious beliefs as well.

Focusing on the Main Ideas

• Traditional African religions shared certain beliefs and provided a guide for living together. *(page 223)*

• Islam played an important role in medieval Africa, but long-held African beliefs and customs still remained strong. *(page 224)*

• The growth of West African empires led to the growth of centralized governments ruled by kings. *(page 227)*

Locating Places
Makkah (MAH•kuh)

Meeting People
Olaudah Equiano (oh•LOW•duh EHK•wee•AHN•oh)
Ibn Battuta (IH•buhn bat•TOO•tah)
Askia Muhammad (ahs•KEE•uh moh•HAH•muhd)

Content Vocabulary
sultan (SUHL•tuhn)
Swahili (swah•HEE•lee)
clan

Academic Vocabulary
vary
accompany (uh•KUHMP•nee)
element (EH•luh•muhnt)
benefit (BEH•nuh•FIHT)

Reading Strategy
Organizing Information Use a diagram to show the characteristics of Swahili culture and language.

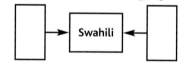

Swahili

NATIONAL GEOGRAPHIC Where & When?

Timbuktu
Mogadishu

1300	1400	1500
1324 Mansa Musa travels to Makkah	**1352** Ibn Battuta arrives in West Africa	**1492** Sunni Ali dies

WH7.4.3 Describe the role of the trans-Saharan caravan trade in the changing religious and cultural characteristics of West Africa and the influence of Islamic beliefs, ethics, and law.

Traditional African Religions

Main Idea Traditional African religions shared certain beliefs and provided a guide for living together.

Reading Connection What questions do most religions try to answer? As you read this section, look for questions answered by traditional African religions.

For centuries, Europeans believed Africans did not have a religion. **Olaudah Equiano** (oh•LOW•duh EHK•wee•AHN•oh), a member of the Igbo, disagreed. The Igbo, he wrote, "believe that there is one Creator of all things, and that he . . . governs events, especially our deaths and captivity."

Most African groups shared the Igbo belief in one supreme god. They understood the Christian and Muslim idea of a single god, but many wanted to continue their own religious practices.

These practices **varied** from place to place. Some groups, like the Nanti in East Africa, thought people could talk directly with their god. Others, like the Igbo, thought their creator could only be spoken to through less powerful gods and goddesses who worked for him.

Even though Africans practiced their religion differently in different places, their beliefs served similar purposes. They provided rules for living and helped people stay in touch with their history.

When relatives died, many Africans believed their spirits stayed with the community. They believed these spirits could talk to the supreme god or help solve problems. As a result, many Africans honored their ancestors.

Reading Check **Explain** What was the role of ancestors in African religion?

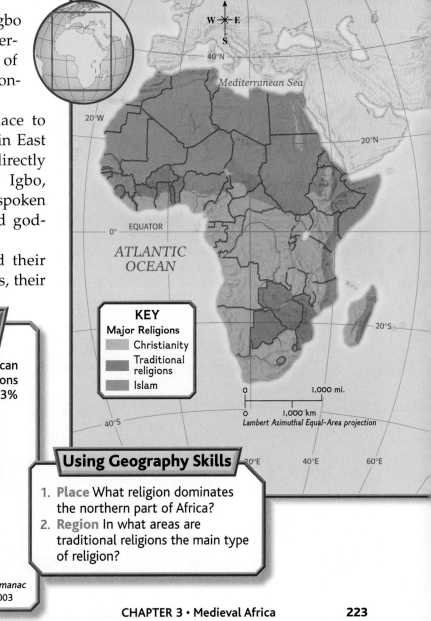

NATIONAL GEOGRAPHIC

African Religions Today

Mediterranean Sea

ATLANTIC OCEAN

KEY
Major Religions
- Christianity
- Traditional religions
- Islam

1,000 mi.
1,000 km
Lambert Azimuthal Equal–Area projection

Using Geography Skills

1. **Place** What religion dominates the northern part of Africa?
2. **Region** In what areas are traditional religions the main type of religion?

Religion in Africa

Traditional African Religions 12.3%

Muslim 40.7%

Christian 46.4%

Other Religions 0.6%

Source: *The World Almanac and Book of Facts*, 2003

WH7.4.3 Describe the role of the trans-Saharan caravan trade in the changing religious and cultural characteristics of West Africa and the influence of Islamic beliefs, ethics, and law. **WH7.4.4** Trace the growth of the Arabic language in government, trade, and Islamic scholarship in West Africa. **WH7.4.5** Describe the importance of written and oral traditions in the transmission of African history and culture.

Islam in Africa

Main Idea Islam played an important role in medieval Africa, but long-held African beliefs and customs still remained strong.

Reading Connection Have you ever changed your ideas because someone you respect has different ideas than you do? Learn how African rulers helped spread Islam and how Arabs and Africans influenced each other.

Ibn Battuta (IH•buhn bat•TOO•tah), a young Arab lawyer from Morocco, set out in 1325 to see the Muslim world. Since the A.D. 600s, the religion of Islam had spread from the Arabian Peninsula to Africa and elsewhere.

Ibn Battuta traveled throughout the lands of Islam for 30 years. He covered a distance of more than 73,000 miles (117,482 km). When Ibn Battuta arrived in West Africa in 1352, Islam had been practiced there for hundreds of years. Yet he soon realized that not all people in West Africa accepted Islam. Many people in the countryside still followed traditional African religions. Islam was popular in the cities where rulers and traders accepted it by choice or because it helped them trade with Muslim Arabs.

Some Muslims complained that Sundiata Keita and Sunni Ali—western Africa's two great empire builders—did not do enough to win people over to Islam. The two leaders were more concerned about stopping rebellions than spreading religion.

Ibn Battuta found things in West Africa that surprised him. He was amazed that

The City of Djenne

Like Timbuktu, the city of Djenne became a center for both trade and Islam. Traders from the deserts to the north and the rain forests to the south met at Djenne, located on the Bani River. The first Great Mosque at Djenne was probably built in the 1200s.
Did all of the people in West Africa accept Islam? Explain.

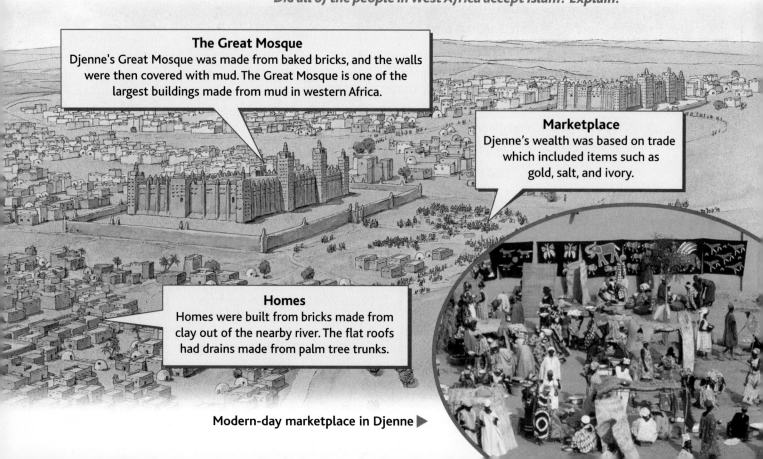

The Great Mosque
Djenne's Great Mosque was made from baked bricks, and the walls were then covered with mud. The Great Mosque is one of the largest buildings made from mud in western Africa.

Marketplace
Djenne's wealth was based on trade which included items such as gold, salt, and ivory.

Homes
Homes were built from bricks made from clay out of the nearby river. The flat roofs had drains made from palm tree trunks.

Modern-day marketplace in Djenne ▶

women did not cover their faces with a veil, as was the Muslim custom. However, he did find that West Africans studied the Quran, the Muslim holy book. "They zealously [eagerly] learn the Quran by heart," he wrote.

Mali and Mansa Musa

Much of what pleased Ibn Battuta was the work of Mansa Musa. Mansa Musa had allowed different religions but was devoted to making Islam stronger. He used the wealth of Mali to build more mosques, or Muslim places of worship. He also set up libraries at Timbuktu, which collected books from all over the Muslim world.

In 1324 Mansa Musa made Mali known to other parts of the world when he set out on a long journey to the city of **Makkah** (MAH•kuh), also known as Mecca. As you read in the chapter on Islam, all Muslims are supposed to make a pilgrimage to the Muslim holy city of Makkah. When Mansa Musa set out on his trip, however, he made sure everybody knew he was the leader of a great empire.

Mansa Musa's caravan had thousands of people, including enslaved people, and 100 pack camels. Each camel carried gold. While in Makkah, Mansa Musa convinced some of Islam's finest architects, teachers, and writers to **accompany** him back to Mali. There they helped spread Islam in West Africa.

Songhai and Askia Muhammad

Sunni Ali, the founder of Songhai, practiced the traditional religion of the Songhai people. However, he declared himself a Muslim to keep the support of townspeople. After Sunni Ali died, his son refused to follow his father's example. One of Sunni Ali's generals, Muhammad Ture, saw a chance to take over the government. With the support of Muslim townspeople, he declared himself

king. In a bloody war, he drove Sunni Ali's family from Songhai. He then took the name Askia, a rank in the Songhai army.

Under **Askia Muhammad** (ahs•KEE•uh moh•HAH•muhd), Songhai built the largest empire in medieval West Africa. He kept local courts in place but told them to honor Muslim laws. He also made Timbuktu an important center of Islamic culture and learning, with a university known throughout the Muslim world. In addition, he set up some 150 schools to teach the Quran.

The empire survived family disputes. But, as you have read, it did not survive the guns of Moroccan invaders. The invasion in 1591 shattered the empire.

Biography

WH7.4.3 Describe the role of the trans-Saharan caravan trade in the changing religious and cultural characteristics of West Africa and the influence of Islamic beliefs, ethics, and law.

WH7.4.4 Trace the growth of the Arabic language in government, trade, and Islamic scholarship in West Africa.

MANSA MUSA
Ruled 1312–1337

Mansa Musa ruled the West African empire of Mali with great skill and organization. Under Mansa Musa's guidance, Mali became a great center of education, commerce, and the arts. Mali was one of the largest empires in the world at the time. In fact, the kingdom was so vast that Mansa Musa once bragged it would take a year to travel from the northern border to the southern border.

Despite Mali's enormous size and wealth, the kingdom was not well-known outside the continent of Africa. Mansa Musa's pilgrimage to Makkah in 1324, however, announced Mali's riches and achievements to the world. Traveling on horseback, Mansa Musa was joined by many people, including 8,000 enslaved people, 100 camels to carry baggage, and 24,000 pounds of gold. Each person carried a staff of gold. According to Egyptian historians and the accounts of observers, Mansa Musa spent so much gold in Cairo, Egypt, that the value of gold dropped in Cairo and did not recover for more than 12 years.

▲ Mansa Musa

Mansa Musa's famous pilgrimage to Makkah brought attention to his kingdom. Mali was included on world maps as early as 1339. Many European nations and kingdoms in North Africa and the Middle East wished to establish trade connections with Mali and gain some of its wealth.

▲ A village in Mali today

Then and Now

Mali was unnoticed by the rest of the world until Mansa Musa's pilgrimage. Is it possible for a present-day country to go unnoticed? Why or why not?

WH7.4.3 Describe the role of the trans-Saharan caravan trade in the changing religious and cultural characteristics of West Africa and the influence of Islamic beliefs, ethics, and law.

WH7.4.4 Trace the growth of the Arabic language in government, trade, and Islamic scholarship in West Africa.

Islam's Impact on Africa Islam had a far-reaching impact on northern and eastern Africa. Africans who accepted Islam also adopted Islamic laws and ideas. Sometimes these changes were opposed by people who favored traditional African ways.

In 1331 Ibn Battuta visited Mogadishu, a trading port on the East African coast. Its **sultan** (SUHL•tuhn), or leader, said in perfect Arabic, "You have honored our country by coming." A moment later, Ibn Battuta heard the sultan speak in **Swahili** (swah•HEE•lee).

The word *Swahili* comes from an Arabic word meaning "people of the coast." By 1331, however, it had come to mean two things: the unique culture of East Africa's coast and the language spoken there.

The Swahili culture and language are a blend of African and Muslim **elements.** African influences came from the cultures of Africa's interior. Muslim influences came from Arab and Persian settlers. The Swahili culture still exists in Africa today.

Islam also advanced learning. Muslim schools drew students from many parts of Africa and introduced the Arabic language to many Africans. These helped pass along African culture and history. Arabic soon became an important language of government and education.

In addition, Islam also influenced African art and buildings. Muslim architects built beautiful mosques and palaces in Timbuktu and other cities.

Reading Check **Explain** How did Askia Muhammad gain control of Songhai?

Web Activity Visit ca.hss.glencoe.com and click on *Chapter 3—Student Web Activities* to learn more about medieval Africa.

Government and Society

Main Idea The growth of West African empires led to the growth of centralized governments ruled by kings.

Reading Connection What makes a system of government effective? Read to learn how African rulers governed their empires.

The loud thumping of drums called the citizens of Ghana to a meeting with the king. Anybody with a complaint could speak. In the royal courtyard, the king sat in an open silk tent. He wore a cap of gold and a jewel-covered robe. Royal officials surrounded him. Guard dogs with gold and silver collars stood watch. Before talking to the king,

▲ The carving above shows a king of Benin. The ivory armband (lower left) was worn by the king during ceremonies. *Why did African kings allow local rulers to keep some power?*

Ghana Profits From Trade

Al Bekri described the way Ghana taxed merchants to increase its own wealth.

"The king [of Ghana] exacts the right of one *dinar* of gold on each donkey-load of salt that enters his country, and two *dinars* of gold on each load of salt that goes out. A load of copper carries a duty of five *mitqals* and a load of merchandise ten *mitqals*. The best gold in the country comes from Ghiaru, a town situated eighteen days' journey from the capital [Kumbi]."

— Abdullah Abu-Ubayd al Bekri, "Ghana in 1067"

▲ Ghana's wealth came from trade caravans.

DBQ Document-Based Question

Which do you think has more worth, a dinar or a mitqal? Why?

subjects poured dust over their heads or fell to the ground. Bowing, they stated their business and waited for the king's reply.

Ruler and Subject

This, said Arab travelers, was how government worked in West Africa. Kings settled arguments, managed trade, and protected the empire. But they expected complete obedience in return.

With the growth of empires, Africans invented new ways to govern themselves. The most successful states, like Ghana, formed some type of central authority. Power usually rested with a king—or, in a few cases, a queen.

Both rulers and people **benefited.** Merchants received favors from the kings,

and the kings received taxes from the merchants. Local rulers kept some power, and the kings in turn received their loyalty. This allowed kingdoms to grow richer and to extend their control over a larger area.

Ghana's Government

The kings of Ghana relied on help from a council of ministers, or group of close advisers. As the empire grew, rulers divided it into provinces. Lesser kings, often conquered leaders, governed each of these areas. Beneath them, district chiefs oversaw smaller districts. Each district usually included a chief's **clan**—a group of people descended from the same ancestor.

Kings held tightly to their power. They insisted that local rulers send their sons to the royal court. They rode through the countryside seeking reports of rebellion. Most important, they controlled trade.

Nobody could trade without the king's permission. Also, nobody could own gold nuggets except the king. People traded only in gold dust. "If kings did otherwise," said one Arab traveler, "gold would become so abundant as practically to lose its value."

One policy of Ghana's government, however, confused outsiders. "It is their custom," exclaimed an Arab writer, "that the kingdom is inherited only by the son of the king's sister." In Arab states, property passed through a man's sons, not the sons of his sister. In Ghana, the throne went to the king's nephew.

What Was Mali's Government Like?

Mali followed Ghana's example but on a larger scale. It had more territory, people, and trade, so royal officials had more responsibilites than in Ghana. One supervised fishing on the Niger. Another looked after the empire's forests. A third oversaw farming, and a fourth managed money.

Most kings divided their kingdoms into provinces, like Ghana. However, Sundiata, the founder of Mali, put his generals in charge of them. People accepted this policy because the generals protected them from invaders. Also, the generals often came from the provinces they ruled.

Mali's other great king, Mansa Musa, rewarded citizens with gold, land, and horses to keep them loyal. He granted military heroes the "National Honor of the Trousers." As one Arab said:

❝ Whenever a hero adds to the lists of his exploits, the king gives him a pair of wide trousers. . . . [T]he greater the number of the knight's [soldier's] exploits, the bigger the size of his trousers. ❞

—Al-Dukhari, as quoted in
Topics in West African History

Because only the king and royal family could wear sewn clothes, this was a big honor indeed. Most people wore only wrapped clothes.

Songhai's Government Songhai built on the traditions of Ghana and Mali. Its founder, Sunni Ali, divided his empire into provinces. However, he never finished setting up his empire. Sunni continually moved, fighting one battle or another.

In 1492 Sunni Ali died mysteriously on a return trip home. Some say he drowned while crossing a stream. Others say his enemies killed him. The next year, general Muhammad Ture seized control of the government. Unlike Sunni Ali, Ture was a loyal Muslim. His religious ideas affected Songhai's government.

 **Reading Check** **Contrast** How was Mali ruled differently from Ghana?

History Online

Study Central Need help understanding African religion and government? Visit **ca.hss.glencoe.com** and click on Study Central.

Section ② Review

Reading Summary

Review the Main Ideas

- Many Africans believed in a single creator and honored the spirits of ancestors.

- Islam became the dominant religion in the kingdoms of West and East Africa.

- The empires of West Africa were ruled by kings who closely controlled trade and divided their lands among lesser chiefs to aid in governing.

What Did You Learn?

1. How did Mansa Musa attempt to strengthen Islam in Mali?

2. How did the kings of Ghana strengthen the government and maintain their power?

Critical Thinking

3. **The Big Ideas** Draw a diagram to show the effects of Islam on Africa. **CA 7RC2.3**

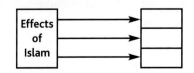

4. **Predict** How might Africa's history be different if Islam had not been introduced? **CA HI2.**

5. **Analyze** How did a strong central authority benefit African kingdoms? In what ways does this reflect modern-day government? **CA 7RC2.0**

6. **Writing Research Reports** Use the library and Internet to research Mansa Musa. Write an essay describing his pilgrimage to Makkah. **CA 7WA2.3**

7. **Analysis** **Understanding Problems** What kinds of problems did Africa's people face during medieval times? Write an essay explaining how Africans tried to solve these problems. **CA HI1.**

Section 3

African Society and Culture

History Social Science Standards

WH7.4 Students analyze the geographic, political, economic, religious, and social structures of the sub-Saharan civilizations of Ghana and Mali in Medieval Africa.

Guide to Reading

Looking Back, Looking Ahead

By the time Europeans came to Africa, people all over the continent had developed complex cultures. For most Africans, life centered on farming villages like the ones you will read about in this section. Here the family formed the basis of society.

Focusing on the Main Ideas

- Despite Africa's great size, its societies shared many common traits. *(page 231)*

- The African slave trade changed greatly when Muslims and Europeans began taking captives from the continent. *(page 233)*

- Enslaved Africans developed rich cultures that influenced many other cultures, including our own. *(page 235)*

Meeting People

Dahia al-Kahina (dah•HEE•uh ahl•kah•HEE•nah)

Nzinga (ehn•ZIHN•GAH)

Content Vocabulary

extended family

matrilineal (MA•truh•LIH•nee•uhl)

oral history

Academic Vocabulary

bond

release (rih•LEES)

Reading Strategy

Compare and Contrast Create a Venn diagram like the one below showing the similarities and differences between the enslavement of Africans in Africa and the enslavement of Africans in Europe.

Enslavement in Africa   Enslavement in Europe

NATIONAL GEOGRAPHIC **Where&When?**

- Timbuktu
- Kilwa
- Great Zimbabwe

A.D. 500	1000	1500

c. A.D. 650
Queen Dahia al-Kahina fights Muslims

c. 1441
First enslaved Africans arrive in Europe

1623
Queen Nzinga fights Portuguese

WH7.4.2 Analyze the importance of family, labor specialization, and regional commerce in the development of states and cities in West Africa.

WH7.4.5 Describe the importance of written and oral traditions in the transmission of African history and culture.

Life in Medieval Africa

Main Idea Despite Africa's great size, its societies shared many common traits.

Reading Connection Have you ever noticed that even though people are different, they all have some things in common? Read to learn why people in different regions of Africa have similar traditions and cultures.

The family formed the basis of African society. People often lived in **extended families,** or families made up of several generations. They included anywhere from ten to hundreds of members.

Many villages, especially Bantu villages, were **matrilineal** (MA•truh•LIH•nee•uhl). They traced their descent through mothers rather than fathers. When a woman married, however, she joined her husband's family. To make up for the loss, her family received gifts—cloth, metal tools, cattle, or goats—from the husband's family.

All families valued children greatly. They saw them as a **bond** between the past and the future. Some people, like the Yoruba of what is today Nigeria, believed an ancestor might be reborn in a child. They also knew children guaranteed that the family would live on.

Education In Africa's villages, education was the responsibility of the family and other villagers. Children learned the history of their people and the skills they would need as adults.

In West Africa, griots, or storytellers, helped in schooling. They kept alive their village's **oral history**—the stories passed down by word of mouth from generation to generation. Many stories included a lesson about living. Lessons also were given through short proverbs. One Bantu proverb stated: "A good deed will make a good neighbor."

What Was the Role of Women? As in other medieval societies, women in Africa acted mostly as wives and mothers. Men had more rights and controlled much of what women did. Visitors to Africa, however, saw exceptions. European explorers were amazed to learn that women served as soldiers in some African kingdoms.

African women also won fame as rulers. In the A.D. 600s, Queen **Dahia al-Kahina** (dah•HEE•uh ahl•kah•HEE•nah) led the fight against the Muslim invasion of her kingdom, which was located about where Mauritania is today. Another woman ruler was Queen **Nzinga** (ehn•ZIHN•GAH), who ruled lands in what are now Angola and Congo. She spent almost 40 years battling Portuguese slave traders in an effort to stop them from enslaving her people and exporting them to America.

Reading Check **Explain** How were Bantu families organized?

▼ This panel shows a family from the Congo at work. *What was an extended family in Bantu society?*

Biography

WH7.4.1 Study the Niger River and the relationship of vegetation zones of forest, savannah, and desert to trade in gold, salt, food, and slaves; and the growth of the Ghana and Mali empires.

WH7.4.3 Describe the role of the trans-Saharan caravan trade in the changing religious and cultural characteristics of West Africa and the influence of Islamic beliefs, ethics, and law.

QUEEN NZINGA
c. 1582–1663

Angolan Warrior-Leader

It was rare in the 1600s for women to take active roles in politics and war, but one African woman—Queen Nzinga of Matamba—was known for her military leadership and political skills. Nzinga was the daughter of the king of the Ndongo people. The Ndongo lived in southwest Africa in what is today called Angola. Nzinga quickly learned archery and hunting. She was intelligent and a natural athlete. Nzinga's father failed to notice his daughter. He was too busy defending the kingdom from the Portuguese, who wanted to buy enslaved Africans and ship them overseas.

▲ **Enslaved Africans in a ship's hold being taken to America.**

Even though she was female, Nzinga knew she could be a strong leader. She did not want to learn the enemy's language, but she soon realized that it could benefit her. She asked a captured priest to teach her Portuguese.

In 1623 Nzinga became queen. She declared all of her territory to be free territory and promised that all enslaved Africans who made it to the kingdom would be free. For nearly 30 years, she led her people in battles against the Portuguese. She allied with other African kingdoms to seal the trade routes used to ship enslaved Africans out of the country. In 1662 she negotiated a peace agreement with the Portuguese. She died the next year at age 81.

◀ **The Portuguese built Elmire Castle on the coast of Ghana to hold enslaved Africans before shipping them overseas.**

Then and Now

Do research to find the name of a modern female leader. Compare her leadership skills to those of Queen Nzinga.

WH7.4.1 Study the Niger River and the relationship of vegetation zones of forest, savannah, and desert to trade in gold, salt, food, and slaves; and the growth of the Ghana and Mali empires.

WH7.4.3 Describe the role of the trans-Saharan caravan trade in the changing religious and cultural characteristics of West Africa and the influence of Islamic beliefs, ethics, and law.

Slavery

Main Idea The African slave trade changed greatly when Muslims and Europeans began taking captives from the continent.

Reading Connection Do you know why the shipment of enslaved Africans to America began? Read to learn about slavery in African society and the beginning of the European slave trade.

In 1441 a Portuguese sea captain sailed down Africa's western coast. His goal was to bring the first African captives back to Portugal. During the voyage, the captain and his 9 sailors seized 12 Africans—men, women, and boys. The ship then sailed back to Portugal. These captives represented only a small portion of a slave trade that would grow into the millions.

How Did Slavery Develop?
Within Africa, Europeans did not invent slavery. For a long time, it had existed throughout the world. In Africa, Bantu chiefs raided nearby villages for captives. These captives became laborers or were **released** for a fee.

Africans also enslaved criminals or enemies taken in war. These enslaved Africans became part of the Saharan trade. However, as long as Africans stayed in Africa, hope of escape still existed. Enslaved Africans might also win their freedom through hard work or by marrying a free person.

The trade in humans also grew as the trade with Muslim merchants increased. The Quran forbade enslavement of Muslims. Muslims, however, could enslave non-Muslims. Arab traders, therefore, began to trade horses, cotton, and other goods for enslaved, non-Muslim Africans.

When Europeans arrived in West Africa, a new market for enslaved Africans opened. Africans armed with European guns began raiding villages to seize captives to sell.

▲ On a slave ship, enslaved people were transported in the dark, crowded spaces of the ship's cargo deck. *Why were enslaved Africans used on Portuguese plantations?*

The European Slave Trade In 1444 a Portuguese ship docked at a port in Portugal. Sailors unloaded the cargo—235 enslaved Africans. Tears ran down the faces of some. Others cried for help. A Portuguese official described the scene:

> 66 But to increase their sufferings still more, . . . was it needful to part fathers from sons, husbands from wives, brothers from brothers. 99
>
> —Gomes Eannes de Zurara, as quoted in *The Slave Trade*

Barely three years had passed since the arrival of the first African captives in Portugal. Some merchants who had hoped to sell gold brought from Africa now sold humans instead. At first, most enslaved Africans stayed in Portugal, working as laborers. This changed when the Portuguese settled the Atlantic islands of Madeira, the Azores, and Cape Verde. There the climate was perfect for growing cotton, grapes, and sugarcane on plantations, or huge farms.

Harvesting sugarcane was hard labor. Planters could not pay high wages to get workers, so they used enslaved Africans. Many Africans had farming skills and the ability to make tools. Enslaved people were not paid and could be fed and kept cheaply. By 1500, Portugal was the world's leading supplier of sugar.

The rest of Europe followed Portugal's example. In the late 1400s, Europeans arrived in the Americas. They set up sugar plantations and brought enslaved Africans across the Atlantic Ocean to work the fields. They also used enslaved people to grow tobacco, rice, and cotton.

✔ Reading Check Analyze How did exploration change the African slave trade?

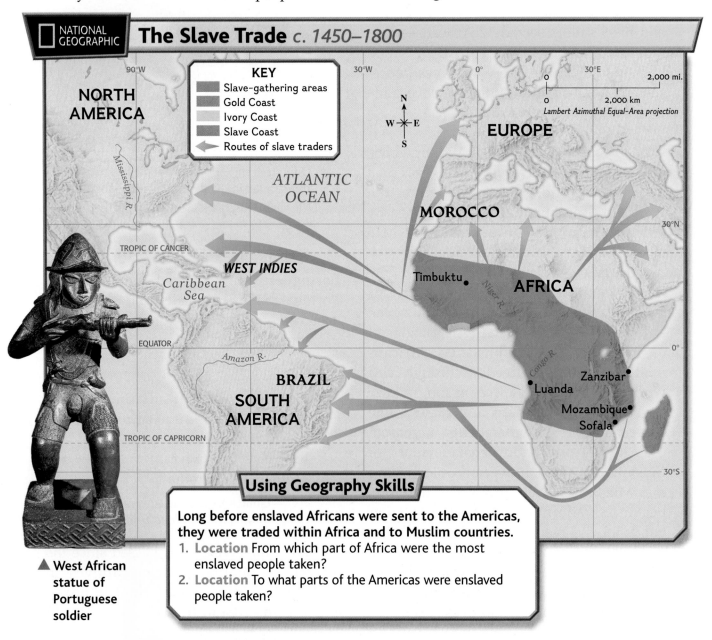

NATIONAL GEOGRAPHIC

The Slave Trade c. 1450–1800

KEY
- Slave-gathering areas
- Gold Coast
- Ivory Coast
- Slave Coast
- → Routes of slave traders

2,000 mi.
2,000 km
Lambert Azimuthal Equal-Area projection

NORTH AMERICA
EUROPE
MOROCCO
AFRICA
ATLANTIC OCEAN
WEST INDIES
Caribbean Sea
Mississippi R.
TROPIC OF CANCER
EQUATOR
Amazon R.
BRAZIL
SOUTH AMERICA
TROPIC OF CAPRICORN
Timbuktu
Niger R.
Congo R.
Luanda
Zanzibar
Mozambique
Sofala
30°N
0°
30°S

Using Geography Skills

Long before enslaved Africans were sent to the Americas, they were traded within Africa and to Muslim countries.
1. **Location** From which part of Africa were the most enslaved people taken?
2. **Location** To what parts of the Americas were enslaved people taken?

▲ West African statue of Portuguese soldier

WH7.4.3 Describe the role of the trans-Saharan caravan trade in the changing religious and cultural characteristics of West Africa and the influence of Islamic beliefs, ethics, and law.

WH7.4.5 Describe the importance of written and oral traditions in the transmission of African history and culture.

African Culture

(Main Idea) **Enslaved Africans developed rich cultures that influenced many other cultures, including our own.**

Reading Connection Do you have any traditions that have been in your family for a long time? Read to learn how Africans took their culture with them when they were enslaved and sent overseas.

"We are almost a nation of dancers, musicians, and poets," declared Olaudah Equiano in describing the Igbo people of West Africa. He might have added artists, weavers, woodcarvers, and metalworkers too. African peoples like the Igbo excelled in many art forms.

When slave traders seized Africans like Equiano from their homelands, they also uprooted their cultures. Africans carried these cultures with them in what has become known as the African Diaspora—the spreading of African people and culture around the world.

People of African descent held on to memories of their cultures and passed them down from generation to generation. The heritage of Africa can be seen and heard in the United States today—not just in the faces and voices of African descendants but in their gifts to our culture.

African Art
Cave paintings are the earliest form of African art we know about. They show people hunting animals, dancing, and doing everyday chores. As in other parts of the world, African art and religion developed hand in hand. Early African cave paintings, as well as later art, almost always had some religious meaning or use. Woodcarvers made masks and statues, for example, to celebrate African religious beliefs. Each carved piece of wood captured some part of the spiritual world.

The Way It Was

Focus on Everyday Life

Kente Cloth *Kente* is the name of a colorful woven cloth. Its name comes from a word that means "basket." The first weavers were mostly men. They used fibers to make cloth that looked like the patterns in baskets. Strips were sewn together to make colorful patterns. *Kente* was worn by tribal chiefs and is still popular today. This African folktale about *kente* cloth has been handed down for generations:

One day two friends walked through a rain forest and saw a spider creating designs in its web. They took the spider web to show their friends, but the web fell apart. They returned the next day to watch as the spider did a weaving dance and spun another web. The friends took their newfound skills to their looms and made colorful cloth they called *kente*.

African women ▶ wearing *kente* cloth

Connecting to the Past
1. Why does the legend suggest that Africans learned to weave *kente* cloth from a spider?
2. Why do you think the first *kente* cloth weavers were mostly men?

African works of art also told stories and served practical purposes. Artists working in wood, ivory, or bronze showed the faces of important leaders, everyday people, and, later, European explorers and traders. Weavers designed cloth similar to cloth still worn today. You may have seen the brightly colored kente cloth of West Africa. Many people wear it today.

Music and Dance Music played a part in almost all aspects of African life. People used it to express their religious feelings or to get through an everyday task, like planting a field.

In many African songs, a singer calls out a line, then other singers repeat it back. Musical instruments, such as drums, whistles, horns, flutes, or banjos, were used to keep the beat.

Africans believed dance allowed the spirits to express themselves. So they used it to celebrate important events such as birth and death. Nearly everybody danced. Lines of men and women swayed and clapped their hands. Individual dancers

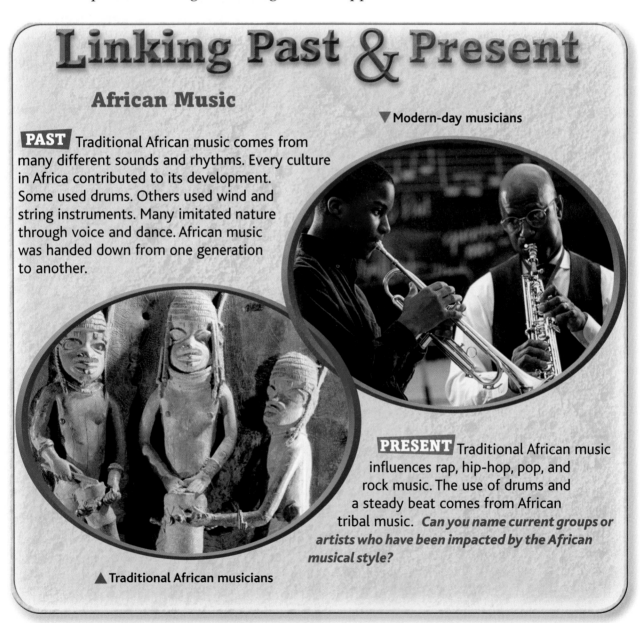

Linking Past & Present

African Music

PAST Traditional African music comes from many different sounds and rhythms. Every culture in Africa contributed to its development. Some used drums. Others used wind and string instruments. Many imitated nature through voice and dance. African music was handed down from one generation to another.

▼ **Modern-day musicians**

PRESENT Traditional African music influences rap, hip-hop, pop, and rock music. The use of drums and a steady beat comes from African tribal music. *Can you name current groups or artists who have been impacted by the African musical style?*

▲ **Traditional African musicians**

leaped and twirled. In the background, drummers sounded out the rhythm.

Enslaved Africans sometimes relied on music to remind them of their homeland. Songs of hardship eventually developed into a type of music that we know today as the blues. Songs of religious faith and hopes for freedom grew into spirituals or gospel songs. Over time, other forms of African-based music developed, such as ragtime, jazz, rock and roll, and, more recently, rap.

Why Was Storytelling Important?

Africans also kept alive their storytelling tradition. A few enslaved Africans escaped and were able to record their stories. Others retold their stories aloud. Those who heard the stories repeated them. They also retold tales taught by griots in the African homeland. Popular stories often told how small

◀ Griots still share the stories and lessons of their ancestors. *What were traditional African stories often about?*

animals, such as turtles and rabbits, outsmarted larger ones.

In more recent times, some African Americans have renewed ties with their past by taking African names or giving them to their children. This also helps keep alive African history and culture.

✓ **Reading Check** **Explain** Why did Africans use dance to celebrate important events?

History Online

Study Central Need help understanding African society and culture? Visit ca.hss.glencoe.com and click on Study Central.

Section 3 Review

Reading Summary

Review the Main Ideas

- Many Africans south of the Sahara lived in small villages. Family was very important, and women had fewer rights than men.

- Africans had kept slaves long before they began to trade enslaved persons to Muslims and Europeans.

- As enslaved Africans were taken to new areas, African culture, including art, music, and storytelling, spread around the world.

What Did You Learn?

1. What was the African Diaspora?

2. What is the earliest form of African art known? Describe some of the subjects portrayed.

Critical Thinking

3. **Organizing Information** Draw a diagram like the one below. Fill in details about African music and dance. **CA 7RC2.0**

African Music and Dance

4. **Analyze** Why do you think storytelling helped keep African culture alive? How did Africans use their stories to teach values and offer hope? **CA HR4.**

5. **Compare** Write an essay comparing the role of music in medieval African society to the role of music in your life today. **CA 7WA2.0**

6. **The Big Ideas** Write a paragraph comparing the reasons Africans, Muslims, and Europeans enslaved people from Africa. **CA 7RC2.0**

7. **Summarize** Write an essay describing the influence of art and music on African culture. **CA 7WA2.5**

Analyzing Primary Sources

African Splendor

WH7.4 Students analyze the geographic, political, economic, religious, and social structures of the sub-Saharan civilizations of Ghana and Mali in Medieval Africa.

The kingdoms of Ghana and Mali grew powerful from the gold and salt trade. In each kingdom, strong leaders arose—some good, some bad. Some kings wanted to amaze and frighten people with their wealth and power. In addition, the kingdom of Mali developed a strong center of learning at Timbuktu.

Read the following passages on pages 238 and 239, and answer the questions that follow.

Camel caravan ▶

Reader's Dictionary

pavilion (puh•VIHL•yuhn): a large tent
page: attendant
clad: clothed

plaited (PLAY•tuhd): woven; braided
ebony (EH•buh•nee): a hard, heavy wood
mitqals: an ancient unit of measure

The King of Ghana

Ghana was one of the first powerful states in Africa south of the Sahara. Its kings lived so that they appeared great to any who saw them. The following quote by a Muslim traveler named Al-Bakri describes the splendor in which King Tenkaminen held court.

"When the king gives audience to his people, to listen to their complaints and to set them to rights, he sits in a **pavilion** around which stand ten **pages** holding shields and gold-mounted swords. On his right hand are the sons of the princes of his empire, splendidly **clad** and with gold **plaited** in their hair. The governor of the city is seated on the ground in front of the king, and all around him are his counselors in the same position. The gate of the chamber is guarded by dogs of an excellent breed. These dogs never leave their place of duty. They wear collars of gold and silver, ornamented with metals. The beginning of a royal audience is announced by the beating of a kind of drum they call *deba*. This drum is made of a long piece of hollowed wood. The people gather when they hear its sound."

—Basil Davidson, *A History of West Africa: To the Nineteenth Century*

The Sultan of Mali

An Arab scholar named Ibn Fadl Allah al Omari describes the West African court and army of Mansa Musa in the 1330s. He refers to Mansa Musa as sultan, *the Arab word for "king."*

The sultan of this kingdom presides in his palace on a great balcony called *bembe* where he has a seat of **ebony** that is like a throne fit for a large and tall person: on either side it is flanked by elephant tusks turned towards each other. His arms stand near him, being all of gold, saber, lance, quiver, bow and arrows. He wears wide trousers made of about twenty pieces [of stuff] of a kind which he alone may wear. . . . His officers are seated in a circle about him, in two rows, one to the right and one to the left; beyond them sit the chief commanders of his cavalry. . . .

The officers of this king, his soldiers and his guard receive gifts of land and presents. Some among the greatest of them receive as much as fifty thousand *mitqals* of gold each year, besides which the king provides them with horses and clothing.

—Al Omari, "Mali in the Fourteenth Century"

White Gold

Salt and gold were what made the kingdoms of Africa rich. Here Ibn Battuta describes the salt city of Taghaza in northern Mali in 1352.

"Its houses and mosques . . . are built of blocks of salt, roofed with camel skins. There are no trees there, nothing but sand. In the sand is a salt mine; they dig for the salt, and find it in thick slabs . . . [They] use salt as a medium of exchange . . . they cut it up into pieces and buy and sell with it. The business done at Taghaza . . . amounts to an enormous figure in terms of hundredweights of gold-dust."

—Basil Davidson, "The Niger to the Nile"

Timbuktu

Timbuktu was a center of trade and learning. The following passage by Leo Africanus describes the city in the 1500s.

"In Timbuktu . . . there are numerous judges, professors, and holy men, all being handsomely maintained by the king, who holds scholars in much honour. Here, too, they sell many handwritten books from North Africa. More profit is made in selling books in Timbuktu than from any other branch of trade."

—Basil Davidson, *A History of West Africa: To the Nineteenth Century*

DBQ Document-Based Questions

The King of Ghana

1. What does the clothing of the princes, dogs, and soldiers tell you about the king's wealth?

The Sultan of Mali

2. What conclusions can you draw about Mansa Musa's power?

3. Why do you think Mansa Musa treated his soldiers so well?

White Gold

4. Why did the people of Taghaza use salt to build their houses?

5. Do you think it rained in Taghaza? Explain.

Timbuktu

6. Do you think that books were valued more than gold and salt in cities that were not centers of learning? Explain.

Read to Write

7. Imagine you have visited an African kingdom during the Middle Ages. Using the primary sources you have just read, write a letter home describing the power of the king and his influence over trade and education.
   `CA 7WA2.1`   `CA HR1.`

Making Comparisons

Compare ancient Rome, early Islam, and medieval Africa by reviewing the chart below. Can you see how people during this time had lives that were very much like yours?

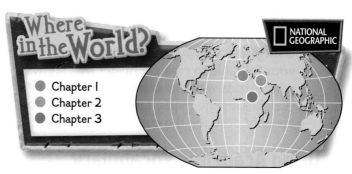

Where in the World?

- Chapter 1
- Chapter 2
- Chapter 3

NATIONAL GEOGRAPHIC

	Ancient Rome	Early Islam	Medieval Africa
	Chapter 1	Chapter 2	Chapter 3
Where did these groups develop?	• Began on Italian peninsula • Won control of Mediterranean world	• Began in Arabia • Arab Empire stretched from North Africa to central Asia	• West Africa; Southern Africa; East Africa
Who were some important people?	• Augustus, ruled 27 B.C.–A.D. 14 • Theodora c. A.D. 500–548	• Muhammad c. A.D. 570–632 • Omar Khayyam A.D. 1048–1131 • Suleiman I, ruled A.D. 1520–1566	• Ibn Battuta, A.D. 1307–1377 • Mansa Musa, ruled A.D. 1312–1332 • Sunni Ali, ruled A.D. 1464–1492 • Queen Nzinga, ruled c. A.D. 1623–1663
Where did most of the people live?	• Farming villages • Major cities included Rome and Alexandria	• Desert oases • Farming villages • Major cities included Makkah and Baghdad	• Farming villages; trading centers, such as Timbuktu and Kilwa

	Ancient Rome Chapter 1 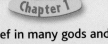	Early Islam Chapter 2	Medieval Africa Chapter 3
What were these people's beliefs?	• Belief in many gods and goddesses • Emperors honored as gods • Many local religions	• Belief in one God (Allah) • Muhammad is final prophet • Major groups: Sunni and Shiite 	• Traditional African religions, Christianity, Islam
What was their government like?	• Rome developed from a republic into an empire • An emperor was the chief leader • Army played role in government 	• Muhammad founded Islamic state • After Muhammad, leaders called caliphs held religious and political power	• Ruled by kings, close advisers, and local officials
What was their language and writing like?	• Latin was official language; Greek spoken in the east of the empire • Many local languages	• Quran written in Arabic • Arabic was Arab Empire's official language • Persian and Turkish also spoken	• Many languages and different writing systems, but much knowledge passed on by oral history
What contributions did they make?	• Introduced ideas about law and government • Developed new styles of building 	• Islam became a world religion • Developed ideas in medicine and mathematics	• Produced tradition of storytelling, dance, music, and sculpture • Developed trade routes across North Africa and supplied salt and gold to Europeans and Arabs
How do these changes affect me? *Can you add any?*	• Latin contributed many words to English language • Rome's idea of a republic followed by governments today	• Islam is a major religion today • Developed algebra • Developed game of chess	• Early Africans passed on musical traditions that led to jazz, rap, gospel, reggae

Unit

The Middle Ages

Why It's Important

Each civilization that you will study in this unit made important contributions to history.

- The Chinese first produced gunpowder, the compass, and printed books.
- The Japanese developed a constitution and new forms of art and poetry.
- The Europeans took the first steps toward representative government.

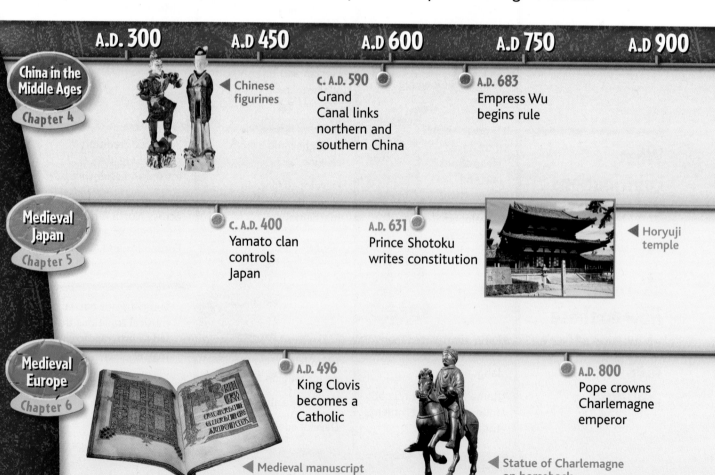

A.D. 300   A.D 450   A.D 600   A.D 750   A.D 900

China in the Middle Ages
Chapter 4

◄ Chinese figurines

C. A.D. 590
Grand Canal links northern and southern China

A.D. 683
Empress Wu begins rule

Medieval Japan
Chapter 5

C. A.D. 400
Yamato clan controls Japan

A.D. 631
Prince Shotoku writes constitution

◄ Horyuji temple

Medieval Europe
Chapter 6

A.D. 496
King Clovis becomes a Catholic

A.D. 800
Pope crowns Charlemagne emperor

◄ Medieval manuscript

◄ Statue of Charlemagne on horseback

NATIONAL GEOGRAPHIC

Where in the World?

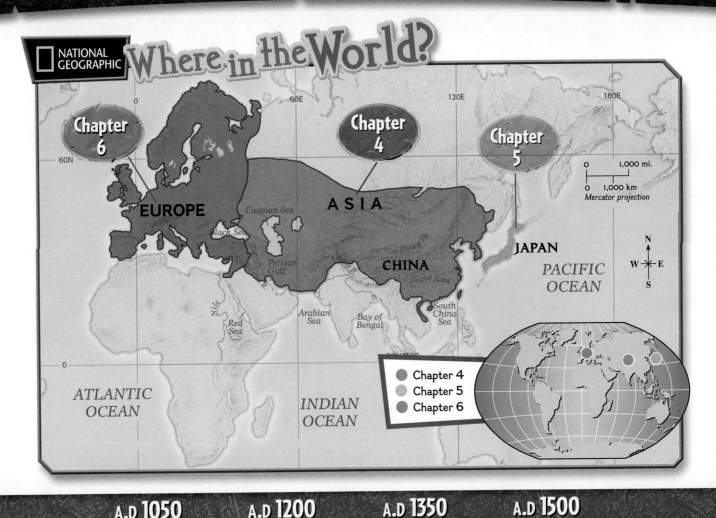

Chapter 6 — EUROPE

Chapter 4 — ASIA

Chapter 5 — JAPAN

0   1,000 mi.
0   1,000 km
Mercator projection

EUROPE

Caspian Sea

Black Sea

Persian Gulf

ASIA

Huang He

CHINA

Chang Jiang

JAPAN

PACIFIC OCEAN

Nile

Red Sea

Arabian Sea

Bay of Bengal

South China Sea

N W E S

ATLANTIC OCEAN

INDIAN OCEAN

● Chapter 4
● Chapter 5
● Chapter 6

A.D 1050   **A.D 1200**   **A.D 1350**   **A.D 1500**

C. A.D. 1000s
Chinese invent movable type

A.D. 1206
Genghis Khan becomes Mongol leader

A.D. 1405
Zheng He begins first of seven overseas voyages

◀ Mongol warrior

C. A.D. 1000
Lady Murasaki Shikibu composes *The Tale of Genji*

▼ Japanese temple in Kyoto

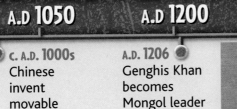

A.D. 1281
Mongols attempt second invasion of Japan

C. A.D. 1450
Civil war divides Japan

Suit of armor worn ▶ by samurai warrior

C. A.D. 1000
Vikings reach North America

A.D. 1215
England's King John signs Magna Carta

A.D. 1492
Ferdinand and Isabella of Spain defeat Moors

◀ Medieval woman spinning wool

Unit

Places to Locate

1 Buddha statue

See China in the Middle Ages
Chapter 4

2 Takamatsu Castle

See Medieval Japan
Chapter 5

4

5

EUROPE

AFRICA

Atlantic Ocean

People to Meet

Prince Shotoku
A.D. 573–621
Japanese leader
Chapter 5, p. 300

Charlemagne
A.D. 742–814
Frankish ruler
Chapter 6, p. 329

Murasaki Shikibu
C. A.D. 973–1025
Japanese writer
Chapter 5, p. 313

ASIA

3 **Todaiji temple**

See Medieval Japan
Chapter 5

4 **Caerphilly Castle**

See Medieval Europe
Chapter 6

5 **Mont St. Michel**

See Medieval Europe
Chapter 6

*Pacific
Ocean*

**Genghis
Khan**

C. A.D. 1167–1227
Mongol conqueror
Chapter 4, p. 271

**Thomas
Aquinas**

A.D. 1225–1274
Christian thinker
Chapter 6, p. 362

Zheng He

A.D. 1371–1433
Chinese admiral
Chapter 4, p. 285

Joan Of Arc

A.D. 1412–1431
French heroine
Chapter 6, p. 368

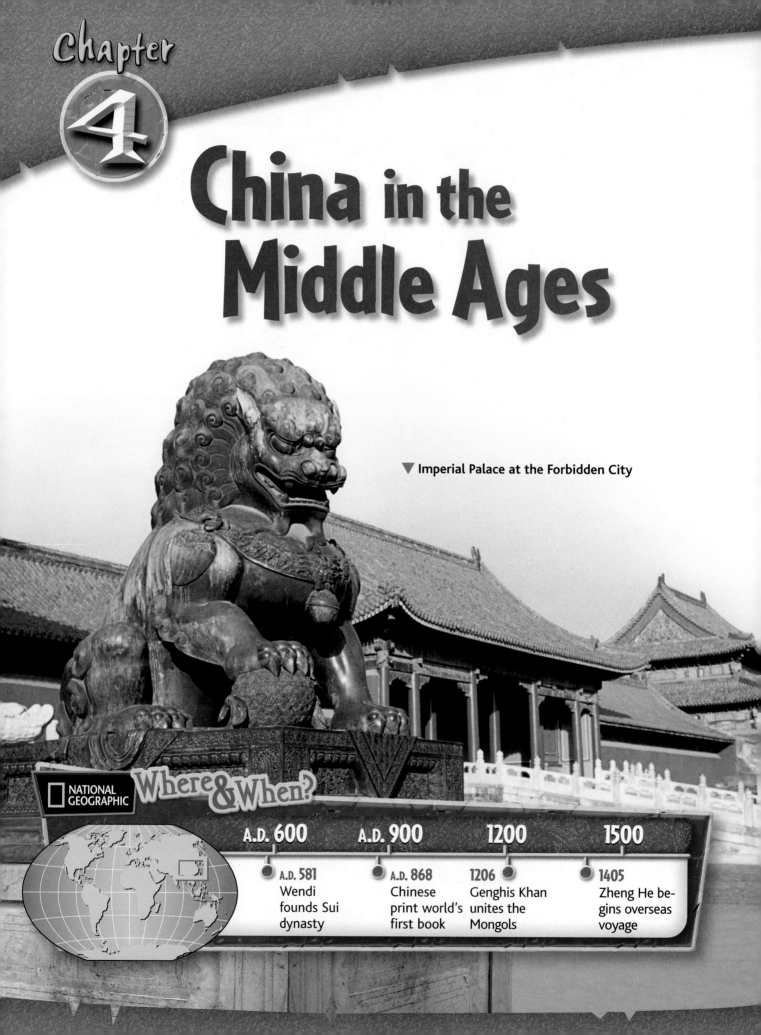

Chapter 4

China in the Middle Ages

▼ Imperial Palace at the Forbidden City

NATIONAL GEOGRAPHIC Where&When?

A.D. 600	A.D. 900	1200	1500
A.D. 581 Wendi founds Sui dynasty	**A.D. 868** Chinese print world's first book	**1206** Genghis Khan unites the Mongols	**1405** Zheng He begins overseas voyage

The Big Ideas

History Online

Chapter Overview Visit ca.hss.glencoe.com for a preview of Chapter 4.

Section 1 China Reunites

Systems of order, such as law and government, contribute to stable societies. During the Middle Ages, Chinese rulers who supported Confucian ideas brought peace, order, and growth to China.

Section 2 Chinese Society

The interaction of different societies brings about the development of new ideas, art, and technology. Farming and trade brought wealth to China. This allowed the Chinese to develop new technology and enjoy a golden age of art and writing.

Section 3 The Mongols in China

All civilizations depend upon leadership for survival. Led by Genghis Khan, the Mongols built a vast empire. Under his son, Kublai Khan, they went on to conquer China as well.

Section 4 The Ming Dynasty

Exploration and trade spread ideas and goods. China's Ming rulers strengthened the government and supported trading voyages that spread Chinese ideas and goods.

 View the Chapter 4 video in the Glencoe Video Program.

Categorizing Information *Make this foldable to help you organize your notes about China in the Middle Ages.*

Step 1 *Fold a sheet of paper in half from side to side, leaving $\frac{1}{2}$ inch tab along the side.*

Leave $\frac{1}{2}$ inch tab here.

Step 2 *Turn the paper and fold it into fourths.*

Fold in half. Then fold in half again.

Reading and Writing *As you read the chapter, identify the main ideas in the chapter. Write these under the appropriate tab.*

Step 3 *Unfold and cut along the top three fold lines.*

This makes four tabs.

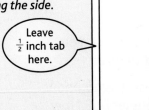

Step 4 *Label as shown.*

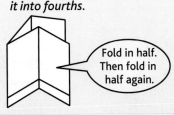

China Reunites | Chinese Society | The Mongols in China | The Ming Dynasty

China in the Middle Ages

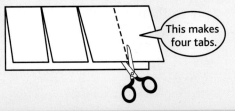

Chapter 4 Get Ready to Read

Making Connections

Reading Skill

1 Learn It!

Making connections means relating what you read to what you already know. Read the excerpts below.

Text-to-self: personal experiences

Have you ever eaten at a Chinese restaurant? How important do you think rice is to the Chinese diet? What kind of foods do you eat every day?

Text-to-world: events in other places

How popular is tea in China today? What is the most popular drink in the United States?

> Farmers also developed new kinds of rice, which grew well in poor soil, produced more per acre, grew faster, and were resistant to disease.
>
> These changes helped farmers grow more and more rice. China's farmers also began to grow tea, which became a popular drink. They made improvements in other crops as well. With more food available, the number of people in China greatly increased.
>
> — *from page 261*

Reading Tip

The better the connection is, the easier it is to remember. Be sure to make connections with memorable ideas or experiences from your life.

Text-to-text: what you have read before

Have you ever read about China's population? How important is the food supply to them today?

2 Practice It!

With a partner, read the following paragraphs. Make a list of the connections you made and compare them to your partner's list. Discuss what things in your lives relate to the story of Marco Polo.

Read to Write ·····
Choose one of the three types of connections that you make most often. Write a brief paragraph explaining why.

One of the most famous European travelers to reach China was Marco Polo (MAHR • koh POH • loh). He came from the city of Venice in Italy. Kublai Khan was fascinated by Marco Polo's stories about his travels. For about 16 years, Polo enjoyed a special status in the country. Kublai sent him on many fact-finding and business trips. For three of those years, Polo ruled the Chinese city of Yangchow. When Polo finally returned to Europe, he wrote a book about his adventures. His accounts of the wonders of China amazed Europeans.

—*from page 273*

**Kublai Khan presents ▶
gift to Marco Polo.**

3 Apply It!

Choose five words or phrases from this chapter that make a connection to something you already know.

China Reunites

History
Social Science Standards

WH7.3 Students analyze the geographic, political, economic, religious, and social structures of the civilizations of China in the Middle Ages.

Guide to Reading

Looking Back, Looking Ahead

You learned in 6th grade that the Han dynasty of China collapsed and China plunged into civil war. As you will read, China eventually reunited. The new dynasties took Chinese civilization to even higher levels.

Focusing on the Main Ideas

- The Sui and Tang dynasties reunited and rebuilt China after years of war. *(page 253)*

- Buddhism became popular in China and spread to Korea and Japan. *(page 256)*

- The Tang dynasty returned to the ideas of Confucius and created a new class of scholar-officials. *(page 258)*

Locating Places

Korea (kuh•REE•uh)
Japan (juh•PAN)

Meeting People

Wendi (WHEHN•DEE)
Empress Wu (WOO)

Content Vocabulary

warlord
economy (ih•KAH•nuh•mee)
reform
monastery (MAH•nuh•STEHR•ee)

Academic Vocabulary

project (PRAH•JEHKT)
seek
medical (MEH•dih•kuhl)

Reading Strategy

Categorizing Information Complete a table like the one below to show the time periods, the most important rulers, and the reasons for the decline of the Sui and Tang dynasties.

	Sui	Tang
Time Period		
Important Rulers		
Reasons for Decline		

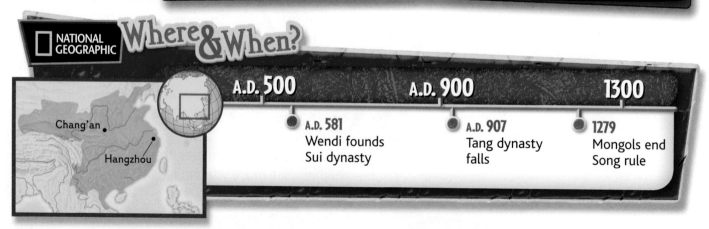

NATIONAL GEOGRAPHIC Where & When?

Chang'an
Hangzhou

A.D. 500	A.D. 900	1300
A.D. 581 Wendi founds Sui dynasty	**A.D. 907** Tang dynasty falls	**1279** Mongols end Song rule

Rebuilding China's Empire

Main Idea The Sui and Tang dynasties reunited and rebuilt China after years of war.

Reading Connection Have you ever thought about how the economy in your town or city works? How do goods get to your local stores? Who makes sure roads are paved? Read to learn how China dealt with these issues.

Earlier you read that China's Han empire ended in A.D. 220. For the next 300 years, China had no central government. It broke into 17 kingdoms. War and poverty were everywhere. Chinese **warlords**—military leaders who run a government—fought with each other while nomads conquered parts of northern China.

While China was absorbed in its own problems, it lost control of some of the groups it had conquered. One of these groups was the people of **Korea** (kuh•REE•uh). They lived on the Korean Peninsula to the northeast of China. The Koreans decided to end Chinese rule of their country. They broke away and built their own separate civilization.

The Reunification of China China finally reunited in A.D. 581. In that year, a general who called himself **Wendi** (WHEHN•DEE) declared himself emperor. Wendi won battle after battle and reunited China by force. He then founded a new short-lived dynasty called the Sui (SWEE).

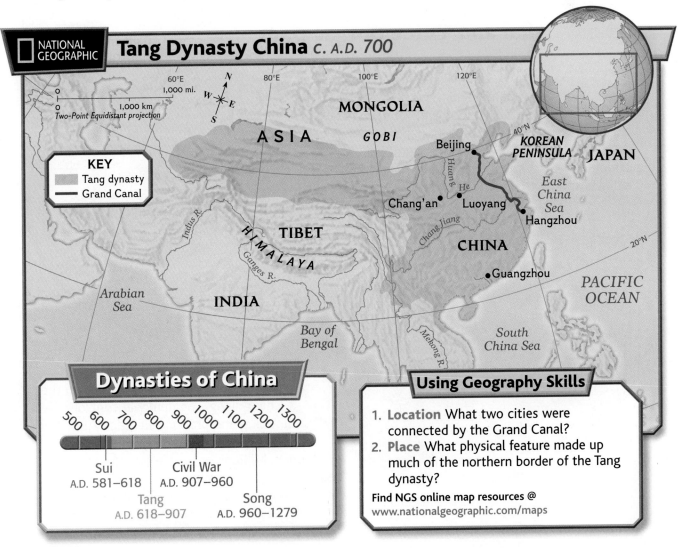

NATIONAL GEOGRAPHIC

Tang Dynasty China C. A.D. 700

KEY
- Tang dynasty
- Grand Canal

Two-Point Equidistant projection

MONGOLIA
ASIA
GOBI
KOREAN PENINSULA
JAPAN
Beijing
Huang He
Chang'an
Luoyang
East China Sea
Hangzhou
TIBET
HIMALAYA
Chang Jiang
CHINA
Indus R.
Ganges R.
Guangzhou
PACIFIC OCEAN
Arabian Sea
INDIA
Bay of Bengal
Mekong R.
South China Sea

Dynasties of China

500 600 700 800 900 1000 1100 1200 1300

Sui
A.D. 581–618

Civil War
A.D. 907–960

Tang
A.D. 618–907

Song
A.D. 960–1279

Using Geography Skills

1. **Location** What two cities were connected by the Grand Canal?
2. **Place** What physical feature made up much of the northern border of the Tang dynasty?

Find NGS online map resources @ www.nationalgeographic.com/maps

After Wendi died, his son Yangdi (YAHNG•DEE) took the Chinese throne. Yangdi wanted to expand China's territory. He sent an army to fight the neighboring Koreans, but the Chinese were badly defeated. At home, Yangdi took on many ambitious building **projects.** For example, the Great Wall had fallen into ruins, and Yangdi had it rebuilt.

Yangdi's greatest effort went into building the Grand Canal. This system of waterways linked the Chang Jiang (Yangtze River) and Huang He (Yellow River). The Grand

History Online

Web Activity Visit ca.hss.glencoe.com and click on *Chapter 4—Student Web Activity* to learn more about China.

Canal became an important route for shipping products between northern and southern China. It helped unite China's economy. An **economy** (ih•KAH•nuh•mee) is an organized way in which people produce, sell, and purchase things.

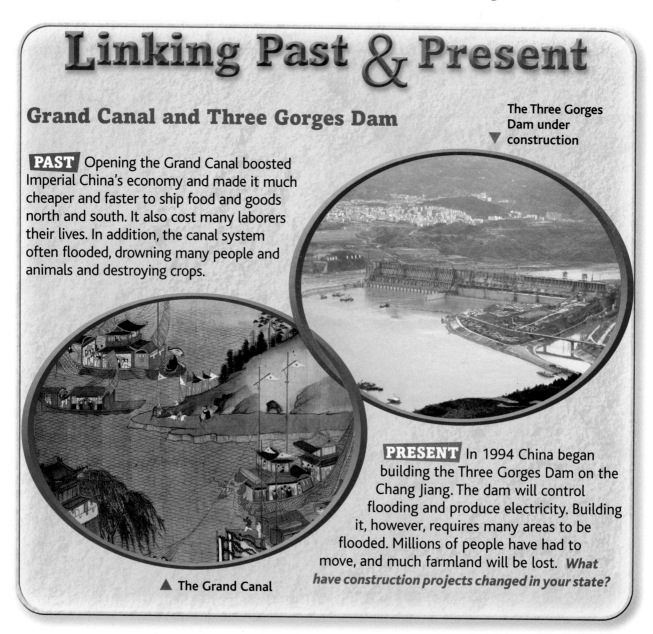

Linking Past & Present

Grand Canal and Three Gorges Dam

The Three Gorges Dam under construction

PAST Opening the Grand Canal boosted Imperial China's economy and made it much cheaper and faster to ship food and goods north and south. It also cost many laborers their lives. In addition, the canal system often flooded, drowning many people and animals and destroying crops.

PRESENT In 1994 China began building the Three Gorges Dam on the Chang Jiang. The dam will control flooding and produce electricity. Building it, however, requires many areas to be flooded. Millions of people have had to move, and much farmland will be lost. *What have construction projects changed in your state?*

▲ The Grand Canal

Yangdi rebuilt China, but he did it by placing stress on the Chinese people. Farmers were forced to work on the Great Wall and the Grand Canal. They also had to pay high taxes to the government for these projects. Finally, the farmers became so angry that they revolted. The army took control and killed Yangdi. With Yangdi gone, the Sui dynasty came to an end.

The Tang Dynasty In A.D. 618 one of Yangdi's generals took over China. He made himself emperor and set up a new dynasty called the Tang (TAHNG). Unlike the short-lived Sui, the Tang dynasty was in power for about 300 years—from A.D. 618 to A.D. 907. The Tang capital at Chang'an became a magnificent city, with about one million people living there.

Tang rulers worked to strengthen China's government. They carried out a number of **reforms,** or changes that brought improvements. The most powerful Tang emperor was named Taizong (TY•ZAWNG). He restored the civil service exam system. Government officials were once again hired based on how well they did on exams rather than on their family connections. Taizong also gave land to farmers and stabilized the countryside.

During the late A.D. 600s, a woman named Wu ruled China as empress. She was the only woman in Chinese history to rule the country on her own. A forceful leader, **Empress Wu** (WOO) added more officials to the government. She also strengthened China's military forces.

Under the Tang, China regained much of its power in Asia and expanded the areas under its control. Tang armies pushed west into central Asia, invaded Tibet, and took control of the Silk Road. They marched into Korea and forced the Korean kingdoms to

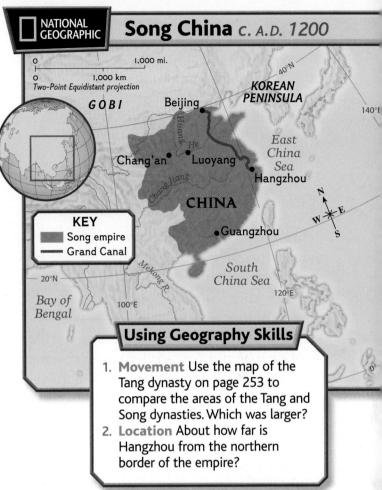

NATIONAL GEOGRAPHIC **Song China** C. A.D. *1200*

GOBI • Beijing • KOREAN PENINSULA • Chang'an • Luoyang • Hangzhou • East China Sea • CHINA • Guangzhou • South China Sea • Bay of Bengal • Mekong R. • Hwang He • Chang Jiang

KEY
Song empire
Grand Canal

Using Geography Skills

1. **Movement** Use the map of the Tang dynasty on page 253 to compare the areas of the Tang and Song dynasties. Which was larger?
2. **Location** About how far is Hangzhou from the northern border of the empire?

pay tribute, a special kind of tax that one country pays to another to be left alone. The Tang also moved south and took control of northern Vietnam.

By the mid-A.D. 700s, however, the Tang dynasty began to have problems. A new group of nomads known as the Turks drove the Tang armies out of central Asia and took control of the Silk Road. This damaged China's economy. Revolts in Tibet and among Chinese farmers at home further weakened the Tang. In A.D. 907 all of this disorder caused the Tang dynasty to collapse.

The Song Dynasty For about 50 years after the fall of the Tang, military leaders ruled China. Then, in A.D. 960, one of the generals declared himself emperor and set up the Song (SOONG) dynasty.

The Song dynasty ruled from A.D. 960 to 1279. This period was a time of prosperity and cultural achievement for China. From the start, however, the Song faced problems that threatened their hold on China. Song rulers did not have enough soldiers to control their large empire. Tibet broke away, and nomads took over much of northern China. For safety, the Song moved their capital farther south to the city of Hangzhou (HAHNG•JOH). Hangzhou was on the coast near the Chang Jiang delta.

▲ Statue of the Buddha, carved about A.D. 460 in the Yun-Kang caves in China.

Reading Check **Explain** How did Wendi unite China?

Buddhism Spreads to China

Main Idea Buddhism became popular in China and spread to Korea and Japan.

Reading Connection Where do you turn when you are having problems? Read to learn why many Chinese turned to Buddhism when China was in trouble.

Traders and missionaries from India brought Buddhism to China in about A.D. 150. At the time, the Han dynasty was already weak. Soon afterward, China collapsed into civil war. People everywhere were dying from war and a lack of food and shelter. It was a time of great suffering. Buddhism taught that people could escape their suffering by following its principles. As a result, many Chinese **seeking** peace and comfort became Buddhists.

Chinese Buddhism Early Tang rulers were not Buddhists, but they allowed Buddhism to be practiced in China. They even

City Life in Tang China

Under the Tang, China grew and was prosperous. Tang cities could be large, with many activities occurring within the city's walls. A city contained many shops and temples. The homes of rich families often had two or three floors. *When did the Tang rule China?*

Musicians and dancers

Farmers selling goods

Civil service examinations

Print shop

Making pottery

supported the building of Buddhist temples. Many Chinese Buddhists became monks and nuns. They lived in places called **monasteries** (MAH•nuh•STEHR•eez), where they meditated and worshiped.

Buddhist temples and monasteries provided services for people. They ran schools and provided rooms and food for travelers. Buddhist monks served as bankers and provided **medical** care.

Not all Chinese people liked Buddhism, however. Many thought that it was wrong for the Buddhist temples and monasteries to accept donations. Others believed that monks and nuns weakened respect for family life because they were not allowed to marry.

In the early A.D. 800s, Tang officials feared Buddhism's growing power. They saw Buddhism as an enemy of China's traditions. In A.D. 845 the Tang had many Buddhist monasteries and temples destroyed. Buddhism in China never fully recovered.

Chinese Buddhism Spreads East
As you read earlier, Korea broke free of China when the Han dynasty fell in A.D. 220. For several hundred years after, Korea was divided into three distinct kingdoms.

In the A.D. 300s, Chinese Buddhists brought their religion to Korea. About A.D. 660, the Koreans united to form one country. After that, with government support, Buddhism grew even stronger in Korea.

Buddhism later spread to the nearby islands of **Japan** (juh•PAN). According to legend, one of Korea's kings wrote to Japan's emperor. The letter contained a statue of the Buddha and Buddhist writings. "This religion is the most excellent of all teachings," the king wrote. As time passed, Buddhism won many followers in Japan as well.

✓ Reading Check **Explain** Why did some Chinese people dislike Buddhism?

The Way It Was

Focus on Everyday Life

Civil Service Exams Proficiency tests and final exams today take a lot of preparation, but they are not as difficult as China's civil service examinations given during the Tang dynasty. Men of almost all ranks tried to pass the exams so they could hold government jobs and become wealthy. Thousands attempted the tests, but only a few hundred people qualified for the important positions.

Chinese boys began preparing for the exams in primary school. After many years of learning to read and write more than 400,000 words and sayings, the boys—now men in their twenties or early thirties—would take the first of three levels of exams. Students traveled to huge testing sites to take the tests. Food and beds were not provided, so they had to bring their own. Many men became sick or insane because of the stress of the tests and the poor conditions under which they were tested.

Students ▶ taking civil service exams

Connecting to the Past
1. How old were the Chinese when they took the tests?
2. Why do you think taking the tests was so stressful for these men?

WH7.3.3 Analyze the influences of Confucianism and changes in Confucian thought during the Song and Mongol periods.
WH7.3.6 Describe the development of the imperial state and the scholar-official class.

New Confucian Ideas

Main Idea The Tang dynasty returned to the ideas of Confucius and created a new class of scholar-officials.

Reading Connection Have you ever seen someone get a reward that he or she did not earn? Read to learn how China's rulers tried to avoid this problem when hiring government officials.

You have already learned about Confucius and his teachings. Confucius and his followers believed that a good government depended on having wise leaders who ruled to benefit the people. The civil service examinations introduced by Han rulers were a product of Confucian ideas. These examinations were supposed to recruit talented government officials.

After the fall of the Han dynasty, no national government existed to give civil service examinations. Confucianism lost much support, and Buddhism with its spiritual message won many followers. Tang and Song rulers, however, brought Confucianism back into favor.

What Is Neo-Confucianism? The Tang dynasty gave its support to a new kind of Confucianism called neo-Confucianism. This new Confucianism was created, in part, to reduce Buddhism's popularity. It taught that life in this world was just as important as the afterlife. Followers were expected to take part in life and help others.

Although it criticized Buddhist ideas, this new form of Confucianism also picked up some Buddhist and Daoist beliefs. For many Chinese, Confucianism became more than a system of rules for being good. It became a religion with beliefs about the spiritual world. Confucian thinkers taught that if people followed Confucius's teachings, they would find peace of mind and live in harmony with nature.

The Song dynasty, which followed the Tang, also supported neo-Confucianism. The Song even adopted it as their official philosophy, or belief system.

Scholar-Officials Neo-Confucianism also became a way to strengthen the government. Both Tang and Song rulers used civil service examinations to hire officials. In doing so, they based the bureaucracy on a merit system. Under a merit system, people are accepted for what they can do and not on their riches or personal contacts.

Primary Source — Defending Confucianism

Han Yü (A.D. 768 to A.D. 824) encouraged the Chinese people to remain faithful to Confucianism.

▲ Han Yü

"What were the teachings of our ancient kings? Universal love is called humanity. To practice this in the proper manner is called righteousness. To proceed according to these is called the Way. . . . They offered sacrifices to Heaven and the gods came to receive them. . . . What Way is this? I say: This is what I call the Way, and not what the Taoists [Daoists] and the Buddhists called the Way. . . ."

—Han Yü, "An Inquiry on The Way" (Tao)

DBQ Document-Based Question

Why does Han Yü think Confucianism should be followed?

The examinations tested job seekers on their knowledge of Confucian writings. To pass, it was necessary to write with style as well as understanding. The tests were supposed to be fair, but only men could take them. Also, only rich people had the money to help their sons study for the tests.

Passing the tests was very difficult. However, parents did all they could to prepare their sons. At the age of four, boys started learning to write the characters of the Chinese language. Later, students had to memorize all of Confucius's writings. If a student recited the passages poorly, he could expect to be hit by his teacher.

After many years of study, the boys took their examinations. Despite all the preparation, only one in five passed. Those who failed usually found jobs helping officials or teaching others. However, they would never be given a government job.

▲ **Chinese scholar-officials on horseback**

Over the years, the examination system created a new wealthy class in China. This group was made up of scholar-officials. Strict rules set the scholar-officials apart from society. At the same time, these scholar-officials began to influence Chinese thought and government well into modern times.

☑ **Reading Check** **Describe** How did Confucianism change in China?

History Online

Study Central Need help understanding the impact of New Confucian ideas? Visit ca.hss.glencoe.com and click on Study Central.

Section 1 Review

Reading Summary
Review the Main Ideas

- While the Sui dynasty was short-lived, the Tang and Song dynasties lasted for hundreds of years and returned power and prosperity to China.

- Buddhism became popular in China and also spread to Korea and Japan.

- A new kind of Confucianism developed in China during the Tang and Song dynasties, and the government used civil service tests to improve itself.

What Did You Learn?

1. What made Buddhism so popular in China?

2. How was neo-Confucianism a response to Buddhism's popularity, and what did it teach?

Critical Thinking

3. **Compare and Contrast** Create a diagram to show how the reigns of Wendi and Yangdi were similar and how they were different. **CA 7RC2.0**

Wendi   Yangdi

4. **The Big Ideas** Which policies of the Tang government helped stabilize China? **CA HI2.**

5. **Cause and Effect** What events led to the fall of the Tang dynasty? **CA HI2.**

6. **Analyze** Why had Confucianism fallen out of favor in China before the Tang and Song dynasties? **CA 7RC2.2**

7. **Reading** **Making Connections** Civil service exams were stressful events. Write a paragraph about a test you had to take. How does your experience compare to China's exams? **CA 7WA2.1**

Chinese Society

Guide to Reading

History Social Science Standards

WH7.3 Students analyze the geographic, political, economic, religious, and social structures of the civilizations of China in the Middle Ages.

Looking Back, Looking Ahead

In the last section, you learned about the rise and fall of the Sui, Tang, and Song dynasties. During those dynasties, China's economy began to grow again. Chinese inventors developed many new technologies, and Chinese artists and writers produced new works that are still admired today.

Focusing on the Main Ideas

- The Tang dynasty strengthened China's economy by supporting farming and trade. *(page 261)*

- The Chinese developed new technologies, such as steelmaking and printing. *(page 262)*

- During the Tang and the Song dynasties, China enjoyed a golden age of art and literature. *(page 264)*

Locating Places
Chang'an (CHAHNG•AHN)

Meeting People
Li Bo (LEE   BOH)
Du Fu (DOO   FOO)

Content Vocabulary
porcelain (POHR•suh•luhn)
calligraphy (kuh•LIH•gruh•fee)

Academic Vocabulary
available (uh•VAY•luh•buhl)
method (MEH•thuhd)

Reading Strategy
Organizing Information Complete a chart like the one below describing the new technologies developed in China during the Middle Ages.

New Technologies

NATIONAL GEOGRAPHIC Where & When?

A.D. 600 — A.D. 900 — 1200

A.D. 618
Tang dynasty takes power

A.D. 868
Chinese print world's first complete book

c. 1150
Chinese sailors are the first to use compass

Chang'an
Hangzhou

A Growing Economy

Main Idea The Tang dynasty strengthened China's economy by supporting farming and trade.

Reading Connection Do you know anyone who drinks tea or wears silk clothing? Both of these goods were first produced in China. Read to learn how farming changed under the Tang dynasty.

When the Han dynasty in China collapsed in the A.D. 200s, it was a disaster for China's economy. As fighting began, cities were damaged and farms were burned. Artisans made fewer goods, farmers grew fewer crops, and merchants had less to trade. Under the Tang dynasty, these problems were solved.

Why Did Farming Improve?

When the Tang rulers took power in A.D. 618, they brought peace to the countryside and gave more land to farmers. As a result, farmers were able to make many advances. They improved irrigation and introduced new ways of growing their crops. Farmers also developed new kinds of rice, which grew well in poor soil, produced more per acre, grew faster, and were resistant to disease.

These changes helped farmers grow more and more rice. China's farmers also began to grow tea, which became a popular drink. They made improvements in other crops as well. With more food **available,** the number of people in China greatly increased. At the same time, more people moved southward, where rice grew abundantly in the Chang Jiang valley. This led to the rise of new cities.

China's Trade Grows Tang rulers also had roads and waterways built. These changes made travel within and outside of China much easier. Chinese merchants were able to increase trade with people in other parts of Asia. The Silk Road, now under Tang control, once again bustled with activity.

▲ A worker removes a tray of silkworms eating mulberry leaves. Eventually the worms will spin cocoons. Workers then collect and unravel the cocoons to make silk thread. *Why do you think silk is still expensive today?*

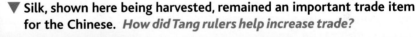

▼ Silk, shown here being harvested, remained an important trade item for the Chinese. *How did Tang rulers help increase trade?*

WH7.3.2 Describe agricultural, technological, and commercial developments during the Tang and Song periods.
WH7.3.5 Trace the historic influence of such discoveries as tea, the manufacture of paper, wood-block printing, the compass, and gunpowder.

One of the items traded by the Chinese was silk fabric. This product gave the road its name and was popular in markets to the west of China. In addition, China traded other products, such as tea, steel, paper, and porcelain. **Porcelain** (POHR•suh•luhn) is made of fine clay and baked at high temperatures. In return, other countries sent China products such as gold, silver, precious stones, and fine woods.

Other trade routes were also established. Roads linked China to central Asia, India, and southwest Asia. In addition, the Tang opened new ports along China's coast to boost trade.

Reading Check **Cause and Effect** How did the new kinds of rice developed in China help its population grow?

New Technology

Main Idea The Chinese developed new technologies, such as steelmaking and printing.

Reading Connection This book is made of paper with letters printed on the paper by a machine. Read to learn how printing was first invented in China during the Tang dynasty.

During the Tang and Song dynasties, new inventions changed China's society. In time, these discoveries spread to other parts of the world.

China Discovers Coal and Steel For most of China's history, people burned wood to heat their homes and cook their food. By the time of the Tang dynasty, wood was

Chang'an's Royal Palace

The Tang capital city of Chang'an may have had a population of one million people at its peak. The city had large blocks that included houses, businesses, and temples set along straight streets. Its layout inspired the design of many later cities. The area containing the royal palace, shown below, was bordered by parklands. *What improvements to agriculture allowed China's population to grow during the Tang dynasty?*

becoming scarce in China. However, the Chinese had discovered that coal could be used to heat things, and soon a coal-mining industry developed.

The Chinese used coal to heat furnaces to high temperatures, which led to another discovery. When iron was produced in hot furnaces heated by coal, the molten iron mixed with carbon from the coal. This created a new, stronger metal known today as steel.

The Chinese used steel to make many things. They made armor, swords, and helmets for their army, but they also made stoves, farm tools, drills, steel chain, and even steel nails and sewing needles.

The Printing Process

Paper had been invented under the Han dynasty. Under the Tang, the manufacture of paper reached new heights. For example, the Tang government printed about 500,000 sheets of paper a year just to assess taxes.

The mass production of paper led to another important Chinese innovation: a **method** for printing books. Before printing, books were copied by hand and were very expensive.

The Chinese began printing in the A.D. 600s. They used blocks of wood on which they cut the characters of an entire page. Ink was placed over the wooden block. Then paper was laid on the block to make a print. Cutting the block took a long time, but the woodblocks could be used again and again to make copies.

Printing allowed for yet another important Chinese invention: paper currency. As both the production of rice increased and trade increased during the Tang dynasty, Chinese merchants needed more money to conduct business. Eventually it became difficult for the Chinese to make enough copper coins to support the economy throughout the empire.

The Way It Was

Science and Inventions

Printing When the Chinese invented movable type, they improved the art of printing. A Chinese author described the work of Pi Sheng:

"He took sticky clay and cut in it characters as thin as the edge of a copper coin. Each character formed as it were a single type. He baked them in the fire to make them hard. He had previously prepared an iron plate and he had covered this plate with a mixture of pine resin, wax, and paper ashes. When he wished to print, he took an iron frame and set it on the iron plate. In this he placed the type, set close together. When the frame was full, the whole made one solid block of type."

—Shên Kua, *Dream Pool Jottings*

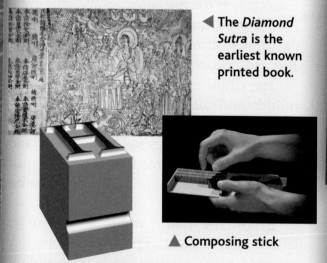

◀ The *Diamond Sutra* is the earliest known printed book.

▲ Composing stick

▲ Movable type block

Connecting to the Past
1. Why do you think Pi Sheng used clay to make his characters?
2. In what instance would woodblock printing have been a better method to use than movable type?

WH7.3.2 Describe agricultural, technological, and commercial developments during the Tang and Song periods.

In 1024, during the Song dynasty, the Chinese decided to print the world's first paper money as a way to help merchants. Paper money helped the economy to expand and cities to grow.

The Chinese soon began printing books. The earliest known printed book dates from about A.D. 868. It is a Buddhist book called the *Diamond Sutra*. The invention of printing was very important. It helped to spread ideas more rapidly.

In the A.D. 1000s, a Chinese printer named Pi Sheng (BEE SHUHNG) invented movable type for printing. With movable type, each character is a separate piece. The pieces can be moved around to make sentences and used again and again. Pi Sheng made his pieces from clay and put them together to produce book pages. However, because written Chinese has so many characters, woodblock printing was easier.

Other Chinese Inventions

The Chinese made gunpowder for use in explosives. One weapon was the fire lance, an ancestor of the gun. It used gunpowder and helped make the Chinese army a strong force. The Chinese also used gunpowder to make fireworks.

The Chinese also built large ships with rudders and sails. About 1150, Chinese sailors began using the compass to help them find their way. This let ships sail farther from land. With these inventions, the Chinese would eventually sail to Indonesia, India, and other places to the west.

Eventually many of these inventions would have a great impact on Europe. For example, block printing made it possible to publish books in large numbers. Gunpowder changed how wars were fought, and the compass encouraged Europeans to explore the world.

Reading Check Analyze Why was the invention of printing so important?

Art and Literature

Main Idea During the Tang and the Song dynasties, China enjoyed a golden age of art and literature.

Reading Connection If you were to choose one poem to read to the class, which poem would it be? Below, you will read a poem that is a Chinese favorite.

The Tang and Song eras were a golden age for Chinese culture. The invention of printing helped to spread Chinese ideas and artwork. Chinese rulers actively supported art and literature, and invited artists and poets to live and work in the capital city of **Chang'an** (CHAHNG•AHN).

What Was Tang Poetry Like? Chinese writers best expressed themselves in poems. In fact, the Tang dynasty is viewed as the great age of poetry in China. Some Tang poems celebrated the beauty of nature, the thrill of seasons changing, and the joy of having a good friend. Other Tang poems expressed sadness for the shortness of life and mourned the cruelty of friends parting.

Li Bo (LEE BOH) was one of the most popular poets of the Tang era. His poems often centered on nature. The poem below by Li Bo is probably the best-known poem in China. For centuries, Chinese schoolchildren have had to memorize it. Its title is "Still Night Thoughts."

> **Moonlight in front of my bed—
> I took it for frost on the ground!
> I lift my eyes to watch the
>   mountain moon,
> lower them and dream of home.**
>
> —Li Bo,
>   "Still Night Thoughts"

Another favorite poet of that time was **Du Fu** (DOO FOO). He was a poor civil servant who had a hard life. Civil war swept

▲ This Chinese landscape was painted in the 1100s. *How were Daoist beliefs depicted in landscapes painted during the Song dynasty?*

▼ Chinese calligraphy

▲ Ink and watercolor drawing on silk

China, and food was hard to find. Du Fu nearly died of starvation. His problems opened his eyes to the sufferings of the common people.

As a result, Du Fu's poems often were very serious. They frequently dealt with issues such as social injustice and the problems of the poor. Du Fu wrote the poem below after a rebellion left the capital city in ruins. It is called "Spring Landscape."

> 66 Rivers and mountains survive
>   broken countries.
> Spring returns. The city grows
>   lush again.
> Blossoms scatter tears thinking of
>   us, and this
> Separation in a bird's cry startles
>   the heart.
>
> Beacon-fires have burned
>   through three months.
> By now, letters are worth ten
>   thousand in gold.
>
> 99
>
> —Du Fu,
>   "Spring Landscape"

Painting in Song China

The painting of landscapes became widespread during the Song dynasty. However, Chinese artists did not try to make exact pictures of the landscapes they were painting. Instead, they attempted to portray the "idea" of the mountains, lakes, and other features of their landscapes. Empty spaces were left in the paintings on purpose. This distinctive style comes from the Daoist belief that a person cannot know the whole truth about something.

Daoist beliefs also can be seen in the way people are portrayed. They are tiny figures, fishing in small boats or wandering up a hillside trail. In other words, the people are living in, but not controlling, nature. They are only a part of the harmony of the natural setting.

Chinese painters often wrote poetry on their works. They used a brush and ink to write beautiful characters called **calligraphy** (kuh•LIH•gruh•fee).

Chinese Porcelain

During the Tang period, Chinese artisans perfected the making of porcelain. Because porcelain later came from

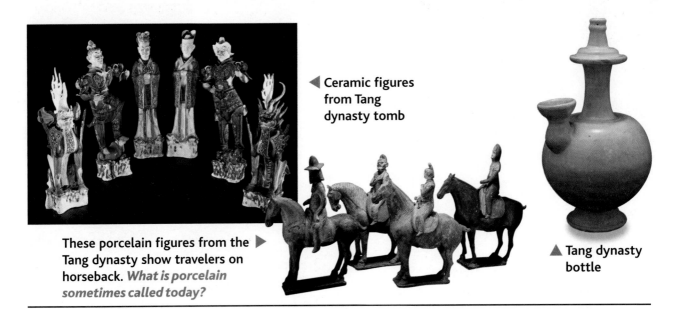

◀ Ceramic figures from Tang dynasty tomb

These porcelain figures from the ▶ Tang dynasty show travelers on horseback. *What is porcelain sometimes called today?*

▲ Tang dynasty bottle

China to the West, people today sometimes call porcelain by the name "china."

Porcelain can be made into plates, cups, figurines, and vases. In A.D. 851 an Arab traveler described the quality of Tang porcelain: "There is in China a very fine clay from which are made vases. . . . Water in these vases is visible through them, and yet they are made of clay."

The technology for making porcelain spread to other parts of the world. It finally reached Europe in the 1700s.

✓ **Reading Check** **Identify** What did Du Fu often write about?

History Online

Study Central Need help understanding the importance of new technology in this period? Visit ca.hss.glencoe.com and click on Study Central.

Section 2 Review

Reading Summary

Review the Main Ideas

• During the Tang dynasty, both farming and trade flourished, and the empire grew much larger than ever before.

• Many important inventions were developed in China during the Tang and Song dynasties, including steel, printing, and gunpowder.

• Chinese literature and arts, including poetry, landscape painting, and porcelain making, reached new heights during the Tang and Song dynasties.

What Did You Learn?

1. What products were traded by China along the Silk Road?

2. What were some of the subjects of Tang poetry?

Critical Thinking

3. **Organizing Information** Draw a chart to describe the new technologies developed in China. **CA 7RC2.0**

Metalworking	
Printing	
Weapons	
Sailing	

4. **Summarize** Describe how farming changed during the Tang dynasty. **CA 7RC2.3**

5. **The Big Ideas** Which Chinese invention do you think is most important? Why? **CA HI2.**

6. **Creative Writing** Reread the poem "Still Night Thoughts" by Li Bo. Then write a short, four-line poem about the view from a window in your school. **CA 7WA2.0**

7. **Analysis** Write a short essay explaining how the invention of printing affected China's economy. **CA HI2.**

Section 3

The Mongols in China

Guide to Reading

Looking Back, Looking Ahead

By A.D. 1200, China had developed a complex society with great achievements in art, literature, and technology. However, an enemy to the North had been building a vast army to invade.

Focusing on the Main Ideas

- Genghis Khan and his sons built the Mongol Empire, which stretched from the Pacific Ocean to Eastern Europe. *(page 268)*

- The Mongols conquered China and created a new dynasty that tried to conquer Japan and began trading with the rest of Asia. *(page 272)*

Locating Places

Mongolia (mahn•GOH•lee•uh)
Gobi (GOH•bee)
Karakorum (KAHR•uh•KOHR•uhm)
Khanbaliq (KAHN•buh•LEEK)
Beijing (BAY•JIHNG)

Meeting People

Genghis Khan
  (GEHNG•guhs KAHN)
Kublai Khan (KOO•BLUH KAHN)
Marco Polo
  (MAHR•koh POH•loh)

Content Vocabulary

tribe
steppe (STEHP)
terror (TEHR•uhr)

Academic Vocabulary

eventual (ih•VEHNT•shuh•wuhl)
encounter (ihn•KOWN•tuhr)

Reading Strategy

Organizing Information Use a diagram like the one below to show the accomplishments of Genghis Khan's reign.

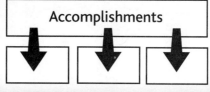

Accomplishments

History Social Science Standards

WH7.3 Students analyze the geographic, political, economic, religious, and social structures of the civilizations of China in the Middle Ages.

NATIONAL GEOGRAPHIC Where&When?

Karakorum
Baghdad   Khanbaliq
          (Beijing)

1200 — 1300 — 1400

1206 Genghis Khan unites Mongols

1271 Kublai Khan becomes China's emperor

1368 Yuan (Mongol) dynasty falls

WH7.3 Students analyze the geographic, political, economic, religious, and social structures of the civilizations of China in the Middle Ages.

WH7.3.5 Trace the historic influence of such discoveries as tea, the manufacture of paper, wood-block printing, the compass, and gunpowder.

The Mongols

Main Idea Genghis Khan and his sons built the Mongol Empire, which stretched from the Pacific Ocean to Eastern Europe.

Reading Connection Have you ever had the chance to ride a horse? For thousands of years, the horse was the most important form of transportation in the world. Read to learn how one people used their skills as horse riders to build a vast empire.

The Mongols lived in an area north of China called **Mongolia** (mahn•GOH•lee•uh). They were made up of **tribes,** or groups of related families, loosely joined together. The Mongols raised cattle, goats, sheep, and horses. They followed their herds as the animals grazed Mongolia's great **steppes** (STEHPS). Steppes are wide, rolling, grassy plains that stretch from the Black Sea to northern China.

From an early period in their history, the Mongols were known for two things. One was their ability to ride horses well. Mongols practically lived on horseback, learning to ride at age four or five. The other skill for which the Mongols were known was the ability to wage war. They could accurately fire arrows at enemies from a distance while charging at them. As they got closer they would attack with spears and swords.

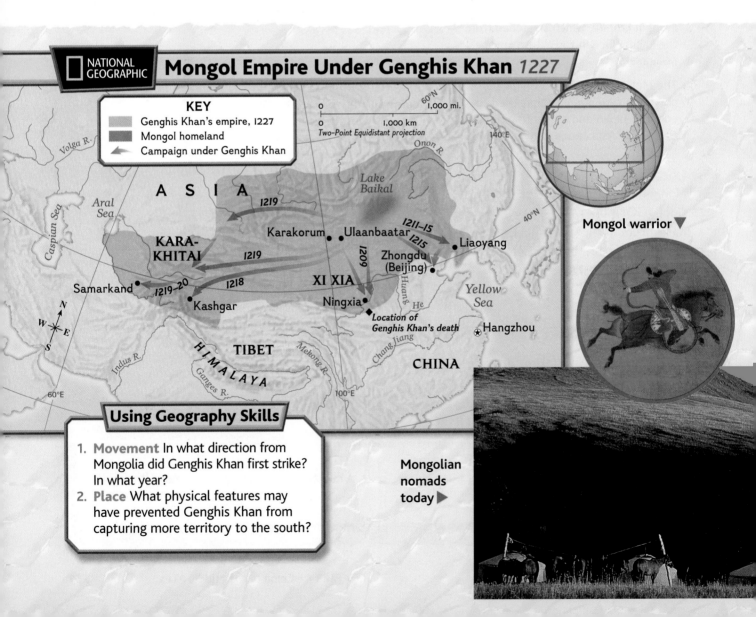

NATIONAL GEOGRAPHIC

Mongol Empire Under Genghis Khan *1227*

KEY
Genghis Khan's empire, 1227
Mongol homeland
Campaign under Genghis Khan

0 — 1,000 mi.
0 — 1,000 km
Two-Point Equidistant projection

Mongol warrior ▼

Using Geography Skills

1. **Movement** In what direction from Mongolia did Genghis Khan first strike? In what year?
2. **Place** What physical features may have prevented Genghis Khan from capturing more territory to the south?

Mongolian nomads today ▶

Who Was Genghis Khan? The man who would unite the Mongols was born in the 1160s. He was named Temujin (teh•MOO•juhn), which means "blacksmith." Temujin showed his leadership skills early. He was still a young man when he began to unite the Mongol tribes.

In 1206 a meeting of Mongol leaders took place somewhere in the **Gobi** (GOH•bee), a vast desert that covers parts of Mongolia and China. At that meeting, Temujin was elected **Genghis Khan** (GEHNG•guhs KAHN), which means "strong ruler." Genghis Khan brought together Mongol laws in a new code. He also created a group of tribal chiefs to help him plan military campaigns. From the time of his election until the end of his life, Genghis Khan fought to conquer the lands beyond Mongolia.

Genghis Khan gathered an army of more than 100,000 warriors. He placed his soldiers into well-trained groups. Commanding them were officers chosen for their abilities, not for their family ties. This approach made the Mongols the most skilled fighting force in the world at that time.

Genghis Khan began building his empire by conquering other people on the steppes. These victories brought him wealth and new soldiers to fill the army.

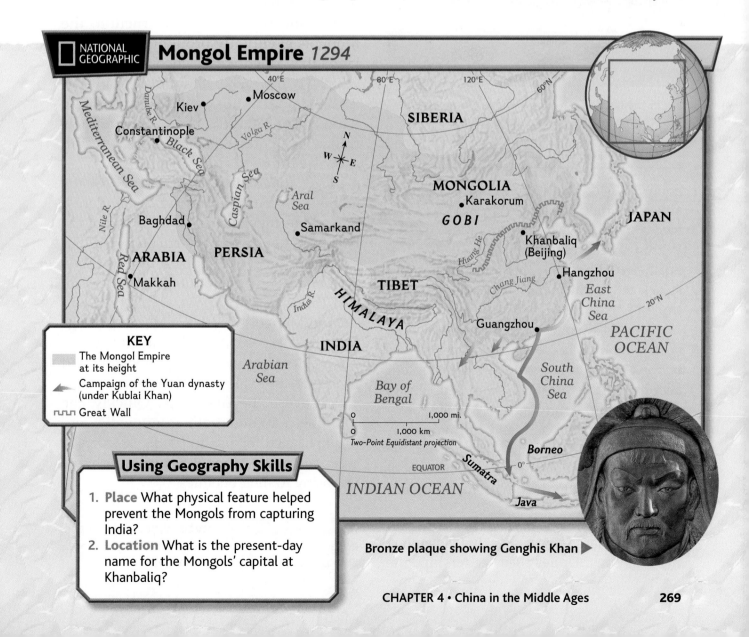

NATIONAL GEOGRAPHIC
Mongol Empire 1294

KEY

- The Mongol Empire at its height
- Campaign of the Yuan dynasty (under Kublai Khan)
- Great Wall

0   1,000 mi.
0   1,000 km
Two-Point Equidistant projection

Using Geography Skills

1. **Place** What physical feature helped prevent the Mongols from capturing India?
2. **Location** What is the present-day name for the Mongols' capital at Khanbaliq?

Bronze plaque showing Genghis Khan ▶

▲ In the battle scene shown here, Mongol troops storm across the Chang Jiang on a bridge made of boats. *After conquering northern China, what areas did the Mongols attack?*

Soon the Mongols were strong enough to attack major civilizations. In 1211 Mongol forces turned east and invaded China. Within three years, they had taken all of northern China. They then moved west and struck at the cities and kingdoms that controlled parts of the Silk Road.

Genghis Khan and his Mongol warriors became known for their cruelty and use of **terror** (TEHR•uhr). Terror refers to violent actions that are meant to scare people into surrendering, or giving up. Mongol warriors attacked, robbed, and burned cities. Within a short time, the Mongols became known for their fierce ways, and many people surrendered to them without fighting.

The Mongol Empire
Genghis Khan died in 1227. His large empire was divided among his four sons. Under their leadership, the empire continued to expand. The Mongols swept into parts of eastern and central Europe. They also conquered much of southwest Asia. In 1258 the famous Muslim city of Baghdad fell to the Mongols. Mongol armies then pushed through Syria and Palestine to Egypt. They were finally stopped by the Muslim rulers of Egypt in 1260.

The Mongols united all of these different territories under their rule. Their empire reached from the Pacific Ocean in the east to Eastern Europe in the west and from Siberia in the north to the Himalaya in the south. It was the largest land empire the world had ever known.

Despite widespread destruction, the Mongols **eventually** brought peace to the lands they ruled. Peace encouraged trade, which helped the Mongols. Many of Asia's trade routes now lay in Mongol hands. The Mongols taxed the products traded over these roads and, as a result, grew wealthy.

The Mongols felt great respect for the advanced cultures they conquered. Sometimes they even adopted some of the beliefs and customs they **encountered.** For example, the Mongols in southwest Asia accepted Islam and adopted Arab, Persian, and Turkish ways.

The Mongols also learned many things from the Chinese. As they battled Chinese troops, they learned about gunpowder and its use as an explosive. They also saw the Chinese use the fire lance. Quickly, the Mongols adopted both gunpowder and the fire lance for use in battle. These new weapons made Mongol armies even more imposing to their enemies.

Reading Check **Analyze** What military and economic reasons explain why the Mongols were able to build an empire so quickly?

Biography

WH7.3 Students analyze the geographic, political, economic, religious, and social structures of the civilizations of China in the Middle Ages.

GENGHIS KHAN
c. A.D. 1167–1227

Mongol Leader

Was Genghis Khan a ruthless warrior who enjoyed causing death and destruction, a skilled leader who improved the lives of those in his empire, or both? Genghis Khan built a huge empire across Asia using loyal, strong, and well-trained warriors. Although the wars he and his sons fought were brutal and bloody, they eventually brought peace and prosperity to most of Asia.

Genghis Khan was named Temujin by his father, the Mongol chief Yisugei. Folklore says Temujin had a large blood clot in his right hand, which meant he was destined to become a great warrior. Temujin grew up in his father's camp along the Onon River in Mongolia.

Temujin's father arranged a marriage for his nine-year-old son. His wife came from another tribe, and the marriage helped bring wealth to his family. Borte, his wife at age ten, was beautiful. Temujin and Borte had four sons when they both became older.

Years later, when his father was killed by the Tartars and his loyal warriors left the tribe, Temujin lost his wealth. His poverty and the disloyalty of his father's soldiers angered him so much that he decided to become a great warrior. Over time, Temujin became Ghengis Khan.

▲ Genghis Khan

"Life is short, I could not conquer the world."
–attributed to Genghis Khan

▲ Genghis Khan's camp

Then and Now

In Mongolia today, Genghis Khan is considered a national hero. What do you think? Was Genghis Khan a villain or a hero?

Mongol Rule in China

Main Idea The Mongols conquered China and created a new dynasty that tried to conquer Japan and began trading with the rest of Asia.

Reading Connection What does it mean to be tolerant? Read to find out how the Mongols used tolerance to rule the Chinese.

In 1260 the Mongols named Genghis Khan's grandson, Kublai, to be the new khan, or ruler. **Kublai Khan** (KOO•BLUH KAHN) continued the Mongol conquest of China that his grandfather had begun. In 1264 Kublai moved his capital from **Karakorum** in Mongolia to **Khanbaliq** in northern China. Today the modern city of **Beijing** (BAY•JIHNG) stands on the site of the Mongols' Chinese capital.

What Did the Mongols Do in China?

In 1271 Kublai Khan decided to become China's next emperor. Within 10 years, the Mongols had conquered southern China and put an end to the Song dynasty. Kublai Khan started the Yuan (YOO•AHN) dynasty. *Yuan* means "beginning," and its name showed that the Mongols wanted to rule China for a long time. But the Yuan dynasty would last only about 100 years. Kublai would rule for 30 of those years.

Kublai Khan gave Mongol leaders the top jobs in China's government, but he knew he needed Chinese scholar-officials to run the government. So he let many of the Chinese keep their government jobs. Later Mongol rulers continued the practice. In 1313 a decree was issued requiring four major texts of Confucian thought to be used in all imperial examinations.

The Mongols were different from the Chinese in many ways. They had their own language, laws, and customs. This kept them separate from Chinese society. The Mongols were rulers at the top of Chinese society, but they did not mix with the Chinese people.

Like many Chinese, the Mongols were Buddhists. They were tolerant, however, of other religions. For example, Kublai Khan invited Christians, Muslims, and Hindus from outside China to practice their faiths and to win converts.

Under Mongol rule, China reached the height of its wealth and power. Its splendor drew foreigners who came to China over the Silk Road. Khanbaliq, the capital, became known for its wide streets, beautiful palaces, and fine homes.

Primary Source — Kublai Khan's Park

Marco Polo recorded a description of the luxury in which Kublai Khan lived.

"[The palace wall] encloses and encircles fully sixteen miles of parkland well watered with springs and streams . . . Into this park there is no entry except by way of the palace. Here the Great Khan keeps game animals of all sorts . . . to provide food for the gerfalcons [large, arctic falcons] and other falcons which he has in here in mew [an enclosure]."

—Marco Polo, "Kublai Khan's Park, c. 1275"

▲ Kublai Khan presents golden tablets to Marco Polo.

DBQ Document-Based Question

Why did Kublai Khan keep game animals—ones hunted for sport or food—in his park?

One of the most famous European travelers to reach China was **Marco Polo** (MAHR•koh POH•loh). He came from the city of Venice in Italy. Kublai Khan was fascinated by Marco Polo's stories about his travels. For about 16 years, Polo enjoyed a special status in the country. Kublai sent him on many fact-finding and business trips. For three of those years, Polo ruled the Chinese city of Yangchow. When Polo finally returned to Europe, he wrote a book about his adventures. His accounts of the wonders of China amazed Europeans.

Trade and Conquest The Mongols ruled a large empire that stretched from China to Eastern Europe. As a result, China prospered from increased overland trade with other areas. The Mongols also continued the shipbuilding of the Song dynasty and expanded seagoing trade. Goods such as silver, spices, carpets, and cotton flowed in from Europe and places in Asia, including Japan, Korea, India, and Southeast Asia. In return, China shipped out tea, silk, and porcelain. Europeans and Muslims also brought Chinese discoveries, such as steel, gunpowder, and the compass, back to their homelands.

The Mongols enlarged China's empire by conquering Vietnam and northern Korea. The rulers of Korea, called the Koryo, remained in power because they accepted Mongol control. The Mongols forced thousands of Koreans to build warships. These ships were used by the Mongols on two separate occasions in attempts to invade Japan. Unfortunately for Kublai Khan, both expeditions ended in failure when huge storms destroyed much of his fleet. You will read more about the Mongol invasions of Japan in the next chapter.

✓ **Reading Check** **Identify** Who founded the Yuan dynasty?

History Online

Study Central Need help with the rise of the Mongol Empire? Visit ca.hss.glencoe.com and click on Study Central.

Section 3 Review

Reading Summary

Review the Main Ideas

- Under leaders such as Genghis Khan and his sons, the Mongol Empire expanded until it stretched from the Pacific Ocean to Eastern Europe and from Siberia south to the Himalaya.

- Kublai Khan conquered China, which led to increased trade between China and other parts of the world.

What Did You Learn?

1. Who was Marco Polo?

2. What areas did the Mongols conquer?

Critical Thinking

3. **Sequencing Information** Draw a time line like the one below. Fill in details to show the Mongols' rise to power in China. **CA CS2.**

```
|----|----|----|----|
c. 1167          1281
Temujin          Mongols
born             conquer
                 China
```

4. **The Big Ideas** How did Ghengis Khan use terror to gain wealth and power for the Mongols? **CA 7RC2.0**

5. **Summarize** How did the Mongols benefit from their contact with the Chinese? **CA HI3.**

6. **Expository Writing** Imagine you are Marco Polo visiting Kublai Khan in Khanbaliq. Write a journal entry describing some of the things you are learning about the Mongol Empire under Kublai Khan. **CA 7WA2.1**

WORLD LITERATURE

CHINA'S BRAVEST GIRL

THE LEGEND OF HUA MU LAN

by Charlie Chin

Before You Read

The Scene: This story takes place in China around A.D. 400.

The Characters: Hua Mu Lan is a brave young woman who disguises herself as a soldier.

The Plot: Hua Mu Lan volunteers to fight in a war in order to protect her father.

Vocabulary Preview

darts: moves quickly

weaves: laces together strands of material

perfumed: scented

yield: to give way

banquet: large feast

Have you ever tried to help or protect a family member or a friend? How did that make you feel? In this story, a daughter makes a true sacrifice to help her father.

As You Read

This exciting tale of Hua Mu Lan's success in battle occurred during the war-filled years between the dynasty of the Han empire and the reunification of China under the Sui empire. The story was known in folklore throughout the ages but did not become popular until it was written down and told across China during the Song dynasty. What did Hua Mu Lan come to represent to the people of China when her story was heard?

The Emperor called for the Pipa[1] player.
"Have him sing a song of old.
I will give him a seat of honor
and a ring of hammered gold."

The Pipa player took his place
and he sang an ancient story,
the legend of young Hua Mu Lan
the girl who won fame and glory.

The sound is click, and again, click click,
young Hua Mu Lan at the loom.[2]
Her fingers fly, the shuttle[3] darts,
as she weaves inside her room.

Last night she saw the notice.
It was posted on the wall.
On it was her father's name.
He must answer the Emperor's call.

The enemy has invaded China.
Our army must prepare to fight.
One man from every household
must be ready by morning light.

---

[1]**Pipa:** a small, guitar-like musical instrument
[2]**loom:** a machine used for weaving threads to make cloth
[3]**shuttle:** a tool used to weave thread together

Her father is old and tired.
His hair is turning white.
She tells him of her plan
as they talk by candlelight.

"I am young and healthy,
and you have no eldest son.
If the Emperor needs a soldier,
then I must be the one."

For love of her elderly father
she will dress in warrior's clothes,
walking and talking like a man,
so no one ever knows.

She travels in the four directions,
preparing for the trip.
She will buy in different towns
the saddle, horse and whip.

The crescent moon spear in her hand,
the willow leaf sword by her side,
her armor is laced and tightened,
her war horse is saddled to ride.

The bravest girl in China
puts away the perfumed comb.
To repay her father's kindness
she will ride away from home.

The banks of the Yellow River
echo the sound of flowing water.
In her heart she hears her father's words,
"Farewell, my faithful daughter."

She joins ten thousand soldiers
camped in the moon-lit snow.
Their tents shine like lanterns
lit by the campfire glow.

The morning light brings the battle.
The invaders take the field.
Enemy arrows find their mark.
China's line begins to yield.

When all seems lost a shout is heard,
"Brave sons of China follow me!"
Warriors wheel and turn about
like the waves of an angry sea.

Cheering troops rally around her.
The enemy line breaks in fear.
Hua Mu Lan's courage wins the day
as she fights with her sword and spear.

She wins in a hundred battles.
Ten years like arrows fly by.
She gains the rank of General.
Her legend will never die.

The Emperor summons his "hero"
to receive from the royal hand
a minister's post and the title
to a nobleman's house and land.

"There is nothing that I desire,
neither wealth nor minister's post.
My duty is to my father.
In old age, he needs me most."

"Give me only a strong camel
and my freedom then to roam.
I will ride the southern road
that leads back to my home."

The news is heard at her father's gate
where colorful lanterns burn.
Her family prepares a feast
to celebrate her return.

She enters as a general.
Her father watches with pride.
She greets her father and mother,
then turns to go inside.

Alone in her room at last,
she sits on her childhood bed.
She takes off the iron helmet
and places flowers on her head.

The ocean hides the oyster.
The oyster hides the pearl.
Bright armor and heavy helmet
hid China's bravest girl.

As she steps into the courtyard,
her comrade says in surprise,
"My general has become a woman.
I can't believe my eyes!"

"We fought shoulder to shoulder.
Our hands gripped sword and spear.
I knew you as a warrior
who was strong and without fear.

"How many times in danger
did you turn to save my life?
We were always the best of friends.
Why not become husband and wife?"

"If I become your wife," she says,
"we will play a different game.
You treat your friends with honor.
Can your wife expect the same?"

"Yes, I will honor you," he says,
"in all I do and say.
Now let's invite the villagers
and set the wedding day."

Red and gold banners adorn the house.
A banquet is prepared for all.
She wears the finest jade[4] and silk
for the wedding in her husband's hall.

The Pipa player sang the last verse
His rewards had been foretold:
for his skill a seat of honor;
for his song a ring of gold.

The legend of young Hua Mu Lan
whose bravery saved her nation
is loved by the Chinese people
and retold each generation.

---

[4]**jade:** a green gemstone

Responding to the Literature

1. Why did Hua Mu Lan's father have to go into battle?

2. How long did Mu Lan stay away from home?

3. **Drawing Conclusions** After reading her story, what do think of the character of Hua Mu Lan? What does the author do to make Mu Lan a sympathetic and heroic character? **CA 7RL3.3**

4. **Understanding Poetry** This story is written in poetry form. How does the presentation of this tale as a poem change the story for the reader? How does the author use poetry to move the story along? After answering these questions, write a short story version of Hua Mu Lan's tale. How does your version differ from the one you have just read? How are they the same? **CA 7RL3.1** **CA 7WA2.1**

5. **Read to Write** Imagine that you are one of Hua Mu Lan's fellow soldiers. How might you have reacted if you found out that she was a woman? Would this change how you viewed her? Write an essay that explains how you would react to the situation. **CA 7WA2.2**

From the California Reading List

Are you interested in amazing events in China, the exciting life of a samurai, or life in medieval Europe? If so, check out these other great books.

Nonfiction

The Great Wall of China by Leonard Everett Fisher recounts the story and construction of this amazing wall. Learn the political and social reasons for its creation and meet several interesting characters in Chinese history. *The content of this book is related to* History–Social Science Standard WH7.3.

Fiction

Mysterious Tales of Japan by Rafe Martin is a collection of scary stories in a Japanese setting. These edge-of-your-seat Japanese tales are filled with mystery and offer a look at the Shinto and Buddhist belief systems. *The content of this book is related to* History–Social Science Standard WH7.5.

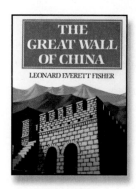

Biography

Images Across the Ages: Japanese Portraits by Dorothy and Thomas Hoobler recounts the lives of important Japanese people. This book includes firsthand accounts from the people who lived during that time. *The content of this book is related to* History–Social Science Standard WH7.5.

Fiction

Catherine, Called Birdy by Karen Cushman, a Newbery Award winner, tells the story of a teenage girl in the thirteenth century. Catherine is determined to marry for love even though her father wants to marry her to the first rich man he can find. This story lets you see into the daily life and family customs of medieval times. *The content of this book is related to* History–Social Science Standard WH7.6.

The Ming Dynasty

Guide to Reading

Looking Back, Looking Ahead

In Section 3, you read about the Mongol conquest. Eventually, the Chinese drove the Mongols out, and a new dynasty arose.

Focusing on the Main Ideas

- Ming rulers strengthened China's government and brought back peace and prosperity. *(page 282)*

- During the Ming dynasty, China sent a fleet to explore Asia and East Africa. *(page 284)*

Locating Places

Nanjing (NAHN•JIHNG)

Portugal (POHR•chih•guhl)

Meeting People

Zhu Yuanzhang
  (JOO   YOO•AHN•JAHNG)

Yong Le (YUNG   LEE)

Zheng He (JUNG   HUH)

Content Vocabulary

treason (TREE•zuhn)

census (SEHN•suhs)

novel (NAH•vuhl)

barbarian (bahr•BEHR•ee•uhn)

Academic Vocabulary

erode (ih•ROHD)

compile (kuhm•PYL)

drama (DRAH•muh)

contact (KAHN•TAKT)

Reading Strategy

Cause and Effect Use a chart like the one below to show cause-and-effect links in China's early trade voyages.

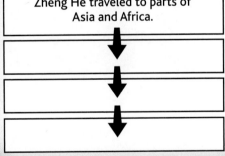

Cause
Zheng He traveled to parts of Asia and Africa.

History Social Science Standards

WH7.3 Students analyze the geographic, political, economic, religious, and social structures of the civilizations of China in the Middle Ages.

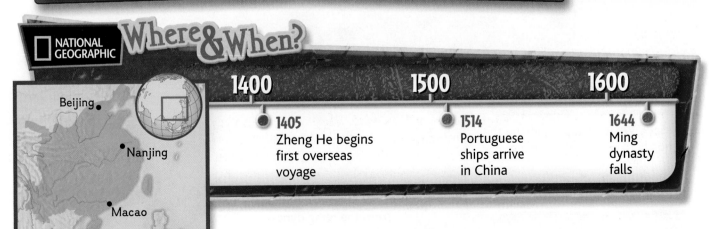

NATIONAL GEOGRAPHIC Where & When?

Beijing
Nanjing
Macao

1400

1500

1600

1405 Zheng He begins first overseas voyage

1514 Portuguese ships arrive in China

1644 Ming dynasty falls

WH7.3 Students analyze the geographic, political, economic, religious, and social structures of the civilizations of China in the Middle Ages.

WH7.3.6 Describe the development of the imperial state and the scholar-official class.

The Rise of the Ming

Main Idea Ming rulers strengthened China's government and brought back peace and prosperity.

Reading Connection Think about all the different things the government does for people. Imagine if you were running the government and had to rebuild the country after a war. What would you do? Read to learn how the Ming rulers in China rebuilt their country after the Mongols left.

Kublai Khan died in 1294. A series of weak rulers followed him, and Mongol power began to **erode.** During the 1300s, problems mounted for the Yuan dynasty. Mongol groups in Mongolia to the north broke away. At the same time, many Chinese resented Mongol controls and wanted their own dynasty.

How Did the Ming Dynasty Begin? A series of rebellions finally drove out the Mongols. In 1368 a rebel leader named **Zhu Yuanzhang** (JOO YOO•AHN•JAHNG) became emperor. Zhu reunited the country and set up his capital at **Nanjing** (NAHN•JIHNG) in southern China. There, he founded the Ming, or "Brilliant," dynasty.

As emperor, Zhu took the name Hong Wu, or the "Military Emperor." He brought back order, but he also proved to be a cruel leader. Hong Wu trusted no one and killed officials he suspected of **treason** (TREE•zuhn), or disloyalty to the government. Hong Wu ruled China for 30 years. When he died in 1398, his son became emperor and took the name of **Yong Le** (YUNG LEE).

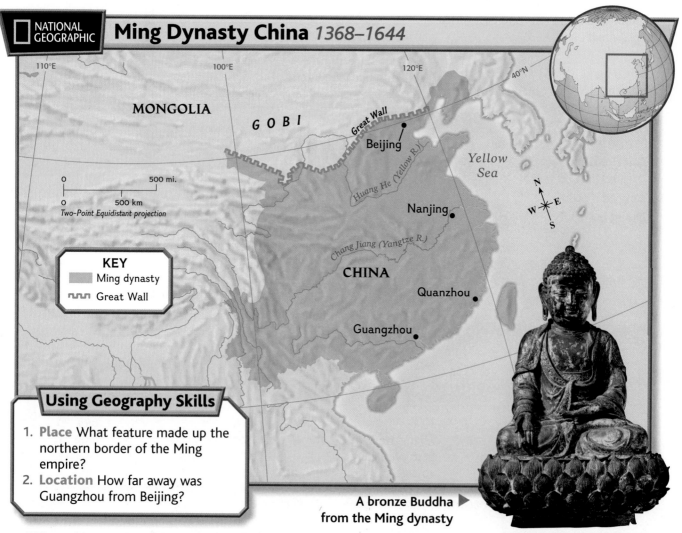

NATIONAL GEOGRAPHIC

Ming Dynasty China *1368–1644*

KEY
- Ming dynasty
- Great Wall

Using Geography Skills

1. **Place** What feature made up the northern border of the Ming empire?
2. **Location** How far away was Guangzhou from Beijing?

► A bronze Buddha from the Ming dynasty

Yong Le worked hard to show that he was a powerful emperor. In 1421 he moved the capital north to Beijing. There, he built a large area of palaces and government buildings known as the Imperial City. The very center of the Imperial City was known as the Forbidden City. Only top officials could enter the Forbidden City because it was home to China's emperors.

The Forbidden City had beautiful gardens and many palaces with thousands of rooms. The emperor and his court lived there in luxury for more than 500 years. The buildings of the Forbidden City still exist. You can visit them if you travel to China.

▲ This image, from a Ming dynasty vase, shows Chinese farmworkers collecting tea.

How Did the Ming Reform China?

Ming emperors made all the decisions, but they still needed officials to carry out their orders. They restored the civil service examinations and made the tests even harder. From time to time, Ming officials **compiled** a **census** (SEHN•suhs), or a count of the number of people. This helped them collect taxes more accurately.

With the strong government of the early Ming emperors providing peace and stability, China's economy began to grow. Hong Wu ordered many of the canals and farms destroyed by the Mongols to be rebuilt and ordered people to move to the new farms. He also ordered new forests to be planted and new roads to be paved.

Agriculture thrived as farmers worked on the new lands and grew more crops. Ming rulers repaired and expanded the Grand Canal so that rice and other goods could again be shipped from southern to northern China. They imported new types of rice from southeast Asia that grew faster. This helped feed the growing number of people living in cities. The Ming also supported the silk industry and encouraged farmers to start growing cotton and weaving cloth. For the first time, cotton became the cloth worn by most Chinese.

Chinese Culture

Chinese culture also advanced under the Ming. As merchants and artisans grew wealthier, they wanted to learn more and be entertained. During the Ming period, Chinese writers produced many **novels** (NAH•vuhls), or long fictional stories. The Chinese also enjoyed seeing **dramas** on stage. These works combined spoken words and songs with dances, costumes, and symbolic gestures.

✓ Reading Check **Identify** What was the Forbidden City?

China Explores the World

Main Idea During the Ming dynasty, China sent a fleet to explore Asia and East Africa.

Reading Connection You probably have heard of Christopher Columbus and his trip to America. Imagine if China had sent ships to America first. Read to learn about Chinese explorations of Asia and East Africa.

Early Ming emperors were curious about the world outside of China. They also wanted to increase China's influence abroad. To reach these goals, Ming emperors built a large fleet of ships. The new ships usually traveled along China's coast. However, they could also sail in the open sea.

Who Was Zheng He? From 1405 to 1431, Emperor Yong Le sent the fleet on seven overseas voyages. The emperor wanted to trade with other kingdoms, show off China's power, and demand that weaker kingdoms pay tribute to China.

The leader of these journeys was a Chinese Muslim and court official named **Zheng He** (JUNG HUH). Zheng He's voyages were quite impressive. His first fleet had 62 large ships, 250 smaller ships, and almost 28,000 men. The largest ship was over 440 feet (134 m) long. That made it more than *five times* as long as the *Santa María* that Christopher Columbus sailed almost 90 years later!

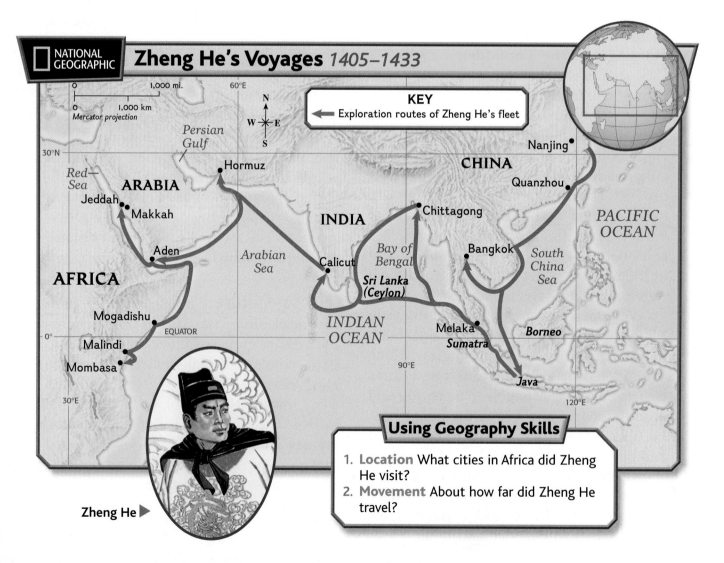

NATIONAL GEOGRAPHIC

Zheng He's Voyages *1405–1433*

KEY

← Exploration routes of Zheng He's fleet

Zheng He ▶

Using Geography Skills

1. **Location** What cities in Africa did Zheng He visit?
2. **Movement** About how far did Zheng He travel?

Biography

WH7.3.4 Understand the importance of both overland trade and maritime expeditions between China and other civilizations in the Mongol Ascendancy and Ming Dynasty.

ZHENG HE

1371–1433

Zheng He ▶

Chinese Navigator

The famous Chinese navigator Zheng He was born in Kunyang in southwest China in 1371. His birth name was Ma He, and he was from a poor Chinese Muslim family. Scholars say that his father and grandfather were honored hajjis—people who successfully made the pilgrimage to Makkah in Arabia. Little did Ma He know that his life would also involve travel. His seven missions across the oceans earned him heroic honors.

His father died when Ma He was little. As a child, Ma He was taken prisoner by the Chinese army. To overcome his sad life, Ma He turned to education. He learned different languages, including Arabic, and studied philosophy and geography. With his language skills and knowledge of the outside world, 10-year-old Ma He became a valuable imperial aide to Chinese officials.

By age 12, he was an assistant to a young prince named Zhu Di. Ma He accompanied the prince on several military missions. The prince, who later became the Emperor Yong Le, became a friend of Ma He. The emperor changed Ma He's name to the honored surname Zheng. Soon after, Zheng He was assigned to lead a fleet of Chinese ships across the Indian Ocean, beginning the career that would make him famous. Zheng He's voyages to new lands opened the door for trade among China, India, and Africa. Many of the Chinese moved abroad to sell Chinese goods. Those who learned and spoke more than one language, like Zheng He, prospered.

> **"We have set eyes on barbarian regions far away."**
> –Zheng He, as quoted in *Chinese Portraits*

Then and Now

What "Made in China" products do you use on a daily basis? Do research to find out what percentage of goods imported to the United States is from China.

▲ Italian missionary Matteo Ricci (left) was one of the most famous Europeans to visit China. He helped in the development of math and science in China during the late 1500s.

Where Did Zheng He Travel?
Zheng He took his first fleet to southeast Asia. In later voyages, he reached India, sailed up the Persian Gulf to Arabia, and even landed in East Africa. In these areas, Zheng He traded Chinese goods, such as silk, paper, and porcelain. He brought back silver, spices, wood, and other goods. From Africa, Zheng He purchased giraffes and other animals for the emperor's zoo.

As a result of Zheng He's voyages, Chinese merchants settled in Southeast Asia and India. There, they not only traded goods but also spread Chinese culture. Chinese merchants at home and abroad grew rich from the trade of the voyages and added to China's wealth.

Despite these benefits, Chinese officials complained that the trips cost too much. They also said that trips were bad for China's way of life because they brought in new ideas from the outside world and helped merchants become rich.

Confucius had taught that people should place loyalty to society ahead of their own desires. To the officials, China's merchants were disobeying this teaching by working to gain money for themselves.

After Zheng He's death in 1433, the Confucian officials persuaded the emperor to stop the voyages. The boats were dismantled, and no more ships capable of long distance ocean travel were allowed to be built. As a result, China's trade with other countries sharply declined. Within 50 years, the shipbuilding technology was forgotten.

The Europeans Arrive in China Chinese officials were not able to cut off all of China's **contacts** with the outside world. In 1514 a fleet from the European country of **Portugal** (POHR•chih•guhl) arrived off the coast of China. It was the first time Europeans had ever sailed to China and the first direct contact between China and Europe since the journeys of Marco Polo.

The Portuguese wanted China to trade with their country. They also wanted to convince the Chinese to become Christians. At the time, the Ming government was not impressed by the Portuguese. China was at the height of its power and did not feel threatened by outsiders. The Chinese thought the Europeans were **barbarians** (bahr•BEHR•ee•uhns), or uncivilized people.

At first, the Chinese refused to trade with the Portuguese, but by 1600, they had allowed Portugal to set up a trading post at the port of Macao (muh•KOW) in southern China. Goods were carried on European ships between Macao and Japan. Still, trade between China and Europe remained limited.

Despite restrictions, ideas from Europe did reach China. Christian missionaries traveled to China on European ships. Many of these missionaries were Jesuits, a special group of Roman Catholic priests. They were highly educated, and their scientific knowledge impressed the Chinese. To get China to accept European ideas, the Jesuits brought with them clocks, eyeglasses, and scientific instruments. Although they tried, the Jesuits did not convert many Chinese.

Why Did the Ming Dynasty Fall? After a long era of prosperity and growth, the Ming dynasty began to decline. Ming emperors had gathered too much power into their own hands. With the emperor having so much control, officials had little desire to make improvements. As time passed, Ming rulers themselves became weak. Greedy officials placed heavy taxes on the peasants, who began to revolt.

As law and order disappeared, a people called the Manchus attacked China's northern border. The Manchus lived to the north-

▲ **This porcelain bowl is from the Ming dynasty.** *Where in China did the Portuguese set up a trading post?*

east of the Great Wall in an area known today as Manchuria. The Manchus defeated Chinese armies and captured Beijing. In 1644 they set up a new dynasty.

✓ Reading Check **Cause and Effect** What caused the Ming dynasty to decline and fall?

Study Central Need help with the rise of the Ming dynasty? Visit ca.hss.glencoe.com and click on Study Central.

Section 4 Review

Reading Summary

Review the Main Ideas

- The Ming dynasty rebuilt and reformed China after the Mongols were driven out. The dynasty restored peace and prosperity to China.

- During the Ming dynasty, China's contacts with the outside world increased as Zheng He led fleets to faraway lands and European ships began arriving in China.

What Did You Learn?

1. What was the purpose of the Forbidden City and where was it located?

2. How did the Chinese react to the arrival of Portuguese traders in 1514?

Critical Thinking

3. **Organizing Information** Draw a diagram like the one below. Fill in details about the achievements of the Ming dynasty. **CA** 7RC2.2

Ming Dynasty Achievements

4. **Cause and Effect** Why did Ming rulers repair and expand the Grand Canal? **CA** 7RC2.3

5. **The Big Ideas** Why did the Emperor Yong Le send Zheng He on his voyages? How did Zheng He's voyages benefit China? **CA** 7RC2.0

6. **Predict** What do you think happened after China tried to limit trade? **CA** HI2.

7. **Persuasive Writing** Imagine you are living in China at the time of Zheng He's voyages. Write a newspaper editorial either for or against the voyages. Describe why you think the voyages are helping or hurting China. **CA** 7WA2.5

Analyzing Primary Sources

WH7.3.2 Describe agricultural, technological, and commercial developments during the Tang and Song periods. **WH7.3.4** Understand the importance of both overland trade and maritime expeditions between China and other civilizations in the Mongol Ascendancy and Ming Dynasty.

A Growing China

In the Middle Ages, China changed dramatically. Improvements in farming techniques helped increase food production and boost the economy. As China's food supply increased, so did its population. For example, from A.D. 750 to A.D. 1100, China's population doubled from about 50 million to 100 million people. Chinese technology, agriculture, and economic activity continued to advance through the Ming dynasty.

Read the following passages and study the photo. Then answer the questions that follow.

▲ Painting of Chinese landscape

Reader's Dictionary

palanquin (PA•luhn•KEEN): a covered vehicle made up of a couch, usually enclosed by curtains, and carried by people on their shoulders

profusion (pruh•FYOO•zhuhn): large amount; abundance

barbarian: foreigner

buffeted (BUH•fuht•uhd): fought against

crags: steep, rugged rocks or cliffs

The Cities of the Song

During the Song dynasty, Chinese cities were transformed. The following is a description of a medicine fair in the city of Chengdu, in the western part of the Song empire in the 1200s.

Coming in a **palanquin** to visit the medicine fair, our bearers' knees are caught in the press of the crowd . . . there is such a **profusion** it cannot be detailed. . . . Mica and frankincense the colour of sparkling crystal, aloe and sandalwood wafting their fragrant scents . . . Some things are costly, . . . others are bitter, . . . some are stale like pemmican and mincemeat pickled in brine, some fresh like dates and chestnuts. Many are products of **barbarian** tribes . . . Merchants have **buffeted** the sea-winds and the waves and foreign merchants crossed over towering **crags** drawn onwards by the profit to be made . . . Here are the rich and powerful with numerous bondservants . . . carriages and horses in grand array, scattering clouds of dust. . . . [They] go home, their bags and boxes bulging.

—Du Zheng, a 13th-century poet, as quoted in *Chronicle of the Chinese Emperors*

Planting Rice

The image to the right depicts Chinese farmers planting rice. Rice is an excellent food crop—it stores well, offers good nutrition, and is easy to cook. During the Middle Ages, the production of rice expanded steadily. Improvements in water pumps and the making of dams allowed farmers to make the land suitable for growing rice.

Chinese Ships

During the Middle Ages, the Chinese developed merchant ships that were the most advanced in the world. The following is a description of Chinese ships during the 1100s.

The ships which sail the Southern Sea and south of it are like houses. When their sails are spread they are like great clouds in the sky. Their rudders are several tens of feet long. A single ship carries several hundred men. It has stored on board a year's supply of grain.

—Zhou Qufei as quoted in
Chronicle of the Chinese Emperors

▲ This image of Chinese farmers was made from a woodcut design. Images like this one were very popular in China during the Middle Ages, but often they were too expensive for people like these farmers to afford.

DBQ Document-Based Questions

The Cities of the Song

1. What kinds of people have come to the medicine fair?

2. How did some of the people who traveled to the medicine fair get there? Why do you think they made such a trip?

Planting Rice

3. Do you think rice farming was easy? Explain. Use the picture to support your answer.

Chinese Ships

4. What do you suppose was the purpose of such ships?

5. What comparisons does the writer make about the ships?

Read to Write

6. Using the primary sources you have just examined, write an essay describing how economic prosperity and the rise of trade during the Middle Ages affected Chinese society. **CA HI2.**

Review Content Vocabulary

Match the word in the first column with its definition in the second column.

___ 1. treason   a. groups of related families loosely joined together

___ 2. warlord   b. change that brings improvement

___ 3. terror   c. disloyalty to the government

___ 4. economy   d. military leader who also runs a government

___ 5. reform   e. a count of the number of people

___ 6. steppe   f. violent actions meant to scare others

___ 7. tribe   g. organized way to buy, sell, and produce

___ 8. census   h. wide grassy plain

Review the Main Ideas

Section 1 • China Reunites

9. What did the Sui and Tang dynasties do to improve China?

10. How did the Tang rulers change China?

Section 2 • Chinese Society

11. How did Tang rulers strengthen China's economy?

12. What kind of technologies did the Chinese develop?

Section 3 • The Mongols in China

13. Why were the Mongols able to build a huge empire?

14. How did the Mongols rule China?

Section 4 • The Ming Dynasty

15. How did the Ming rulers affect China?

16. Why did the Portuguese want to explore Africa and Asia?

Critical Thinking

17. **Analyze** How did the return of Confucianism affect Chinese society and government? **CA HI3.**

18. **Predict** How would China be different today if Tang rulers had not tried to stop Buddhism in A.D. 845? **CA HI4.**

19. **Hypothesize** The Mongols built a vast empire, but the Yuan dynasty lasted only about 100 years. Create a hypothesis that might explain this situation. **CA HR1.**

Geography Skills

Study the map below and answer the following questions.

20. **Location** What was the length of the Grand Canal? **CA CS3.**

21. **Human/Environment Interaction** What part of Asia did the Tang control that helped China's trade? **CA CS3.**

22. **Region** What geographic features helped the Tang dynasty expand? **CA CS3.**

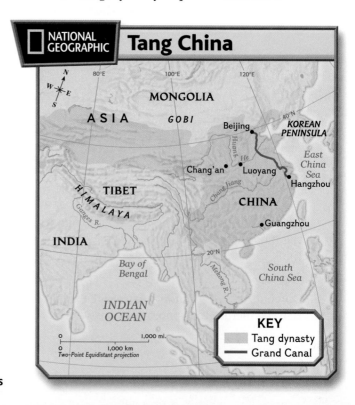

NATIONAL GEOGRAPHIC **Tang China**

KEY
Tang dynasty
Grand Canal

Read to Write

23. **The Big Ideas** **Persuasive Writing** Imagine you are a Portuguese merchant. You have just traveled to China to persuade the Chinese people to trade with your country. Create a script detailing the dialogue that would take place between you and a representative of the Chinese government. **CA 7WA2.5**

24. **Using Your FOLDABLES** On your foldable, add details to the main headings in Section 2. Think about how the changes and arts described there might have had an impact on people's lives. Write a story about a family whose life is affected by these changes. Illustrate your story. **CA HI1.**

Using Academic Vocabulary

25. All the words in the chart below are verbs. Complete the chart by changing them into past tense verbs.

Term	Past Tense
encounter	
contact	
seek	
erode	
compile	

Linking Past and Present

26. **Expository Writing** Write a short essay that describes similarities and differences between the Imperial City of the Ming dynasty and the United States capital, Washington, D.C. **CA 7WA2.0**

Understanding Change

27. When the Portuguese traders first went to China, they were not quickly accepted. Write an essay that describes why they were not accepted and how that eventually changed. Be sure to discuss the role of trade and its benefits in China. **CA HI2.**

Building Citizenship

28. **Writing Research Reports** How did neo-Confucianism strengthen government in China? How does the use of a merit system reflect the way that jobs in the U.S. government are given? How is it different? **CA 7WA2.3**

Reviewing Skills

29. **Reading Skill** **Making Connections** The voyages of Zheng He introduced China to many other cultures. His journeys took him to parts of Asia, Africa, and the Middle East. Use your local library and the Internet to identify other important explorers who have helped cultures learn about one another. Explain your findings in a short essay. **CA 7WA2.3**

30. **Analysis Skill** **Understanding Perspective** Major exploration and trade was stopped by Chinese leaders in 1433. Write a letter to the emperor explaining why you think this is a good or bad decision. What are the benefits of exploration and trade with the outside world? What possible harm can come from opening a country's borders to foreigners? **CA HR5.**

 Standards Practice

Select the best answer for each of the following questions.

31 What helped the Chinese economy to improve during the Tang dynasty?

   A wars and lower taxes

   B farming and trade

   C wars and farming

   D exploration and education

32 The Tang and Song dynasties encouraged the Chinese people to practice

   A neo-Confucianism.

   B Buddhism.

   C Confucianism.

   D Daoism.

Medieval Japan

Kinkaku Temple in Kyoto, Japan ▼

A.D. **300**	A.D. **700**	**1100**	**1500**
c. A.D. 300 Yayoi people organize into clans	**A.D. 646** Taika reforms strengthen emperor's powers	**1192** Rule by shoguns begins	**c. 1300s** Noh plays first performed

The Big Ideas

Chapter Overview Visit ca.hss.glencoe.com for a preview of Chapter 5.

 Early Japan

Physical geography plays a role in how civilizations develop. Japan's islands and mountains have shaped its history. The Japanese developed their own unique culture but looked to China as a model.

 Shoguns and Samurai

Conflict often brings about great change. Japan's emperors lost power to military leaders. Warrior families and their followers fought each other for control of Japan.

 Life in Medieval Japan

Religion influences how civilization develops and culture spreads. The religions of Shinto and Buddhism shaped Japan's culture. Farmers, artisans, and merchants brought wealth to Japan.

 **View the Chapter 5 video in the Glencoe Video Program.**

FOLDABLES™ Study Organizer

Categorizing Information *Make this foldable to help you organize information about the history and culture of medieval Japan.*

Step 1 *Mark the midpoint of the side edge of a sheet of paper.*

Draw a mark at the midpoint

Step 2 *Turn the paper and fold in each outside edge to touch at the midpoint. Label as shown.*

Step 3 *Open and label your foldable as shown.*

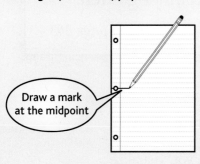

Reading and Writing *As you read the chapter, organize your notes by writing the main ideas with supporting details under the appropriate heading.*

Visualizing

Reading Skill

1 Learn It!

Visualize by forming mental images of the text as you read. Imagine how the text descriptions look, sound, feel, smell, or taste. Look for any pictures or diagrams on the page that may help you add to your understanding. Read the following passage and answer the questions that follow.

The city of Nara looked much like China's capital of Chang'an, only smaller. It had broad streets, large public squares, government offices, Buddhist temples, and Shinto shrines. Nobles and their families lived in large, Chinese-style homes. The typical home of a noble had wooden walls, a heavy tile roof, and polished wooden floors. It also included an inner garden.

— *from page 303*

- What part of the city can you best visualize? Why?
- How do you picture the nobles' houses of the city?
- What words helped you visualize the city and the houses?

Reading Tip

Forming your own mental images will help you remember what you read.

2 Practice It!

Read the following paragraph. As you read, use the underlined details to form a picture in your mind.

> Unlike Shinto shrines, Buddhist temples were built in the <u>Chinese style.</u> They had <u>massive tiled roofs held up by thick, wooden pillars.</u> The temples were <u>richly decorated.</u> They had <u>many statues, paintings,</u> and <u>altars.</u>
>
> Around their buildings, the Japanese created <u>gardens</u> designed to <u>imitate nature in a miniature form.</u> Some of these <u>gardens</u> had <u>carefully placed rocks, raked sand, and a few plants.</u>
>
> —*from pages 311–312*

Read to Write

Visualizing helps you organize ideas in your head before you write, especially when using graphic organizers. Read **The First Settlers** in Section 1. Use a table to write two facts about each group who settled Japan.

Based on the description above, try to visualize how a Japanese Buddhist temple may have looked. Now look at the photo to the right.

- How closely does it match your mental picture?
- Now reread the passage and look at the picture again. Did your ideas change?
- What other words would you use to describe the picture?
- Compare your image with what others in your class visualized. Discuss how your mental picture differed from theirs.

▼ A Zen monk sits in a Japanese rock garden.

3 Apply It!

Read the chapter and list three subjects or events that you were able to visualize. Make a rough sketch or drawing showing what you visualized.

Section

1

Early Japan

**History
Social Science
Standards**

WH7.5 Students
analyze the geographic,
political, economic,
religious, and social
structures of the
civilizations of Medieval
Japan.

Guide to Reading

Looking Back, Looking Ahead

During the Middle Ages, another civilization developed in East Asia. It arose on the islands of Japan off the coast of the Korean Peninsula.

Focusing on the Main Ideas

- Japan's mountains and islands isolated Japan and shaped its society. *(page 297)*

- Japan was settled by people who came from northeast Asia. They were organized into clans and ruled by warriors. *(page 298)*

- Prince Shotoku created Japan's first constitution and borrowed many ideas from China. *(page 299)*

- The Japanese religion called Shinto was based on nature spirits. *(page 301)*

Meeting People

Jimmu (jeem•mu)
Shotoku (shoh•TOH•koo)

Locating Places

Japan (juh•PAN)
Hokkaido (hah•KY•doh)
Honshu (HAHN•shoo)
Shikoku (shih•KOH•koo)
Kyushu (kee•OO•shoo)

Content Vocabulary

clan (KLAN)
constitution
(KAHN•stuh•TOO•shuhn)
animism (A•nuh•MIH•zuhm)
shrine (SHRYN)

Academic Vocabulary

occur (uh•KUHR)
portion (POHR•shuhn)

Reading Strategy

Organizing Information Create a diagram to show the basic beliefs of the Shinto religion.

Shinto Religion

NATIONAL GEOGRAPHIC Where&When?

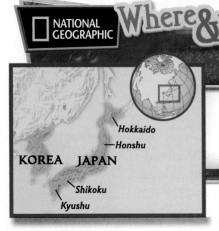

KOREA JAPAN
Hokkaido
Honshu
Shikoku
Kyushu

A.D. 300	A.D. 500	A.D. 700

c. A.D. 300
Yayoi people organize into clans

c. A.D. 550
Yamoto clan rules most of Japan

A.D. 646
Taika reforms strengthen emperor's powers

Japan's Geography

Main Idea Japan's mountains and islands isolated Japan and shaped its society.

Reading Connection Have you ever been in a place with no television, radio, or telephone? How would you feel if you did not know what was going on outside your home? Read to learn how Japan's geography isolated the Japanese and shaped their society.

Japan (juh•PAN) is a chain of islands that stretches north to south in the northern Pacific Ocean. Japan's islands number more than 3,000, and many of them are tiny. For centuries, most Japanese have lived on the four largest islands: **Hokkaido** (hah•KY•doh), **Honshu** (HAHN•shoo), **Shikoku** (shih•KOH•koo), and **Kyushu** (kee•OO•shoo).

Like China, much of Japan is covered by mountains. In fact, the islands of Japan are actually the tops of mountains that rise from the floor of the ocean. About 188 of Japan's mountains are volcanoes. Many earthquakes **occur** in Japan because the islands lie in an area where parts of the earth's surface often shift.

Because of Japan's mountains, only about 20 percent of its land can be farmed. Throughout Japan's history, local armies often fought over the few patches of fertile

▼ **Mount Fuji is an important national symbol.**
How did the region's mountains affect early settlement in Japan?

farmland. Just as in ancient Greece, the rugged terrain forced many Japanese to turn to the sea for a living. Early on, they settled in villages along the coast and fished for food. Fish and seafood are still an important element in the Japanese diet.

The sea surrounding Japan's islands made it easy for people in ships to travel along the coast and from island to island. It encouraged people to become merchants, traveling from village to village with goods to trade. The vast ocean around Japan's islands, however, kept the Japanese people isolated, or separate, from the rest of Asia. As a result, Japan developed its own intensely independent society with its own religion, art, literature, and government.

✓ **Reading Check** **Describe** How did Japan's geography shape its society?

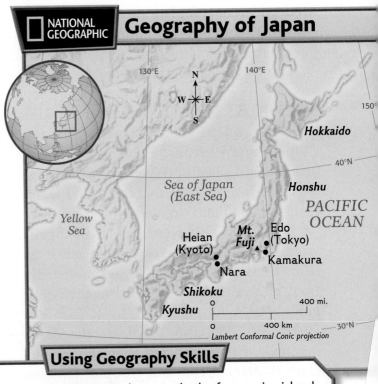

NATIONAL GEOGRAPHIC
Geography of Japan

Hokkaido

Sea of Japan (East Sea)

Honshu

PACIFIC OCEAN

Yellow Sea

Heian (Kyoto)

Mt. Fuji

Edo (Tokyo)

Kamakura

Nara

Shikoku

Kyushu

400 mi.

400 km

Lambert Conformal Conic projection

Using Geography Skills

1. **Regions** List, from north to south, the four major islands that make up Japan.
2. **Location** What body of water separates Japan from mainland Asia?

Find NGS online map resources @ www.nationalgeographic.com/maps

The First Settlers

Main Idea Japan was settled by people who came from northeast Asia. They were organized into clans and ruled by warriors.

Reading Connection Do you have many relatives? Do your relatives all come together to do things? Read to learn how the early Japanese people were organized into groups made up of people who were all related to each other.

Japan's earliest people probably came from northeast Asia between 30,000 B.C. and 10,000 B.C. At that time, Japan was joined to the Asian continent by land. These early people hunted animals and gathered wild plants. They used fire and stone tools, and they lived in pits dug into the ground.

Who Were the Yayoi? About 300 B.C., a new group of people appeared in Japan. Modern archaeologists have named this culture Yayoi (YAH•yoy), after the place in Japan where they first dug up its artifacts.

The Yayoi were the ancestors of the Japanese people. They introduced farming to Japan and practiced a number of skills that they might have learned from the Chinese and Koreans. They made pottery on a potter's wheel and grew rice in paddies. A paddy is a rice field that is flooded when rice is planted and drained for the harvest.

The Yayoi also were skilled in metal-working. They made axes, knives, and hoes from iron, and swords, spears, and bells from bronze. Bells were used in their religious rituals.

By A.D. 300, the Yayoi, or the early Japanese, had organized themselves into **clans** (KLANZ). A clan is a group of families related by blood or marriage. Yayoi clans were headed by a small group of warriors. Under the warriors were the rest of the people—farmers, artisans, and servants of the warriors. The clan's warrior chiefs pro-tected the people in return for a **portion** of the rice harvest each year.

The Yayoi buried their chiefs in large mounds known as *kofun*. Made of dirt, these tombs were filled with personal belongings, such as pottery, tools, weapons, and armor. Many of the tombs were as big as Egypt's pyramids. The largest tomb still stands today. It is longer than five football fields and at least eight stories high.

Who Are the Yamato? During the A.D. 500s, a clan called the Yamato became strong enough to rule most of Japan. The other clans still held their lands, but they gave their loyalty to the Yamato chief.

Yamato chiefs claimed that they were descended from the sun goddess and, therefore, had a right to rule Japan. Japanese legend states that a Yamato leader named **Jimmu** (jeem•mu) took the title "emperor of heaven." He founded a line of rulers in Japan that has never been broken. Akihito (AH•kee•HEE•toh), who is Japan's emperor today, is one of his descendants.

Reading Check **Identify** What do historians know about the rise of the Yamato?

Bronze bell from the ▶ Yayoi people

Yayoi pottery ▼

WH7.5.1 Describe the significance of Japan's proximity to China and Korea and the intellectual, linguistic, religious, and philosophical influence of those countries on Japan.

WH7.5.2 Discuss the reign of Prince Shotoku of Japan and the characteristics of Japanese society and family life during his reign.

Prince Shotoku's Reforms

Main Idea Prince Shotoku created Japan's first constitution and borrowed many ideas from China.

Reading Connection When you try something new, are you tempted to use what someone else has done as a model? Read to find out how Shotoku used China as a model for his reforms in Japan.

About A.D. 600, a Yamato prince named **Shotoku** (shoh•TOH•koo) took charge of Japan on behalf of his aunt, the empress Suiko (swee•koh). He wanted to create a strong government, and he looked to China as an example of what to do. You remember that in China, a powerful emperor ruled with the help of trained officials chosen for their abilities.

To reach this goal for Japan, Shotoku created a **constitution** (KAHN•stuh•TOO•shuhn), or a plan of government. Shotoku's constitution gave all power to the emperor, who had to be obeyed by the Japanese people. He also created a bureaucracy and gave the emperor the power to appoint all the officials. The constitution listed rules for working in the government. The rules were taken from the ideas of Confucius.

Shotoku also wanted Japan to learn from China's brilliant civilization. He sent officials and students to China to study. The Japanese not only learned about Buddhist teachings but also absorbed a great deal about Chinese art, medicine, and philosophy, much of which came through Korea.

Shotoku ordered Buddhist temples and monasteries to be built throughout Japan. One of them, called Horyuji (HOHR•yoo•JEE), still stands. It is Japan's oldest temple and the world's oldest surviving wooden building.

After Shotoku, other officials continued to make Japan's government look like China's. In A.D. 646 the Yamato began the

Primary Source — Japan's New Constitution

This is part of the constitution created by Shotoku.

"Harmony is to be cherished, and opposition for opposition's sake must be avoided as a matter of principle. . . .

When an imperial command is given, obey it with reverence. The sovereign is likened to heaven, and his subjects are likened to earth. With heaven providing the cover and earth supporting it, the four seasons proceed in orderly fashion, giving sustenance to all that which is in nature. If earth attempts to overtake the functions of heaven, it destroys everything.

Cast away your ravenous desire for food and abandon your covetousness [envy] for material possessions. If a suit is brought before you, render a clear-cut judgement. . . .

Punish that which is evil and encourage that which is good."

—Prince Shotoku,
"The Seventeen Article Constitution"

DBQ Document-Based Question

To what are the emperor and his subjects compared?

Taika, or Great Change. They divided Japan into provinces, or regional districts, all run by officials who reported to the emperor. In addition, all land in Japan came under the emperor's control.

Clan leaders could direct the farmers working the land, but they could not collect taxes anymore. Instead, government officials were to gather part of the farmers' harvest in taxes for the emperor. Together with Shotoku's reforms, this plan created Japan's first strong central government.

✓ **Reading Check** **Identify** What Chinese ideas influenced Prince Shotoku?

Biography

PRINCE SHOTOKU

A.D. 573–621

▲ Statue believed to be of Prince Shotoku

Prince Shotoku was born into the powerful Soga family, as the second son of Emperor Yomei. Shotoku's real name is Umayado, which means "the prince of the stable door." According to legend, Shotoku's mother gave birth to him while she was inspecting the emperor's stables. During Shotoku's childhood, Japan was a society of clans, or large extended families. There was fighting between Shotoku's own Soga family and their rival, the Mononobe family. The Soga and Mononobe clans were Japan's two most powerful families, and each wanted to rule Japan.

Shotoku was a very bright, articulate child. He learned about Buddhism from one of his great uncles. He then studied with two Buddhist priests and became devoted to Buddhism.

At the age of 20, Shotoku became Japan's crown prince. The early teachings of Buddhism strongly influenced his leadership. He introduced political and religious reforms that helped build a strong central government in Japan modeled after China. At the request of his aunt, the empress, Shotoku often spoke about Buddhism and the process of enlightenment. He also wrote the first book of Japanese history.

When Prince Shotoku died, the elderly people of the empire mourned as if they had lost a dear child of their own. A written account describes their words of grief: "The sun and moon have lost their brightness; heaven and earth have crumbled to ruin: henceforward, in whom shall we put our trust?"

▲ The Horyuji temple, built by Prince Shotoku

Then and Now

Think of a recent leader or other public figure whose death caused people to mourn as if they knew that person well. Who is it? Why do you think people identified with that person? Why did the Japanese identify so closely with Shotoku?

WH7.5.1 Describe the significance of Japan's proximity to China and Korea and the intellectual, linguistic, religious, and philosophical influence of those countries on Japan.
WH7.5.4 Trace the development of distinctive forms of Japanese Buddhism.

What Is Shinto?

◀ Shinto priests

Main Idea The Japanese religion called Shinto was based on nature spirits.

Reading Connection Today we know the importance of protecting the environment. Why is nature important to us? Read to learn why the early Japanese thought nature was important.

Like many ancient peoples, the early Japanese believed that all natural things are alive, even the winds, the mountains, and the rivers. They believed that all of these things have their own spirits. This idea is called **animism** (A•nuh•MIH•zuhm). When people needed help, they asked the nature spirits, whom they called *kami,* to help them.

To honor the *kami,* the Japanese worshiped at **shrines** (SHRYNZ), or holy places. There, priests, musicians, and dancers performed rituals for people who asked the

gods for a good harvest, a wife or a child, or some other favor.

These early Japanese beliefs developed into the religion of Shinto. The word *Shinto* means "way of the spirits," and many Japanese still follow Shinto today. Followers believe the *kami* will help only if a person is pure. Many things, such as illness, cause spiritual stains that must be cleansed by bathing and other rituals before praying.

 **Explain** How did the Japanese honor the *kami?*

History Online

Study Central Need help with early people in Japan? Visit ca.hss.glencoe.com and click on Study Central.

Section 1 Review

Reading Summary

Review the Main Ideas

- Japan's mountainous islands contain little land for farming, leading many people to turn to the sea for a living.

- Japan was settled by people from northeast Asia, organized into clans and ruled by warriors.

- While ruling Japan, Prince Shotoku made the emperor a strong ruler and set up a government similar to China's.

- Japan's first religion, Shinto, was based on the idea of nature spirits called *kami.*

What Did You Learn?

1. What skills did the Yayoi practice that they may have learned from the Chinese and Koreans?

2. What is a clan?

Critical Thinking

3. **Sequencing Information** Draw a time line. Fill in dates and information about early Japan. **CA CS2.**

```
|——+——+——+——+——+——|
300 B.C.              A.D. 646
```

4. **The Big Ideas** How did the Japanese use their surroundings to survive? **CA CS3.**

5. **Analyze** How did Shotoku strengthen Japan's government? **CA 7RC2.3**

6. **Writing Summaries** Imagine you are visiting Japan in the A.D. 300s. Write a letter to a friend summarizing what you have learned about the Shinto religion. **CA 7RC2.0; 7WA2.5**

7. **Reading Visualizing** Reread the first three paragraphs of Section 1. Does the description give you an idea of what Japan looks like? Write a short essay describing what you saw as you read. **CA 7RC2.0; 7WA2.0**

Shoguns and Samurai

Guide to Reading

History Social Science Standards

WH7.5 Students analyze the geographic, political, economic, religious, and social structures of the civilizations of Medieval Japan.

Looking Back, Looking Ahead

In the last section, you learned how Japan's leaders looked to China as a model of government. As you have learned, warlords sometimes took over parts of China. Japan had similar problems.

Focusing on the Main Ideas

- During the A.D. 700s, Japan built a strong national government at Nara, and Buddhism became a popular religion. *(page 303)*

- Japan's civilian government and the emperor came to be dominated by military rulers known as shoguns. *(page 304)*

- As the shogun's power weakened, Japan broke into warring kingdoms run by rulers known as daimyo. *(page 307)*

Locating Places
Heian (HAY•ahn)
Kamakura (kah•MAH•kuh•RAH)

Meeting People
Minamoto Yoritomo (mee•nah• moh•toh   yoh•ree•toh•moh)
Ashikaga Takauji (ah•shee•kah• gah   tah•kow•jee)

Content Vocabulary
samurai (SA•muh•RY)
shogun (SHOH•guhn)
daimyo (DY•mee•OH)
vassal (VA•suhl)
feudalism (FYOO•duhl•IH•zuhm)

Academic Vocabulary
role (ROHL)
conduct (KAHN•DUHKT)

Reading Strategy

Showing Relationships Create a diagram to show the relationship between daimyo and samurai.

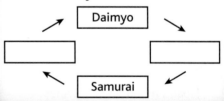

Daimyo

Samurai

NATIONAL GEOGRAPHIC Where&When?

Heian (Kyoto) **JAPAN**
KOREA   •Kamakura
Nara

A.D. 700 — **1100** — **1500**

A.D. 794
Japan's capital moved to Heian

1192
Rule by shoguns begins

1477
Civil war ends in Japan

WH7.5.1 Describe the significance of Japan's proximity to China and Korea and the intellectual, linguistic, religious, and philosophical influence of those countries on Japan.

WH7.5.4 Trace the development of distinctive forms of Japanese Buddhism.

Nara Japan

Main Idea During the A.D. 700s, Japan built a strong national government at Nara, and Buddhism became a popular religion.

Reading Connection Do you know people who got their jobs because they were friends with the boss or because the boss knew their families? Read to learn how Japan's emperor chose people for government jobs.

In the early A.D. 700s, Japan's emperors built a new capital city called Nara. For the next 100 years, Nara was the center of government and religion in Japan. Because of Nara's importance, the history of Japan during the A.D. 700s is called the Nara Period.

The city of Nara looked much like China's capital of Chang'an, only smaller. It had broad streets, large public squares, government offices, Buddhist temples, and Shinto shrines. Nobles and their families lived in large, Chinese-style homes. The typical home of a noble had wooden walls, a heavy tile roof, and polished wooden floors. It also included an inner garden.

The Emperor's Government

At Nara, Japanese emperors added to the changes begun by Prince Shotoku. They organized government officials into ranks, or levels of importance from top to bottom. However, unlike China, Japan did not use examinations to hire officials. Instead, the emperor gave the jobs to nobles from powerful families. Once a person was appointed to a job, he could pass on his office to his son or other relatives. For their services, top government officials received estates, or large farms. They also were given farmers to work the land.

The emperor's power came from his control of the land and its crops. To measure Japan's wealth, the government carried out a census. It counted all the people in the country. Census takers also compiled a list of the lands on which people lived and worked. Based on the census results, all people who held land from the emperor had to pay taxes in rice or silk. The men counted in the census had to serve in the army.

Buddhism Spreads in Japan

At the same time that the emperor's government was growing strong, Buddhism became popular in Japan. Buddhism came to Japan from Korea in the A.D. 500s. Japanese government officials and nobles were the first to accept the new religion. Then, during the A.D. 600s and A.D. 700s, Buddhism spread rapidly among the common people. It soon became a major religion in Japan and had an important **role** in government and society.

As Buddhism became more powerful, nobles who were not Buddhists began to oppose the religion. Soon, those who backed Buddhism and those who opposed it were fighting for control of the government.

▲ Built in the early A.D. 600s, the Horyuji temple in Nara, Japan, is the oldest wooden building in the world.

WH7.5.3 Describe the values, social customs, and traditions prescribed by the lord-vassal system consisting of *shogun*, *daimyo*, and *samurai* and the lasting influence of the warrior code throughout the twentieth century.
WH7.5.6 Analyze the rise of a military society in the late twelfth century and the role of the samurai in that society.

In A.D. 770 a Buddhist monk who served in the government tried to seize the throne and become emperor. He was stopped by the emperor's family and leading nobles.

Frightened by this encounter, the emperor and his family briefly turned away from Buddhism. Do you remember how the government in China attacked Buddhist monasteries when they became strong? In Japan, instead of attacking the Buddhists, the emperor simply decided to leave Nara and its many Buddhist monks.

✓ Reading Check **Explain** How did Buddhist ideas affect Japan's government?

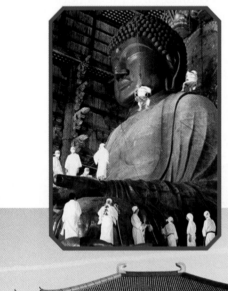

◀ Inside the Todaiji temple is Japan's largest statue of the Buddha. It is made of copper and gold, weighs 250 tons, and is nearly 50 feet tall.

▲ The Todaiji temple was first built in A.D. 752 to serve as the head temple for Buddhism in Japan. It is the world's largest wooden building. This reconstruction was built in 1692.

The Rise of the Shogun

Main Idea Japan's civilian government and the emperor came to be dominated by military rulers known as shoguns.

Reading Connection Every leader promises certain things to the people in return for their support. In the United States, what promises do politicians make to win votes? Read to learn how Japan's nobles increased their power by giving land in return for people's support.

In A.D. 794, Emperor Kammu of Japan began building a new capital city called **Heian** (HAY•ahn). This city later became known as Kyoto (kee•OH•toh). Like Nara, Heian was modeled on the Chinese city of Chang'an. It remained the official capital of Japan for more than 1,000 years.

The Government Weakens During the A.D. 800s, the emperor's power diminished. Why did this happen? After a time of strong emperors, a number of weak emperors came to the throne. Many of these emperors were still only children, and court officials known as regents had to govern for them. A regent is a person who rules for an emperor who is too young or too sick to rule. When the emperors grew up, however, the regents refused to give up their power.

Most regents came from a clan called the Fujiwara. Under the Fujiwara, Japan's emperors were honored, but they no longer had real power. Instead of ruling, these emperors spent time studying Buddhism or writing poetry in their palace at Heian.

History Online

Web Activity Visit ca.hss.glencoe.com and click on *Chapter 5—Student Web Activity* to learn more about medieval Japan.

As the Fujiwara grew wealthy and powerful in Heian, other powerful nobles gained control of much of the land in the provinces of Japan. This happened because the government gave the nobles lands as a way to pay them for their work. At the same time, new lands were settled as Japan's empire expanded. The nobles who settled farmers on these lands were allowed to keep the lands.

To keep the nobles happy, the government let them stop paying taxes, but it put them in charge of governing the lands under their control. In order to govern their lands, the nobles began collecting more taxes from the peasants working the land.

Who Were the Samurai? To protect their lands and enforce the law, nobles formed private armies. To create their armies, they gave land to warriors who agreed to fight for them. These warriors became known as **samurai** (SA•muh•RY).

In battle, samurai fought on horseback with swords, daggers, and bows and arrows. They wore armor made of leather or steel scales laced together with silk cords. Their helmets had horns or crests, and they wore masks designed to be terrifying.

The word *samurai* means "to serve." The samurai lived by a strict code of **conduct.** It was called Bushido, or "the way of the warrior." This code demanded that a samurai be devoted to his master as well as courageous, loyal, and honorable. Samurai were not supposed to care for wealth. They regarded merchants as lacking in honor.

Pledged to these principles, a samurai would rather die in battle than betray his lord. He also did not want to suffer the disgrace of being captured in battle. The distinct sense of loyalty that set apart the samurai continued into modern times. During World War II, many Japanese soldiers fought to the death rather than accept defeat or capture. Since that conflict, the Japanese have turned away from the military beliefs of the samurai.

What Is a Shogun? By the early 1100s, the most powerful Japanese families had begun fighting each other using their samurai armies. They fought over land and to gain control over the emperor and his government.

In 1180 the Gempei War began. The Gempei War was a civil war between the two most powerful clans: the Taira family

Japanese Samurai

A samurai's helmet was often individually decorated.

A samurai usually carried two swords. The longer one was called the *katana*, the shorter one was the *wakizashi*.

The *naginata* was a blade mounted on a long handle. It was used against cavalry.

A samurai's armor was made from scales of metal or leather, brightly painted, and laced together with silk or leather.

▲ At first, most samurai fought on horseback. Later samurai were foot soldiers who fought with a variety of weapons. *What was the samurai code of conduct called?*

and the Minamoto family. In 1185 the Minamoto forces defeated the Taira in a sea battle near the island of Shikoku.

The leader of the Minamoto was a man named **Minamoto Yoritomo** (mee• nah•moh•toh   yoh•ree•toh•moh). In the Japanese language, a person's family name comes first, followed by the personal name. Yoritomo was the commander of the Minamoto armies. After Yoritomo won the Gempei War, the emperor worried that the Minamoto family would try to replace the Yamato family as the rulers of Japan. He decided it would be better to reward Yoritomo to keep him loyal.

Primary Source

Bushido Code

This passage describes the samurai's Bushido.

"It is further good fortune if . . . [a servant] had wisdom and talent and can use them appropriately. But even a person who is good for nothing . . . will be a reliable retainer [servant] if only he has the determination to think earnestly of [respect and admire] his master. Having only wisdom and talent is the lowest tier [level] of usefulness."

—Yamamoto Tsunetomo, *Hagakure: The Book of the Samurai*

◀ Samurai armor

DBQ Document-Based Question

How powerful is a samurai's determination to respect and admire his master?

In 1192 the emperor gave Yoritomo the title of **shogun** (SHOH•guhn)—commander of all of the emperor's military forces. This decision created two governments in Japan. The emperor stayed in his palace at Heian with his bureaucracy. He was still officially the head of the country, but he had no power. Meanwhile the shogun set up his own government at his headquarters in **Kamakura** (kah•MAH•kuh•RAH), a small seaside town. This military government was known as a shogunate. Japan's government was run by a series of shoguns for the next 700 years.

Yoritomo proved to be a ruthless ruler. He killed most of his relatives, fearing that they would try to take power from him. Yoritomo and the shoguns after him appointed high-ranking samurai to serve as advisers and to run the provinces. Bound by an oath of loyalty, these samurai lords ruled Japan's villages, kept the peace, and gathered taxes. They became the leading group in Japanese society.

The Mongols Attack In the late 1200s, the Kamakura shogunate faced its greatest test. In 1274 and again in 1281, China's Mongol emperor Kublai Khan sent ships and warriors to invade Japan. Both times, the Mongols were defeated because violent Pacific storms smashed many of their ships. The Mongol troops who made it ashore were defeated by the Japanese.

The victorious Japanese named the typhoons *kamikaze* (KAH•mih•KAH•zee), or "divine wind," in honor of the spirits they believed had saved their islands. Much later, during World War II, Japanese pilots deliberately crashed their planes into enemy ships. They were named kamikaze pilots after the typhoons of the 1200s.

Reading Check **Identify** Who was the shogun, and why was he important?

The Daimyo Divide Japan

Main Idea   As the shogun's power weakened, Japan broke into warring kingdoms run by rulers known as daimyo.

Reading Connection Have you ever been promised something and then been upset when the promise was broken? Read to learn how Japan's shogun lost power because the samurai felt he had broken his promises.

The Kamakura shogunate ruled Japan until 1333. By that time, many samurai had become resentful. Over the years, as samurai divided their lands among their sons, the piece of land each samurai owned became smaller and smaller. Without enough land, many samurai became poor. By the 1300s, they had begun to feel that they no longer owed the shogun loyalty because he had not given them enough land.

In 1331 the emperor rebelled, and many samurai came to his aid. The revolt succeeded, but the emperor was not able to gain control of Japan because he too refused to give more land to the samurai. Instead, a general named **Ashikaga Takauji** (ah•shee•kah•gah   tah•kow•jee) turned against the emperor and made himself shogun in 1333. A new government known as the Ashikaga shogunate began.

The Ashikaga shoguns proved to be weak rulers, and revolts broke out across Japan. The country soon divided into a number of small territories. These areas were headed by powerful military lords known as **daimyo** (DY•mee•OH).

The daimyo pledged loyalty to the emperor and the shogun. However, they ruled their lands as if they were independent kingdoms. To protect their lands, the daimyo created their own local armies made up of samurai warriors, just as other nobles had done in the past.

The Way It Was

Focus on Everyday Life

Samurai The path to becoming a samurai was difficult and dangerous. Mothers in samurai families began teaching their sons Bushido at a young age. They taught their sons to place bravery, honor, and loyalty above all else. Each young warrior knew and could recite from memory the brave feats of his samurai ancestors.

For centuries, young samurai lived apart from their families in the castle of their lord or in the barracks of their lord's town. Beginning in the 1800s, samurai schools were built. At the age of 10, boys began training in martial arts and studying other subjects, such as math and astronomy. By age 16, many were warriors.

Painting of a ▶ samurai hero

Connecting to the Past
1. What lessons was the mother of a samurai responsible for teaching her young son?
2. Do you think soldiers today have a code of conduct similar to Bushido? Explain.

Many samurai became **vassals** (VA•suhlz) of a daimyo. That is, a samurai gave an oath of loyalty to his daimyo and promised to serve him in times of war. In return, each daimyo gave land to his samurai warriors—more land than they had been given by the shogun. This bond of loyalty between a lord and a vassal is known as **feudalism** (FYOO•duhl•IH•zuhm). In the next chapter, you will learn about a similar form of feudalism that arose in Europe during the Middle Ages.

With the breakdown of central government, Japan's warriors fought each other. From 1467 to 1477, the country suffered through the disastrous Onin War. During this conflict, the city of Kyoto (Heian) was almost completely destroyed.

For 100 years after the Onin War, a series of weak shoguns tried to reunite Japan. Powerful daimyo, however, resisted their control. Fighting spread throughout the country. The violence finally brought down the Ashikaga shogunate in 1567. By that time, only a handful of powerful daimyo remained. Each of these daimyo was eager to defeat his rivals and rule all of Japan.

▲ The Takamatsu castle was built in 1590. It sits on the edge of a sea and was once surrounded by moats, gates, and towers for protection.

Reading Check **Analyze** Why were shoguns unable to regain control of Japan after the Onin War?

History Online
Study Central Need help understanding the role of the samurai and shogun? Visit ca.hss.glencoe.com and click on Study Central.

Section 2 Review

Reading Summary

Review the Main Ideas

- During the Nara Period, the emperor's power grew, and Buddhism spread among Japan's common people.

- Over time, the Japanese emperors lost power to nobles and their armies of samurai. Eventually a military ruler, called a shogun, ruled the country.

- In the 1400s and 1500s, the shoguns lost power, and military lords, called daimyo, divided Japan into a number of small territories.

What Did You Learn?

1. What was a shogun? Who was the first shogun, and how did he gain his position of power?

2. What prevented the Mongol conquest of Japan?

Critical Thinking

3. **Organizing Information** Draw a diagram like the one below. Add details about the samurai, such as their weapons, dress, and beliefs. **CA 7RC2.0**

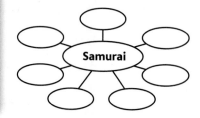

Samurai

4. **Describe** Describe events that led to the growth of Buddhism in Japan. **CA 7RC2.2**

5. **Explain** Why did the power of the Japanese emperors decline during the A.D. 800s? **CA HI2.**

6. **The Big Ideas** How was Japan's culture and society affected by war and conflict? **CA 7RC2.3**

7. **Persuasive Writing** Create a plan for government that allows the emperor, the shogun, the daimyo, and the samurai to work together. Write an essary defending your plan and explaining why it will work. **CA 7WA2.4**

Life in Medieval Japan

Guide to Reading

Looking Back, Looking Ahead

In the last section, you learned how shoguns and samurai ruled Japan. During that time, the Japanese suffered from many wars. However, Japan's economy continued to grow, and its people produced beautiful art, architecture, and literature.

Focusing on the Main Ideas

• Buddhism and Shinto shaped much of Japan's culture. These religions affected Japanese art, architecture, novels, and plays. *(page 310)*

• Some Japanese nobles, merchants, and artisans grew wealthy during the shogun period, but the lives of women remained restricted in many areas of life. *(page 314)*

Locating Places
Kyoto (kee•OH•toh)

Meeting People
Murasaki Shikibu (MUR•uh•SAH•kee shee•kee•boo)

Content Vocabulary
sect (SEHKT)
martial arts (MAHR•shuhl)
meditation (MEH•duh•TAY•shuhn)
calligraphy (kuh•LIH•gruh•fee)
tanka (TAHNG•kuh)
guild (GIHLD)

Academic Vocabulary
involve (ihn•VAHLV)
reveal (rih•VEEL)
contribute (kuhn•TRIH•byuht)

Reading Strategy
Summarizing Information Complete a diagram like the one below describing the role of women in the families of medieval Japan.

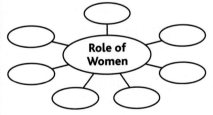

Role of Women

History Social Science Standards

WH7.5 Students analyze the geographic, political, economic, religious, and social structures of the civilizations of Medieval Japan.

NATIONAL GEOGRAPHIC Where & When?

1000   1200   1400

c. 1000 Lady Murasaki Shikibu writes *The Tale of Genji*

c. 1100s Zen Buddhism spreads in Japan

c. 1300s Noh plays first performed

JAPAN

KOREA

Heian (Kyoto)

Japanese Religion and Culture

Main Idea Buddhism and Shinto shaped much of Japan's culture. These religions affected Japanese art, architecture, novels, and plays.

Reading Connection Have you ever seen paintings, sculptures, and works of literature that have religious subjects or messages? In medieval Japan, the religions of Shinto and Buddhism greatly influenced the arts.

During the Middle Ages, many Japanese artists, scribes, traders, and diplomats visited China. Through them, great cultural exchange occurred. Much of this affected the Japanese upper class, especially in areas of government and philosophy. The Chinese also influenced literature, science, and religion.

Throughout the Middle Ages, religion was a part of everyday life for the Japanese. Most Japanese came to believe in both Buddhism and Shinto, and worshiped at Shinto shrines and Buddhist temples. To them, each religion met different needs. Shinto was concerned with daily life, while Buddhism prepared people for the life to come. During the Middle Ages, Buddhist ideas inspired many Japanese to build tem-

▲ A Zen monk meditates beside a Japanese rock garden.

ples, produce paintings, and write poems and plays.

Pure Land Buddhism
As you have already learned, Mahayana Buddhism began in India and spread to China and Korea. By the time Buddhism reached Japan, it had developed into many different **sects** (SEHKTS), or smaller religious groups.

One of the most important sects in Japan was Pure Land Buddhism. Pure Land Buddhism was a type of Mahayana Buddhism. It won many followers in Japan because of its message about a happy life after death. Pure Land Buddhists looked to Lord Amida, a buddha of love and mercy. They believed Amida had founded a paradise above the clouds. To get there, all they had to do was have faith in Amida and chant his name.

What Is Zen Buddhism?
Another important Buddhist sect in Japan was Zen. Buddhist monks brought Zen to Japan from China during the 1100s. Zen taught that people could find inner peace through self-control and a simple way of life.

Followers of Zen learned to control their bodies through **martial arts** (MAHR•shuhl), or sports that **involved** combat and self-defense. This appealed to the samurai, who trained to fight bravely and fearlessly.

Followers of Zen Buddhism also practiced **meditation** (MEH•duh•TAY•shuhn). In meditation, a person sat cross-legged and motionless for hours, with the mind cleared of all thoughts and desires. Meditation helped people to relax and find inner peace.

Art and Architecture
During the Middle Ages, the Japanese borrowed artistic ideas from China and Korea. Later they went on to develop their own styles. The arts of Japan **revealed** the Japanese love of beauty and simplicity.

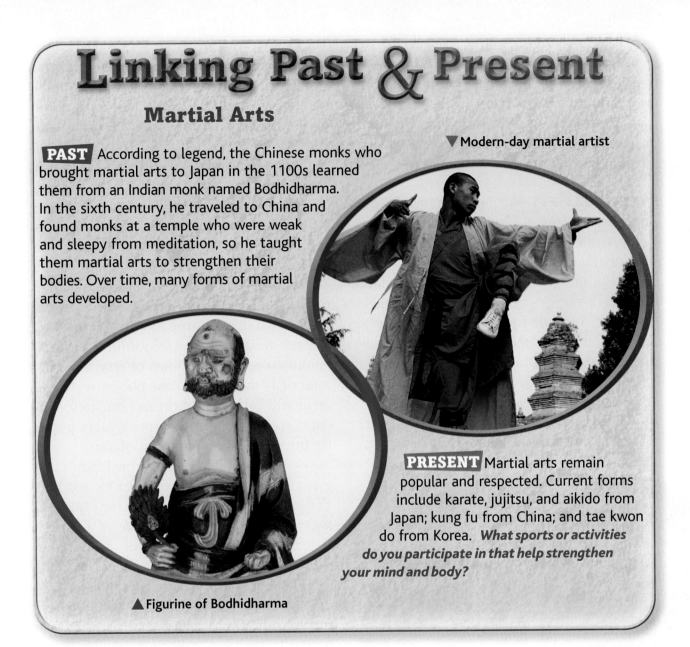

Linking Past & Present

Martial Arts

PAST According to legend, the Chinese monks who brought martial arts to Japan in the 1100s learned them from an Indian monk named Bodhidharma. In the sixth century, he traveled to China and found monks at a temple who were weak and sleepy from meditation, so he taught them martial arts to strengthen their bodies. Over time, many forms of martial arts developed.

▼ **Modern-day martial artist**

PRESENT Martial arts remain popular and respected. Current forms include karate, jujitsu, and aikido from Japan; kung fu from China; and tae kwon do from Korea. *What sports or activities do you participate in that help strengthen your mind and body?*

▲ **Figurine of Bodhidharma**

During the Middle Ages, artisans in Japan made wooden statues, furniture, and household items. On many of their works, they used a shiny black and red coating called lacquer. From the Chinese, Japanese artists learned to do landscape painting. Using ink or watercolors, they painted images of nature or battles on paper scrolls or on silk. Japanese nobles at the emperor's court learned to fold paper to make decorative objects. This art of folding paper is called origami. They also arranged flowers. Buddhist monks and the samurai turned tea drinking into a beautiful ceremony.

Builders in Japan used Chinese or Japanese designs. Shinto shrines were built in the Japanese style near a sacred rock, tree, or other natural feature. Usually a shrine was a wooden building, with a single room and a roof made of rice straw. People entered the shrine through a sacred gate called a torii (TOHR•ee).

Unlike Shinto shrines, Buddhist temples were built in the Chinese style. They had massive tiled roofs held up by thick, wooden pillars. The temples were richly decorated. They had many statues, paintings, and altars.

Around their buildings, the Japanese created gardens designed to imitate nature in a miniature form. Some of these gardens had carefully placed rocks, raked sand, and a few plants. They were built this way to create a feeling of peace and calmness.

Poems and Plays During the A.D. 500s, the Japanese borrowed China's writing system. They wrote their language in Chinese picture characters that stood for whole words. Because the Japanese and Chinese languages were so different, the Japanese found it difficult to use these characters. Then, in the A.D. 800s, they added symbols that stood for sounds, much like the letters of an alphabet. This addition made reading and writing much easier.

Calligraphy (kuh•LIH•gruh•fee), the art of writing beautifully, was much admired in Japan. Every well-educated person was expected to practice it. It was thought that a person's handwriting revealed much about his or her education, social standing, and character.

During the Middle Ages, the Japanese wrote poems, stories, and plays. Japan's oldest form of poetry was the **tanka** (TAHNG•kuh). It was an unrhymed poem of five lines. Tanka poems capture nature's beauty and the joys and sorrows of life.

By the 1600s, a new form of poetry had fully developed from the tanka tradition. Called haiku, this form was popularized by Matsuo Basho, a man of samurai descent. Haiku consisted of 3 lines of words with a total of 17 syllables. These poems were colorful and full of emotion and imagery. This short style of poetry became widely popular throughout the Japanese islands.

Women living in Heian wrote Japan's first great stories around A.D. 1000. One woman, Lady **Murasaki Shikibu** (MUR•uh•SAH•kee shee•kee•boo), wrote *The Tale of Genji*. It describes the adventures of a Japanese prince. Some people believe the work is the world's first novel, or long fictional story.

About 200 years later, Japan's writers turned out stirring tales about warriors in battle. The greatest collection was *The Tale of Heike*. It describes the fight between the Taira and the Minamoto clans.

The Japanese also created plays. The oldest type of play is called Noh. Created during the 1300s, Noh plays were used to teach Buddhist ideas. Noh plays were performed on a simple, bare stage. The actors wore masks and elaborate robes. They danced, gestured, and chanted poetry to the music of drums and flutes.

▲ Noh masks like these were often carved from a single piece of wood and were lightweight so an actor could wear it for several hours. *Why were Noh plays performed?*

Reading Check Analyze How are martial arts and meditation connected to Zen Buddhism's principle of self-control?

Biography

WH7.5.5 Study the ninth and tenth centuries' golden age of literature, art, and drama and its lasting effects on culture today, including Murasaki Shikibu's *Tale of Genji*.

▲ Murasaki Shikibu

MURASAKI SHIKIBU

c. A.D. 973–1025

Murasaki Shikibu was a great novelist and poet of the Japanese Heian period. She was one of the first modern novelists. Murasaki became famous for writing *The Tale of Genji,* but her work also included a diary and over 120 poems.

Murasaki was born into the Fujiwara clan, a noble family but not a rich family. Her father was a scholar and a governor. Murasaki's mother and older sister died when she was a child. Traditionally, children were raised by the mother and her family, but Murasaki's father decided to raise his daughter himself. He broke another custom by educating his daughter in Chinese language and literature, subjects reserved for boys.

Murasaki married and had a daughter, but her husband died after only a few years of marriage. Around that time, Murasaki began writing *The Tale of Genji* and working as an attendant to Empress Akiko. She based the novel on life at court, which she knew about through her father's job and her own life. Much about Murasaki's life—and life at the emperor's palace—is revealed in her diary. This excerpt describes the preparations for a celebration honoring the birth of a new prince:

"Even the sight of the lowest menials [servants], chattering to each other as they walked round lighting the fire baskets under the trees by the lake and arranging the food in the garden, seemed to add to the sense of occasion. Torchbearers stood everywhere at attention and the scene was as bright as day."

—Murasaki Shikibu,
The Diary of Lady Murasaki

▲ Scene from
The Tale of Genji

Then and Now

Do you keep a diary? What might you and your classmates record in a diary that would be useful to people a few centuries from now?

Economy and Society

Main Idea Some Japanese nobles, merchants, and artisans grew wealthy during the shogun period, but the lives of women remained restricted in many areas of life.

Reading Connection What determines whether a person is wealthy or poor? Read to find what contributed to the growing wealth of Japan.

Under the shoguns, Japan not only developed its arts but also produced more goods and grew richer. However, only a small number of Japanese benefited from this wealth. This group included the emperor, the nobles at his court, and leading military officials. A small but growing class of merchants and traders also began to prosper. Most Japanese were farmers who remained poor.

Farmers and Artisans Much of Japan's wealth came from the hard work of its farmers. Japanese farmers grew rice, wheat, millet, and barley. Some had their own land, but most lived and worked on the daimyo estates. Despite hardships, life improved for Japan's farmers during the 1100s. They used a better irrigation process and planted more crops. As a result, they could send more food to the markets that were developing in the towns.

At the same time, the Japanese were producing more goods. Artisans on the daimyo estates began making weapons, armor, and tools. Merchants sold these items in town markets throughout Japan. New roads made travel and trade much easier. As trade increased, each region focused on making goods that it could best produce. These goods included pottery, paper, textiles, and lacquered ware. All of these new products helped Japan's economy grow.

The capital, **Kyoto** (kee•OH•toh), became a major center of production and trade. Many artisans and merchants settled there. They formed groups called **guilds** (GIHLDZ) (or *za* in Japanese) to protect and increase their profits. The members of these guilds relied on a wealthy daimyo to protect them from rival artisans. They sold the daimyo goods that he could not get from his country estates.

Japan's wealth also came from increased trade with Korea, China, and Southeast Asia. Japanese merchants exchanged lacquered goods, sword blades, and copper for silk, dyes, pepper, books, and porcelain.

◀ **This painting shows Japanese farmers working the land.**
What were some crops grown by medieval Japanese farmers?

The Role of Women During the Middle Ages, a Japanese family included grandparents, parents, and children in the same household. A man headed the family. A woman was expected to obey her father, husband, and son. In wealthy families, parents arranged the marriages of their children to increase the family's wealth.

In early Japan, about the time of Prince Shotoku, wealthy women enjoyed a high position in society. There were several women rulers, and women could own property. When Japan became a warrior society with samurai and daimyo, upper-class women lost these freedoms.

In farm families, women had a greater say in whom they married. However, they worked long hours in the fields. In addition, they cooked, spun and wove cloth, and cared for their children. In towns, wives of artisans and merchants helped with family businesses and ran their homes.

Despite the lack of freedom, some women managed to **contribute** to Japan's culture in remarkable ways. These talented women gained fame as artists, writers, and even warriors. In *The Tale of the Heike,* one female samurai named Tomoe is described this way:

> ❝ **Tomoe was indescribably beautiful; the fairness of her face and the richness of her hair were startling to behold. Even so, she was a fearless rider and a woman skilled with the bow. Once her sword was drawn, even the gods . . . feared to fight against her. Indeed, she was a match for a thousand.** ❞
>
> —Heike Monogatori,
> *The Tale of the Heike*

✓ **Reading Check** **Identify** Which groups in Japan benefited from the country's wealth?

History Online

Study Central Need help with Japanese culture? Visit ca.hss.glencoe.com and click on Study Central.

Section 3 Review

Reading Summary

Review the Main Ideas

• In medieval Japan, several forms of Buddhism, along with Shinto, were practiced, and the arts, architecture, and literature flourished.

• During the time of the shoguns, Japan's economy grew stronger. In the family, women lost some of their freedoms as Japan became a warrior society.

What Did You Learn?

1. How did the Shinto and Buddhist religions meet different needs in Japan?

2. What were Noh plays, and how were they performed?

Critical Thinking

3. **Organizing Information** Draw a table to show the characteristics of Pure Land Buddhism and Zen Buddhism. **CA** 7RC2.0

Pure Land Buddhism	Zen Buddhism

4. **The Big Ideas** How did religion influence Japan's culture? Which religion had the most influence? Why? **CA** HI2.

5. **Analyze** Why do you think women lost some of their freedoms when Japan became a warrior society? **CA** 7RC2.2

6. **Analysis** **Analyzing Sources** What do Japanese novels, plays, and poems tell us about medieval Japan's society? What forms of writing reflect our society today? **CA** HR4.

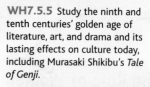

WH7.5.5 Study the ninth and tenth centuries' golden age of literature, art, and drama and its lasting effects on culture today, including Murasaki Shikibu's *Tale of Genji*.

Japanese Society and Art

People in medieval Japan used symbols and images to explain their ideas about life. This was reflected in their literature, even in works about normal, everyday things.

Read the passages on pages 316 and 317, and answer the questions that follow.

Painting of a Samurai ▶

Reader's Dictionary

measure (MEH • zhuhr): amount or portion

plea (PLEE): request

haze (HAYZ): light fog

twilight (TWY • LYT): before dark but after sunset

fragile (FRA • juhl): easily broken

Noh Drama: *Taniko*

Noh stories often conveyed images and ideas by having the chorus talk while the main character acted out the scene. In the following passage from the play Taniko, a young boy wishes to accompany his teacher on a dangerous pilgrimage to pray for his sick mother.

TEACHER.

. . . [Y]our son says he is going to come with us. I told him he could not leave you when you were ill and that it would be a difficult and dangerous road. I said it was quite impossible for him to come. But he says he must come to pray for your health. What is to be done?

MOTHER.

I have listened to your words. I do not doubt what the boy says,—that he would gladly go with you to the mountains: (*to the* BOY) but since the day your father left us I have had none but you at my side . . . Give back the **measure** of my love. Let your love keep you with me.

BOY.

This is all as you say. . . . Yet nothing shall move me from my purpose. I must climb this difficult path and pray for your health in this life.

CHORUS.

They saw no **plea** could move him. . . .
The mother said,
"I have no strength left;
If indeed it must be,
Go with the Master."

—Zenchiku, *Taniko*

Haiku

Haiku is a poem made up of seventeen syllables. The poems are intended to create a visual image in a very short space. The following are some haiku written by Matsuo Basho. The English translations do not always have seventeen syllables.

On the Road to Nara
Oh, these spring days!
 A nameless little mountain,
  wrapped in morning **haze!**

Clouds
Clouds come from time to time—
 and bring to men a chance to rest
  from looking at the moon.

The End of Summer
The beginning of fall:
 the ocean, the rice fields—
  one green for all!

—Harold G. Henderson, *An Introduction to Haiku*

The Tale of Genji

The Tale of Genji *is the story of a young man searching for the meaning of life. In this passage, Genji is sorrowful, for he does not have the companionship of the woman he loves. He shares his thoughts with two companions.*

"Very little in this life has really satisfied me, and despite my high birth I always think how much less fortunate my destiny has been than other people's. The Buddha must have wanted me to know that the world slips away from us and plays us false. I who long set myself to ignore this truth have suffered in the **twilight** of my life so awful and so final a blow that I have at last seen the extent of my failings, but while no attachments bind me any longer, it will be a fresh sorrow to leave you both behind, when I now know you so much better than before. Ties like ours are **fragile**. Oh, I know that I should not feel this way!"

—Murasaki Shikibu, *The Tale of Genji*

▲ **Murasaki Shikibu**

DBQ Document-Based Questions

Noh Drama: Taniko

1. Why does the boy want to go on the pilgrimage?
2. Why do you think the boy decided to go pray for his mother rather than stay with her?

Haiku

3. What images are presented in the first haiku?
4. In the second poem, what seems to be implied about the purpose of clouds?
5. In the third poem, what does "one green for all" mean?

The Tale of Genji

6. What does Genji mean when he says that the Buddha is trying to teach him that the world slips away?
7. Why is Genji sad about leaving the two companions?

Read to Write

8. Using all three primary sources, write an essay describing different Japanese ideas about life. How do you think the writer of the haiku would react to *The Tale of Genji*?
   `CA 7WA2.2` `CA HR5.`

Review Content Vocabulary

Write the key term that completes each sentence.

a. tanka   e. shogun
b. daimyo   f. guilds
c. clans   g. samurai
d. sects   h. meditation

1. The ___ was the military leader of Japan.

2. Many artisans and merchants formed ___ for protection and profit.

3. The Yayoi formed ___ that were headed by a small group of warriors.

4. In ___, a person clears the mind of all thoughts and desires.

5. The ___ is an unrhymed poem of five lines.

6. Each vassal gave an oath of loyalty to his ___.

7. The private armies of Japanese nobles were made up of ___.

8. Buddhism was divided into many different ___.

Review the Main Ideas

Section 1 • Early Japan

9. How did geography shape Japanese society?

10. How did Shotoku use Chinese government and culture as a model?

Section 2 • Shoguns and Samurai

11. Describe the roles of shoguns.

12. What happened when the shogun's power weakened?

Section 3 • Life in Medieval Japan

13. How did religion shape Japan's culture?

14. How did the shogun period affect different groups of Japanese people?

Critical Thinking

15. **Analyze** Why were the early Japanese people so independent? **CA 7RC2.0**

16. **Contrast** What were the major differences between the reign of the shogun and the rule of the daimyo? **CA HI2.**

Geography Skills

Study the map below and answer the following questions.

17. **Place** Which of the four major Japanese islands has been home to the country's major cities? **CA CS3.**

18. **Human/Environment Interaction** How did Japan's geography and location help it become a center of production and trade? **CA CS3.**

19. **Location** Identify present-day countries, states, or provinces that are made up largely of islands. How are they similar to and different from the Japanese islands? **CA CS3.**

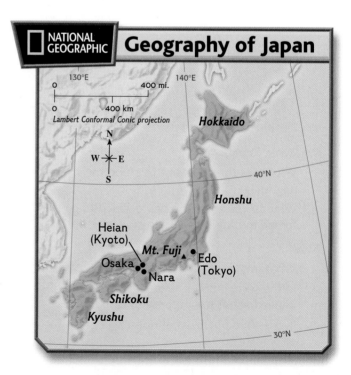

NATIONAL GEOGRAPHIC

Geography of Japan

Read to Write

20. **The Big Ideas** **Writing Research Reports**
Review this chapter and conduct research to gather information about the Mongols' attack on the Kamakura shogunate. Write an essay describing how this attack affected Japan. What major changes occurred? **CA 7WA2.3**

21. **Using Your** **FOLDABLES** Write a poem, series of journal entries, or short story using the main ideas and supporting details from your completed foldable. **CA 7WA2.1**

Using Academic Vocabulary

22. Using the words below, write a short essay summarizing the events discussed in Section 2. Be sure to include details about the rise of shoguns and daimyo, and the role of the samurai.

portion	conduct
occur	involve
role	contribute

Linking Past and Present

23. **Analyzing Art** Japanese art, architecture, and literature reflected the Japanese love of beauty and simplicity. What values are reflected in present-day art? **CA HR4.**

Reviewing Skills

24. **Reading Skill** **Visualizing** Read the following excerpt from page 305 in Section 2:

> In battle, samurai fought on horseback with swords, daggers, and bows and arrows. They wore armor made of leather or steel scales laced together with silk cords. Their helmets had horns or crests, and they wore masks designed to be terrifying.

What do you imagine as you read this passage? What words or phrases help you create a mental picture of the samurai warrior? Now look at the drawing of the samurai at the bottom of that page. How does it compare to the image you visualized? Write a short essay explaining the similarities and differences. **CA 7RC2.1**

25. **Analysis Skill** **Analyzing Primary Sources**
Reread the biography of Murasaki Shikibu on page 313. What kinds of things may have influenced how she wrote about palace life? How would some of these same events seem different to another person, such as a servant or the emperor? **CA HR4.; HR5.**

Standards Practice

Use the map below to answer the following question.

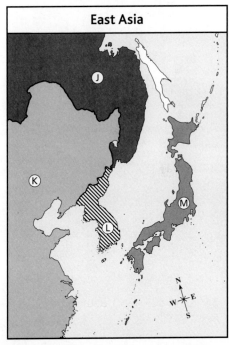

East Asia

26 Which areas on the map represent Japan's neighboring countries of China and Korea?

A M & K

B L & M

C K & L

D J & M

Medieval Europe

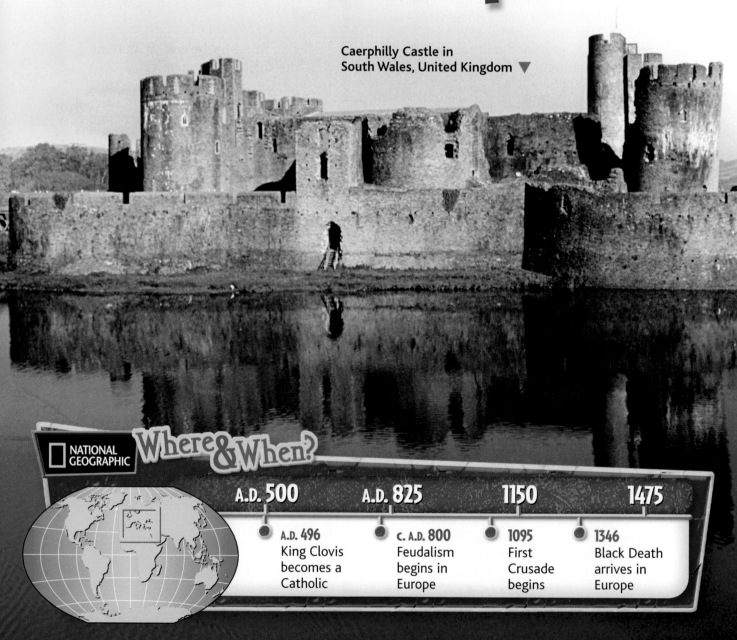

Caerphilly Castle in
South Wales, United Kingdom ▼

NATIONAL GEOGRAPHIC **Where & When?**

A.D. 500	A.D. 825	1150	1475
A.D. 496 King Clovis becomes a Catholic	**C. A.D. 800** Feudalism begins in Europe	**1095** First Crusade begins	**1346** Black Death arrives in Europe

The Big Ideas

History Online

Chapter Overview Visit
ca.hss.glencoe.com for a
preview of Chapter 6.

 Section 1 **The Early Middle Ages**

The interaction of different societies brings about the development of new ideas, art, and technology. During the Middle Ages, Western Europe built a new civilization based on Christian, Roman, and Germanic ways.

 Section 2 **Feudalism**

Different social, economic, and political classes can exist in a society. A new social and governmental structure called feudalism arose in Europe.

 Section 3 **Kingdoms and Crusades**

Studying the past helps to understand the present. The kingdoms of Europe, especially England, established new systems of government that influence modern democratic thought.

 Section 4 **The Church and Society**

Religion influences how civilization develops and how culture spreads. Religion in medieval Europe helped to shape European culture.

 Section 5 **The Late Middle Ages**

Conflict often brings about great change. Disease and war took the lives of millions of people in the late Middle Ages.

View the Chapter 6 video in the Glencoe Video Program.

Sequencing Information *Make this foldable to help you sequence important events that occurred in medieval Europe.*

Step 1 *Fold two sheets of paper in half from top to bottom. Cut each in half.*

Cut along the fold lines.

Step 2 *Turn and fold the four pieces in half from top to bottom.*

Reading and Writing
As you read the chapter, write the important events and dates that occurred in medieval Europe on each section of your time line.

Step 3 *Tape the ends of the pieces together (overlapping the edges slightly) to make an accordion time line.*

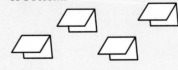
Pieces of tape

 6 Get Ready to Read

Making Inferences

Reading Skill

1 Learn It!

You naturally make inferences about things you read, see, and hear every day. To make inferences means to "read between the lines" or to draw conclusions that are not directly stated. By drawing upon your prior knowledge and experience, you are able to interpret clues and details. Read this paragraph about Europe's geography from Section 1.

> Now that **Rome no longer united people**, Europe's geography began to play a more significant role in shaping events. Europe is a continent, but it is also a very large peninsula made up of many smaller **peninsulas**.
>
> — *from page 325*

Use this think-through chart to help you make inferences.

Text	Question	Inference
Rome no longer united people	What happened to the Roman Empire?	Had it declined? Who was now in control? Was there another major empire?
geography began to play a more important role in shaping events	What kind of role?	How can geography affect events? How important has geography been at other times or places in history?
	What type of events?	What sort of events could have been affected and how? Trade? Wars? Movements of peoples?
peninsulas	What is special about peninsulas?	Is it because they are surrounded by water? Are they tough to access or easy to defend? Were only peninsulas important? How about mountains or rivers?

Reading Tip

Making inferences sometimes involves using other reading skills, such as questioning and predicting.

2 Practice It!

Read the paragraph below and pay attention to highlighted words. Create your own think-through chart to help you make further inferences about life in feudal times. You might want to use a chart similar to the one on the previous page, with the same labels: *Text, Questions,* and *Inference.* Read pages 338–340 to see if your inferences were correct.

Read to Write · · · ·
Read **Who Was Thomas Aquinas?** in Section 4. Write down the inferences you can make about the kind of person you think Thomas Aquinas was. Read the **Biography** of Thomas Aquinas on page 362 to see if your inferences were correct.

Knights followed certain rules called the code of chivalry (SHIH • vuhl • ree). A knight was expected to obey his lord, to be brave, to show respect to women of noble birth, to honor the church, and to help people. A knight was also expected to be honest and to fight fairly against his enemies. The code of chivalry became the guide to good behavior. Many of today's ideas about manners come from the code of chivalry.

— *from page 338*

▲ **Medieval knight on horseback**

3 Apply It!

Inferring can help you understand an author's viewpoint. With a partner, read the excerpt from the Magna Carta on page 349. Discuss inferences you can make about the author.

Guide to Reading

Looking Back, Looking Ahead

After the fall of Rome came a period called the Middle Ages, or medieval times. It is a fitting name for the period that lies between ancient and modern times.

Focusing on the Main Ideas

- Geography influenced where medieval Europeans settled and what they did. *(page 325)*

- The Franks, Angles, and Saxons of Western Europe built new societies and defended them against Muslims, Magyars, and Vikings. *(page 326)*

- The Catholic Church spread Christianity through Western Europe. *(page 331)*

Meeting People

Clovis (KLOH•vuhs)
Charles Martel (mahr•TEHL)
Charlemagne (SHAHR•luh•MAYN)
Gregory VII
Henry IV

Locating Places

Aachen (AH•kuhn)
Scandinavia (SKAN•duh•NAY•vee•uh)
Holy Roman Empire

Content Vocabulary

fjord (fee•AWRD)
missionary (MIH•shuh•NEHR•ee)
excommunicate (EHK•skuh•MYOO•nuh•KAYT)
concordat (kuhn•KAWR•DAT)

Academic Vocabulary

significant (sihg•NIH•fih•kuhnt)
instance (IHN•stuhns)
enable (ih•NAY•buhl)
exclude (ihks•KLOOD)

Reading Strategy

Organizing Information Create a table to show the major accomplishments of medieval leaders.

Leader	Major Accomplishments

History Social Science Standards

WH7.6 Students analyze the geographic, political, economic, religious, and social structures of the civilizations of Medieval Europe.

NATIONAL GEOGRAPHIC Where & When?

A.D. 500	A.D. 800	1100

A.D. 496 King Clovis becomes Catholic

A.D. 800 Charlemagne is crowned by pope

c. 1050 Most people in Western Europe are Catholic

SCANDINAVIA
BRITAIN
Aachen • HOLY ROMAN EMPIRE
• Rome
SPAIN

WH7.6.1 Study the geography of Europe and the Eurasian land mass, including their location, topography, waterways, vegetation, and climate and their relationship to ways of life in Medieval Europe.

The Geography of Europe

Main Idea Geography influenced where medieval Europeans settled and what they did.

Reading Connection If you wanted to go sledding or swimming, where would you go? Your answer will be based partly on geography. Read to learn how geography shaped life for people in Europe during the Middle Ages.

The Roman Empire had united all the land surrounding the Mediterranean Sea. When the last Roman emperor in the West fell from power in A.D. 476, that unity was lost. Western Europe was divided into many kingdoms as wave after wave of Germanic invaders swept south and west, conquering large areas of Europe.

Now that Rome no longer united people, Europe's geography began to play a more **significant** role in shaping events. Europe is a continent, but it is also a very large peninsula made up of many smaller peninsulas. As a result, most of Europe lies within 300 miles (483 km) of an ocean or a sea. This encouraged trade and fishing and helped Europe's economy to grow.

Rivers also played an important role in Europe. The Rhine, Danube, Vistula, Volga, Seine, and Po Rivers made it easy to travel into the interior of Europe and encouraged people to trade.

The seas and rivers provided safety as well as opportunities for trade. The English Channel, for **instance,** separated Britain and Ireland from the rest of Europe. As a result,

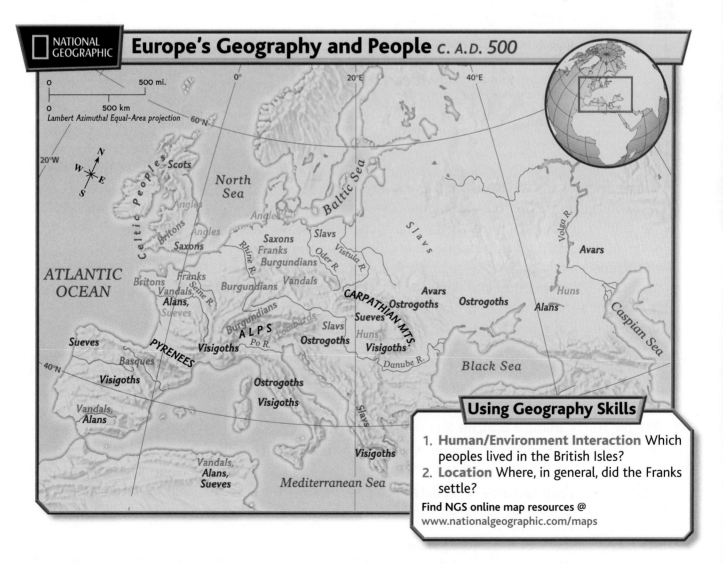

NATIONAL GEOGRAPHIC

Europe's Geography and People c. A.D. 500

Using Geography Skills

1. **Human/Environment Interaction** Which peoples lived in the British Isles?
2. **Location** Where, in general, did the Franks settle?

Find NGS online map resources @ www.nationalgeographic.com/maps

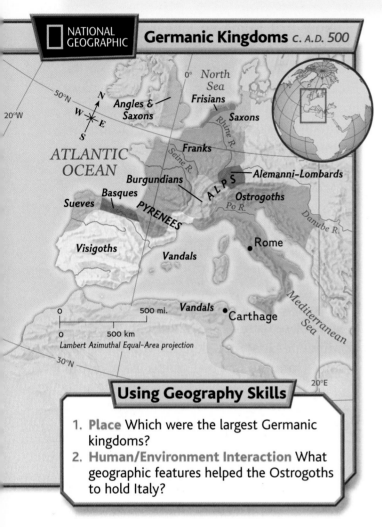

NATIONAL GEOGRAPHIC

Germanic Kingdoms C. A.D. 500

Using Geography Skills

1. **Place** Which were the largest Germanic kingdoms?
2. **Human/Environment Interaction** What geographic features helped the Ostrogoths to hold Italy?

The Germanic Kingdoms

Main Idea The Franks, Angles, and Saxons of Western Europe built new societies and defended them against Muslims, Magyars, and Vikings.

Reading Connection Have you ever moved to a new place? What adjustments did you have to make? Read to learn how the Germanic peoples who invaded Europe had to adjust to the lands they occupied.

After Rome fell, Western Europe was divided into many kingdoms. These kingdoms developed different societies based on their locations. The Visigoths in Spain and the Ostrogoths in Italy were close to the center of the old Roman Empire. As a result, they adopted many Roman ways. People farther from Rome held on to more of their Germanic traditions.

In Britain as the empire began to weaken, Roman culture eroded quickly. In the A.D. 300s, the Roman legions in Britain began heading home to fight Germanic invaders. By the early A.D 400s, the Romans had pulled out of England. Soon the Angles and Saxons invaded Britain from Denmark and Germany. In time, they became the Anglo-Saxons.

When the Angles and Saxons conquered southeastern Britain, they pushed aside the people living there. These people were called the Celts (KEHLTS). Some Celts fled north and west to the mountains. Others went to Ireland. Scottish, Welsh, and Irish people today are descendants of the Celts.

Who Were the Franks? During the A.D. 400s, a Germanic people called the Franks settled the area that is now France. In A.D. 496 King **Clovis** (KLOH•vuhs) of the Franks became a Catholic. This won him the support of the Romans living in his kingdom. Before long, nearly all of the Franks became Catholic.

people there were sheltered from the many wars fought on Europe's mainland. They were able to develop their own distinct ways of life. Within Europe, wide rivers like the Rhine also kept people separated and **enabled** different cultures to develop.

Europe also has many mountain ranges. In the east, the Carpathians cut off what is now Ukraine and Russia from southeast Europe. In the middle, the Alps separated Italy from central Europe. To the southwest, the Pyrenees isolated Spain and Portugal. The mountains, like the rivers, made it difficult for one group to rule all of Europe and encouraged the development of independent kingdoms.

✓ Reading Check **Identify** What did Europe's seas and rivers provide for its people?

After Clovis died, his sons divided the kingdom among themselves. Later, their sons divided these kingdoms even further. These kings often fought over land. While they fought, the nobles under them took over many royal duties. The most important of these nobles was called the "mayor of the palace." By A.D. 700, the mayors were giving out land, settling disputes, and fighting their own wars.

Of all the mayors, the most powerful was **Charles Martel** (mahr•TEHL). He wanted to unite all the Frankish nobles under his rule. The Catholic Church wanted to restore order in the lands of the Western Roman Empire and was willing to support Germanic rulers who were Catholic. The pope—the head of the Catholic Church—offered his support to Charles Martel.

First, however, Martel had to defend Europe from invasion. In A.D. 711 a Muslim army from North Africa conquered Spain. Later, Muslim forces invaded southern France. In A.D. 732 Charles Martel led the Franks against the Muslims. He defeated them at the Battle of Tours. This stopped the Muslim advance, and Christianity remained Europe's major religion.

When Charles Martel died, his son Pepin (PEH•puhn) became mayor of the palace. With the help of the pope and most Frankish nobles, Pepin became the new king of the Franks. When a Germanic group called the Lombards threatened the pope, Pepin took his army into Italy and defeated them. He donated the land he had conquered to the pope. The pope ruled these lands as if he were a king, and they became known as the Papal States.

Who Was Charlemagne? After Pepin died, his son Charles became king. Like his father, Charles went to the aid of the pope when the Lombards tried to regain their territory. He also invaded eastern Germany and defeated the Saxons. He ordered them to convert to Christianity. He then invaded Spain and gained control of the northeastern corner from the Muslims.

By A.D. 800, Charles's kingdom had grown into an empire. It covered much of western and central Europe. Charles's

The Crowning of Charlemagne

◄ In A.D. 800 the pope crowned Charlemagne "Emperor of the Romans," officially creating a new Roman Empire. *How large was Charlemagne's empire in A.D. 800?*

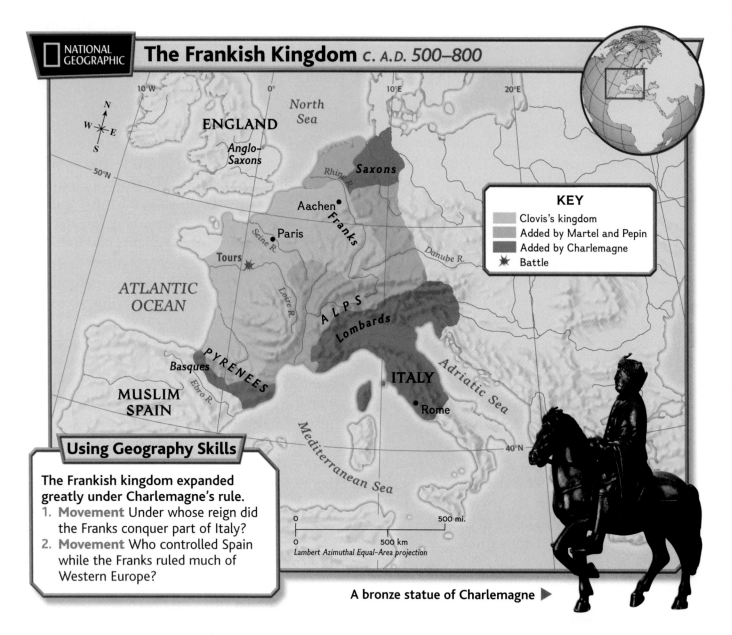

The Frankish Kingdom C. A.D. 500–800

KEY

- Clovis's kingdom
- Added by Martel and Pepin
- Added by Charlemagne
- ✳ Battle

North Sea

ENGLAND

Anglo-Saxons

Saxons

Rhine R.

Aachen

Franks

Paris

Seine R.

Tours

Loire R.

ALPS

Danube R.

Lombards

ATLANTIC OCEAN

PYRENEES

Basques

Ebro R.

MUSLIM SPAIN

ITALY

Rome

Adriatic Sea

Mediterranean Sea

0   500 mi.

0   500 km

Lambert Azimuthal Equal-Area projection

Using Geography Skills

The Frankish kingdom expanded greatly under Charlemagne's rule.

1. **Movement** Under whose reign did the Franks conquer part of Italy?
2. **Movement** Who controlled Spain while the Franks ruled much of Western Europe?

A bronze statue of Charlemagne ▶

conquests earned him the name of **Charlemagne** (SHAHR•luh•MAYN), or Charles the Great.

The pope was impressed with Charlemagne. On Christmas day in A.D. 800, Charlemagne was worshiping at the church of St. Peter in Rome. After the service, the pope placed a crown on Charlemagne's head and declared him the new Roman emperor. Charlemagne was pleased but also concerned. He did not want people to think the pope had the power to choose who was emperor.

Charlemagne made **Aachen** (AH•kuhn) the capital of his empire. To uphold his

laws, he set up courts throughout the empire. Nobles called counts ran the courts. To keep the counts under control, Charlemagne sent out inspectors called "the lord's messengers" to make sure the counts conducted their duties properly.

Unlike other earlier Frankish rulers, Charlemagne was an advocate of education. He had tried late in life to learn to write and wanted his people to be educated too. He asked a scholar named Alcuin (AL•kwuhn) to start a school in one of the royal palaces. Alcuin trained the children of government officials. His students studied religion, Latin, music, literature, and arithmetic.

Biography

CHARLEMAGNE
A.D. 742–814

Charles the Great (Charlemagne) became king of the Franks at age 29. He married and divorced many different women and had at least 18 children.

Charlemagne was an intelligent person. He studied many subjects and especially enjoyed astronomy. He could speak many languages, including German and Latin. He also could read but had trouble writing. Einhard, the king's historian and scribe, wrote that Charlemagne "used to keep tablets under his pillow in order that at leisure hours he might accustom his hand to form the letters; but as he began these efforts so late in life, they met with ill success."

Charlemagne was disappointed to learn that the Franks were not as educated as the people of Britain and Ireland. In A.D. 782 he arranged for several famous scholars to come to his capital in Aachen and create a school in the royal palace. During his reign, schools opened throughout his empire, and many people were educated.

▲ Charlemagne

◀ The Palatine Chapel at Charlemagne's palace in Aachen

"No one shall . . . be kept back from the right path of justice by . . . fear of the powerful."

—Charlemagne, as quoted in "The World of Charlemagne"

Then and Now

Charlemagne realized the importance of education. He arranged reading and writing lessons for his people. What types of school programs does our government fund?

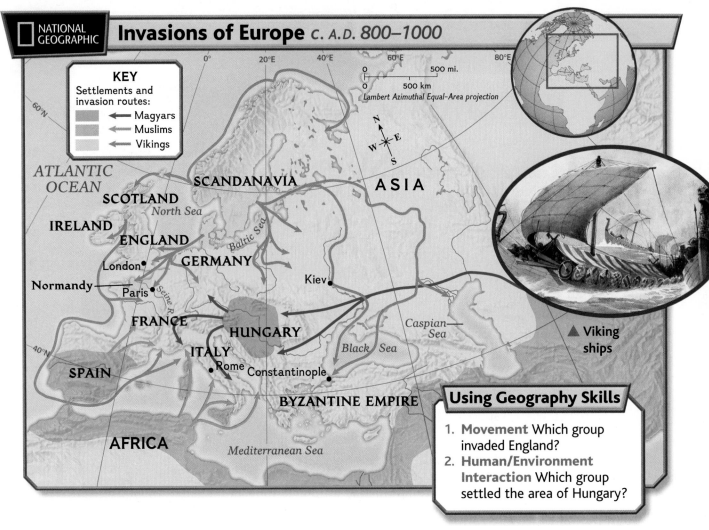

Invasions of Europe C. A.D. 800–1000

KEY
Settlements and invasion routes:
← Magyars
← Muslims
← Vikings

ATLANTIC OCEAN

SCANDANAVIA

ASIA

SCOTLAND

North Sea

IRELAND

ENGLAND

Baltic Sea

London

GERMANY

Normandy

Paris

Seine R.

Kiev

FRANCE

HUNGARY

Caspian Sea

ITALY

Rome

Black Sea

Constantinople

SPAIN

BYZANTINE EMPIRE

AFRICA

Mediterranean Sea

500 mi.
500 km
Lambert Azimuthal Equal-Area projection

▲ Viking ships

Using Geography Skills

1. **Movement** Which group invaded England?
2. **Human/Environment Interaction** Which group settled the area of Hungary?

Europe Is Invaded After Charlemagne died in A.D. 814, his empire did not last long. His son Louis was not a strong leader, and after Louis died, Louis's sons divided the empire into three kingdoms.

These three kingdoms were weakened further by a wave of invaders who swept across Europe in the A.D. 800s and A.D. 900s. From the south came Muslims, who raided France and Italy from Spain and North Africa. From the east came the Magyars, a nomadic people who had settled in Hungary. From **Scandinavia** (SKAN•duh•NAY•vee•uh) came the Vikings, whose raids terrified all of Europe.

Scandinavia is in northern Europe. Norway, Sweden, and Denmark are all part of Scandinavia today. Much of Scandinavia has a long, jagged coastline. It has many **fjords** (fee•AWRDS), or steep-sided valleys that are inlets of the sea. The Viking people lived in villages in the fjords. They were known as the Norsemen, or "north men."

Scandinavia has little farmland. This forced the Vikings to rely on the sea for food and trade. They became expert sailors and built sturdy boats called longboats. These boats could survive the rough Atlantic and also navigate shallow rivers.

In the A.D. 700s and A.D. 800s, the Vikings began raiding Europe, probably because their population had grown too big to support itself at home. The word *viking* comes from their word for raiding. They robbed villages and churches, carrying off

WH7.6.2 Describe the spread of Christianity north of the Alps and the roles played by the early church and by monasteries in its diffusion after the fall of the western half of the Roman Empire. WH7.6.4 Demonstrate an understanding of the conflict and cooperation between the Papacy and European monarchs (e.g., Charlemagne, Gregory VII, Emperor Henry IV). WH7.6.8 Understand the importance of the Catholic church as a political, intellectual, and aesthetic institution (e.g., founding of universities, political and spiritual roles of the clergy, creation of monastic and mendicant religious orders, preservation of the Latin language and religious texts, St. Thomas Aquinas's synthesis of classical philosophy with Christian theology, and the concept of "natural law").

grain, animals, and anything else of value. They even conquered part of western France. This area was named Normandy, after the Norsemen who ruled it.

The Holy Roman Empire
The raids by Muslims, Magyars, and Vikings helped to destroy the Frankish kingdoms. In the A.D. 900s, the eastern Frankish kingdom, which became known as Germany, was divided into many tiny states ruled by counts, dukes, and other nobles. In A.D. 911 a group of these nobles sought to unite Germany by electing a king. The king did not have much power, however, because the nobles wanted to remain independent.

One of the stronger kings of Germany was Otto I (AH•toh). He fought the Magyars and sent troops into Italy to protect the pope. To reward Otto for his help, the pope declared him emperor of the Romans in A.D. 962. Otto's territory, which included most of Germany and northern Italy, became known as the **Holy Roman Empire.**

Most of the emperors of the Holy Roman Empire were not very powerful. Two of the strongest ones, Frederick I and Frederick II, tried to unite northern Italy and Germany under a single ruler with a strong central government in the 1100s and 1200s. The popes fought against these plans because they did not want the emperor to control them. They banded together with Italy's cities to resist the emperors' forces. As a result, both Germany and Italy remained divided into small kingdoms until the 1800s.

✓ Reading Check **Explain** Who were the Vikings, and why did they raid Europe?

The Rise of the Catholic Church

Main Idea The Catholic Church spread Christianity through Western Europe.

Reading Connection Do you have a goal that you would devote your life to reaching? Read to learn the goals of the Catholic Church in the early Middle Ages.

Both religion and geography contributed to shaping life in Europe. By the time the Western Roman Empire collapsed, Christianity had become the official religion of Rome. After the Roman government fell apart, the Roman Catholic Church began to play an important role in the growth of a new civilization in Western Europe.

Why Were Monks Important? At the time Rome fell, much of northwest Europe was not yet Christian. One exception was Ireland. In the A.D. 400s, a priest named Patrick traveled to Ireland, where he spread the Christian message and set up churches and monasteries. For

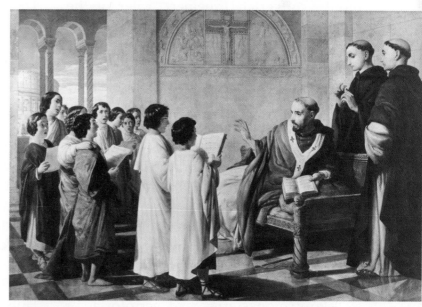
▲ Pope Gregory I is shown teaching boys the songs that became known as Gregorian chants. *Which area of northwest Europe had accepted Christianity before the fall of the Western Roman Empire?*

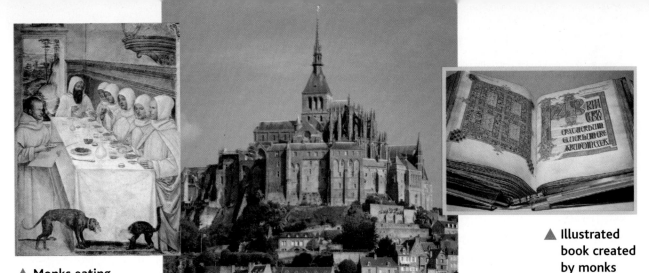

▲ Monks eating together in a monastery

▲ The monastery at Mont St. Michel in France is a beautiful work of architecture that took several hundred years to complete. *How did monasteries help local people in Europe?*

▲ Illustrated book created by monks

several hundred years, Irish monks played an important role in preserving Roman learning and passing it on to the people of Europe.

Patrick's success inspired others, including Pope Gregory I, or Gregory the Great. Gregory I was pope from A.D. 590 to A.D. 604. He wanted all of Europe to become Christian, and he asked monks to become **missionaries** (MIH•shuh•NEHR•eez)—people who are sent out to teach their religion.

In A.D. 597 Gregory sent 40 monks to southern Britain to teach Christianity. The monks converted Ethelbert, ruler of the kingdom of Kent. Ethelbert allowed the missionaries to build a church in his capital city of Canterbury. Meanwhile, Irish monks brought Christianity to northern Britain. By A.D. 800, monks were spreading Christianity throughout Europe. Most people in Western Europe had become Catholics by 1050.

Monasteries played an important role in medieval Europe. Monks schooled people, provided food and rest to travelers, and offered medical care for the sick. They taught carpentry and weaving and developed better methods of farming. They also helped to preserve knowledge.

Many monasteries had scriptoria, or writing rooms, where monks made copies of important works. The monks copied Christian writings, including the Bible, as well as works of Roman and Greek writers. The literary efforts of these monks helped to preserve the Latin language.

Over time, monasteries began to play a role in Europe's politics. Monks took a vow of poverty, wore simple clothes, and ate simple food, but their monasteries could make money. Each monastery produced goods and owned land, and over time many of them became wealthy. The leader of a monastery is called an abbot (A•buht), and many abbots became involved in politics. They served as advisers to kings and acted as rulers of the lands near their monasteries.

Why Is Gregory VII Important? The growing role of Church leaders in Europe's politics caused many arguments over who was in charge. Kings wanted Church leaders to obey them, while the pope claimed he could crown kings.

In 1073 **Gregory VII** was elected pope. He wanted to stop nobles and kings from interfering in Church affairs. He issued a decree, or order, forbidding kings from appointing high-ranking Church officials.

The pope's decree angered **Henry IV,** the Holy Roman emperor. For many years, the Holy Roman emperor had appointed bishops in Germany. Without them, Henry IV risked losing power to the nobles.

Henry refused to obey Gregory. He declared that Gregory was no longer pope. Gregory then stated that Henry was no longer emperor. He **excommunicated** (EHK•skuh•MYOO•nuh•KAY•tuhd) Henry. This means to **exclude** a person from church membership. Catholics believed that if they were excommunicated, they could not go to heaven.

When the German nobles defended the pope, Henry backed down. He traveled to Italy and stood barefoot in the snow outside the pope's castle asking to be forgiven. Gregory forgave Henry, but the German nobles still chose a new king. When Gregory accepted the new king as emperor, Henry went to war. He captured Rome and named a new pope. Gregory's allies drove out Henry's forces, but the dispute was not resolved.

In 1122 a new pope and the German king finally agreed that only the pope could choose bishops, but only the emperor could give them jobs in the government. This deal, called the Concordat of Worms, was signed in the city of Worms. A **concordat** (kuhn•KAWR•DAT) is an agreement between the pope and the ruler of a country.

By the time Innocent III became pope in 1198, the Catholic Church was at the height of its power. Innocent was able to control kings. If a ruler did not obey, Innocent would excommunicate him or issue an interdict (IHN•tuhr•DIHKT) against the ruler's people. An interdict forbids priests from providing Christian rituals to a group of people. The pope anticipated that by using an interdict, local people would pressure their ruler to obey.

✓ **Reading Check** **Contrast** How did Gregory VII and Henry IV disagree?

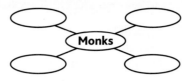

History Online

Study Central Need help understanding Europe in the early Middle Ages? Visit ca.hss.glencoe.com and click on Study Central.

Section ❶ Review

Reading Summary

Review the Main Ideas

- During the Middle Ages, Europe's geography affected where people lived, their ways of life, and their relations with other people.

- The Angles and Saxons invaded Britain, the Franks created an empire in Western Europe, and the Saxons created a German kingdom that became the Holy Roman Empire.

- Monks helped spread Christianity throughout Europe, and the Catholic Church became strong in the early Middle Ages.

What Did You Learn?

1. Why is the Battle of Tours significant?

2. Why were monasteries important to medieval Europe?

Critical Thinking

3. **Summarizing Information** Draw a diagram like the one below. Use it to describe the role of monks in medieval Europe. **CA 7RC2.0**

```
  ◯       ◯
       Monks
  ◯       ◯
```

4. **Analyze** How did Charlemagne support education? **CA 7RC2.0**

5. **The Big Ideas** What ideas did monks help spread across Europe? **CA HI2.**

6. **Asking Questions** If you were asked to interview Henry IV, what three questions would you ask him? **CA HR1.**

7. **Reading** **Making Inferences** Create a think-through chart that lists the important groups that invaded Europe and the possible effect that they had on the continent. What conclusions can you draw about the influences of these groups? **CA 7WA2.5**

Feudalism

Guide to Reading

History Social Science Standards

WH7.6 Students analyze the geographic, political, economic, religious, and social structures of the civilizations of Medieval Europe.

Looking Back, Looking Ahead

In the last section, you read how the Vikings spread fear and destruction throughout Europe. During the Middle Ages, people looked to nobles to protect them.

Focusing on the Main Ideas

- Feudalism developed in Europe in the Middle Ages. It was based on landowning, loyalty, and the power of armored knights on horseback. *(page 335)*

- Knights followed a code of chivalry and lived in castles, while peasants lived in simple houses and worked hard all year long. *(page 338)*

- Increased trade led to the growth of towns and cities and the rise of guilds and city governments. *(page 340)*

Locating Places
Venice (VEH•nuhs)
Flanders (FLAN•duhrz)

Content Vocabulary
feudalism (FYOO•duhl•IH•zuhm)
vassal (VA•suhl)
fief (FEEF)
knight (NYT)
serf (SUHRF)
guild (GIHLD)

Academic Vocabulary
shift (SHIHFT)
process (PRAH•SEHS)

Reading Strategy

Compare and Contrast Complete a Venn diagram like the one below showing the similarities and differences between serfs and slaves.

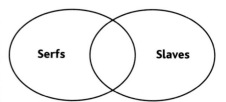

Serfs   Slaves

NATIONAL GEOGRAPHIC **Where & When?**

SCANDINAVIA
ENGLAND
Bruges• HOLY ROMAN
FRANCE   EMPIRE
               •Venice
SPAIN   •Rome
         ITALY

A.D. **800**   **1000**   **1200**

c. A.D. **800s**
Feudalism
begins in Europe

c. **1100**
Flanders and
Italy trade
goods regularly

c. **1200**
Guilds are
widespread
in Europe

What Is Feudalism?

Main Idea Feudalism developed in Europe in the Middle Ages. It was based on landowning, loyalty, and the power of armored knights on horseback.

Reading Connection What would it be like to live in a country where the government has fallen apart? Read to learn how the fall of Charlemagne's government changed life for people in the Middle Ages.

When Charlemagne's grandfather, Charles Martel, needed an army to fight the Muslims invading France, he began giving estates—large farms—to nobles willing to fight for him. The nobles used the resources generated by the estates to obtain horses and weapons. Although Martel did not realize it, he was using a new way of organizing society that would eventually spread across most of Europe.

When Charlemagne's empire collapsed, Western Europe lost its last strong central government. Landowning nobles became more and more powerful. They gained the right to collect taxes and to impose laws on the people on their estates. When invaders attacked Europe, the peasants, or farmers, could not rely on kings. Instead, they looked to nobles for protection.

During the A.D. 800s, this **shift** of power from kings to nobles led to a new order known as **feudalism** (FYOO•duhl•IH•zuhm). Under feudalism, landowning nobles governed and protected the people in return for services, such as fighting in a noble's army or farming the land.

By A.D. 1000, the kingdoms of Europe were divided into thousands of feudal territories. Some of these territories were large, but most were smaller than the city-states of ancient Greece. At the center of each, however, was not a city but a noble's castle, or fortress.

The Role of Vassals and Knights

Feudalism was based on bonds of loyalty and duty among nobles. Nobles were both lords and vassals. A **vassal** (VA•suhl) was a noble who served a lord of higher rank. In return, the lord protected the vassal.

The tie between a lord and his vassal was made known in a public ceremony. The vassal put his hands together and placed them between the hands of his lord. Then the vassal swore "to keep faith and loyalty to you against all others."

Kings and queens

Lords and ladies

Knights

Peasants and serfs

▲ Under feudalism each level of society had duties to the groups above and below it. *Which group in the diagram served as vassals to the lords and ladies?*

A vassal showed his loyalty by serving in his lord's army. In return for the vassal's military service, a lord granted his vassal land. The land granted to a vassal was known as a **fief** (FEEF). Vassals governed the people who lived on their fiefs.

These vassals were **knights** (NYTS), or warriors in armor who fought on horseback. Until the A.D. 700s, nobles in Western Europe mostly fought on foot. They wore coats of mail—armor made from metal links—and carried swords and shields. In the A.D. 700s, a new innovation, the stirrup, made it possible for an armored man to sit on a horse and charge while holding a lance, a long heavy spear. Knights would charge enemies, spearing them with their lances. From the A.D. 700s to the 1200s, armored knights on horseback were the most powerful soldiers in Europe.

Europe was not the only place with a feudal society. As you remember from Chapter 5, Japan had a similar system between A.D. 800 and 1500. Powerful nobles owed only a loose loyalty to the Japanese emperor. The nobles primarily relied on samurai. Like knights, the samurai owed loyalty to their lords, the daimyo, and provided military service for them. Also like knights in Europe, the samurai wore armor and fought on horseback.

What Was the Manorial System? The lands on the fiefs of the Middle Ages were called manors. The lords ruled the manor, and peasants worked the land. Some peasants were freemen, who paid fees to the noble for the right to farm the land. They had rights under the law and could move whenever and wherever they wished.

Most peasants, however, were **serfs** (SUHRFS). Serfs could not leave the manor, own property, or marry without the lord's approval. Lords even had the right to try

A Medieval Manor

A medieval manor usually consisted of the lord's manor house or castle, the surrounding fields, and a peasant village. While minor knights or nobles would own only one manor, more powerful lords might own several. A powerful lord would spend time at each of his manors during the year.
What duty did lords have to their serfs?

Fields
In the spring, serfs planted crops such as summer wheat, barley, oats, peas, and beans. Crops planted in the fall included winter wheat and rye. Women often helped in the fields.

serfs in their own court. Serfs were not enslaved, however. Lords could not sell the serfs or take away the land given to serfs to support themselves. Lords also had a duty to protect their serfs, providing them the safety they needed to grow crops.

Serfs worked long hours on the lord's land and performed services for the lord. They spent three days working for the lord and the rest of the week growing food for themselves. They also had to give a portion of their own crops to the lord and pay him for the use of the village's mill, bread oven, and winepress.

It was not easy for serfs to gain their freedom. One way was to run away to the towns. If a serf remained in a town for more than a year, he or she was considered free. By the end of the Middle Ages, serfs in many kingdoms were also allowed to buy their release.

How Did Farming Improve? During the Middle Ages, Europeans invented new technology that helped increase the amount of crops they could grow. Perhaps the most important was a heavy wheeled plow with an iron blade. It easily turned over Western Europe's dense clay soils.

Another important invention was the horse collar. The horse collar made it possible for a horse to pull a plow. Horses could pull plows much faster than oxen, allowing peasants to plant more crops and produce more food.

Castle
Castles were built in a variety of forms and were usually designed to fit the landscape.

Church
Village churches often had no benches. Villagers sat on the floor or brought stools from home.

Serf's Home
Serfs had little furniture. Tables were made from boards stretched across benches, and most peasants slept on straw mattresses on the floor.

WH7.6.3 Understand the development of feudalism, its role in the medieval European economy, the way in which it was influenced by physical geography (the role of the manor and the growth of towns), and how feudal relationships provided the foundation of political order.

Europeans also found new ways to harness water and wind power. Europe's many rivers powered water mills that ground grain into flour. Where rivers were not available, windmills were used for grinding grains, pumping water, and cutting wood.

Peasants also learned to grow more food by rotating crops on three fields instead of two. The rotation kept soil fertile. One field was planted in fall and another in spring. The third field was left unplanted. The three-field system meant that only one-third, rather than one-half, of the land was unused at any time. As a result, more crops could be grown. Greater food production allowed the population to expand.

✓ Reading Check **Explain** How could a noble be both a lord and a vassal?

▲ Nobles celebrated special occasions with large feasts, which included many courses of meats, fruits, and vegetables. *What were the wife's duties when a nobleman went off to war?*

Life in Feudal Europe

Main Idea Knights followed a code of chivalry and lived in castles, while peasants lived in simple houses and worked hard all year long.

Reading Connection Have you heard the phrase "knight in shining armor"? Read to learn why these words apply to how a knight acted as well as how he dressed.

During the Middle Ages, nobles were the most powerful people in Europe. Great lords had much more wealth and land than ordinary knights. However, their belief in the feudal system united lords and knights in defending their society.

How Did Nobles Live? Knights followed certain rules called the code of chivalry (SHIH•vuhl•ree). A knight was expected to obey his lord, to be brave, to show respect to women of noble birth, to honor the church, and to help people. A knight was also expected to be honest and to fight fairly against his enemies. The code of chivalry became the guide to good behavior. Many of today's ideas about manners come from the code of chivalry.

When noblemen went to war, their wives or daughters ran the manors. This was no small job because manors had many officials and servants. Keeping track of the household's accounts took considerable skill. The lady of a manor also had to oversee the storing of food and other supplies needed to run the household.

The center of the manor was a castle. At first, castles were built of wood. Later, they were built of stone. A castle had two basic parts. One was a human-made or

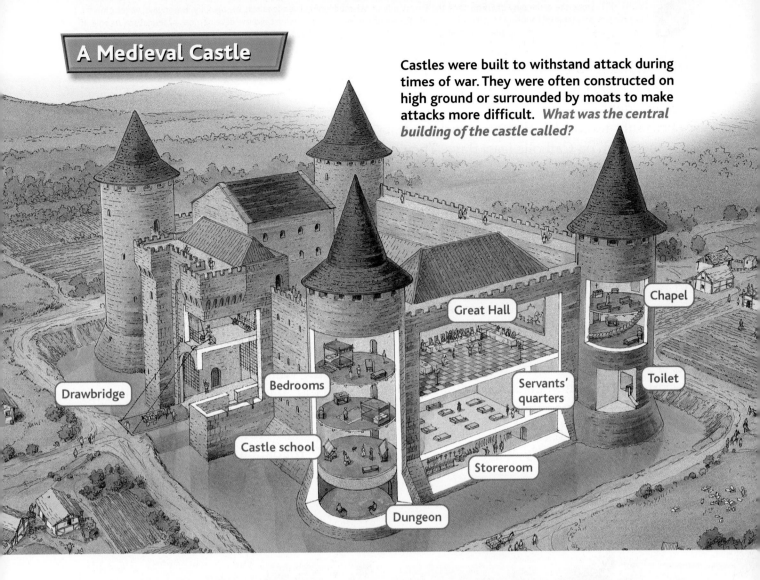

A Medieval Castle

Castles were built to withstand attack during times of war. They were often constructed on high ground or surrounded by moats to make attacks more difficult. *What was the central building of the castle called?*

Drawbridge

Bedrooms

Castle school

Dungeon

Great Hall

Servants' quarters

Storeroom

Chapel

Toilet

naturally steep-sided hill called a motte (MAHT). The bailey was an open space next to the motte. High stone walls encircled the motte and bailey. The keep, or central building of the castle, was built on the motte.

The keep had a number of stories. The basement housed storerooms for tools and food. On the ground floor were kitchens and stables, and above the ground floor was a great hall. Here the people of the household ate and sometimes slept, and the lord of the castle held court and received visitors. Smaller rooms opened off the great hall. They included chapels, toilets, and bedrooms with huge curtained beds.

In the later Middle Ages, nobles owned more jewelry, better clothes, and exotic spices. They also built more elaborate castles with thicker walls, more towers, finer furniture, and richer decoration.

What Was Peasant Life Like?
The homes of peasants were much simpler. They lived in wood-frame cottages plastered with clay. Their roofs were thatched with straw. The houses of poorer peasants had a single room. Better cottages had a main room for cooking and eating and another room for sleeping.

The climate of Europe required peasants to work year-round. They harvested grain in August and September. In October they prepared the ground for winter crops. In November they slaughtered livestock and salted the meat to keep it for winter. In February and March, they plowed the land for planting oats, barley, peas, and beans. In

WH7.6.1 Study the geography of Europe and the Eurasian land mass, including their location, topography, waterways, vegetation, and climate and their relationship to ways of life in Medieval Europe. **WH7.6.3** Understand the development of feudalism, its role in the medieval European economy, the way in which it was influenced by physical geography (the role of the manor and the growth of towns), and how feudal relationships provided the foundation of political order.

early summer they weeded the fields, sheared the sheep, and tended small vegetable gardens.

Peasants took a break from work and went to church on Catholic feast days. They celebrated more than 50 feast days each year. The most important were Christmas and Easter. On feast days and at Sunday worship, the village priest taught them the basic elements of Christian belief.

Peasant women worked in the fields and raised children at the same time. They also gathered and prepared their family's food. Each day they mixed bread dough and baked it in community ovens. Bread was a basic staple of the medieval diet. Peasants ate it with vegetables, milk, nuts, and fruits. Sometimes they added eggs or meat, and they often had ale to drink.

Reading Check **Identify** What was the code of chivalry?

Trade and Cities

Main Idea Increased trade led to the growth of towns and cities and the rise of guilds and city governments.

Reading Connection What effect would a new shopping mall have on your community? Read to learn how the growth of trade and the rise of cities changed the way people lived and worked in medieval Europe.

When the Roman Empire collapsed, almost all trade in Western Europe came to an end. Bridges and roads fell into disrepair. Law and order vanished. Money was no longer used. Most people spent their lives in the villages where they were born.

By 1100, feudalism had made Europe safer, and new technology enabled people to produce more food and goods. Nobles repaired roads, arrested bandits, and enforced the law. As a result, trade resumed.

Medieval City Life

◀ This scene shows a market in a medieval town. *Which area became the center of trade for northern Europe?*

A mayor of London from the early 1200s ▶

As trade increased, towns grew larger, and several cities became wealthy from trade. For example, the city of **Venice** (VEH•nuhs) and other Italian cities began trading with the Byzantine Empire and soon became the center of trade in the Mediterranean. Meanwhile, towns in **Flanders** (FLAN•duhrz)—which today is part of Belgium—became the center of trade for northern Europe. This area was known for its woolen cloth. Merchants from England, Scandinavia, France, and the Holy Roman Empire met there to trade their goods for wool.

By 1100, Flanders and Italy were exchanging goods regularly. To encourage this trade, the counts of Champagne in northern France began holding trade fairs. Northern European merchants exchanged furs, tin, honey, and wool for cloth and swords from northern Italy and silks, sugar, and spices from Asia.

During the early Middle Ages, people bartered, or traded goods for other goods. As trade increased, demand for gold and silver coins rose. Slowly, people began using money again to purchase goods. Merchants set up banks to manage the use of money.

How Were Cities Governed? Towns were often located on land owned by lords. This meant the towns were under their control. However, townspeople needed freedom to trade and wanted to make their own laws. In exchange for paying taxes, people in towns were granted certain basic rights by their lords. These included the right to buy and sell property and the freedom from having to serve in the army.

Over time, medieval towns set up their own governments. Only males who had been born in the city or who had lived there for a certain length of time were citizens. In

▲ Medieval streets were narrow and often contained wastewater and garbage. *Why was fire a major threat in medieval cities?*

▼ A stained glass window showing the arms, or symbol, of a blacksmiths' group

many cities, these citizens elected a city council. The council served as judges, city officials, and lawmakers. Candidates from the wealthiest and most powerful families usually won the elections.

Crafts and Guilds

Trade encouraged manufacturing. People produced cloth, metalwork, shoes, and other goods right in their houses. Over time, these craftspeople organized **guilds** (GIHLDZ), or business groups. By 1200, tanners, carpenters, bakers, and almost every other type of craftspeople had guilds. The rise of towns and guilds created a new middle class in medieval Europe. People in the middle class were not lords, vassals, or serfs. They did not own land, but they did have some wealth and freedom.

Craft guilds set standards for quality in products. They decided how goods were to be made and set prices. Guilds also decided who could join a trade and the **process** they had to follow to do so.

A person could become an apprentice around the age of 10. An apprentice learned a trade from a master craftsperson who provided room and board but no wages. After five to seven years of service, the apprentice

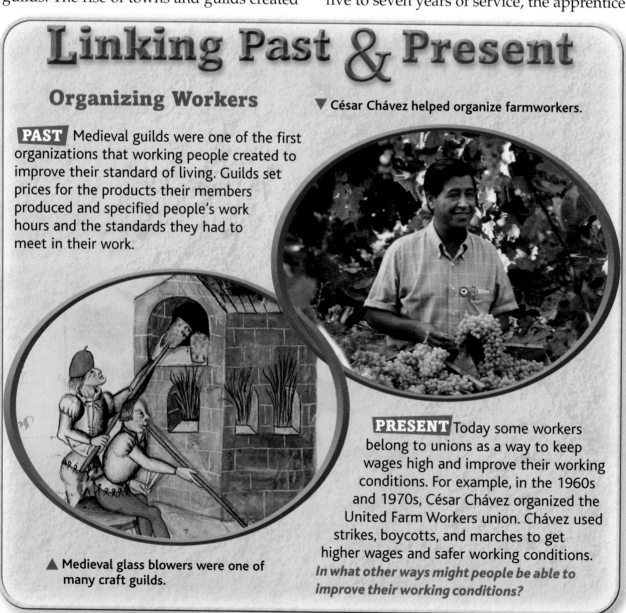

Linking Past & Present

Organizing Workers

PAST Medieval guilds were one of the first organizations that working people created to improve their standard of living. Guilds set prices for the products their members produced and specified people's work hours and the standards they had to meet in their work.

▼ César Chávez helped organize farmworkers.

PRESENT Today some workers belong to unions as a way to keep wages high and improve their working conditions. For example, in the 1960s and 1970s, César Chávez organized the United Farm Workers union. Chávez used strikes, boycotts, and marches to get higher wages and safer working conditions.

In what other ways might people be able to improve their working conditions?

▲ Medieval glass blowers were one of many craft guilds.

became a journeyman and worked for wages. To become a master, a journeyman had to produce a masterpiece—an outstanding example of the craft.

▲ **This painting shows a medieval woman spinning wool as her husband warms himself by the fire.** *What were some responsibilities of women in medieval cities?*

What Was City Life Like?

Medieval cities had narrow, winding streets. Wooden houses were crowded against one another, and the upper stories were built out over the streets. Candles and fireplaces were used for light and heat. As a result, medieval cities could be destroyed rapidly once a fire started.

The cities were often dirty and smelly. Wood fires in people's homes and shops filled the air with ashes and smoke. Brewers, dyers, and poor people who could not afford wood burned cheap coal, polluting the air even more. Butchers and tanners dumped animal wastes into the rivers.

City women ran their households, prepared meals, raised their children, and managed the family's money. Often they helped their husbands in their trades. Sometimes when a master craftsperson died, his widow carried on his trade. Some women developed their own trades to earn extra money. Many women became brewers, weavers, and hatmakers.

✔ **Reading Check** **Analyze** How did guilds change the way goods were made and sold?

History Online

Study Central Need help understanding feudalism? Visit ca.hss.glencoe.com and click on Study Central.

Section 2 Review

Reading Summary

Review the Main Ideas

- Under feudalism, Europe was divided into thousands of territories held by nobles with the lands worked by serfs.

- During the Middle Ages, nobles lived in large castles, while serfs lived in small wood cottages.

- As medieval trade increased, towns grew and craftspeople organized guilds.

What Did You Learn?

1. What was a vassal?

2. Describe the system of crop rotation used in the later Middle Ages, and explain how it increased the amount of food being grown.

Critical Thinking

3. **The Big Ideas** Draw a chart to compare the duties and obligations of lords, knights, and serfs. **CA 7RC2.3**

Lords	Knights	Serfs

4. **Summarize** Explain the shift of power from kings to nobles during the Middle Ages. **CA 7RC2.0**

5. **Cause and Effect** How did an increase in trade lead to the growth of towns and cities? **CA HI2.**

6. **Conclude** What were guilds, and why were they important? **CA 7RC2.2**

7. **Analysis** **Economics Connection** How did the shift from a barter system to a money system change medieval Europe's economy? **CA HI6.**

You Decide . . .

WH7.6.3 Understand the development of feudalism, its role in the medieval European economy, the way in which it was influenced by physical geography (the role of the manor and the growth of towns), and how feudal relationships provided the foundation of political order.

Feudalism: Good or Bad?

Feudalism was the major social and political order in medieval Europe. It developed as power passed from kings to local lords.

Good?

Feudalism brought together two powerful groups: lords and vassals. The lords gave vassals land in return for military and other services. Feudalism was a help to Western Europeans for the following reasons:

- Feudalism helped protect communities from the violence and warfare that broke out after the fall of Rome and the collapse of strong central government in Western Europe. Feudalism secured Western Europe's society and kept out powerful invaders.

- Feudalism helped restore trade. Lords repaired bridges and roads. Knights arrested bandits, enforced laws, and made it safe to travel.

- Feudalism benefited lords, vassals, and peasants. Lords gained a dependable fighting force in their vassals. Vassals received land for their military service. Peasants were protected by their lords. The lord built mills, blacksmith shops, and woodworking shops.

- Feudal ceremonies, oaths, and contracts required lords and vassals to be faithful and to carry out their duties. These agreements later helped shape the development of European governments.

- Feudalism did not allow one person or organization to become too powerful. Power was shared. This led to European ideas about limited government, constitutions, and civil rights.

◀ Serfs working the land

◀ Landowning nobles often served as knights.

to many wars among lords. Feudalism protected Western Europe from outside invaders, but it did not bring peace to a region.

- Lords or vassals often placed their personal interests over the interests of the areas they ruled. Feudal lords had complete power in their local areas and could make harsh demands on their vassals and peasants.

- Feudalism did not treat people equally or let them move up in society. A person born a serf was supposed to remain a serf, just as a person born a lord received special treatment without earning it.

- Most peasants were serfs. They were not allowed to leave their lord's lands. Serfs had to work three days each week as a payment to the lords or vassals for allowing them to farm for themselves on other days. The serfs were restricted in movement and even daily activities because they could not leave the land without permission.

Bad?

Feudalism did not always work as well in real life as it did in theory, and it caused many problems for society.

- Feudalism provided some unity and security in local areas, but it often did not have the strength to unite larger regions or countries. Small feudal governments could not afford big projects, such as building aqueducts, sewers, or fleets of ships, that might benefit society.

- Because there was no strong central government to enforce laws fairly, it was easy to use force, violence, and lies to get one's way. This led

You Be the Historian

Checking for Understanding

1. Do you think feudalism helped or hurt Western Europe's development? **CA HR5.**

2. Is there any way feudal lords could have worked their lands without using serfs? **CA 7RC2.0**

3. Imagine you live in a feudal society. Write an autobiographical story about your life as a lord, vassal, or serf and your relationship with the other two groups. Your entries should show feudalism as either a good or bad order. **CA 7WA2.1**

Kingdoms and Crusades

Guide to Reading

History Social Science Standards

WH7.6 Students analyze the geographic, political, economic, religious, and social structures of the civilizations of Medieval Europe.

Looking Back, Looking Ahead

In the last section, you read about how Western Europeans lived during the Middle Ages. This section describes the political changes.

Focusing on the Main Ideas

- England developed a system in which the king's power was shared with Parliament. *(page 347)*

- French kings called the Capetians conquered lands held by the English in western France and set up France's first parliament. *(page 350)*

- After the Mongols destroyed the Kievan state, the rulers of Moscow built a new Russian state. *(page 351)*

- Crusaders from Europe captured Jerusalem but were later driven out by the Muslims. *(page 352)*

Locating Places

Normandy (NAWR•muhn•dee)
Kiev (KEE•EHF)
Moscow (MAHS•koh)

Meeting People

William the Conqueror
King John
Philip II (FIH•luhp)
Saladin (SA•luh•DEEN)

Content Vocabulary

grand jury
trial jury
clergy (KLUHR•jee)

Academic Vocabulary

guarantee (GAR•uhn•TEE)
document (DAH•kyuh•muhnt)
nonetheless (NUHN•thuh•LEHS)

Reading Strategy

Cause and Effect Complete a diagram to show the causes and effects of the Crusades.

Causes		Effects

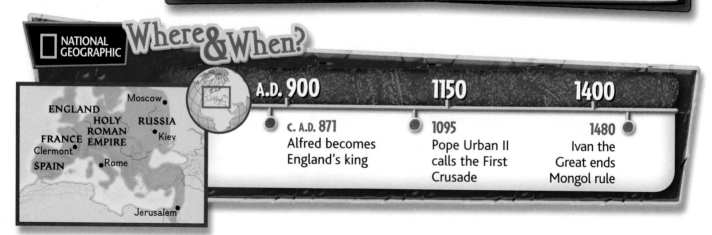

NATIONAL GEOGRAPHIC **Where & When?**

ENGLAND
HOLY
ROMAN   RUSSIA
FRANCE EMPIRE
Clermont
SPAIN   •Rome
Moscow•
•Kiev

Jerusalem•

A.D. 900 — 1150 — 1400

C. A.D. 871
Alfred becomes England's king

1095
Pope Urban II calls the First Crusade

1480
Ivan the Great ends Mongol rule

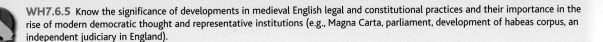

WH7.6.5 Know the significance of developments in medieval English legal and constitutional practices and their importance in the rise of modern democratic thought and representative institutions (e.g., Magna Carta, parliament, development of habeas corpus, an independent judiciary in England).

England in the Middle Ages

Main Idea England developed a system in which the king's power was shared with Parliament.

Reading Connection Do you know anyone who has had to go to court or has served on a jury? Read to learn how these institutions began in medieval England.

In section one, you learned that Germanic peoples called the Angles and Saxons invaded Britain in the early A.D. 400s. They took over much of the country from the Celts and set up many small kingdoms. In the late A.D. 800s, Vikings attacked Britain. King Alfred of Wessex, later known as Alfred the Great, united the Anglo-Saxon kingdoms and drove away the Vikings. Alfred's united kingdom became known as "Angleland," or England.

Alfred ruled England from A.D. 871 to A.D. 899. He founded schools and hired scholars to rewrite Latin books in the Anglo-Saxon language. However, the Anglo-Saxon kings who came after him were weak rulers.

Who Was William the Conqueror? In the A.D. 900s, the Vikings conquered part of western France across the English Channel from England. This region came to be called **Normandy** (NAWR•muhn•dee), after the Vikings, or Norsemen, who ruled it. By the middle of the A.D. 1000s, Normandy was ruled by William, a descendant of the Viking ruler who had conquered Normandy. William was also a cousin of King Edward of England.

When Edward died, a noble named Harold Godwinson claimed England's throne. However, William believed that he, not Harold, should be king of England. Accompanied by his army of knights, William landed in England in 1066. They defeated Harold and his foot soldiers at the Battle of Hastings. William was then crowned king of England and became known as **William the Conqueror.**

▼ **This painting of the Battle of Hastings shows Norman knights on horseback led by William the Conqueror attacking the English foot soldiers.** *What area did William rule before he attacked England?*

At first the Anglo-Saxons resisted William's rule. He had to find a way to stop Anglo-Saxon revolts and to control his own soldiers. He did so by giving land to his Norman knights. Then he made them swear loyalty to him as ruler of England.

William wanted to know all about his new kingdom. So he took the first census in Europe since Roman times. This census was known as the Domesday Book. It counted people, manors, and farm animals.

The Normans who ruled England brought Europe's customs to England.

Under William's rule, officials and nobles spoke French. Ordinary Anglo-Saxons still spoke their own language, which later became English. As more and more Normans and Anglo-Saxons married, their ways of doing things merged into a new English culture.

Henry II and the Common Law

The power of the English king increased under Henry II. Henry ruled England from 1154 to 1189. Henry utilized the law courts to increase his power. He set up a central court

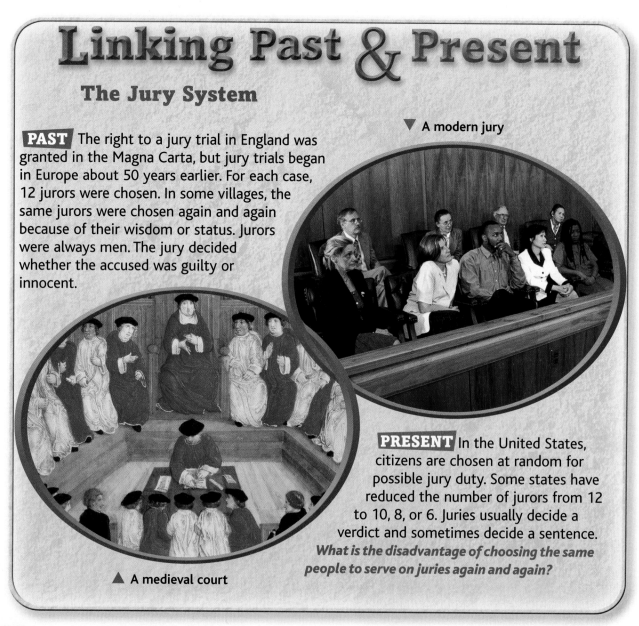

Linking Past & Present

The Jury System

PAST The right to a jury trial in England was granted in the Magna Carta, but jury trials began in Europe about 50 years earlier. For each case, 12 jurors were chosen. In some villages, the same jurors were chosen again and again because of their wisdom or status. Jurors were always men. The jury decided whether the accused was guilty or innocent.

▼ A modern jury

▲ A medieval court

PRESENT In the United States, citizens are chosen at random for possible jury duty. Some states have reduced the number of jurors from 12 to 10, 8, or 6. Juries usually decide a verdict and sometimes decide a sentence.

What is the disadvantage of choosing the same people to serve on juries again and again?

with trained lawyers and judges. Then he appointed circuit judges, who traveled across the country hearing cases. He also established a body of common law, or law that was the same throughout the whole kingdom.

Henry set up juries to handle arguments over land. In time, two kinds of juries developed. The **grand jury** decided whether people should be accused of a crime. The **trial jury** decided whether an accused person was innocent or guilty.

What Was the Magna Carta?

Henry's son John became king of England in 1199. **King John** raised taxes in England and punished his enemies without trials. Many English nobles resented the king's power. They refused to obey him unless he agreed to **guarantee** certain rights.

The nobles met with King John at a meadow called Runnymede in 1215. There they forced John to sign a **document** of rights called the Magna Carta, or the Great Charter. The Magna Carta took away some of the king's powers. He could no longer collect taxes unless a group called the Great Council agreed. Freemen accused of crimes had the right to fair trials by their peers, or equals.

Based on these ideas, England went on to develop the concept of habeas corpus that is still important in modern democratic countries. Habeas corpus protects a person from being imprisoned indefinitely without a trial.

The Magna Carta also stated that the king and vassals both had certain rights and duties. The Magna Carta was important because it helped to establish the idea that people have rights and that the power of the government should be limited.

In the 1200s, another English king, Edward I, called for a meeting of people

Primary Source

Magna Carta

This excerpt from the Magna Carta describes the right to a trial by jury:

"No free man shall be taken, imprisoned, disseised [seized], outlawed, banished, or in any way destroyed, nor will We proceed against or prosecute him, except by the lawful judgment of his peers and by the law of the land."

—Magna Carta

King John signing the Magna Carta ▲

DBQ Document-Based Question

Why do you think this part of the Magna Carta is important?

from different parts of England. Their job was to advise him and help him make laws. This gathering, called the Parliament, was an important step toward representative government. At first, Parliaments were made up of two knights from every county, two people from every town, and all high-ranking nobles and church officials. Later, Parliament divided into two houses. High-ranking nobles and church officials met as the House of Lords. Knights and townspeople met as the House of Commons.

Reading Check **Explain** How did the Magna Carta affect the king's power?

The Kingdom of France

Main Idea French kings called the Capetians conquered lands held by the English in western France and set up France's first parliament.

Reading Connection Has a poll ever been taken in your class? Read to find out how one French king found out what his people were thinking.

In A.D. 843 Charlemagne's empire was divided into three parts. The western part eventually became the kingdom of France. In A.D. 987 Frankish nobles chose Hugh Capet to be their king. Hugh was the first of the Capetian (kuh•PEE•shuhn) kings of France. The Capetians controlled the area around Paris (PAR•uhs), the capital. Many French nobles had more power than the kings did. This began to change when **Philip II** (FIH•luhp) became king of France.

Philip ruled from 1180 to 1223. When he took the throne, England's king ruled parts of western France. Philip went to war against England and conquered most of these territories. As a result, French kings gained more land and became more powerful.

Philip IV, called Philip the Fair, ruled from 1285 to 1314. In 1302 he met with representatives from the three estates, or classes, of French society. The first estate was the **clergy** (KLUHR•jee), or people who had been ordained as priests. Nobles made up the second estate, and townspeople and peasants were the third estate. This meeting began the Estates-General, France's first parliament. It was the first step in France toward representative government.

Reading Check **Describe** How did King Philip II bring power back to French kings?

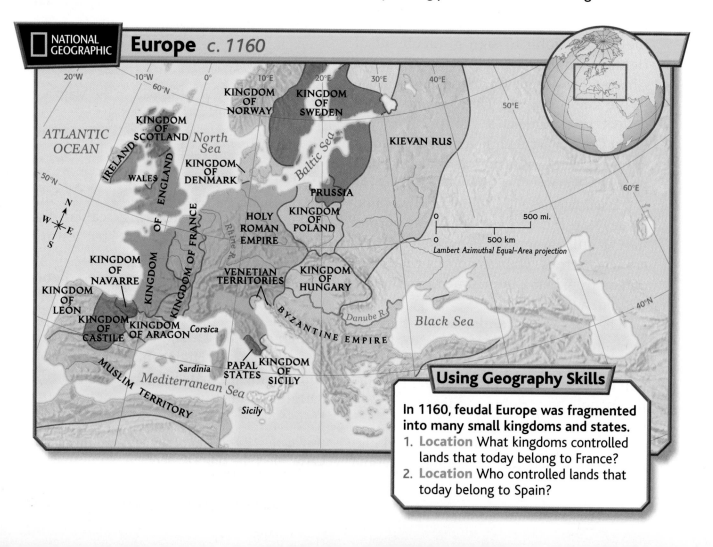

NATIONAL GEOGRAPHIC

Europe c. 1160

ATLANTIC OCEAN

KINGDOM OF NORWAY
KINGDOM OF SWEDEN
KINGDOM OF SCOTLAND
North Sea
IRELAND
WALES
KINGDOM OF ENGLAND
KINGDOM OF DENMARK
Baltic Sea
KIEVAN RUS
PRUSSIA
KINGDOM OF FRANCE
Rhine R.
HOLY ROMAN EMPIRE
KINGDOM OF POLAND
KINGDOM OF NAVARRE
VENETIAN TERRITORIES
KINGDOM OF HUNGARY
KINGDOM OF LEÓN
KINGDOM OF CASTILE
KINGDOM OF ARAGON
Corsica
BYZANTINE EMPIRE
Danube R.
Black Sea
MUSLIM TERRITORY
Sardinia
PAPAL STATES
KINGDOM OF SICILY
Mediterranean Sea
Sicily

500 mi.
500 km
Lambert Azimuthal Equal-Area projection

Using Geography Skills

In 1160, feudal Europe was fragmented into many small kingdoms and states.
1. **Location** What kingdoms controlled lands that today belong to France?
2. **Location** Who controlled lands that today belong to Spain?

Eastern Europe and Russia

Main Idea After the Mongols destroyed the Kievan state, the rulers of Moscow built a new Russian state.

Reading Connection Why do you think some of the cities in your state grew large while others stayed small? Read to learn how the cities of Kiev and Moscow grew to become the centers of large Slavic states.

About A.D. 500, a people called the Slavs organized villages in Eastern Europe. In time, the Slavs divided into three major groups: the southern, western, and eastern Slavs. The southern Slavs became the Croats, Serbs, and Bulgarians. The western Slavs became the Poles, Czechs, and Slovaks. The eastern Slavs became the Ukrainians (yoo•KRAY•nee•uhnz) and Russians (RUH•shuhnz).

What Was the Kievan Rus?

In the late A.D. 700s, Vikings began moving into the Slavs' territory from the north. Over time, the Vikings became rulers of the Slavs. The Slavs called their Viking rulers the Rus. The Vikings and Slavs intermarried and blended into one people.

Around A.D. 900, a Viking leader named Oleg created a Rus state around the city of **Kiev** (KEE•EHF). Called the Kievan Rus, this state was really a group of small territories.

The growth of the Kievan Rus attracted missionaries from the Byzantine Empire. One Rus ruler, Vladimir, married the Byzantine emperor's sister. He became an Eastern Orthodox Christian and declared his people Eastern Orthodox.

Kiev Falls to the Mongols

About 1240, the Mongols swept into the Kievan Rus. The Slavs called the Mongols "Tatars" because one of the Mongol tribes was the Tata people. The Mongols destroyed nearly all the major cities and killed many people.

The only major city to survive the Mongol attack was Novgorod. The city's rulers paid tribute to the Mongols, and accepted the Mongols as their rulers. Although the Mongols spared Novgorod, the city faced attacks from Germans and Swedes. Led by Alexander Nevsky, the Slavs of Novgorod defeated the Swedes and Germans. The Mongol khan rewarded Nevsky with the title of grand duke.

The Rise of Moscow Although the Mongols had caused great damage, the Slavs **nonetheless** recovered, and the city of **Moscow** (MAHS•koh) began to grow. Moscow was located at the crossroads of several important trade routes. Alexander Nevsky's son Daniel and his descendants became Moscow's rulers.

The rulers of Moscow married women from the ruling families in other Slavic towns. They also fought wars to expand Moscow's territory. Moscow became even more important when it became the headquarters for the Russian branch of the Eastern Orthodox Church.

In 1462 Ivan III became the ruler of Moscow. He married Sophia, the niece of the last Byzantine emperor. Afterward, Ivan began living in the style of an emperor. He had architects build fine palaces and large cathedrals in the Kremlin—the fortress at the center of Moscow. He even began calling himself czar. Czar was a shortened version of Caesar. In Russian, *czar* means "emperor."

Ivan III lived up to his title. In 1480 he finally drove the Mongols out of Russia. Then he expanded his territory to the north and west. When Ivan III died in 1505, the Russians were well on the way toward building a vast empire.

Reading Check Cause and Effect Why was Alexander Nevsky important?

The Crusades

Main Idea Crusaders from Europe captured Jerusalem but were later driven out by the Muslims.

Reading Connection Have you ever put all your energy into making something important happen? Read to learn why Europeans thought capturing the city of Jerusalem was important.

During the Middle Ages, the Byzantine Empire in the East came under attack. In 1071 an army of Muslim Turks defeated the Byzantines and seized control of most of the Byzantine lands in Asia Minor.

The Byzantine emperor did not have enough money or troops to drive out the Turks. In desperation, he asked the pope to help him defend his Christian empire against the Muslim invaders.

In 1095 Pope Urban II spoke before a large crowd in eastern France. He asked Europe's lords to launch a crusade, or holy war, against the Muslim Turks. He urged them to capture Jerusalem and free the Holy Land where Jesus had lived from the Muslims. The pope explained why the crusade was needed:

> 66 Jerusalem is the navel [center] of the world. . . . This is the land which the Redeemer [Jesus] of mankind illuminated by his coming. . . . This royal city, situated in the middle of the world, is now held captive by his enemies. . . . It looks and hopes for freedom; it begs unceasingly that you will come to its aid. 99
>
> —Pope Urban II,
> as quoted in *The Discoverers*

As the pope spoke, the excited crowd cried out, "It is the will of God, it is the will of God." The Crusades had begun.

Early Victories Several thousand soldiers on horseback and as many as ten thousand on foot headed east. Many of them wore a red cross on their clothes as a sign of their obedience to the pope's call.

In 1098 the First Crusade captured Antioch in Syria. From there, the crusaders entered Palestine, reaching Jerusalem in 1099. After a bloody fight, they stormed the city, killing Muslims, Jews, and Christians alike.

In the painting above, Pope Urban II calls for a crusade against the Muslims. At right, the crusaders attack Jerusalem with siege towers and catapults. *What was the pope's goal for the crusade?*

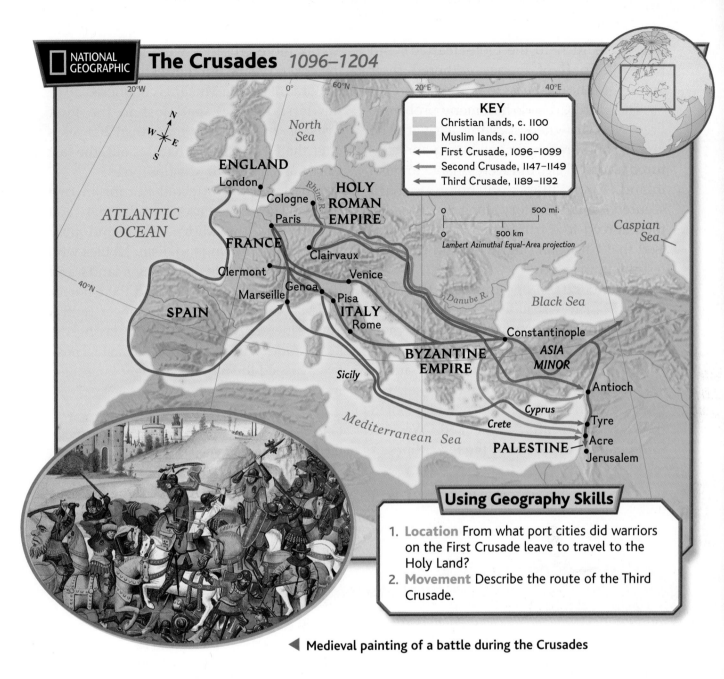

NATIONAL GEOGRAPHIC
The Crusades 1096–1204

KEY
Christian lands, c. 1100
Muslim lands, c. 1100
First Crusade, 1096–1099
Second Crusade, 1147–1149
Third Crusade, 1189–1192

500 mi.

500 km

Lambert Azimuthal Equal-Area projection

Using Geography Skills

1. **Location** From what port cities did warriors on the First Crusade leave to travel to the Holy Land?
2. **Movement** Describe the route of the Third Crusade.

◀ Medieval painting of a battle during the Crusades

Having driven the Muslims from the region, the crusaders created four states: the Kingdom of Jerusalem in Palestine, the county of Edessa and the principality of Antioch in Asia Minor, and the county of Tripoli where Lebanon is located today. These four states were surrounded by Muslims and depended on the Italian cities of Genoa, Pisa, and Venice for supplies.

The Muslims fought back, however, and in 1144 they captured Edessa. In response, European rulers sent another crusade to regain the lost lands. This Second Crusade, however, was a total failure.

In 1174 a Muslim named **Saladin** (SA•luh•DEEN) became ruler of Egypt. He united Muslims and declared war against the Christian states the crusaders had built. Saladin proved to be a brilliant commander. He defeated the Christians and captured Jerusalem in 1187.

The fall of Jerusalem led to the Third Crusade. Emperor Frederick of the Holy Roman Empire, King Richard I of England, (known as Richard the Lion-Hearted), and King Philip II of France gathered their armies and headed east to fight Saladin.

The Third Crusade had many problems. Frederick drowned crossing a river. The English and French arrived by sea and captured a coastal city but were unable to push inland. After Philip went home, Richard secured a small territory along the coast. He then agreed to a truce after Saladin promised that Christian pilgrims could travel to Jerusalem in safety.

Around 1200, Pope Innocent III called for a Fourth Crusade. Merchants from Venice used the crusade to weaken their trading rival, the Byzantine Empire. They convinced the crusaders to attack Constantinople, the Byzantine capital. For three days, the crusaders burned and looted the city. The attack shocked Western Europeans and weakened the Byzantines.

Six more crusades were launched over the next 60 years, but they achieved very little. Gradually, the Muslims conquered all of the territory they had lost to the First Crusade. In 1291, a bit more than 200 years after the First Crusade had set out, the last Christian city fell to Muslim forces.

The Crusades affected Europe in two ways. They increased trade between Europe and the Middle East, and they helped break down feudalism. Nobles who joined the Crusades sold their lands and freed their serfs. This reduced their power and enabled kings to build stronger central governments. Kings also began taxing the new trade with the Middle East. These taxes helped them build stronger kingdoms in Western Europe.

Reading Check **Compare and Contrast** What did the First Crusade accomplish? What did the Third Crusade accomplish?

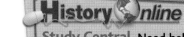

History Online

Study Central Need help with the impact of the Crusades? Visit ca.hss.glencoe.com and click on Study Central.

Section 3 Review

Reading Summary

Review the Main Ideas

- The English king granted rights to his people in the Magna Carta and established a parliament.

- French kings regained French territories from the English and, like the English, created a parliament.

- Russia had its beginnings in the territories of the Kievan Rus and Moscow.

- West Europeans launched crusades to capture Jerusalem and Palestine from the Muslims.

What Did You Learn?

1. What is the significance of the Battle of Hastings?

2. What groups developed from the three major divisions of Slavs in Eastern Europe?

Critical Thinking

3. **Organizing Information** Draw a chart to list the kings of England and France and their achievements. **CA 7RC2.0**

King/Country	Achievements

4. **The Big Ideas** How has the Magna Carta influenced modern government? **CA HI2.**

5. **Summarize** Describe the development of England's Parliament, and discuss its role in changing government. **CA HI3.**

6. **Explain** Why did cities such as Venice flourish as a result of the Crusades? **CA 7RC2.2**

7. **Writing Reports** Use your local library to research how the Crusades changed feudalism. Write a research report describing this effect. **CA 7WA2.3**

Section 4

The Church and Society

Guide to Reading

Looking Back, Looking Ahead

Kings and popes had a powerful effect on the lives of medieval people, as did religion. In this section, you will learn how religion in medieval Europe shaped its culture.

Focusing on the Main Ideas

• The Catholic Church played an important role in medieval Europe and used its power to uphold its teachings. **(page 356)**

• Church and government leaders supported learning and the arts in medieval Europe. **(page 360)**

Locating Places

Bologna (buh•LOH•nyuh)

Meeting People

Francis of Assisi (uh•SIHS•ee)

Thomas Aquinas
(TAH•muhs   uh•KWY•nuhs)

Content Vocabulary

mass

heresy (HEHR•uh•see)

anti-Semitism
(AN•tih•SEH•muh•TIH•zuhm)

theology (thee•AH•luh•jee)

scholasticism
(skuh•LAS•tuh•SIH•zuhm)

vernacular (vuhr•NA•kyuh•luhr)

Academic Vocabulary

job

demonstrate (DEH•muhn•STRAYT)

obtain (uhb•TAYN)

Reading Strategy

Organizing Information Complete a Venn diagram to show the similarities and differences between Romanesque and Gothic cathedrals.

Romanesque Cathedrals / Gothic Cathedrals

History Social Science Standards

WH7.6 Students analyze the geographic, political, economic, religious, and social structures of the civilizations of Medieval Europe.

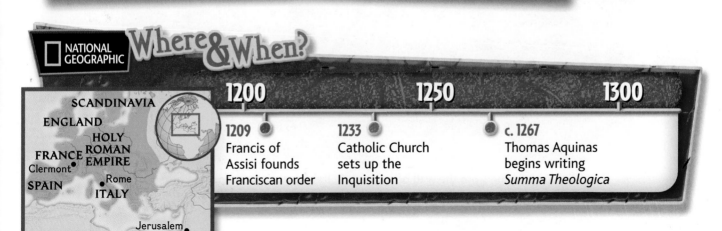

NATIONAL GEOGRAPHIC Where & When?

1200	1250	1300
1209 Francis of Assisi founds Franciscan order	**1233** Catholic Church sets up the Inquisition	**c. 1267** Thomas Aquinas begins writing *Summa Theologica*

SCANDINAVIA
ENGLAND
HOLY ROMAN EMPIRE
FRANCE
Clermont
SPAIN
Rome
ITALY
Jerusalem

WH7.6.6 Discuss the causes and course of the religious Crusades and their effects on the Christian, Muslim, and Jewish populations in Europe, with emphasis on the increasing contact by Europeans with cultures of the Eastern Mediterranean world.
WH7.6.8 Understand the importance of the Catholic church as a political, intellectual, and aesthetic institution (e.g., founding of universities, political and spiritual roles of the clergy, creation of monastic and mendicant religious orders, preservation of the Latin language and religious texts, St. Thomas Aquinas's synthesis of classical philosophy with Christian theology, and the concept of "natural law").

Religion and Society

Main Idea The Catholic Church played an important role in medieval Europe and used its power to uphold its teachings.

Reading Connection Have you ever noticed how many things in society have been influenced by religion? What examples can you give? Read to learn about the important role religion played in the lives of people living in the Middle Ages.

Between 1050 and 1150, a strong wave of religious feeling swept across Western Europe. As a result, more monasteries were built, and new religious orders, or groups of priests, monks, and nuns, were started.

New Religious Orders
The Cistercian (sihs•TUHR•shuhn) order was founded in 1098. Cistercian monks farmed the land as well as worshiped and prayed. They developed many new farming techniques that helped Europeans grow more crops. The most famous Cistercian monk was Bernard of Clairvaux (klar•VOH). Bernard helped promote the Second Crusade. He also advised the pope and defended the poor.

Many women entered convents between A.D. 1000 and 1200. Most of them were from noble families. They included widows and women unable or unwilling to marry. Women who were scholars found convents ideal places for study and writing.

Most educated women in medieval Europe were nuns. One famous woman was Hildegard of Bingen (HIHL•duh•GAHRD uhv BIHNG•uhn). She headed a convent in Germany and was one of the very few women who wrote music for the Church.

▲ This religious painting from the wall of a church in Italy depicts the pope and other Christian leaders, a number of saints, and Jesus ruling over all. *How did Cistercian monks aid European society?*

Until the 1200s, most people in religious orders stayed in their monasteries separate from the world. They lived a simple life of prayer and hard work. In the 1200s, several new religious orders were created. The men in these religious orders were called friars. The word *friar* comes from a Latin word for "brother."

Friars were different from monks. They did not stay in their monasteries. Instead, they went out into the world to preach. Friars lived by begging. They could not own property or keep any personal wealth.

The first order of friars was founded by **Francis of Assisi** (uh•SIHS•ee) in 1209. These friars became known as Franciscans. They lived in towns and taught Christianity to the people. In addition, the Franciscans helped the poor and served as missionaries.

A Spanish priest named Dominic de Guzmán founded another group of friars called the Dominicans. The Dominicans' goal was to defend Church teachings. Dominican friars spent years in study so they could defend their faith when preaching to well-educated people.

The Role of Religion Throughout medieval Western Europe, daily life revolved around the Catholic Church. Priests ran schools and hospitals. They also recorded births, performed weddings, and conducted burials. On Sundays and holy days, people went to **mass**—or the Catholic worship service.

During mass, medieval Christians took part in Church rituals called sacraments. The most important sacrament was communion, in which people took bread and wine to remind them of Jesus' death on the cross for their sins. Only clergy could give people the sacraments.

Many Christians also prayed to saints. Saints were holy men and women who had died and were believed to be in heaven.

Primary Source — The Franciscan Way of Life

Francis of Assisi recorded instructions for living in the Franciscan order. This passage is about the nature of love.

"Blessed that friar who loves his brother as much when he is sick and can be of no use to him as when he is well and can be of use to him. Blessed that friar who loves and respects his brother as much when he is absent as when he is present and who would not say anything behind his back that he could not say charitably [nicely] to his face."

—Francis of Assisi, as quoted in "Admonitions"

Francis of Assisi ▶

DBQ Document-Based Question

Does Francis of Assisi think that love for another person should be constant or changing? How do you know?

Their presence before God enabled the saints to ask favors for people who prayed to them.

Of all the saints, Mary, the mother of Jesus, was the most honored. Many churches were named for her. Several French churches carried the name *Notre Dame*, or "Our Lady," in honor of Mary.

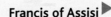

History Online

Web Activity Visit ca.hss.glencoe.com and click on *Chapter 6—Student Web Activity* to learn more about the Middle Ages.

Medieval Christians also believed that God blessed pilgrims, or religious travelers who journeyed to holy places. The holiest place was Jerusalem in the Middle East.

What Was the Inquisition?

The Catholic Church was very powerful in medieval society, and most of its leaders wanted everyone to accept the Church's teachings. Church leaders feared that if people stopped believing Church teachings, it would weaken the Church and endanger people's chances of getting into heaven.

Using its power, the Church tried to put an end to **heresy** (HEHR•uh•see), or a religious belief that conflicts with Church teachings. At first, it tried to stop the spread of heresy by sending friars like the Dominicans to preach the Church's message. Then, in 1233, the pope established a court called the Inquisition (IHN•kwuh•ZIH•shuhn), or Church court. To Church leaders, heresy was a crime against God. The Inquisition's job was to try heretics, or people suspected of heresy.

People brought before the Inquisition were urged to confess their heresy and to ask forgiveness. When they confessed, the Inquisition punished them and then allowed them to return to the Church. People who refused to confess could be tortured until they admitted their heresy. Those who did not confess were considered guilty. The Inquisition turned them over to political leaders, who could execute them.

How Were the Jews Treated?

Church leaders persecuted Jews as actively as they punished heretics. Many Europeans hated Jews for refusing to become Christians. Others hated them because many Jews were moneylenders who charged interest. At that time, Christians believed charging interest was a sin.

▲ This painting shows an accused heretic being questioned by the Inquisition. *What happened to people who refused to confess to the Inquisition?*

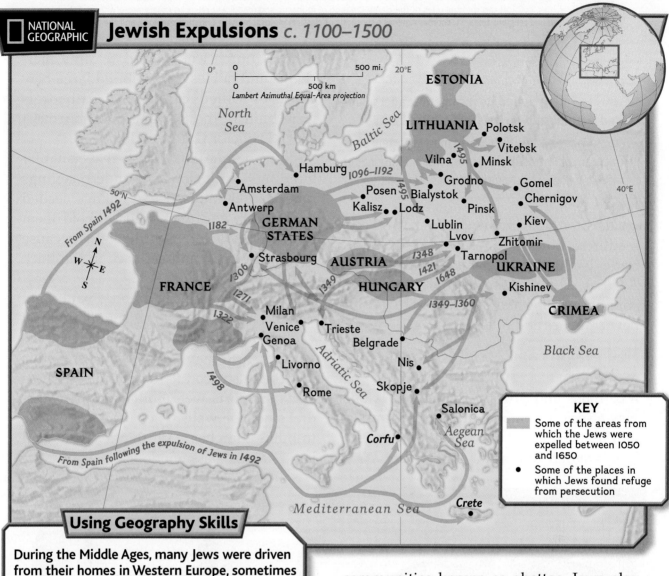

NATIONAL GEOGRAPHIC

Jewish Expulsions c. 1100–1500

KEY

Some of the areas from which the Jews were expelled between 1050 and 1650

• Some of the places in which Jews found refuge from persecution

Using Geography Skills

During the Middle Ages, many Jews were driven from their homes in Western Europe, sometimes from areas where their families had lived for generations.

1. **Movement** From where did many of the Jews who moved to Eastern Europe come?
2. **Movement** Where did many of the Jews expelled from Spain settle?

When disease or economic problems hurt society, people blamed the Jews. Jews became scapegoats—people who are blamed for other people's troubles. Hatred of Jews is known as **anti-Semitism** (AN•tih•SEH•muh•TIH•zuhm).

Anti-Semitism in the Middle Ages took horrible forms. Christian mobs attacked and killed thousands of Jews. Governments made Jews wear special badges or clothing. In some places, Jews had to live in separate communities known as ghettos. Jews also lost the right to own land and to practice certain trades. This was why many of them had to become peddlers and moneylenders, **jobs** that Christians despised.

Beginning in the 1100s, European rulers began driving out their Jewish subjects. England expelled Jews in 1290. France expelled groups of Jews in 1306 and 1394. By 1350, some German cities also forced Jews to leave. Many of these Jews settled in Eastern European countries. Over the years, the Jews of Eastern Europe established thriving communities based on their religious traditions.

Reading Check **Contrast** How did the main goal of the Franciscans differ from the main goal of the Dominicans?

WH7.6.8 Understand the importance of the Catholic church as a political, intellectual, and aesthetic institution (e.g., founding of universities, political and spiritual roles of the clergy, creation of monastic and mendicant religious orders, preservation of the Latin language and religious texts, St. Thomas Aquinas's synthesis of classical philosophy with Christian theology, and the concept of "natural law").

Medieval Culture

Main Idea Church and government leaders supported learning and the arts in medieval Europe.

Reading Connection What are the most important parts of American culture today? Read to learn about the kinds of things that made up the culture of medieval Europe.

As strong governments arose, people in medieval Europe felt safer. As a result, trade, banking, and businesses prospered. A good economy meant more money to support learning and the arts and to pay for new churches and other buildings.

Medieval Art and Architecture Europe experienced a building boom in the A.D. 1000s and 1100s. Architecture is one way a society **demonstrates** what is important to its culture. In the Middle Ages, religion was an important part of life. As a result, Church leaders and wealthy merchants and nobles paid to build large new churches called cathedrals. Cathedrals were built in the Romanesque (ROH•muh•NEHSK) style or Gothic style.

Romanesque churches were rectangular buildings with long, rounded ceilings called barrel vaults. These ceilings needed huge pillars and thick walls to hold them up. Windows let in little light because they were small and set back in the thick walls.

Gothic cathedrals had ribbed vaults and pointed arches instead of rounded barrel vaults. This allowed Gothic churches to be taller than Romanesque churches. Gothic churches also used flying buttresses. These stone supports were built onto the cathedral's outside walls. They made it possible to build churches with thinner walls and large stained glass windows.

Medieval Church Architecture

Early Christian churches (above) were often rectangular with flat roofs, like some Roman buildings. Romanesque churches (top right) had rounded barrel vault ceilings, eliminating the flat roof. Gothic cathedrals, such as St. Etienne in Bourges (right), used flying buttresses on the exterior to hold up the tall ceiling inside. *Who paid for cathedrals to be built?*

Stained glass windows were picture Bibles for Christians who could not read. The pieces of stained glass often formed scenes from Jesus' life and teachings. They also let in sunlight, which came to symbolize the divine light of God.

The First Universities

Two of the first European universities were in **Bologna** (buh•LOH•nyuh), Italy, and Paris, France. Masters, or teachers, were also teaching at Oxford, England by 1096. Oxford University was founded in 1231.

Universities were created to educate and train scholars. They were like the guilds that trained craftspeople. In fact, *university* comes from a Latin word for "guild." In medieval universities, students studied grammar, logic, arithmetic, geometry, music, and astronomy. Students did not have books because books were rare before the European printing press was created in the 1400s.

University students studied their subjects for four to six years. Then a committee of teachers gave them an oral exam. If the students passed, they were given their degree.

After **obtaining** a basic degree, a student could go on to earn a doctor's degree in law, medicine, or **theology** (thee•AH•luh•jee)—the study of religion and God. Earning a doctor's degree could take 10 years or more.

Who Was Thomas Aquinas?

Beginning in the 1100s, a new way of thinking called **scholasticism** (skuh•LAS•tuh•SIH•zuhm) began to change the study of theology. Followers used reason to explore questions of faith. A Dominican friar and priest named **Thomas Aquinas** (TAH•muhs uh•KWY•nuhs) was scholasticism's greatest champion. He is best known for combining Church teachings with the ideas of Aristotle.

Europeans had forgotten about Aristotle after Rome fell and his works had been lost.

▲ **This medieval art shows students in a university classroom.** *What were some of the subjects studied in medieval universities?*

In the 1100s, however, Muslim and Jewish scholars reintroduced Aristotle to Europe using copies of his books that had been preserved in Muslim libraries. Aristotle's ideas upset many Christian thinkers because he used reason, not faith, to arrive at his conclusions about the meaning of life.

In the 1200s, Thomas Aquinas wrote several works explaining that Aristotle would have agreed with many Christian teachings. About 1267, Aquinas began writing *Summa Theologica*, or a summary of knowledge on theology. In this book, Aquinas asked hard questions such as "Does God exist?"

Aquinas wrote about government as well as theology, with an emphasis on the idea of natural law. People who believe in natural law think that some laws are part of human nature. These laws do not have to be made by governments.

Aquinas claimed that natural law gave people certain rights that the government should not take away. These included the right to live, to learn, to worship, and to reproduce. Aquinas's writings on natural law have influenced governments to the present day. His ideas have contributed in part to our belief that people have rights that government cannot take away.

Biography

WH7.6.8 Understand the importance of the Catholic church as a political, intellectual, and aesthetic institution (e.g., founding of universities, political and spiritual roles of the clergy, creation of monastic and mendicant religious orders, preservation of the Latin language and religious texts, St. Thomas Aquinas's synthesis of classical philosophy with Christian theology, and the concept of "natural law").

THOMAS AQUINAS
1225–1274

Thomas Aquinas was born in 1225 in his family's castle between Rome and Naples, Italy. His parents, Countess Theodora and Count Landulf of Aquino, were from noble families. At age five, Aquinas began school at Monte Cassino, a Benedictine monastery where his uncle was the abbot. Monastic schools required students to learn many subjects, including grammar, speech, mathematics, science, and music. When he was older, Aquinas studied at the University of Naples.

Aquinas joined the Dominican friars around 1244, against the wishes of his family. As a new Dominican, he studied in Paris under Albertus Magnus (Albert the Great). Both Aquinas and Albertus greatly admired the ideas of Aristotle.

Aquinas spent the next few decades studying, teaching, and writing. He lived in Paris, Rome, and other cities in France and Italy and taught theology. He wrote about the Bible, groups within the Church, and the ideas of philosophers. *Summa Theologica* best explains how Aquinas combines Aristotle's ideas with those of the Church. He began writing his *Summa Theologica* around 1267 and worked on it until his death.

In 1274 the pope asked Aquinas to travel to France to attend the Council of Lyons. Even though he was not in good health, he set out for the French city. He became very sick along the way. Aquinas wanted to live out his last days in a monastery, so he was taken to a Cistercian abbey in the town of Fossanova, where he died on March 7, 1274.

▲ Thomas Aquinas

> ## "The happy man in this life needs friends."
> –St. Thomas Aquinas,
> *Summa Theologiae*

Aquinas's ideas were respected during his lifetime, and as time passed they became even more important. His writings influenced governments and the Roman Catholic Church. He was made a saint in 1323.

◀ Monte Cassino monastery

Then and Now

The writings of Thomas Aquinas influenced governments and religions for a long time after his death. Which present-day writers or leaders do you think have ideas that will influence people for centuries to come?

Medieval Literature During the Middle Ages, educated people throughout Europe generally spoke or wrote in Latin. The Church used Latin in its worship, and university teachers taught in Latin.

In addition to Latin, each region had its own local language that people used every day. This everyday language is called the **vernacular** (vuhr•NA•kyuh•luhr). The vernacular included early versions of Spanish, French, English, Italian, and German.

During the 1100s, new literature was written in the vernacular. Educated people enjoyed vernacular literature, especially troubadour (TROO•buh•DOHR) poetry. These poems were about love.

Another type of vernacular literature was the heroic epic. In heroic epics, bold knights fight for kings and lords. An early example of a heroic epic is *The Song of Roland*, written in French about 1100.

In *The Song of Roland,* a brave knight named Roland fights for Charlemagne against the Muslims. Roland sounds his horn for Charlemagne to help him, but it is too late for him to be saved:

> ❝ **The Count Rollanz [Roland], with sorrow and with pangs,**
> **And with great pain sounded his olifant [horn]:**
> **Out of his mouth the clear blood leaped and ran,**
> **About his brain the very temples cracked.**
> **Loud is its voice, that horn he holds in hand;**
> **Charlès [Charlemagne] hath heard, where in the pass he stands,**
> **And Neimès [a commander] hears, and listen all the Franks.** ❞
>
> —*The Song of Roland*

✓ **Reading Check** **Explain** What is natural law?

Study Central Need help with the roles of the church and society? Visit ca.hss.glencoe.com and click on Study Central.

Section 4 Review

Reading Summary

Review the Main Ideas

- In the Middle Ages, new religious orders developed to spread Christianity. Nonbelievers and people of other faiths were mistreated.

- In medieval Europe, a number of universities opened, large Christian churches known as cathedrals were built, and European languages developed.

What Did You Learn?

1. What is theology?

2. What is vernacular language, and what were common vernacular languages in medieval times?

Critical Thinking

3. **Compare and Contrast** Draw a Venn diagram like the one below. Use it to describe the similarities and differences between Cistercians, Franciscans, and Dominicans. **CA 7RC2.0**

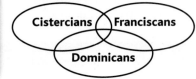

4. **Summarize** How did the Inquisition treat the people brought before it? **CA 7RC2.2**

5. The Big Ideas How did Christian beliefs result in a resettlement of Jews? Where did many Jews settle in the Middle Ages? **CA HI2.**

6. **Explain** What were Thomas Aquinas's beliefs about the government? **CA 7RC2.0**

7. **Persuasive Writing** Write a letter to a medieval university telling why you would like to become a student there. Include the subjects you would like to study. **CA 7WA2.4**

The Late Middle Ages

Guide to Reading

History Social Science Standards

WH7.6 Students analyze the geographic, political, economic, religious, and social structures of the civilizations of Medieval Europe.

Looking Back, Looking Ahead

In previous sections, you learned about the politics, religion, and culture of much of medieval Europe. In this section, you will find out about the disasters and conflicts of the late Middle Ages.

Focusing on the Main Ideas

- A terrible plague, known as the Black Death, swept through Europe in the 1300s, killing millions. *(page 365)*

- Western Europe was devastated by war in the 1300s and 1400s, as England and France fought each other and Spain and Portugal fought against the Muslims. *(page 367)*

Meeting People

Joan of Arc

Isabella of Castile (ka•STEEL)

Ferdinand of Aragon (AR•uh•GAHN)

Locating Places

Crécy (kray•SEE)

Orléans (AWR•lay•AHN)

Content Vocabulary

plague (PLAYG)

Reconquista (RAY•kohn•KEES•tuh)

Academic Vocabulary

approximate (uh•PRAHK•suh•muht)

abandon (uh•BAN•duhn)

Reading Strategy

Summarizing Information Complete a table like the one below showing the path of the Black Death in Europe and Asia.

Time Period	Affected Areas
1330s	
1340s	
1350s	

NATIONAL GEOGRAPHIC — Where & When?

London
Paris
Orléans
Granada
SICILY

1300

1400

1500

1346 The Black Death arrives in Europe

1429 Joan of Arc inspires the French

1492 The Spanish defeat the Muslims and expel the Jews

WH7.6.7 Map the spread of the bubonic plague from Central Asia to China, the Middle East, and Europe and describe its impact on global population.

The Black Death

Main Idea A terrible plague, known as the Black Death, swept through Europe in the 1300s, killing millions.

Reading Connection Have you ever been given a shot to prevent the flu or to protect you from another disease? Read to learn what happened in Europe before modern medicine could control contagious diseases.

The Middle Ages in Europe reached a high point during the 1200s. In the 1300s, however, disaster struck. A terrible **plague** (PLAYG), known as the Black Death, swept across Europe and Asia. A plague is a disease that spreads quickly and kills many people. Most scientists think the Black Death was bubonic plague—a disease caused by a type of bacteria carried by fleas. These fleas infested black rats, and in the Middle Ages, these rats were everywhere.

The Black Death probably began somewhere in the Gobi, a desert in central Asia. It had been around for centuries, but in the 1300s, it began to spread farther and more quickly than ever before. Scientists are still not sure why this occurred.

Historians believe the Mongol Empire was partly responsible for the plague spreading so fast. The empire covered all the land from Eastern Europe through central Asia to China. The Mongols opened up trade between China, India, the Middle East, and Europe. They encouraged the use of the Silk Road and other trade routes.

By the early 1300s, more goods were being shipped across central Asia than ever before. This made it possible for the Black Death to spread rapidly, as caravans infested with rats carried it from city to city.

The first outbreak took place in China in 1331. It erupted there again in 1353. The

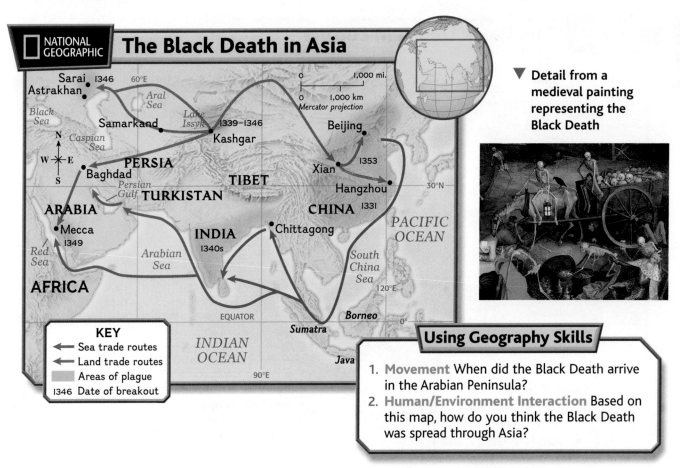

NATIONAL GEOGRAPHIC

The Black Death in Asia

KEY
← Sea trade routes
← Land trade routes
   Areas of plague
1346 Date of breakout

▼ Detail from a medieval painting representing the Black Death

Using Geography Skills

1. **Movement** When did the Black Death arrive in the Arabian Peninsula?
2. **Human/Environment Interaction** Based on this map, how do you think the Black Death was spread through Asia?

disease killed between 40 and 60 million people, cutting China's population nearly in half. The disease appeared in India in the 1340s and reached Makkah, deep inside Muslim lands, in 1349. In the meantime, it also spread to Europe.

The Black Death appeared in Europe in 1346 at the city of Caffa on the Black Sea. Caffa was a trade colony controlled by Italian merchants from the city of Genoa. Their ships carried the plague to Sicily in October 1347. From there it spread into Europe. By the end of 1349, it had spread through France and Germany and had arrived in England. By 1351, it had reached Scandinavia, Eastern Europe, and Russia. **Approximately** 19–38 million Europeans—nearly one out of every two people—died of the Black Death between 1347 and 1351.

People at the time did not know why the plague happened. Some people thought God was punishing them. Others blamed the Jews. For this reason, the Germans expelled many Jews from some of their cities.

The death of so many people in the 1300s turned Europe's economy upside down. Trade declined, and wages rose sharply because workers were few and in demand. At the same time, fewer people meant less demand for food, and food prices fell.

Landlords found they had to pay workers more and charge lower rents. Some peasants bargained with their lords to pay rent instead of owing services. This meant that they were no longer serfs. In this way, the plague, like the Crusades, helped to weaken the feudal system and change European society.

✓ **Reading Check** **Identify** How many Europeans died of the plague between 1347 and 1351?

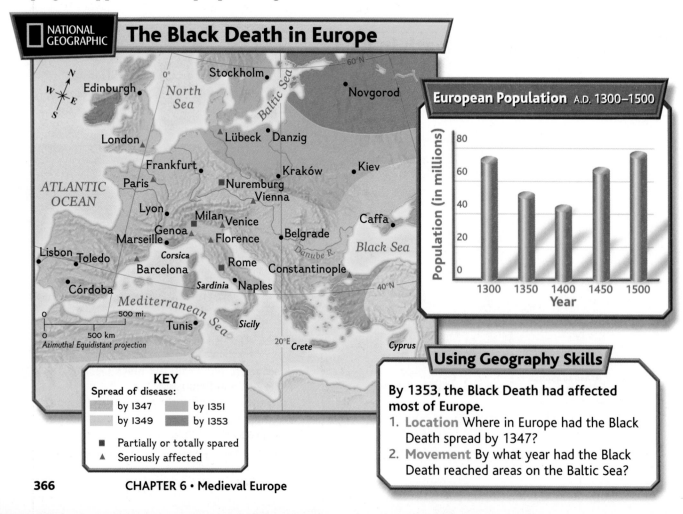

NATIONAL GEOGRAPHIC

The Black Death in Europe

European Population A.D. 1300–1500

KEY
Spread of disease:
- by 1347
- by 1351
- by 1349
- by 1353

■ Partially or totally spared
▲ Seriously affected

Using Geography Skills

By 1353, the Black Death had affected most of Europe.
1. **Location** Where in Europe had the Black Death spread by 1347?
2. **Movement** By what year had the Black Death reached areas on the Baltic Sea?

WH7.6 Students analyze the geographic, political, economic, religious, and social structures of the civilizations of Medieval Europe.
WH7.6.9 Know the history of the decline of Muslim rule in the Iberian Peninsula that culminated in the Reconquista and the rise of Spanish and Portuguese kingdoms.

A Troubled Continent

Main Idea Western Europe was devastated by war in the 1300s and 1400s, as England and France fought each other and Spain and Portugal fought against the Muslims.

Reading Connection Have you ever had a hero you looked up to? Read to learn what happened when a young peasant girl became a hero to the French people.

The bubonic plague was not Europe's only problem in the late Middle Ages. The English and French went to war with each other, while the Spanish and Portuguese fought to drive out the Muslims who had conquered them centuries before.

The Hundred Years' War

In Section 3, you learned that William of Normandy became king of England in 1066, although he still ruled Normandy. French kings wanted to drive the English out of Normandy. English kings claimed a right to the land, and in 1337 the English king Edward III declared himself king of France. This angered the French even more. War began, and it lasted for over 100 years.

The first major battle of the Hundred Years' War took place at **Crécy** (kray • SEE) after Edward invaded France. English archers defeated the French army and forced the French king to give up some of his kingdom.

Under a new king, however, the French slowly won back their land. Then in 1415 Henry V of England went on the attack. England's archers again won the battle and restored English control of northern France.

Who Was Joan of Arc?

Charles, the prince who ruled southern France, wanted to take back the north. In 1429 a French peasant girl named Joan was brought to him. She told him that her favorite saints had urged her to free France. Joan's honesty persuaded Charles to let her go with a French army to

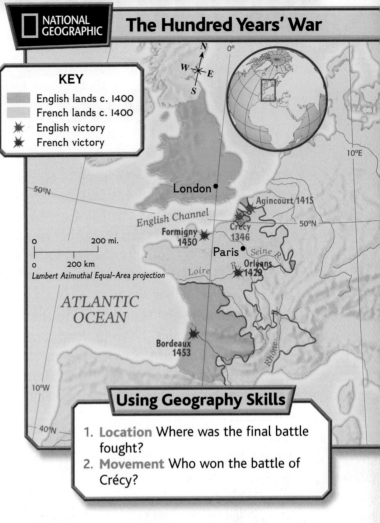

NATIONAL GEOGRAPHIC

The Hundred Years' War

KEY
- English lands c. 1400
- French lands c. 1400
- ✴ English victory
- ✴ French victory

London
Agincourt 1415
English Channel
Crécy 1346
Formigny 1450
Paris
Seine R.
Orléans 1429
Loire
ATLANTIC OCEAN
Bordeaux 1453
Rhône

Lambert Azimuthal Equal-Area projection
200 mi.
200 km

Using Geography Skills

1. **Location** Where was the final battle fought?
2. **Movement** Who won the battle of Crécy?

Orléans (AWR • lay • AHN). Joan's faith stirred the soldiers, and they took the city.

Shortly after, with Joan at his side, Charles was declared king. A few months later, however, the English captured Joan. They handed her over to the Inquisition, which had her burned at the stake. She later became known as **Joan of Arc.**

The French finally defeated the English in 1453. The king had spent almost all of his money, but the war strengthened French devotion to their country. French kings used that spirit to develop a strong government.

The Hundred Years' War also took a toll on the English and their economy. In addition, a civil war known as the Wars of the Roses, broke out among the nobles over who should be king. The winner, Henry Tudor, became King Henry VII.

JOAN OF ARC
1412–1431

Jeanne d'Arc—better known as Joan of Arc—was born January 6, 1412, in the village of Domremy in eastern France. Joan was the youngest of five children. When she was 13, she began having visions of saints telling her to attend church and to be a good person. As time passed, the voices began telling her to speak with Charles VII about her ability to help France. After three attempts, she was finally allowed to see the leader. Charles spoke with Joan and had her questioned by doctors and priests. All of them believed Joan was a good person and was telling the truth.

Joan was sent with the French army to the city of Orléans, which was surrounded by the English. Everywhere she went, Joan carried a banner with religious pictures on it. She rode at the front of the troops, giving them directions and encouragement. The troops came to believe God was on their side. Inspired by Joan, they fought harder and better than ever before. They defeated the English at Orléans and began driving them out of France.

"Courage! Do not fall back."
–Joan of Arc

Joan of Arc on horseback

In 1430 Joan said the saints revealed to her that she would soon be captured. In late May, she was seized by the English and charged with heresy and improper dress—for the soldier's uniform she wore as army commander. Joan was found guilty and told that if she admitted her crimes, she would not be executed. She insisted she had done nothing wrong and was executed on May 30, 1431. Almost two decades later, an investigation into the matter found Joan innocent of all charges. In 1920 she was made a saint by the Roman Catholic Church.

Then and Now

Joan was tried and found guilty, even though many people felt she was innocent. She was also denied many rights during her trial. What prevents this from happening today in the United States?

Spain and Portugal Fight the Muslims

During the Middle Ages, Muslims ruled most of Spain and Portugal. These two lands make up the Iberian Peninsula. Most of the peninsula's people, however, were Christians. Some were also Jews.

The Muslims developed a rich culture in Spain and Portugal. They built beautiful mosques and palaces, such as the Alhambra in the southern kingdom of Granada. They also founded schools where Muslims, Jews, and Christians studied together. Most Christians, however, opposed Muslim rule. Their struggle to take back the Iberian Peninsula was called the *Reconquista* (RAY•kohn•KEES•tuh), or "reconquest."

By the 1200s, the Christians had set up three kingdoms: Portugal in the west, Castile in the center, and Aragon on the Mediterranean coast. Over the next 200 years, the Muslims slowly lost ground, until all that remained was Granada in the south.

In 1469 Princess **Isabella of Castile** (ka•STEEL) married Prince **Ferdinand of Aragon** (AR•uh•GAHN). Within 10 years, they became king and queen and joined their lands into one country called Spain. Ferdinand and Isabella wanted all of Spain to be Catholic, and they began to pressure the Jews to convert.

To escape persecution, some Jews became Christians. Ferdinand and Isabella, however, believed many still secretly practiced Judaism. So they set up the Spanish Inquisition. The Spanish Inquisition tried and tortured thousands of people charged with heresy. In 1492 Ferdinand and Isabella forced Jews to convert or leave Spain.

Next the king and queen turned to the Muslims. In 1492 Spain's armies conquered Granada. Ten years later, Muslims had to convert or leave. Most **abandoned** Spain for North Africa.

Reading Check **Cause and Effect** What caused the Hundred Years' War?

Study Central Need help with the late Middle Ages? Visit ca.hss.glencoe.com and click on Study Central.

Section 5 Review

Reading Summary

Review the Main Ideas

- A plague, known as the Black Death, killed millions of people in Europe and Asia and greatly changed Europe's economy and society.

- Wars between England and France weakened those countries' economies, and Spain became a united Catholic country.

What Did You Learn?

1. How was the Black Death spread?

2. Who was Joan of Arc, and why is she important?

Critical Thinking

3. **Understanding Cause and Effect** Draw a diagram like the one below. Fill in some of the effects of the Black Death on Europe. **CA HI2.**

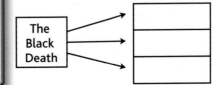

4. **The Big Ideas** How did the Hundred Years' War affect the countries involved? **CA 7RC2.3**

5. **Summarize** Describe the history of Spain and Portugal during the Middle Ages. **CA 7RC2.0**

6. **Writing Research Reports** Do you think the removal of the Jews and Muslims from Spain was a wise policy? Use your local library to research information about these events. Write an essay explaining your answer. **CA 7WA2.3**

Analyzing Primary Sources

Medieval Life

WH7.6.5 Know the significance of developments in medieval English legal and constitutional practices and their importance in the rise of modern democratic thought and representative institutions (e.g., Magna Carta, parliament, development of habeas corpus, an independent judiciary in England). **WH7.6.7** Map the spread of the bubonic plague from Central Asia to China, the Middle East, and Europe and describe its impact on global population.

During the Middle Ages, religion played a key role in how people looked at the world. Whether discussing a battle, creating governmental policy, or planning the final moments of a person's life, Europeans based many of their views on their religions.

Read the passages on pages 370 and 371, and answer the questions that follow.

King John signing ▶
the Magna Carta

Reader's Dictionary

exploits: deeds; adventures

audaciously (aw•DAY•shuhs•lee): boldly

perpetuity (PUHR•puh•TOO•uh•tee): time without end

unimpaired: left alone

contagious (kuhn•TAY•juhs): something that spreads quickly

pestilence (PEHS•tuh•luhns): plague

parson: a church leader

sacrament of penance: holy rite in which a person confesses his or her sins and is forgiven

---

The Epic of *Beowulf*

Beowulf is one of the earliest poems written in Old English, written some time in the A.D. 700s. It tells the story of a conflict between good and evil. In the following passage, Hrothgar, leader of the Danes, thanks Beowulf for killing the monster Grendel.

"Now Beowulf, best of men, I will cherish you in my heart as a son. . . . It is often enough that I have given a reward for less, and honoured with my gifts a meaner soldier and a lesser fighter. But by your **exploits** you have established your fame

for ever. May God reward you with good fortune, as He has done up to now."

Beowulf replied: "When we **audaciously** took on the might of the unknown we fought and discharged our task with the greatest goodwill. . . . The evildoer is burdened with sins and will live none the longer. . . . The guilty wretch must now wait for the last judgement, and the sentence of almighty God."

—*Beowulf*, David Wright, trans.

The Magna Carta

The Magna Carta gave common people some freedoms and increased the power of the nobles by limiting the powers of the king. Through this document, it is clear that religion played an important role in shaping English politics.

(1) FIRST, THAT WE HAVE GRANTED TO GOD, and by this present charter have confirmed for us and our heirs in **perpetuity,** that the English Church shall be free, and shall have its rights undiminished, and its liberties **unimpaired.** . . .

TO ALL FREE MEN OF OUR KINGDOM we have also granted, for us and our heirs for ever, all the liberties written out below. . . .

(8) No widow shall be compelled to marry, so long as she wishes to remain without a husband. . . .

(20) For a trivial offence, a free man shall be fined only in proportion to the degree of his offence. . . .

(30) No sheriff, royal official, or other person shall take horses or carts for transport from any free man, without his consent. . . .

(40) To no one will we sell, to no one deny or delay right or justice.

(41) All merchants may enter or leave England unharmed and without fear, and may stay or travel within it, by land or water, for purposes of trade. . . .

—Magna Carta

The Black Death

The Black Death was a terrible plague that swept through Europe and Asia in the mid-1300s. It killed nearly 50 percent of Europe's population. The following is a letter that the bishop of Bath and Wells wrote to parish priests in 1349.

The **contagious pestilence** of the present day, which is spreading far and wide, has left many parish churches without **parson** or priest to care for the parishioners. Since no priests can be found who are willing, . . . to take . . . care of these aforesaid places, nor to visit the sick and administer to them the sacraments of the church, we understand that many people are dying without the **sacrament of penance.** [Therefore] . . . persuade all men, in particular, those who are now sick or should feel sick in the future, that, if they are on the point of death and cannot secure the services of a priest, then they should make confession to each other . . . or if no man is present, then even to a woman.

—Robert S. Gottfried, *The Black Death*

DBQ Document-Based Questions

The Epic of Beowulf
1. According to the passage, how are the good rewarded and the guilty punished?
2. What does Beowulf believe will happen to Grendel at the last judgement?

The Magna Carta
3. By using the phrase "free man," who does the Magna Carta not cover?
4. What complaints might the people have had that the Magna Carta attempted to fix?

The Black Death
5. Why did people die without receiving the sacrament of penance?
6. What did the bishop recommend to correct the situation?
7. What do the bishop's words tell you about the status of women in England at this time?

Read to Write
8. Using examples from each of the sources, describe how religion influenced different aspects of life in medieval Europe. **CA CS1.**

Review Content Vocabulary

Match the word in the first column with its definition in the second column.

___ 1. fief   a. worked their own land and a lord's land

___ 2. serf   b. the study of religion

___ 3. concordat   c. people ordained as priests

___ 4. clergy   d. land granted to a vassal

___ 5. heresy   e. agreement between the pope and the ruler of a country

___ 6. theology   f. a belief different from Church teachings

Review the Main Ideas

Section 1 • The Early Middle Ages

7. Which peoples invaded Europe in the Middle Ages?

8. How did the Catholic Church affect medieval Europe?

Section 2 • Feudalism

9. What was the basis for wealth and power in medieval Europe?

10. What was the result of increased trade?

Section 3 • Kingdoms and Crusades

11. What changes in England were steps toward representative government?

12. Which groups fought with each other in the Crusades? Why were they fighting?

Section 4 • The Church and Society

13. How did the Catholic Church use its power to uphold its teachings?

14. Why did learning and the arts flourish in medieval Europe?

Section 5 • The Late Middle Ages

15. Describe the Black Death and its effects.

16. Which European nations were at war during the 1300s and 1400s?

Critical Thinking

17. **Cause and Effect** What improvements in farming led to an increase in the production of food? **CA HI2.**

18. **Compare** What did Alfred the Great and William the Conqueror succeed in doing? **CA 7RC2.0**

19. **Analyze** According to Thomas Aquinas, how does natural law limit the power of government? **CA 7RC2.2**

Geography Skills

Study the map below and answer the following questions.

20. **Location** On which river was the battle of Orléans fought? **CA CS3.**

21. **Interaction** Which side do you think had an advantage, based on the map? Consider the land held and geography. **CA CS3.**

22. **Place** Why were most battle sites near the English Channel? **CA CS3.**

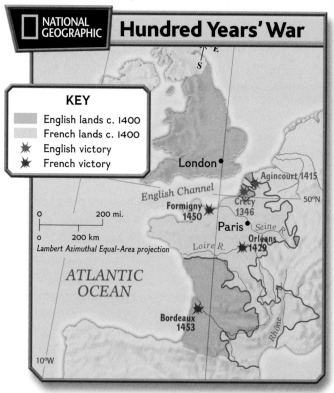

NATIONAL GEOGRAPHIC **Hundred Years' War**

KEY
English lands c. 1400
French lands c. 1400
✹ English victory
✹ French victory

Read to Write

23. **The Big Ideas** **Writing Summaries** The feudal system divided medieval society into different classes. Look over Section 2. Write a summary of the important people, events, and ideas that helped to create these different classes. Use the summary to explain why feudalism was important to medieval Europe. **CA 7WA2.5**

24. **Using Your** **FOLDABLES** Choose one major medieval European event from your foldable and write a paragraph that predicts how history would have been different if that event had not occurred. **CA HI2.**

Using Academic Vocabulary

25. Complete the chart below to fill in the missing tense of each word.

Past Tense	Present Tense
	enable
excluded	
	shift
	process
guaranteed	
	document
obtained	
demonstrated	
	approximate
	abandon

Linking Past and Present

26. **Comparing** Describe how present-day universities compare to medieval ones, such as those in Bologna, Paris, and Oxford. In your description, explain what it would be like to have to learn without the use of books. **CA HI2.**

Reviewing Skills

27. **Analysis Skill** **Comparing Cultures** Write an essay comparing feudalism in Europe and Japan. Use the text in Chapters 5 and 6 as well as sources from the library and Internet to research the similarities and differences. **CA HI3.**

28. **Reading Skill** **Making Inferences** Reread page 349 describing the importance of the Magna Carta. What inferences can you make about the future English government from the text? What are the possible benefits to England's people? Imagine that you are living in the 1200s. Write a newspaper article describing the Magna Carta's effect on your life and the lives of people you know. Use your local library to find more information about the Magna Carta and its significance. **CA 7WA2.3**

Standards Practice

Read the passage below and answer the following questions.

> No free man shall be taken, imprisoned, disseised [seized], outlawed, banished, or in any way destroyed, nor will We proceed against or prosecute him, except by the lawful judgment of his peers and by the law of the land.

29 The above passage comes from which influential document?

A the Constitution

B the Concordat of Worms

C the Song of Roland

D the Magna Carta

30 What act of justice is this passage describing?

A illegal searches

B Miranda rights

C trial by jury

D freedom of speech

Making Comparisons

Compare civilizations of the Middle Ages by reviewing the information below. Can you see how the peoples of these civilizations had lives that were very much like yours?

Where in the World?
- Chapter 4
- Chapter 5
- Chapter 6

NATIONAL GEOGRAPHIC

	China in the Middle Ages Chapter 4	Medieval Japan Chapter 5	Medieval Europe Chapter 6
Where did these civilizations develop?	• Mainland of East Asia 	• Islands off coast of East Asia	• Northwestern Europe and Mediterranean area
Who were some important people in these civilizations?	• Taizong, ruled A.D. 627–649 • Empress Wu, ruled A.D. 684–705 • Kublai Khan, ruled A.D. 1271–1294 • Zheng He, A.D. 1371–1433	• Prince Shotoku, A.D. 573–621 • Murasaki Shikibu, C. A.D. 973–1025 • Minamoto Yoritomo, A.D. 1147–1199 • Ashikaga Takauji, A.D. 1305–1358	• Charlemagne, ruled A.D. 768–814 • William the Conqueror, ruled A.D. 1066–1087 • Thomas Aquinas, A.D. 1225–1274 • Joan of Arc, A.D. 1412–1431
Where did most of the people live?	• Farming villages and towns along major rivers	• Fishing and farming villages in coastal plains area	• Farming villages on estates located on plains; trading centers in Italy and Flanders

	China in the Middle Ages *Chapter 4*	Medieval Japan *Chapter 5*	Medieval Europe *Chapter 6*
What were these people's beliefs?	• Confucianism, Daoism, Buddhism	• Shintoism, Buddhism	• Roman Catholic with small numbers of Jews and Muslims
What was their government like?	• Emperors ruled with the help of scholar-officials selected by exams	• Emperors ruled in name but power held by military leaders	• Feudal territories united into kingdoms
What was their language and writing like?	• Chinese: symbols standing for objects are combined to represent ideas	• Japanese: characters standing for ideas as well as symbols representing sounds	• Many languages derived from Latin and Germanic
What contributions did they make?	• Civil service based on merit; invented movable type, gunpowder, and the compass	• Developed ideas based on harmony with nature	• Developed universities and representative government
How do these changes affect me? *Can you add any?*	• The Chinese invented fireworks, the compass, and printed books	• Japanese warriors developed martial arts, such as jujitsu and karate	• Medieval Europeans passed on Christian ideas and a system of banking

Unit 3

A Changing World

Why It's Important

Each chapter you will study in this unit describes important developments in history.

- Renaissance and Reformation thinkers and artists supported the individual.
- Native Americans built a network of trade routes.
- Explorers and mercantilism brought the world closer together.
- People during the Enlightenment developed ideas about freedom and democracy.

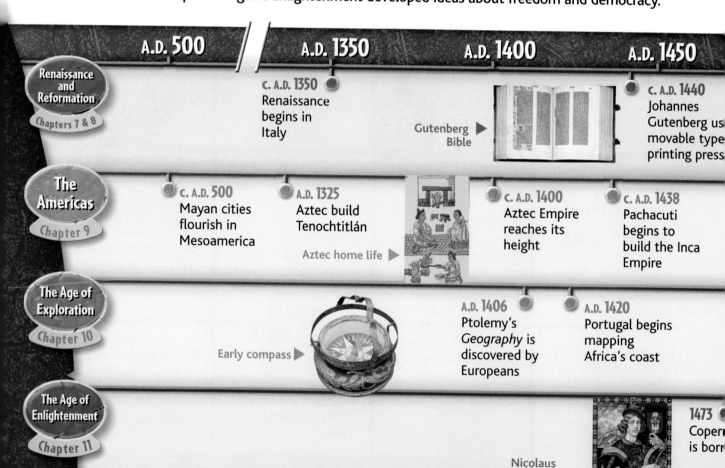

A.D. 500 | A.D. 1350 | A.D. 1400 | A.D. 1450

Renaissance and Reformation
Chapters 7 & 8

C. A.D. 1350
Renaissance begins in Italy

Gutenberg Bible ▶

C. A.D. 1440
Johannes Gutenberg us[es] movable type [for] printing press

The Americas
Chapter 9

C. A.D. 500
Mayan cities flourish in Mesoamerica

A.D. 1325
Aztec build Tenochtitlán

Aztec home life ▶

C. A.D. 1400
Aztec Empire reaches its height

C. A.D. 1438
Pachacuti begins to build the Inca Empire

The Age of Exploration
Chapter 10

Early compass ▶

A.D. 1406
Ptolemy's *Geography* is discovered by Europeans

A.D. 1420
Portugal begins mapping Africa's coast

The Age of Enlightenment
Chapter 11

Nicolaus Copernicus ▶

1473
Coper[nicus] is bor[n]

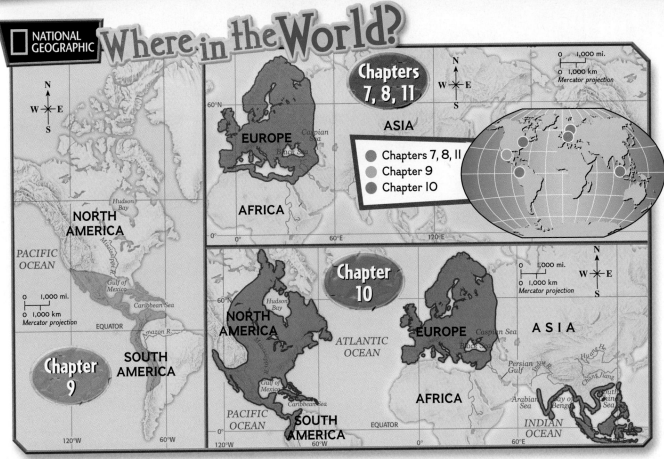

NATIONAL GEOGRAPHIC
Where in the World?

Chapters 7, 8, 11
- Chapters 7, 8, 11
- Chapter 9
- Chapter 10

Chapter 10

Chapter 9

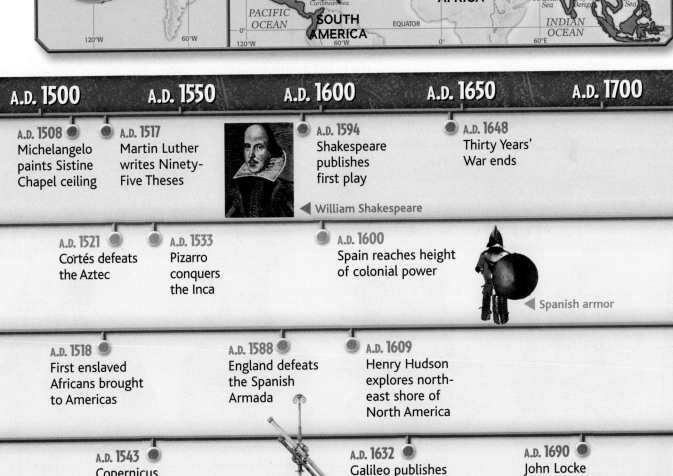

A.D. **1500**	A.D. **1550**	A.D. **1600**	A.D. **1650**	A.D. **1700**

A.D. **1508**
Michelangelo paints Sistine Chapel ceiling

A.D. **1517**
Martin Luther writes Ninety-Five Theses

A.D. **1594**
Shakespeare publishes first play

◄ William Shakespeare

A.D. **1648**
Thirty Years' War ends

A.D. **1521**
Cortés defeats the Aztec

A.D. **1533**
Pizarro conquers the Inca

A.D. **1600**
Spain reaches height of colonial power

◄ Spanish armor

A.D. **1518**
First enslaved Africans brought to Americas

A.D. **1588**
England defeats the Spanish Armada

A.D. **1609**
Henry Hudson explores north-east shore of North America

A.D. **1543**
Copernicus presents a new view of the universe

Galileo's telescope ▶

A.D. **1632**
Galileo publishes his ideas on astronomy

A.D. **1690**
John Locke develops theory of government

Places to Locate

1 Sistine Chapel

See The Renaissance
Chapter 7

2 Wittenberg

See The Reformation
Chapter 8

NORTH
AMERICA

*Atlantic
Ocean*

Pacific Ocean

SOUTH
AMERICA

3

People to Meet

Pachacuti

Ruled A.D. 1438–1471
Inca ruler
Chapter 9, page 463

**Leonardo
da Vinci**

A.D. 1452–1519
**Italian artist
and scientist**
Chapter 7, page 396

**Martin
Luther**

A.D. 1483–1546
**German Protestant
leader**
Chapter 8, page 427

**Hernán
Cortés**

A.D. 1485–1547
Spanish conqueror
Chapter 9, page 475

3 Machu Picchu

See The Americas
Chapter 9

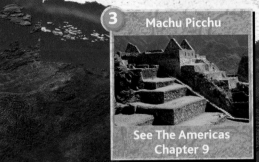

4 Portuguese lighthouse

See The Age of
Exploration Chapter 10

5 Versailles

See The Age of Enlight-
enment Chapter 11

ASIA

EUROPE

AFRICA

*Indian
Ocean*

**Catherine
de' Medici**

A.D. 1519–1589
French queen
Chapter 8, page 438

Elizabeth I

Ruled A.D. 1558–1603
English queen
Chapter 10, page 496

John Locke

A.D. 1632–1704
**English political
thinker**
Chapter 11, page 527

**Isaac
Newton**

A.D. 1642–1727
**English
mathematician**
Chapter 11, page 521

Chapter 7

The Renaissance

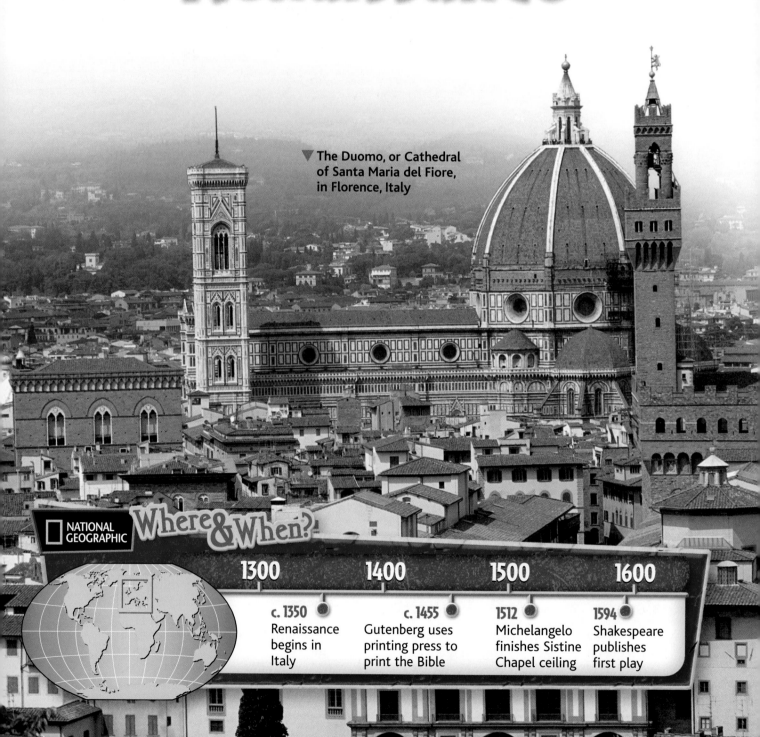

▼ The Duomo, or Cathedral of Santa Maria del Fiore, in Florence, Italy

NATIONAL GEOGRAPHIC Where & When?

1300	1400	1500	1600
c. 1350 Renaissance begins in Italy	**c. 1455** Gutenberg uses printing press to print the Bible	**1512** Michelangelo finishes Sistine Chapel ceiling	**1594** Shakespeare publishes first play

History Online

Chapter Overview Visit ca.hss.glencoe.com for a preview of Chapter 7.

The Big Ideas

Section 1 The Renaissance Begins

Exploration and trade spread ideas and goods. The Italian city-states grew wealthy through trade. This wealth led to new values and new art.

Section 2 New Ideas and Literature

Studying the past helps to understand the present. Renaissance thinkers looked to the ancient Greeks and Romans to develop a new way of understanding the world. Renaissance thinking influenced many aspects of society, including art and literature, and is still important today.

Section 3 Renaissance Art

The interaction of different societies brings about the development of new ideas, art, and technology. The Italian artists developed Renaissance ideas of art and architecture and spread their ideas to northern Europe.

 View the Chapter 7 video in the Glencoe Video Program.

FOLDABLES™ Study Organizer

Categorizing Information *Make the following foldable to organize information about the ideas and creative works of the Renaissance.*

Step 1 *Collect two sheets of paper and place them about one inch apart.*

Keep the edges straight.

Step 2 *Fold the bottom edges of the paper to form four tabs.*

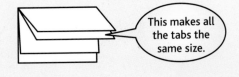

This makes all the tabs the same size.

Step 3 *When all the tabs are the same size, crease the paper to hold the tabs in place and staple the sheets together. Turn the paper and label each tab as shown.*

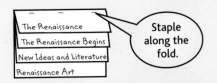

The Renaissance
The Renaissance Begins
New Ideas and Literature
Renaissance Art

Staple along the fold.

Reading and Writing *As you read, use your foldable to write down important concepts and events that occurred during the Renaissance. Write facts on each appropriate tab.*

7 Get Ready to Read

Questioning

Reading Skill

1 Learn It!

Asking questions helps you to understand what you read. As you read, think about the questions you would like answered. Often you can find the answer in the next paragraph or section. Learn to ask good questions by asking *who, what, when, where, why,* and *how* about the main ideas, people, places, and events. Read the passage below and the highlighted questions.

What subjects had the Greeks and Romans studied that became of interest again?

> In some ways the Renaissance was a rebirth of interest in the same subjects the Greeks and Romans had studied. After the horrible years of the Black Death, Europeans began looking to the past when times seemed better. They wanted to learn how to make their own society better.
>
> — *from page 385*

What was the Black Death, and how long did it last? What do you already know about it?

How did Europeans think they could improve society?

Reading Tip

As you read, turn headings into questions.

2 Practice It!

Read the paragraph below about Renaissance art, and then read the directions that follow.

> During the Renaissance, wealthy Italian families and church leaders paid artists to create paintings, sculptures, and buildings for display throughout their cities. The pope himself funded many works of art to decorate the Vatican. Renaissance artists followed the models of the ancient Romans and Greeks but expressed humanist ideas.
>
> — *from page 409*

Read to Write

Write a *What If* paragraph based on what you read in this chapter. For example, *what if* the Renaissance had not spread outside of Italy? Your paragraph should answer your *What If* question.

Practice using the question words: *who, what, where, when, why,* and *how.* Make a chart like the one below. Using each question word in the first column, ask a question about the paragraph above. Then reread the section to find the answers.

	Question	Answer
Who		
What		
Where		
When		
Why		
How		

▲ Painting by Jan van Eyck

3 Apply It!

Read the text in Section 2 about Renaissance humanism. Write four questions about the passage. Share your questions with another student and discuss possible answers.

Section 1

The Renaissance Begins

Guide to Reading

History Social Science Standards

WH7.8 Students analyze the origins, accomplishments, and geographic diffusion of the Renaissance.

Looking Back, Looking Ahead

Previously, you learned about life in medieval Europe. In this section, you will learn why Europeans became interested in art and learning as they left the Middle Ages behind.

Focusing on the Main Ideas

- The wealthy urban society of the Italian city-states brought a rebirth of learning and art to Europe. *(page 385)*

- Italy's location helped its city-states grow wealthy from trade and banking, but many of the cities fell under the control of strong rulers. *(page 387)*

- Unlike medieval nobles, the nobles of the Italian city-states lived in cities and were active in trade, banking, and public life. *(page 390)*

Locating Places
Florence (FLAWR•uhns)
Venice (VEH•nuhs)

Meeting People
Marco Polo (MAHR•koh   POH•loh)
Medici (MEH•duh•chee)
Niccolò Machiavelli (NEE•koh•LOH MA•kee•uh•VEH•lee)

Content Vocabulary
Renaissance (REH•nuh•SAHNS)
secular (SEH•kyuh•luhr)
doge (DOHJ)
diplomacy (duh•PLOH•muh•see)

Academic Vocabulary
network (NEHT•WUHRK)
publish (PUH•blihsh)
expert (EHK•SPUHRT)

Reading Strategy
Summarizing Information Complete a chart like the one below showing the reasons Italian city-states grew wealthy.

Wealth Grows in City-States

NATIONAL GEOGRAPHIC Where & When?

1350 — **c. 1350** Renaissance begins in Italy

1450 — **1434** Medici family begins rule of Florence

1550 — **1513** Machiavelli writes *The Prince*

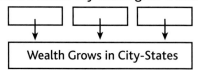

Genoa • Venice • Florence • Rome

The Italian Renaissance

Main Idea The wealthy urban society of the Italian city-states brought a rebirth of learning and art to Europe.

Reading Connection Hollywood makes many of the world's movies. Why is it the center of the movie industry? Read to learn why the city-states of Italy became the center of art during the Renaissance.

Renaissance (REH•nuh•SAHNS) means "rebirth." The years from about 1350 to 1550 in European history are called the Renaissance because there was a rebirth of interest in art and learning.

In some ways the Renaissance was a rebirth of interest in the same subjects the Greeks and Romans had studied. After the horrible years of the Black Death, Europeans began looking to the past when times seemed better. They wanted to learn how to make their own society better.

During the Renaissance, Europeans also began to stress the significance of the individual. They began to believe that people could make an impact and change the world for the better.

People were still very religious during the Renaissance, but they also began to celebrate human achievements. People became more **secular** (SEH•kyuh•luhr). This means they were more interested in this world than in religion and getting to heaven.

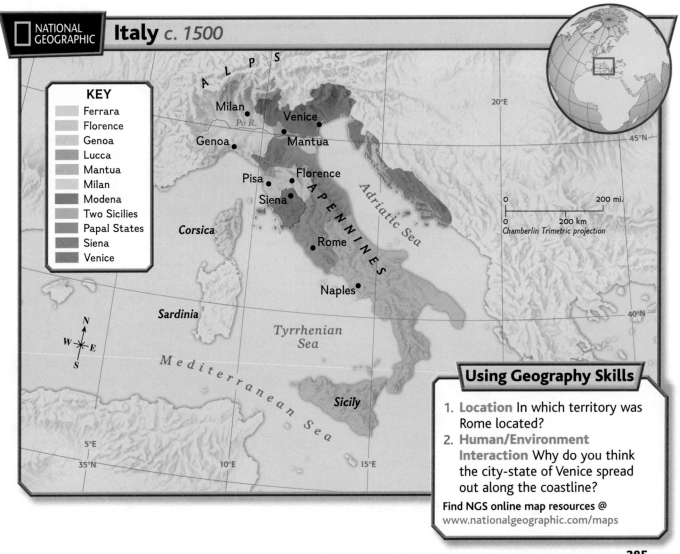

NATIONAL GEOGRAPHIC

Italy c. 1500

KEY
- Ferrara
- Florence
- Genoa
- Lucca
- Mantua
- Milan
- Modena
- Two Sicilies
- Papal States
- Siena
- Venice

ALPS

Milan
Po R.
Venice
Genoa
Mantua
Pisa
Florence
Siena
APENNINES
Corsica
Rome
Naples
Sardinia
Tyrrhenian Sea
Mediterranean Sea
Sicily
Adriatic Sea

20°E
45°N
40°N
5°E
10°E
15°E
35°N

0   200 mi.
0   200 km
Chamberlin Trimetric projection

Using Geography Skills

1. **Location** In which territory was Rome located?
2. **Human/Environment Interaction** Why do you think the city-state of Venice spread out along the coastline?

Find NGS online map resources @ www.nationalgeographic.com/maps

Why did the Renaissance begin in Italy? First of all, Italy had been the center of the Roman Empire. Ruins and art surrounded the Italians and reminded them of their past. It was only natural that they became interested in Greek and Roman art and tried to make their own art as good.

Another reason the Renaissance began in Italy was because by the 1300s, Italy's cities had become very wealthy. This enabled them to pay painters, sculptors, architects, and other artists to produce new works.

A third reason was because the region was still divided into many small city-states. **Florence** (FLAWR•uhns), **Venice** (VEH•nuhs), Genoa, Milan, and Rome were some of the most important cities of the Renaissance.

The Italian city-states competed with each other. This helped bring about the Renaissance. Wealthy nobles and merchants wanted artists to produce works that increased the fame of their cities.

In most of Europe, the vast majority of people lived in the country, including the knights and nobles who owned estates. In Italy's city-states, the population was becoming more urban. That means more people were living in the city, rather than in the country. So many people living together in a city meant more customers for artists and more money for art.

The large number of people living in cities also led to more discussion and sharing of ideas about art. Just as the city-states of ancient Greece had produced many great works of art and literature, so too did urban society in Italy.

Reading Check **Explain** Why did the Renaissance start in Italy?

Florence Cathedral

Florence, Italy, was one of the centers of the Renaissance. The Florence Cathedral, better known as the Duomo, became a symbol of the city, as well as one of the finest examples of Renaissance architecture and engineering. *What were other important Italian Renaissance cities?*

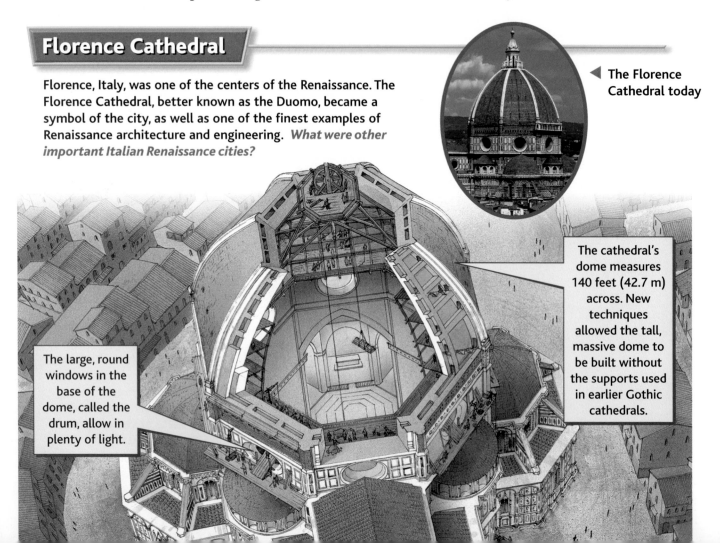

◄ The Florence Cathedral today

The cathedral's dome measures 140 feet (42.7 m) across. New techniques allowed the tall, massive dome to be built without the supports used in earlier Gothic cathedrals.

The large, round windows in the base of the dome, called the drum, allow in plenty of light.

WH7.8.2 Explain the importance of Florence in the early stages of the Renaissance and the growth of independent trading cities (e.g., Venice), with emphasis on the cities' importance in the spread of Renaissance ideas.

WH7.8.3 Understand the effects of the reopening of the ancient "Silk Road" between Europe and China, including Marco Polo's travels and the location of his routes.

The Rise of Italy's City-States

Main Idea Italy's location helped its city-states grow wealthy from trade and banking, but many of the cities fell under the control of strong rulers.

Reading Connection Do you have a bank account? What are banks for? Read to learn how banking helped to make the Italian city-states wealthy and powerful.

During the Middle Ages, no ruler was able to unite Italy into a single kingdom. There were several reasons for this. First of all, the Roman Catholic Church did everything it could to stop the rise of a powerful kingdom in Italy. Church leaders were afraid that if a strong ruler united Italy, that same ruler would be able to control the pope and the Church.

At the same time, the city-states that developed in Italy were about equal in strength. They fought many wars and often captured territory from each other, but no state was able to defeat all the others.

Probably the most important reason the city-states stayed independent was because they became very wealthy. With their great wealth, they could build large fleets and hire people to fight in their armies. A person who fights in an army for money is called a mercenary. The city-states also loaned money to the kings of Europe. The kings left the city-states alone so they could borrow more money in the future.

Italy's City-States Grow Wealthy

The Italian city-states obtained their wealth through trade. The geography of the long Italian peninsula meant that most of the city-states had a coastline and ports where merchant ships could dock. They also had a prime location on the Mediterranean Sea. Spain and France lay to the west, and the Byzantine and Ottoman Empires lay to the east. North Africa was only a short trip to the south.

From the Byzantines, Turks, and Arabs, the Italians bought Chinese silk and Indian spices and sold them to people in Western Europe for very high prices. At the same time, from the Spanish, French, Dutch, and English, they bought goods such as wool, wine, and glass that they could sell in the Middle East. The Italian cities also had many skilled artisans, who could take raw materials the merchants bought and make goods that could be sold for high prices.

Geography was not the only reason for the success of the Italians. Several events led to trade becoming even more important in the city-states. First, the Crusades brought Italian merchants into contact with Arab merchants. Second, the rise of the Mongol Empire united almost all of Asia into one vast trade **network.**

The Mongols encouraged trade and protected the Silk Road from China to the Middle East. This made it cheaper and easier for caravans to transport goods from China

▲ **This painting shows a wealthy Italian family during the Renaissance.** *How did competition between the city-states lead to great works of art?*

and India to Muslim and Byzantine cities. As more and more silk and spices were transferred from Asia, the price of these goods fell. More Europeans could afford the luxuries, and demand for the items greatly increased. In turn, business for Italian merchants continued to grow.

Who Was Marco Polo?

Europeans were fascinated with Asia and its goods after reading a book written by **Marco Polo** (MAHR•koh POH•loh), a merchant from the city of Venice. In the 1270s, Marco Polo accompanied his father and uncle on an amazing journey to China. They set off to meet Kublai Khan, the ruler of the Mongol Empire.

When the Polo family finally made it to the khan's court, the great emperor was impressed with Marco Polo. He sent Marco Polo on business all over China. Marco Polo asked many questions and learned more about Asia than any other European.

When he returned to Europe, he **published** a book about his travels. His stories helped increase interest in China and made many people want to buy China's goods.

The Wealth of Florence

No city was more famous in the Renaissance than Florence. It was the first to grow wealthy, and it produced many famous artists. It sat on the banks of the Arno River surrounded by beautiful hills. It was walled and had many tall towers for defense. Its people were known for their love of elegant clothing.

At first, Florence's wealth came from trading cloth, especially wool. The city's merchants sailed to England to get sheep's wool. Artisans in Florence then wove it into fine fabrics. Florentines also found another way to make money—banking.

With goods pouring into Italy from around the world, merchants needed to

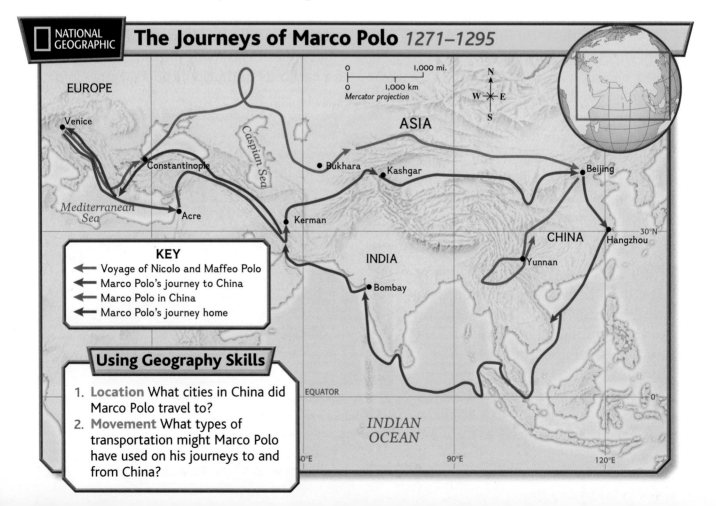

NATIONAL GEOGRAPHIC

The Journeys of Marco Polo 1271–1295

EUROPE

Venice

Constantinople

Caspian Sea

Bukhara

Kashgar

ASIA

Beijing

30°N

Hangzhou

CHINA

Mediterranean Sea

Acre

Kerman

INDIA

Yunnan

Bombay

EQUATOR

0°

INDIAN OCEAN

1,000 mi.
1,000 km
Mercator projection

KEY
← Voyage of Nicolo and Maffeo Polo
← Marco Polo's journey to China
← Marco Polo in China
← Marco Polo's journey home

Using Geography Skills

1. **Location** What cities in China did Marco Polo travel to?
2. **Movement** What types of transportation might Marco Polo have used on his journeys to and from China?

The Ducal Palace today ▶

▲ **This painting from Renaissance Italy shows the busy pier and the Ducal Palace in Venice.** *What industry provided some of Venice's wealth?*

know the value of coins from different countries. Florentine bankers became the **experts.** They used the florin, the gold coin of Florence, to measure the value of other money. Bankers also began lending money and charging interest. Florence's richest family, the **Medici** (MEH•duh•chee), were bankers. They had branch banks as far away as London.

The Rise of Venice

The wealthiest city-state of all was Venice, where Marco Polo was born. Venice is at the northern end of the Adriatic Sea. The Venetians were great sailors and shipbuilders. They built their city on many small, swampy islands just off the coast. Early Venetians learned how to drive long wooden poles into mud to support their buildings.

Instead of paving roads, the Venetians cut canals through their swampy islands and used boats to move about. Even today, many of the streets in the older parts of Venice are canals and waterways. Gondolas—a type of long, narrow boat—still carry people along these canals.

Some of Venice's wealth came from building ships. Artisans worked on ships at a shipyard known as the Arsenal. Teams of workers cut the wood, shaped it into hulls, caulked (or sealed) the wood, and made sails and oars. Sometimes Venetians needed ships quickly. When the Turks tried to take a Venetian colony in the Mediterranean, the Arsenal built 100 ships in only two months to prepare for battle.

✓ **Reading Check** **Describe** How did Florence and the Medici family become so wealthy?

The Urban Noble

Main Idea Unlike medieval nobles, the nobles of the Italian city-states lived in cities and were active in trade, banking, and public life.

Reading Connection How does our society measure wealth? Before the Renaissance, wealth was based on the amount of land a person owned. Read to learn how that changed during the Renaissance.

The wealthy men of the Italian city-states were a new type of leader—the urban noble. Before this time, European nobles got their wealth from land, not trade. In fact, they looked down on trade and believed themselves to be above the town merchants.

In the Italian city-states, old noble families moved to the cities. They mixed with wealthy merchants and decided that money from trade was just as good as money from land.

Meanwhile, wealthy merchants copied the manners and lifestyle of noble families. Soon, the sons and daughters of nobles and rich merchants were marrying each other. Eventually, the old nobles and wealthy merchant families blended together to become the upper class of the city-states.

How Were Italian City-States Run? At first, many of the city-states were republics. A republic is a government controlled by its citizens. Not everyone was a citizen, however, only the artisans and merchants who had membership in the city's guilds.

From your study of the ancient Romans, you might recall that when their cities faced war or rebellion, they gave power to a dictator. The Italian city-states did something similar. In many cases, the cities were ruled by one powerful man who ran the government.

In Venice, the head of state was the duke, or **doge** (DOHJ). At first, the doge had great power over his council of nobles. Later, he lost power to a small group of nobles.

In Florence, the powerful Medici family gained control of the government in 1434. The Medici ran Florence for many decades. Lorenzo de' Medici ruled the city from 1469 to 1492. Known as "the Magnificent," Lorenzo used his wealth to support artists, architects, and writers. Many of Italy's Renaissance artists owed their success to his support.

Politics in Italy was complicated. Within each city, the rulers had to keep the poor from

Primary Source

The Prince

In Machiavelli's masterpiece, he explains his theories about human nature.

"You should consider then, that there are two ways of fighting, one with laws and the other with force. The first is properly a human method, the second belongs to beasts. But as the first method does not always suffice [meet your needs], you sometimes have to turn to the second. Thus a prince must know how to make good use of both the beast and the man."

—Niccolò Machiavelli,
The Prince

▲ Niccolò Machiavelli

DBQ Document-Based Question

Why must a good leader know more than one way to fight?

rebelling and prevent other wealthy people from seizing power. They had to make deals with merchants, bankers, landlords, church leaders, and mercenaries. At the same time, they had to deal with the leaders of the other city-states.

To deal with the other states around them, the Italians developed **diplomacy** (duh•PLOH•muh•see). Diplomacy is the art of negotiating, or making deals, with other countries. Each city-state sent ambassadors to live in the other city-states and act as representatives for their city. Many of the ideas of modern diplomacy first began in Italy.

How could a ruler guarantee that he would stay in power? **Niccolò Machiavelli** (NEE•koh•LOH MA•kee•uh•VEH•lee), a diplomat in Florence, tried to answer this question when he wrote *The Prince* in 1513. Machiavelli claimed that people were greedy and self-centered. Rulers should not

▲ This palace served as a government building in Rome for hundreds of years. *What form of government did many of the city-states have at first?*

try to be good, he argued. Rather, they should do whatever is necessary to keep power and protect their city, including killing and lying. Today when we say someone is being Machiavellian, we mean they are being tricky and not thinking about being good.

✓ **Reading Check** **Compare** How were medieval and Renaissance nobles different?

History Online

Study Central Need help with the rise of Italian city-states? Visit ca.hss.glencoe.com and click on Study Central.

Section 1 Review

Reading Summary
Review the Main Ideas

- A rebirth of learning called the Renaissance began in wealthy Italian city-states in the 1300s.

- Italian city-states, including Florence and Venice, grew wealthy through trade, manufacturing, and banking.

- In the Italian city-states, a noble's wealth was based on trade, rather than the amount of land owned.

What Did You Learn?

1. Why is the era from 1350 to 1550 in Europe called the Renaissance?

2. Why did the Renaissance begin in Italy?

Critical Thinking

3. **Organizing Information** Draw a diagram like the one below. Add details about the characteristics of the Italian Renaissance. **CA 7RC2.0**

Italian Renaissance

4. **The Big Ideas** How did Italian city-states gain their wealth? How did it affect society in the city-states? **CA HI6.**

5. **Summarize** Describe the governments of the Renaissance Italian city-states. **CA 7WA2.5**

6. **Persuasive Writing** Write a letter to a Renaissance newspaper telling why you agree or disagree with Machiavelli's ideas. **CA 7WA2.4** **CA HR4.**

7. **Reading** Questioning Write three questions about topics in the section. Reread the section, answering the questions as you go. **CA HR1.**

You Decide . . .

WH7.8.2 Explain the importance of Florence in the early stages of the Renaissance and the growth of independent trading cities (e.g., Venice), with emphasis on the cities' importance in the spread of Renaissance ideas.

The Value of City-States

During the Renaissance, Italy was divided into more than 20 city-states. Some people think that the city-state form of government was a good idea. The leaders and wealthy nobles of the city-states encouraged the arts and sciences. This produced masterpieces by Michelangelo, Raphael, Leonardo, and others. Would this rebirth of arts and sciences have happened if Italy's independent city-states had not existed?

Other people, such as Girolamo Savonarola, were against the city-state form of government. After the fall of the Medici family in Florence, Savonarola spoke out in favor of a new type of leadership:

"I tell you that you must select a good form for your new government, and above all no one must think of making himself head if you wish to live in liberty."

—Girolamo Savonarola,
"This Will Be Your Final Destruction"

Examine the advantages and disadvantages of the city-state form of government. Then decide whether you think this type of government is generally good or bad.

Advantages:

- Because of their independent governments, each territory on the Italian peninsula was able to have its own culture.

- Some city-states were led by wealthy families, but most were led by a single leader. Almost all supported cultural and scientific advancement. The competition among city-states also encouraged the development of art and science.

- City-state rulers helped preserve the values and teachings of the ancient Greeks and Romans. They gave their own artists, architects, scholars, and writers opportunities to study classical works and interpret them in their own ways.

▲ A detail from the ceiling of the Sistine Chapel painted by Michelangelo

▲ **Renaissance nobles**

- Many citizens liked their city-state and wanted to help it. This encouraged patriotism.
- Some rulers were generous to the citizens of their city-states. For example, Duke Federigo da Montefeltro (1422–1482), a popular ruler in Urbino, built schools, hospitals, churches, and a library with his own money. He was known for talking to the commoners and helping the poor.
- The city-states helped bring an end to feudalism by making merchants, as well as landowners, wealthy and by ending the relationship between lords and vassals.

Disadvantages:

- Many city-states were led by one man. The common people were often mistreated until they revolted and threw out their leaders. This happened to Florence's Medici family in 1527.
- The divided city-states were weaker than a united Italy would have been, so they were often invaded by foreign groups.
- Smaller territories did not always have enough soldiers to defend their cities and land. They hired mercenaries—generals and armies from outside their city—to help them fight. Sometimes mercenaries took over the city-states that had hired them.
- Because many Italians were poor, there were noticeable class differences in the city-states. These differences often led to bloody conflicts between the social classes.
- Wealthy families often battled each other for control of the city-states.
- Some city-state rulers became even wealthier by overseeing banking and trade. These leaders lived in luxury, while many citizens were very poor.

You Be the Historian

Checking for Understanding

1. Do you think that the art of the Renaissance would have been created if Italy had not been divided into individual city-states? Why or why not? **CA HI3.**
2. Do you think Italian artists had more artistic freedom under this form of government? Why or why not? **CA HI2.**
3. Would you have enjoyed living during the Renaissance? Would you have wanted to be a ruler, noble, artist, or commoner? Write a story from the viewpoint of someone living during the Renaissance. **CA 7WA2.1**

Guide to Reading

History Social Science Standards

WH7.8 Students analyze the origins, accomplishments, and geographic diffusion of the Renaissance.

Looking Back, Looking Ahead

In Section 1, you learned about the growth of Italian city-states. In this section, you will learn how the wealth of the city-states led to a new way of understanding the world, called humanism.

Focusing on the (Main Ideas)

- Humanists studied the Greeks and Romans, which greatly affected how they thought. *(page 395)*

- During the Renaissance, people began to write poetry, plays, and novels in their own language, and the development of the printing press helped spread their works. *(page 397)*

Meeting People

Leonardo da Vinci (LEE•uh•NAHR• doh duh VIHN•chee)

Dante Alighieri (DAHN•tay A•luh• GYEHR•ee)

Johannes Gutenberg (yoh•HAHN• uhs GOO•tuhn•BUHRG)

William Shakespeare (SHAYK•SPIHR)

Locating Places

Canterbury (KAN•tuhr•BEHR•ee)

Content Vocabulary

humanism (HYOO•muh•NIH• zuhm)

vernacular (vuhr•NA•kyuh•luhr)

Academic Vocabulary

debate (dih•BAYT)

credit (KREH•diht)

Reading Strategy

Organizing Information Create a chart listing people who contributed to Renaissance literature.

Contributor	Role in Renaissance Literature

NATIONAL GEOGRAPHIC Who & When?

1300

c. 1307 Dante begins writing *Divine Comedy*

1450

1455 Johannes Gutenberg uses printing press to print the Bible

1600

1594 Shakespeare publishes first play

WH7.8.1 Describe the way in which the revival of classical learning and the arts fostered a new interest in humanism (i.e., a balance between intellect and religious faith). **WH7.8.5** Detail advances made in literature, the arts, science, mathematics, cartography, engineering, and the understanding of human anatomy and astronomy (e.g., by Dante Alighieri, Leonardo da Vinci, Michelangelo di Buonarroti Simoni, Johann Gutenberg, William Shakespeare).

Renaissance Humanism

Main Idea Humanists studied the Greeks and Romans, which greatly affected how they thought.

Reading Connection Have you ever tried to draw a copy of a painting you like? Is it harder to copy what other people have done or to come up with new ideas for your own pictures? Read to learn how Renaissance artists borrowed ideas from the past but also tried to be original.

In the 1300s, a new way of understanding the world developed in medieval Europe. This new approach was called **humanism** (HYOO•muh•NIH•zuhm). It was based on the values of the ancient Greeks and Romans. Humanists believed that the individual and human society were important. Humanists did not abandon religious faith, but they emphasized a balance between faith and reason. Their new ideas encouraged men to be active in their cities and achieve great things.

Ancient Works Become Popular
In the 1300s, Italians began to study early Roman and Greek works. For most of the Middle Ages, Western Europeans knew little about ancient Greek and Roman writings. When they went on the Crusades, however, they opened trade with the Middle East and began to get information from the Arabs. Arab scholars knew classic Greek and Roman works very well. In addition, when the Turks conquered Constantinople in 1453, many Byzantine scholars left and moved to Venice or Florence.

One famous scholar of the ancient works was Francesco Petrarch (PEH•TRAHRK). Petrarch was a poet and scholar who lived in the 1300s. He studied Roman writers like Cicero and wrote biographies of famous Romans.

Petrarch encouraged Europeans to search for Latin manuscripts in monasteries all over Europe. In time, his efforts paid off and new libraries were built to keep the documents. The largest was the Vatican Library in Rome.

Italians studied more than ancient books. They studied the old buildings and statues all around them. All over Rome, one could see workers in the process of cleaning broken columns and statues. Italian artists eagerly studied the proportions of the ancient works. If they knew how long a statue's arms were compared to its height, they would be able to understand why it looked so perfect.

Ancient Greek manuscript on Archimedes ▼

◄ **Francesco Petrarch has been called the father of Italian Renaissance humanism.** *How did Petrarch contribute to the preservation of Roman knowledge?*

395

WH7.8.5 Detail advances made in literature, the arts, science, mathematics, cartography, engineering, and the understanding of human anatomy and astronomy (e.g., by Dante Alighieri, Leonardo da Vinci, Michelangelo di Buonarroti Simoni, Johann Gutenberg, William Shakespeare).

LEONARDO DA VINCI
1452–1519

Leonardo was born in Vinci, Italy, to a peasant woman named Caterina. Shortly after Leonardo's birth, she left the boy in the care of his father. By the time Leonardo was 15 years old, his father knew his son had artistic talent. He arranged for Leonardo to become an apprentice to the famous painter Andrea del Verrocchio.

By 1472, Leonardo had become a master in the painters' guild of Florence. He worked in Florence until 1481, and then he went to the city of Milan. There he kept a large workshop and employed many apprentices. During this time, Leonardo began keeping small pads of paper tucked in his belt for sketching. Later he organized the drawings by theme and assembled the pages into notebooks.

Seventeen years later, Leonardo returned to Florence, where he was welcomed with great honor. During this time, Leonardo painted some of his masterpieces. He also made scientific studies, including dissections, observations of the flight of birds, and research on the movement of water currents.

In 1516 Leonardo accepted an invitation to live in France. The king admired Leonardo and gave him freedom to pursue his interests. During the last three years of his life, Leonardo lived in a small house near the king's summer palace. He spent most of his time sketching and working on his scientific studies.

▲ Leonardo da Vinci

> **"Nothing can be loved or hated unless it is first known."**
>
> –Leonardo da Vinci

▲ The *Mona Lisa* by Leonardo da Vinci

Then and Now

Leonardo's curiosity fueled his creativity and interest in science. What invention created in the last 100 years do you think would impress Leonardo the most? Why?

WH7.8.4 Describe the growth and effects of new ways of disseminating information (e.g., the ability to manufacture paper, translation of the Bible into the vernacular, printing). WH7.8.5 Detail advances made in literature, the arts, science, mathematics, cartography, engineering, and the understanding of human anatomy and astronomy (e.g., by Dante Alighieri, Leonardo da Vinci, Michelangelo di Buonarroti Simoni, Johann Gutenberg, William Shakespeare).

How Did Humanism Affect Society?

Humanist scholars studied the Greeks and Romans to increase their knowledge of many different topics. They were curious about everything, including plants and animals, human anatomy and medicine, and the stars and planets.

Their study of mathematics helped them in many subjects. For instance, advances in engineering and better use of mathematics allowed the artist Filippo Brunelleschi to build the dome of the Florence cathedral in the 1430s. Later, after Arab traders brought gunpowder to Europe from China, European engineers used it to develop new kinds of weapons.

One of the best Renaissance scientists was also a great artist, **Leonardo da Vinci** (LEE•uh•NAHR•doh duh VIHN•chee). Leonardo dissected corpses to learn anatomy and studied fossils to understand the world's history. He was also an inventor and an engineer.

Most of what we know about Leonardo comes from his notebooks. Leonardo filled their pages with sketches of his scientific and artistic ideas. Centuries before the airplane was invented, Leonardo drew sketches of a glider, a helicopter, and a parachute. Other sketches show a version of a military tank and a scuba diving suit.

Humanist ideas also led to advances in cartography, or the art of making maps, and in science. By studying the ideas of the ancient Greek geographers, such as Ptolemy, and the Arab geographer, al-Idrisi, Europeans began producing better maps and charts. This allowed them to trade better and to explore new areas of the world.

✔ **Reading Check** **Explain** How did Renaissance thinkers view ancient writings?

Changes in Literature

Main Idea During the Renaissance, people began to write poetry, plays, and novels in their own language, and the development of the printing press helped spread their works.

Reading Connection Have you ever seen a book in a foreign language? Could you understand it? Read to find out how Renaissance writers began to write in their own language to help spread their works.

During the Renaissance, educated people wrote in "pure" Latin, the Latin used in ancient Rome. Petrarch thought classical Latin was the best way to write, but when

Leonardo's Inventions

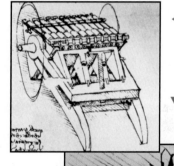

◀ A multibarreled artillery piece

▼ A helicopter-like flying machine

◀ Cross section of a palace with subways for carriages

he wanted to write poems to the woman he loved, he wrote in the **vernacular** (vuhr•NA•kyuh•luhr). The vernacular is the everyday language people speak in a region—Italian, French, or German, for example. When authors began writing in the vernacular, many more people could read their work.

HISTORY MAKERS

Movable Type c. 1450

Johannes Gutenberg, a German goldsmith, built a printing press modeled after a winepress. Once the press was completed, Gutenberg spent two years printing his first book. For each page, he set metal letters in a frame, rolled ink over the frame, and pressed the frame against paper. Around 1455, he completed printing what is now known as the Gutenberg Bible, or the 42 Line Bible. This was the first book printed using movable metal type, sparking a revolution in publishing and reading.

▼ Gutenberg Bible

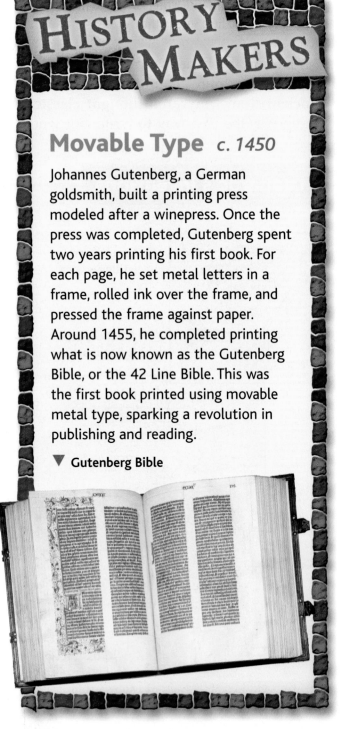

In the early 1300s, **Dante Alighieri** (DAHN•tay A•luh•GYEHR•ee), a poet of Florence, wrote one of the world's greatest poems in the vernacular. It is called *The Divine Comedy.* As a young man, Dante was involved in politics, but when noble families began fighting over power, he had to leave Florence. That was when he wrote his long poem—more than 14,000 lines. *The Divine Comedy* tells the gripping tale of the main character's journey from hell to heaven.

Another important writer who used the vernacular was Chaucer. Chaucer wrote in English. In his famous book, *The Canterbury Tales,* he describes 29 pilgrims traveling to the city of **Canterbury** (KAN•tuhr•BEHR•ee). The book describes the levels of English society, from the nobles at the top to the poor at the bottom. The English Chaucer used in his writing is the ancestor of the English we speak today.

The Printing Press Spreads Ideas
The printing press was a key to the spread of humanist ideas throughout Europe. In the early 1450s, **Johannes Gutenberg** (yoh•HAHN•uhs GOO•tuhn•BUHRG) developed a printing press that used movable metal type. This type of printing press made it possible to print many books much more quickly. With more books available, more people learned to read. Scholars could read one another's works and **debate** their ideas in letters. Ideas grew and spread more quickly than ever before in Europe.

The Chinese had already invented movable type, but it did not work well with their large alphabet of characters. For Europeans, the printing press was a big improvement. It was easy to use with linen paper, another Chinese invention.

Gutenberg's Bible, printed in the 1450s, was the first European book produced on the new press. Soon books flooded Europe.

Approximately 40,000 books were published by 1500. Half of these were religious works like the Bible or prayer books.

The printing press helped spread many ideas throughout Europe, not just religious ideas. Literature was printed, and with the invention of the printing press, books like Ptolemy's *Geography* were widely sold.

Who Was William Shakespeare?
In England, the Renaissance occurred in writing and theater more than in art. The Renaissance began in England in the later 1500s, during the rule of Elizabeth I. It is often referred to as the Elizabethan era.

The greatest writer of the era was **William Shakespeare** (SHAYK•spihr). Shakespeare was born in 1564. He was an actor and a poet but is best known for his plays. He wrote all kinds of plays during his lifetime. Some of his greatest tragedies include *Hamlet, Macbeth,* and *Romeo and Juliet.* In each tragedy, the main characters'

flaws cause their downfall. Among Shakespeare's most famous comedies are *A Midsummer Night's Dream, Twelfth Night,* and *Much Ado About Nothing.* His best-known historical plays include *Henry V* and *Richard III.* These plays, along with many others, made Shakespeare one of the most well-known playwrights in England.

The works of playwrights such as Shakespeare were popular enough to be printed during the Renaissance. This was a change in how the printing press was used. Until then, most printed works had been religious books.

In 1594 the first William Shakespeare play, *Titus Andronicus,* was published. Shakespeare had five more plays published in the next five years, but it was not until 1598 that he was given **credit** for his early published works.

Shakespeare wrote continuously until his death in 1616. Seven years after his death, the first complete collection of his

Globe Theater

William Shakespeare's plays were performed at the Globe Theater in London. It could hold about 3,000 people. Plays were performed every day of the week except Sunday. Performances occurred during the day, since the theater had no lights. *When did the Renaissance spread to northern Europe and England?*

Flags announced the type of play. White flags meant comedies, black flags meant tragedies, and red flags stood for history plays.

Wealthy and important people sat beneath the covered section.

Poor commoners, called groundlings, stood on the ground for the show. They often brought fruit and vegetables to throw at actors they did not like.

work appeared. This enormous book contained 35 plays and was so large and expensive that only the wealthiest people in England could afford to buy it. Shakespeare remains one of the best-known and most popular writers today.

What Did Cervantes Write? Another influential writer during the Renaissance was the Spanish author Miguel de Cervantes (mee•GEHL day suhr•VAN•TEEZ). Cervantes was born in 1547. He wrote numerous plays and works of fiction, including *Novelas ejemplares (The Exemplary Novels)* in 1613.

Cervantes was not widely known, however, until the publication of his most influential piece, *Don Quixote de la Mancha.* The novel, published in 1604, made Cervantes extremely popular in Spain. The book tells the story of a country gentleman who searches for adventure in life. It looks at the difference between what people hope life can be and what life actually is like.

In the story, the hero Don Quixote and his companion Sancho Panza have many adventures. Don Quixote dreams of himself as a medieval knight and tries to live according to the medieval code of chivalry. Many people think that he is a fool. He makes many mistakes, yet he continues to live according to his dreams.

After it was published, the novel became famous throughout Europe. People eagerly read the book for its humor and insight. Cervantes died in 1616. His works, like Shakespeare's, are read throughout the world to this day.

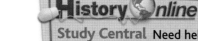 **Reading Check** **Explain** What was the benefit of writing in the vernacular?

History Online

Study Central Need help understanding Renaissance humanism and literature? Visit ca.hss.glencoe.com and click on Study Central.

Section 2 Review

Reading Summary

Review the Main Ideas

• Humanists changed medieval ideas by studying the Greeks and Romans.

• New poetry, plays, and novels written in the vernacular appeared during the Renaissance and were widely read after Gutenberg invented the printing press.

What Did You Learn?

1. Explain the beliefs of humanists during the Renaissance.

2. How did writers make their work more available to the general public?

Critical Thinking

3. **The Big Ideas** Create a diagram like the one below. Fill in information about ancient texts and ideas that people used in the Renaissance. **CA 7WA2.3**

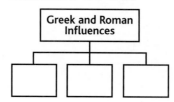

Greek and Roman Influences

4. **Evaluate** Why was the printing press important? **CA HI2.**

5. **Science Connection** Describe Leonardo da Vinci's scientific contributions. **CA 7RC2.2**

6. **Explain** How were the ideals of the Renaissance expressed in England? Provide examples in your answer. **CA 7RC2.0**

7. **Writing Research Reports** Use your local library to research William Shakespeare. Write an essay that describes what his life was like. **CA 7WA2.3**

A MIDSUMMER NIGHT'S DREAM

By William Shakespeare,
Adapted by E. Nesbit

Before You Read

The Scene: This story takes place in Athens, Greece, during a legendary time when magical creatures lived among humans.

The Characters: Hermia and Lysander are in love. Demetrius loves Hermia, and Helena loves Demetrius. Oberon and Titania are the king and queen of the fairies.

The Plot: Hermia and Lysander run away to be married. Demetrius follows them because he loves Hermia. Helena follows Demetrius because she loves him. The fairies they encounter try to use magic to help the four humans.

Vocabulary Preview

betrayed: gave to an enemy

mortal: human

quarrel: argument

glade: grassy, open space in a forest

suitor: one who wants to marry another

bade: asked

scheme: plan

Have you ever tried to help someone but made the situation worse? In this story, fairies attempt to help four young people traveling through the woods, but their efforts do not go as planned.

As You Read

Keep in mind that William Shakespeare wrote this story as a play. E. Nesbit rewrote the story in paragraph form to make it shorter and easier to read. While you are reading, think about what the story would be like if it were performed as a play.

Hermia and Lysander were [in love]; but Hermia's father wished her to marry another man, named Demetrius.

Now in Athens, where they lived, there was a wicked law, by which any girl who refused to marry according to her father's wishes, might be put to death. . . .

Lysander of course was nearly mad with grief, and the best thing to do seemed to him for Hermia to run away to his aunt's house at a place beyond the reach of that cruel law; and there he would come to her and marry her. But before she started, she told her friend, Helena, what she was going to do.

Helena had been Demetrius' sweetheart long before his marriage with Hermia had been thought of, and being very silly, like all jealous people, she could not see that it was not poor Hermia's fault that Demetrius wished to marry her instead of his own lady, Helena. She knew that if she told Demetrius that Hermia was going, as she was, to the wood outside Athens, he would follow her, "and I can follow him, and at least I shall see him," she said to herself. So she went to him, and betrayed her friend's secret.

Now this wood where Lysander was to meet Hermia, and where the other two had decided to follow them, was full of fairies,[1] as most woods are, if one only had the eyes to see them, and in this wood on this night were the King and Queen of the fairies, Oberon and Titania. Now fairies are very wise people, but now and then they can be quite as foolish as mortal folk. Oberon and Titania, who might have been as happy as the days were long, had thrown away all their joy in a foolish quarrel. . . .

So, instead of keeping one happy Court and dancing all night through in the moonlight, as is fairies' use, the King with his attendants wandered through one part of the wood, while the Queen with hers kept state in another. And the cause of all this trouble was a little Indian boy

---

[1]**fairies:** imaginary beings, usually having small human form and magic powers

whom Titania had taken to be one of her followers. Oberon wanted the child to follow him and be one of his fairy knights; but the Queen would not give him up.

On this night, in a glossy moonlight glade, the King and Queen of the fairies met.

"Ill[2] met by moonlight, proud Titania," said the King.

"What! jealous, Oberon?" answered the Queen. "You spoil everything with your quarreling. Come, fairies, let us leave him. I am not friends with him now."

"It rests with you to make up the quarrel," said the King. "Give me that little Indian boy, and I will again be your humble servant and suitor."

"Set your mind at rest," said the Queen. "Your whole fairy kingdom buys not that boy from me. Come fairies."

And she and her train rode off down the moonbeams.[3]

"Well, go your ways," said Oberon. "But I'll be even with you before you leave this wood."

Then Oberon called his favorite fairy, Puck. Puck was the spirit of mischief. . . .

"Now," said Oberon to this little sprite,[4] "fetch me the flower called Love-in-idleness. The juice of that little purple flower laid on the eyes of those who sleep will make them when they wake to love the first thing they see. I will put some of the juice of that flower on my Titania's eyes, and when she wakes, she will love the first thing she sees, were it lion, bear, or wolf, or bull, or meddling monkey, or a busy ape."

_____

[2]**ill:** causing suffering or distress
[3]**moonbeams:** rays of light from the moon
[4]**sprite:** fairy

"I should like some good dry oats," said the clown—for his donkey's head made him desire donkey's food—"and some hay to follow."

"Shall some of my fairies fetch you new nuts from the squirrel's house?" asked the Queen.

"I'd rather have a handful or two of good dried peas," said the clown. "But please don't let any of your people disturb me, I am going to sleep."

Then said the Queen, "And I will wind thee in my arms."

And so when Oberon came along he found his beautiful Queen lavishing kisses and endearments on a clown with a donkey's head. And before he released her from the enchantment, he persuaded her to give him the little Indian boy he so much desired to have. Then he took pity on her, and threw some juice of the disenchanting flower on her pretty eyes; and then in a moment she saw plainly the donkey-headed clown she had been loving, and knew how foolish she had been.

Oberon took off the [donkey's] head from the clown, and left him to finish his sleep with his own silly head lying on the thyme and violets.

Thus all was made plain and straight again. Oberon and Titania loved each other more than ever. Demetrius thought of no one but Helena, and Helena had never had any thought of anyone but Demetrius. As for Hermia and Lysander, they were as loving a couple as you could meet in a day's march, even through a fairy-wood. So the four [mortals] went back to Athens and were married; and the fairy King and Queen live happily together in that very wood at this very day.

Responding to the Literature

1. How did Demetrius and Lysander fall in love with Helena?

2. How did the story get its title, *A Midsummer Night's Dream?*

3. **Understanding Form** How would this story have been different as a play? What are the benefits to performing it as a play? What are the difficulties? **C**

4. **Predict** What do you think might have happened if Oberon had not interfered with the conflict among the four young people? **CA 7RL3.2**

5. **Read to Write** What lesson do you think William Shakespeare was trying to tell in this story? What have each of the main characters learned at the end of the story? Write an essay explaining your answers. **CA 7WA2.2**

Reading on Your Own...

Are you interested in reading more about the Renaissance,
the Reformation, or the adventures of the Age of Exploration?
If so, check out these other great books.

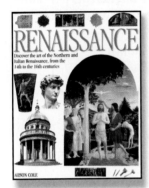

Nonfiction

Renaissance by Alison Cole offers a glimpse into the Renaissance period.
You will explore artwork, paintings, and sculptures created by the most
famous artists in the world. *The content of this book is related to*
History–Social Science Standard WH7.8.

Historical Fiction

A Murder for Her Majesty by Beth Hilgartner tells the story of a young girl
who witnesses the murder of her father and hides in the cathedral, disguising
herself as a boy in the choir. There she encounters mystery and adventure as
she finds clues about her father's death. *The content of this book is related to*
History–Social Science Standard WH7.9.

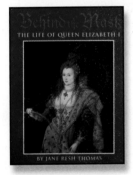

Biography

Behind the Mask: The Life of Queen Elizabeth I by Jane Resh Thomas
recounts the life of this amazing young English queen. Follow Elizabeth as she
overcomes many obstacles to maintain her power and right as queen. *The con-*
tent of this book is related to *History–Social Science Standard WH7.9.*

Nonfiction

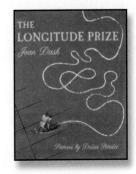

The Longitude Prize by Joan Dash tells of the dangers of early sailing and an
amazing invention that changed the world. The story follows the inventor and
his innovative clock that could survive the wild seas. *The content of this book is*
related to *History–Social Science Standard WH7.11.*

Renaissance Art

History
Social Science Standards
WH7.8 Students analyze the origins, accomplishments, and geographic diffusion of the Renaissance.

Guide to Reading

Looking Back, Looking Ahead
New ideas about art created a whole new way of painting and sculpture. In this section, you will learn about how artists in Italy created the Renaissance and how their ideas spread in Europe.

Focusing on the Main Ideas
• Renaissance artists used new techniques to produce paintings that showed people in an emotional and realistic way. **(page 409)**

• Renaissance ideas and art spread from Italy to northern Europe. **(page 412)**

Locating Places
Flanders (FLAN•duhrz)

Meeting People
Sandro Botticelli (SAHN•droh BAH•tuh•CHEH•lee)
Raphael Sanzio (RA•fee•uhl SAHNT•syoh)

Michelangelo Buonarroti (MY•kuh•LAN•juh•LOH BWAW•nahr•RAW•tee)
Titian (TIH•shuhn)
Jan van Eyck (van EYEK)
Albrecht Dürer (AHL•brehkt DUR•uhr)

Content Vocabulary
chiaroscuro (kee•AHR•uh•SKYUR•oh)
fresco (FREHS•koh)

Academic Vocabulary
differentiate (DIHF•uh•REHN•shee•AYT)
perspective (puhr•SPEHK•tihv)

Reading Strategy
Organizing Information Create a diagram to show features of Renaissance art.

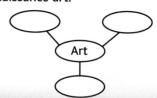

National Geographic — Who & When?

1400

c. 1494 Leonardo begins painting *The Last Supper*

1500

1512 Michelangelo finishes painting Sistine Chapel

1576 Titian, the great Venetian painter, dies

1600

Artists in Renaissance Italy

Main Idea Renaissance artists used new techniques to produce paintings that showed people in an emotional and realistic way.

Reading Connection Have you ever had trouble making your drawings look real and three-dimensional? Read to learn how Renaissance artists learned to make their art look natural and real.

During the Renaissance, wealthy Italian families and church leaders paid artists to create paintings, sculptures, and buildings for display throughout their cities. The pope himself funded many works of art to decorate the Vatican. Renaissance artists followed the models of the ancient Romans and Greeks but expressed humanist ideas.

What Was New About Renaissance Art?

If you compare medieval and Renaissance paintings, you will see major differences in their styles. When a medieval artist depicted the birth of Jesus, he wanted to remind Christians about their belief that Jesus was born to save the world. Because of this, medieval artists did not try to make their works look truly realistic. Instead, their images were intended to have a more symbolic meaning that viewers were supposed to interpret.

Renaissance artists **differentiated** their work from medieval artists in many ways. For example, instead of focusing on symbols, Renaissance artists tried to show people as they would appear in real life. They also tried to show people's emotions. A Renaissance artist painting a scene of the birth of Jesus might try to show how tender Mary looked with her tiny baby.

Renaissance painters also used new techniques. The most innovative was **perspective**. Perspective is a method that makes a drawing or painting look three-

Comparing Art

Cimabue's *Maesta* (left) is a typical medieval painting. Its main subjects, Mary and the baby Jesus, are larger than the rest. In contrast, Renaissance paintings, such as Botticelli's *Madonna of the Eucharist* (right), show people as more lifelike and three-dimensional. *How else do the two paintings differ?*

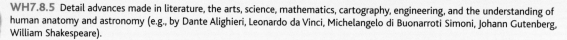

WH7.8.5 Detail advances made in literature, the arts, science, mathematics, cartography, engineering, and the understanding of human anatomy and astronomy (e.g., by Dante Alighieri, Leonardo da Vinci, Michelangelo di Buonarroti Simoni, Johann Gutenberg, William Shakespeare).

The Way It Was

Focus on Everyday Life

The Life of a Renaissance Artist If a young boy in Renaissance Italy wanted to be an artist, he would become an apprentice at a workshop run by an established artist. The main job of apprentices was preparing materials. Apprentices used minerals, spices, egg yolk, and other everyday materials to mix paints. They readied wax and clay for sculpture modeling. Eventually, apprentices became assistants. Talented assistants could become masters of their own workshops.

Master artists could afford to have workshops because of the patronage system in Italy. Patrons—people who pay to support someone else's work—would commission, or hire, an artist to complete a project.

▲ Renaissance painter and apprentice

Connecting to the Past

1. What was the main job of apprentices?
2. Does the patronage system or the apprentice system exist today? If so, in what fields?

The Renaissance Spreads

Main Idea Renaissance ideas and art spread from Italy to northern Europe.

Reading Connection If you were a Canadian artist, would your painting look different than if you lived in Arizona? Read to learn how the Renaissance changed as it moved into northern Europe.

In the late 1400s, the Renaissance spread to northern Europe. The Northern Renaissance refers to the art in places we know today as Belgium, Luxembourg, Germany, and the Netherlands. Like Italian artists, northern artists wanted their works to have greater realism, but they used different methods. One important method they developed was oil painting. First developed in **Flanders** (FLAN•duhrz)—a region that is in northern Belgium today—oils let artists paint intricate details and surface textures, like the gold braid on a gown.

Who Was Van Eyck? Jan van Eyck

(van EYEK) was a master of oil painting. In fact, some credit him with having created this method of painting. Van Eyck learned how to mix and blend his oil paints to create brilliant colors. Some thought the colors in his work sparkled like jewels or stained glass.

In one of his best-known paintings, a newly married couple stands side by side in a formal bedroom. Van Eyck showed every fold in their rich gowns and every detail of the chandelier above their heads. The painting is also visually appealing because of the balance in color and space between the couple and the other objects in the room.

The Engravings of Dürer Albrecht

Dürer (AHL•brehkt DUR•uhr) of Germany is perhaps one of the greatest artists of the Northern Renaissance. Dürer was able to master both perspective and fine detail. He is considered a master painter but is best known for his engravings. An engraving is made from an image carved on metal, wood, or stone. Ink is applied to the surface, and then the image is printed on paper.

Dürer printed many copies of his engravings and sold them throughout Germany, earning him great wealth. His *Four Horsemen of the Apocalypse* is an example of a woodcut, or a print made from a wood engraving. The image draws on a passage from the Bible. Like many artists, Dürer interpreted the passage and drew upon his creative abilities to create a strong visual image. The woodcut depicts four horsemen riding to announce the end of the world.

✔ **Reading Check** **Compare** How did the Northern Renaissance differ from the Italian Renaissance?

▲ Dürer's *Four Horsemen of the Apocalypse*

History Online

Study Central Need help understanding Renaissance humanism and literature? Visit ca.hss.glencoe.com and click on Study Central.

Section 3 Review

Reading Summary

Review the Main Ideas

- Renaissance artists used chiaroscuro and perspective to produce paintings that showed people in an emotional and realistic way.

- Renaissance ideas and art spread from Italy to northern Europe where artists such as Van Eyck and Dürer became popular.

What Did You Learn?

1. Explain the artistic techniques of perspective and chiaroscuro.

2. What were some of the important artists and ideas to come out of the Northern Renaissance?

Critical Thinking

3. **Summarizing Information** Draw a chart like the one below. Use it to describe the artistic work and techniques of each artist listed. **CA 7RC2.0**

Leonardo da Vinci	
Michelangelo	
Jan van Eyck	
Albrecht Dürer	

4. **The Big Ideas** How did artists differentiate their work from medieval art? What new techniques did they use? **CA HI2.**

5. **Descriptive Writing** Choose a painting or sculpture shown in this section. In a short essay describe the work and explain how it demonstrates Renaissance techniques or characteristics. **CA 7WA2.0**

6. **Analysis** **Creating Maps** Create a map that shows the different countries that were influenced by the Renaissance. Color each country to show how far the Renaissance spread. **CA CS3.**

Analyzing Primary Sources

WH7.8.5 Detail advances made in literature, the arts, science, mathematics, cartography, engineering, and the understanding of human anatomy and astronomy (e.g., by Dante Alighieri, Leonardo da Vinci, Michelangelo di Buonarroti Simoni, Johann Gutenberg, William Shakespeare).

Renaissance Art

Renaissance artists borrowed heavily from Greek and Roman works. They studied the ancient artists for ideas on proportion and presentation. However, as the ideas of humanism began to spread, Renaissance artists began to approach art in new and different ways. These included the use of perspective, emotion, and shadow.

Examine the images on pages 414 and 415, and answer the questions that follow.

▲ Renaissance artist and thinker Leonardo da Vinci

Reader's Dictionary

Calumny (KA•luhm•nee): lie that hurts reputation

King Midas: king in Greek mythology known for being just

Deceit (dih•SEET): lying or trickery

Remorse: feeling bad about doing something wrong

Calumny by Botticelli

In this painting Botticelli used Greek and Roman imagery to tell a symbolic story. The people in the painting represent emotions or ideas. In the center **Calumny,** preceded by Jealousy (pointing), drags Innocence to be judged by **King Midas.** The figures speaking into the king's ears are Suspicion and **Deceit.** The hooded figure on the left represents **Remorse.**

Holy Family With Lamb
by Raphael

*R*aphael's work is a great example of Renaissance harmony and balance. He places the holy family in a pastoral, realistic setting, making them seem more human.

Pietà
by Michelangelo

*M*ichelangelo's Pietà, showing Mary holding Jesus just after his death, demonstrates exceptional realism and emotion. It was one of the first statues to show a realistic view of death. The overall beauty of the work gives it a sense of the divine.

DBQ Document-Based Questions

Calumny *by Botticelli*

1. How does the figure of Remorse convey this emotion?
2. What do you think Suspicion and Deceit are saying? Why?

Holy Family With Lamb *by Raphael*

3. Raphael used contrasting colors to direct the viewer's eyes to the baby Jesus. What other things in the painting direct your eyes there?
4. The New Testament refers to Jesus as the Lamb of God. How did Raphael show this idea?

Pietà *by Michelangelo*

5. How does the Pietà demonstrate the Renaissance ideas of perspective and emotion?
6. How does the artist portray both the religious and human sides of Mary?

Read to Write

7. How do these works of art reflect the ideas of Renaissance artists that you have studied in this chapter on pages 409–411? **CA HR4.**

Review Content Vocabulary

Write **True** beside each true statement. Replace the word in italics to make false statements true.

___ 1. The *doge* was the leader of Venice.

___ 2. In order to reach more people, Petrarch wrote in *English.*

___ 3. Balancing faith and reason was an important part of being a *humanist.*

___ 4. Italian city-states used *seminaries* to make deals with each other.

___ 5. Using *florin,* artists could draw more realistic images.

___ 6. Artists used *chiaroscuro* to soften edges in their works.

Review the Main Ideas

Section 1 • The Renaissance Begins

7. What was responsible for the new values and art of the Renaissance?

8. How did Italian city-states use their location to gain wealth?

9. What made nobles of the Renaissance different from nobles of previous times?

Section 2 • New Ideas and Literature

10. How were the humanists inspired by the ancient Greeks and Romans?

11. What invention helped spread literature throughout Europe? How?

Section 3 • Renaissance Art

12. What new techniques did Renaissance artists develop?

13. Renaissance art and ideas began in Italy. Where did they spread from there?

Critical Thinking

14. **Making Connections** Research Niccolò Machiavelli's theories of government. What governments today reflect Machiavelli's political philosophy? **CA HI2.**

15. **Predict** Do you think the Italian city-states would have been famous centers of wealth and art during the Renaissance without banking? **CA HI6.**

16. **Compare and Contrast** How was art of the Italian Renaissance similar to and different from art of the Northern Renaissance? **CA 7RC2.2**

Geography Skills

Study the map below and answer the following questions.

17. **Place** What geographical advantage does Venice have over Milan? **CA CS3.**

18. **Place** Why might Mantua have been disadvantaged in terms of trade? **CA CS3.**

19. **Movement** If you traveled from the city of Florence to the city of Venice, in what direction would you be going? **CA CS3.**

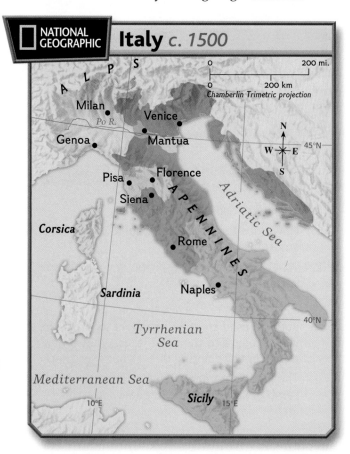

NATIONAL GEOGRAPHIC

Italy c. 1500

Read to Write

20. **The Big Ideas** **Narrative Writing** Research the life of merchants or shopkeepers before and during the Renaissance. Write a short story describing the lifestyle and position of the group you chose. How did their lives change when the Renaissance began? **CA 7WA2.1**

21. **Using Your FOLDABLES** Use information from your foldable to create a collage. Choose one of the tabs from your foldable and create a colorful, detailed group of images that best represent the people and ideas that were important during the Renaissance.

Using Academic Vocabulary

22. Choose the word in Column A that most closely matches a word in Column B.

A	B
network	print
expert	separate
publish	professional
debate	system
credit	argument
differentiate	recognition

Linking Past and Present

23. **Understanding Influences** Renaissance artists, architects, and writers were greatly influenced by the ancient Greeks and Romans. Do you think people in those professions today are equally influenced by the Greeks and Romans. Why or why not? **CA HI2.**

Reviewing Skills

24. **Reading Skill Questioning** Look back through Chapter 7. Make a list of artists or writers who interest you. In order to learn more about these people, write two to three questions for each person. Use your textbook and other resources to answer these questions. **CA HR1.**

25. **Analysis Skill Understanding the Past** The discovery of ancient Greek and Roman manuscripts during the Renaissance greatly influenced European artists and thinkers. Use your local library and the Internet to find out about more recent discoveries, such as the Rosetta Stone or the Dead Sea Scrolls, that have influenced the way we think about history. Write an essay explaining the significance of the discovery. **CA HI5.**

Standards Practice

Select the best answer for each of the following questions.

26 **The invention of the printing press**

 A encouraged new artistic methods in painting.

 B spread humanist ideas.

 C helped people sell their goods in markets.

 D was based on early Greek and Roman ideas.

27 **During the Renaissance, Italy's wealth was based on**

 A the sale of artwork.

 B the spread of humanism.

 C trade and banking.

 D the power of the Church.

28 **Chiaroscuro was used**

 A in writing.

 B in government.

 C in painting.

 D in the printing press.

Chapter 8

The Reformation

Wittenberg Cathedral in ▶
Wittenberg, Germany

NATIONAL GEOGRAPHIC Where&When?

1500	1525	1550	1600

1517
Martin Luther writes Ninety-Five Theses

1536
Calvin publishes *Institutes of the Christian Religion*

1545
Pope Paul III opens the Council of Trent

The Big Ideas

History Online

Chapter Overview Visit
ca.hss.glencoe.com for a
preview of Chapter 8.

Section 1 The Reformation Begins

Religion influences how civilization develops and how culture spreads.
Martin Luther and other reformers broke from the Catholic Church
and began a new Christian movement that came to be called
Protestantism.

Section 2 The Reformation Spreads

All civilizations depend upon leadership for survival. John Calvin's
Protestant teachings spread across Europe and into North America.
Meanwhile, Henry VIII declared himself the head of the Church in
England.

Section 3 The Counter-Reformation

Conflict often brings about great change. While the Catholic Church
attempted to carry out reforms known as the Counter-
Reformation, Catholics and Protestants fought bloody religious
wars across Europe.

 View the Chapter 8 video in the Glencoe Video Program.

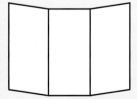

FOLDABLES™
Study Organizer

Summarizing Information *Make this foldable and use it to organize note cards
with information about the Reformation.*

Step 1 *Fold a horizontal
sheet of paper (11" x 17")
into thirds.*

Step 2 *Fold the bottom edge up two inches and
crease well. Glue the outer edges of the tab to
create three pockets.*

Glue
here.

Glue
here.

Reading and Writing
*As you read the chapter,
summarize key facts
about the Reformation on
note cards or on quarter
sheets of paper. Organize
your notes by placing
them in your pocket
foldable inside the
appropriate pockets.*

Step 3 *Label the pockets
as shown. Use these
pockets to hold notes taken
on index cards or quarter
sheets of paper.*

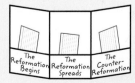

The
Reformation
Begins

The
Reformation
Spreads

The
Counter-
Reformation

Identifying Cause and Effect

Reading Skill

1 Learn It!

Learning to identify causes and effects helps you understand how and why things happen in history. A *cause* is the reason why something happens. The result of what happens is called an *effect*. Use graphic organizers to help you sort and understand causes and effects in your reading. Read the following passage, and then see how the information can be sorted.

> By the 1300s, many people believed the Church had problems. It taxed people heavily, and some bishops behaved like they were kings. They built palaces, spent money on fine art, and made sure that their relatives had good jobs. In many villages, priests could barely read or give a good sermon.
>
> — *from page 423*

Reading Tip

A single cause can have several effects. A single effect can also be the result of several causes.

CAUSE

Church had problems—only concerned with money and power

EFFECTS

heavily taxed the people

clergy behaved and spent money like kings

used position to get family jobs

less concerned with religion

2 Practice It!

History is often a chain of causes and effects. The result, or effect, of one event can also be the cause of another effect. Read the passage called **The Church Tries to Reform Itself** from Section 3 on page 436. Then use the graphic organizer below or create your own to show the chain of causes and effects explained in the passage.

Read to Write ⋯⋯

Choose a major event from the chapter. Then write a brief paragraph explaining what caused this event.

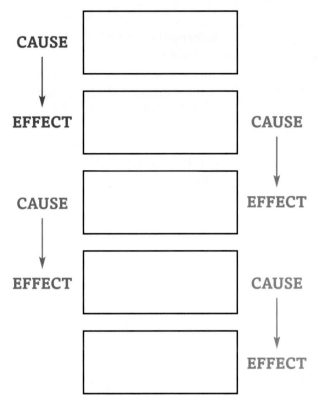

CAUSE

EFFECT   **CAUSE**

CAUSE   **EFFECT**

EFFECT   **CAUSE**

                              EFFECT

▼ **The Council of Trent**

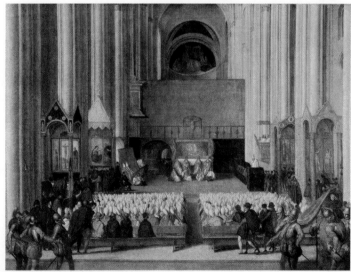

3 Apply It!

Identify causes and effects in the history of the Reformation as you read the chapter. Find at least five causes and their effects, and create graphic organizers to record them.

The Reformation Begins

Guide to Reading

Looking Back, Looking Ahead

During the Middle Ages, all of Western Europe's Christians were Catholic. The movement called the Reformation, however, questioned Catholic beliefs and power.

Focusing on the Main Ideas

- The reforms of Martin Luther led to the creation of new Christian churches. *(page 423)*

- Political leaders often supported Protestantism because they wanted more power. *(page 428)*

Locating Places
Wittenberg (WIH•tuhn•BUHRG)

Meeting People
Martin Luther

Desiderius Erasmus (DEHS•ih•DIHR•ee•uhs ih•RAZ•muhs)

John Wycliffe (WIH•KLIHF)

William Tyndale (TIHN•duhl)

Content Vocabulary
Reformation (REH•fuhr•MAY•shuhn)

indulgence (ihn•DUHL•juhns)

denomination (dih•NAH•muh•NAY•shuhn)

Academic Vocabulary
conclude (kuhn•KLOOD)

energy (EH•nuhr•jee)

resource (REE•SOHRS)

convert (kuhn•VUHRT)

Reading Strategy
Cause and Effect Create a diagram to show some of the causes for the Reformation.

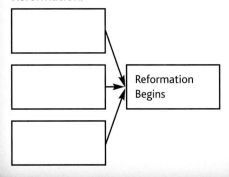

Reformation Begins

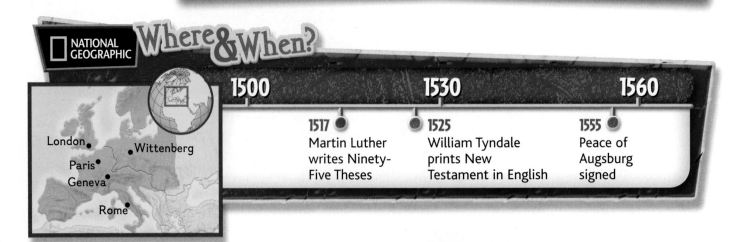

NATIONAL GEOGRAPHIC Where & When?

London • Wittenberg • Paris • Geneva • Rome

1500 — **1530** — **1560**

1517 Martin Luther writes Ninety-Five Theses

1525 William Tyndale prints New Testament in English

1555 Peace of Augsburg signed

Calls for Church Reform

Main Idea The reforms of Martin Luther led to the creation of new Christian churches.

Reading Connection Can you think of any reformers in the United States? Read to learn how some Europeans set out to reform the Catholic Church and ended up starting a new church instead.

In 1517 a young monk named **Martin Luther** challenged the Roman Catholic Church. He publicly argued that the pope could not decide what a person had to do to get into heaven. Eventually, his challenge to the pope's authority led to the creation of new churches in Western Europe.

At first, Luther only wanted to reform the Catholic Church. This is why we call these events the **Reformation** (REH•fuhr•MAY•shuhn). The Reformation was the beginning of a movement in Christianity known as Protestantism. By the end of the Reformation, many new Christian churches had appeared in Europe.

What Ideas Led to the Reformation? In the last chapter, you read about humanism. When humanism spread to northern Europe, it led to a new movement in Christianity called Christian humanism. Its chief leader was a scholar and clergyman named **Desiderius Erasmus** (DEHS•ih•DIHR•ee•uhs ih•RAZ•muhs).

Erasmus wrote that human beings could use their reason to become better Christians and thereby improve the Church. He studied ancient Christian works for inspiration.

One of Erasmus's goals was to translate the Bible into the vernacular. He wanted a farmer working in the fields to be able to stop and read the Bible. Erasmus also believed that it was important for people to be good in their everyday lives. It was not enough to participate in religious activities, like going to church on Sunday. Erasmus was also critical of people who did whatever they could, good or bad, just to make money. He even criticized members of the clergy who had personal ambitions of earning money.

The Church Upsets Reformers By the 1300s, many people believed the Church had problems. It taxed people heavily, and some bishops behaved like they were kings. They built palaces, spent money on fine art, and made sure that their relatives had good jobs. In many villages, priests could barely read or give a good sermon.

Many Catholics became angry at the Church's focus on money. One Church practice that especially angered them was the selling of indulgences. An **indulgence** (ihn•DUHL•juhns) reduced the Church's punishment for a sin. The Church had given out indulgences before, but it did not

▲ Desiderius Erasmus, the most famous Christian humanist, criticized the wealth and power of Catholic leaders. *What change did Erasmus want to make to the Bible?*

423

▲ This painting shows indulgences being sold in a village marketplace. *Why was the Church selling indulgences?*

▲ Indulgence box

enable people to better understand how they should live their lives, so he translated many passages into English for his followers to use. After Wycliffe died, his followers finished translating the Bible, creating the first English edition. Their work influenced preachers and religious teaching throughout England.

The Englishman **William Tyndale** (TIHN•duhl) also believed people needed an English translation of the Bible. Unlike Wycliffe and his followers, who had used Latin sources, Tyndale used the ancient Hebrew and Greek texts for his translation. He began printing his English edition of the New Testament in 1525.

Tyndale also wrote several works in defense of the Reformation. Because of this, he was executed in 1536 for heresy. Even though he had been labeled a heretic, his translation was considered to be of high value. It later became the basis for other English translations. The most famous is the Authorized King James Version of the Bible published in 1611, still in common use today.

Who Was Martin Luther?
Martin Luther became one of the most famous men in history. His break with the Catholic Church led to a revolution in Christianity. Why would a religious man disagree with his faith? First of all, Luther was angered by the conduct of Church leaders. Secondly, he was worried about his own soul.

When Luther went to Rome on a pilgrimage, he was shocked at the behavior of the Roman clergy. Back home in Germany, he taught at a university in the town of **Wittenberg** (WIH•tuhn•BUHRG). He worried

usually sell them. In the 1500s, however, the pope needed money to repair the church of St. Peter's in Rome. To obtain the money, he sold indulgences for the project.

The sale of indulgences outraged Martin Luther. He was also angry at Church leaders who allowed people to think an indulgence was a pardon for sin. The idea of selling God's forgiveness seemed unholy to him.

Martin Luther was not the first person to contradict the pope. As early as the 1370s, an English priest named **John Wycliffe** (WIH•KLIHF) had preached that Christians needed only to recognize Jesus Christ as a power above them, not the pope.

Wycliffe and Luther both challenged the pope's power, but they had something else in common—their respect for the Bible. Wycliffe wanted everyone to read the Bible. He thought that studying it directly would

about the Church's problems and also about his own soul. With the plague killing people all around him, it is not surprising that Luther worried about whether he would go to heaven when he died.

The Church said that Luther would go to heaven if he had faith in God and showed it by doing good works and receiving the sacraments. Still Luther worried that this was not true. He prayed and fasted as he searched for answers to his questions. He prayed so long that sometimes he fell unconscious on the cold church floor.

Luther found his answers by studying the Bible. He **concluded** that only faith, not good works, brought salvation. He believed that salvation was a gift from God, not something earned by doing good works.

In 1517, when the Church began selling indulgences, Luther was astonished. How could the Church tell peasants that buying an indulgence would save them? He angrily prepared a list of 95 arguments against indulgences and sent them to his bishop. Some accounts say that Luther also nailed them to the door of Wittenberg Cathedral for everyone to read. The list became known as the Ninety-Five Theses. Thousands of copies were printed and read all across the German kingdoms.

Revolt Leads to New Churches At first the Church did not take Luther very seriously. Soon, though, Church leaders saw that Luther was dangerous. If people believed Luther, they would rely on the Bible, not priests. Who would need priests if the sacraments were not needed to get to heaven?

The pope and Luther argued for several years, but Luther refused to change his position. Finally, the pope excommunicated Luther. This meant Luther was no longer a member of the Church and could no longer receive the sacraments.

▲ Martin Luther began the Reformation when he made public his Ninety-Five Theses. *How did the Catholic Church react to Luther's actions?*

Luther's ideas soon led to the creation of a new **denomination** (dih•NAH•muh•NAY•shuhn), or organized branch of Christianity. It was known as Lutheranism and was the first Protestant denomination.

Lutheranism has three main ideas. The first is that faith in Jesus, not good works, brings salvation. The second is that the Bible is the final source for truth about God, not a church or its priests. Finally, Lutheranism said that the church was made up of all its believers, not just the clergy.

Peasant Revolts Luther's debate with the pope was so famous that even peasants in the countryside had heard about it. The life

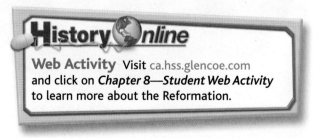

History Online

Web Activity Visit ca.hss.glencoe.com and click on *Chapter 8—Student Web Activity* to learn more about the Reformation.

of a peasant had always been hard, but in the 1520s, it was terrible. The crops had been poor for several years. On top of that, noble landowners increased the taxes that peasants had to pay.

Because of their suffering, Luther's ideas stirred the peasants to revolt. If Luther had a right to rebel against an unjust pope, then the peasants must have a right to stand up to greedy nobles. Like Luther, they based their ideas on the Bible. One leader said the peasants would no longer work for the nobles, "unless it should be shown us from the Gospel that we are serfs."

When the nobles did not give in, huge revolts broke out. It was not long, however, before the peasants were defeated. The nobles had better weapons and horses and won easily, killing thousands of peasants.

Luther sympathized with the peasants, but hated the violence. In his sermons Luther criticized nobles for their treatment of the peasants, but he stressed to the peasants that God had set the government above them and they must obey it.

Reading Check **Cause and Effect** What was the result of the Church's decision to sell indulgences in 1517?

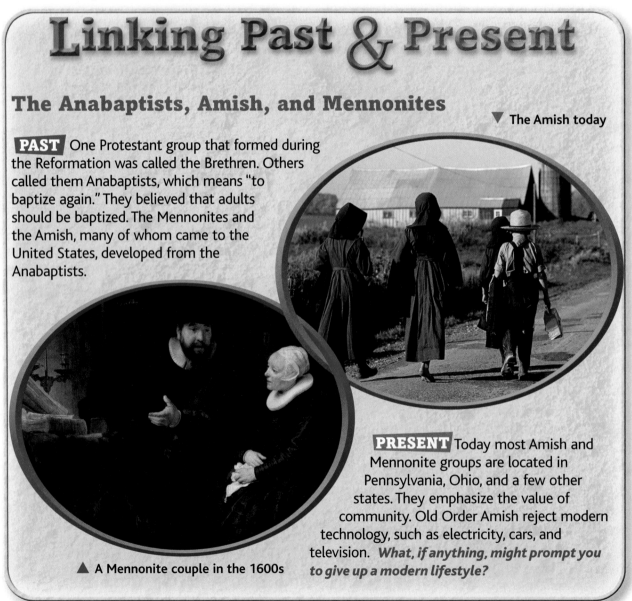

Linking Past & Present

The Anabaptists, Amish, and Mennonites

▼ The Amish today

PAST One Protestant group that formed during the Reformation was called the Brethren. Others called them Anabaptists, which means "to baptize again." They believed that adults should be baptized. The Mennonites and the Amish, many of whom came to the United States, developed from the Anabaptists.

PRESENT Today most Amish and Mennonite groups are located in Pennsylvania, Ohio, and a few other states. They emphasize the value of community. Old Order Amish reject modern technology, such as electricity, cars, and television. *What, if anything, might prompt you to give up a modern lifestyle?*

▲ A Mennonite couple in the 1600s

Biography

MARTIN LUTHER
1483–1546

Long before Martin Luther struggled with the Catholic Church, he faced difficult issues. Luther was born in Eisleben, Germany, in 1483 to a family of miners. Both his parents beat Luther as a child. Luther later said his father's beatings caused him to feel bitter and hateful toward his family.

To avoid his abusive home life, Luther went to schools away from home. At his father's urging, he considered studying law but instead earned a Bachelor of Arts degree in philosophy in 1502.

Later, Luther entered a monastery to separate himself from his abusive past. In 1505 he traveled to Erfurt and became a monk. He then went to Wittenberg in 1508 and stayed with a group of Augustinians. There he continued his study of theology.

Luther was a determined young man. Although he was a priest, he began to question the practices of the Catholic Church. His reforms resulted in a break with the Church. In 1525 he married a former nun named Katharine von Bora. They had six children and lived in a former monastery.

▲ Martin Luther

> **"He who gives to a poor man, or lends to a needy man, does better than if he bought pardons."**
>
> –Martin Luther, "The Ninety-five Theses (1517)"

▲ Wittenberg today

Although known for his hot temper—which cost him many friendships—Luther and his wife cared for as many as 20 orphans whose parents died from the plague. In his later years, Luther enjoyed gardening and music, and continued his lifelong love of writing. He died in 1546, probably of a heart attack.

Then and Now

Martin Luther was willing to stand up for his beliefs, even if that meant offending people. Can you think of anyone in the news who has shown that same willingness?

WH7.9.2 Describe the theological, political, and economic ideas of the major figures during the Reformation (e.g., Desiderius Erasmus, Martin Luther, John Calvin, William Tyndale).

WH7.9.4 Identify and locate the European regions that remained Catholic and those that became Protestant and explain how the division affected the distribution of religions in the New World.

Politics and Lutheranism

Main Idea Political leaders often supported Protestantism because they wanted more power.

Reading Connection Under the U.S. Constitution, the government cannot favor any one religion. Read to learn what happened during the Reformation when kings decided what faith people had to follow.

In the past, there had been thinkers who challenged Catholic beliefs, but the Church always remained in control. In the 1500s, however, changes occurred that allowed Protestantism to take hold. Protestantism succeeded in part because some of Europe's kings realized they could increase their power by supporting Lutheranism against the Catholic Church.

You read earlier about the Holy Roman Empire, which covered much of central Europe. The heart of the empire was made up of about 300 small German kingdoms. In 1519 Charles V became the Holy Roman Emperor. His empire included the lands of the Holy Roman Empire, as well as all of Spain, the Netherlands, parts of Italy, and territories in the Americas.

The Reformation created challenges for Charles V. His chief political rival was Francis I, the king of France. Francis I, like Charles V, worked **energetically** to stop the growth of Protestantism. However, he also fought many wars with the Holy Roman Empire. This drained his finances and military **resources.**

Charles V also faced trouble from the rulers in his own realm. The local rulers and nobles of the Holy Roman Empire were concerned about Charles V's power. They did not want a strong central ruler. They wanted to rule their own small kingdoms with as little interference as possible.

Many German rulers became Lutherans for religious and political reasons. By doing so, their kingdom became Lutheran. After breaking with the Catholic Church, these rulers seized lands owned by Catholic monasteries in their kingdoms. Now they, not the Church, benefited from the income earned from those lands.

At the same time, when the Catholic Church left a kingdom, it meant the kingdom no longer paid taxes to the Church. Rulers could impose their own church taxes and keep the money for themselves. This made rulers who became Protestants stronger and the Church weaker.

NATIONAL GEOGRAPHIC
Holy Roman Empire 1520

KEY
Holy Roman Empire

0   300 mi.
0   300 km
Lambert Azimuthal Equal-Area projection

NORWAY

NORTH
SEA

SCOTLAND
IRELAND
ENGLAND
DENMARK
TEUTONIC ORDER
North Sea
POLAND
Bohemia
ATLANTIC OCEAN
Netherlands
FRANCE
Swiss Confed.
Austria
HUNGARY
Milan
VENICE
OTTOMAN EMPIRE
Savoy
Genoa
Papal States
Florence
PORTUGAL
SPAIN
NAPLES
Mediterranean Sea
20°E

Using Geography Skills

1. **Location** What were some of the areas that made up the Holy Roman Empire?
2. **Movement** Why might it have been difficult for one ruler to control the Holy Roman Empire?

Find NGS online map resources @
www.nationalgeographic.com/maps

This challenged the power of the pope in Rome. The pope did what he could to stop Lutheranism in Germany. However, Charles V ruled a great deal of Italy, and the pope considered him a threat as well. Because of this, the pope supported Francis I of France over Charles V. The emperor attacked Rome to show his authority. As Charles V strengthened his hold on Italy, the papacy's power eroded.

Charles V eventually went to war with the German rulers who **converted** to Lutheranism, but he was unable to defeat them. In 1555 the fighting ended with the Peace of Augsburg. This agreement let each German ruler decide whether his kingdom would be Lutheran or Catholic. As a result most of northern Germany became Protestant, while the south stayed Catholic.

▲ This painting by Titian shows the Emperor Charles V riding into battle in Germany. *What agreement did Charles make to end the fighting with German rulers?*

✔️ **Reading Check** **Explain** Why did many German princes support Martin Luther's ideas?

History Online

Study Central Need help understanding the beginning of the Reformation? Visit ca.hss.glencoe.com and click on Study Central.

Section 1 Review

Reading Summary

Review the Main Ideas

• Many Christians, including Martin Luther, believed the Catholic Church was becoming corrupt. This led people to leave the Church and create new Christian churches.

• Many European rulers and nobles supported Luther's reforms for political as well as religious reasons.

What Did You Learn?

1. What were indulgences, and why did they become controversial?

2. What were the Ninety-Five Theses?

Critical Thinking

3. **Organizing Information** Draw a diagram like the one below to list the three main ideas of Lutheranism. **CA 7RC2.0**

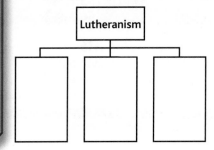

4. **The Big Ideas** How did Erasmus use humanism to shape Christian ideas? How did he use religious works to spread the ideas of humanism? **CA HI2.**

5. **Explain** How did the Catholic Church lose power in Europe? Why? **CA 7RC2.3**

6. **Analyze** How did Germany's peasants react to Luther's teachings, and what was Luther's response? **CA HI2.**

7. **Reading** **Identifying Cause and Effect** What major ideas or events influenced Martin Luther's view of the Catholic Church? How did his ideas change the Church? **CA 7RC2.3**

Section 2

The Reformation Spreads

History Social Science Standards
WH7.9 Students analyze the historical developments of the Reformation.

Guide to Reading

Looking Back, Looking Ahead
As you have learned, Martin Luther's ideas contributed to the rise of Protestantism. In this section, you will learn about the ideas of John Calvin as well as how the Reformation changed England.

Focusing on the (Main Ideas)
- John Calvin's Protestant teachings spread across Europe and into North America. *(page 431)*
- Henry VIII created the Anglican Church in England. *(page 432)*

Locating Places
Geneva (juh•NEE•vuh)
London (LUHN•duhn)

Meeting People
John Calvin
Henry VIII
Mary I
Elizabeth I

Content Vocabulary
theology (thee•AH•luh•jee)
predestination (pree•DEHS•tuh•NAY•shuhn)
annul (uh•NUHL)

Academic Vocabulary
clarify (KLAR•uh•FY)
consent (kuhn•SEHNT)

Reading Strategy
Organizing Information Complete a table to show the major impact of rulers on the English Reformation.

Ruler	Impact

NATIONAL GEOGRAPHIC **Who & When?**

1520

1540

1560

c. 1534 Henry VIII sets up the Church of England

c. 1536 Calvin publishes *Institutes of the Christian Religion*

c. 1555 Mary I persecutes Protestants in England

WH7.9.2 Describe the theological, political, and economic ideas of the major figures during the Reformation (e.g., Desiderius Erasmus, Martin Luther, John Calvin, William Tyndale).

WH7.9.3 Explain Protestants' new practices of church self-government and the influence of those practices on the development of democratic practices and ideas of federalism.

Calvin and Calvinism

Main Idea John Calvin's Protestant teachings spread across Europe and into North America.

Reading Connection Are there some things you are sure are true? Read to learn how some Protestants developed a faith where everyone agreed that some people were going to heaven and others were not.

Who Was John Calvin? John Calvin was

born in France in the early 1500s. When he was old enough, he went to Paris to study **theology** (thee•AH•luh•jee). Theology is the study of questions about God.

Although Calvin lived in France, he began to hear about the ideas of Martin Luther. Secretly, Calvin began to read about Luther at his college. The more Calvin read, the more he was convinced by Luther's new perspective on religion.

Eventually, Calvin left Paris because it became too dangerous to talk about Lutheranism. Once he dared to return to his hometown, but he was arrested and spent months in a damp jail. Calvin finally found safety in **Geneva** (juh•NEE•vuh), Switzerland, a Protestant city. There his powerful preaching convinced many people to follow him.

What Is Calvinism? In 1536 Calvin pub-

lished a book called *Institutes of the Christian Religion*. This book describes Calvin's ideas. It became very influential among Protestants. Calvinism became the basis of many Protestant churches, including the churches of Puritans and Presbyterians in England and Scotland.

Calvin's main idea was that God's will is absolute and decides everything in the world in advance. God has decided who will go to heaven and who will not. This belief is called **predestination** (pree•DEHS• tuh•NAY•shuhn), meaning that no matter

what people do, the outcome of their life is already planned.

Most Calvinists decided that they were probably among the saved. To prove it, they worked hard, behaved well, and obeyed the laws of their towns. In this way, Calvinism helped promote a stable society.

Another important idea of Calvinism is that neither kings nor bishops should control the Church. Calvinists believed that congregations should choose their own elders and ministers to run the church.

This innovative idea had a strong impact on England and on many of the English settlers in America. The idea that a congregation could choose its own leaders

Primary Source Knowledge of God

John Calvin's writings helped Europeans accept Protestantism.

"What help is it . . . to know a God with whom we have nothing to do? Rather, our knowledge should serve first to teach us fear and reverence [respect]; secondly, with it as our guide and teacher, we should learn to seek every good from him, and having received it, to credit it to his account. . . . Again, you cannot behold him clearly unless you acknowledge him to be the fountainhead [source of life] and source of every good."

▲ John Calvin

—John Calvin, *Institutes of the Christian Religion*

DBQ Document-Based Question

According to Calvin, what is needed for believers to understand God clearly?

WH7.9.2 Describe the theological, political, and economic ideas of the major figures during the Reformation (e.g., Desiderius Erasmus, Martin Luther, John Calvin, William Tyndale). **WH7.9.3** Explain Protestants' new practices of church self-government and the influence of those practices on the development of democratic practices and ideas of federalism. **WH7.9.4** Identify and locate the European regions that remained Catholic and those that became Protestant and explain how the division affected the distribution of religions in the New World.

helped build support for the idea that people should elect their political leaders.

In the colonies, this developed into an important democratic principle. When the Founders of the United States wrote the Declaration of Independence, they used these ideas, in part, to **clarify** their arguments. For instance, they stated that people are governed by **consent** and have the right to choose their own leaders.

This principle also developed into the idea of federalism, or the idea that power should be divided between local governments and a central government. This idea can be traced, in part, to the idea that local churches can manage their own affairs while belonging to a larger organization.

✓ **Reading Check** **Compare** How did Calvin's ideas differ from those of Luther?

The English Reformation

Main Idea Henry VIII created the Anglican Church in England.

Reading Connection You have probably heard about the Pilgrims. Do you know why they left England to come here? Read to learn why some Protestants left England for America during the Reformation.

In the history of England, no king is more famous than **Henry VIII.** He ruled England from 1509 to 1547. Henry married six queens, of which two were divorced and two were beheaded. He imprisoned bishops and nobles in the Tower of **London** (LUHN•duhn) for disagreeing with him. Eventually, they were all beheaded. One reason Henry VIII is England's most famous king is because his decisions brought the Reformation to England.

The Tower of London

The Tower of London was built in 1078. During the Middle Ages, it was used as a royal residence. At the time of Henry VIII, many people were jailed and executed in the Bloody Tower and buried in the Chapel of St. Peter. Today, the Tower of London houses the British royal family's crown jewels. *Why did Henry VIII imprison many people in the Tower of London?*

Henry VIII ▼

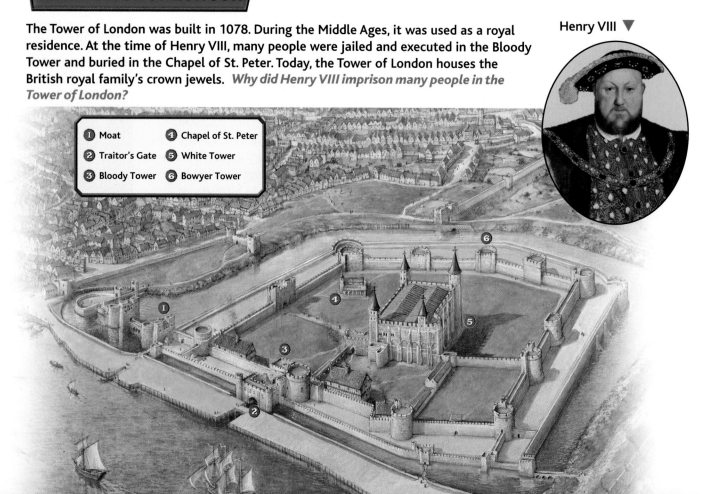

1. Moat
2. Traitor's Gate
3. Bloody Tower
4. Chapel of St. Peter
5. White Tower
6. Bowyer Tower

Henry VIII Starts His Own Church Henry was a member of the Tudor family. In the 1400s, before the Tudors came to the throne, England's nobles had fought over who should be king. Henry was determined to keep the Tudors on the throne.

To do this he needed a son to succeed him, but Henry had no son. His wife Catherine had given birth to one surviving daughter. Henry asked the pope to **annul** (uh•NUHL), or cancel, his marriage to Catherine.

An annulment is not the same as a divorce. If the pope annulled the marriage, it would be as if the marriage had never happened. It would mean that Henry could find a new wife to give birth to sons. Those sons would be heirs to the throne, not the daughter Catherine had given him.

Popes had annulled marriages before, but this time the pope refused. Catherine was the daughter of Ferdinand and Isabella of Spain. Spain was the strongest Catholic kingdom at that time, and the pope did not want to make Catherine's family angry.

Henry decided to have the archbishop of Canterbury—the highest bishop in England—annul the marriage. In response, the pope excommunicated Henry from the Church. Henry fought back. In 1534 he had Parliament pass the Act of Supremacy. This act declared the king, not the pope, to be the head of the Church in England.

Henry ordered all the priests and bishops in England to accept him as the new head of their church. Some refused and were killed. The most famous was Sir Thomas More, who was executed in 1535. Henry then seized the Catholic Church's land in England and gave portions of it to his nobles. This kept the nobles loyal. If they ever let the Catholic Church regain power in England, they would have to give up their land.

Mary I (above) attempted to restore the Catholic religion in England, and she married Philip II (right), the Catholic king of Spain. *Why was Mary I known as "Bloody Mary"?*

Who Was Bloody Mary? The Church of England came to be known as the Anglican Church. It kept most of the rituals and sacraments of the Catholic Church. However, many English Catholics did not want to abandon Catholicism. They backed Henry and Catherine's daughter Mary when she became Queen **Mary I** in 1553. Mary had been raised Catholic and wanted to make England a Catholic kingdom again.

Mary restored the Catholic Church in England in 1555 and arrested Protestants who opposed her. In her struggle to make England Catholic again, Mary burned 300 people at the stake. The English were horrified and called her "Bloody Mary."

Mary ruled about five years, then died. Her half-sister Elizabeth took over the throne, becoming Queen **Elizabeth I.** Elizabeth was a Protestant. She restored the

Anglican Church and went on to become one of the greatest rulers in English history.

How Did Calvinism Affect England?

Although the Catholics were defeated, the religious tensions continued. By the late 1500s, the ideas of John Calvin had reached England. Many educated people read Calvin's works and became convinced that he was right. They began to demand that the Anglican Church give up its Catholic ways of doing things. These reformers became known as Puritans because they wanted to purify the Anglican Church of Catholic ideas.

Puritans began to form their own congregations. These congregations were independent. They made their own decisions about what their congregations should and should not do. They did not report to a bishop of the Anglican Church, and they chose their own ministers.

Queen Elizabeth I tolerated the Puritans, but when James I became king in 1603, the Puritans faced harder times. The king headed the Anglican Church and appointed its leaders. The leaders, in turn, chose the priests for the congregations. James believed that by choosing their own ministers, the Puritans were challenging the king's power.

James I and the king who came after him, Charles I, persecuted the Puritans. They shut down Puritan churches and jailed Puritan leaders. Many Puritans decided to move to America to practice their religion freely. There they founded colonies that eventually became the states of Massachusetts, Connecticut, New Hampshire, and Rhode Island.

✓ **Reading Check** **Cause and Effect** Why did Henry VIII create the Anglican Church?

History Online

Study Central Need help understanding Calvinism or the English Reformation? Visit ca.hss.glencoe.com and click on Study Central.

Section 2 Review

Reading Summary

Review the Main Ideas

- John Calvin created new Protestant teachings that spread across Europe and into North America.

- The Anglican Church began in England due to a reformation led by Henry VIII.

What Did You Learn?

1. What were John Calvin's basic beliefs about God's will?

2. What prompted Henry VIII to create his own church?

Critical Thinking

3. **Organizing Information** Create a chart like the one below showing England's rulers during the Reformation and their religious policies. **CA CS2.**

| Henry VIII | ▶ | ▶ | ▶ | ▶ | Charles I |

4. **Comparing** How did Calvin's ideas differ from those of Martin Luther? **CA 7RC2.0**

5. **The Big Ideas** Write a short essay comparing how Queen Elizabeth I and James I dealt with the Puritans. Which leader do you think made England stronger? Why? **CA 7RC2.3**

6. **Determining Cause and Effect** How did people react to the idea of predestination? How did people who believed in the idea behave? **CA 7RC2.3**

7. **Analysis** **Understanding Changes** Write an essay explaining how Henry VIII and Calvinism changed religion and politics in England. **CA CS1.; HI2.**

The Counter-Reformation

Guide to Reading

Looking Back, Looking Ahead
In the last two sections, you learned about the rise of Protestantism. In this section, you will read about the Catholic Church's attempts at reform and the struggle between Europe's Protestants and Catholics.

Focusing on the Main Ideas
- Catholics and Protestants fought religious wars across Europe. **(page 436)**

- During the Reformation and Counter-Reformation, the power of kings increased. At the same time, Catholic kingdoms began sending missionaries overseas to convert people to Christianity. **(page 440)**

Locating Places
Trent
Navarre (nuh•VAHR)
Paris

Meeting People
Ignatius of Loyola (ihg•NAY•shuhs loy•OH•luh)
Huguenot (HYOO•guh•NAHT)
King Ferdinand
Queen Isabella
Maimonides (my•MAH•nuh•DEEZ)
Francis Xavier (ZAYV•yuhr)

Content Vocabulary
seminary (SEH•muh•NEHR•ee)
heresy (HEHR•uh•see)
divine right

Academic Vocabulary
contradict (KAHN•truh•DIHKT)
impact (IHM•PAHKT)
philosophy (fuh•LAH•suh•fee)
eliminate (ih•LIH•muh•NAYT)

Reading Strategy
Cause and Effect Create a diagram to show the results of the Catholic Church's attempts at reform.

Reform	→	Result

History Social Science Standards
WH7.9 Students analyze the historical developments of the Reformation.

NATIONAL GEOGRAPHIC Where & When?

London
Paris
Trent
Rome

1550 — 1600 — 1650

c. 1545 Pope Paul III opens the Council of Trent

c. 1598 Edict of Nantes allows French Protestants right to worship

c. 1648 Thirty Years' War ends

Biography

WH7.9.4 Identify and locate the European regions that remained Catholic and those that became Protestant and explain how the division affected the distribution of religions in the New World. **WH7.9.5** Analyze how the Counter Reformation revitalized the Catholic church and the forces that fostered the movement (e.g., St. Ignatius of Loyola and the Jesuits, the Council of Trent).

CATHERINE DE' MEDICI
1519–1589

▲ Catherine de' Medici

Catherine de' Medici was an Italian woman who played an important role in French history during the Reformation. She was born in Florence to Lorenzo de' Medici and Madeleine de la Tour d' Auvergne. Catherine was orphaned as a baby and was raised by relatives. At age 14, Catherine was married to Henry, a French prince. Catherine took Italian artists, musicians, writers, and dancers with her to the French court. She was never fully accepted in France, however, because she was Italian and was not from a royal family.

In 1547 Catherine's husband became King Henry II. After he died in a jousting accident in 1559, their three oldest sons—Francis II, Charles IX, and Henry III—succeeded each other as king. Although Catherine was no longer queen, she still had much influence over her sons.

Catherine is blamed for many of the conflicts between French Catholics and French Protestants, called Huguenots. In 1568 she outlawed freedom of worship. In 1572 Catherine arranged the murder of a Huguenot adviser. His death sparked the Saint Bartholomew's Massacre, which resulted in the deaths of about 6,000 Huguenots. Catherine was not always opposed to Huguenots. In fact, she arranged the marriage of her daughter Margaret to Henry of Navarre, a former Protestant Huguenot who became King Henry IV of France.

Views on Catherine's accomplishments are mixed. Some blame her entirely for the French religious wars. Others remember her efforts to protect her sons. Still others remember her as a Renaissance woman because she supported the arts, added to the royal library, and sponsored a dance and theater pageant that is considered to be the first ballet. Catherine died in 1589 of pneumonia.

> **"God and the world will have reason to be satisfied with me."**
> –Catherine de' Medici,
> *Biography of a Family*

Then and Now

If Catherine de' Medici were running for political office today, do you think she would be a popular candidate? Why or why not?

What Was the Thirty Years' War? The worst religious war of the Reformation era was fought in the Holy Roman Empire in the 1600s. The war began in Bohemia, today known as the Czech Republic, when Protestant nobles rebelled against their Catholic king.

The war lasted 30 years, from 1618 to 1648, and quickly became a war of kingdoms. France, Sweden, Denmark, England, and the Netherlands sent troops to help the Protestants, while Spain and the Holy Roman Empire backed the Catholics. The war weakened Spain and helped make France one of Europe's most powerful countries.

The Reformation in Spain

The ideas of Luther and Calvin never became very popular in Spain. Still, when Protestants began fighting in Europe, it had a dramatic **impact** on Spain. Spanish rulers became suspicious of Protestant countries and of anyone in Spain who was not Catholic.

When the Reformation began, Spain was still a young nation. It had been founded in 1469 when **King Ferdinand** and **Queen Isabella** married and joined their two kingdoms. These monarchs wanted a strong nation. They felt that all their subjects should be Catholic, because that would keep the people loyal and united.

When Ferdinand and Isabella began to rule, many Muslims still lived in Spain. As you read in earlier chapters, Muslims ruled Spain from about A.D. 700 to 1200. The Muslims had made non-Muslims pay special taxes and limited their rights, but they did not seek to kill or expel nonbelievers. Jews, for example, found life in Muslim Spain better than other places in Europe where they had been persecuted.

Muslim Spain during the Middle Ages was a golden age for both Muslim and

▲ This photo shows the Alhambra, a Muslim palace and fortress in Granada, Spain. *What happened to Spanish Muslims after Ferdinand and Isabella took power?*

Maimonides ▶

Jewish thinkers, poets, artists, and scientists. A doctor and lawyer named Averroës, or Ibn Rushd, helped advance scientific and medical knowledge. He also wrote commentaries on Aristotle.

The Muslims built universities and encouraged learning. They studied the ancient Greek and Roman texts on nature and added to them. They expanded European knowledge of the medicinal properties of plants and medicine in general. They also studied geography and developed one of the first maps for sea travel. Technological advancements included windmills and the manufacturing of paper.

The most famous Jewish scholar in Spain was **Maimonides** (my•MAH•nuh•DEEZ). Maimonides wrote books on religion, medicine, and law. His books on Jewish oral law earned him great respect.

Jewish poets in Spain include Solomon ibn Gabirol. He wrote poems about love, nature, and religion. Ibn Gabirol's religious poetry is used in some Jewish ceremonies.

WH7.9.4 Identify and locate the European regions that remained Catholic and those that became Protestant and explain how the division affected the distribution of religions in the New World.

WH7.9.6 Understand the institution and impact of missionaries on Christianity and the diffusion of Christianity from Europe to other parts of the world in the medieval and early modern periods; locate missions on a world map.

His books of **philosophy** influenced many European philosophers.

In 1492 Ferdinand and Isabella ordered all Jews and Muslims to convert to Catholicism or leave the country. To ensure religious unity, they also set up the Spanish Inquisition to investigate people's beliefs. A similar inquisition was established in Portugal by King John III in 1536.

The Spanish and Portuguese Inquisitions were Catholic courts, similar to the one the Catholic Church had set up in Europe to investigate heresy. These inquisitions were much crueler. Charges of heresy were made just to **eliminate** enemies. Horrible tortures were invented to force confessions of guilt. The head of the Spanish Inquisition, Tomás de Torquemada (TAWR • kuh • MAH • duh), executed some 2,000 Spaniards.

Reading Check **Identify** What deal earned Henry of Navarre the French throne?

Legacy of the Reformation

Main Idea During the Reformation and Counter-Reformation, the power of kings increased. At the same time, Catholic kingdoms began sending missionaries overseas to convert people to Christianity.

Reading Connection Do you think spreading democracy is important? Read to learn how Catholic missionaries tried to spread their religion to other people in the world.

The Reformation and the Counter-Reformation had an intense impact on the world. In Europe, the political and economic power of the Catholic Church was greatly diminished. At the same time, kings continued to gain greater power and authority.

Kings also solidified their power among their own nobles. Kings began to claim that they ruled by **divine right**. This meant that their authority was granted to them directly

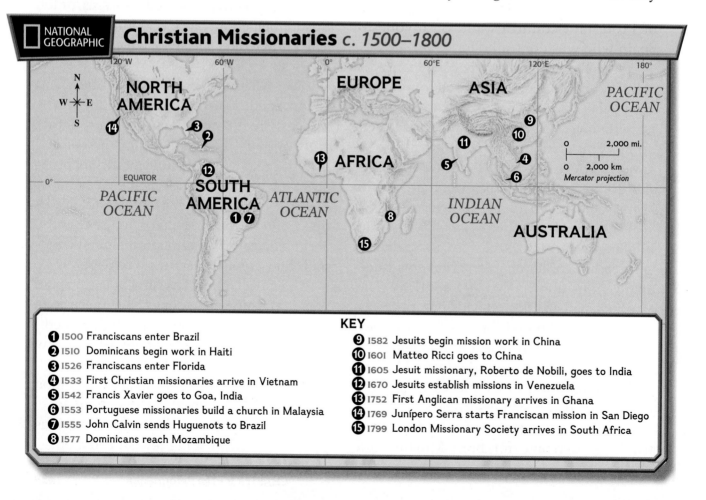

NATIONAL GEOGRAPHIC — Christian Missionaries c. 1500–1800

KEY

- ❶ 1500 Franciscans enter Brazil
- ❷ 1510 Dominicans begin work in Haiti
- ❸ 1526 Franciscans enter Florida
- ❹ 1533 First Christian missionaries arrive in Vietnam
- ❺ 1542 Francis Xavier goes to Goa, India
- ❻ 1553 Portuguese missionaries build a church in Malaysia
- ❼ 1555 John Calvin sends Huguenots to Brazil
- ❽ 1577 Dominicans reach Mozambique
- ❾ 1582 Jesuits begin mission work in China
- ❿ 1601 Matteo Ricci goes to China
- ⓫ 1605 Jesuit missionary, Roberto de Nobili, goes to India
- ⓬ 1670 Jesuits establish missions in Venezuela
- ⓭ 1752 First Anglican missionary arrives in Ghana
- ⓮ 1769 Junípero Serra starts Franciscan mission in San Diego
- ⓯ 1799 London Missionary Society arrives in South Africa

from God, not through the papacy. This idea was particularly influential in France under the reign of Louis XIV.

When the Counter-Reformation began, many Catholics were committed to spreading their faith. As part of this new energy and determination, Catholic kingdoms began sending missionaries overseas to the Americas and Asia. French and Spanish Jesuits were among the most active missionaries in the 1500s and 1600s.

The first Jesuit missionary to Japan, **Francis Xavier** (ZAYV•yuhr), arrived in 1549. The Japanese at first welcomed the Jesuits. By 1600, the Jesuits had converted thousands of Japanese to Christianity.

Eventually, however, the Jesuits lost favor in Japan. They clashed with people who believed in Buddhism and Shintoism. The Japanese shogun, or military ruler, banned Christianity in Japan and expelled all missionaries.

Spanish missionaries had much greater success in the Philippine Islands. Most of the people there eventually became Catholic. Today the Philippines is the only Asian country with a Catholic majority. French missionaries tried to convert the people of Vietnam but were expelled by Vietnam's emperor.

The spread of the Catholic faith also shows another result of the Reformation. European nations had divided. Some supported Protestantism, others Catholicism. This division was spread to the world through each nation's missionary efforts.

In the Americas, for example, Catholic missionaries had great success in Central and South America. These areas remain heavily Catholic today. Meanwhile, Puritans and other Protestants settled colonies in North America.

✓ **Reading Check** **Identify** In what parts of the world did Catholic missionaries teach?

History Online

Study Central Need help understanding the Counter-Reformation? Visit ca.hss.glencoe.com and click on Study Central.

Section 3 Review

Reading Summary
Review the Main Ideas

- Across Europe, religious wars between Catholics and Protestants were fought in the 1500s and 1600s while the Spanish monarchs tried to make Spain an exclusively Catholic country.

- The power of kings grew while Catholic missionaries tried to spread their religion to Asia and America.

What Did You Learn?

1. What was the Council of Trent, and what did it accomplish?

2. Why was the Edict of Nantes important?

Critical Thinking

3. **Organizing Information** Draw a chart like the one below. Fill in details listing ways the Catholic Church tried to counter the Reformation. **CA 7RC2.0**

Church's Policies

4. **Analyze** How did the Reformation affect the world outside of Europe? **CA HI2.**

5. **The Big Ideas** How did the religious wars and conflicts affect France and Spain? **CA 7RC2.2**

6. **Explain** How were Muslims and Jews treated in Spain during the golden age? How were they treated after Catholics took control? **CA HI2.**

7. **Writing Summaries** Write a short essay summarizing the history of Catholicism in Spain from the 1400s to the 1600s. **CA 7WA2.5**

Analyzing Primary Sources

WH7.9.2 Describe the theological, political, and economic ideas of the major figures during the Reformation (e.g., Desiderius Erasmus, Martin Luther, John Calvin, William Tyndale).

A Church Divided

During the Reformation, Martin Luther separated from the Catholic Church. He believed that the Bible was the ultimate source of truth, and that faith did not require works to be saved. John Calvin took Luther's ideas even further. He believed in predestination. However, many people remained faithful to the Catholic Church and actively preached the Catholic message. These events led to a period of spiritual and political turmoil.

Read the passages on pages 442 and 443, and answer the questions that follow.

▲ **Martin Luther at Wittenberg cathedral**

Reader's Dictionary

remit: release from guilt

canons (KA•nuhns): traditions

letters of pardon: the granting of an indulgence

preordain: determine in advance

immutable: unchangeable

bridegroom: a man about to be or just married

Martin Luther's Ninety-Five Theses

I*n his Ninety-Five Theses, Martin Luther protested against many practices of the pope and the Catholic Church. These were printed and circulated throughout Europe.*

5. The Pope has neither the will nor the power to **remit** any penalties except those which he has imposed by his own authority, or by that of the **canons.**

6. The Pope has no power to remit any guilt, except by declaring and warranting it to have been remitted by God; or at most by remitting cases reserved for himself; in which cases, if his power

were [disregarded], guilt would certainly remain. . . .

21. Thus those preachers of indulgences are in error who say that by the indulgences of the Pope a man is freed and saved from all punishment. . . .

32. Those who believe that, through **letters of pardon,** they are made sure of their own salvation will be eternally damned along with their teachers.

37. Every true Christian, whether living or dead, has a share in all the benefits of Christ and of the Church, . . . even without letters of pardon.

45. Christians should be taught that he who sees any one in need, and, passing him by, gives money for pardons, is not purchasing for himself the indulgences of the Pope but the anger of God. . . .

—Martin Luther, "The Ninety-five Theses"

Calvin and Predestination

While Luther preached the importance of faith, John Calvin believed that both Luther and the Catholic Church were incorrect about who could be saved. The following passage by Calvin describes some of his doctrines.

By predestination we mean the eternal decree of God, by which he determined with himself whatever he wished to happen with regard to every man. All are not created on equal terms, but some are **preordained** to eternal life, others to eternal damnation. . . .

We say, then, that Scripture clearly proves this much, that God by his eternal and **immutable** counsel determined once for all those whom it was his pleasure one day to admit to salvation, and those whom, on the other hand, it was his pleasure to doom to destruction. We maintain that this counsel, as regards the elect, is founded on his free mercy, without any respect to human worth, while those whom he dooms to destruction are excluded from access to life by a just and blameless . . . judgment.

—John Calvin, "Predestination: Institutes of the Christian Religion"

Saint Ignatius of Loyola

In order to fight Protestantism, the Catholic Ignatius Loyola founded a new religious order. He insisted on certain principles:

▲ St. Ignatius of Loyola

First Rule. The first: All judgment laid aside, we ought to have our mind ready and prompt to obey, in all, the true Spouse of Christ our Lord, which is our holy Mother the Church Hierarchical [Roman Catholic].

Thirteenth Rule. To be right in everything, we ought always to hold that the white which I see, is black, if the Hierarchical Church so decides it, believing that between Christ our Lord, the **Bridegroom**, and the Church, His Bride, there is the same Spirit which governs and directs us for the salvation of our souls.

—St. Ignatius Loyola, *Spiritual Exercises*

DBQ Document-Based Questions

Martin Luther's Ninety-Five Theses

1. The pope eventually excommunicated Martin Luther. Use the theses presented here to explain why you think this happened.

2. What does Luther say is a use for money that will please God?

Calvin and Predestination

3. According to Calvin, how much does an individual's worth influence whether or not he or she is saved?

4. Calvin used the term "predestination" to describe the teachings in this primary source. Based on what you have read, define "predestination."

Saint Ignatius of Loyola

5. What does Saint Ignatius compare the Roman Catholic Church and Jesus Christ to? Explain.

6. What reason does Saint Ignatius give for his belief that Catholics should obey the Church completely?

Read to Write

7. Suppose that you are an artist of the Reformation and you have been commissioned by Saint Ignatius to portray his vision of a good church. In addition, Luther and Calvin have asked you to create paintings that depict the beliefs of Lutheranism and Calvinism. Write a description of what your paintings would look like. **CA HR4.**

Review Content Vocabulary

Write the vocabulary word that completes each sentence. Write a sentence for each unused word.

a. indulgence   d. predestination

b. denomination   e. seminary

c. theology   f. heresy

___ 1. Lutheranism is a(n) ____ of Christianity.

___ 2. _____ is the belief that God decides who goes to heaven before they are born.

___ 3. In the 1500s, Catholics could buy a(n) ____ to reduce the penalty for a sin.

___ 4. The Jesuits fought against ____.

Review the Main Ideas

Section 1 • The Reformation Begins

5. What happened when Martin Luther tried to reform the Catholic Church?

6. How did some political leaders try to strengthen their power?

Section 2 • The Reformation Spreads

7. How were John Calvin's religious ideas spread to North America?

8. Why did Henry VIII separate himself and England from the Catholic Church?

Section 3 • The Counter-Reformation

9. Where did major religious conflicts occur between Catholics and Protestants?

10. How did the Reformation affect the power of the Catholic Church?

Critical Thinking

11. **Identify** What two things led Luther to challenge the Catholic Church? **CA 7RC2.2**

12. **Explain** Who fought the Thirty Years' War? What was the result? **CA 7RC2.0**

13. **Analyze** Why was the excommunication of Henry VIII a powerful message from the Catholic Church? How did Henry react to his excommunication? **CA HR5.**

Geography Skills

Study the map below and answer the following questions.

14. **Identify** Which religious group was most predominant in England? **CA CS3.**

15. **Location** Where are the Calvinists located? **CA CS3.**

16. **Movement** Which group is located in England, Scotland, and Ireland? **CA CS3.**

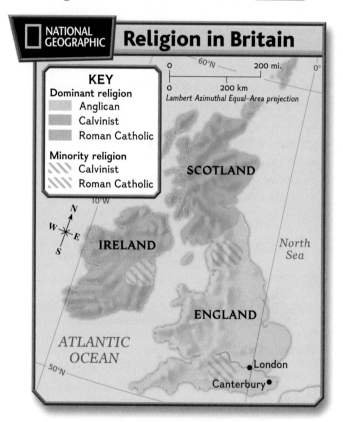

NATIONAL GEOGRAPHIC **Religion in Britain**

KEY

Dominant religion
- Anglican
- Calvinist
- Roman Catholic

Minority religion
- Calvinist
- Roman Catholic

Lambert Azimuthal Equal-Area projection

0   200 mi.

0   200 km

SCOTLAND

IRELAND

North Sea

ENGLAND

ATLANTIC OCEAN

London

Canterbury

Read to Write

17. **The Big Ideas** Understanding Cause and Effect Choose one of the countries mentioned in this chapter. Use your local library to research the changes that occurred in that country during the Reformation. Write an essay explaining those changes. **CA 7WA2.3**

18. **Using Your** **FOLDABLES** Use the information from your foldable to write a series of questions about the chapter. Work with a classmate to answer all of your questions and help review the chapter. **CA HR1.**

Using Academic Vocabulary

19. Choose the words from the list below that have the same prefix. What is this prefix? Look the word up in a dictionary to find out its meaning. Then write a sentence for each of the selected words.

conclude   consent
resource   contradict
convert   impact
clarify

Building Citizenship

20. **Making Connections** Write an essay that explains how religious beliefs of the Reformation affected people's ideas about their rights. How are these ideas reflected in our own society? **CA HI2.**

Economics Connection

21. **Understanding Points of View** How did the Catholic Church use indulgences to increase its wealth and power? Do research to find out some of the main reasons why the Church began to charge for indulgences in the 1500s. Also include information on why people did not support the Church's use of indulgences. **CA 7WA2.3** **CA HR5.**

Reviewing Skills

22. **Reading Skill** **Identifying Cause and Effect** After the Reformation and Counter-Reformation, Catholic kingdoms sent missionaries across the world. Use your local library and the Internet to research how those missionaries affected the world. Choose one place where missionaries went, and write an essay that describes how the missionaries affected the culture. Be sure to use examples from your research. **CA 7WA2.4**

23. **Analysis Skill** **Distinguishing Fact and Opinion** Read the following excerpt from Martin Luther's Ninety-Five Theses. According to Luther, is a letter of pardon, or indulgence, necessary? Is Luther's statement about indulgences a fact or an opinion? Why? **CA HR2.**

"37. Every true Christian, whether living or dead, has a share in all the benefits of Christ and of the Church, . . . even without letters of pardon. . . .

45. Christians should be taught that he who sees any one in need, and, passing him by, gives money for pardons, is not purchasing for himself the indulgences of the Pope but the anger of God . . ."

—Martin Luther, "Ninety-five Theses"

Standards Practice

Select the best answer for each of the following questions.

24 **Martin Luther criticized the Catholic Church for**

A siding with the Protestants.

B not supporting the pope.

C refusing to pay taxes.

D the behavior of its leaders.

25 **During the Spanish Inquisition, which groups were expelled from Spain?**

A Jews and Protestants

B peasants and serfs

C Jews and Muslims

D Muslims and Lutherans

The Americas

▼ The ruins of Machu Picchu near Cuzco, Peru

NATIONAL GEOGRAPHIC Where & When?

c. 1500 B.C.	A.D. 500	A.D. 1000	A.D. 1500
c. 1200 B.C. Olmec build an empire in Mexico	A.D. 500 Mayan cities flourish in Mesoamerica	c. A.D. 1250 Aztec arrive in central Mexico	A.D. 1492 Columbus reaches the Americas

The Big Ideas

History Online

Chapter Overview Visit ca.hss.glencoe.com for a preview of Chapter 9.

 Section 1

The First Americans

Physical geography plays a role in how civilizations develop. The first people in the Americas arrived thousands of years ago. Farming led to the growth of civilizations in what is now Mexico, Central America, and Peru.

 Section 2

Life in the Americas

Different social, economic, and political classes can exist in a society. The Maya, Aztec, and many other Native American civilizations developed in North and South America. These societies were organized with powerful kings and social classes.

 Section 3

The Fall of the Aztec and Inca Empires

Conflict often brings about great changes. Spanish explorers and soldiers were drawn to the riches of Native American civilizations. Using horses and guns, they defeated the Aztec and Inca Empires in the early A.D. 1500s.

 View the Chapter 9 video in the Glencoe Video Program.

FOLDABLES™
Study Organizer

Organizing Information *Make this foldable to help you organize information about the history and culture of the Americas.*

Step 1 *Take two sheets of paper and place them about 1 inch apart.*

Keep the edges straight.

Step 2 *Fold up the bottom edges of the paper to form four tabs.*

This makes all the tabs the same size.

Step 3 *When all the tabs are the same size, crease the paper to hold the tabs in place and staple the sheets together. Label each tab as shown.*

The Americas
The First Americans
Life in the Americas
Fall of the Empires

Staple along the fold.

Reading and Writing
As you read the chapter, write the main ideas presented in each of the three sections on the tabs of your foldable. Note details that support the main ideas.

Comparing and Contrasting

Reading Skill

1 Learn It!

To compare and contrast information, look for similarities and differences. Some comparison signal words are *same, at the same time, like,* and *still*. Contrast signal words may include *some, others, different, however, rather, yet, but,* and *or*. Read the passage below about Mayan writing. Then look at the questions that follow.

1) Mayan written language is being compared to that of the Egyptians.

3) *Like* signals a comparison, and *however* signals a contrast.

> The Maya also invented a written language to record numbers and dates. Like the Egyptians, the Maya used a system of hieroglyphics. Symbols represented sounds, words, or ideas. Only nobles could read them, however. After Mayan civilization collapsed, nobody could read them.
>
> — *from page 458*

2) The similarities are highlighted in blue and the contrasts in green.

Reading Tip

As you read, use a graphic organizer to sort the information you find when comparing or contrasting.

Ask yourself these questions as you compare and contrast:
1) What is being compared or contrasted?
2) Which characteristics can be compared or contrasted?
3) How are they similar? How are they different?
4) Are there any signal words to help you recognize comparisons or contrasts?

2 Practice It!

Read the passage below from page 447. Then read Section 3 and follow the directions.

Read to Write
Read Section 1 of this chapter. Then write a short paragraph comparing and contrasting two civilizations in the Americas.

> Spanish explorers and soldiers were drawn to the riches of Native American civilizations. Using horses and guns, they defeated the Aztec and Inca Empires in the early A.D. 1500s.
>
> —*from page 447*

Create a chart like the one below to list the similarities and differences between how each conquistador confronted the Aztec and the Inca. In the first column, fill in the characteristics to compare and contrast. Then describe each characteristic in the second and third columns.

Characteristic	Cortés and the Aztec	Pizarro and the Inca

▲ Spanish armor

3 Apply It!

Choose three pairs of subjects from the chapter to compare and contrast. List the similarities and differences using a graphic organizer such as the one above.

The First Americans

Guide to Reading

Looking Back, Looking Ahead
While Western Europe rebuilt itself after the fall of Rome, diverse cultures thrived in the Americas.

Focusing on the Main Ideas
• People came to the Americas during the Ice Age, and about 10,000 years ago, farming began in Mesoamerica. *(page 451)*

• The first civilizations in America were based on farming and trade. *(page 453)*

Locating Places
Beringia (buh•RIHN•jee•uh)

Mesoamerica (MEH•zoh•uh•MEHR•ih•kuh)

Teotihuacán (TAY•oh•TEE•wuh•KAHN)

Yucatán Peninsula (YOO•kuh•TAN)

Cuzco (KOOS•koh)

Meeting People
Olmec (OHL•MEHK)

Maya (MY•UH)

Toltec (TOHL•TEHK)

Moche (MOH•cheh)

Inca (IHNG•kuh)

Content Vocabulary
glacier (GLAY•SHUHR)

monopoly (muh•NAH•puh•lee)

Academic Vocabulary
environment (ihn•VY•ruhn•muhnt)

design (dih•ZYN)

Reading Strategy
Summarizing Information Create a chart to show the characteristics of the Olmec and Moche.

	Location	Dates	Lifestyle
Olmec			
Moche			

History Social Science Standards

WH7.7 Students compare and contrast the geographic, political, economic, religious, and social structures of the Meso-American and Andean civilizations.

NATIONAL GEOGRAPHIC Where & When?

Teotihuacán
Cuzco

| 2000 B.C. | | 500 B.C. | | A.D. 1000 |

c. 1200 B.C. Olmec build an empire in Mexico

c. A.D. 500 Mayan cities flourish in Mesoamerica

A.D. 1100 Inca found city of Cuzco

Farming Begins in Mesoamerica

Main Idea People came to the Americas during the Ice Age, and about 10,000 years ago, farming began in Mesoamerica.

Reading Connection What would our lives be like if people never learned to farm? Read to learn how farming made civilization possible in Mesoamerica.

We know people came to America a long time ago, but how did they get here? Today, America is not connected by land to the rest of the world, but in the past it was. Scientists have studied the earth's geography during the Ice Age—a period when temperatures dropped sharply. At that time, much of the earth's water froze into huge sheets of ice, or **glaciers** (GLAY•shuhrz).

As the ice froze and the seas fell, an area of dry land was exposed between Asia and Alaska. Scientists call this land bridge **Beringia** (buh•RIHN•jee•uh), after Vitus Bering, a famous European explorer. They think that people in Asia followed the animals they were hunting across this land bridge into the Americas. By testing the age of bones and tools at ancient campsites, scientists estimate that the first people arrived between 15,000 to 40,000 years ago.

When the Ice Age ended about 10,000 years ago, the glaciers melted and released water back into the seas. The land bridge to America disappeared beneath the waves.

Hunting and Gathering Hunters in the Americas were constantly on the move seeking food. They fished and gathered nuts, fruits, or roots. They also hunted massive prey, such as the woolly mammoth, antelope, caribou, and bison.

It took several hunters to kill a woolly mammoth, which could weigh as much as 9 tons. These big animals provided meat, hides for clothing, and bones for tools.

As the Ice Age ended, some animals became extinct, or disappeared from the earth. Other animals found ways to survive the change in **environment.** The warm weather, however, opened new opportunities to early Americans.

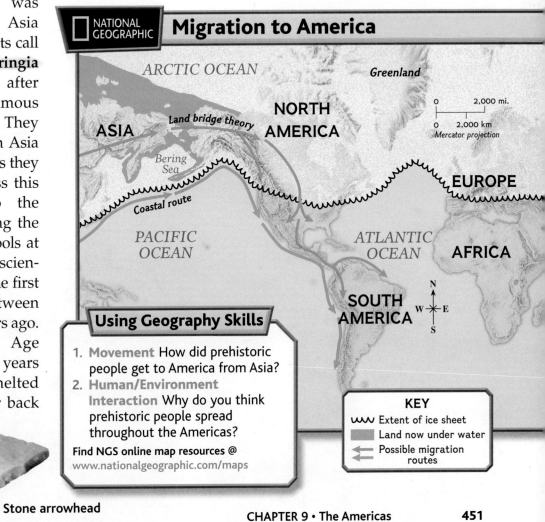

NATIONAL GEOGRAPHIC

Migration to America

ARCTIC OCEAN · Greenland · NORTH AMERICA · Land bridge theory · ASIA · Bering Sea · EUROPE · Coastal route · PACIFIC OCEAN · ATLANTIC OCEAN · AFRICA · SOUTH AMERICA

0 2,000 mi. · 0 2,000 km · Mercator projection

Using Geography Skills

1. **Movement** How did prehistoric people get to America from Asia?
2. **Human/Environment Interaction** Why do you think prehistoric people spread throughout the Americas?

Find NGS online map resources @ www.nationalgeographic.com/maps

KEY
ᨠᨠ Extent of ice sheet
▨ Land now under water
⇐ Possible migration routes

◀ Stone arrowhead

The Agricultural Revolution in America

The first Americans were hunter-gatherers, but as the Ice Age ended and the climate warmed, people in America made an amazing discovery. They learned that seeds could be planted and they would grow into crops that people could eat.

Farming began in **Mesoamerica** (MEH•zoh•uh•MEHR•ih•kuh) 9,000 to 10,000 years ago. *Meso* comes from the Greek word for "middle." This region includes lands stretching from the Valley of Mexico to Costa Rica in Central America.

The region's geography was ideal for farming. Much of the area had a rich, volcanic soil and a mild climate. Rains fell in the spring, helping seeds to sprout. They decreased in the summer, allowing crops to ripen for harvest. Then, in the autumn, the rains returned, soaking the soil for the next year's crop.

The first crops grown in the Americas included pumpkins, peppers, squash, gourds, and beans. It took longer to develop corn, which grew as a wild grass. Early plants produced a single, one-inch cob. After hundreds of years, the early Americans finally learned how to cross corn with other grasses to get bigger cobs and more cobs per plant. With this discovery, corn, also known as maize, became the most important food in the Americas.

✓ **Reading Check** **Summarize** How did the agricultural revolution begin in America?

The First Americans

Working in groups, hunters could bring down large prey, such as a woolly mammoth. *Why do you think early hunters preferred to hunt large animals such as mammoths instead of smaller animals?*

Early American Civilizations

Main Idea The first civilizations in America were based on farming and trade.

Reading Connection Have you ever traded something you had with your friend for something you wanted? Read to find out how early American civilizations traded goods to get what they needed.

Growing corn and other crops allowed Mesoamericans to form more complex societies. Around 1200 B.C., a people called the **Olmec** (OHL•MEHK) built a far-reaching trading empire. This was Mesoamerica's first civilization. It lasted about 800 years.

Who Were the Olmec?

The Olmec enjoyed rich farming resources, but they lacked other raw materials. They traded salt and beans with inland peoples to get jade for jewelry and obsidian, or volcanic glass, to make sharp-edged knives. They traded hematite, a shiny volcanic stone, to make polished mirrors and basalt to carve gigantic stone heads.

The Olmec used the region's many rivers as highways for trade, but eventually, the inland peoples seized control of the trade. One of these groups built the first planned city in the Americas. Known as **Teotihuacán** (TAY•oh•TEE•wuh•KAHN), or

History Online

Web Activity Visit ca.hss.glencoe.com and click on *Chapter 9—Student Web Activity* to learn more about the Americas.

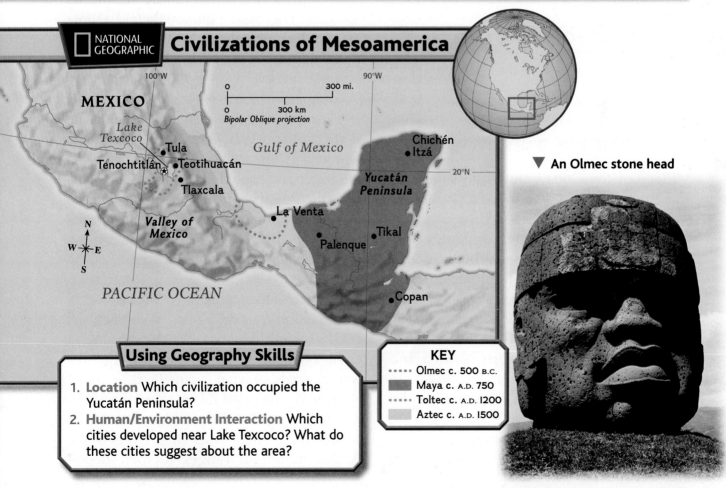

NATIONAL GEOGRAPHIC

Civilizations of Mesoamerica

MEXICO

Lake Texcoco

Tula

Ténochtitlán • Teotihuacán

Tlaxcala

Gulf of Mexico

Chichén Itzá

Yucatán Peninsula

La Venta

Valley of Mexico

Palenque

Tikal

PACIFIC OCEAN

Copan

300 mi.

300 km

Bipolar Oblique projection

100°W

90°W

20°N

N
W E
S

▼ An Olmec stone head

Using Geography Skills

1. **Location** Which civilization occupied the Yucatán Peninsula?
2. **Human/Environment Interaction** Which cities developed near Lake Texcoco? What do these cities suggest about the area?

KEY

········ Olmec c. 500 B.C.

▓ Maya c. A.D. 750

········ Toltec c. A.D. 1200

░ Aztec c. A.D. 1500

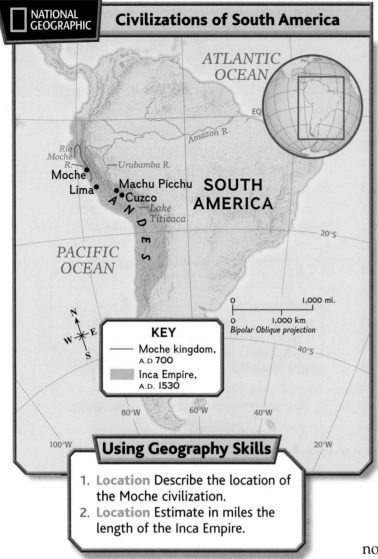

Civilizations of South America

NATIONAL GEOGRAPHIC

ATLANTIC OCEAN

EQ

Amazon R.

Río Moche R.
Urubamba R.
Moche
Lima
Machu Picchu
Cuzco
Lake Titicaca

SOUTH AMERICA

20°S

PACIFIC OCEAN

KEY
— Moche kingdom, A.D 700
▨ Inca Empire, A.D. 1530

0   1,000 mi.
0   1,000 km
Bipolar Oblique projection

40°S

80°W   60°W   40°W   20°W
100°W

Using Geography Skills

1. **Location** Describe the location of the Moche civilization.
2. **Location** Estimate in miles the length of the Inca Empire.

"Place of the Gods," the city reached its height around A.D. 400. It had a population of over 120,000 people.

As Teotihuacán's power spread, a people called the **Maya** (MY•uh) built another civilization in the steamy rain forests of the **Yucatán Peninsula** (YOO•kuh•TAN). They, too, traded throughout Mesoamerica. The Maya used their central location to reach into what is now southern Mexico and Central America.

Teotihuacán and the Mayan cities hit their peaks in the A.D. 400s and A.D. 500s. Then, around A.D. 600, Teotihuacán started to decline. No one is sure why this occurred.

Some experts conclude that overpopulation drained the city of food and resources. Others blame a long drought, or period without rain. Still others say that the poor people rebelled against their rich rulers. Whatever the reason, by A.D. 750, the city had been destroyed.

The Mayan civilization lasted about 200 years longer. But it also came to a mysterious end. The Maya abandoned their cities, and by the A.D. 900s, the cities lay deserted, hidden in a thick tangle of vines.

The Rise of the Aztec As the Maya left their cities, a people called the **Toltec** (TOHL•TEHK) built a city called Tula in a prime location northwest of where Mexico City is today. From Tula, they conquered lands all the way to the Yucatán Peninsula.

The Toltec rulers tightly controlled trade. They held a **monopoly** (muh•NAH•puh•lee), or sole right, to the trade in obsidian. As a result, the Toltec kept other people from making weapons to challenge them.

Around A.D. 1200, invaders from the north captured Tula. One group of invaders, who called themselves the Aztec, admired the Toltec and copied their ways. Aztec warriors then took control of the region's trade and built a huge empire. When Europeans arrived in the A.D. 1500s, the Aztec ruled approximately five million people.

The Moche and Inca South of Mesoamerica, other civilizations developed along the west coast of South America. The **Moche** (MOH•cheh) civilization developed in the dry coastal desert of what is now Peru.

The Moche ruled this region from about A.D. 100 to A.D. 700. They **designed** and built canals that carried water from rivers in the Andes mountain ranges to their desert homeland. Because of this irrigation, the Moche suffered no shortage of food. They ate corn, squash, beans, and peanuts. They also hunted llamas and guinea pigs and fished in the nearby Pacific Ocean.

The Moche did not have a written language. Instead, their culture's story is documented through artwork. Pottery often showed animals that were important to the Moche, such as the llama. The llama served as a pack animal, carrying goods for long-distance trade. It also provided meat for food and wool for weaving.

For all their achievements, however, the Moche never expanded much beyond their homeland. The first empire in South America was built by another people called the **Inca** (IHNG•kuh).

The Incan homeland lay in the Andes mountain ranges of present-day Peru. They chose to live in high river valleys, often

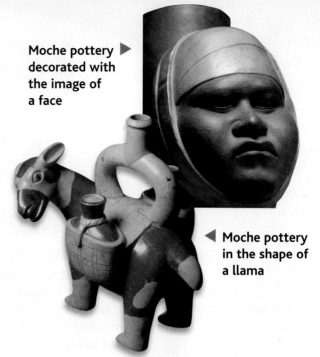

► Moche pottery decorated with the image of a face

◄ Moche pottery in the shape of a llama

above 10,000 feet (3,048 m). Over time, the Inca built the biggest empire in the ancient Americas. It centered around the capital of **Cuzco** (KOOS • koh), founded in A.D. 1100.

✓ **Reading Check** **Explain** What do historians think caused Teotihuacán's collapse?

History Online

Study Central Need help understanding early Mesoamerican civilizations? Visit ca.hss.glencoe.com and click on Study Central.

Section 1 Review

Reading Summary
Review the Main Ideas

- The first Americans were most likely hunter-gatherers who came from Asia across a land bridge.

- A number of civilizations developed in the Americas, including the Olmec, Maya, Toltec, and Aztec in Central America and Mexico, and the Moche and Inca in South America. All were dependent on farming.

What Did You Learn?

1. Why was Mesoamerica's geography ideal for farming?

2. How did the Toltec keep other people from challenging them?

Critical Thinking

3. **Summarizing Information** Draw a chart like the one below. Add details about the early peoples of Mesoamerica and South America. **CA 7RC2.2**

Mesoamerica	South America

4. **Summarize** How did the first people come to the Americas, and how did they live once they were here? **CA 7WA2.5**

5. **The Big Ideas** How did geography shape the development of the Moche civilization? **CA CS3.**

6. **Analyze** Use your local library to research some of the possible explanations for the decline of Teotihuacán and Mayan cities. Then write an essay defending the explanation you think is correct. **CA 7WA2.4**

7. **Reading** Comparing and Contrasting Review the descriptions of hunter gatherers and farmers on pages 451–52. Create a graphic organizer comparing these two groups. **CA 7RC2.3**

Life in the Americas

Guide to Reading

Looking Back, Looking Ahead

In Section 1, you read about the rise of the first civilizations in the Americas. The first Americans had to use whatever natural resources the land had to offer. As a result, they developed many different cultures suited to where they lived.

Focusing on the Main Ideas

- The Maya created a civilization of city-states and thrived in Mesoamerica's rain forest. *(page 457)*

- The Maya developed a society and culture based on their religion. *(page 458)*

- The Aztec moved into the Valley of Mexico where they created an empire based on conquest and war. *(page 460)*

- To unite their huge empire, Incan rulers set up a highly organized government and society. *(page 462)*

Meeting People
Jasaw Chan K'awiil I (KAH•weel)
Pachacuti (PAH•chah•KOO•tee)

Locating Places
Petén (peh•TEHN)
Tenochtitlán (tay•NAWCH•teet•LAHN)
Machu Picchu (MAH•choo•PEE•choo)

Content Vocabulary
sinkhole (sihngk•hohl)
alliance (uh•LY•uhns)
codices (KOH•duh•SEEZ)
quipu (KEE•poo)

Academic Vocabulary
source (SOHRS)
cooperate (koh•AH•puh•RAYT)
previous (PREE•vee•uhs)

Reading Strategy
Organizing Information Use a pyramid to show the Incan classes.

History Social Science Standards

WH7.7 Students compare and contrast the geographic, political, economic, religious, and social structures of the Meso-American and Andean civilizations.

NATIONAL GEOGRAPHIC Where & When?

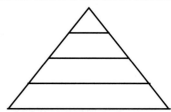

Tenochtitlán
Cuzco

A.D. 1250	A.D. 1350	A.D. 1450
c. A.D. 1250 Aztec arrive in central Mexico	**A.D. 1325** Aztec build Tenochtitlán	**c. A.D. 1438** Pachacuti starts to build Inca Empire

The Mayan People

Main Idea The Maya created a civilization of city-states and thrived in Mesoamerica's rain forest.

Reading Connection What would it be like to live in a jungle? Read to learn how the Maya adapted to life in the jungles of Mesoamerica.

In A.D. 1839 an American lawyer named John Lloyd Stevens and an English artist named Frederick Catherwood slashed their way into the tangled Yucatán rain forest. There they found the vine-covered ruins of an ancient city.

Stevens and Catherwood learned that the people who had built the city were called the Maya. The Maya are the ancestors of millions of Native Americans who still live in present-day Mexico, Guatemala, Honduras, El Salvador, and Belize.

At first glance, it looked like the Maya had settled in one of the worst spots on Earth. They picked the **Petén** (peh•TEHN), the Mayan word for "flat region." Located in present-day Guatemala, the Petén's dense forests nearly blocked out the sun.

The Maya saw what others missed. Swamps and sinkholes gave them a year-round **source** of water. The **sinkholes** (sihngk•hohlz)—areas where the earth has collapsed—connected the Maya with a huge system of underground rivers.

Even with a ready water supply, only an organized culture could have succeeded in building cities and fields in the Petén. The effort required **cooperation** among many people, which could only be accomplished by having an organized government.

Like the ancient Greeks and Mesopotamians, Mayan civilization was divided into city-states. Each Mayan city-state was ruled by a king who was also leader of the army. Leadership passed from one king to the next, and the city-states often fought with each other.

Reading Check **Identify** What was the main advantage of living in a tropical rain forest?

The City of Tikal

▼ The city of Tikal was one of the largest and oldest Mayan cities. Huge temples and monuments were spread throughout the city. The area that you see here was the main religious center of the city. *Why did the Maya build cities in the rain forest?*

Temple II today ▶

1. Temple of the Masks (Temple II)
2. North Acropolis
3. Temple of the Giant Jaguar (Temple I)
4. Stelae
5. Great Plaza
6. Ball Court

WH7.7.2 Study the roles of people in each society, including class structures, family life, warfare, religious beliefs and practices, and slavery. **WH7.7.4** Describe the artistic and oral traditions and architecture in the three civilizations. **WH7.7.5** Describe the Meso-American achievements in astronomy and mathematics, including the development of the calendar and the Meso-American knowledge of seasonal changes to the civilizations' agricultural systems.

Mayan Culture

Main Idea The Maya developed a society and culture based on their religion.

Reading Connection Did you ever wonder why people need calendars? Read to learn how the Maya developed calendars and math to help them farm.

Mayan rulers said they were descended from the sun and claimed to rule as god-kings. They expected people to serve them and to build huge monuments to honor them. A good example of this is the pyramid built for **Jasaw Chan K'awiil I** (KAH•weel) at Tikal.

Life in Mayan Cities As god-kings, Mayan rulers taught their subjects how to please the gods. One way was human sacrifice. When the Maya marched into battle, they wanted captives more than they wanted land. During times of drought, Mayan priests offered the captives to Chac, the god of rain and sunlight. The Maya believed Chac lived in the waters below the sinkholes. Captives were often thrown into these watery pits to earn the Chac's favor.

The Maya usually only sacrificed captives from the elite classes of conquered peoples. These included the king, the warriors, and the owners of large estates. Most enslaved people were farmers, however. These captives were typically held by the Mayan elite. They were used for heavy labor or household chores.

The Maya believed that the gods controlled everything that happened on Earth. As a result, religion was at the core of Mayan life. A huge pyramid with a temple at the top towered over every city. Priests, who claimed to know what the gods wanted, set up a strict class system in which everyone had a place.

Royal Mayan women often married into royal families who lived in distant Mayan city-states. This practice strengthened trade. It also helped form **alliances** (uh•LY•uhns•uhs), or political agreements between people or states to work together.

Women played a significant role in the Mayan city-states. In one Mayan carving, a woman wears a war headdress and rides atop a platform carried by soldiers, which shows she had military influence. In the city-state of Calakmul, at least two women served as all-powerful queens. One of them may have helped to found the city.

Mayan cities also had ball courts. This game was similar to basketball, except that players could not use their hands to throw the ball. They used their hips to propel a ball through stone rings high above the ground. The game had deadly results. The losing team was sacrificed to the gods.

Mayan Science and Writing Mayan rulers relied on their priests for advice. The priests thought gods revealed their plans through the movements of the sun, moon, and stars, so they studied the sky closely.

By watching the sky, the priests learned about astronomy and developed a 365-day calendar. They used it to predict eclipses and to schedule religious festivals, plantings, and harvests. To chart the passage of time, the Maya developed a complex system of mathematics. They invented a method of counting based on 20.

The Maya also invented a written language to record numbers and dates. Like the Egyptians, the Maya used a system of hieroglyphics. Symbols represented sounds, words, or ideas. Only nobles could read them, however. After Mayan civilization collapsed, nobody could read them. Only recently have scholars begun to unlock the stories told by the hieroglyphics.

Reading Check **Explain** How did the Maya treat enslaved people?

Biography

WH7.7.2 Study the roles of people in each society, including class structures, family life, warfare, religious beliefs and practices, and slavery.

WH7.7.4 Describe the artistic and oral traditions and architecture in the three civilizations.

JASAW CHAN K'AWIIL I
Ruled A.D. 682–734

When Jasaw Chan K'awiil began his rule in A.D. 682, the Mayan city-state of Tikal was weak and struggling. Its temples and other buildings were falling into disrepair, and the people were dominated by their great rival city, Calakmul.

Things began to improve in A.D. 695 when Jasaw defeated the armies of Calakmul in battle. Jasaw held a celebration a month later to honor the gods and himself. Tikal began to prosper again, and Jasaw spent the next 40 years rebuilding and strengthening his city-state.

Although Jasaw had been victorious, he spent only part of his time expanding his control over the region. Instead, most of his efforts went toward helping his people and restarting building projects in Tikal.

Jasaw's efforts teach us a great deal about Mayan art, architecture, and customs. For example, he built the famous pyramid in Tikal. The huge structure was 154 feet (47 m) in height and served as both a temple and as Jasaw's tomb. In the room at the top of the structure, carvings depicted Jasaw's victories and mythological scenes. Jasaw wears clothing similar to the ancient leaders of Tikal to show that he was as great as they were. Other images were carved on bones and on other buildings. They show events from Mayan mythology and history praising Tikal's rulers.

One piece of art was of great importance: the effigy, or image, of the god that armies carried into battle. This god was supposed to be the special god of that city. When Jasaw defeated Calakmul, he captured the image of their city's god. The people of Tikal thought this meant that their god was more powerful than the others. Jasaw ordered the story of this great accomplishment to be carved on his pyramid so everyone would remember what he had done.

Jasaw began to rebuild Tikal during his reign, but most of the great building projects and military expansion of the city occurred under the reign of his son. Nevertheless, it could not have happened without Jasaw's efforts.

▲ A stone monument showing Jasaw Chan K'awiil I

Then and Now

The Maya emphasized religion and the accomplishments of their rulers in their art and architecture. What do people use as subjects for art today? Why?

WH7.7.1 Study the locations, landforms, and climates of Mexico, Central America, and South America and their effects on Mayan, Aztec, and Incan economies, trade, and development of urban societies. **WH7.7.2** Study the roles of people in each society, including class structures, family life, warfare, religious beliefs and practices, and slavery. **WH7.7.3** Explain how and where each empire arose and how the Aztec and Incan empires were defeated by the Spanish. **WH7.7.4** Describe the artistic and oral traditions and architecture in the three civilizations. **WH7.7.5** Describe the Meso-American achievements in astronomy and mathematics, including the development of the calendar and the Meso-American knowledge of seasonal changes to the civilizations' agricultural systems.

The Aztec

Main Idea The Aztec moved into the Valley of Mexico where they created an empire based on conquest and war.

Reading Connection Why do you think some countries try to conquer other countries? Read to learn why the Aztec people conquered their neighbors.

The warlike Aztec nomads who arrived in the Valley of Mexico about A.D. 1250 were anything but welcome. One king granted the Aztec a patch of snake-filled land. He expected the deadly serpents to destroy them. Instead, the Aztec feasted on roasted snakes and eventually built their own kingdom.

The Aztec Government The Aztec had wandered for years in search of a home that they believed their sun god—the feathered serpent Quetzalcoatl (KWEHT•suhl•kuh•WAH•tuhl)—had promised them. According to legend, the Aztec would know they had found this place when an eagle "screams and spreads its wings, and eats . . . the serpent."

In A.D. 1325, they took shelter on a soggy, swampy island in Lake Texcoco (tehs•KOH•koh). There an eagle greeted them from its perch on a prickly pear cactus. It tore apart a snake dangling from its beak. The Aztec believed they had found their home.

Priests, speaking for the gods, told the Aztec what to do next: build a great city. Workers toiled day and night. They dug soil from the lake bottom to build bridges to the mainland. They built floating gardens, piling soil on rafts anchored to the lake bottom.

The Aztec called their new city **Tenochtitlán** (tay•NAWCH•teet•LAHN), which means "place of the prickly pear cactus." As

Tenochtitlán

At the center of Tenochtitlán was a walled ceremonial area. It contained temples, schools and the priests' houses. *What ceremonial act took place at the top of the Great Temple?*

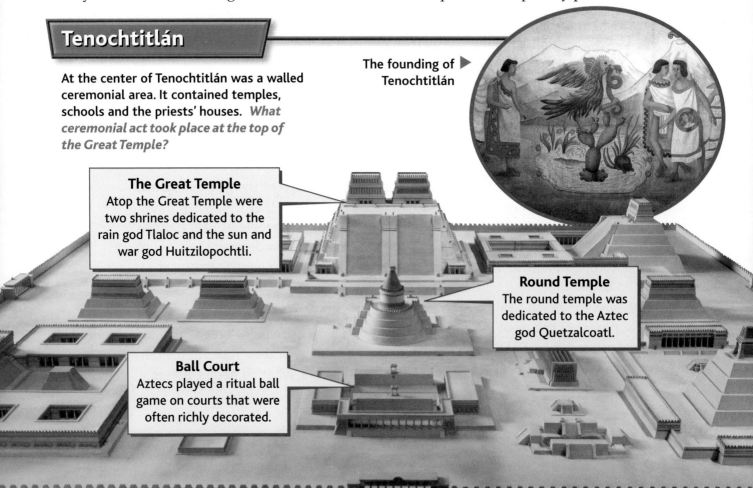

▶ The founding of Tenochtitlán

The Great Temple
Atop the Great Temple were two shrines dedicated to the rain god Tlaloc and the sun and war god Huitzilopochtli.

Round Temple
The round temple was dedicated to the Aztec god Quetzalcoatl.

Ball Court
Aztecs played a ritual ball game on courts that were often richly decorated.

Aztec Daily Life

Aztec homes were simple and built for usefulness rather than beauty. *How do you think the Aztec used each of the household items shown here?*

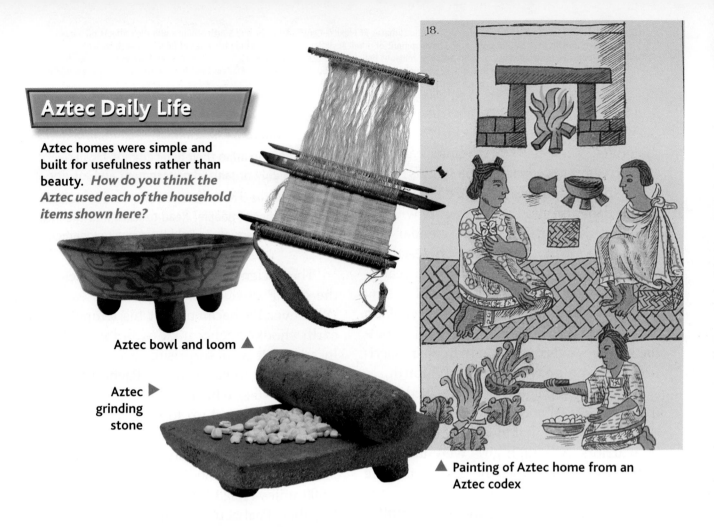

Aztec bowl and loom ▲

Aztec ► grinding stone

▲ Painting of Aztec home from an Aztec codex

the city rose from the marshes, the Aztec dreamed of conquest and wealth. They wanted to collect tribute, or payment for protection, from conquered peoples.

To fulfill their goal, the Aztec turned to strong kings who claimed descent from the gods. A council of warriors, priests, and nobles picked each king from the royal family. The council usually chose the last king's son, but not always. They expected a king to prove himself by leading troops into battle.

Life in the Aztec Empire The king, or emperor, was at the top of Aztec society. The rest of the population fell into four classes: nobles, commoners, unskilled laborers, and enslaved people. Commoners formed the largest group, working as farmers, artisans, or traders. They could join the noble class by performing one act of bravery in war. They, or their children if the soldier died, received land and the rank of noble.

Among the important responsibilities of the priests was preserving the religion, history, and poetry of the people. To record their religion and history, the Aztec made books that historians refer to as **codices** (KOH•duh•SEEZ). Aztec codices were painted on deerskin, cloth, or paper made from the bark of fig trees. The Aztec produced so many books that they used the equivalent of nearly 500,000 sheets of paper per year.

Each Aztec book, or codex, was a single strip, up to 40 feet (12 m) long, that was folded in a zig-zag pattern to make a book. Pages were read from top to bottom and consisted of brightly painted images and pictograms showing events and people in Aztec history. Most of these Aztec books were lost after the Spanish conquered the Aztec and broke up their empire. Those that survive provide historians with much information about Aztec life.

WH7.7.1 Study the locations, landforms, and climates of Mexico, Central America, and South America and their effects on Mayan, Aztec, and Incan economies, trade, and development of urban societies. **WH7.7.2** Study the roles of people in each society, including class structures, family life, warfare, religious beliefs and practices, and slavery. **WH7.7.3** Explain how and where each empire arose and how the Aztec and Incan empires were defeated by the Spanish. **WH7.7.4** Describe the artistic and oral traditions and architecture in the three civilizations.

Like the Maya, the Aztec also developed a calendar. In fact, the Aztec had two different calendars. They used a religious calendar with 260 days to keep track of religious rituals and festivals. They also had a 365-day calendar for daily use and to keep track of when to plant and harvest crops. This calendar was divided into 18 months with 20 days each and a special 5-day week at the end of the year.

In serving their gods, the Aztec saw death as honorable. Those worthy of an afterlife included soldiers who died in battle, captives who gave their lives in sacrifice, and women who died in childbirth.

From an early age, children learned about the glories of war and their duties as an Aztec. Boys were taught that they had been born to be warriors. Although girls were taught to stay in the home, those who gave birth were honored as heroes by Aztec society.

To honor their gods, the Aztec built a huge pyramid in the center of Tenochtitlán. Known as the Great Temple, it rose 135 feet (41 m) high and had more than 100 steps. Thousands of victims were taken to the top, where they were sacrificed to the gods.

Tenochtitlán became the largest city of any in Mesoamerica. At its height, it may have held some 400,000 people, with a million more in other cities and villages under Aztec control. Supporting such a high population was a challenge for the Aztec considering that much of the region was unsuitable for agriculture.

The Aztec accomplished this by heavy use of irrigation, fertilization, and by draining water from swamps. They even drained lakes, turning **previously** water-filled regions into highly productive agricultural areas. The large empire also encouraged trade and paid for government and military actions through taxes and conquest.

✓ Reading Check) **Describe** How could commoners move into the noble class?

Life in the Inca Empire

Main Idea) **To unite their huge empire, Incan rulers set up a highly organized government and society.**

Reading Connection Have you ever tried to organize a large number of people? Read to learn how the Inca organized their society to hold their empire together.

The ancient Inca blamed earthquakes on the god Pachacamac, "Lord of the earth." Whenever Pachacamac lost his temper, the earth shook. Pachacamac was the highest Incan god. It is not surprising that the greatest Incan leader took the name **Pachacuti** (PAH•chah•KOO•tee), which means "Earthshaker."

Pachacuti lived up to his name. Starting around A.D. 1438, Pachacuti and his son, Topa Inca, built the largest ancient empire in the Americas. It stretched north to south about 2,500 miles (4,023 km). To hold his empire together, Pachacuti set up a strong central government but let local rulers stay in power. To ensure their loyalty, he took their sons to Cuzco for training.

Pachacuti united the empire in other ways too. He required people to learn Quechua (KEH•chuh•wuh), the language spoken by the Inca. He also designed a network of roads that covered about 25,000 miles (40,234 km).

The large system of roads helped the Inca overcome the challenges of climate and geography. The coastal deserts and the high, rugged mountains and volcanoes made trade and transport difficult. Roads helped them move goods and information quickly.

The Inca also developed agricultural techniques. They used irrigation and fertilizers to improve the land. Incan engineers developed terraced farming, or a series of ridges built into a mountainside that created level farmland. In addition, the Inca herded llama as cattle. With these food resources, they developed healthy urban cities.

Biography

PACHACUTI
Ruled 1438–1471

Pachacuti was the son of the eighth Inca king, Viracocha. In 1438 an enemy from the north attacked the capital city, Cuzco. Viracocha fled, but Pachacuti stayed behind to defend the city and defeat the enemy. Because of his victory, Pachacuti became king.

At first, Pachacuti concentrated on expanding the Inca Empire. When he wanted to conquer a kingdom, he first sent messengers to tell the local rulers all the benefits of being part of the Inca Empire and then asked them to join willingly. If they accepted, they were treated with respect and given some rights. If they refused, the Inca attacked with brutal force.

Pachacuti next turned his attention to rebuilding Cuzco. He was the first to use white granite as a building material. No mortar was needed to hold the granite stones together because the sides of each piece were cut accurately and fit closely together.

Pachacuti built an estate for himself called Machu Picchu. It was made of white granite and was located thousands of feet high in the Andes. Recent research suggests that Machu Picchu was used not only as a home for the royal family, but also as a center for celebrations and ceremonial gatherings.

▲ Pachacuti

> **"I was born as a flower of the field . . ."**
> —Pachacuti, as quoted in
> *History of the Incas*

According to legend translated from a sacred text, Pachacuti became very sick when he was an elderly man. He called all of his relatives to his bedside. He divided his possessions among them and then made a speech with instructions for his burial.

Then and Now

How can a nation today get another nation to do something without threatening war?

▲ Machu Picchu

An Organized Society The Inca believed the sun god Inti protected Cuzco, the Incan capital. The rulers called themselves "sons of the sun." They and their wives, known as Coyas, were at the top of society.

The head priest and top commander of the army were just below the royal family. Next came regional army leaders. Below them were temple priests, army commanders, and skilled workers. At the bottom were farmers, herders, and soldiers.

The Inca further divided society into 12 job categories. Every man, woman, and child over age five had work to do. Young girls, for example, were baby-sitters, while young boys chased birds from gardens.

What Was Incan Culture Like?
The Inca rarely honored their gods with human sacrifice. They turned to sacrifice only in times of trouble, such as during earthquakes, or on special occasions. To please their gods, the Inca built large works of stone. They had no system of writing, no wheels, and no iron tools. Yet they built places like **Machu Picchu** (MAH•choo PEE•choo), a retreat for Incan kings.

Building large structures required the Inca to develop a method for doing mathematical calculations. The Inca used a **quipu** (KEE•poo), a rope with knotted cords of different lengths and colors. Each knot represented a number or item. Quipu was also used to keep records. Like the Aztec, the Inca relied on oral tradition to pass on most of their wisdom and knowledge.

The Inca were also skilled engineers. Workers fit stones so tightly together that a knife could not slip between them. Because the Inca used no mortar, the stone blocks could slide up and down without collapsing during earthquakes.

Reading Check Explain How did Pachacuti make sure local leaders would be loyal to him?

History Online

Study Central Need help understanding the Maya, Aztec, or Inca? Visit ca.hss.glencoe.com and click on Study Central.

Section 2 Review

Reading Summary
Review the Main Ideas

- In the rain forests of Central America, the Maya developed a civilization divided into city-states.
- The Maya developed a complex society and culture based on their religion.
- A fierce warrior people, the Aztec created a strong empire in central Mexico.
- In the Andes, the Inca created the largest empire in the Americas.

What Did You Learn?

1. How did Pachacuti maintain the empire he built?

2. What were the different groups that made up Aztec society?

Critical Thinking

3. **Compare and Contrast** Draw a Venn diagram and use it to compare Aztec and Incan society. **CA 7RC2.0**

Aztec Society / Incan Society

4. **Science Link** How did the Maya use astronomy? **CA HI2.**

5. **Drawing Conclusions** Why do you think the Inca assigned specific jobs to people? Is this a good idea for a society? Explain. **CA 7RC2.3**

6. **Analysis Understanding Narratives** Reread the Aztec story of the founding of Tenochtitlán on pages 460–461. Do you know if this story is true? What parts do you think are true? What information would you need to verify the story? **CA HR3.; HI5.**

THE FLOOD

By Pleasant DeSpain

Before You Read

The Scene: This story takes place in early America, in a part of present-day Mexico.

The Characters: A young Huichol man and his pet dog.

The Plot: The young man is a farmer in a Huichol village. He has trouble growing his crops and asks the advice of the Earth Goddess.

Vocabulary Preview

maneuver: a clever or skillful action

unceasing: never-ending

deluge: a flood

recede: to move or back away

embrace: a hug

Have you ever had to move? In this story a young man is faced with a life away from all of the things and people that he knows.

WORLD LITERATURE

As You Read

The flood story is a classic tale that appears in many religious texts. From Noah in the Bible to Hindu and Buddhist stories, floods are often responsible for changing the face of the earth and the people who live on it. How does the flood affect the people in this story?

Long before the Spanish came to the place now called Mexico, the first people to inhabit the land were the Huichol.[1] They lived in caves, and grew maize,[2] pumpkins, and beans.

Life was hard. Life was peaceful.

One of the Huichol was a strong young man who lived apart from the families. One morning, the youth awoke to find a black female dog guarding his cave entrance. He tried to shoo her away. She licked his hand, wagged her tail, and refused to leave.

"Earth Goddess must have sent me this gift," he said aloud, "and I give thanks."

Soon after, the Huichol leaders told the youth it was time to marry and have a family. He agreed, saying, "I'll raise one more maize crop. Then I'll be ready."

Day after day, he labored in his field, tilling the hard earth and planting precious seeds. He returned to the field each morning only to discover his work undone. The ground was packed hard again, and the seeds were carefully piled at the field's edge.

"Earth Goddess!" he cried. "What have I done? Please tell me."

An ancient woman with bright eyes appeared before him. She supported her bent body with a mesquite[3]-wood branch. She beckoned him to lean down to hear her whispered words.

"The flood of all floods is soon to come. It will cover the earth. Every person, creature, and plant will drown. You alone have been chosen to live."

"How will I survive?"

"Chop down the largest tree at the edge of your field and cut it into thick planks. Use the planks to build a watertight box with a strong lid. Make it large enough for you and the black dog I sent you. Place seven seeds of each in the box—maize,

---

[1]**Huichol:** early settlers in Mexico, related to the Aztec people
[2]**maize:** corn
[3]**mesquite:** a thorny, deep rooted tree

pumpkin, and bean. Do not delay. The rain begins in seven days."

So saying, Earth Goddess vanished.

The young man did as he was told, and on the morning of the seventh day, the box was finished. He wrapped the seeds in broad leaves and carefully packed them in a clay jar. After sealing the jar with beeswax, he called to the black dog. She jumped into the box without hesitation. Finally, he climbed in and maneuvered the heavy lid into place. No light crept in through the wooden joints. The box was watertight.

It began to rain. The sky opened wide and poured an unceasing ocean of fresh water upon the land. The deluge was complete.

The wooden box rose high on the new waves and bobbed and flowed wherever swift currents carried it. The man and dog fell into a deep and profound sleep. The rain, as well as their sleep, continued for seven years.

At the end of the seven years, the rain stopped falling. The bright sun came out and the waters began to recede. Several days later, the box came to rest on a mountaintop. The man and dog awoke. He pushed the lid aside and they climbed out of the box.

Earth Goddess appeared before them with her mesquite-wood staff. Wherever she pointed, trees, forests, birds, animals, and creatures of all kinds appeared. When again the earth was alive and green, she vanished.

The youth cut down tall trees, moved heavy rocks, and planted three fields with the seven seeds of each—maize, pumpkin, and bean. He worked hard and the crops

The Fall of the Aztec and Inca Empires

Guide to Reading

History Social Science Standards

WH7.7 Students compare and contrast the geographic, political, economic, religious, and social structures of the Meso-American and Andean civilizations.

Looking Back, Looking Ahead

As the 1400s drew to a close, people in the Americas and Europe knew nothing of each other. This changed when Europeans began exploring the world and searching for trade routes to Asia.

Focusing on the Main Ideas

- Spanish conquerors were able to defeat the Aztec using horses and guns. *(page 471)*
- The riches of the Aztec Empire led other Spanish conquerors to seek their fortunes in South America. *(page 476)*

Meeting People

Christopher Columbus

Hernán Cortés (ehr•NAHN kawr•TEHZ)

Montezuma II (MAHN•tuh•ZOO•muh)

Malintzin (mah•LIHNT•suhn)

Francisco Pizarro (fran•SIHS•koh puh•ZAHR•oh)

Locating Places

Hispaniola (HIHS•puh•NYOH•luh)

Extremadura (EHK•struh•muh•DUR•uh)

Content Vocabulary

conquistador (kahn•KEES•tuh•DAWR)

treason (TREE•zuhn)

Academic Vocabulary

finance (FY•nans)

generate (JEH•nuh•RAYT)

Reading Strategy

Cause and Effect Create a diagram to show the reasons Cortés was able to conquer the Aztec.

Cortés Conquers the Aztec

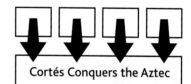

Where & When?

NATIONAL GEOGRAPHIC

Tenochtitlán
Cuzco

1450   1500   1550

1492 Christopher Columbus reaches the Americas

1521 Cortés defeats Aztec

1533 Francisco Pizarro conquers the Inca

Spain Conquers Mexico

Main Idea Spanish conquerors were able to defeat the Aztec using horses and guns.

Reading Connection Think of decisions that you have already made today. Read to learn how the decisions made by two people—a Spanish conqueror and an Aztec king—changed the course of history.

In 1492 the Aztec appeared unbeatable. Around 250,000 people lived in Tenochtitlán, making it the largest city in the Americas—if not the world. In just a few short years, however, people from Europe would destroy their empire.

Columbus Arrives in America

As you learned previously, by the 1400s several strong European kingdoms had developed in Western Europe. Those kingdoms knew that money could be made if they could find a way to trade with the countries of East Asia without having to deal with the Muslim kingdoms in between.

One by one, the people of Western Europe took to the sea to find a route to Asia. The first were the Portuguese, who began mapping Africa's eastern coast, hoping to find a way around Africa.

Next were the Spaniards, who decided to **finance** a trip by an Italian sea captain named **Christopher Columbus.** Columbus convinced Spain's rulers that he could reach Asia by sailing west across the Atlantic Ocean. He had no idea that two continents blocked his way.

Columbus set sail with three ships in August 1492. In October, he landed on an island in the Caribbean Sea. Columbus believed that he had arrived in Asia. He traveled farther into the Caribbean and landed on the island of **Hispaniola** (HIHS•puh•NYOH•luh), which is today Haiti and the Dominican Republic.

He then returned home carrying colorful parrots, some gold and spices, and several Native American captives. His success astonished and pleased Spain's rulers, and they consented to pay for another trip.

Columbus Returns

Columbus set out again in 1493. This time, he came to conquer, bringing soldiers to help him. In the spring of 1494, the Spanish landed on Hispaniola.

▲ In the painting above, Christopher Columbus is depicted arriving in the Americas. *Why did Columbus sail west across the Atlantic?*

The Taino who lived on Hispaniola got their first look at the **conquistadors** (kahn•KEES•tuh•DAWRZ), the soldier-explorers sent to the Americas by Spain. What they saw frightened them. Armor-clad men rode on armor-clad horses. Snarling dogs ran by their sides. In a show of power, the soldiers fired guns that spit out flames and lead balls.

Soldiers claimed the island for Spain. Then they enslaved the Taino and forced them to work for the Spanish. Spain now had a foothold in the Americas.

Who Was Hernán Cortés? Christopher Columbus sailed to the Americas four times. His voyages inspired many poor nobles to go to the Americas to seek their fortunes.

Many came from the part of Spain known as the **Extremadura** (EHK•struh•muh•DUR•uh). This region's poor soil, blistering hot summers, and icy winters held little chance for wealth. One of these nobles was 19-year-old **Hernán Cortés** (ehr•NAHN kawr•TEHZ).

Linking Past & Present

Chocolate

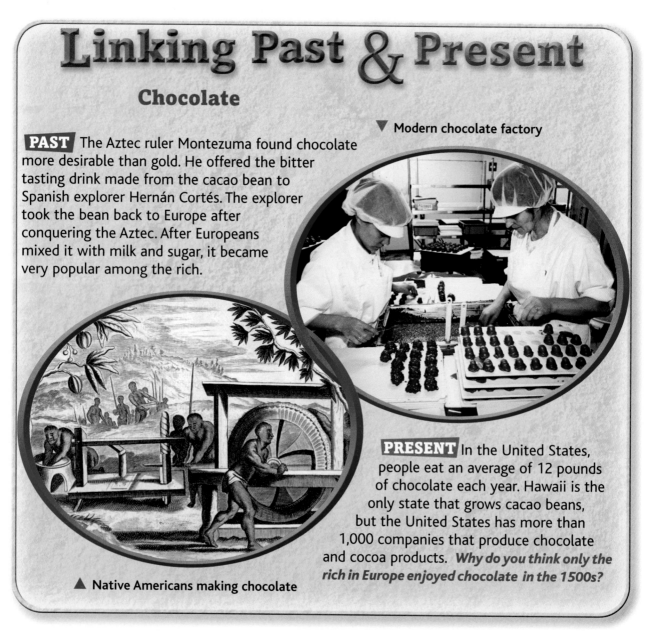

PAST The Aztec ruler Montezuma found chocolate more desirable than gold. He offered the bitter tasting drink made from the cacao bean to Spanish explorer Hernán Cortés. The explorer took the bean back to Europe after conquering the Aztec. After Europeans mixed it with milk and sugar, it became very popular among the rich.

▼ Modern chocolate factory

PRESENT In the United States, people eat an average of 12 pounds of chocolate each year. Hawaii is the only state that grows cacao beans, but the United States has more than 1,000 companies that produce chocolate and cocoa products. *Why do you think only the rich in Europe enjoyed chocolate in the 1500s?*

▲ Native Americans making chocolate

As a teenager, Cortés had a choice of three jobs: priest, lawyer, or soldier. Cortés picked soldier. In 1504 he set out for Hispaniola. In 1511 he took part in the Spanish invasion of Cuba. His courage and energy impressed the Spanish commander, who gave Cortés control over several Native American villages and the goods they **generated.**

Six years later, smallpox swept across Cuba, killing thousands of Native Americans. The Spanish commander asked Cortés to find new people who could be forced to work for the Spanish. Cortés knew just where to look.

Earlier that year, a ship sent to explore the coast of the Yucatán returned to Cuba. Unlike earlier search parties, the soldiers did not fight with the Maya who lived there. Instead a group of Maya paddled out to greet them. As one soldier recalled:

> **❝** They brought gold cast in bars . . . a beautiful gold mask, a figurine [statue] of a man with a half mask of gold, and a crown of gold beads. **❞**
>
> —Juan Díaz, as quoted in "Conquest and Aftermath"

The Spanish needed to hear no more. Cortés made plans to sail. On February 18, 1519, Cortés set sail for Mexico.

Cortés Invades Mexico When Cortés arrived, the Aztec emperor was **Montezuma II** (MAHN•tuh•ZOO•muh), also called Moctezuma. Montezuma expected the invaders. In a dream, he looked into a mirror and saw a huge army headed over the mountains. "What shall I do?" cried the emperor. "Where shall I hide?"

The Spanish Fight the Aztec

▼ Aztec warriors carried clubs edged with obsidian and wore colorful costumes made of animal skins and feathers. They were no match for armored Spanish soldiers with swords, guns, and cannons. *Besides weapons and horses, what else did the Spanish bring to America that helped them defeat the Aztec?*

▲ Spanish armor

▲ Spanish sword

◄ Aztec warrior

▼ Aztec shield

▲ Aztec war club

The Aztec Defeat

This excerpt describes the aftermath of Cortés's victory.

"Broken spears lie in the roads; we have torn our hair in our grief. The houses are roofless now, and their walls are red with blood. . . . We have pounded our hands in despair against the adobe walls, for our inheritance, our city, is lost and dead. The shields of our warriors were its defense, but they could not save it."

—author unknown, from *The Broken Spears*, edited by Miguel Leon-Portilla

▲ Battle scene between Aztec and Spanish soldiers

DBQ Document-Based Question

The Aztec felt that their lost city was their inheritance. What does that mean?

The dreaded invasion began in April 1519 when Cortés stepped onto a beach near present-day Veracruz. He came with 550 soldiers, 16 horses, 14 cannons, and a few dogs. How could such a small force conquer a huge warrior empire?

First, Cortés knew how to use Spanish horses and guns to shock Native Americans. In a display of power, he forced thousands of Tabascans (tuh•BAS•kuhnz), a people living in Mesoamerica, to surrender. Second, the Tabascans gave Cortés another weapon—a Mayan woman named **Malintzin** (mah•LIHNT•suhn). She spoke both Mayan and Nahuatl (NAH•WAH•tuhl), the language of the Aztec.

Speaking through a Spaniard who knew Mayan, Malintzin described the Aztec Empire to Cortés. She also told Cortés that many of the people the Aztec ruled hated the Aztec. Acting as a translator, she helped Cortés form alliances.

Finally, Cortés benefited from invisible allies—germs that carried diseases, such as measles and smallpox. These diseases would eventually kill more Aztec than the Spanish swords.

Cortés Defeats the Aztec The Spaniards marched 400 miles (644 km) to reach Tenochtitlán, the Aztec capital. At first, Montezuma was afraid to attack the Spanish. The Aztec believed in a light-skinned god named Quetzalcoatl who had left long ago and promised to return someday. Montezuma was afraid Cortés was the god returning home.

As Cortés marched closer, Montezuma decided to ambush the Spanish troops. Cortés learned of the plan and attacked first, killing 6,000 people. In November 1519, the Spaniards marched into Tenochtitlán. To prevent the Aztec from rebelling, Cortés took Montezuma hostage. He then ordered the Aztec to stop sacrificing people.

Cortés's orders angered the Aztec, who planned a rebellion. Fighting erupted, and the Spanish killed thousands of Aztec. Montezuma tried to stop the fighting, but he too was killed. Outnumbered, the Spanish fought their way out of the city and took refuge in the nearby hills with their allies.

While Cortés prepared a second attack, smallpox broke out in Tenochtitlán. Greatly weakened, the Aztec were no match for the Spanish and their allies. In June 1521, the Spanish destroyed the Aztec capital.

✓ Reading Check **Explain** Why was Cortés able to defeat the Aztec?

Biography

Montezuma ▶

MONTEZUMA II
1480–1520
HERNÁN CORTÉS
1485–1547

Although Montezuma II became known as the emperor who let the Spanish capture the Aztec Empire, most of his years as a ruler had been very successful. Montezuma Xocoyotl was the youngest son of Emperor Axacayatl. Aztec leadership was not hereditary, so after Axacayatl's death a man named Ahuitzotl was selected emperor. Montezuma was in his early twenties when he was chosen emperor. He became a popular leader. He led his armies in battle and won over 40 battles against kingdoms south of the Aztec Empire. His one major mistake was in his dealings with the Spanish conquistadors.

Leading the Spanish march into the Aztec Empire in 1519 was a 34-year-old Spaniard named Hernán Cortés. Cortés was born in the province of Extremadura, Spain. At age 19, Cortés left the university and boarded a ship for the Spanish lands in America. He was determined to make his fortune.

In 1511, Spanish troops led by Diego Velázquez conquered Cuba. Cortés took part in the invasion, and his courage impressed Velázquez. He rewarded Cortés by giving him control of several Native American villages. Six years later, smallpox swept across Cuba, killing thousands of Native Americans.

Velázquez asked Cortés to lead an expedition to the Yucatán Peninsula to find people who could be forced to work for the Spanish. He was also asked to investigate reports of a wealthy civilization there. On February 18, 1519, Cortés set sail for Mexico. After conquering the Aztec, Cortés served as Governor General of New Spain. He returned to Spain a very wealthy man and died near the city of Seville in 1547.

◀ Hernán Cortés

Then and Now

Because of their encounter in war, the names of Montezuma and Cortés often appear together in history books. What two leaders today do you think will be paired in future history books? Why?

WH7.7.3 Explain how and where each empire arose and how the Aztec and Incan empires were defeated by the Spanish.

Pizarro Conquers the Inca

Main Idea The riches of the Aztec Empire led other Spanish conquerors to seek their fortunes in South America.

Reading Connection Have you ever done anything because you have seen other people do it and succeed? Read to learn how another conquistador followed the example of Cortés and conquered the Inca.

In 1513 Vasco Núñez de Balboa (VAHS•koh NOON•yays day bal•BOH•uh) led a band of soldiers across the jungle-covered mountains of present-day Panama. Native Americans said that if Balboa traveled south along a western sea, he would find a great empire filled with gold.

Balboa found the sea, known today as the Pacific Ocean. However, he never found the golden empire. A jealous Spanish official in Panama falsely charged him with **treason** (TREE•zuhn), or disloyalty to the government, and ordered him beheaded.

Francisco Pizarro (fran•SIHS•koh puh•ZAHR•oh), who marched with Balboa, took up the search. Pizarro could not write his name, but he knew how to fight. Like Balboa and Cortés, Pizarro came from the harsh Extremadura. Unlike his neighbors, however, he was not of noble birth.

At age 16, Pizarro fled a job herding pigs to fight in Italy. In 1502 he arrived in the Americas. After helping to explore Panama, he became a wealthy landowner. But Pizarro longed to find the golden empire.

Pizarro and the Inca By the 1530s, the Inca thought they ruled most of the world. Two threats from the north soon proved they did not. The Inca could do nothing to stop the southward spread of smallpox. They also failed to scare away Pizarro, who led 160 adventurers up the mountains to the Incan homeland.

The Inca tried to ignore him, but Pizarro, now in his 50s, would not leave. He raided Incan storehouses and fired guns at villagers. The Incan emperor, Atahualpa (AH•tuh•WAHL•puh), thought Pizarro was crazy or a fool. How could this man stand up to an army of 80,000 Incan warriors?

Atahualpa misjudged Pizarro. The Spaniard had an advantage. The Inca knew little about the Europeans, but Pizarro knew a lot about Native Americans. He had spent more than 30 years fighting them. In addition, his good friend Hernán Cortés had given him a detailed look at the

Primary Source

Incan Record Keeping

A Spanish conquistador wrote about aspects of Incan culture.

"At the beginning of the new year the rulers of each village came to Cuzco, bringing their quipus, which told how many births there had been during the year, and how many deaths. In this way the Inca and the governors knew which of the Indians were poor, the women who had been widowed, whether they were able to pay their taxes, and how many men they could count on in the event of war, and many other things they considered highly important."

—Pedro de Cieza de Léon, *The Second Part of the Chronicle of Peru*

▲ Quipu

DBQ Document-Based Question

Quipus were used to calculate records and building plans. How else do you think the Inca might have used quipus?

conquest of the Aztec. In late 1532, Pizarro decided on a plan so bold that even Cortés might not have risked it.

Pizarro Defeats the Inca Spanish messengers invited Atahualpa to a meeting. Atahualpa agreed but made two errors. He left most of his huge army behind. He believed that his 5,000 bodyguards were enough protection. He also decided, based on Pizarro's small force, that the Inca needed no weapons.

When they met, Pizarro wasted no time in asking the emperor to give up his gods. When Atahualpa laughed at his request, Pizarro ordered an attack. Cannons roared, trumpets blared, and sword-swinging soldiers shrieked battle cries. Pizarro then seized Atahualpa and dragged him off the battlefield.

Atahualpa tried to buy his freedom. He offered to fill his jail cell with gold and a nearby room with silver for his release. Pizarro agreed.

Atahualpa kept his part of the bargain. Pizarro did not. He charged the emperor with many crimes: plotting a rebellion, worshiping false gods, having too many wives, and more. In 1533 a military court found the emperor guilty and sentenced him to death.

To reward Pizarro, the Spanish king made him governor of Peru. Pizarro then chose a new emperor for the Inca, but the emperor had to follow Pizarro's orders.

Pizarro's conquest of Peru opened most of South America to Spanish rule. Spain controlled a vast territory covering 375,000 square miles (975,000 sq km) with almost 7 million inhabitants. It was on its way to building the world's first global empire.

Reading Check **Explain** How did Pizarro fail to keep his promise to Atahualpa?

Study Central Need help understanding the fall of the Aztec and Inca? Visit ca.hss.glencoe.com and click on Study Central.

Section 3 Review

Reading Summary

Review the Main Ideas

- Christopher Columbus arrived in the Americas and claimed lands there for Spain. With a small army, Spanish conquistador Hernán Cortés conquered Montezuma and the Aztec capital of Tenochtitlán.

- In Peru, a small Spanish force led by Francisco Pizarro captured the Inca Empire.

What Did You Learn?

1. Why did Cortés sail from Cuba to Mexico in search of the Aztec?

2. What was Pizarro's advantage over the Inca?

Critical Thinking

3. **Sequencing Information** Draw a time line like the one shown. Fill in events related to Cortés's capture of Tenochtitlán. **CA CS2.**

1517: Spanish ship brings back gold from Yucatán

4. **Predict** How might the history of the Aztec people be different without the legend of the Aztec god Quetzalcoatl? **CA HI2.**

5. **The Big Ideas** **Explain** How did Spain benefit from the conquests of Cortés and Pizarro? How did these conquests change Spain's power in the world? **CA 7RC2.3**

6. **Narrative Writing** Imagine you are an Aztec or an Inca seeing a Spanish conquistador for the first time. Write a short story describing what you have observed. **CA 7WA2.1**

Analyzing Primary Sources

WH7.7.3 Explain how and where each empire arose and how the Aztec and Incan empires were defeated by the Spanish.

The Power of Kings

The people in the Americas believed that their rulers were important and powerful men. In some instances, their rulers had absolute control over their people and greatly influenced their daily lives.

Read the following passages and study the image on pages 478 and 479, and answer the questions that follow.

Montezuma ▶

Reader's Dictionary

finery (FY•nuh•ree): fancy clothes and jewelry

installed: placed in

plunder: stolen goods, usually during war

van: troops at the front

litter: a couch carried by servants on which a leader sits

Arrival of the Spaniards

A *few Aztec descriptions of the Spanish conquest still exist. This selection describes the meeting of Montezuma and Cortés.*

The Spaniards arrived . . . near the entrance to Tenochtitlan . . .

[Montezuma] now arrayed himself in his **finery,** preparing to go out to meet them. . .

. . . Then he hung the gold necklaces around their necks and gave them presents of every sort as gifts of welcome. . . .

. . . Then [Montezuma] stood up to welcome Cortes; he came forward, bowed his head low and addressed him in these words: "Our lord, you are weary. The journey has tired you, but now you have arrived on the earth. You have come to your city, Mexico. . . ."

When the Spaniards were **installed** in the palace, they asked [Montezuma] about the city's resources. . . .

When they entered the hall of treasures, it was as if they had arrived in Paradise. . . . All of [Montezuma's] possessions were brought out: fine bracelets, necklaces with large stones, ankle rings with little gold bells, the royal crowns and all the royal finery—everything that belonged to the king. . . . They seized these treasures as if they were their own, as if this **plunder** were merely a stroke of good luck.

—author unknown, from *The Broken Spears*, edited by Miguel Leon-Portilla

Welcoming a New King

The Mayan painting shown below comes from a Mayan tomb. It shows a procession of musicians playing various instruments. The people are shown celebrating the choosing of the heir to the throne.

Incan Wealth

In 1532 Spanish troops led by Pizarro confronted the Incan emperor Atahualpa. The following excerpt describes what happened.

Soon the **van** of the enemy began to enter the open space. First came a squadron of Indians dressed in a livery of different colors, like a chessboard. They advanced, removing the straws from the ground and sweeping the road. Next came three squadrons in different dresses, dancing and singing. Then came a number of men with armor, large metal plates, and crowns of gold and silver. Among them was Atahualpa in a **litter** lined with plumes of macaws' feathers of many colors and adorned with plates of gold and silver. Many Indians carried it on their shoulders on high. . . .

A priest offered Atahualpa a Bible, but Atahualpa, angry at how his people had been treated, threw it to the ground.

Then the Governor [Pizarro] put on a jacket of cotton, took his sword and dagger . . . Then the guns were fired off, the trumpets were sounded, and the troops, both horse and foot, sallied forth. . . . The horsemen rode them down, killing and wounding, and following in pursuit. The infantry made so good an assault upon those that remained that in a short time most of them were put to the sword.

—Francisco de Xeres,
Narrative of the Conquest of Peru

DBQ Document-Based Questions

Arrival of the Spaniards

1. Who did Montezuma think that Cortés was? How did this affect Montezuma's interaction with him?

2. How did Cortés treat Montezuma? Give examples from the passage.

Welcoming a New King

3. What kinds of instruments do you think the musicians are playing?

4. Why do you think someone would place this image in a tomb?

Incan Wealth

5. What does this story tell you about the wealth and power of the Incan emperor?

6. Did the Spanish seem frightened by Atahualpa's power? Why not?

Read to Write

7. How do each of these sources demonstrate the important role the ruler played?
CA HR5.

Review Content Vocabulary

Match the word in the first column with its definition in the second column. Write the letter of the definition in the blank.

____ 1. monopoly   a. disloyalty, usually to a state or nation

____ 2. glacier   b. having the sole right to something

____ 3. sinkhole   c. Incan counting device

____ 4. quipu   d. soldier-explorer

____ 5. treason   e. huge sheet of ice

____ 6. conquistador   f. areas of collapsed earth

Review the Main Ideas

Section 1 • The First Americans

7. When did the first people arrive in the Americas? How did they obtain food?

8. What led to the development of civilizations in Mexico, Central America, and Peru?

Section 2 • Life in the Americas

9. How was the Mayan civilization organized? Who were its leaders?

10. How did the Maya use astronomy?

Section 3 • The Fall of the Aztec and Inca Empires

11. Which groups of Europeans were the first to take control of land in the Americas?

12. What happened after the riches of the Aztec Empire became known?

Critical Thinking

13. **Infer** Why do you think the Mayan civilization came to an end? **CA 7RC2.0**

14. **Analyze** Why was it so important for Cortés to have Aztec people helping him? How did he use the knowledge gained from them to defeat Montezuma? **CA HI2.**

15. **Predict** What do you think would have happened if the Inca had seen Pizarro as a threat from the beginning? **CA 7RC2.3**

Geography Skills

Study the map below and answer the following questions.

16. **Human/Environment Interaction** Why do you think the Inca built stone walls in parts of Cuzco? **CA CS3.**

17. **Place** What natural defenses existed around Cuzco? **CA CS3.**

18. **Movement** What do the roads leading out of Cuzco reveal about the contact between the capital city and the rest of the empire? **CA CS3.**

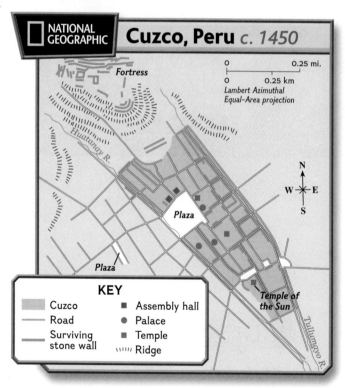

NATIONAL GEOGRAPHIC **Cuzco, Peru** c. 1450

Lambert Azimuthal Equal-Area projection

KEY
- Cuzco
- Road
- Surviving stone wall
- ■ Assembly hall
- ● Palace
- ■ Temple
- \\\\\ Ridge

Read to Write

19. **The Big Ideas** **Writing Summaries** Write a summary of what life was like in Mesoamerica before Europeans arrived. Then write a summary of what happened after the Europeans arrived. Use these summaries to write an essay describing the changes that occurred in the Americas in the 1500s. **CA 7WA2.5**

20. **Using Your FOLDABLES** Create an outline map of the Americas on poster board, a dry erase board, or a blackboard. The map should be big enough for the entire class to work together. Take turns labeling each country and the location of each civilization from your chapter. Then use your foldables to write facts about each civilization on the map. **CA CS3.**

Using Academic Vocabulary

21. Match the words in Column A with a word or phrase in Column B.

A	B
environment	work together
source	support with money
cooperate	create
previous	surroundings
finance	occurs earlier
generate	origin

Economic Connection

22. **Persuasive Writing** Imagine that you are a Native American during the time of the Spanish conquests. Write a letter to the conquistadors persuading them to trade with your culture rather than conquer it. Your letter should give examples of ways the Europeans and Native Americans can learn from each other. Be sure to state the benefits that trade would bring to both sides. **CA 7WA2.4** **CA HI6.**

Reviewing Skills

23. **Reading Skill** **Comparing and Contrasting** Create a chart like the one below to compare the Maya and Aztec cultures. Use what you learned from the chapter to provide information for the chart. **CA 7RC2.2**

	Maya	Aztec
Government		
Daily Life		
Science		
Art		

24. **Analysis Skill** **Recognizing Changes** The discovery of an ancient Mayan city in the Yucatán rain forest led to new information and a better understanding of the Mayan people. Write a research paper that explains the significance of this discovery. What new things did the world learn about the Maya? What artifacts provided this information? How did the chance discovery change the way historians view ancient American civilizations? Use your local library or Internet to find out information about this discovery and others that helped historians learn about early Native American cultures. **CA HI4.; HI5.**

Standards Practice

Select the best answer for each of the following questions.

25 The Mesoamerican people formed permanent, complex societies because they

A learned to grow corn and other crops.

B conquered nearby civilizations.

C were protected from the influences of trade.

D learned to make weapons.

26 Sporting events, pyramid construction, and the development of a 365-day calendar revolved around what aspect of Mayan life?

A human sacrifice

B warrior training

C a strict class system

D religion

The Age of Exploration

A lighthouse stands among the ruins ▶
of Prince Henry the Navigator's school
of navigation in Algarve, Portugal.

NATIONAL GEOGRAPHIC *Where&When?*

1400	1475	1550	1625
1420 Portugal begins mapping Africa's coast	**1492** Columbus reaches the Americas	**1520** Magellan's crew sails around the world	**1588** England defeats the Spanish Armada

Chapter Overview Visit ca.hss.glencoe.com for a preview of Chapter 10.

The Big Ideas

 ## Europe Explores the World

The interaction of different societies brings about the development of new ideas, art, and technology. In the 1400s, many trade routes collapsed. At the same time, Europeans learned new technologies from Asia and the Arab world and invented some of their own. This led to an age of exploration.

 ## Trade and Empire

The interaction of different societies brings about the development of new ideas, art, and technology. Exploration led to the creation of new empires. It also encouraged the development of new ideas in commerce.

 ## A Global Exchange

Exploration and trade spread ideas and goods. European exploration and trade spread new goods and ideas throughout the world. This had both positive and negative effects.

View the Chapter 10 video in the Glencoe Video Program.

FOLDABLES™ Study Organizer

Organizing Information *Make this foldable to help you organize and analyze information by asking yourself questions about the Age of Exploration.*

Step 1 *Fold three sheets of paper in half from top to bottom.*

Step 2 *On each folded paper, make a cut 1 inch from the side on the top flap.*

Cut 1 inch from the edge through the top flap only.

Step 3 *Place the folded papers one on top of the other. Staple the three sections together and label the top three tabs: Europe Explores the World, Trade and Empire, A Global Exchange.*

Staple here.

Europe Explores the World

Reading and Writing *As you read the chapter, write the main ideas for each section under the appropriate tabs of your foldable. Then write one statement for each tab that summarizes all of the main ideas in that tab.*

Chapter 10 Get Ready to Read

Monitoring

1 Learn It!

A key strategy to help you improve your reading is monitoring, or finding your reading strengths and weaknesses. As you read, monitor yourself to make sure that the text makes sense. Discover different monitoring techniques that you can use at different times, depending on the type of text and situation. Read the following paragraph and the examples of monitoring.

Sometimes reading ahead will help you understand the meaning. Cartography is defined in the text immediately following the term.

Do you recognize these terms? Have you ever used longitude and latitude to read a globe or map?

With the invention of the printing press, books like Ptolemy's could be printed and sold all over Europe. Ptolemy's theories about cartography, or the science of mapmaking, were very influential. His basic system of longitude and latitude is still used today.

— *from page 488*

What do you remember about the emergence of printing? Check back in the book to help you remember.

Do you know who Ptolemy was? The index may show you where to find more information about him.

Reading Tip

A useful monitoring strategy is to slow down or speed up your reading, depending on the text.

- If the text does not make sense, reread what you do not understand. Reading the text before or after the passage may help.
- Look at related graphs, charts, illustrations, or photographs on the page.
- Think about what you already know about the text, based on what you may have read, seen, or experienced.

2 Practice It!

The paragraph below appears in Section 2. Read the passage and answer the questions that follow. Discuss your answers with other students to see how they monitor their reading.

> Mercantilism encouraged Europeans to set up trading posts and colonies in Asia and North America. By the end of the 1500s, Spain had set up a colony in the Philippines. The Spanish shipped silver to the Philippines from America and then used it to buy Asian spices and silk for sale in Europe.
>
> —*from page 497*

- What questions do you still have after reading?
- Do you understand all the words in the passage?
- Did you read the passage differently than you would have read a short story or a newspaper article? How do you read various types of text differently?
- Did you have to stop reading often? Is the reading the appropriate level for you?

Read to Write

As you reread a section from this chapter, monitor yourself to see how well you understand. Then describe in a short paragraph what kind of strategies are most helpful to you before, during, and after you read.

▼ **Ships of the Dutch East India Company**

3 Apply It!

Identify one paragraph in each section of the chapter that is difficult to understand. Discuss each paragraph with a partner to improve your understanding.

Europe Explores the World

Guide to Reading

History **Social Science Standards**

WH7.11 Students analyze political and economic change in the sixteenth, seventeenth, and eighteenth centuries (the Age of Exploration, the Enlightenment, and the Age of Reason).

Looking Back, Looking Ahead

You have learned how Italy's cities grew rich from trade. In the 1400s, other European states began exploring the world in search of wealth.

Focusing on the Main Ideas

- In the 1400s, trade, technology, and the rise of strong kingdoms led to a new era of exploration. *(page 487)*

- While the Portuguese explored Africa, the Spanish, English, and French explored America. *(page 489)*

Locating Places
Azores (AY•ZOHRZ)
Madeira (muh•DIHR•uh)
Hispaniola (HIHS•puh•NYOH•luh)
Strait of Magellan (muh•JEH•luhn)
Newfoundland (NOO•fuhn•luhnd)
St. Lawrence River (LAWR•uhns)

Meeting People
Vasco da Gama (VAS•koh duh GA•muh)
Christopher Columbus
Magellan (muh•JEH•luhn)
John Cabot (KA•buht)
Jacques Cartier (ZHAHK kahr•TYAY)

Content Vocabulary
astrolabe (AS•truh•LAB)
compass (KUHM•puhs)
caravel (KAR•uh•VEHL)
cartography (kahr•TAH•gruh•fee)

Academic Vocabulary
fund
locate

Reading Strategy
Cause and Effect Complete a diagram like the one below showing why Europeans began to explore.

☐ → ☐ → ☐

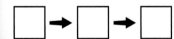

NATIONAL GEOGRAPHIC **Where & When?**

NORTH AMERICA   EUROPE   CHINA   AFRICA   INDIA   SOUTH AMERICA

1400	1475	1550
1420 Portugal begins mapping Africa's coast	**1492** Columbus reaches the Americas	**1520** Magellan's crew sails around the world

WH7.11.1 Know the great voyages of discovery, the locations of the routes, and the influence of cartography in the development of a new European worldview.

WH7.11.2 Discuss the exchanges of plants, animals, technology, culture, and ideas among Europe, Africa, Asia, and the Americas in the fifteenth and sixteenth centuries and the major economic and social effects on each continent.

Europe Gets Ready to Explore

Main Idea In the 1400s, trade, technology, and the rise of strong kingdoms led to a new era of exploration.

Reading Connection Do you like traveling to places that you have never been to? Read to learn why Western Europeans set off to explore the world.

In the 1400s and 1500s, nations in Western Europe began exploring the world. They soon gained control of the Americas and parts of India and Southeast Asia as well. Why did they begin exploring in the 1400s? Many events generated just the right conditions for exploration.

Trade With Asia

As you have read, in the Middle Ages, Europeans began buying vast amounts of spices, silks, and other goods from Asia. In the 1400s, however, it became harder to get those goods.

First of all, the Mongol Empire had collapsed. The Mongols had kept the Silk Road running smoothly. When their empire collapsed, local rulers along the Silk Road imposed new taxes on merchants. This made Asian goods more expensive.

Next, the Ottoman Turks conquered the Byzantine Empire and blocked Italian merchants from entering the Black Sea. The Italians had trading posts on the coast of the Black Sea where they bought goods from Asia. Now, they could no longer reach them. They had to trade with the Turks instead, and this drove prices even higher.

Europeans still wanted the spices and silks of East Asia. Anyone who could find a way to get them cheaply would make a lot of money. Merchants began looking for a route to East Asia that bypassed the Middle East. If they could not get there by land, maybe they could get there by sea.

◀ Early compass

▲ European explorers and traders began to use smaller, faster ships called caravels in the 1400s. *What advantage did triangular sails offer a ship?*

Astrolabe ▲

New Technology

Even though the Europeans wanted to go exploring, they could not do it without the right technology. The Atlantic Ocean was too dangerous and difficult to navigate.

By the 1400s, they had the technology they needed. From the Arabs, Europeans learned about the astrolabe and the compass. The **astrolabe** (AS•truh•LAB) was an ancient Greek device that could be used to find latitude. The **compass** (KUHM•puhs), invented by the Chinese, helped navigators find magnetic north.

Even with these new tools, the Europeans needed better ships. In the 1400s, they began using triangular sails developed by the Arabs. These sails let a ship zigzag into the wind.

The rise of towns and trade helped make governments stronger. Rulers could tax the trade in their kingdoms and then use the money to build armies and navies. Using their new power and resources, they were able to build strong central governments.

By the end of the 1400s, four strong kingdoms—Portugal, Spain, France, and England—had been developed in Europe. They had harbors on the Atlantic Ocean and were anxious to find a sea route to Asia. The question was where to go.

Did Maps Encourage Exploration? By the 1400s, most educated people in Europe knew the world was round, but they only had maps of Europe and the Mediterranean. When the Renaissance began, however, people began to study ancient maps as well as books written by Arab scholars.

Twelve hundred years earlier, a Greek-educated Egyptian geographer named Claudius Ptolemy had drawn maps of the world. His book *Geography* was discovered by Europeans in 1406 and printed in 1475.

With the invention of the printing press, books like Ptolemy's could be printed and sold all over Europe. Ptolemy's theories about **cartography** (kahr•TAH•gruh•fee), or the science of mapmaking, were very influential. His basic system of longitude and latitude is still used today.

European cartographers also began reading a book written by al-Idrisi, an Arab geographer. Al-Idrisi had published a book in 1154 showing the parts of the world known to Muslims. By studying the works of al-Idrisi and Ptolemy, Europeans learned the geography of East Africa and the Indian Ocean. If they could find a way around Africa, they could get to Asia.

Reading Check **Summarize** What were the main reasons the Europeans began exploring the world in the 1400s?

▲ Prince Henry's school for navigation helped make possible the discovery of new water routes and new lands. Here, Prince Henry is shown watching for the return of his ships. *What types of professionals did Prince Henry invite to his research center?*

They also began building ships with many masts and smaller sails to make their ships go faster. A new type of rudder made steering easier. In the 1400s, these inventions came together in a Portuguese ship called the caravel. With ships like the **caravel** (KAR•uh•VEHL), Europeans could begin exploring the world.

The Rise of Strong Nations Even with new technology, exploration was still expensive and dangerous. For most of the Middle Ages, Europe's kingdoms were weak and could not **fund** exploration. This situation began to change in the 1400s.

Exploring the World

Main Idea While the Portuguese explored Africa, the Spanish, English, and French explored America.

Reading Connection Have you ever done something daring or tried something new not knowing how it would turn out? Read to learn how European explorers took chances and went places no Europeans had ever been before.

By the early 1400s, Europeans were ready to explore. England and France were still fighting each other, however, and Spain was still fighting the Muslims. This gave Portugal the chance to explore first.

Who Was Henry the Navigator? In 1419
Prince Henry of Portugal, known as "Henry the Navigator," set up a research center in southern Portugal. He invited sailors, cartographers, and shipbuilders to come and help him explore the world.

In 1420 Portugal began mapping Africa's coastline and trading with Africa's kingdoms. It also seized the **Azores** (AY•ZOHRZ), **Madeira** (muh•DIHR•uh), and Cape Verde islands. Soon after, the Portuguese discovered sugarcane would grow on the islands.

Sugar was very valuable in Europe. To work their sugarcane fields, the Portuguese began bringing enslaved Africans to the islands. This was the beginning of a slave trade that would eventually bring millions of enslaved people to the Americas as well.

In 1488 the Portuguese explorer Bartolomeu Dias reached the southern tip of Africa. Nine years later, **Vasco da Gama** (VAS•koh duh GA•muh) rounded the tip of Africa, raced across the Indian Ocean, and landed on India's coast. A water route to East Asia had at last been **located.**

Santa María

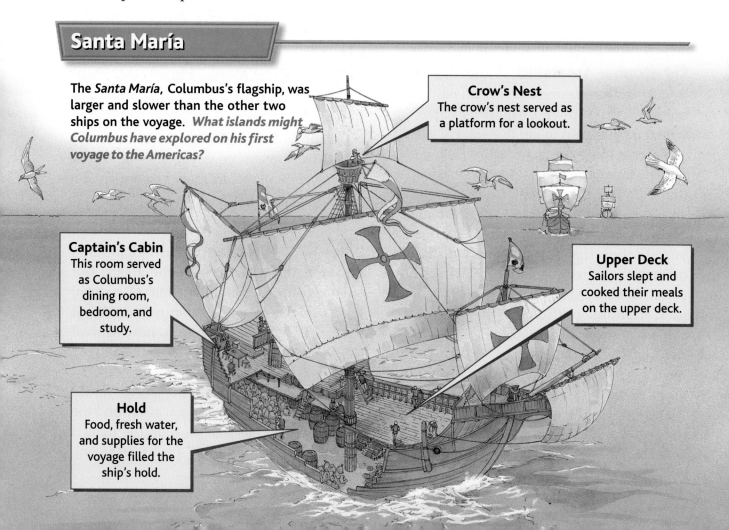

The *Santa María*, Columbus's flagship, was larger and slower than the other two ships on the voyage. *What islands might Columbus have explored on his first voyage to the Americas?*

Crow's Nest
The crow's nest served as a platform for a lookout.

Captain's Cabin
This room served as Columbus's dining room, bedroom, and study.

Upper Deck
Sailors slept and cooked their meals on the upper deck.

Hold
Food, fresh water, and supplies for the voyage filled the ship's hold.

European Exploration of the World

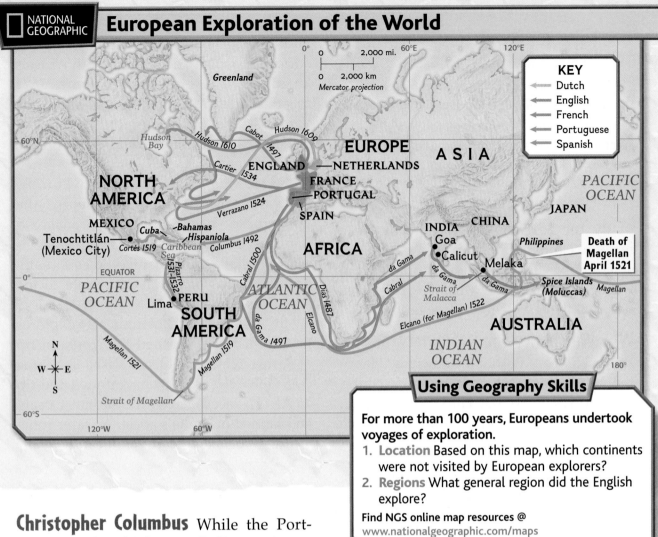

KEY
- Dutch
- English
- French
- Portuguese
- Spanish

Greenland

Hudson 1610

Hudson 1609

Cabot 1497

Hudson Bay

EUROPE

ASIA

PACIFIC OCEAN

NORTH AMERICA

Cartier 1534

ENGLAND — NETHERLANDS

FRANCE

PORTUGAL

SPAIN

Verrazano 1524

JAPAN

MEXICO

Cuba

Bahamas

Hispaniola

CHINA

INDIA

Goa

Calicut

Philippines

Death of Magellan April 1521

Tenochtitlán (Mexico City)

Cortés 1519

Caribbean Sea

Columbus 1492

da Gama

Melaka

EQUATOR

Cabral 1500

AFRICA

da Gama

Strait of Malacca

da Gama

Spice Islands (Moluccas)

Magellan

PACIFIC OCEAN

Pizarro 1531–1532

Lima

PERU

SOUTH AMERICA

da Gama 1497

ATLANTIC OCEAN

Dias 1487

Cabral

Elcano (for Magellan) 1522

AUSTRALIA

Elcano

INDIAN OCEAN

Magellan 1521

Magellan 1519

N W E S

Strait of Magellan

120°W   60°W

Using Geography Skills

For more than 100 years, Europeans undertook voyages of exploration.

1. **Location** Based on this map, which continents were not visited by European explorers?
2. **Regions** What general region did the English explore?

Find NGS online map resources @ www.nationalgeographic.com/maps

Christopher Columbus While the Portuguese explored Africa, an Italian navigator named **Christopher Columbus** came up with a daring plan to get to Asia. He would sail across the Atlantic Ocean.

Columbus needed someone to finance the trip. The rulers of Portugal, England, and France all turned him down. Finally in 1492 Ferdinand and Isabella of Spain said yes. Earlier that year, they had finally driven the Muslims out of Spain. They could now afford to pay for exploration.

Columbus outfitted three ships: the *Santa María*, the *Niña*, and the *Pinta*. In 1492 they left Spain and headed west. As the weeks passed, the crew grew desperate. Finally they sighted land, probably the island of San Salvador. Columbus claimed the land for Spain and then explored Cuba and **Hispaniola** (HIHS•puh•NYOH•luh).

Columbus thought he was in Asia. He conducted three more voyages to the region but never realized he had arrived in the Americas. Eventually, Europeans realized they had reached two huge continents.

Who Was Magellan? Many Spaniards explored the Americas in the 1500s, but only Ferdinand **Magellan** (muh•JEH•luhn) tried to finish what Columbus had set out to do. In 1520 he left Spain and headed west to sail around the Americas and then all the way to Asia.

Magellan sailed south along South America. Finally, he found a way around the continent. The passage he found is named the **Strait of Magellan** (muh•JEH•luhn).

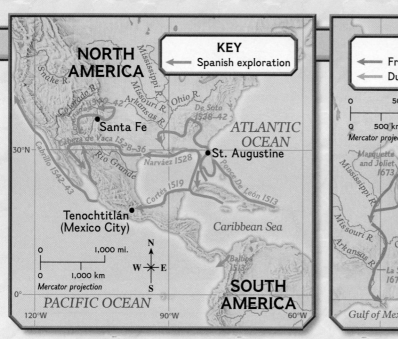

NORTH AMERICA

KEY
⬅ Spanish exploration

Snake R.

Colorado R.

Missouri R.

Ohio R.

Arkansas R.

Mississippi R.

De Soto 1539–42

• Santa Fe

Cabeza de Vaca 1528–36

30°N

Cabrillo 1542–43

Rio Grande

Narváez 1528

ATLANTIC OCEAN

• St. Augustine

Ponce De León 1513

Cortés 1519

Tenochtitlán (Mexico City) •

Caribbean Sea

Balboa 1513

0   1,000 mi.

0   1,000 km
Mercator projection

N W E S

0°

PACIFIC OCEAN

120°W   90°W   60°W

SOUTH AMERICA

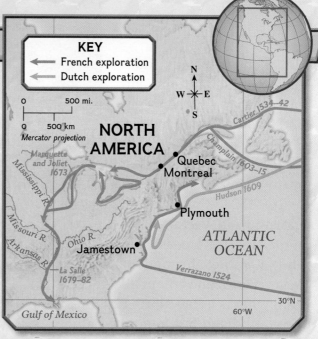

KEY
⬅ French exploration
⬅ Dutch exploration

0   500 mi.

0   500 km
Mercator projection

N W E S

NORTH AMERICA

Marquette and Joliet 1673

Mississippi R.

Missouri R.

Arkansas R.

Ohio R.

La Salle 1679–82

Cartier 1534–42

Champlain 1603–15

• Quebec
Montreal

Hudson 1609

• Plymouth

• Jamestown

ATLANTIC OCEAN

Verrazano 1524

Gulf of Mexico

60°W   30°N

Important European Explorers

Christopher Columbus

Voyages: 1492, 1493, 1498, 1502

First European to sail west searching for a water route to Asia

Vasco da Gama

Voyage: 1497–1499

First European to sail around the south of Africa and reach India

Ferdinand Magellan

Voyage: 1519–1522

Led the first expedition to sail completely around the world

Jacques Cartier

Voyages: 1534, 1535, 1541

Explored the St. Lawrence River

Henry Hudson

Voyages: 1607, 1608, 1609, 1610

Explored the Hudson River and Hudson Bay

After passing through the stormy strait, his ship entered a vast sea. It was so peaceful, or pacific, that he named the sea the Pacific Ocean.

Magellan then headed west. His sailors nearly starved and had to eat leather, sawdust, and rats. Finally, after four months at sea, they reached the Philippines. After local people killed Magellan, his crew continued west across the Indian Ocean, around Africa, and back to Spain. They became the first known people to circumnavigate (SUHR•kuhm•NA•vuh•GAYT), or sail around, the world.

The First English and French Explorers

As the news spread about Columbus's journey, England decided to search for a northern route to Asia. In 1497 an English ship commanded by **John Cabot** (KA•buht) headed across the Atlantic.

Cabot encountered a large island he named **Newfoundland** (NOO•fuhn•luhnd).

He then traveled south along the coast of present-day Canada but did not find a path through to Asia. Cabot disappeared on his second trip and was never heard from again.

In 1524 France sent Giovanni da Verrazano to map America's coast and find a route through to Asia. Verrazano mapped from what is today North Carolina north to Newfoundland but found no path to Asia.

Ten years later, the French tried again. This time they sent **Jacques Cartier** (ZHAHK kahr•TYAY). Cartier sailed past Newfoundland and entered the **St. Lawrence River** (LAWR•uhns). After two more trips, France stopped exploring. By the mid-1500s,

▲ **The St. Lawrence River today**

French Protestants and Catholics were fighting a civil war. There was no more exploring until it was settled.

✓ **Reading Check** **Identify** Who was the first European to sail to India? Whose crew was first to sail around the world?

History Online

Study Central Need help understanding European explorers? Visit ca.hss.glencoe.com and click on Study Central.

Section 1 Review

Reading Summary

Review the Main Ideas

- Rising prices of Asian goods, increased wealth from trade, strong central governments, new sailing technology and maps, and Renaissance attitudes caused Europeans to begin exploring the world in the 1400s.

- Portugal found a route around Africa to India, Spain began building an empire in America, and England and France sent explorers to America and Asia.

What Did You Learn?

1. What was a caravel, and why was it important?

2. Describe the accomplishments of Ferdinand Magellan.

Critical Thinking

3. **Organize Information** Draw a chart like the one below. Use it to name the explorers discussed in this section, the country they sailed for, and the places they explored. **CA 7RC2.0**

Explorer	Country Sailed For	Area Explored

4. **Persuasive Writing** Which explorer do you think accomplished the most? Why? Write an essay defending your position. **CA 7WA2.4**

5. **The Big Ideas** What knowledge and inventions of other cultures did Europeans use in their explorations? How did they help the explorers? **CA HI2.**

6. **Reading** Monitoring Write a 10-question multiple choice test to help you review the important information in this section. Exchange tests with a classmate. **CA HR1.**

Guide to Reading

Looking Back, Looking Ahead
One effect of European exploration was the creation of new empires. At the same time, a commercial revolution occurred as companies engaged in early forms of capitalism.

Focusing on the Main Ideas
- The Spanish and Portuguese built new empires by establishing colonies in the Americas. *(page 494)*

- To increase trade, Europeans set up colonies and created joint-stock companies. *(page 497)*

Locating Places
Netherlands (NEH•thuhr•luhnz)
Moluccas (muh•LUH•kuhz)

Meeting People
Henry VIII
Elizabeth I
Pedro Alvares Cabral (PAY•throo AHL•vahr•ihs kuh•BRAHL)

Content Vocabulary
mercantilism (MUHR•kuhn•TUH•LIH•zuhm)
export (EHK•SPOHRT)
import (IHM•POHRT)
colony (KAH•luh•nee)
commerce (KAH•muhrs)
invest (ihn•VEHST)
capitalism (KA•puh•tuhl•IHZ•uhm)

Academic Vocabulary
primary (PRY•MEHR•ee)
aid
anticipate (an•TIH•suh•PAYT)

Reading Strategy
Cause and Effect Complete a diagram like the one below showing what led to the rise of modern capitalism.

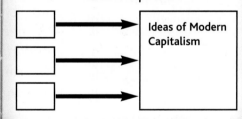

Ideas of Modern Capitalism

History Social Science Standards
WH7.11 Students analyze political and economic change in the sixteenth, seventeenth, and eighteenth centuries (the Age of Exploration, the Enlightenment, and the Age of Reason).

NATIONAL GEOGRAPHIC **Where & When?**

1500	1550	1600
1500 Cabral takes control of Indian Ocean trade	**c. 1550** Portuguese plantations set up in Brazil	**1588** England defeats the Armada
		1619 Dutch arrive in Java

NORTH AMERICA · EUROPE · CHINA · INDIA · AFRICA · SOUTH AMERICA

WH7.11 Students analyze political and economic change in the sixteenth, seventeenth, and eighteenth centuries (the Age of Exploration, the Enlightenment, and the Age of Reason). **WH7.11.3** Examine the origins of modern capitalism; the influence of mercantilism and cottage industry; the elements and importance of a market economy in seventeenth-century Europe; the changing international trading and marketing patterns, including their locations on a world map; and the influence of explorers and map makers.

Europe's Empires

Main Idea The Spanish and Portuguese built new empires by establishing colonies in the Americas.

Reading Connection Have you ever been to a store that did not have what you wanted and then bought something else instead? Read to learn how the Spanish hoped to find spices and silk in the Americas but found gold and silver instead.

As you have learned previously, Spain and Portugal built vast empires by establishing colonies in the Americas and trading posts in Asia in the 1500s. To create these empires, they first had to conquer the Aztec and Inca.

The Fall of the Aztec and Inca

As you read in Chapter 9, when the Spanish conquistadors arrived, both the Aztec and Inca ruled large empires. The Aztec empire ruled more than five million people. To support this population, they designed complex farming methods, built irrigation systems, and drained swamps. They also made advances in science, developed a calendar, and built impressive buildings and bridges.

As you have learned, the Inca also ruled a vast empire, stretching thousands of miles through the Andes. To govern effectively, they built a huge network of roads covering about 25,000 miles. Their buildings reveal highly advanced engineering skills. They used no mortar to hold their stone blocks together, yet their buildings could survive earthquakes.

Both the Inca and the Aztec were expert metalworkers and had great quantities of precious metals. These included silver and gold. They also commanded large, well-organized armies. Nonetheless, neither could fight well against the steel swords and guns of the Spanish troops led by Cortés and Pizarro.

The Spanish had another advantage. They carried diseases with them. Among these were whooping cough, smallpox, and the measles. These diseases proved especially deadly to the Native Americans because they had never been exposed to them before. The result was devastating. Millions of people died, and much of their native culture vanished as well.

Spain and Portugal's Empires

After the Spanish conquered the Aztec and Inca, they set up governments to rule the region. The

NATIONAL GEOGRAPHIC — Empires in America

KEY
Portuguese territory c. 1500
Spanish territory c. 1500

120°W   60°W
60°N

NORTH AMERICA

N
W — E
S

MEXICO   ATLANTIC OCEAN
West Indies

EQUATOR
0°

PACIFIC OCEAN

BRAZIL
SOUTH AMERICA

0   2,000 mi.
0   2,000 km
Mercator projection

Using Geography Skills

1. **Location** Which country controlled the most territory in the Americas?
2. **Region** What geographical traits did the territories of Spain and Portugal have in common?

Aztec Empire became New Spain, and the Inca Empire became New Castile. The Spanish appointed local governors who reported to the king. The **primary** responsibility of these governors was to mine gold and silver and send as much as possible back home to Spain. Vast amounts of gold and silver began to flow to Europe from Spain's empire in America.

The Spanish did not rule all of the Americas. A large portion of South America was controlled by the Portuguese. They called this region Brazil.

Unlike the Spanish, the Portuguese colonists focused on producing one specific cash crop—sugarcane. As you learned previously, sugarcane is used to produce sugar, a product that had become very popular in Europe by that time.

Beginning around 1550, the Portuguese set up large sugarcane plantations along the Brazilian coast. They then began bringing enslaved people from Africa to Brazil to work on the plantations. Soon more than half the population of Brazil had come from Africa.

Spain Fights England
In the meantime, England had become Spain's enemy. As you have read, in 1534 King **Henry VIII** of England broke from the Catholic Church and made his kingdom Protestant. By the 1560s, the Dutch had converted to Protestantism too, even though they were part of Spain's empire at that time. Spain was strongly Catholic and tried to stop Protestantism in the **Netherlands** (NEH • thuhr • luhnz). When the Dutch people rebelled against Spain, England came to their **aid.**

To help the Dutch, Queen **Elizabeth I** of England let English privateers attack Spanish ships. Privateers are privately owned ships that have a license from

▲ To defeat the Spanish Armada, the English sent ships that had been set on fire toward the Spanish warships. *Why was the defeat of the Spanish Armada important?*

the government to attack ships of other countries. People nicknamed the English privateers "sea dogs." They raided the Spanish treasure ships that were bringing gold back from America.

England's raids frustrated Philip II, the king of Spain. In 1588 he sent a huge fleet known as the Spanish Armada to invade England. In July 1588, the Armada headed into the English Channel—the narrow body of water between England and Europe.

The Spanish ships, called galleons, were large and had many guns, but they were hard to steer. The smaller English ships moved much more quickly than the galleons. Their attacks forced the Armada to retreat north. There a great storm arose and broke up the Armada.

The defeat of the Spanish Armada was an important event. The Spanish were still strong, but England now had the power to stand up to them. This encouraged the English and Dutch to begin exploring both Asia and North America. Soon afterward they began establishing colonies in North America as well.

Reading Check Explain How did the arrival of the Spanish change the Americas?

Biography

ELIZABETH I
1533–1603

Elizabeth I was one of the most popular British rulers—but she was more loved by the people of England than by her father, King Henry VIII. Elizabeth's young life was filled with change and sadness. She was born to Henry VIII and his second wife, Anne Boleyn. The king was upset when Elizabeth was born, because he wanted a boy to inherit the throne.

When Elizabeth became queen, she surrounded herself with intelligent advisers. Together they turned England into a strong, prosperous country. Elizabeth supported Protestantism in England and in the rest of Europe. She sent aid to the French Huguenots and Protestants in Scotland and the Netherlands. She worked well with Parliament but called few sessions during her reign. She was a skilled writer and speaker and won the love and support of the English people.

▲ **Queen Elizabeth I**

> **"I have the heart and stomach of a king and of a king of England, too."**
> —Elizabeth I, "Armada Speech"

Elizabeth never married, which was unusual at that time. Many men were interested in marrying her, but she turned down their proposals. One reason Elizabeth probably remained single was to maintain control of the government at a time when most rulers were men. She also used her status to the advantage of England. Many prominent men wanted to marry her, and she sometimes threatened to marry someone's enemy in order to get him to do what she wanted.

Elizabeth's personality also influenced England's society. She loved horse riding, dances, parties, and plays. Her support of the arts resulted in the development of new English literature and music. Elizabeth was so popular by the time of her death that the date she became queen was celebrated as a national holiday for 200 years.

Then and Now

Even though Queen Elizabeth I had an unhappy childhood, she overcame it to become one of England's most popular leaders. Today England's Queen Elizabeth II has also faced sad situations. Research her life and write a short essay comparing her life to the life of Elizabeth I.

WH7.11.2 Discuss the exchanges of plants, animals, technology, culture, and ideas among Europe, Africa, Asia, and the Americas in the fifteenth and sixteenth centuries and the major economic and social effects on each continent. **WH7.11.3** Examine the origins of modern capitalism; the influence of mercantilism and cottage industry; the elements and importance of a market economy in seventeenth-century Europe; the changing international trading and marketing patterns, including their locations on a world map; and the influence of explorers and map makers.

The Commercial Revolution

Main Idea To increase trade, Europeans set up colonies and created joint-stock companies.

Reading Connection Do you know anyone who works at home? Read to learn how merchants in the 1600s gave people jobs at home and changed the world trade system.

While Spain built its empire in America, Portugal began building a trading empire in Asia. In 1500, shortly after Vasco da Gama's trip, the Portuguese sent 13 ships back to India. Led by **Pedro Alvares Cabral** (PAY•throo AHL•vahr•ihs kuh•BRAHL), the Portuguese fought a war against the Muslim merchants in the Indian Ocean.

After defeating the Arab fleet, the Portuguese built trading posts in India, China, Japan, the Persian Gulf, and in the **Moluccas** (muh•LUH•kuhz), or Spice Islands of Southeast Asia. From these bases, they controlled most of southern Asia's sea trade.

What Is Mercantilism?
As Europeans watched Spain and Portugal grow wealthy from their empires, they tried to figure out how they had become rich. They came up with the idea of **mercantilism** (MUHR•kuhn•TUH•LIH•zuhm). Mercantilism is the idea that a country gains power by compiling a large supply of gold and silver.

Mercantilists believe the way to do this is to **export** (EHK•SPOHRT), or sell to other countries, more goods than you **import** (IHM•POHRT), or buy from them. If you export more than you import, more gold and silver flows in from other countries than goes out.

Mercantilists also thought countries should set up colonies. A **colony** (KAH•luh•nee) is a settlement of people living in a new territory controlled by their home country. Colonists are supposed to produce goods their country does not have at home. That

▲ **These ships sailed for the Dutch East India Company.** *Which European nation did the Dutch replace in the spice trade?*

way, the home country will not have to import those goods from other countries.

Trade Empires in Asia Mercantilism encouraged Europeans to set up trading posts and colonies in Asia and North America. By the end of the 1500s, Spain had set up a colony in the Philippines. The Spanish shipped silver to the Philippines from America and then used it to buy Asian spices and silk for sale in Europe.

In the 1600s, English and French merchants landed in India and began trading with the people there. In 1619 the Dutch built a fort on the island of Java, in what is now Indonesia. They slowly excluded the Portuguese from the spice trade.

What Are Joint-Stock Companies?
In the 1600s, new ways of doing business developed in Europe. Historians call this the "commercial revolution." **Commerce** (KAH•muhrs) is the buying and selling of goods in large amounts over long distances.

To trade long distance, merchants needed a lot of money. They had to buy goods, store them in warehouses, and transport them over land and sea. They had to know what people in distant lands wanted to buy and what prices were like there.

In other words, European merchants were making decisions based on the concept of supply and demand. Demand refers to what people want to buy and how much they are willing to pay for it. Supply refers to things people want to sell and the price at which they can afford to sell it.

If people want a certain good very much, the demand is high, and if there is very little of the good available, the price will be high too—because people will pay a lot of money to get it. If manufacturers make a lot of a particular good and people do not want it, the price will be low to get people to purchase the surplus.

Merchants usually tried to find goods that were cheap in one place and in high demand in another place. They then moved the goods from where they were cheap to where prices were high. This process enabled them to make a profit on the trade.

The rise of commerce created a new type of businessperson called an entrepreneur. Entrepreneurs **invest** (ihn•VEHST), or put money into a project. Their goal is to make even more money when the project is done.

Many projects were so large that a group of entrepreneurs had to come together and form a joint-stock company. A joint-stock company is a business that people can invest in by buying a share of the company. These shares are called stocks.

What Was Cottage Industry? To trade over a long distance, merchants need a large supply of goods. They also have to buy goods at low prices so they can make money selling them at higher prices.

By the 1600s, merchants had become frustrated with artisans who charged too

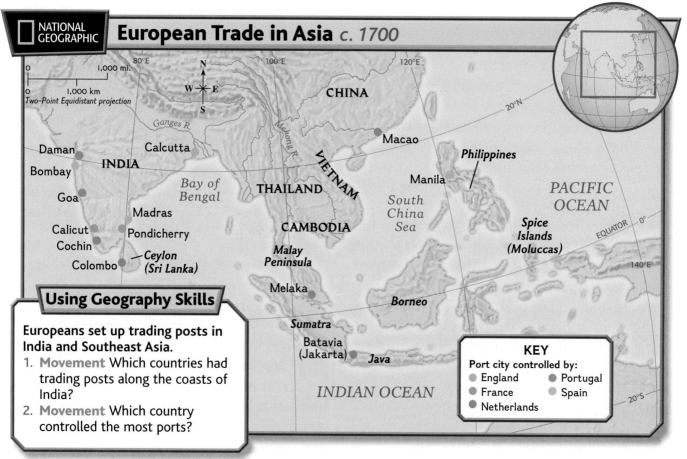

NATIONAL GEOGRAPHIC

European Trade in Asia *c.* 1700

Using Geography Skills

Europeans set up trading posts in India and Southeast Asia.

1. **Movement** Which countries had trading posts along the coasts of India?
2. **Movement** Which country controlled the most ports?

KEY
Port city controlled by:
- England
- France
- Netherlands
- Portugal
- Spain

much and worked too slowly. So merchants began asking peasants to make goods for them. In particular, they asked the peasants to make wool cloth.

The peasants were happy to make extra money and glad to find jobs they could do in their homes. Merchants would buy wool and give it to the peasants. This system is often called the "cottage industry," because the small houses where peasants lived were called cottages.

The rise of joint-stock companies and the cottage industry were important contributions to early capitalist society. **Capitalism** (KA•puh•tuhl•IHZ•uhm) is a system in which people, rather than governments, own property and make goods. Individuals and private companies owned by individuals decide what products to buy and sell.

Although these early ventures in capitalism were directed by individuals and companies, they were supported by governments. This was especially true in England and Holland, where merchants were particularly active in creating new commercial opportunities. Governments **anticipated** that helping entrepreneurs grow their business would bring in more tax money to the government. As a result, northern European seaports became very successful as trade expanded commercial opportunities.

By the mid-1600s, both England and Holland began supporting Jewish entrepreneurs. Many European Jews had become merchants because they were not allowed to own land. As you recall, many cities in Europe had expelled Jews during the Middle Ages. By allowing them to return to England and Holland, these countries benefited from the experience and wealth these Jewish entrepreneurs had to offer.

☑ Reading Check **Explain** How did merchants raise the money for overseas trade?

Study Central Need help understanding the commercial revolution? Visit ca.hss.glencoe.com and click on Study Central.

Section 2 Review

What Did You Learn?

1. What contributed to the fall of the Aztec and Incan people?

2. How did mercantilism lead to the establishment of colonies?

Critical Thinking

3. **Organizing Information** Use a graphic organizer like the one below to identify the causes of the commercial revolution. **CA CS2.**

Commercial Revolution

4. **The Big Ideas** What new economic ideas encouraged countries to build trade empires? **CA HI2.**

5. **Persuasive Writing** Write an essay in which you support or reject the decision by Queen Elizabeth I to use privateers to fight Spanish ships. **CA 7WA2.4**

6. **Analysis** **Economics Connection** How did joint-stock companies help merchants overcome the high costs of overseas trade? **CA HI6.**

Reading Summary

Review the Main Ideas

- The Spanish and Portuguese built large empires in the Americas where they used Native Americans and enslaved Africans to grow sugarcane and mine gold and silver.

- Europeans built trading posts in Asia following the ideas of mercantilism while a commercial revolution led to the rise of joint-stock companies and cottage industry.

You Decide . . .

 WH7.11.2 Discuss the exchanges of plants, animals, technology, culture, and ideas among Europe, Africa, Asia, and the Americas in the fifteenth and sixteenth centuries and the major economic and social effects on each continent.

Exploration and Trade: Good or Bad for the World?

Beginning in the 1400s, Europeans began exploring Africa, Asia, and the Americas and greatly increased their trade with other parts of the world. Was this exploration and trade good for the world?

Yes

Many historians and economists believe that European trade and exploration was good for the world. They argue that people in one part of the world often had solutions to problems that people in other parts of the world were still struggling to solve. Some of the major benefits and advantages of exploration and trade include the following:

- Exploration led to more accurate maps. This made travel safer and increased knowledge of the world's geography.

▼ **Columbus arriving in the Americas**

- Trade led to a sharing of technology. The Europeans obtained the compass, gunpowder, porcelain, and silk from Asia. The Asians received glass products, woolen cloth, wine, telescopes, and eyeglasses from Europe.

- Foods such as the potato from the Americas and rice from Asia helped reduce famine in the world. Salt from Africa helped preserve food so it could be shipped long distances.

- European ideas about democracy and individual rights eventually spread to the world and helped improve many societies.

- Trade produced more wealth for all societies involved. Although only a few people became rich, trade improved the standard of living for many people in each society.

- Exploration and trade brought more cultures into contact with each other. It increased people's knowledge of other people in the world. Although it took many centuries, this helped promote tolerance and acceptance of diversity.

▲ French explorers battling natives

No

While many historians and economists think that European exploration and trade was good for the world, many others argue that the problems and costs outweigh the benefits. Some of the major problems include the following:

- Exploration and trade spread many diseases to parts of the world where the people had no resistance. These diseases killed millions of people.

- Trade in sugarcane and exploration of Africa led to the rise of the European slave trade. Millions of Africans were enslaved and transported to the Americas to work on plantations.

- European ideas and technology greatly changed traditional societies in America, Asia, and Africa. Many people lost their traditional ways of life.

- European trade led to the rise of colonies and empires. Many local people were conquered by the Europeans and forced to work for European landowners.

- European colonies and trade changed the economy in many societies. Local people made goods for trade and no longer produced goods they needed for themselves.

One historian wrote:
"Just twenty-one years after Columbus' first landing in the Caribbean, the vastly populous island that the explorer had renamed Hispaniola was effectively desolate; nearly 8,000,000 people . . . had been killed by violence, disease, and despair. [W]hat happened on Hispaniola was the equivalent of more than fifty Hiroshimas. And Hispaniola was only the beginning."
—David E. Stannard, *American Holocaust*

What do you think? Did the Age of Exploration benefit the world or cause more problems than it solved?

You Be the Historian

Checking for Understanding

1. Which benefit from exploration and trade do you think is the most important? Explain your answer. **CA 7RC2.3**

2. What does Stannard mean when he compares the impact of Columbus's visit on Hispaniola to "more than fifty Hiroshimas"? **CA HR4.; HR5.**

3. What arguments would a European have used to defend exploration? What arguments would an Asian or African have made against it? Write two fictional narratives, one from a European viewpoint and one from an African or Asian viewpoint, that show the two sides. **CA 7WA2.1** **CA HR5.**

A Global Exchange

Guide to Reading

History Social Science Standards

WH7.11 Students analyze political and economic change in the sixteenth, seventeenth, and eighteenth centuries (the Age of Exploration, the Enlightenment, and the Age of Reason).

Looking Back, Looking Ahead

European exploration and trade led to an exchange of goods and ideas throughout the world. This had both positive and negative consequences.

Focusing on the Main Ideas

• Exploration and trade led to a worldwide exchange of products, people, and ideas.
(page 503)

• While the global exchange had a positive impact in many ways, it also created problems.
(page 504)

Locating Places

Argentina (AHR•juhn•TEE•nuh)
Great Plains
Caribbean (KAR•uh•BEE•uhn)

Content Vocabulary

Columbian Exchange
pampas (PAM•puhz)
East India Company
Dutch East India Company

Academic Vocabulary

transfer (trans•FUHR)
positive (PAH•zuh•tihv)

Reading Strategy

Organizing Information Create a chart like the one below showing the positive and negative effects of the global exchange.

The Global Exchange	
Positive Effects	Negative Effects

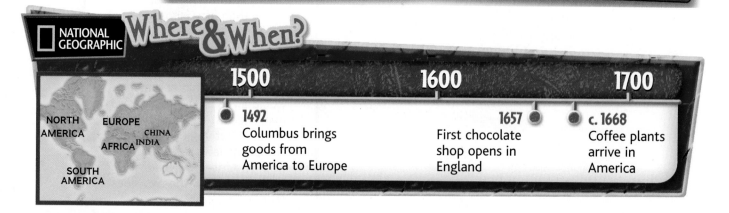

NATIONAL GEOGRAPHIC Where & When?

1500

1492
Columbus brings goods from America to Europe

1600

1657
First chocolate shop opens in England

1700

c. 1668
Coffee plants arrive in America

NORTH AMERICA EUROPE CHINA AFRICA INDIA SOUTH AMERICA

The Columbian Exchange

Main Idea Exploration and trade led to a worldwide exchange of products, people, and ideas.

Reading Connection Have you ever eaten rice or wheat bread? Neither rice nor wheat grew in America when Columbus arrived here. Read to learn how the movement of goods and people between America and the rest of the world caused great changes.

After the Age of Exploration, the economies of Europe, Africa, Asia, and America changed. As Europe traded with the world, a global exchange of people, goods, technology, ideas, and even diseases began. We call this **transfer** the **Columbian Exchange,** after Christopher Columbus who began it by bringing back goods from America to Europe in 1492.

Two important foods—corn and potatoes—were taken to Europe from North America. Corn was used to feed animals. Larger, healthier animals resulted in more meat, leather, and wool. The potato also had a significant impact. Europeans discovered that if they planted potatoes instead of grain, about four times as many people could live off the same amount of land.

Other American foods, such as squash, beans, and tomatoes, also made their way to Europe. Tomatoes greatly changed cooking in Italy, where tomato sauces became very popular. Chocolate was a popular food from Central America. By mixing it with milk and sugar, Europeans created a sweet that is still popular today. The first chocolate shop in England opened in 1657.

Some American foods, such as chili peppers and peanuts, were taken to Europe, but they also made their way to Asia and Africa where they became popular. Both Europeans and Asians also began smoking tobacco, an American plant.

Many European and Asian grains, such as wheat, oats, barley, rye, and rice, were planted in the Americas. Many tropical fruits, such as bananas, were brought to America, as was coffee. Coffee, which

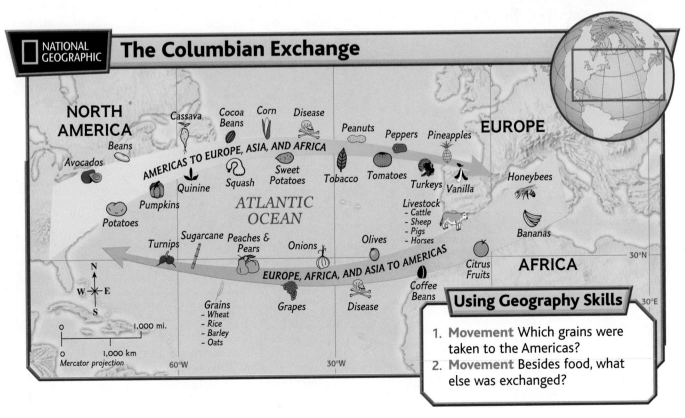

NATIONAL GEOGRAPHIC **The Columbian Exchange**

NORTH AMERICA

Cassava • Cocoa Beans • Corn • Disease • Beans • Avocados • Quinine • Squash • Sweet Potatoes • Pumpkins • Potatoes • Turnips • Sugarcane • Peaches & Pears • Onions

AMERICAS TO EUROPE, ASIA, AND AFRICA

ATLANTIC OCEAN

Peanuts • Peppers • Pineapples • EUROPE • Tobacco • Tomatoes • Turkeys • Vanilla • Honeybees • Livestock - Cattle - Sheep - Pigs - Horses • Bananas • Olives • Citrus Fruits • AFRICA • Coffee Beans

EUROPE, AFRICA, AND ASIA TO AMERICAS

Grains - Wheat - Rice - Barley - Oats • Grapes • Disease

N W E S

0   1,000 mi.
0   1,000 km
Mercator projection   60°W   30°W

30°N
30°E

Using Geography Skills

1. **Movement** Which grains were taken to the Americas?
2. **Movement** Besides food, what else was exchanged?

comes from southwest Asia, was first planted in the Americas about 1668. Eventually, large coffee and banana farms employed thousands of workers in Central and South America.

New animals, including pigs, sheep, cattle, and chickens, were brought to North America. The Europeans began raising cattle on the plains of North America and the **pampas** (PAM•puhz), or grassy plains, of **Argentina** (AHR•juhn•TEE•nuh). European horses changed the lives of Native Americans on the **Great Plains** of North America. Horses provided a faster way to move from place to place. As a result, Native Americans began hunting buffalo as their main food source.

The great exchange of food products dramatically increased the world's food supply. This, in turn, helped increase the world's population.

Reading Check **Describe** Describe the Columbian exchange.

Problems With the Exchange

Main Idea While the global exchange had a positive impact in many ways, it also created problems.

Reading Connection Have you heard about insects from other countries that hurt American crops? Read to learn how the global exchange created many new problems for people around the world.

Not everything exchanged between Europe and America was **positive.** You read earlier that Europeans carried germs that could kill Native Americans. European diseases caused widespread outbreaks in the Pacific islands as well. Between 1500 and 1800, historians estimate that as many as 100 million people died from European diseases.

In addition to disease, Europeans introduced new species of plants and animals. In some instances this hurt the local environment. Many species do not cause problems in their native habitat. However, when

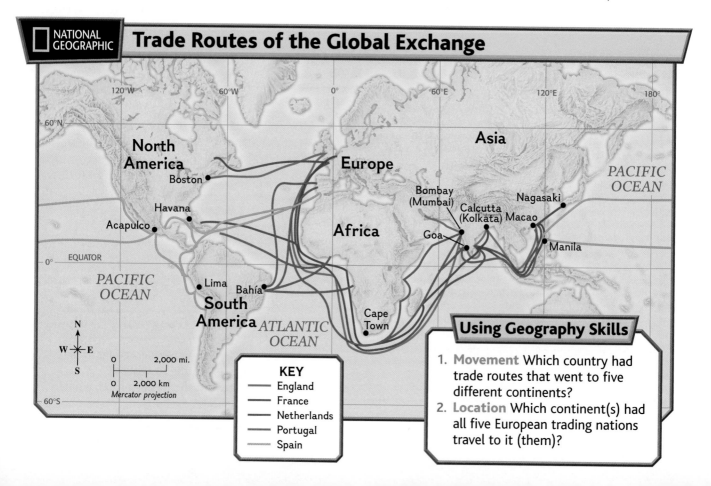

NATIONAL GEOGRAPHIC

Trade Routes of the Global Exchange

KEY
— England
— France
— Netherlands
— Portugal
— Spain

Using Geography Skills

1. **Movement** Which country had trade routes that went to five different continents?
2. **Location** Which continent(s) had all five European trading nations travel to it (them)?

introduced to a new region, some plants and animals can damage the area.

This problem still exists today. For example, in the early 2000s the Asian carp had escaped the ponds where it had been kept in the United States. It quickly grew out of control and threatened to overwhelm other fish species located along major rivers and lakes.

You have also read about the destruction that occurred among the Aztec and Inca following the Spanish conquests. Although the Spanish established new governments and new societies, their presence weakened or eliminated many native cultures.

European empires also caused a huge shift of people throughout the world. Many of them were colonists moving from Europe to America. Millions of people, however, were forcibly moved. After Europeans began growing sugarcane in the **Caribbean** (KAR•uh•BEE•uhn), they enslaved millions of Africans and moved them to the Americas.

Europeans also changed Asian society. With their guns and powerful ships, the Europeans easily defeated Arab fleets and Indian princes. Across Asia, the Europeans forced local rulers to let them set up trading posts. Within a short time, the **East India Company** of England had built an empire in India, and the **Dutch East India Company** had built an empire in Indonesia.

European contact with Japan also changed that society. Using guns and cannons imported from Europe, a new shogun was finally able to defeat the daimyo, or the feudal lords, and reunite Japan. In addition, Europeans spread their religion and their political and economic philosophies. This helped create unity and cooperation in many areas, especially those under European control.

✔ **Reading Check** **Explain** How did the global exchange create problems?

History Online

Study Central Need help understanding the global exchange? Visit ca.hss.glencoe.com and click on Study Central.

Section 3 Review

Reading Summary
Review the Main Ideas

• European exploration and trade brought about a global exchange of goods and other items, including plants, animals, technology, and diseases.

• While the global exchange had many positive effects on the world, it also caused many problems.

What Did You Learn?

1. Name two important foods that come from the Americas. Why were they important?

2. What sometimes happens when new plants and animals are introduced in an area?

Critical Thinking

3. **Organize Information** Draw a diagram showing items traded between Europe and the rest of the world. **CA 7RC2.2**

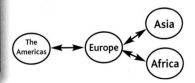

4. **The Big Ideas** Pick a food or good from the global exchange. Use your local library and the Internet to research how it spread around the world. **CA 7WA2.3**

5. **Analyze** How did foods imported from the Americas benefit Europe? Identify some of those foods. **CA 7RC2.0**

6. **Persuasive Writing** Write an essay explaining whether or not you think the Columbian Exchange was beneficial to the world. **CA 7WA2.4**

Analyzing Primary Sources

WH7.11.1 Know the great voyages of discovery, the locations of the routes, and the influence of cartography in the development of a new European worldview.

European Explorers

In the 1400s and 1500s, several European countries sent out explorers to map the world and find sea routes to Asia. They soon found a sea route around Africa to India and learned that two continents lay to the west across the Atlantic. With this knowledge, European goals changed. They began sending out ships to trade with Asia, to build empires, and to spread Christianity.

Read the passages on pages 506 and 507, and then answer the questions that follow.

▲ European explorers used caravels to travel the world.

Reader's Dictionary

conceive: gain

idolater (eye•DAH•luh•tuhr): person who worships idols

samorin: ambassador to the king

Columbus in America

On returning from his voyage to the Americas, Christopher Columbus wrote a letter describing the island of Hispañiola.

[The people of this island] refuse nothing that they possess, if it be asked of them; on the contrary, they invite any one to share it and display as much love as if they would give their hearts. They are content with whatever trifle of whatever kind that may be given to them, whether it be of value or valueless. I forbade that they should be given things so worthless as fragments of broken crockery, scraps of broken glass and lace tips, although when they were able to get them, they fancied that they possessed the best jewel in the world. So it was found that for a [leather strap] a sailor received gold to the weight of two and a half castellanos, and others received much more for other things which were worth less. . . . I gave them a thousand handsome good things, which I had brought, in order that they might **conceive** affection for us and, more than that, might become Christians and be inclined to the love and service of Your Highnesses [king and queen of Spain] . . . and strive to collect and give us of the things which they have in abundance and which are necessary to us.

They do not hold any creed nor are they **idolaters;** but they all believe that power and good are in the heavens and were very firmly convinced that I, with these ships and men, came from the heavens.

—The Journals of Christopher Columbus, Cecil Jane, trans.

Vasco da Gama in Africa

In 1497 King Manuel I of Portugal sent Vasco da Gama to find a sea route to India. Below, Da Gama describes the land of Mozambique in eastern Africa, where his fleet stopped briefly on the way to India.

"The men of the land are copper-colored, well-built, and follow the religion of Mohammed. They speak the language of the Moors. Their clothes are made of fine cotton and linen fabric with many brightly colored and richly embroidered stripes. . . . They are traders and do business with the white Moors, including four ships that were anchored at port and loaded with gold, silver, fabrics, nutmeg, pepper, ginger, silver rings adorned with many pearls, seed pearls, and rubies—things also worn by the men of this country. It appeared to us, according to what they told us, that all these things had been imported, that it was the Moors who brought them, except for the gold; and that farther on, in the direction we were heading, there was more. Stones, seed pearls, and spices were so abundant, they said, that it wasn't even necessary to barter for them: you could gather them by the basketful."

—Francois Bellec, *Unknown Lands*

Portugal's Empire

Vasco da Gama did indeed find India and returned to Portugal triumphant with his ships full of valuable goods. The Portuguese immediately set out to establish a trade empire based on the following plan.

"If Pedro Alvares Cabral does not manage to obtain the friendship and proof of loyalty from the *samorin* of Calicut, he should declare war and then pursue it. . . . [If] these people are so determined to follow their errors, by refusing to accept the words of the [true] Faith, denying the law of peace that must unite men and exist among them to conserve the human race, and creating obstacles and hindrances to the exercise of trade and exchange, we must then, by fire and sword, wage a cruel war. The captains have abundant and clear instructions on these points."

—Francois Bellec, *Unknown Lands*

Vasco da Gama ▶

DBQ Document-Based Questions

Columbus in America

1. List several of the most likely reasons that the natives of Hispaniola were so pleasant to the Spaniards.

2. How did the Spanish soldiers take advantage of the natives?

Vasco da Gama in Africa

3. What can you conclude about the economic status of the people of Mozambique? Explain.

4. After his visit to Mozambique, do you think da Gama wanted to continue on to find India? Why or why not?

Portugal's Empire

5. According to the Portuguese court, why do the people of Calicut deserve to have war waged against them?

Read to Write

6. The readings suggest that spreading religion was a reason for journeying to new lands, and for going to war. Based on these passages, do you think this was the main goal? Explain.
   CA HR4.

Review Content Vocabulary

Write the key term that completes each sentence in the blank.

a. export

b. astrolabe

c. Columbian Exchange

d. mercantilism

e. cartography

1. Rulers who supported _____ tried to get gold and build colonies.

2. European explorers used a(n) _____ to help them find latitude.

3. The art of mapmaking is _____.

4. Goods were traded from the Americas to Europe and back in the _____.

5. Wealthy traders wanted to _____ more than they imported.

Review the Main Ideas

Section 1 • Europe Explores the World

6. What caused Europeans to explore other parts of the world?

7. Which European nations were first to explore and conquer other parts of the world?

Section 2 • Trade and Empire

8. How were the Americas divided between Spain and Portugal?

9. How did the Europeans increase trade?

Section 3 • A Global Exchange

10. What new goods entered Europe after the establishment of the Columbian Exchange?

11. What were some of the problems with the global exchange?

Critical Thinking

12. **Analyze** Do you think the Portuguese or the Spanish found the better route to East Asia by sea? **CA 7RC2.0**

13. **Predict** How successful do you think the colonies would have been without the use of enslaved people? **CA HI2.**

14. **Making Connections** How did the introduction of horses into the Americas change the way the native people lived? Do you think this was a change for the better? Why or why not? **CA 7RC2.3**

Geography Skills

Study the map below and answer the following questions.

15. **Place** Which city in Europe was the first to receive the potato as part of the Columbian Exchange? **CA CS3.**

16. **Movement** Why do you think so much time passed before the potato arrived in Sweden and Finland? **CA CS3.**

17. **Movement** Does it appear from the map that trade between nations followed a strict pattern? Why or why not? **CA CS3.**

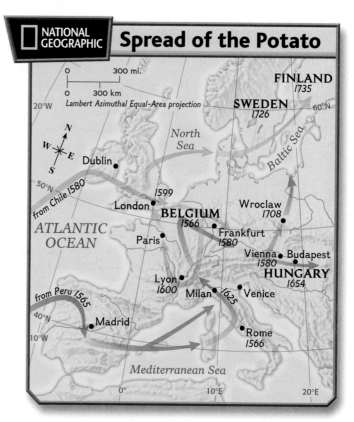

NATIONAL GEOGRAPHIC **Spread of the Potato**

0 — 300 mi.
0 — 300 km
Lambert Azimuthal Equal-Area projection

FINLAND 1735
SWEDEN 1726
Dublin
North Sea
Baltic Sea
from Chile 1580
London 1599
BELGIUM 1566
Wroclaw 1708
ATLANTIC OCEAN
Paris
Frankfurt 1580
Vienna 1580 Budapest
HUNGARY 1654
from Peru 1565
Lyon 1600
Milan 1625
Venice
Madrid
Rome 1566
Mediterranean Sea

Read to Write

18. **The Big Ideas** **Writing Research Reports**
Write a report describing the ideas and inventions European explorers used to map the world and establish the global exchange. How did the exchange of ideas shape the worldwide trade system? Use information from the text as well as other research to support your report. **CA 7WA2.3**

19. **Using Your FOLDABLES** Work with your classmates to create a quiz that tests your knowledge of the Age of Exploration. Use the information from your foldables to create questions about European exploration, trade and the building of empires, and the global exchange. **CA HR1.**

Using Academic Vocabulary

Replace each of the underlined words with the word that best fits in its place.

20. It is not always easy to <u>locate</u> something that you have lost.
    a. forget   b. find   c. remember

21. His <u>primary</u> job as a chef was to make people dinner.
    a. main   b. only   c. easiest

22. The Red Cross offers <u>aid</u> to sick and hurt people.
    a. medicine   b. help   c. money

23. He reacted <u>positively</u> when he received an A on the test.
    a. sadly   b. eagerly   c. happily

Economic Connections

24. **Summarizing** Write a detailed summary describing the development of the economic systems that helped to increase trade and profit in Europe. **CA 7WA2.5**

Reviewing Skills

25. **Analysis Skill** **Understanding Problems and Solutions** Write a brief essay describing the problems facing Europeans in the 1400s and how they overcame those problems through inventions and exploration. The essay should trace the development of exploration and trade from the 1400s to the global exchange of the 1600s. **CA H11.**

26. **Reading Skill** **Monitoring** Write five questions you would ask to help you better understand the information in the following paragraph. **CA 7RC2.0** **CA HR1.**

> To help the Dutch, Queen Elizabeth I of England let English privateers attack Spanish ships. Privateers are privately owned ships that have a license from the government to attack ships of other countries. People nicknamed the English privateers "sea dogs." They raided the Spanish treasure ships that were bringing gold back from America.

—from page 495

Standards Practice

Use the map below to answer the following question.

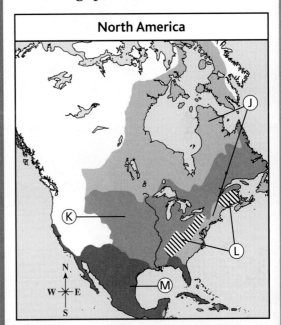

North America

27 **The Spanish controlled which area of North America by 1750?**

A J

B K

C L

D M

The Age of Enlightenment

◀ A statue of Louis XIV on horseback outside of the palace of Versailles in France

NATIONAL GEOGRAPHIC Where & When?

1650	1700	1750	1800

1687
Isaac Newton states laws about motion and gravity

1690
John Locke writes about people's rights

1748
Montesquieu describes separation of powers

1776
Declaration of Independence is signed

The Big Ideas

History Online
Chapter Overview Visit ca.hss.glencoe.com for a preview of Chapter 11.

Section 1 The Scientific Revolution

Studying the past helps to understand the present. Scientific ideas and discoveries gave Europeans a new way to understand the universe.

Section 2 The Ideas of the Enlightenment

Systems of order, such as law and government, contribute to stable societies. During the 1700s, many Europeans believed that reason could be used to make government and society better.

Section 3 Politics and the Enlightenment

Studying the past helps to understand the present. The ideas of the Enlightenment played a role in both the American Revolution and the French Revolution, and brought about many other changes that still affect our world today.

 View the Chapter 11 video in the Glencoe Video Program.

Organizing Information *Make this foldable to help you compare and contrast the ideas of the Scientific Revolution and the Enlightenment.*

Step 1 *Fold a sheet of paper in half from side to side.*

Fold it so the left edge is about $\frac{1}{2}$ inch from the right edge.

Step 2 *Turn the paper and fold it into thirds.*

Step 3 *Unfold and cut the top layer only along both folds.*

This will make three tabs.

Step 4 *Label as shown.*

The Age of Enlightenment
Science | New Ideas | Politics

Reading and Writing *As you read the chapter, write notes under each appropriate tab of your foldable. Be sure to use main ideas and key terms to help you organize your notes.*

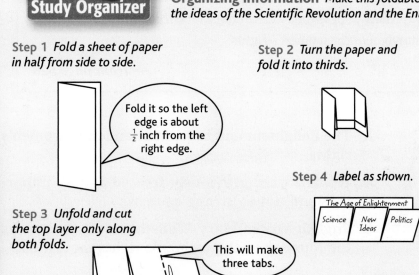

Taking Notes

1 Learn It!

The best way for you to remember information is to write it down, or take notes. Good note-taking is useful for studying and research. When you are taking notes, it is helpful to:

- phrase the information in your own words
- restate ideas in short, memorable phrases
- stay focused on main ideas and only the most important supporting details

See the example of note-taking using the paragraph below.

> (A) The Enlightenment raised questions about the role of women in society. Previously, many male thinkers claimed that women were less important than men and had to be controlled and protected. By the 1700s, however, women thinkers began calling for women's rights. The most powerful supporter of women's rights was the English writer Mary Wollstonecraft. . . . Many people today credit her as the founder of the modern movement for women's rights. (B) (C)
>
> — *from page 529*

Reading Tip

Finish reading before you begin taking notes.

A. The Enlightenment brought attention to women's rights.

B. Women were previously treated as less important and not as strong as men.

C. English writer Mary Wollstonecraft is seen as the founder of the women's rights movement.

2 Practice It!

Make note-taking easier by using a chart to help you organize information clearly. Write the main ideas in the left column. Then write at least two supporting details for each main idea in the right column. Read the text from Section 1 of this chapter under the heading **The Scientific Revolution,** pages 515–517. Then take notes using a chart, such as the one below.

pages 515–517

Read to Write ·····

Choose an important scientist, philosopher, or thinker from the chapter. Do further research, using at least three sources and taking notes as you read. Use your notes to write a brief report.

Main Idea	Supporting Details
	1.
	2.
	3.
	4.
	5.
	1.
	2.
	3.
	4.
	5.

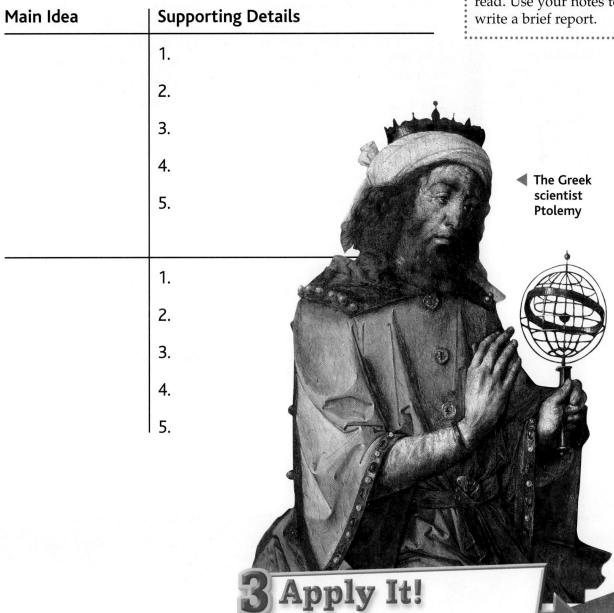

◀ The Greek scientist Ptolemy

3 Apply It!

As you read this chapter, make a chart with important dates, names, places, and events as main ideas. Under each main idea, list at least two supporting details from your reading.

The Scientific Revolution

Guide to Reading

History Social Science Standards

WH7.10 Students analyze the historical developments of the Scientific Revolution and its lasting effect on religious, political, and cultural institutions.

Looking Back, Looking Ahead

One result of the Renaissance was a new interest in science. During the 1600s, people began to observe, experiment, and reason to find new knowledge.

Focusing on the Main Ideas

- The thinkers of the ancient world developed early forms of science and passed this knowledge to later civilizations. *(page 515)*

- European interest in astronomy led to new discoveries and ideas about the universe and Earth's place in it. *(page 517)*

- The Scientific Revolution led to new discoveries in physics, medicine, and chemistry. *(page 519)*

- Using the scientific method, Europeans of the 1600s and 1700s developed new ideas about society based on reason. *(page 522)*

Meeting People
Ptolemy (TAH•luh•mee)
Copernicus (koh•PUHR•nih•kuhs)
Kepler (KEH•pluhr)
Galileo (GA•luh•LEE•oh)
Newton (NOO•tuhn)
Descartes (day•KAHRT)

Content Vocabulary
theory (THEE•uh•ree)
rationalism (RASH•nuh•LIH•zuhm)
scientific method
hypothesis (hy•PAH•thuh•suhs)

Academic Vocabulary
investigate (ihn•VEHS•tuh•GAYT)
approach (uh•PROHCH)

Reading Strategy
Compare and Contrast Use a diagram like the one below to show the similarities and differences in the views of Ptolemy and Copernicus.

Ptolemy   Copernicus

NATIONAL GEOGRAPHIC **Where & When?**

1500	1600	1700
1543 Copernicus supports sun-centered solar system	**1632** Galileo publishes work supporting Copernicus's ideas	**1687** Isaac Newton states laws about motion and gravity

London
Paris
Florence
Rome

The Scientific Revolution

Main Idea The thinkers of the ancient world developed early forms of science and passed this knowledge to later civilizations.

Reading Connection Have you ever taught a skill or passed on an idea to a younger brother or sister? Read in this chapter how the scientific ideas of early thinkers were passed on to later generations.

From earliest times, people have been curious about the world around them. Thousands of years ago, people began to use numbers, study the stars and planets, and watch the growth of plants and animals. These activities were the beginnings of science. Science is any organized study of the natural world and how it works.

Early Scientists
Early civilizations developed different kinds of science to solve practical problems. Among the first sciences were mathematics, astronomy, and medicine. Mathematics was used for record keeping and building projects. Astronomy helped people keep time and figure out when to plant and harvest crops. Early civilizations also developed medical practices, such as surgery, acupuncture, and the use of herbs, for treating illnesses.

The ancient Greeks left behind a large amount of scientific knowledge. They believed that reason was the only way to understand nature. As they studied the world, they developed theories. A **theory** (THEE•uh•ree) is an explanation of how or why something happens. A theory is based on what you can observe about something. It may not be correct, but it seems to fit the facts.

In ancient Greece, the Greek philosopher Aristotle observed nature and compiled vast amounts of information about plants, animals, and the environment. He then took the facts he gathered and classified them, or arranged them into groups, based on their similarities and differences.

The Greeks made many important scientific advances, but their approach to science had some problems. For example, they did not experiment, or test, new ideas to see if they were true. Many of their conclusions were false because they were based on "common sense" instead of experiments.

For example, in the A.D. 100s, the Egyptian-born astronomer **Ptolemy** (TAH•luh•mee) stated that the sun and the planets moved around the earth in circular paths. After all, it did seem like the earth was the center of the universe. Astronomers in Europe accepted Ptolemy's geocentric, or Earth-centered, theory for more than 1,400 years.

Science During the Middle Ages
In Roman times, people continued to accept the scientific knowledge of the Greeks. During the Middle Ages, most Europeans were more interested in theology, or the study of God, than in the study of nature. For scientific knowledge, they relied on Greek and Roman writings and saw no need to **investigate** the facts or to make their own observations. Many of these ancient works, however, were either lost or poorly preserved.

Meanwhile, Arabs and Jews in the Islamic Empire preserved much of the science of the Greeks and Romans. They carefully copied many Greek and Roman works into the Arabic language. They also came into contact with the science of the Persians and the Indian system of mathematics.

Arabic and Jewish scientists made advances of their own in areas such as mathematics, astronomy, and medicine. However, in spite of these achievements, scientists in the Islamic world did not experiment or develop the instruments necessary to advance their scientific knowledge.

During the 1100s, European thinkers became involved in science again as a result of their contacts with the Islamic world. Major Islamic scientific works were brought to Europe and translated into Latin. The Hindu-Arabic system of numbers also spread to Europe, where it eventually replaced Roman numerals.

Christian thinkers, such as Thomas Aquinas, tried to show that Christianity and reason could go together. During the 1100s, Europeans began building new universities. These universities would play an important role in the growth of science.

As you have read, in the 1300s the ideas of the Renaissance humanists developed into a new way of understanding the world. Humanists borrowed ideas from the ancient Greeks and Romans and combined them with ideas based on reason and ideas based on faith.

Humanist ideas then spread across Europe, aided by the invention of the printing press. This invention continued to play an important role in spreading ideas during the 1600s and 1700s.

In the meantime, the humanist **approach** to science and reason led to other inventions during the Renaissance. These helped bring about the Age of Exploration that you read about in Chapter 10. Better charts, maps, and navigational instruments helped explorers reach different parts of the world in the 1400s and 1500s.

A New View of the Universe

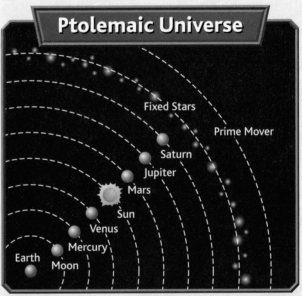

Ptolemaic Universe

Fixed Stars

Prime Mover

Saturn

Jupiter

Mars

Sun

Venus

Mercury

Earth Moon

The astronomical theory of Ptolemy (left) placed Earth at the center of the universe (above). His theory was accepted for more than a thousand years. *According to the diagram, how many planets besides Earth were known at the time of Ptolemy?*

WH7.10.1 Discuss the roots of the Scientific Revolution (e.g., Greek rationalism; Jewish, Christian, and Muslim science; Renaissance humanism; new knowledge from global exploration). **WH7.10.2** Understand the significance of the new scientific theories (e.g., those of Copernicus, Galileo, Kepler, Newton) and the significance of new inventions (e.g., the telescope, microscope, thermometer, barometer).

The voyages of exploration helped Europe become the world leader in commerce and trade. They also added to Europe's scientific knowledge. Explorers mapped the oceans and continents, and new kingdoms and countries were located. Scientists gathered and classified new knowledge about plants, animals, and diseases in different parts of the world.

By the 1500s, various developments in Europe had come together to increase European interest in science. As more and more people began to study science, many new discoveries were made. This era, when Europeans became interested in science again, is known as the Scientific Revolution.

✓ **Reading Check** **Describe** Describe scientific knowledge during the Middle Ages.

A Revolution in Astronomy

Main Idea European interest in astronomy led to new discoveries and ideas about the universe and Earth's place in it.

Reading Connection What would people on Earth think if life were discovered on other planets? Read to see how Europeans reacted to new discoveries about the universe.

During the 1500s, European thinkers began to abandon the old scientific ideas. They increasingly understood that advances in science could only come through mathematics and experimentation. This new way of thinking led to a revolution, or sweeping change, in the way Europeans understood science and the search for knowledge. Astronomy was the first science affected by

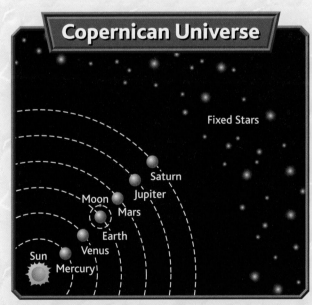

Copernican Universe

Fixed Stars

Saturn
Jupiter
Moon
Mars
Earth
Venus
Sun
Mercury

Nicolaus Copernicus (right), a Polish mathematician, believed that the sun was at the center of the universe. His model (above) placed Earth and the other planets in orbits around the sun. *Why did Europeans again become interested in science in the 1100s?*

the Scientific Revolution. New discoveries brought changes in the way Europeans saw the universe. They challenged traditional thinking that God had made the earth as the center of the universe.

Who Was Copernicus? Leading the Scientific Revolution was a Polish mathematician named Nicolaus **Copernicus** (koh•PUHR•nih•kuhs). In 1543 Copernicus released a book called *On the Revolutions of the Heavenly Spheres.* He disagreed with Ptolemy's view that the earth was the center of the universe. Copernicus believed that Ptolemy's theory

was too complicated. Instead, he developed a simpler heliocentric, or sun-centered, theory of the universe. Copernicus's theory stated that the Sun, not Earth, was the center of the universe. The planets moved in circular paths around the Sun.

Kepler's Revolution The next step forward in astronomy was taken by a German astronomer named Johannes **Kepler** (KEH•pluhr). He supported Copernicus's theory but also made corrections to it. Kepler added the idea that the planets move in ellipses (ih•LIHP•SEEZ), or oval paths, rather than circular

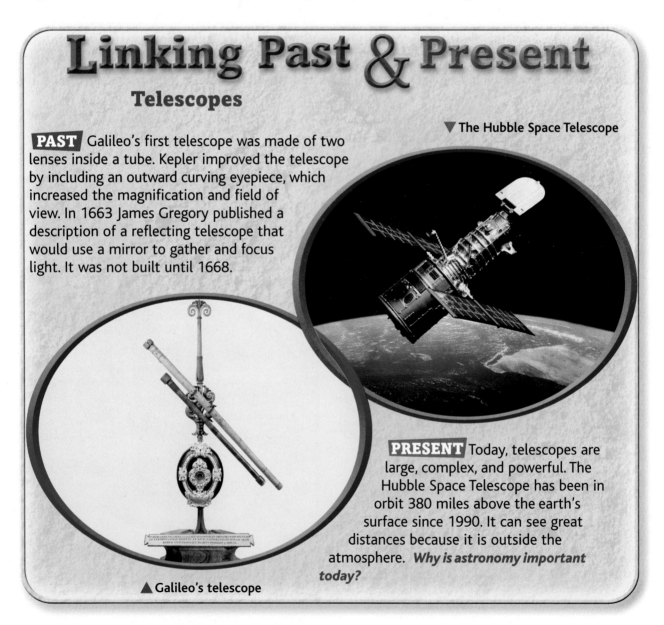

Linking Past & Present

Telescopes

PAST Galileo's first telescope was made of two lenses inside a tube. Kepler improved the telescope by including an outward curving eyepiece, which increased the magnification and field of view. In 1663 James Gregory published a description of a reflecting telescope that would use a mirror to gather and focus light. It was not built until 1668.

▼ The Hubble Space Telescope

PRESENT Today, telescopes are large, complex, and powerful. The Hubble Space Telescope has been in orbit 380 miles above the earth's surface since 1990. It can see great distances because it is outside the atmosphere. *Why is astronomy important today?*

▲ Galileo's telescope

WH7.10.2 Understand the significance of the new scientific theories (e.g., those of Copernicus, Galileo, Kepler, Newton) and the significance of new inventions (e.g., the telescope, microscope, thermometer, barometer).

ones. His theory made it easier to explain the movements of the planets. It also marked the beginning of modern astronomy.

Who Was Galileo? An Italian scientist named Galileo Galilei made the third great breakthrough in the Scientific Revolution. **Galileo** (GA•luh•LEE•oh) believed that new knowledge could come through experiments that were carefully carried out. For example, Galileo challenged Aristotle's idea that the heavier the object is, the faster it falls to the ground. Galileo's experiments proved that Aristotle was wrong. Objects fall at the same speed regardless of their weight.

Galileo also realized that scientific instruments could help humans better explore the natural world. He improved instruments, such as the clock and telescope. With the telescope, Galileo found clear evidence supporting Copernicus's view that Earth revolves around the Sun.

Galileo also played an important role in the development of new scientific instruments. In 1593 he invented a water thermometer that, for the first time, allowed temperature changes to be measured. Galileo's assistant, Evangelista Torricelli, then used the element called mercury to build the first barometer, an instrument that measures air pressure.

When Galileo published his ideas in 1632, his work was condemned by the Roman Catholic Church. The Catholic Church held to the geocentric, or Earth-centered, view of the universe, believing that it was taught in the Bible. The pope ordered Galileo to come to Rome to be tried for heresy. Church threats finally forced Galileo to withdraw many of his statements. Nonetheless, Galileo's ideas spread throughout Europe and changed people's views about the universe.

✓ **Reading Check** **Explain** How did Galileo prove Copernicus's theory?

New Scientific Discoveries

Main Idea The Scientific Revolution led to new discoveries in physics, medicine, and chemistry.

Reading Connection Think about all the facts you know about medicine. For example, you know your heart pumps blood, your lungs breathe air, and your body is made of cells. Read to learn how scientists of the 1600s and 1700s made discoveries we often take for granted today.

Throughout the 1600s and 1700s, the Scientific Revolution continued to spread. Many new discoveries were made in physics, medicine, and chemistry.

Who Is Isaac Newton? Despite continuing scientific breakthroughs, the ideas of Copernicus, Kepler, and Galileo needed to be brought together as one system. This feat was accomplished by an English mathematician named Isaac **Newton** (NOO•tuhn).

According to tradition, Newton was sitting in his garden one day when he watched an apple fall to the ground. The

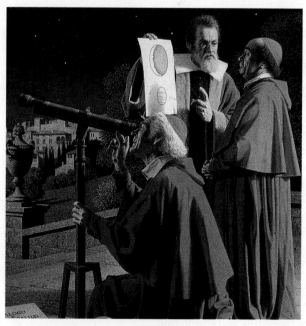

▲ In this painting, Galileo presents his astronomical findings to the Catholic clergy. *How did Galileo respond to the Church's condemnation of his work in astronomy?*

CHAPTER 11 • The Age of Enlightenment   **519**

apple's fall led him to the idea of gravity, or the pull of the earth and other bodies on objects at or near their surfaces.

In a book called *Principia*, published in 1687, Newton stated his laws, or well-tested theories, about the motion of objects in space and on Earth. The most significant was the universal law of gravitation. It explains that the force of gravity holds the entire solar system together by keeping the sun and the planets in their orbits. Newton's ideas led to the rise of modern physics, or the study of physical properties such as matter and energy.

Medicine and Chemistry Sweeping changes were made in medicine in the 1500s and 1600s. Since Roman times, European doctors had relied on the teachings of the Greek physician Galen. Galen wanted to study the human body, but he was only allowed to dissect, or cut open, animals.

In the 1500s, however, a Flemish doctor named Andreas Vesalius began dissecting dead human bodies for research. In 1543 Vesalius published *On the Structure of the Human Body*. In this work, Vesalius presented a detailed account of the human body that replaced many of Galen's ideas.

Other breakthroughs in medicine took place. In the early 1600s, William Harvey, an English doctor, proved that blood flowed through the human body. In the mid-1600s, an English scientist named Robert Hooke began using a microscope, and he soon discovered cells, the smallest structures of living material.

Beginning in the 1600s, European scientists developed new ideas in chemistry. Chemistry is the study of natural substances and how they change. In the mid-1600s, Robert Boyle, an Irish scientist, proved that all substances are made up of basic elements that cannot be broken down.

European scientists of the 1700s also developed ways to study gases. They discovered hydrogen, carbon dioxide, and oxygen. By 1777, Antoine Lavoisier (AN•twahn luhv•WAH•zee•AY) of France had proven that materials need oxygen to burn. Marie Lavoisier, also a scientist, contributed to her husband's work.

✓ Reading Check **Identify** According to Newton, what force held the planets in orbit?

The Scientific Revolution

Scientist	Nation	Discoveries
Nicolaus Copernicus (1473–1543)	Poland	Earth orbits the Sun; Earth spins on its axis
Galileo Galilei (1564–1642)	Italy	other planets have moons
Johannes Kepler (1571–1630)	Germany	planets have elliptical orbits
William Harvey (1578–1657)	England	heart pumps blood
Robert Hooke (1635–1703)	England	cells
Robert Boyle (1627–1691)	Ireland	air is made of gases
Isaac Newton (1642–1727)	England	gravity; laws of motion; calculus
Antoine Lavoisier (1743–1794)	France	how materials burn

Understanding Charts

During the Scientific Revolution, scientists made discoveries in many fields, such as astronomy and medicine.
1. What did William Harvey discover?
2. **Identify** Which scientists' discoveries dealt with chemistry?

History Online

Web Activity Visit ca.hss.glencoe.com and click on *Chapter 11—Student Web Activity* to learn more about early science.

Biography

WH7.10.2 Understand the significance of the new scientific theories (e.g., those of Copernicus, Galileo, Kepler, Newton) and the significance of new inventions (e.g., the telescope, microscope, thermometer, barometer).

SIR ISAAC NEWTON
1642–1727

Isaac Newton was born into a farming family on December 25, 1642, in Woolsthorpe, England. His father died before Newton was born. His mother remarried when he was three years old. His new stepfather did not want the boy to live with them, so Newton's grandmother raised him.

Newton earned a degree from Trinity College, part of Cambridge University, in 1664. He planned to work for the university, but from 1664 to 1666, it closed because of the plague. Newton spent the next two years in his hometown. While there, he developed his theory of gravity, invented a new kind of mathematics called calculus, and discovered that white light is made up of all other colors of light.

Newton returned to Cambridge, earned a master's degree, and was appointed to several positions there. His life was very stressful because many scientists questioned his calculations. These criticisms made Newton reluctant to publish his discoveries, but eventually he did. His book *Principia* is considered one of the greatest scientific books ever written. In it, Newton describes his three laws of motion and his ideas about gravity.

During his life, Newton won many awards for his discoveries. In 1705 he became the first scientist ever to be knighted by the English king.

▲ Newton analyzing light rays

> **"If I have seen farther, it is by standing upon the shoulders of giants."**
> –Isaac Newton, in a letter to Robert Hooke

▲ Trinity College today

Then and Now

Newton's findings were criticized by some scientists of his time. Do research to find a scientific discovery made in the last 50 years that others have questioned or criticized. Describe your findings to the class.

The Triumph of Reason

Main Idea Using the scientific method, Europeans of the 1600s and 1700s developed new ideas about society based on reason.

Reading Connection What do modern scientists do in their laboratories? Read to understand how methods of scientific research changed Europeans' understanding of human society in the 1600s and 1700s.

As scientists made new discoveries, European thinkers began to apply science to society. For these thinkers, science had proven that the physical universe followed natural laws. By using their reason, people could learn how the universe worked. Using this knowledge, people also could solve existing human problems and make life better.

Descartes and Reason One of the most important scientific thinkers was the Frenchman René **Descartes** (day•KAHRT). In 1637 he wrote a book called *Discourse on Method*. In this book, Descartes began with the problem of knowing what is true. To Descartes, one fact seemed to be beyond doubt—his own existence. Descartes clarified this idea by the phrase, "I think, therefore I am."

In his work, Descartes claimed that mathematics was the source of all scientific truth. In mathematics, he said, the answers were always true. This was because mathematics began with simple, obvious principles and then used logic to move gradually to other truths. Today, Descartes is viewed as the founder of modern **rationalism** (RASH•nuh•LIH•zuhm). This is the belief that reason is the chief source of knowledge.

What Is the Scientific Method?

Scientific thought was also influenced by English thinker Francis Bacon, who lived from 1561 to 1626. Bacon believed that ideas based on tradition should be put aside. He developed the **scientific method**, an orderly way of collecting and analyzing evidence. It is still the process used in scientific research today.

The scientific method is made up of several steps. First a scientist begins with careful observation of facts and then tries to find a **hypothesis** (hy•PAH•thuh•suhs), or an explanation of the facts. Through experiments, the scientist tests the hypothesis under all possible conditions to see if it is true. Finally, if repeated, experiments show that the hypothesis is true, and then it is considered a scientific law.

Struggles of Faith Because the Scientific Revolution led many people to rely more on reason than faith, it diminished the power and influence of Christian churches. This was particularly true with the Roman Catholic Church. However, Christianity did not cease to exist. Missionaries continued to

The Microscope

- Eyepiece
- Lenses
- Light source
- Focusing screw
- Specimen holder

▲ An early microscope used by Robert Hooke to discover cells

gain converts throughout the world, and church membership continued to increase in many areas.

Although scientists supported reason as a way of gaining knowledge, many continued to believe in God. They argued that God had created the universe according to mathematical laws. God then allowed the universe to run itself by these laws. This religious approach is called deism.

Isaac Newton was foremost among the deist scientists. He believed that God had created natural laws that could not be explained in any other way. For example, he believed that the force of gravity was a scientific law. However, he believed it could not exist unless God had made it. In this way, religion coexisted with reason during the Scientific Revolution.

Reading Check **Explain** What is the scientific method?

The Scientific Method

Observe some aspect of the universe.

↓

Hypothesize about what you observed.

↓

Predict something based on your hypothesis.

↓

Test your predictions through experiments and observation.

↓

Modify hypothesis in light of results.

Understanding Charts

The scientific method is still important today.
1. What is the next step after predictions are tested through experiments and observation?
2. **Conclude** Why is the scientific method necessary to create scientific law?

History Online

Study Central Need help understanding the Scientific Revolution? Visit ca.hss.glencoe.com and click on Study Central.

Section 1 Review

Reading Summary

Review the Main Ideas

- The thinkers of the ancient world developed early forms of science and passed this knowledge to later generations.

- European interest in science led to new discoveries and ideas about the universe and Earth's place in it.

- The Scientific Revolution led to new discoveries in physics, medicine, and chemistry.

- Descartes invented rationalism, and Bacon developed the scientific method.

What Did You Learn?

1. Who was Copernicus, and what was the heliocentric theory?

2. Describe Francis Bacon's beliefs about scientific reasoning.

Critical Thinking

3. **Summarize** Draw a diagram like the one below. Add details to show some of the new ideas developed during the Scientific Revolution. **CA 7RC2.0**

Ideas From Scientific Revolution

4. **Science Connection** Explain Kepler's view of the solar system. **CA 7RC2.2**

5. **Analyze** Why did the Church condemn Galileo's astronomical findings? **CA 7RC2.2**

6. **The Big Ideas** Write an essay describing how astronomy changed from the time of Ptolemy to the time of Galileo. **CA 7RC2.3**

7. **Reading** Taking Notes List the main ideas in Section 1 and take notes on them. Use these notes to write a short essay on the section. **CA 7WS1.3**

The Ideas of the Enlightenment

Guide to Reading

 **History Social Science Standards**

WH7.10 Students analyze the historical developments of the Scientific Revolution and its lasting effect on religious, political, and cultural institutions.

WH7.11 Students analyze political and economic change in the sixteenth, seventeenth, and eighteenth centuries (the Age of Exploration, the Enlightenment, and the Age of Reason).

Looking Back, Looking Ahead

As you have read, the Scientific Revolution led to new discoveries. At the same time, it also led to many new ideas about government and society.

Focusing on the Main Ideas

• During the 1700s, many Europeans believed that reason could be used to make government and society better. *(page 525)*

• The Enlightenment was centered in France, where thinkers wrote about changing their society and met to discuss their ideas. *(page 528)*

Meeting People

Thomas Hobbes (HAHBZ)

John Locke

Baron Montesquieu (MAHN•tuhs• KYOO)

Voltaire (vohl•TAR)

Denis Diderot (dee•DROH)

Mary Wollstonecraft (WUL•stuhn• KRAFT)

Content Vocabulary

natural law

social contract

separation of powers

Academic Vocabulary

error (EHR•uhr)

topic (TAH•pihk)

advocate (AD•vuh•kuht)

Reading Strategy

Summarizing Information Complete a table like the one below showing the major ideas of Enlightenment thinkers.

Thinkers	Ideas

NATIONAL GEOGRAPHIC **Who & When?**

1700

1690 John Locke writes about people's rights

1750

1748 Montesquieu describes separation of powers

1800

1792 Mary Wollstonecraft calls for women's rights

WH7.10.3 Understand the scientific method advanced by Bacon and Descartes, the influence of new scientific rationalism on the growth of democratic ideas, and the coexistence of science with traditional religious beliefs. WH7.11.4 Explain how the main ideas of the Enlightenment can be traced back to such movements as the Renaissance, the Reformation, and the Scientific Revolution and to the Greeks, Romans, and Christianity. WH7.11.5 Describe how democratic thought and institutions were influenced by Enlightenment thinkers (e.g., John Locke, Charles-Louis Montesquieu, American founders). WH7.11.6 Discuss how the principles in the Magna Carta were embodied in such documents as the English Bill of Rights and the American Declaration of Independence.

New Ideas About Politics

Main Idea During the 1700s, many Europeans believed that reason could be used to make government and society better.

Reading Connection What makes people get along with each other? Do they need rules, a strong leader, or to learn to work together? Read to learn how thinkers in Europe answered these questions.

During the 1700s, European thinkers were impressed by scientific discoveries in the natural world. They believed that reason could also uncover the scientific laws that governed human life. Once these laws were known, thinkers said, people could use the laws to make society better.

As the Scientific Revolution advanced, many educated Europeans came to believe that reason was a much better guide than faith or tradition. To them, reason was a "light" that revealed **error** and showed the way to truth. As result, the 1700s became known as the Age of Enlightenment.

European thinkers during the Enlightenment believed they were entering a new era of thought and ideas. Even so, they knew that many of their ideas came from older traditions. The Greeks had looked at nature and seen patterns that could be observed. Greek philosophers, such as Plato, Aristotle, and Socrates, had all stressed reason and analysis. The Enlightenment thinkers were also influenced by the Romans. Many laws and ideas of government had come from the Romans, who had emphasized systems of order.

The use of reason during the Renaissance and the critical thinking of religious writers during the Reformation had helped bring about the Scientific Revolution. In turn, the Renaissance, Reformation, and Scientific

▲ This illustration is from the title page of Hobbes's *Leviathan*. *What sort of government did Hobbes support in* Leviathan?

Revolution helped bring about the Enlightenment. Christianity also played a role in shaping Enlightenment ideas. Some writers during the Enlightenment rejected Christianity. They compared their own methods for gaining knowledge to religion in order to determine which method they thought worked best.

During the Enlightenment, political thinkers tried to apply reason and scientific ideas to government. They claimed that there was a **natural law,** or a law that applied to everyone and could be understood by reason. As early as the 1600s, two English thinkers—Thomas Hobbes and John Locke—used natural law to develop very different ideas about how government should work.

Who Was Thomas Hobbes? Thomas
Hobbes (HAHBZ) wrote about English government and society. During his life, England was torn apart by civil war. Supporters of King Charles I fought those who backed

The Separation of Powers

The ideas of the French writer Baron Montesquieu were influential in shaping British and American ideas about government.

▲ Montesquieu

"Again, there is no liberty, if the judiciary power be not separated from the legislative and executive. Were it joined with the legislative, the life and liberty of the subject would be exposed to arbitrary control; for the judge would be then the legislator. Were it joined to the executive power, the judge might behave with violence and oppression."

—Montesquieu, *The Spirit of Laws*

DBQ Document-Based Question

According to Montesquieu, why should judges be independent?

---

they needed to obey a government that had the power of a leviathan, or sea monster. To Hobbes, this meant the rule of a king because only a strong ruler could give people direction.

Why Is John Locke Important? Another English thinker, **John Locke,** contradicted Hobbes. Locke used natural law to affirm basic democratic ideas such as citizens' rights and the need for government to be answerable to the people.

During Locke's life, another English king, James II, wanted to set up an absolute monarchy against Parliament's wishes. In 1688 war threatened, and James fled the country. Parliament then asked Mary, James's daughter, and her husband, William, to take the throne. This event came to be called the "Glorious Revolution."

In return for the English throne, William and Mary agreed to a Bill of Rights. The document guaranteed all English people basic rights, like those the Magna Carta had given to the nobles. For instance, people had the right to a fair trial by jury and to freedom from cruel punishment for a crime.

In 1690 John Locke explained many of the ideas of the Glorious Revolution in a book called *Two Treatises of Government.* Locke argued against the absolute rule of one person. He stated that government should be based on natural law. This law, said Locke, gave all people from their birth certain natural rights. Among them were the right to life, the right to liberty, and the right to own property.

Locke believed that the purpose of government is to protect these rights. All governments, he said, were based on a **social contract,** or an agreement between rulers and the people. If a ruler took away people's rights, the people had a right to revolt and set up a new government.

Parliament. Charles I wanted to have absolute, or total, power as king. Parliament demanded a greater role in running England.

The fighting eventually led to Charles's execution. This event shocked Thomas Hobbes, who was a strong supporter of the monarchy. In 1651 Hobbes wrote a book called *Leviathan.* In this work, Hobbes argued that natural law made absolute monarchy the best form of government.

According to Hobbes, humans were naturally selfish and violent. They could not be trusted to make their own decisions. Left to themselves, people would make life "nasty, brutish, and short." Therefore, Hobbes said,

Biography

WH7.11.5 Describe how democratic thought and institutions were influenced by Enlightenment thinkers (e.g., John Locke, Charles-Louis Montesquieu, American founders).

JOHN LOCKE
1632–1704

John Locke was born in Somerset, England. His father was a lawyer but also served as a cavalry soldier. Using his military connections, he arranged for his son John to get a good education. Locke studied classical languages, grammar, philosophy, and geometry at Oxford University. To Locke, the courses were not exciting, so he turned to his true interests—science and medicine.

After graduating, Locke went to work for governments in Europe. He continued to study science and philosophy. He particularly liked the work of Descartes. In 1671 Locke began recording his own ideas about how people know things. Nineteen years later, he published his ideas in *An Essay Concerning Human Understanding.* In this book, Locke argued that people's minds are blank when they are born and that society shapes what people think and believe. This idea meant that if people could make society better, it would also make people better.

▲ John Locke

"**Law is not to abolish or restrain, but to preserve and enlarge freedom.**"

–John Locke, *Two Treatises of Government*

In 1683 Locke fled to Holland after the English government began to think his political ideas were dangerous. During that time, he was declared a traitor and was not able to return until after the Glorious Revolution of 1688. It was at that time that he wrote his famous *Two Treatises of Government.* Soon afterward, Locke retired to Essex. There he enjoyed frequent visits from Sir Isaac Newton and other friends until his death in 1704.

▲ William and Mary being crowned following the Glorious Revolution

Then and Now

Give examples of how Locke's ideas have influenced our lives and ideas.

Who Was Montesquieu?

England's government was admired by thinkers in France. They liked it better than their own absolute monarchy. In 1748 **Baron Montesquieu** (MAHN•tuhs•KYOO), a French thinker, published a book called *The Spirit of Laws*.

In this book, Montesquieu said that England's government was the best because it had a separation of powers. **Separation of powers** means that power is divided among the branches of government: executive, legislative, and judicial. The legislative branch makes the laws, and the executive branch enforces them. The judicial branch interprets the laws. Separating these powers keeps government from becoming too powerful and threatening people's rights.

✓ **Reading Check** **Explain** How did Baron Montesquieu want government organized?

The French Philosophes

Main Idea The Enlightenment was centered in France, where thinkers wrote about changing their society and met to discuss their ideas.

Reading Connection What role do writers play in the United States today? Read on to find out what effect writers had on Europe during the Enlightenment.

During the 1700s, France became the major center of the Enlightenment. As the Enlightenment spread, thinkers in France and elsewhere became known by the French name *philosophe* (FEE•luh•ZAWF), which means "philosopher." Most philosophes were writers, teachers, journalists, and observers of society.

The philosophes wanted to use reason to change society. They attacked superstition, or unreasoned beliefs. In addition,

▲ During the Enlightenment, upper-class nobles held gatherings of writers, artists, and government officials in their homes to discuss new ideas. *How did the philosophes spread their ideas?*

Voltaire▶

they also disagreed with Church leaders who opposed new scientific discoveries. The philosophes believed in both freedom of speech and the individual's right to liberty. They used their skills as writers to spread their ideas across Europe.

Who Was Voltaire?

The greatest thinker of the Enlightenment was François-Marie Arouet, known simply as **Voltaire** (vohl•TAR). Born in a middle-class family, Voltaire wrote many novels, plays, letters, and essays that brought him fame and wealth.

Voltaire became known for his strong dislike of the Roman Catholic Church. He blamed Church leaders for keeping knowledge from people in order to maintain the Church's power. Voltaire also opposed the government supporting one religion and forbidding others. He thought people should be free to choose their own beliefs. Voltaire, like many philosophes, supported deism.

Who Was Diderot?

Denis Diderot (dee•DROH) was the French philosophe who did the most to spread Enlightenment ideas. With the help of friends, Diderot published a large, 28-volume encyclopedia. His project, which began in the 1750s, took about 20 years to complete.

The *Encyclopedia* included a wide range of **topics,** such as science, religion, government, and the arts. It became an important weapon in the philosophes' fight against traditional ways. Many articles attacked superstition and supported freedom of religion. Others called for changes that would make society more just and caring.

The Enlightenment and Women

The Enlightenment raised questions about the role of women in society. Previously, many male thinkers claimed that women were less important than men and had to be

controlled and protected. By the 1700s, however, women thinkers began calling for women's rights. The most powerful supporter of women's rights was the English writer **Mary Wollstonecraft** (WUL•stuhn•KRAFT). She sought to eliminate inequality in education between men and women. Many people today credit her as the founder of the modern movement for women's rights.

In 1792 Mary Wollstonecraft wrote a book called *A Vindication of the Rights of Woman.* In this work, she claimed that all humans have reason. Because women have reason, they should have the same rights as men. Women, Wollstonecraft said, should have equal rights in education, the workplace, and in political life.

Rousseau's Social Contract

By the late 1700s, some European thinkers were starting to criticize Enlightenment ideas. One of these thinkers was Jean-Jacques Rousseau (zhahn zhahk ru•SOH).

Rousseau claimed that **advocates** of the Enlightenment relied too much on reason. Instead, people should pay more attention to their feelings. According to Rousseau, human beings were naturally good, but civilized life corrupted them. To improve themselves, he thought people should live simpler lives closer to nature.

▲ **Rousseau**

In 1762 Rousseau published a book called *The Social Contract.* In this work, Rousseau presented his political ideas. A workable government, he said, should be based on a social contract. This is an agreement in which everyone in a society agrees to be governed by the general will, or what society as a whole wants.

✔ **Reading Check** Compare and Contrast
Compare Voltaire's ideas to those of Rousseau.

History Online

Study Central Need help understanding the Enlightenment? Visit ca.hss.glencoe.com and click on Study Central.

Section 2 Review

Reading Summary

Review the Main Ideas

- In the 1700s, many Europeans thought reason could make government and society better. Hobbes, Locke, and Montesquieu developed ideas about how to improve government.

- Enlightenment thinkers, such as Voltaire, Diderot, and Rousseau, described ways to make society better.

What Did You Learn?

1. Who were the French philosophes?

2. What was the *Encyclopedia,* and what message did it attempt to deliver to its readers?

Critical Thinking

3. **Organizing Information** Draw a chart to list the thinkers of the Enlightenment and their accomplishments. **CA 7RC2.0**

Thinker	Accomplishments

4. **The Big Ideas** Why did Enlightenment thinkers believe that reason could be used to make government and society better? **CA 7RC2.3**

5. **Conclude** Which of the Enlightenment thinkers discussed in this section do you think had the most impact on modern society? Explain your answer. **CA HI2.**

6. **Civics Link** Describe how beliefs about people and government during the Enlightenment are reflected in our government today. **CA HI2.**

Section 3 Politics and the Enlightenment

Guide to Reading

Looking Back, Looking Ahead
You have learned how people during the Scientific Revolution and the Enlightenment emphasized reason. This concept continues to impact our world today.

Focusing on the Main Ideas
- Many of Europe's monarchs who claimed to rule by the will of God tried to model their countries on Enlightenment ideas. *(page 532)*
- The American and French people staged revolutions based on Enlightenment ideas. *(page 534)*
- The ideas of the Enlightenment continue to influence the world today. *(page 539)*

Meeting People
Louis XIV (LOO•ee)
Frederick II
Catherine II
George Washington
Thomas Jefferson

Locating Places
Prussia (PRUH•shuh)
Austria (AWS•tree•uh)
St. Petersburg (PEE•tuhrz•BUHRG)

Content Vocabulary
absolutism (AB•suh•LOO•TIH•zuhm)
representative government (REH•prih•ZEHN•tuh•tihv)
constitution (KAHN•stuh•TOO•shuhn)
popular sovereignty (SAH•vuh•ruhn•tee)
estate (ihs•TAYT)
bourgeoisie (BURZH•WAH•ZEE)

Academic Vocabulary
tension (TEHN•shuhn)

Reading Strategy
Cause and Effect Complete a cause-and-effect diagram showing how Enlightenment ideas led to the American Revolution and the French Revolution.

History Social Science Standards
WH7.11 Students analyze political and economic change in the sixteenth, seventeenth, and eighteenth centuries (the Age of Exploration, the Enlightenment, and the Age of Reason).

NATIONAL GEOGRAPHIC Where & When?

St. Petersburg
London
Moscow
Paris
Berlin
Vienna

1650	1750	1850

1643 Louis XIV becomes king

1740 Frederick the Great becomes Prussia's king

1776 American Revolution begins

1789 French Revolution begins

The Age of Absolutism

Main Idea Many of Europe's monarchs who claimed to rule by the will of God tried to model their countries on Enlightenment ideas.

Reading Connection If you were given the chance to be a leader, how would you treat the people you ruled? As you read, think about the power of Europe's kings and queens during the 1600s and 1700s.

During the 1600s and 1700s, many European thinkers favored limits on government power. However, powerful kings and queens ruled most of Europe. This system was known as **absolutism** (AB•suh•LOO•TIH•zuhm). In this system, monarchs held absolute, or total, power. They claimed to rule by divine right, or by the will of God. This meant that rulers did not answer to their people, but rather to God alone.

However, as the Enlightenment spread, many of Europe's absolute rulers turned to philosophes for help in making their governments work better. At the same time,

▲ Louis XIV shows the plans for his palace at Versailles. *Why is Louis XIV important?*

however, they did not want to lose any of their power. Historians used to call these rulers enlightened despots. Despots are rulers who hold total power.

Louis XIV: France's Sun King During the 1600s, France was one of Europe's strongest nations. In 1643 **Louis XIV** (LOO•ee) came to the throne. As king, Louis XIV was the most celebrated absolute monarch. His reign of 72 years—the longest in European history—set the style for Europe's kings and queens. Louis was known as the Sun King, the source of light for all of his people.

Louis relied on a bureaucracy, but he was the source of all political authority in France. He is said to have boasted, "I am the State." Louis's army fought and won wars to expand France's territory, but these conflicts were costly in money and soldiers to France. The king's constant wars and excessive spending weakened France and the monarchy.

Frederick the Great During the 1600s and 1700s, Germany was a collection of over 300 separate states. Of these states, two—**Prussia** (PRUH•shuh) and **Austria** (AWS•tree•uh)—became great European powers.

The most famous Prussian ruler was **Frederick II,** also called Frederick the Great. He ruled from 1740 to 1786. As Prussia's king, Frederick strengthened the army and fought wars to gain new territory for Prussia. He also tried to be an enlightened ruler. He supported the arts and learning and tried to carry out enlightened reforms. He permitted his people to speak and publish more freely. He also consented to greater religious toleration.

Austria's Hapsburg Rulers By the 1700s, the other powerful German state, Austria, ruled a large empire of many different

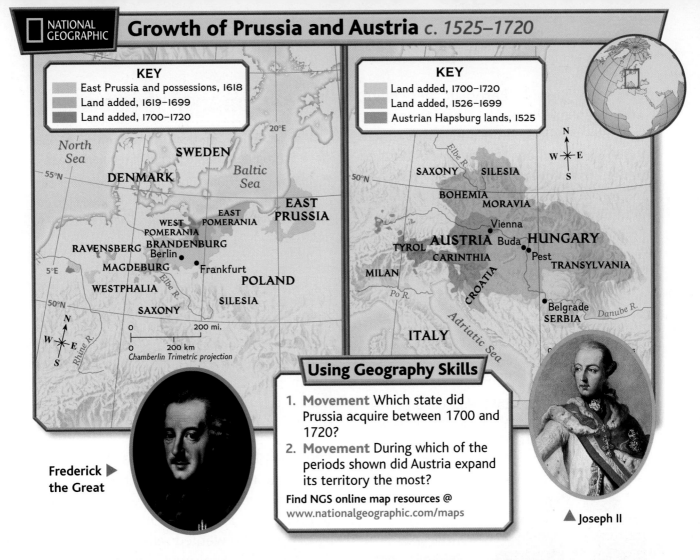

KEY
- East Prussia and possessions, 1618
- Land added, 1619–1699
- Land added, 1700–1720

KEY
- Land added, 1700–1720
- Land added, 1526–1699
- Austrian Hapsburg lands, 1525

Frederick ▶ the Great

Using Geography Skills

1. **Movement** Which state did Prussia acquire between 1700 and 1720?
2. **Movement** During which of the periods shown did Austria expand its territory the most?

Find NGS online map resources @ www.nationalgeographic.com/maps

▲ Joseph II

peoples, languages, and cultures. This vast Austrian empire spread over much of central and southeastern Europe. It was ruled by a family known as the Hapsburgs.

In 1740 a young Hapsburg princess named Maria Theresa became Austria's ruler. Energetic and talented, Maria Theresa worked hard to improve the lot of Austria's serfs, who worked for the nobles. She also tried to make government work better.

After Maria Theresa died in 1780, her son, Joseph II, became ruler. Joseph II admired Enlightenment philosophies. He freed the serfs, made land taxes equal for nobles and farmers, and allowed books to be published freely. Despite his efforts, most of Joseph's reforms failed. The nobles opposed Joseph's changes, and he was forced to back down. However, the former serfs, now farmers, were allowed to keep their freedom.

Russia's Peter I and Catherine II To the east of Austria stretched the vast empire of Russia. As you read previously, Russia was ruled by all-powerful rulers known as czars. One of the most powerful czars was Peter I, also known as Peter the Great. During his reign from 1689 to 1725, Peter tried to make Russia into a strong and up-to-date European power. He began reforms to make the government work more smoothly.

Peter also improved Russia's military and expanded Russia's territory westward to the Baltic Sea. In 1703 he founded a city called **St. Petersburg** (PEE•tuhrz•BUHRG) in this area. A few years later, Russia's capital was moved to St. Petersburg from Moscow.

After Peter died, conflict erupted among Russia's nobles. Then, in 1762 a German princess named **Catherine II** came to the throne of Russia. Early in her reign, Catherine was devoted to Enlightenment ideas. She studied about and wrote letters to the philosophes. She even considered freeing the serfs, but a serf uprising changed her mind. In the end, she allowed the nobles to treat the serfs as they pleased.

Under Catherine, Russia gained even more land and increased its power in Europe. As a result, Catherine became known as "the Great." However, by 1796, the year Catherine died, the ideas of liberty and equality had spread across Europe. These ideas seriously threatened the rule of powerful kings and queens.

Reading Check **Explain** How did the ideas of absolute monarchs conflict with the ideas of Enlightenment thinkers?

◀ **Russia grew powerful under Peter the Great.** *How did Peter try to make Russia a European power?*

Catherine the ▶ **Great studied Enlightenment ideas.**

Revolution and Enlightenment

Main Idea The American and French people staged revolutions based on Enlightenment ideas.

Reading Connection Do you like to make your own decisions, without someone else telling you what to do? Read to find out why the American colonies wanted to make decisions without British interference.

Previously, you learned that Spain and Portugal built colonies in the Americas in the 1500s. Beginning in the 1600s, the English began setting up their own colonies in the Americas. While the Spanish had settled in the Caribbean, Mexico, and South America, England's colonies were primarily in North America.

The English Settle in America English settlers came to North America for many reasons. Merchants set up some English colonies to make money. Others were set up by people who wanted religious freedom.

England's colonies grew rapidly because of economic problems in England. Many people in England wanted to move to America because their landlords had evicted them from their farms. In America, they had a chance to own land for themselves. Still others came because they were unemployed and needed jobs.

By the early 1700s, the English had created colonies along the coast of North America. These colonies had different societies, but they had one thing in common: they wanted to govern themselves.

Self-Government in America The tradition of self-government began early in the English colonies. To attract more settlers, the head of the Virginia Company, an English joint-stock company, gave the colonists in Virginia the right to elect burgesses. Burgesses were representatives chosen from among the men who owned land. The first House of Burgesses met in 1619. It was patterned after the English Parliament and voted on laws for the Virginia colony.

The House of Burgesses set an example for **representative government** (REH•prih•ZEHN•tuh•tihv), or a government in which people elect representatives to make laws and conduct government. It was not long before other colonies set up their own legislatures as well.

A year after the Virginia House of Burgesses met, a group of Puritans called the Pilgrims arrived in North America. They began their own tradition of self-government. Before going ashore, the Pilgrims signed an agreement called the Mayflower Compact. They agreed to rule themselves by choosing their own leaders and making their own laws.

Over the years, several of the English colonies drew up **constitutions** (KAHN•stuh•TOO•shuhnz), or written plans of government. These documents let the colonists elect assemblies and protected their rights.

The Road to War

For many years, Great Britain allowed the American colonies to run their own local affairs. Between 1756 and 1763, however, the French and British fought for control of the Americas. The British won, but at great financial expense. When the British decided to impose new taxes on the American colonies to pay for the war, the colonists became frustrated. The colonists believed that only their local assemblies had the right to impose taxes.

This conflict eventually led to violence, more taxes, harsher laws, and rising **tension** between the two sides. Finally, in September 1774, delegates from 12 colonies met in Philadelphia. They called themselves the First Continental Congress. The Congress

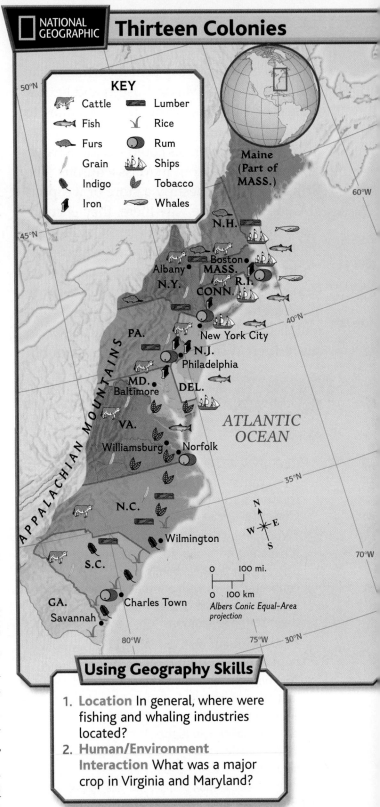

NATIONAL GEOGRAPHIC Thirteen Colonies

KEY

Cattle		Lumber	
Fish		Rice	
Furs		Rum	
Grain		Ships	
Indigo		Tobacco	
Iron		Whales	

Maine (Part of MASS.)

N.H.
Albany • Boston
N.Y. MASS.
CONN. R.I.
New York City
PA.
N.J.
Philadelphia
MD. DEL.
Baltimore
VA.
Williamsburg • Norfolk

ATLANTIC OCEAN

N.C.
Wilmington
S.C.
GA. Charles Town
Savannah

APPALACHIAN MOUNTAINS

0   100 mi.
0   100 km
Albers Conic Equal-Area projection

Using Geography Skills

1. **Location** In general, where were fishing and whaling industries located?
2. **Human/Environment Interaction** What was a major crop in Virginia and Maryland?

spoke out against various British policies and called for their repeal.

Colonial leaders, however, continued to debate about what to do. Some, like George Washington of Virginia, hoped to settle the differences with Great Britain. Others, like Samuel Adams of Massachusetts and Patrick Henry of Virginia, wanted the colonies to become independent.

Before the colonists could decide what to do, fighting broke out in Massachusetts. The British set out to destroy a store of weapons at Concord. On the way there, they encountered colonial troops at Lexington and fought the first battle of the American Revolution.

In May 1775, the Second Continental Congress met in Philadelphia. **George Washington** was named head of a new colonial army. The Congress then tried again to settle their differences with Great Britain.

They appealed to King George III, who refused to cooperate. More and more Americans began to think that independence was the only answer.

The Declaration of Independence
On July 4, 1776, the Congress issued the Declaration of Independence. Written by **Thomas Jefferson** of Virginia, the Declaration stated that the colonies were separating from Great Britain and forming a new nation, the United States of America.

In the Declaration, Jefferson borrowed the ideas of John Locke to explain why the colonists were founding a new nation.

Primary Source

The Declaration of Independence

On July 4, 1776, Congress approved the Declaration of Independence. The preamble—the first part of the document—explains Congress's reason for issuing the declaration:

"When in the Course of human events, it becomes necessary for one people to dissolve the political bands which have connected them with another. . . . they should declare the causes which impel them to the separation."

The document also explained that people have certain basic rights:

"We hold these truths to be self-evident, that all men are created equal, that they are endowed by their Creator with certain unalienable Rights, that among these are Life, Liberty and the pursuit of Happiness."

—Declaration of Independence, July 4, 1776

DBQ Document-Based Question

Why do you think the Congress thought they had to issue a written declaration of independence?

▲ Benjamin Franklin, John Adams, and Thomas Jefferson, shown left to right, worked together to write the Declaration of Independence.

▲ The American leaders who met in Philadelphia in 1787 and wrote the United States Constitution were some of the nation's greatest political minds. *What sort of system of government did the Constitution create?*

Previously, you learned about Locke's idea that people have the right to overthrow governments that violate their rights. The Declaration stated that "all men are created equal" and have certain God-given rights. It said that King George III had violated colonists' rights, so they had the right to rebel.

The Declaration also drew from earlier English documents, such as the Magna Carta and the English Bill of Rights. Both documents established the idea that governments are not all-powerful and that rulers had to obey the laws and treat citizens fairly.

The United States Constitution For many years, the colonists fought to obtain their freedom. In 1783 Great Britain finally recognized American independence. At first the United States was a confederation, or a loose union of independent states. Its plan of government was a document called the Articles of Confederation. The Articles created a national government, but the states held most powers. It soon became clear that the Articles were too weak to deal with the new nation's problems.

In 1787, 55 delegates met in Philadelphia to change the Articles. Instead, they decided to write a constitution for an entirely new national government. The new United States Constitution set up a federal system in which powers were divided between the national government and the states. Following the ideas of Montesquieu, power in the national government was divided between executive, legislative, and judicial branches. A system called checks and balances enabled each branch to limit the powers of the other branches.

Under the Constitution, the United States was a republic with an elected president instead of a king. Elections held in 1789 made George Washington the first president of the United States. That same year, a Bill of Rights was added to the U.S. Constitution. The Bill of Rights set out certain rights the government could not violate. These rights included freedom of religion, speech, and press, and the right to trial by jury.

The U.S. Constitution was also shaped by Enlightenment principles. One of these is **popular sovereignty** (SAH•vuh•ruhn•tee), or the idea that government receives its powers from the people. Another is limited government, or the idea that a government may use only those powers given to it by the people.

The French Revolution Begins The same Enlightenment ideas that led to the American Revolution also influenced France. In the 1700s, French kings ruled with absolute power. Nobles had many privileges and lived in great wealth. Most people, however, were poor, had little education, and struggled to make a living.

The French people were divided into three **estates** (ihs•TAYT), or classes. The First Estate was the Catholic clergy, or church officials. They did not pay taxes, and they received money from church lands. The Second Estate was the nobles. They filled the highest posts in government and the military. Like the clergy, the nobles were free from taxes. They lived in luxury at the king's court and owned large areas of land.

Everyone else in France belonged to the Third Estate. At the top of this group was the **bourgeoisie** (BURZH•WAH•ZEE), or the middle classes. They included merchants, bankers, doctors, lawyers, and teachers. Next were the city workers—artisans, day laborers, and servants. At the bottom were the peasants, who made up more than 80 percent of the French people.

Members of the Third Estate were excluded from government affairs, but they paid the country's taxes. As Enlightenment ideas about freedom and justice spread, the Third Estate came to resent more and more the privileges of the nobles and clergy.

In 1789, the members of the Third Estate decided they had had enough. They had seen the British colonists in America revolt and gain their freedom. Many members of the Third Estate were aware of the American Declaration of Independence. They decided to hold an assembly to design

The Way It Was

Focus on Everyday Life

Music of the Enlightenment The 1700s was one of the greatest musical periods in history. Before this time, almost all music was religious in nature and was limited to church performances. During the Enlightenment, music was played in theaters for the first time, and some of the new pieces were not religious.

▲ A string quartet

Many types of music existed in the 1700s. Sonatas were performed with one instrument and a piano, and string quartets were played with four instruments. Concertos and symphonies were longer and involved an orchestra. Operas were full-scale theatrical performances using vocal and instrumental music.

Baroque music emphasized drama and emotion. Johann Sebastian Bach and George Frederick Handel composed baroque music. Bach composed

WH7.11.5 Describe how democratic thought and institutions were influenced by Enlightenment thinkers (e.g., John Locke, Charles-Louis Montesquieu, American founders).

a new constitution so that they, too, could have rights and privileges. A revolt began, and people around the countryside became terrified.

To calm the people, the assembly passed new laws that ended the privileges of both the clergy and nobles. It also issued the Declaration of the Rights of Man and the Citizen. The Declaration drew Enlightenment ideas from the American Declaration of Independence, which had borrowed from the Magna Carta. The French Declaration transferred the powers of government to the people.

Within a few years, the French people had overthrown their king and established a new government. The French Revolution had begun.

Reading Check **Explain** Why did the colonists decide to separate from Great Britain and create a new nation?

The Enlightenment's Legacy

Main Idea The ideas of the Enlightenment continue to influence the world today.

Reading Connection Think about how you make decisions. Do you consider the various reasons for and against something before deciding? Read to find out how the rationalist approach of the Enlightenment continues today.

As you have learned, the ideas of the Enlightenment had a profound impact on the world. Enlightenment ideas changed the way people thought and acted and how they viewed the world.

The Enlightenment also changed the course of history in many countries. For some people, it led them to emphasize reason over faith or tradition. For others, the rational approach to knowledge helped them better understand the world but did not break their faith.

many pieces of music that are still popular today. Handel wrote many operas, but he is best known for *Messiah*, an oratorio, or religious composition that mixes voices, orchestra, and organ.

Classical music emerged in the mid-1700s. Classical composers, inspired by the ancient Greeks and Romans, emphasized balance, harmony, and stability. Franz Joseph Haydn and Wolfgang Amadeus Mozart wrote classical music. Haydn's use of instruments made the symphony more popular. Mozart composed a large number of musical pieces that remain popular today.

Wolfgang Amadeus Mozart ▼

▲ Johann Sebastian Bach

Connecting to the Past
1. What is the difference in tone between baroque and classical music?
2. What factors allowed music to thrive during the 1700s?

New Rights in America Enlightenment principles sometimes took many years to change government. For instance, the United States was not as democratic as it is today. When the country was founded, women and African Americans could not vote. Ideas inspired by the Enlightenment, such as equality under the law, eventually led to positive changes. Sometimes these changes came through war. Other times they resulted from peaceful discussion and demonstrations.

Martin Luther King, Jr., is a prime example of how Enlightenment principles brought about change. King was an important civil rights leader in the United States during the 1950s and 1960s. During this period in U.S. history, many African Americans were treated differently than white people. There were laws in parts of the United States that kept African Americans and white Americans segregated, or separate, from each other.

King believed that all people should have an equal opportunity to make their way in the United States. He also believed that people's success should depend on their abilities. Although King often spoke to people's hearts, his arguments were also based on the Enlightenment ideas of reason and human rights.

Human Rights The idea of human rights is a concern of people throughout the world today. Many countries came together after World War II to create an international organization called the United Nations. This organization was formed to encourage countries to settle disagreements peacefully and to support human rights worldwide. The United Nations sends representatives throughout the world to try to accomplish these goals.

Generally, people in the United States today try to solve problems through the democratic process rather than through force. Americans have not always succeeded in resolving their differences peacefully, but there is widespread agreement that a democratic government that respects individual rights and freedoms is the best form of government. This is an Enlightenment idea.

In many other countries, the government leaders are changed only through

Primary Source

Declaration of the Rights of Man and the Citizen

On August 26, 1789, the French National Assembly approved 17 articles that stated their basic freedoms. Three of the articles are listed below.

2. The aim of every political association is the preservation of the natural . . . rights of man. These rights are liberty, property, security, and resistance to oppression [hardship].

9. Every man being presumed innocent until he has been proven guilty, . . .

11. The free communication of ideas and opinions is one of the most precious of the rights of man; every citizen can then freely speak, write, and print. . . .

—Declaration of the Rights of Man and the Citizen (August 1789)

▲ Declaration of the Rights of Man and the Citizen

DBQ Document-Based Question

Which freedoms do Articles 2, 9, and 11 protect?

violence. This was the case in ancient Rome and in France during the French Revolution. In the United States, and in many other countries today, change in leadership occurs through a peaceful election process.

Technology and Trade The Enlightenment principle of applying rationalism to science and technology is still important today. Many great discoveries have been generated by utilizing the scientific method. Examples of important inventions include automobiles, telephones, electrical appliances, airplanes and spaceships, computers, and many new medicines to fight diseases.

One reason so many new technologies have been developed is capitalism—an economic system where people can own private property and run their own businesses. Today capitalism is one of the most important economic systems in the world. Companies in many different countries compete with each other. Trade between countries is greater than ever before.

When Columbus set sail hoping to find a new trade route to China, he had no idea he was helping launch the Age of Exploration. Similarly, the Age of Exploration helped begin an economic revolution that furthered the rise of capitalism. Over 500 years ago, exploration, trade, and an interest in science and discovery began to build the world that we live in today.

Reading Check **Explain** How did Martin Luther King, Jr., use Enlightenment principles?

History Online

Study Central Need help understanding the legacy of the Enlightenment? Visit ca.hss.glencoe.com and click on Study Central.

Section 3 Review

Reading Summary

Review the Main Ideas

- In the 1700s, Europe was ruled by absolute monarchs, several of whom tried to implement some reforms based on Enlightenment ideas.

- The ideas of the Enlightenment helped to cause revolutions in America and in France and also influenced the U.S. Constitution.

- The Enlightenment led to a widespread belief in democracy and human rights and to a commitment to science and reason that continues to shape the world today.

What Did You Learn?

1. What was absolutism?

2. What is representative government, and what was one of the first examples?

Critical Thinking

3. **Sequencing Information** Create a chart like the one below. Fill in information about where and when each of the rulers reigned.

Louis XIV	Frederick II	Maria Theresa	Peter I & Catherine II

4. **The Big Ideas** How did the ideas and events of the Enlightenment influence the Declaration of Independence? **CA HI2.**

5. **Describe** How did absolute rulers use the ideas of the Enlightenment to better or change their countries? Were they successful? **CA 7RC2.0**

6. **Summarize** Write an essay summarizing the effect of Enlightenment ideas on Europe. **CA 7WA2.5**

7. **Analysis** **Conclude** Write a letter to the editor giving your opinion on either the Declaration of Independence, or the French Declaration of the Rights of Man and the Citizen. Describe the political ideas in the document and state whether you agree or disagree with those ideas. **CA HR5.**

Analyzing Primary Sources

WH7.11.5 Describe how democratic thought and institutions were influenced by Enlightenment thinkers (e.g., John Locke, Charles-Louis Montesquieu, American founders).

The Age of Enlightenment

The philosophers of the Enlightenment wanted to build a better society than the one in which they lived. Many of their essays described how government should work and how people should treat one another.

Read the passages on pages 542 and 543, and answer the questions that follow.

▲ Jean-Jacques Rousseau

Reader's Dictionary

sovereign (SAH•vuh•ruhn): supreme

multitude: great number of people

oblige (uh•BLYJ): require

mutual: shared; common

body politic: political body

premises (PREH•muhs•ehs): place; location

indifferent: unconcerned

divulging (duh•VUHLJ•ihng): revealing

The Social Contract

J*ean-Jacques Rousseau published* The Social Contract *in 1762. The piece discussed people's relationship to government.*

. . . [Each] person, in making a contract, as it were, with himself, finds himself doubly committed, first, as a member of the **sovereign** body in relation to individuals, and secondly as a member of the state in relation to the sovereign. . . .

As soon as the **multitude** is united thus in a single body, no one can injure any one of the members without attacking the whole, still less injure the whole without each member feeling it. Duty and self-interest thus equally **oblige** the two . . . parties to give each other **mutual** aid. . . .

For every individual as a man may have a private will contrary to, or different from, the general will that he has as a citizen. His private interest may speak with a very different voice from that of the public interest; . . . and . . . he might seek to enjoy the rights of a citizen without doing the duties of a subject. The growth of this kind of injustice would bring about the ruin of the **body politic** . . .

There is often a great difference between [individual will] and the general will; the general will studies only the common interest while the [individual will] studies private interest.

—Jean-Jacques Rousseau, *The Social Contract*

Encyclopedia

The philosophes were interested in acquiring knowledge. One of them, Denis Diderot, led a team in compiling a 28-volume encyclopedia. In defining the word encyclopedia, *Diderot focuses on how important it is to share knowledge.*

ENCYCLOPÉDIE, f. n. *(Philosophy)*. This word means the *interrelation of all knowledge*. . . . In truth, the aim of an encyclopédie is to collect all the knowledge scattered over the face of the earth, to present its general outlines and structure to the men with whom we live, and to transmit this to those who will come after us, so that the work of past centuries may be useful to the following centuries, that our children, by becoming more educated, may at the same time become more virtuous and happier. . . .

It would be desirable for the government to authorize people to go into the factories and shops, to see the craftsmen at their work, to question them, to draw the tools, the machines, and even the **premises**. . . .

I know that this feeling is not shared by everyone. These are narrow minds, deformed souls, who are **indifferent** to the fate of the human race and who are so enclosed in their little group that they see nothing beyond its special interest. . . . What is the good of **divulging** the knowledge a nation possesses, its private transactions, its inventions, its industrial processes, its resources, its trade secrets, its enlightenment, its arts, and all its wisdom? Are not these the things to which it owes a part of its superiority over the rival nations that surround it? This is what they say . . . instead of enlightening the foreigner, we could spread darkness over him . . . so that we could dominate more securely over everyone? These people do not realize that they occupy only a single point on our globe and that they will endure only a moment in its existence. To this point and to this moment they would sacrifice the happiness of future ages and that of the entire human race.

—Denis Diderot, "Encyclopédie"

▲ Nobles discuss Enlightenment ideas.

DBQ Document-Based Questions

The Social Contract

1. What is the difference between general will and the individual will?

2. Why is it important for the individual to keep in mind the general will, instead of concentrating only on the individual will?

Encyclopedia

3. According to Diderot, why is it important to create the *Encyclopédie?*

4. Why did some people say it was a bad idea to create the *Encyclopédie?* How did Diderot respond to this?

Read to Write

5. Rousseau argues that people should not let their individual interests interfere with the interests of the common good. Would Diderot have agreed with Rousseau? Give examples from both passages that prove your opinion. **CA HR5.**

Review Content Vocabulary

Write the key term that completes each sentence.

    a. constitution
    b. the scientific method
    c. separation of powers
    d. absolutism
    e. theory
    f. natural law

1. Louis XIV and Frederick the Great ruled under the system of _____.

2. Locke and Hobbes used _____ to help develop their ideas.

3. Francis Bacon developed _____.

4. Scientists develop a(n) _____ to explain how or why something happens.

5. Montesquieu believed _____ was needed for good government.

6. A(n) _____ is a written plan for government.

Review the Main Ideas

Section 1 • The Scientific Revolution

7. How did European thinkers develop new ideas?

8. How did the interest in astronomy lead to new information about the earth?

9. In what areas were significant scientific discoveries made?

Section 2 • The Ideas of the Enlightenment

10. How did Thomas Hobbes and John Locke disagree?

11. Who were the philosophes, and what did they want to accomplish?

Section 3 • Politics and the Enlightenment

12. How did the Enlightenment affect Europe's rulers?

13. What are some of the ways that the ideas of the Enlightenment still affect us today?

Critical Thinking

14. **Explain** How did Copernicus, Kepler, Galileo, and Newton each add to our understanding of the universe? **CA HI2.**

15. **Analyze** How did the ideas of the Enlightenment influence the rise of democracy? **CA 7RC2.3**

Geography Skills

16. **Movement** In what years did Austria gain the most territory? **CA CS3.**

17. **Human/Environment Interaction** What natural features probably helped the Austrian Empire increase its ability to trade as it grew? **CA CS3.**

18. **Location** Use a map of modern-day Europe to find out which countries made up part of the Austrian Empire. **CA CS3.**

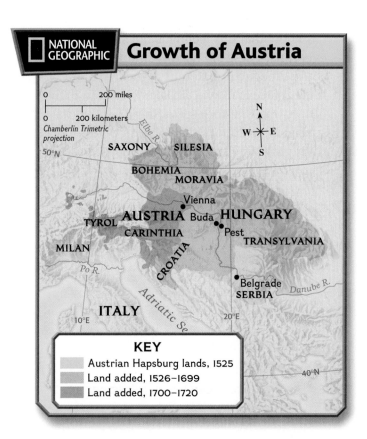

NATIONAL GEOGRAPHIC

Growth of Austria

0 200 miles
0 200 kilometers
Chamberlin Trimetric projection

KEY
Austrian Hapsburg lands, 1525
Land added, 1526–1699
Land added, 1700–1720

Read to Write

19. **The Big Ideas** **Writing Research Reports**
Write a brief essay describing Montesquieu's beliefs about government and explaining how they are reflected in the U.S. Constitution. Use your local library and the Internet to find information to support your essay. **CA 7WA2.3**

20. **Using Your FOLDABLES** Use the information from your foldable to write a short summary of the main ideas of the Enlightenment and the Scientific Revolution. Use this summary to help you write an essay explaining how these ideas affected society. **CA 7WA2.5**

Using Academic Vocabulary

Read each of the following sentences. Change the underlined word in each sentence to make sure that it is grammatically correct.

21. During the Renaissance, many scientists and thinkers used a humanist <u>approached</u> in their work.

22. There was more than one <u>topics</u> covered in Denis Diderot's *Encyclopedia*.

23. Mary Wollstonecraft was an <u>advocating</u> for women's rights.

24. The desire for freedom and independence led to many <u>tension</u> moments between England and the colonies in North America.

Building Citizenship

25. **Making Connections** Mary Wollstonecraft is often considered the founder of the modern women's rights movement. Use your local library to find information about Wollstonecraft's impact on women's rights. Write an essay describing her influence during the Enlightenment and today. **CA 7WA2.3** **CA HI2.**

Linking Past and Present

26. **Analyze** The music, art, and literature of the Enlightenment reflected people's views during that time. Write an essay describing how present-day music, art, and literature reflect people's feelings about society. Give examples to support your opinion.
CA 7WA2.0

Reviewing Skills

27. **Reading Skill** **Taking Notes** Create a chapter study guide by making a two-column chart that lists each main idea and details that support that main idea. **CA 7WS1.3**

28. **Analysis Skill** **Recognizing Change** Using information from the chapter, as well as your own research, write an essay discussing the ideas of Enlightenment thinkers and their effect on the rise of democracy in Europe and America. **CA 7WA2.3** **CA HI3.**

 Standards Practice

Select the best answer for each of the following questions.

29 **The Enlightenment thinker Baron Montesquieu believed that a government would not become too powerful if the government**

A was ruled by an honorable king.

B obeyed Parliament's laws.

C had a separation of powers.

D was based on natural law.

30 **John Locke's belief that all people have certain natural rights influenced the writing of which important document?**

A the Magna Carta

B the Declaration of Independence

C the English Bill of Rights

D the Mayflower Compact

Making Comparisons

Compare early modern times by reviewing the information below. Can you see how the people who lived during this period had lives that were very much like yours?

	Renaissance and Reformation Chapters 7 & 8	The Americas Chapter 9	Age of Exploration Chapter 10	Age of Enlightenment Chapter 11
Where did the events in these chapters take place?	• Europe	• North America • Central America • Caribbean islands • South America	• Western Europe • North America • Africa • South Asia • Southeast Asia	• Europe • North America
Who were some important people?	• Leonardo da Vinci A.D. 1452–1519 • Martin Luther A.D. 1483–1546 • Queen Isabella (Spain), ruled A.D. 1474–1504	• Pachacuti, ruled A.D. 1438–1471 • Montezuma II, ruled A.D. 1502–1520 • Atahualpa, ruled A.D. 1525–1533	• Christopher Columbus A.D. 1451–1506 • Queen Elizabeth I (England), ruled A.D. 1558–1603	• Francis Bacon A.D. 1561–1626 • Galileo Galilei A.D. 1564–1642 • John Locke A.D. 1632–1704
Where did most people live?	• City-states (Italy) • Commercial cities (London, Paris) • Farming villages	• Hunter-gatherers • Farming villages • Cities (Cuzco and Tenochtitlán)	• Port cities (Lisbon, Amsterdam) • Overseas settlements and plantations	• Cities • Farming villages
What were people's beliefs?	• Northern Europe: Protestant • Southern Europe: Roman Catholic • Jewish communities	• Traditional Native American religions	• Europeans spread Christianity overseas	• Deism introduced in Europe and America

	Renaissance and Reformation Chapters 7 & 8	The Americas Chapter 9	Age of Exploration Chapter 10	Age of Enlightenment Chapter 11
What was government like?	• Italian city-states ruled by wealthy families • Most European areas ruled by kings, princes, and nobles	• Local groups ruled by chiefs and councils • Powerful emperors or kings (Maya, Aztec, and Inca)	• Monarchies • Control of overseas territories through colonies	• Divine right of kings • English king's powers are limited, representative government spreads • United States founded as a republic
What role did language and writing play?	• Printed books helped spread knowledge • Vernacular used in Protestant worship • Latin remains language of Catholic Church	• Native Americans spoke hundreds of languages • Mayan and Aztec languages written in hieroglyphics • Inca had no written language	• Meeting of cultures meant spread of knowledge about languages • European languages brought by settlers to overseas colonies	• Studied ancient Greek and Roman texts as well as ideas of Jews and Muslims • Developed new ideas about science and philosophy
What contributions were made?	• Furthered education • Created lifelike art • Different religions existed side by side	• Developed trade networks and methods of farming and building	• Used new technologies to explore the world • Mercantilism leads to early forms of capitalism	• Reason seen as a way to truth • General rules developed for scientific study • New ideas about government
How are we affected today? Can you add any examples?	• Renaissance and Reformation Europeans passed on practice of printing books	• Native Americans passed on foods (corn, chocolate, potatoes)	• Foods and supplies available through worldwide trade	• Supported rights that we enjoy today • Scientific tools (microscope, telescope) and vaccines for disease developed

547

Appendix

What Is an Appendix?

An appendix is the additional material you often find at the end of books. The following information will help you learn how to use the Appendix in Discovering Our Past: Medieval and Early Modern Times.

SkillBuilder Handbook

The **SkillBuilder Handbook** offers you information and practice using critical thinking and social studies skills. Mastering these skills will help you in all your courses.

California Standards Handbook

Take time to review what you have learned in this book by using the **California Standards Handbook.** The handbook lists all the content standards listed in each chapter and challenges you with questions about them.

Glossary

The **Glossary** is a list of important or difficult terms found in a textbook. Since words sometimes have other meanings, you may wish to consult a dictionary to find other uses for the term. The glossary gives a definition of each term as it is used in the book. The glossary also includes page numbers telling you where in the textbook the term is used.

Spanish Glossary

The **Spanish Glossary** contains everything that an English glossary does, but it is written in Spanish. A Spanish glossary is especially important to bilingual students, or those Spanish-speaking students who are learning the English language.

Gazetteer

The **Gazetteer** (GA•zuh•TIHR) is a geographical dictionary. It lists some of the largest countries, cities, and several important geographic features. Each entry also includes a page number telling where this place is talked about in your textbook.

Index

The **Index** is an alphabetical listing that includes the subjects of the book and the page numbers where those subjects can be found. The index in this book also lets you know that certain pages contain maps, graphs, photos, or paintings about the subject.

Acknowledgements and Photo Credits

This section lists photo credits and/or literary credits for the book. You can look at this section to find out where the publisher obtained the permission to use a photograph or to use excerpts from other books.

Test Yourself

Find the answers to these questions by using the Appendix on the following pages.

1. What is a *minaret?*
2. Where exactly is Rome located?
3. On what page can I find out about Confucianism?
4. What skill is discussed on page 555?
5. What main standard is explained on page 569?

SkillBuilder Handbook

Contents

Finding the Main Idea

Why Learn This Skill?

Understanding the main idea allows you to grasp the whole picture and get an overall understanding of what you are reading. Historical details, such as names, dates, and events, are easier to remember when they are connected to a main idea.

1 Learning the Skill

Follow these steps when trying to find the main idea:

- Read the material and ask, "Why was this written? What is its purpose?"

- Read the first sentence of the first paragraph. The main idea of a paragraph is often found in the topic sentence. The main idea of a large section of text is often found in a topic paragraph.

- Identify details that support the main ideas.

- Keep the main idea clearly in your mind as you read.

2 Practicing the Skill

Read the paragraph at the top of the next column that describes how the culture of the world is changing. Answer the questions, and then complete the activity that follows. If you have trouble, use the graphic organizer to help you.

Cultural diffusion has increased as a result of technology. Cultural diffusion is the process by which a culture spreads its knowledge and skills from one area to another. Years ago, trade—the way people shared goods and ideas—resulted in cultural diffusion. Today communication technology, such as television and the Internet, links people throughout the world.

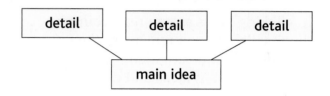

1. What is the main idea of this paragraph?

2. What are some details that support that main idea?

3. Do you agree or disagree with the main idea presented above? Explain.

4. Practice the skill by reading three paragraphs in your textbook and identifying their main ideas.

3 Applying the Skill

Bring a newspaper or magazine to class. With a partner, identify the main ideas in three different articles. Then describe how other sentences or paragraphs in the article support the main idea.

Taking Notes and Outlining

Why Learn This Skill?

If you asked someone for his or her phone number or e-mail address, how would you best remember it? Most people would write it down. Making a note of it helps you remember. The same is true for remembering what you read in a textbook.

1 Learning the Skill

Taking notes as you read your textbook will help you remember the information. As you read, identify and summarize the main ideas and details and write them in your notes. Do not copy material directly from the text.

Using note cards—that you can reorder later—can also help. First write the main topic or main idea at the top of the note card. Then write the details that support or describe that topic. Number the cards to help you keep them in order.

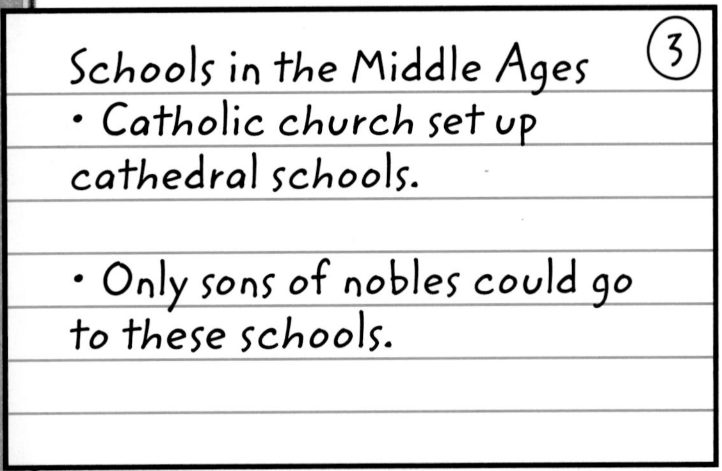

Schools in the Middle Ages ③
• Catholic church set up cathedral schools.

• Only sons of nobles could go to these schools.

You also may find it helpful to use an outline when writing notes. Outlining can help you organize your notes in a clear and orderly way.

First read the material to identify the main ideas. In this textbook, section headings and subheadings provide clues to the main ideas. Supporting details can then be placed under each heading. Each level of an outline must contain at least two items. The basic pattern for outlines is as follows:

Main Topic
  I. First idea or item
  II. Second idea or item
    A. first detail
    B. second detail
      1. subdetail
      2. subdetail
  III. Third idea or item
    A. first detail
    B. second detail

2 Practicing the Skill

Look back at Chapter 2, Section 1. Outline the main ideas of the section as shown above.

3 Applying the Skill

Use the outline that you created in step 2 to write a paragraph with a main idea and at least three supporting details.

Reading a Time Line

Why Learn This Skill?

Have you ever had to remember events and their dates in the order in which they happened? A time line is an easy way to make sense of the flow of dates and events. It is a simple diagram that shows how dates and events relate to one another. On most time lines, years are evenly spaced. Events on time lines are placed beside the date they occurred.

1 Learning the Skill

To read a time line, follow these steps:

- Find the dates on the opposite ends of the time line. They show the period of time that the time line covers.

- Note the equal spacing between dates on the time line.

- Study the order of events.

- Look to see how the events relate to each other.

2 Practicing the Skill

Examine the time line below. It shows major events in the history of ancient Rome. Then answer the questions and complete the activity that follows.

1. When does the time line begin? When does it end?

2. What major event happened around 146 B.C.?

3. How long was Rome ruled by emperors?

4. What happened to Rome around A.D. 500?

3 Applying the Skill

List 10 key events found in Unit 1 and the dates on which these events took place. Write the events in the order in which they occurred on a time line.

Ancient Rome

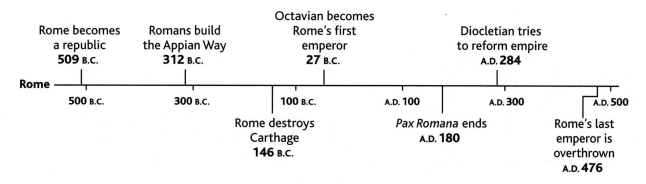

Rome becomes a republic
509 B.C.

Romans build the Appian Way
312 B.C.

Octavian becomes Rome's first emperor
27 B.C.

Diocletian tries to reform empire
A.D. **284**

Rome ——
500 B.C.   **300** B.C.   **100** B.C.   A.D. **100**   A.D. **300**   A.D. **500**

Rome destroys Carthage
146 B.C.

Pax Romana ends
A.D. **180**

Rome's last emperor is overthrown
A.D. **476**

Sequencing and Categorizing Information

Why Learn This Skill?

Sequencing means placing facts in the order in which they happened. *Categorizing* means organizing information into groups of related facts and ideas. Both actions help you deal with large quantities of information in an understandable way.

1 Learning the Skill

Follow these steps to learn sequencing and categorizing skills:

- Look for dates or clue words that provide you with a chronological order: *in 2004, the late 1990s, first, then, finally, after the Great Depression,* and so on.

- Sequencing can be seen in unit and chapter time lines or on graphs where information covers several years.

- If the sequence of events is not important, you may want to categorize the information instead. To categorize information, look for topics and facts that are grouped together or have similar characteristics. If the information is about farming, one category might be *tools of farming*.

- List these categories, or characteristics, as the headings on a chart.

- As you read, look for details. Fill in these details under the proper categories on the chart.

2 Practicing the Skill

Read the paragraph below and then answer the questions that follow.

Buddhism started in India about 500 B.C. but was mostly driven out by 300 B.C. The religion of Islam also influenced India's history. In the A.D. 700s, Muslims from southwest Asia brought Islam to India. In the 1500s, they founded the Mogul empire and ruled India for the next 200 years.

1. What information can be organized by sequencing?
2. What categories can you use to organize the information? What facts could be placed under each category?

3 Applying the Skill

Look at the Geographic Dictionary on pages 104 and 105. Record any terms that would fit into the category "bodies of water." Also, find two newspaper or magazine articles about an important local issue. Sequence or categorize the information on note cards or in a chart.

Recognizing Point of View

Why Learn This Skill?

If you say, "Cats make better pets than dogs," you are expressing a point of view. You are giving your personal opinion. Knowing when someone is giving you his or her personal point of view can help you judge the truth of what is being said.

1 Learning the Skill

Most people have feelings and ideas that affect their point of view. A person's point of view is often influenced by his or her age, background, or position in a situation.

To recognize point of view, follow these steps:

- Identify the speaker or writer and examine his or her views on an issue. Think about his or her position in life and relationship to the issue.

- Look for language that shows an emotion or an opinion. Look for words such as *all, never, best, worst, might,* or *should.*

- Examine the speech or writing for imbalances. Does it have only one viewpoint? Does it fail to provide equal coverage of other viewpoints?

- Identify statements of fact. Factual statements usually answer the *Who? What? When?* and *Where?* questions.

- Determine how the person's point of view is reflected in his or her statements or writing.

2 Practicing the Skill

Read the following statement about wildlife in Africa, and answer the questions below.

Mountain gorillas live in the misty mountain forests of East Africa. Logging and mining, however, are destroying the forests. Unless the forests are protected, all of the gorillas will lose their homes and disappear forever. As a concerned African naturalist, I must emphasize that this will be one of the worst events in Africa's history.

1. What problem is the speaker addressing?
2. What reasons does the speaker give for the loss of the forests?
3. What is the speaker's point of view about the problem facing the gorillas in East Africa?

3 Applying the Skill

Choose a "Letter to the Editor" from a newspaper. Summarize the issue being discussed and the writer's point of view about that issue. State what an opposing point of view to the issue might be. Describe who might hold this other viewpoint in terms of their age, occupation, and background.

Distinguishing Fact From Opinion

Why Learn This Skill?

Suppose a friend says, "Our school's basketball team is awesome. That's a fact." Actually, it is not a fact; it is an opinion. Knowing how to tell the difference between a fact and an opinion can help you analyze the accuracy of political claims, advertisements, and many other kinds of statements.

1 Learning the Skill

A **fact** answers a specific question such as: What happened? Who did it? When and where did it happen? Why did it happen? Statements of fact can be checked for accuracy and proven.

An **opinion,** on the other hand, expresses beliefs, feelings, and judgments. It may reflect someone's thoughts, but it cannot be proven. An opinion often begins with a phrase such as *I believe, I think, probably, it seems to me,* or *in my opinion.*

To distinguish between facts and opinions, ask yourself these questions:

- Does this statement give specific information about an event?

- Can I check the accuracy of this statement?

- Does this statement express someone's feelings, beliefs, or judgment?

- Does it include phrases such as *I believe,* superlatives, or judgment words?

2 Practicing the Skill

Read each statement below. Tell whether each is a fact or an opinion, and explain how you arrived at your answer.

(1) The Han dynasty ruled China from 202 B.C. to A.D. 220.

(2) The Han dynasty was a much better dynasty than the Qin dynasty.

(3) The Han divided the country into districts to be better able to manage such a large area.

(4) The government should not have encouraged support for arts and inventions.

(5) The Han kept very good records of everything they did, which helps historians today learn about them.

(6) Han rulers chose government officials on the basis of merit rather than birth.

(7) No other ruling family in the world can compare with the Han dynasty of China.

(8) Han rulers should have defended the poor farmers against the harsh actions of wealthy landowners.

3 Applying the Skill

Read one newspaper article that describes a political event. Find three statements of fact and three opinions expressed in the article.

Analyzing Library and Research Resources

Why Learn This Skill?

Imagine that your teacher has sent you to the library to write a report on the history of ancient Rome. Knowing how to choose good sources for your research will help you save time in the library and write a better report.

1 Learning the Skill

Not all sources will be useful for your report on Rome. Even some sources that involve topics about Rome will not always provide the information you want. In analyzing sources for your research project, choose items that are nonfiction and that contain the most information about your topic.

When choosing research resources ask these questions:

• Is the information up-to-date?

• Does the index have several pages listed for the topic?

• Is the resource written in a way that is easy to understand?

• Are there helpful illustrations and photos?

2 Practicing the Skill

Look at the following list of sources. Which would be most helpful in writing a report on the history of ancient Rome? Explain your choices.

(1) A travel guide to Italy today

(2) A guide to early Roman art and architecture

(3) A children's storybook about ancient Europe

(4) A history of ancient Greece

(5) A study of the rise and fall of the Roman Empire

(6) A book on modern republican ideas

(7) A biographical dictionary of ancient rulers of the world

(8) An atlas of the world

3 Applying the Skill

Go to your local library or use the Internet to create a bibliography of sources you might use to write a report on the history of ancient Rome. List at least five sources.

▲ **Roman mosaic showing gladiators in battle**

Analyzing Primary Source Documents

Why Learn This Skill?

Historians determine what happened in the past by combing through bits of evidence to reconstruct events. These types of evidence—both written and illustrated—are called primary sources. Examining primary sources can help you understand history.

1 Learning the Skill

Primary sources are sources that were created in the historical era being studied. They can include letters, diaries, photographs and pictures, news articles, legal documents, stories, literature, and artwork.

To analyze primary sources, ask yourself the following questions:

- What is the item?
- Who created it?
- Where did it come from?
- When was it created?
- What does it reveal about the topic I am studying?

2 Practicing the Skill

The primary source that follows was written by a Spanish conquistador around the early 1500s. He wrote about the Incan culture and what he observed about their counting methods using a quipu. Read his account and then answer the questions that follow.

At the beginning of the new year the rulers of each village came to Cuzco, bringing their quipus, which told how many births there had been during the year, and how many deaths. In this way the Inca and the governors knew which of the Indians were poor, the women who had been widowed, whether they were able to pay their taxes, and how many men they could count on in the event of war, and many other things they considered highly important.

Pedro de Cieza de Leon,
The Second Part of the Chronicle of Peru.

1. What is the main topic?
2. Who used the quipus and for what were they used?
3. What kinds of things were counted by the Incan leaders?
4. Why was the number of men important to them?

3 Applying the Skill

Find a primary source from your past—a photo or newspaper clipping. Explain to the class what it shows about that time in your life.

Building a Database

Why Learn This Skill?

A database is a collection of information stored in a computer or on diskette files. It runs on software that organizes large amounts of information in a way that makes it easy to search and make any changes. It often takes the form of a chart or table. You might build databases to store information related to a class at school or your weekly schedule.

1 Learning the Skill

To create a database using word-processing software, follow these steps:

• Enter a title identifying the type of information in your document and file names.

• Determine the set of specific points of information you wish to include. As the database example on this page shows, you might want to record data on the imports and exports of specific countries.

• Enter the information categories along with country names as headings in a columned chart. Each column makes up a *field*, which is the basic unit for information stored in a database.

• Enter data you have collected into the *cells*, or individual spaces, on your chart.

• Use your computer's sorting feature to organize the data. For example, you might alphabetize by country name.

• Add, delete, or update information as needed. Database software automatically adjusts the cells in the chart.

2 Practicing the Skill

On a separate sheet of paper, answer the following questions referring to the database on this page.

1. What type of information does the database contain?

2. What related fields of information does it show?

3. The author learns that Canada also exports clothing, beverages, and art to the United States. Is it necessary to create a new database? Explain.

3 Applying the Skill

Build a database to help you keep track of your school assignments. Work with four fields: Subject, Assignment Description, Due Date, and Completed Assignments. Be sure to keep your database up-to-date.

U.S. International Commerce			
Country	Japan	United Kingdom	Canada
Exports to U.S.	Engines, rubber goods, cars, trucks, buses	Dairy products, beverages, petroleum products, art	Wheat, minerals, paper, mining machines
Value of Exports to U.S.	$128 billion	$35.2 billion	$232.6 billion
Imports from U.S.	Meat, fish, sugar, tobacco, coffee	Fruit, tobacco, electrical equipment	Fish, sugar, metals, clothing
Value of Imports from U.S.	$67.3 billion	$42.8 billion	$199.6 billion

Summarizing

Why Learn This Skill?

Imagine you have been assigned a long chapter to read. How can you remember the important information? Summarizing information—reducing large amounts of information to a few key phrases—can help you remember the main ideas and important facts.

1 Learning the Skill

To summarize information, follow these guidelines when you read:

- Separate the main ideas from the supporting details. Use the main ideas in a summary.

- Use your own words to describe the main ideas. Do not copy the selection word for word.

- If the summary is almost as long as the reading selection, you are including too much information. The summary should be very short.

2 Practicing the Skill

To practice the skill, read the paragraph below. Then answer the questions that follow.

In early West Africa's villages, education was carried out by the family and other villagers. Children learned the history of their people and the skills needed as adults. Griots, or storytellers, helped in schooling. They kept alive an oral history—the stories passed down from generation to generation. Many stories included a lesson about living. Lessons also were given through short proverbs. One Bantu proverb stated: "A good deed will make a good neighbor." Grandparents and other older people also kept oral histories alive.

1. What are the main ideas of this paragraph?
2. What are the supporting details?
3. Write a brief summary of two or three sentences that will help you remember what the paragraph is about.

3 Applying the Skill

Read a newspaper or short magazine article. Summarize the article in one or two sentences.

Evaluating a Web Site

Why Learn This Skill?

The Internet has grown to become a necessary household and business tool as more people use it. With so many Web sites available, how do you know which one will be the most helpful to you? You must look at the details, so you do not waste valuable time in Web searches.

1 Learning the Skill

The Internet is a valuable research tool. It is easy to use, and it often provides fast, up-to-date information. The most common use of the Internet by students is in doing research. However, some Web site information is not really accurate or reliable.

When using the Internet to do research, you must evaluate the information very carefully. When evaluating the Web site, ask yourself the following questions:

- Do the facts on the site seem accurate?

- Who is the author or sponsor of the site, and what is that person's or organization's reason for maintaining it?

- Does the site information explore a subject in-depth?

- Does the site contain links to other useful resources?

- Is the information easy to read and access?

2 Practicing the Skill

To practice the skill, find three Web sites on the shoguns or samurai of Japan. Follow these steps and write your explanation.

1. Evaluate how useful these sites would be if you were writing a report on the topic.
2. Choose which one is the most helpful.
3. Explain why you chose that site.

3 Applying the Skill

If your school had a Web site, what kind of information would be on it? Write a paragraph describing this site.

A Japanese samurai warrior ▶

Understanding Cause and Effect

Why Learn This Skill?

You know if you watch television instead of completing your homework, you probably will not get a good grade. The cause—not doing homework—leads to the effect—not getting a good grade.

1 Learning the Skill

A *cause* is any person, event, or condition that makes something happen. What happens as a result is known as an *effect*.

These guidelines will help you identify cause and effect.

- Identify two or more events.

- Ask questions about why events occur.

- Look for "clue words" that alert you to cause and effect, such as *because, led to, brought about, produced,* and *therefore.*

- Identify the outcome of events.

2 Practicing the Skill

As you read the following passage, record cause-and-effect connections in a chart or graphic organizer.

Around A.D. 1000 Europe's economy began to revive. Changes in agriculture increased the production of food. Trade grew through annual fairs, and an economy based on money and banking developed. Merchants and artisans founded guilds to regulate trade and protect their own interests. Guilds set standards for the craftspeople's membership, training, quality, and prices.

The money economy created a new wealthy middle class. This class gained political power that led to the decline of feudalism. The rising middle class also influenced the growth of art, literature, and universities. Movements of thought, such as scholasticism, developed.

3 Applying the Skill

Look again at the chapter you are currently reading. Choose a major event that is described and list its causes.

◀ Market in a medieval town

Making Comparisons

Why Learn This Skill?

Suppose you want to buy a portable CD player, and you must choose among three models. To make this decision, you would probably compare various features of the three models, such as price, sound quality, size, and so on. By making comparisons, you will figure out which model is best for you. In the study of world history, you often compare people or events from one time period with those from a different time period.

1 Learning the Skill

When making comparisons, you examine and identify two or more groups, situations, events, or documents. Then you identify any similarities (ways they are alike) and differences (ways they are different). For example, the chart on this page compares the characteristics of two ancient civilizations.

When making comparisons, apply the following steps:

- Decide what items will be compared. Clue words such as *also, as well as, like, same as,* and *similar to* can help you identify things that are being compared.

- Determine which characteristics you will use to compare them.

- Identify similarities and differences in these characteristics.

2 Practicing the Skill

To practice the skill, analyze the information on the chart at the bottom of this page. Then answer these questions.

1. What items are being compared?
2. What characteristics are being used to compare them?
3. In what ways were the early Byzantine and Islamic civilizations similar? In what ways were they different?
4. Suppose you wanted to compare the two civilizations in more detail. What are some of the characteristics you might use?

3 Applying the Skill

Think about two sports that are played at your school. Make a chart comparing such things as: where the games are played, who plays them, what equipment is used, and other details.

Early Byzantine and Islamic Civilizations

Cultural Characteristic	Byzantine Empire	Islamic Empire
Homeland	Greece	Arabia
Political Organization	Emperors	Caliphs (religious leaders)
Official Language	Greek	Arabic
Religion	Eastern Christianity	Islam
Main Occupations	Farmers, traders, artisans	Traders, herders, artisans
A Main Contribution	Religious architecture	Medicine and mathematics

Making Predictions

Why Learn This Skill?

In history you read about people making difficult decisions based on what they think *might* happen. By making predictions yourself, you can get a better understanding of the choices people make.

1 Learning the Skill

As you read a paragraph or section in your book, think about what might come next. What you think will happen is your *prediction.* A prediction does not have a correct or incorrect answer. Making predictions helps you to carefully consider what you are reading.

To make a prediction, ask yourself:

- What happened in this paragraph or section?

- What prior knowledge do I have about the events in the text?

- What similar situations do I know of?

- What do I think might happen next?

- Test your prediction: read further to see if you were correct.

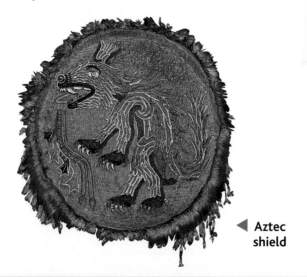

◀ Aztec shield

2 Practicing the Skill

To practice the skill, read the following paragraph about the Aztec Empire. Then answer the questions.

The Aztec of ancient Mexico built the strongest empire of any Native American group. They mined gold, silver, and other goods for trade. In building their empire, they conquered many other Native American groups. The Aztec fought their enemies using wooden weapons with stone blades.

In the 1500s, a Spanish army seeking gold heard about the Aztec and their riches. Led by Hernán Cortés, the Spaniards were helped by enemies of the Aztec. Armed with steel swords, muskets, and cannons, the Spaniards moved towards the Aztec capital.

1. Choose the outcome below that is most likely to occur between the Aztec and Spaniards.

   a. The Spaniards will avoid the Aztec altogether.

   b. The two groups will become friends.

   c. The Spaniards will conquer the Aztec.

   d. The Aztec will conquer the Spaniards.

2. Explain why you chose the answer you did.

3 Applying the Skill

Watch a television show or a movie. Halfway through the show, write your prediction of how it will end on a piece of paper. At the end of the show, check your prediction.

Drawing Inferences and Conclusions

Why Learn This Skill?

Suppose your teacher brought an artifact to class and a classmate exclaimed, "That came from Greece, didn't it?" You might infer that your classmate had an interest in Greece.

1 Learning the Skill

To *infer* means to evaluate information and arrive at a *conclusion*. Social studies writers do not always spell out everything in the text. When you make inferences you "read between the lines." You must then use the available facts and your own knowledge of social studies to draw a conclusion.

Use the following steps to help draw inferences and make conclusions:

- Read carefully for stated facts and ideas.

- Summarize the information and list the important facts.

- Apply related information that you may already know to make inferences.

- Use your knowledge and insight to develop some conclusions about these facts.

2 Practicing the Skill

Read the passage below and answer the questions.

As the Scientific Revolution advanced, many educated Europeans came to believe that reason—sound thinking—was a much better guide than faith or tradition. To them, reason was a "light" that revealed error and showed the way to truth. As a result, the 1700s became known as the Age of Enlightenment.

1. What topic is the writer describing?
2. What facts are given?
3. What can you infer about the Scientific Revolution?
4. What conclusions can you draw about how Enlightenment thinkers felt about religion?

3 Applying the Skill

Read one of the biographies in this text. What can you infer about the life of the person described? Draw a conclusion about whether or not you would like to meet this person.

▼ An Enlightenment gathering

Recognizing Economic Indicators

Why Learn This Skill?

Every day, business and government leaders are faced with the challenge of trying to predict what will happen to the economy in the coming months and years. To help these leaders in making decisions, economists, or scientists who study the economy, have developed ways to measure an economy's performance. These ways are called economic indicators.

1 Learning the Skill

Economic indicators are statistics, or numbers, that tell how well the economy is doing and how well the economy is going to do in the future. They include the number of jobless, the rate at which prices rise over a period of time, and the amount of goods and services that are produced and sold. Each month, the U.S. Department of Commerce gathers data for 78 economic indicators covering all aspects of the state of the United States economy. The chart below lists some common terms for economic indicators that you may read about.

▲ Prices on the stock market often rise or fall based on changes in economic indicators.

2 Practicing the Skill

Start an Economics Handbook. Using a dictionary, look up each economic term listed on this chart. Write a definition for each term in your Economics Handbook.

3 Applying the Skill

Think about one of the countries you have read about in this text that has grown to be wealthy. Using the terms that you just defined, write a paragraph describing that country's wealth.

Economic Indicators

Term	Definition
Saving	
Income	
Expenditure	
Consumption	
Inflation	
Debt	
Gross Domestic Product (GDP)	
Interest Rates	
Credit	
Export	
Import	

Interpreting Political Cartoons

Why Learn This Skill?

Political cartoonists use art to express political opinions. Their work appears in newspapers, magazines, books, and on the Internet. Political cartoons are drawings that express an opinion. They usually focus on public figures, political events, or economic or social conditions. A political cartoon can give you a summary of an event or circumstance and the artist's opinion in a quick and entertaining manner.

1 Learning the Skill

To interpret a political cartoon, follow these steps:

- Read the title, caption, or conversation balloons. Most cartoons will carry at least one of these elements. They help you identify the subject of the cartoon.

- Identify the characters or people shown. They may be caricatures, or unrealistic drawings that exaggerate the characters' physical features.

- Identify any symbols shown. Symbols are things that stand for something else. An example is the American flag that is a symbol of our country. Commonly recognized symbols may not be labeled. Unusual symbolism will be labeled.

- Examine the actions in the cartoon—what is happening and why?

- Identify the cartoonist's purpose. What statement or idea is he or she trying to get across? Decide if the cartoonist wants to persuade, criticize, or just make people think.

2 Practicing the Skill

On a separate sheet of paper, answer these questions about the political cartoon below.

1. What is the subject of the cartoon?
2. What words give clues as to the meaning of the cartoon?
3. What item seems out of place?
4. What message do you think the cartoonist is trying to send?

3 Applying the Skill

Bring a news magazine to class. With a partner, analyze the message in each political cartoon that you find.

California Standards Handbook

GRADE 7

Dear Student and Family,

After you complete each chapter, take time to review what you have learned by using this handbook. **The California Standards Handbook** lists all of the California History-Social Science content standards covered in each chapter of the book. In addition, a brief review of the content and page numbers where the content can be found are included. Test your knowledge of each major standard by answering the questions that appear in each of the red boxes.

Remember, the importance of the knowledge and skills you gain this year will extend well beyond your classroom. After all, you learn about the world's history not simply to know names and dates, but to become a well-informed citizen of the United States and the world.

Contents

WH7.1

What Is the Standard? ➡ Where Can I Find It?

WH7.1 Students analyze the causes and effects of the vast expansion and ultimate disintegration of the Roman Empire.

➡ **Chapter 1,** covers standard WH7.1, including problems caused by the expanding empire as well as Rome's collapse and the rise of the Byzantine Empire. **(See pp. 132–69.)**

WH7.1.1 Study the early strengths and lasting contributions of Rome (e.g., significance of Roman citizenship; rights under Roman law; Roman art, architecture, engineering, and philosophy; preservation and transmission of Christianity) and its ultimate internal weaknesses (e.g., rise of autonomous military powers within the empire, undermining of citizenship by the growth of corruption and slavery, lack of education, and distribution of news).

➡ **Chapter 1, Section 1** The Romans made significant advances in building techniques, literature, science and engineering. **(See pp. 136–43.)**

➡ **Chapter 1, Sections 1 and 2** In the A.D. 200s, Rome began to experience political, social, economic, and military problems that would eventually lead to its collapse. **(See pp. 144–51; 154–55.)**

➡ **Chapter 1, Section 2** Roman ideas including government and architecture as well as the spread of Christianity still influence us today. **(See pp. 152–53.)**

WH7.1.2 Discuss the geographic borders of the empire at its height and the factors that threatened its territorial cohesion.

➡ **Chapter 1, Section 1 and 2** Rome eventually could not protect the borders of its vast empire, and invading armies began breaking the empire apart. **(See pp. 136–51.)**

WH7.1.3 Describe the establishment by Constantine of the new capital in Constantinople and the development of the Byzantine Empire, with an emphasis on the consequences of the development of two distinct European civilizations, Eastern Orthodox and Roman Catholic, and their two distinct views on church-state relations.

➡ **Chapter 1, Section 3** Years after Constantine founded Constantinople the Emperor Justinian's military efforts and law codes helped make the Byzantine Empire strong. **(See pp. 156–60; 163–67.)**

➡ **Chapter 1, Section 3** The Eastern Orthodox and Roman Catholic Church each had different roles and relationships with the states in which they had influence. **(See pp. 161–62.)**

Standards Practice

1 Roman engineers were known for
- **A** building the Grand Canal.
- **B** building aqueducts.
- **C** inventing the compass.
- **D** developing a printing press.

2 Constantinople became an important city because it
- **A** sat on the crossroads of trade.
- **B** was the capital of France.
- **C** was located near Babylon.
- **D** was the world center of Christianity.

WH7.2

What Is the Standard? ➡ Where Can I Find It?

WH7.2 Students analyze the geographic, political, economic, religious, and social structures of the civilizations of Islam in the Middle Ages.

Chapter 2 covers standard WH7.2, including geographic features such as the desert in Arabia, the rise and spread of Islam, and the economic and social aspects of Islamic civilization. **(See pp. 170–201.)**

WH7.2.1 Identify the physical features and describe the climate of the Arabian peninsula, its relationship to surrounding bodies of land and water, and nomadic and sedentary ways of life.

Chapter 2, Section 1 Arabia is a desert surrounded by seas, mountains, and rivers/valleys. Civilizations arose in these valleys. **(See pp. 174–76.)**

Chapter 2, Section 1 Different styles of living arose in Arabia. Many were nomadic, some were sedentary. **(See pp. 174–76.)**

WH7.2.2 Trace the origins of Islam and the life and teachings of Muhammad, including Islamic teachings on the connection with Judaism and Christianity.

Chapter 2, Section 1 The prophet Muhammad brought the message of Islam to the people of Arabia. **(See pp. 176–78.)**

Chapter 2, Section 1 Muslims share common beliefs with Christians and Jews. **(See p. 179.)**

Chapter 2, Section 2 Muslims view Christians and Jews as "People of the Book." **(See p. 184.)**

WH7.2.3 Explain the significance of the Qur'an and the Sunnah as the primary sources of Islamic beliefs, practice, and law, and their influence in Muslims' daily life.

Chapter 2, Section 1 The Quran provided guidelines for Muslims' lives and the governments of Muslim states. **(See pp. 179–80.)**

Chapter 2, Section 1 The Sunna is the name given to customs based on Muhammad's words and deeds and covers all areas of daily life. **(See p. 180.)**

WH7.2.4 Discuss the expansion of Muslim rule through military conquests and treaties, emphasizing the cultural blending within Muslim civilization and the spread and acceptance of Islam and the Arabic language.

Chapter 2, Section 1 By raising an army and signing treaties, Muhammad gained control of most of Arabia. **(See pp. 176–77.)**

Chapter 2, Section 2 The Rightly Guided Caliphs expanded Islam throughout southwest Asia. **(See pp. 181–83.)**

Chapter 2, Section 2 The Umayyad empire spread Islam and Arabic through preaching, conquests, and trade. **(See pp. 183–84.)**

Chapter 2, Section 2 First the Abbasids, then the Seljuks conquered Muslim kingdoms and established new rules in southwest Asia. **(See pp. 185–86.)**

Chapter 2, Section 2 Later Muslim empires spread in Asia, Africa, and Europe, especially the Ottomans. **(See pp. 187–89.)**

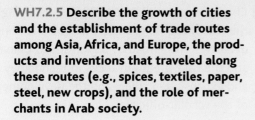

WH7.2

WH7.2.5 Describe the growth of cities and the establishment of trade routes among Asia, Africa, and Europe, the products and inventions that traveled along these routes (e.g., spices, textiles, paper, steel, new crops), and the role of merchants in Arab society.

➡ **Chapter 2, Section 2** The Abbasids built a new city, Baghdad, that prospered from trade. **(See pp. 185–86.)**

➡ **Chapter 2, Section 3** Cities arose along trade routes through Arabia. **(See pp. 190–92.)**

➡ **Chapter 2, Section 3** Muslims also established trade routes from Indonesia to Spain and built new cities along these routes. **(See p. 191.)**

➡ **Chapter 2, Section 3** Muslim merchants brought many new products to India, including paper and gunpowder. **(See pp. 190–91.)**

➡ **Chapter 2, Section 3** New Muslim cities became places of learning. **(See pp. 191–93.)**

WH7.2.6 Understand the intellectual exchanges among Muslim scholars of Eurasia and Africa and the contributions Muslim scholars made to later civilizations in the areas of science, geography, mathematics, philosophy, medicine, art, and literature.

➡ **Chapter 2, Section 3** Scholars in Muslim lands saved much of the learning of the ancient world. **(See p. 194.)**

➡ **Chapter 2, Section 3** Muslims made important progress in science, mathematics, architecture, and medicine, such as perfecting the astrolabe and discovering how disease spreads. **(See pp. 193–97.)**

Standards Practice

1 The earliest followers of Islam came from

   A Makkah's wealthy merchants and religious leaders.

   B monks and nuns living in the desert.

   C Makkah's poor.

   D Makkah's Jewish tribes.

2 The Quran was important because it

   A controlled the Muslim economy.

   B provided maps of the area.

   C set out the teachings of Islam.

   D was a biography of Muhammad.

3 How did Muslim rulers contribute to the growth of trade?

   A They abolished all taxes on trade goods.

   B They kept detailed records of business deals.

   C They forced many farmers to become merchants.

   D They provided merchants with coins.

4 Who were the moguls?

   A Muslim warriors from northern India

   B European merchants

   C Muslim scholars

   D Muslim scientists

WH7.3

What Is the Standard? ➡ **Where Can I Find It?**

WH7.3 **Students analyze the geographic, political, economic, religious, and social structures of the civilizations of China in the Middle Ages.**	**Chapter 4** covers standard WH7.3, including the rise of the Tang, Song, Mongol, and Ming dynasties, the spread of Buddhism to China and the East, great advances in technology and expansion in trade, and the development of the scholar-officials. (See pp. 248–91.)
WH7.3.1 **Describe the reunification of China under the Tang Dynasty and reasons for the spread of Buddhism in Tang China, Korea, and Japan.**	**Chapter 4, Section 1** Wendi reunified China through conquest. Soon Yangdi established the Tang dynasty. (See pp. 252–56.) **Chapter 4, Section 1** Missionaries spread Buddhism to China and Korea, where it had an important influence on culture. Later it spread to Japan. (See pp. 256–57.)
WH7.3.2 **Describe agricultural, technological, and commercial developments during the Tang and Song periods.**	**Chapter 4, Section 2** Under the Tang, new irrigation and crop-growing techniques were developed and trade increased through the Silk Road. (See pp. 260–62.) **Chapter 4, Section 2** New inventions affected both Tang and Song societies. (See pp. 262–263.) **Chapter 4, Section 2** In addition to literary developments, the Chinese invented porcelain, which greatly aided trade. (See pp. 264–66.)
WH7.3.3 **Analyze the influences of Confucianism and changes in Confucian thought during the Song and Mongol periods.**	**Chapter 4, Section 1** Neo-Confucianism developed under the Tang dynasty. (See pp. 258–59.) **Chapter 4, Section 1** In both the Tang and Song dynasties, Neo-Confucianism led to the rise of scholar-officials and civil service exams. (See pp. 258–59.) **Chapter 4, Section 3** The Mongols continued the use of scholar-officials. (See pp. 272–73.)
WH7.3.4 **Understand the importance of both overland trade and maritime expeditions between China and other civilizations in the Mongol Ascendancy and Ming Dynasty.**	**Chapter 4, Section 3** The Mongols expanded trade along the Silk Road and on sea, trading goods such as silver, spices, carpets, and cotton. (See pp. 267–73.) **Chapter 4, Section 4** Zheng He built a massive fleet for trade and discovery. (See pp. 284–87.)

WH7.3

What Is the Standard? → Where Can I Find It?

WH7.3.5 Trace the historic influence of such discoveries as tea, the manufacture of paper, wood-block printing, the compass, and gunpowder.

→ **Chapter 4, Section 2** Tea became a popular drink in China. (See p. 261.)

→ **Chapter 4, Section 2** Major inventions influenced Chinese society. Some of these included the use of coal to make steel, the printing press and paper, gunpowder, and the compass. (See pp. 262–64.)

→ **Chapter 4, Section 3** The Mongols created powerful armies equipped with gunpowder weapons and were able to conquer China. (See pp. 267–70.)

WH7.3.6 Describe the development of the imperial state and the scholar-official class.

→ **Chapter 4, Section 1** Both Tang and Song rulers used civil service examinations to hire officials. (See pp. 256–57.)

→ **Chapter 4, Section 1** Civil service exams led to the rise of a new wealthy class in China. (See pp. 256–57.)

→ **Chapter 4, Section 4** Ming emperors made all the decisions in government, but they restored the civil service exams. (See pp. 281–83.)

Standards Practice

1 **Which invention spread from China to other parts of the world?**

A wheel
B gunpowder
C banking
D arch

2 **Who was Genghis Khan?**

A A ruler of China during the Han dynasty
B A Mongol leader who conquered an empire
C A trader along the Silk Road
D A Chinese leader who sent out fleets of ships

3 **What effect did civil service examinations have on China?**

A It created a new wealthy class of scholar-officials.
B It led to the creation of a constitutional monarchy.
C It shifted control from the emperor to officials in the provinces.
D It strengthened the hold of Buddhism on the emperor's court.

4 **To make steel, the Chinese used**

A rice paper.
B granite.
C wood.
D coal.

California Standards Handbook

California Standards Handbook   **573**

WH7.4

What Is the Standard? ➡ Where Is It Covered?

WH7.4 Students analyze the geographic, political, economic, religious, and social structures of the sub-Saharan civilizations of Ghana and Mali in Medieval Africa.

Chapter 3 covers standard WH7.4, including the rise of the Ghana and Mali empires, the importance of regional trade of gold and salt, and the spread of Islam in Africa. (See pp. 202–41.)

WH7.4.1 Study the Niger River and the relationship of vegetation zones of forest, savannah, and desert to trade in gold, salt, food, and slaves; and the growth of the Ghana and Mali empires.

Chapter 3, Section 1 Africa's varied climate includes the civilization-supporting Niger River. (See pp. 206–08.)

Chapter 3, Section 1 West Africa grew rich through trade of various goods across deserts, savannahs, and along rivers. (See pp. 209–12.)

Chapter 3, Section 1 Both Ghana and Mali depended on salt and gold trade in the Niger River valley. (See pp. 209–12.)

Chapter 3, Section 3 Queen Nzinga fought to halt the trade of slaves. (See pp. 231–32.)

Chapter 3, Section 3 The slave trade across the Sahara expanded when the Portuguese arrived in ships and established ports. (See pp. 233–34.)

WH7.4.2 Analyze the importance of family, labor specialization, and regional commerce in the development of states and cities in West Africa.

Chapter 3, Section 1 Control of trade routes allowed powerful kingdoms to arise in Africa. (See pp. 209–14.)

Chapter 3, Section 3 Although in villages African society was matrilineal, women had fewer rights than men. (See pp. 231–32.)

Chapter 3, Section 3 Education in villages was carried out by the family and other villagers. (See p. 231.)

WH7.4.3 Describe the role of the trans-Saharan caravan trade in the changing religious and cultural characteristics of West Africa and the influence of Islamic beliefs, ethics, and law.

Chapter 3, Section 2 Before the coming of Islam and Christianity, Africans had their own religious practices. (See pp. 222–23.)

Chapter 3, Section 2 Traders spread Islam to West Africa, where it played an important role, especially in the Mali and Songhai empires. (See pp. 224–29.)

Chapter 3, Section 3 The trans-Saharan slave trade spread slavery through Africa. (See pp. 233–34.)

Chapter 3, Section 3 The slave trade spread local traditions throughout Africa. (See pp. 235–37.)

WH7.4

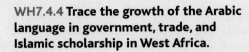

What Is the Standard? ➡ Where Is It Covered?

WH7.4.4 Trace the growth of the Arabic language in government, trade, and Islamic scholarship in West Africa.

➡ **Chapter 3, Section 2** Especially under the Mali and Songhai, Africans built libraries and universities and expanded trade. (See pp. 224–27.)

➡ **Chapter 3, Section 2** The Arabic language and Arabic ideas of government and trade influenced the development of countries in Africa. (See pp. 227–29.)

WH7.4.5 Describe the importance of written and oral traditions in the transmission of African history and culture.

➡ **Chapter 3, Section 1** Storytellers called griots passed on African history. (See p. 211.)

➡ **Chapter 3, Section 2** With the establishment of libraries, Africans recorded and preserved their history. (See pp. 224–27.)

➡ **Chapter 3, Section 3** Griots were important in preserving oral history. (See p. 231.)

➡ **Chapter 3, Section 3** Enslaved Africans kept their culture alive through storytelling. (See p. 237.)

Standards Practice

1 **The rulers of Ghana became rich by**

A building canals that linked various parts of their kingdom.

B controlling trade in silver.

C taxing traders passing through Ghana.

D seizing the wealth of the mosques.

2 **What two items increased trade in West Africa?**

A water and gold

B salt and camels

C water and camels

D salt and gold

3 **Which of the following is true about Arabic language in West Africa?**

A Arabic was the language of royal courts only.

B Arabic was taught to many Africans in Muslim schools.

C Arabic was the language of trade and commerce only.

D Arabic replaced Swahili as the major language of West Africa.

4 **Traders spread what religion to West Africa?**

A Islam

B Buddhism

C Shintoism

D Daoism

WH7.5

What Is the Standard? ➡ Where Is It Covered?

WH7.5 Students analyze the geographic, political, economic, religious, and social structures of the civilizations of Medieval Japan.	➤ **Chapter 5** covers standard WH7.5, including feudal society, the rise of Japanese forms of Buddhism, and great works of literature and art. **(See pp. 292–319.)**
WH7.5.1 Describe the significance of Japan's proximity to China and Korea and the intellectual, linguistic, religious, and philosophical influence of those countries on Japan.	➤ **Chapter 5, Section 1** Japan's geography isolated its society. **(See pp. 296–98.)** ➤ **Chapter 5, Section 1** Under Shotoku, the Japanese borrowed culturally from China and Korea, including the use of trained officials in government and the rise of Buddhism in Japan. **(See pp. 299–300.)** ➤ **Chapter 5, Section 1** The early Japanese followed a religion called Shinto. **(See p. 301.)** ➤ **Chapter 5, Section 2** The Japanese capital Nara was designed on the style of China's Chang'an. **(See pp. 302–03.)** ➤ **Chapter 5, Section 2** Buddhism came to Japan through Korea. **(See pp. 303–04.)** ➤ **Chapter 5, Section 3** Japanese forms of Buddhism led to new styles of art, architecture, and the rise of martial arts in Japan. **(See pp. 309–13.)**
WH7.5.2 Discuss the reign of Prince Shotoku of Japan and the characteristics of Japanese society and family life during his reign.	➤ **Chapter 5, Section 1** Prince Shotoku created a strong government in Japan based on the Chinese model. **(See pp. 299–300.)** ➤ **Chapter 5, Section 1** Shotoku helped spread Buddhism throughout Japan. Under him, Japan also borrowed Chinese ideas of art, medicine, and philosophy. **(See pp. 299–300.)** ➤ **Chapter 5, Section 3** Under Shotoku and later rulers, family life was very important. Although women had many restrictions, they made important contributions to society. **(See pp. 313–15.)**
WH7.5.3 Describe the values, social customs, and traditions prescribed by the lord-vassal system consisting of *shogun*, *daimyo*, and *samurai* and the lasting influence of the warrior code throughout the twentieth century.	➤ **Chapter 5, Section 2** To defend their lands, nobles used faithful warriors called samurai who followed a code of conduct. At the same time, military commanders called shoguns gained power over government. **(See pp. 304–06.)** ➤ **Chapter 5, Section 2** After the samurai revolted from the shogun, military lords called daimyo used samurai to control small regions. **(See pp. 307–08.)**

WH7.5

What Is the Standard? ➡ Where Is It Covered?

WH7.5.4 Trace the development of distinctive forms of Japanese Buddhism.	➡ **Chapter 5, Section 1** Before the Japanese followed Buddhism, they practiced a religion called Shinto. (See p. 301.) ➡ **Chapter 5, Section 2** Buddhism became very popular in Japan, but some officials rejected it. (See pp. 302–04.) ➡ **Chapter 5, Section 3** Two popular sects of Buddhism in Japan were Pure Land Buddhism and Zen. (See pp. 309–11.)
WH7.5.5 Study the ninth and tenth centuries' golden age of literature, art, and drama and its lasting effects on culture today, including Murasaki Shikibu's *Tale of Genji*.	➡ **Chapter 5, Section 3** Japanese artists developed unique works of art in wooden statues and furniture and by using watercolors for paints. (See pp. 310–12.) ➡ **Chapter 5, Section 3** Japanese literature and drama include Noh plays and tanka and haiku poetry. Murasaki Shikibu's *Tale of Genji* may be the world's first novel. (See pp. 312–13.)
WH7.5.6 Analyze the rise of a military society in the late twelfth century and the role of the samurai in that society.	➡ **Chapter 5, Section 2** By using samurai, nobles helped create a military society in Japan. Eventually military leaders called shoguns would control the government. (See pp. 304–06.)

Standards Practice

1 **Bushido, the code of the samurai, demanded that a warrior must**

- A seek his own safety during battle
- B die in battle rather than betray his lord
- C take an oath of loyalty to the constitution
- D pray and give alms to the local temple

2 **Samurai could be recognized by their**

- A great height.
- B manner of walking.
- C clothing.
- D religious medal.

3 **Every well-educated Japanese was expected to practice which art form?**

- A Bushido
- B Shinto
- C calligraphy
- D dancing

4 **Japanese artisans and merchants fomed**

- A guilds.
- B churches.
- C farms.
- D armies.

WH7.6

What Is the Standard? ➡ Where Is It Covered?

WH7.6 **Students analyze the geographic, political, economic, religious, and social structures of the civilizations of Medieval Europe.**

Chapter 6 covers Standard WH7.6, including the rise of feudalism, the importance of the Catholic Church, new political and social ideas, the Crusades, advances in art and architecture, and the plague. (See pp. 320–73.)

WH7.6.1 **Study the geography of Europe and the Eurasian land mass, including their location, topography, waterways, vegetation, and climate and their relationship to ways of life in Medieval Europe.**

Chapter 6, Section 1 The geography of Europe includes many rivers, mountains, and peninsulas, all of which influenced the rise of civilization. (See pp. 324–26.)
Chapter 6, Section 2 Abundant waterways led to the rise of towns and guilds. (See pp. 340–43.)

WH7.6.2 **Describe the spread of Christianity north of the Alps and the roles played by the early church and by monasteries in its diffusion after the fall of the western half of the Roman Empire.**

Chapter 6, Section 1 After the fall of Rome, Christianity spread through Europe largely through monks sent by popes as missionaries. (See pp. 331–32.)

WH7.6.3 **Understand the development of feudalism, its role in the medieval European economy, the way in which it was influenced by physical geography (the role of the manor and the growth of towns), and how feudal relationships provided the foundation of political order.**

Chapter 6, Section 2 During the A.D. 800s, a shift in power from kings to nobles and vassals developed into feudalism. The manorial system also developed with peasants and freemen working the land for nobles. (See pp. 334–40, 344–45.)
Chapter 6, Section 2 Some towns were controlled by lords, while others were controlled by local governments and guilds. (See pp. 340–43.)

WH7.6.4 **Demonstrate an understanding of the conflict and cooperation between the Papacy and European monarchs (e.g., Charlemagne, Gregory VII, Emperor Henry IV).**

Chapter 6, Section 1 A Germanic people called the Franks helped defend the pope and spread Christianity. (See pp. 326–31.)
Chapter 6, Section 1 Charlemagne was crowned emperor by the pope in 800. Later, Gregory VII tried to stop Henry IV from interfering in Church affairs. (See pp. 327–31.)

WH7.6.5 **Know the significance of developments in medieval English legal and constitutional practices and their importance in the rise of modern democratic thought and representative institutions (e.g., Magna Carta, parliament, development of habeas corpus, an independent judiciary in England).**

Chapter 6, Section 3 Although English kings had established the principles of common law, the nobles forced King John to sign the Magna Carta to give them greater freedoms and rights. (See pp. 346–49.)

WH7.6

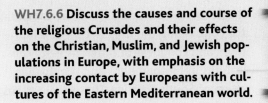

What Is the Standard? → Where Is It Covered?

WH7.6.6 Discuss the causes and course of the religious Crusades and their effects on the Christian, Muslim, and Jewish populations in Europe, with emphasis on the increasing contact by Europeans with cultures of the Eastern Mediterranean world.

→ **Chapter 6, Section 3** The Crusades began to free the Holy Land from Muslim control. Many Christians, Muslims, and Jews were killed. Despite early victories, the Crusaders eventually lost Jerusalem. (See pp. 352–54, 358–59.)

→ **Chapter 6, Section 3** The Crusades increased trade between Europe and the Middle East and helped break down feudalism. (See pp. 352–54.)

WH7.6.7 Map the spread of the bubonic plague from Central Asia to China, the Middle East, and Europe and describe its impact on global population.

→ **Chapter 6, Section 5** The bubonic plague began in Central Asia and spread to Europe and China. It devastated the population in both parts of the world. (See pp. 364–66.)

WH7.6.8 Understand the importance of the Catholic church as a political, intellectual, and aesthetic institution (e.g., founding of universities, political and spiritual roles of the clergy, creation of monastic and mendicant religious orders, preservation of the Latin language and religious texts, St. Thomas Aquinas's synthesis of classical philosophy with Christian theology, and the concept of "natural law").

→ **Chapter 6, Section 1** Monks spread Christianity and helped preserve Latin. (See pp. 331–33.)

→ **Chapter 6, Section 4** In Medieval Europe, daily life revolved around the Catholic Church, while new religious orders developed. (See pp. 355–59.)

→ **Chapter 6, Section 4** New styles of art and architecture arose, the first universities developed and Thomas Aquinas worked to understand Classical philosophy with Christian theology. (See pp. 360–63.)

WH7.6.9 Know the history of the decline of Muslim rule in the Iberian Peninsula that culminated in the Reconquista and the rise of Spanish and Portuguese kingdoms.

→ **Chapter 6, Section 5** Conflict erupted all over Europe in the late Middle Ages. In Spain, Christians engaged in the *Reconquista* to force Muslims out of the peninsula. This helped the rise of Spain and Portugal. (See pp. 367–69.)

Standards Practice

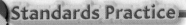

1 **How did monks affect European society during the Middle Ages?**

A They set up feudalism.

B They helped to train armies for battle.

C They harvested crops.

D They helped preserve knowledge.

2 **The Crusades affected Europe by**

A increasing trade with the east.

B strengthening feudalism

C causing the plague

D unifying England with France.

WH7.7

What Is the Standard? → Where Can I Find It?

WH7.7 Students compare and contrast the geographic, political, economic, religious, and social structures of the Meso-American and Andean civilizations.	**Chapter 9** covers standard WH7.7, comparing and contrasting the rise, spread, development, and conquest of different early civilizations in Mesoamerica and the Andean region of South America. These civilizations include Olmec, Maya, Aztec, Moche, and Inca. (See pp. 446–81.)
WH7.7.1 Study the locations, landforms, and climates of Mexico, Central America, and South America and their effects on Mayan, Aztec, and Incan economies, trade, and development of urban societies.	**Chapter 9, Section 1** Early peoples in the Americas changed from hunting and gathering to settling large civilizations. (See pp. 450–53.)
	Chapter 9, Sections 1 and 2 The Maya built a trading civilization of city-states based in the rain forests of the Yucatán Peninsula in Meso-America. (See pp. 453–54, 456–59.)
	Chapter 9, Sections 1 and 2 The Aztec capital of Tenochtitlán was a center of a vast trading empire in central Mexico. In rural areas, Aztec farmers used irrigation and drainage to grow crops. (See pp. 454, 460–62.)
	Chapter 9, Sections 1 and 2 A system of roads increased trade and united the Inca Empire. The Inca used irrigation and terraced farming to improve the land and developed healthy urban cities. (See pp. 454–55, 462–64.)
WH7.7.2 Study the roles of people in each society, including class structures, family life, warfare, religious beliefs and practices, and slavery.	**Chapter 9, Section 2** The Maya believed in many gods, saw their kings as divine, and practiced human sacrifice. Their priests set up a strict class system, in which war captives worked the land as slaves. Women played a large role in Mayan society. (See pp. 456–59.)
	Chapter 9, Section 2 Strong Aztec kings headed a society of four classes that honored many gods and engaged in conquests. (See pp. 460–62.)
	Chapter 9, Section 2 Inca rulers set up a strong central government but let local rulers stay in power. The society of the Inca was highly organized, including rulers and their families at the top, army leaders, priests, and skilled workers in the middle, and farmers, herders, and soldiers at the bottom. (See pp. 462–64.)

WH7.7

What Is the Standard? → Where Is It Covered?

WH7.7.3 Explain how and where each empire arose and how the Aztec and Incan empires were defeated by the Spanish.	**Chapter 9, Section 1** Warlike nomadic Aztecs settled in central Mexico and built the city of Tenochtitlán. (See pp. 460–61.) **Chapter 9, Section 1** The Inca built the largest empire in the Americas, located in the Andes ranges of South America. (See p. 462.) **Chapter 9, Section 3** Spanish forces under Hernán Cortés conquered the Aztec. Disease killed more Aztec than Spanish swords. (See pp. 470–75.) **Chapter 9, Section 3** Francisco Pizarro used treachery and weapons to conquer the Inca Empire (See pp. 476–77.)
WH7.7.4 Describe the artistic and oral traditions and architecture in the three civilizations.	**Chapter 9, Section 2** The Maya excelled in building and carving. The Maya also developed a written language to record numbers and dates. (See pp. 456–59.) **Chapter 9, Section 2** The Aztec built pyramid-temples to honor the gods, used oral tradition and later codices to pass on their culture. (See pp. 460–62.) **Chapter 9, Section 2** The Inca built roads and large structures and kept records on ropes with knotted cords. They relied on oral tradition to pass on knowledge. (See pp. 462–64.)
WH7.7.5 Describe the Meso-American achievements in astronomy and mathematics, including the development of the calendar and the Meso-American knowledge of seasonal changes to the civilizations' agricultural systems.	**Chapter 9, Section 2** The Maya produced a calendar to predict eclipses and to schedule festivals, plantings, and harvests. They also invented a system of counting based on 20. (See p. 458.) **Chapter 9, Section 2** The Aztec developed two different calendars, one for planning festivals, the other for agriculture. (See pp. 461–62.)

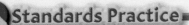

Standards Practice

1 Why did Mayan warriors carry out conquests?

  A to gain control of more land

  B to find places that had a lot of water

  C to find women to marry

  D to acquire captives to sacrifice

2 On whom did Hernán Cortés rely to defeat the Aztec?

  A the Inca

  B Native American allies

  C the Olmec

  D African Americans opposed to slavery

WH7.8

What Is the Standard? ➡️ Where Can I Find It?

WH7.8 **Students analyze the origins, accomplishments, and geographic diffusion of the Renaissance.**

➡️ **Chapter 7** covers standard WH7.8, including the beginnings of the Renaissance in the city-states of Italy, the accomplishments of Renaissance artists, writers and thinkers, and the spread of the Renaissance from Italy to other parts of Europe (See pp. 380–417.)

WH7.8.1 Describe the way in which the revival of classical learning and the arts fostered a new interest in humanism (i.e., a balance between intellect and religious faith).

➡️ **Chapter 7, Section 1** The Renaissance was a rebirth of interest in the same subjects the Greeks and Romans studied. (See pp. 384–86.)

➡️ **Chapter 7, Section 2** Renaissance humanism was based on classical values, but did not abandon religious faith. It emphasized a balance between faith and reason and the study of classical works. (See pp. 394–97.)

WH7.8.2 Explain the importance of Florence in the early stages of the Renaissance and the growth of independent trading cities (e.g., Venice), with emphasis on the cities' importance in the spread of Renaissance ideas.

➡️ **Chapter 7, Section 1** The Renaissance began and developed in Florence, Venice, and other prosperous trading city-states that used their wealth to support the arts and promote new ideas (See pp. 385–89.)

➡️ **Chapter 7, Section 1** Wealthy urban nobles and merchants were involved in shaping the politics, government, and diplomacy of city-states. (See pp. 390–93.)

WH7.8.3 Understand the effects of the reopening of the ancient "Silk Road" between Europe and China, including Marco Polo's travels and the location of his routes.

➡️ **Chapter 7, Section 1** The Mongols united almost all of Asia into a vast trade network, increasing the flow of goods between China and western regions. The prices of luxury goods fell, increasing demand in Europe and bringing new wealth to Italian merchants. (See pp. 387–88.)

➡️ **Chapter 7, Section 1** Marco Polo's travels in China sparked European interest in the East and its products. (See p. 388.)

WH7.8.4 Describe the growth and effects of new ways of disseminating information (e.g., the ability to manufacture paper, translation of the Bible into the vernacular, printing).

➡️ **Chapter 7, Section 2** European authors in the early 1300s began writing in the vernacular, enabling many more people to read their works. Beginning in the mid-1400s, Gutenberg's moveable type printing press, combined with the use of linen paper, increased the availability of books (especially vernacular Bibles) and the spread of new ideas. (See pp. 397–400.)

WH7.8

What Is the Standard? ➡ Where Is It Covered?

WH7.8.5 Detail advances made in literature, the arts, science, mathematics, cartography, engineering, and the understanding of human anatomy and astronomy (e.g., by Dante Alighieri, Leonardo da Vinci, Michelangelo di Buonarroti Simoni, Johann Gutenberg, William Shakespeare).

➡ **Chapter 7, Section 2** The arts and sciences flourished during the Renaissance. Scientists, such as Leonardo da Vinci, Johannes Gutenberg, advanced studies in the fields of mathematics, physics, anatomy, engineering, and mapmaking. Literary figures, such as Dante Alighieri and William Shakespeare, produced vernacular literature that probed deeply into the human character. **(See pp. 396–406.)**

➡ **Chapter 7, Section 3** Italian Renaissance artists, such as Michelangelo Buonarrotti and Leonardo da Vinci, used perspective and other techniques to lend realism to their works. **(See pp. 408–12.)**

➡ **Chapter 7, Section 3** Spreading to northern Europe, the Renaissance brought realism to the arts there, although different methods, such as oil painting, were used. **(See pp. 412–13.)**

Standards Practice

1 Why did Florence become the first major center of the Renaissance?

A Popes lived there and used church funds to support the arts.

B The Medici family used wealth from the cloth trade and banking to support the arts.

C Italian kings founded schools in Florence that drew scholars from the rest of Europe.

D Ruling doges used wealth from sea trade to fund artists and writers.

2 Renaissance humanism balanced

A faith and reason.

B love and religion.

C faith and adventure.

D adventure and love.

3 In what way was Renaissance art different from the art of medieval Europe?

A Renaissance art portrayed secular subjects instead of religious ones.

B The Church, rather than secular rulers, supported the arts.

C Renaissance painters made their works more realistic by using perspective.

D Renaissance artists painted flat images instead of ones that looked three-dimensional.

4 Gutenberg's printing press was important because

A it was the first printing press.

B it printed only in German.

C it made books more available.

D it made Gutenberg wealthy.

WH7.9

What Is the Standard? ➡ Where Can I Find It?

What Is the Standard?	Where Can I Find It?
WH7.9 Students analyze the historical developments of the Reformation.	**Chapter 8** covers standard WH7.9, including the causes of the Reformation and Counter-Reformation, the wars that resulted in a divided Europe, and the spread of Christian ideas throughout the world. (See pp. 418–45.)
WH7.9.1 List the causes for the internal turmoil in and weakening of the Catholic church (e.g., tax policies, selling of indulgences).	**Chapter 8, Section 1** Humanist ideas about various Church policies, including the sale of indulgences, led some clergy to want to reform the Church. (See pp. 422–27.)
WH7.9.2 Describe the theological, political, and economic ideas of the major figures during the Reformation (e.g., Desiderius Erasmus, Martin Luther, John Calvin, William Tyndale).	**Chapter 8, Section 1** Various leaders developed important ideas that led to the Reformation. Erasmus believed in using reason to become a better Christian. William Tyndale pushed for an English Bible to make it more accessible. Martin Luther argued against the sale of indulgences. (See pp. 422–27.) **Chapter 8, Section 1** Many kings used Luther's ideas to break with the Catholic Church and earn income from their lands. (See pp. 428–29.) **Chapter 8, Section 2** John Calvin's ideas of predestination led to other new churches. (See pp. 430–32.) **Chapter 8, Section 2** Henry VIII created the Church of England. Later, religious conflict would lead to civil war in England. (See pp. 432–34.)
WH7.9.3 Explain Protestants' new practices of church self-government and the influence of those practices on the development of democratic practices and ideas of federalism.	**Chapter 8, Section 2** Calvinist ideas that congregations should choose their own leaders had a strong impact on the English settlers in America and later influenced the rise of democratic principles. (See pp. 430–32.) **Chapter 8, Section 2** Calvinist ideas led to the rise of Puritans in England. They eventually founded colonies in the Americas. (See p. 434.)
WH7.9.4 Identify and locate the European regions that remained Catholic and those that became Protestant and explain how the division affected the distribution of religions in the New World.	**Chapter 8, Section 1** Most of northern Germany became Protestant, while most of southern Germany remained Catholic. (See pp. 428–29.) **Chapter 8, Section 2** England broke from the Catholic Church. Many of its Protestant peoples settled in North America. (See pp. 432–34.)

WH7.9

What Is the Standard? ➤ Where Is It Covered?

	Chapter 8, Section 3 Religious wars between Protestants and Catholics divided Europe. Germanic areas tended to be Protestant while Latin areas tended to be Catholic. These countries spread their faith to the Americas and elsewhere. **(See pp. 435–41.)**
WH7.9.5 Analyze how the Counter Reformation revitalized the Catholic church and the forces that fostered the movement (e.g., St. Ignatius of Loyola and the Jesuits, the Council of Trent).	**Chapter 8, Section 3** The Catholic Church tried to halt the spread of Protestantism through the Counter-Reformation. The Pope established a church council at Trent to discuss how to deal with the Reformation. The Jesuits, founded by Ignatius of Loyola, devoted their energies to preserving the Church. **(See pp. 435–40.)**
WH7.9.6 Understand the institution and impact of missionaries on Christianity and the diffusion of Christianity from Europe to other parts of the world in the medieval and early modern periods; locate missions on a world map.	**Chapter 8, Section 3** The Reformation had a profound impact on the world. Missionaries spread Christianity as far as Japan and the Philippines in the East. In the Americas, they established Protestant and Catholic regions. **(See pp. 440–41.)**
WH7.9.7 Describe the Golden Age of cooperation between Jews and Muslims in medieval Spain that promoted creativity in art, literature, and science, including how that cooperation was terminated by the religious persecution of individuals and groups (e.g., the Spanish Inquisition and the expulsion of Jews and Muslims from Spain in 1492).	**Chapter 8, Section 3** Before the Reformation in Spain, Muslims had built universities and, along with many Jewish scholars and writers, had advanced learning and philosophy. However, when Catholic rulers unified Spain in 1492, they ordered Muslims and Jews to convert to Catholicism or leave the country. **(See pp. 439–40.)**

Standards Practice

1 How did Calvinism contribute to the later growth of democracy?

A Calvinists elected a president to lead all of their churches.

B Calvinist congregations chose their own leaders.

C Calvinist ministers called for complete separation of church and state.

D Calvinist theologians taught that all religions were pathways to the one God.

2 Which of the following was a result of the Council of Trent?

A The Catholic mass was celebrated in vernacular languages instead of Latin.

B Popes and church councils were to share power in governing the Church.

C Schools called seminaries were set up to train priests.

D Relations between Catholics and Protestants improved.

WH7.10

What Is the Standard? → Where Can I Find It?

What Is the Standard?	Where Can I Find It?
WH7.10 Students analyze the historical developments of the Scientific Revolution and its lasting effect on religious, political, and cultural institutions.	**Chapter 11, Sections 1 and 2** cover standard WH7.10, including how the thinkers of the Scientific Revolution built on ancient, medieval, and Renaissance ideas, developed new ways of examining truth, and created new technologies. (See pp. 510–23.)
WH7.10.1 Discuss the roots of the Scientific Revolution (e.g., Greek rationalism; Jewish, Christian, and Muslim science; Renaissance humanism; new knowledge from global exploration).	**Chapter 11, Section 1** During the Scientific Revolution, scientists looked to Classical philosophers to understand the scientific approach to new ideas. They were also influenced by Christian, Muslim, and Jewish scientists. (See pp. 514–17.) **Chapter 11, Section 1** Thinkers at this time began to abandon older ideas in favor of mathematics and experimentation. (See pp. 517–19.)
WH7.10.2 Understand the significance of the new scientific theories (e.g., those of Copernicus, Galileo, Kepler, Newton) and the significance of new inventions (e.g., the telescope, microscope, thermometer, barometer).	**Chapter 11, Section 1** New theories about astronomy by Copernicus, Kepler, and Galileo, along with new inventions, expanded our understanding of the universe. (See pp. 517–19.) **Chapter 11, Section 1** Newton's ideas led to the rise of modern physics. Other scientists made advances in medicine and chemistry. (See pp. 519–21.)
WH7.10.3 Understand the scientific method advanced by Bacon and Descartes, the influence of new scientific rationalism on the growth of democratic ideas, and the coexistence of science with traditional religious beliefs.	**Chapter 11, Section 1** European thinkers believed science was a source of truth. Such thinkers included Descartes and Bacon. (See pp. 522–23.) **Chapter 11, Section 2** The Scientific Revolution helped spur the ideas of the Enlightenment. (See pp. 524–28.)

Standards Practice

1 **Why did the Roman Catholic Church condemn Galileo?**

A Galileo's theory of relativity was against church teaching.

B He did not believe in miracles.

C He challenged the belief that the earth was the center of the universe.

D He dissected human bodies.

2 **What is the scientific method?**

A an orderly way of collecting and analyzing evidence

B the study of the solar system

C the use of mathematical instruments

D the study of foreign languages

WH7.11

What Is the Standard?	Where Can I Find It?
WH7.11 Students analyze political and economic change in the sixteenth, seventeenth, and eighteenth centuries (the Age of Exploration, the Enlightenment, and the Age of Reason).	**Chapter 10** covers standard WH7.11, including the voyages of discovery, the good and bad aspects of the Columbian Exchange, and the beginnings of capitalism. (See pp. 482–509.) **Chapter 11, sections 2 and 3** cover standard WH7.11, including the scientific reasoning of the Enlightenment and the growing democratic principles that influenced the American Declaration of Independence. (See pp. 524–45.)
WH7.11.1 Know the great voyages of discovery, the locations of the routes, and the influence of cartography in the development of a new European worldview.	**Chapter 10, Section 1** Trade through the Silk Road brought new ideas and technologies to Europe. These helped Europeans expand their knowledge of cartography and their understanding of the world. (See pp. 486–88.) **Chapter 10, Section 1** Europeans began voyages of discovery and trade around Africa to East Asia as well as to the Americas. (See pp. 489–92.)
WH7.11.2 Discuss the exchanges of plants, animals, technology, culture, and ideas among Europe, Africa, Asia, and the Americas in the fifteenth and sixteenth centuries and the major economic and social effects on each continent.	**Chapter 10, Section 1** Trade with Asia helped Europeans expand their knowledge and technologies, such as the compass and caravel. (See pp. 486–88.) **Chapter 10, Section 2** Global trade spread goods such as spices and helped ideas and systems such as capitalism spread. (See pp. 497–501.) **Chapter 10, Section 3** The Columbian Exchange spread many goods and ideas, but diseases killed millions of Native Americans and destroyed some societies. (See pp. 500–05.)
WH7.11.3 Examine the origins of modern capitalism; the influence of mercantilism and cottage industry; the elements and importance of a market economy in seventeenth-century Europe; the changing international trading and marketing patterns, including their locations on a world map; and the influence of explorers and map makers.	**Chapter 10, Section 2** Europeans developed world empires by conquering peoples in the Americas and establishing global trade patterns. (See pp. 493–95.) **Chapter 10, Section 2** A commercial revolution developed as countries used mercantilism to get rich. As trade and profits increased, people started joint-stock companies. This led to the rise of a market economy and capitalism. (See pp. 497–99.)

WH7.11

What Is the Standard? ➡ Where Can I Find It?

WH7.11.4 Explain how the main ideas of the Enlightenment can be traced back to such movements as the Renaissance, the Reformation, and the Scientific Revolution and to the Greeks, Romans, and Christianity.

Chapter 11, Section 2 Enlightenment thinkers drew from the Greeks and Romans to develop ideas about reason as a source of knowledge, as well as government. Further, the use of reason and critical thinking during the Renaissance, Reformation, and Scientific Revolution, all contributed to the Enlightenment. **(See pp. 524–28, 531–34.)**

WH7.11.5 Describe how democratic thought and institutions were influenced by Enlightenment thinkers (e.g., John Locke, Charles-Louis Montesquieu, American founders).

Chapter 11, Section 2 Locke argued that people had natural rights. Montesquieu believed in a separation of powers. **(See pp. 525–28.)**

Chapter 11, Section 2 French philosophes continued the search for knowledge and pushed for democratic principles. Among them, Rousseau argued that people gave government power through a social contract. **(See pp. 528–30.)**

Chapter 11, Section 3 Democratic principles from the Enlightenment led settlers in North America to declare independence from Britain and establish a democratic government. **(See pp. 534–39.)**

Chapter 11, Section 3 The ideas of the Enlightenment changed the way people thought, and its legacy still influences us today. **(See pp. 539–41.)**

WH7.11.6 Discuss how the principles in the Magna Carta were embodied in such documents as the English Bill of Rights and the American Declaration of Independence.

Chapter 11, Section 3 Both the Magna Carta and English Bill of Rights established the idea that governments are not all-powerful and that rulers had to obey the laws and treat citizens fairly. These influenced the writers of the Declaration of Independence. **(See pp. 534–39.)**

Standards Practice

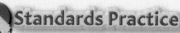

1 **What river in the Americas was explored and mapped by Frenchman Jacques Cartier?**

  A the Amazon River in South America

  B the St. Lawrence River in present-day Canada

  C the Mississippi River in central North America

  D the Rio Grande between present-day Mexico and the United States

2 **England's John Locke used natural law to**

  A explain how the universe worked.

  B defend the idea of absolute monarchy.

  C promote the spread of Christianity.

  D make government accountable to citizens.

California Standards Handbook Answer Key

The answers for the California Standards Handbook are listed below. Use this answer key to check your understanding of the material covered in the grade 7 social studies course.

WH7.1

1 B
2 A

WH7.2

1 C
2 C
3 D
4 A

WH7.3

1 B
2 B
3 A
4 D

WH7.4

1 C
2 D
3 B
4 A

WH7.5

1 B
2 C
3 C
4 A

WH7.6

1 D
2 A

WH7.7

1 D
2 B

WH7.8

1 B
2 A
3 C
4 C

WH7.9

1 B
2 C

WH7.10

1 C
2 A

WH7.11

1 B
2 D

Glossary

This glossary includes all the yellow highlighted and boldfaced vocabulary words from your text. Content vocabulary (those words highlighted in yellow in your text) are words that relate to history content. Academic vocabulary (those words **boldfaced** in your text) are words that will help you understand all of your school subjects. Academic vocabulary is shown with an asterisk (*).

A

*abandon to leave or give up completely (p. 369)

absolutism system of rule in which monarchs held total power and claimed to rule by the will of God (p. 532)

*accompany to go with or join someone as a companion (p. 225)

*advocate a person who supports a theory or cause (p. 530)

*aid to provide help (p. 495)

alliance political agreement between people or countries to work together (p. 458)

anatomy the study of body structure (p. 141)

animism belief that all natural things are alive and have their own spirits (p. 301)

annul to cancel (p. 433)

*anticipate to expect something to happen a certain way (p. 499)

anti-Semitism hatred of Jews (p. 359)

*approach a particular way of dealing with something or someone (p. 516)

*approximate an estimate that is almost exact (p. 366)

aqueduct human-made channel built to carry water (p. 141)

astrolabe a device used to find latitude at sea (p. 487)

*available easy to get (p. 261)

B

barbarian uncivilized person (p. 286)

barter to exchange goods without using money (p. 146)

bazaar marketplace (p. 192)

* benefit something that does good or is helpful to someone (p. 228)

* bond a link uniting things or people together (p. 231)

bourgeoisie the French middle class; part of the Third Estate class system (p. 538)

C

caliph important Muslim political and religious leader (p. 182)

calligraphy beautiful handwriting; the art of producing beautiful handwriting (pp. 265, 312)

capitalism a system in which people, rather than governments, own property and make goods (p. 499)

caravan group of traveling merchants and animals (p. 175)

caravel an early type of Portuguese ship (p. 488)

cartography the science of map making (p. 488)

census a count of the number of people (p. 283)

chiaroscuro a painting technique that creates softened edges by using light and dark (p. 410)

clan group of families related by blood or marriage (pp. 228, 298)

* clarify to make something easier to understand (p. 432)

clergy religious officials, such as priests, given authority to conduct religious services (p. 350)

codices books, often made of deerskin, cloth, or bark, that the Aztec used to record their religion and history (p. 461)

colony settlement in a new territory that keeps close ties with its homeland (p. 497)

Columbian Exchange the global exchange of people, goods, technology, ideas, and diseases that began after Christopher Columbus' voyages (p. 503)

commerce the buying and selling of goods in large amounts over long distances (p. 497)

compass a device used to find direction when traveling (p. 487)

* **compile** to collect into a list or group (p. 283)

* **conclude** to decide on something by reasoning and investigating (p. 425)

concordat agreement between the pope and the ruler of a country (p. 333)

* **conduct** a person's actions and behavior (p. 305)

conquistador Spanish conqueror or soldier in the Americas (p. 472)

* **consent** to approve of what is done (p. 432)

* **consider** to think of something in a certain way (p. 152)

constitution written plan of government (pp. 299, 535)

* **contact** to meet or interact with others (p. 286)

* **contradict** to say the opposite of what someone else has said (p. 436)

* **contribute** to add to something (p. 315)

* **convert** to change from one belief to another (p. 429)

* **cooperate** to work together to get something done (p. 457)

* **credit** to publicly acknowledge someone for his or her work or effort (p. 399)

crier announcer who calls Muslim believers to prayer five times a day (p. 197)

daimyo powerful military lord in feudal Japan (p. 307)

* **debate** to present the reasons for and against a subject (p. 398)

* **demonstrate** to make a public display (p. 360)

denomination an organized branch of Christianity (p. 425)

* **design** to create something for a specific purpose (p. 454)

* **devote** to focus one's time and energy on a particular subject (p. 186)

dhow an Arab sailboat (p. 214)

* **differentiate** to see the differences between two things (p. 409)

* **diminish** to become gradually less or smaller (p. 211)

diplomacy the art of negotiating with other countries (p. 391)

* **distinct** to be very different from others (p. 139)

divine right a belief in early Europe that a king's authority to rule was granted by God, not the people (p. 440)

* **document** a written or printed paper giving proof of something or information about something (p. 349)

doge the head of the state in Venice (p. 390)

* **drama** a story told by actors who pretend to be characters in the story (p. 283)

Dutch East India Company Dutch trading empire in Indonesia (p. 505)

East India Company English trading empire in India (p. 505)

Glossary

economy organized way in which people produce, sell, and buy goods and services (p. 254)

***element** each of the parts of which something is made up (p. 227)

***eliminate** to get rid of something (p. 440)

***emphasis** special importance given to something (p. 140)

***enable** to make something possible or easy to do (p. 326)

***encounter** to meet unexpectedly (p. 270)

***energy** to be very active and motivated (p. 428)

***environment** all of the factors in our surroundings that influence the ability for a plant, animal, or human to survive (p. 451)

***erode** to wear away slowly (p. 282)

***error** a false belief or statement (p. 525)

estate a social class in France (p. 538)

***eventual** some time later or in the future (p. 270)

***exclude** to keep out of a group (p. 333)

excommunicate to declare that a person or group no longer belongs to a church (p. 333)

***expert** a person with special skill in, or knowledge of, a subject (p. 389)

export to sell to another country (p. 497)

extended family family group including several generations as well as other relatives (p. 231)

F

***fee** money paid for a service (p. 210)

feudalism political system based on bonds of loyalty between lords and vassals (pp. 308, 335)

fief under feudalism, the land a lord granted to a vassal in exchange for military service and loyalty (p. 336)

***finance** to provide money for something (p. 471)

fjord steep-sided valley that is an inlet of the sea (p. 330)

fresco a painting done on wet plaster with watercolor paint (p. 410)

***fund** money available for a specific purpose (p. 488)

G

***generate** to create something (p. 473)

glacier huge sheet of ice (p. 451)

grand jury group that decided whether there was enough evidence to accuse a person of a crime (p. 349)

griot storyteller (p. 211)

***guarantee** a promise that some condition will be fulfilled (p. 349)

guild medieval business group formed by craftspeople and merchants (pp. 314, 342)

H

heresy belief that differs from or contradicts the accepted teachings of a religion (pp. 358, 436)

humanism Renaissance movement based on the values of the ancient Greeks and Romans, such as that individuals and human society were important (p. 395)

hypothesis proposed explanation of the facts (p. 522)

I

***image** an object or statue made to look like a person or thing (p. 161)

Glossary

*impact to have a strong effect on someone or something (p. 439)

import to buy from another country (p. 497)

*impose to force someone to accept or do something (p. 189)

indulgence a pardon from the Catholic Church for a person's sins (p. 423)

inflation period of rapidly increasing prices (p. 146)

*innovate to do something a new way (p. 194)

*instance to mention as an example (p. 325)

*intense an extreme degree (p. 175)

invest to put money into a project (p. 498)

*investigate to closely examine facts to find the truth (p. 515)

*involve to have something included or to be a part of something (p. 310)

*job work a person regularly does for pay (p. 359)

knight a noble warrior who fought on horseback in the Middle Ages (p. 336)

*locate to look for and find a place or object (p. 489)

martial arts sports, such as judo and karate, that involve combat and self-defense (p. 310)

mass Catholic worship service (p. 357)

matrilineal refers to a group that traces descent through mothers rather than fathers (p. 231)

*medical dealing with medicine and doctors (p. 257)

meditation practice of quiet reflection to clear the mind and find inner peace (p. 310)

mercantilism the idea that a country gains power by building up its supply of gold and silver (p. 497)

*method a procedure for doing something (p. 263)

minaret tower of a mosque from which the crier calls believers to prayer five times a day (p. 197)

missionary person who travels to carry the ideas of a religion to others (p. 332)

monastery religious community where monks live and work (p. 257)

monopoly control of all (or almost all) trade or production of a certain good (p. 454)

mosaic picture made from many bits of colored glass, tile, or stone (p. 164)

mosque Muslim house of worship (p. 192)

natural law law that applies to everyone and can be understood by reason (p. 525)

*network a system of routes connecting several cities (p. 387)

*nonetheless achieving a goal in spite of the odds against success (p. 351)

novel long fictional story (p. 283)

oasis green area in a desert fed by underground water (p. 175)

Glossary

*obtain to gain something, usually by planning or effort (p. 361)

*occur to happen (p. 297)

ode poem that expresses strong emotions about life (p. 140)

oral history the stories passed down from generation to generation (p. 231)

pampas grassy plains (p. 504)

Pax Romana ("Roman Peace") long era of peace and safety in the Roman Empire (p. 137)

*perspective a technique of painting a picture so that objects seem to have depth and distance (p. 409)

*philosophy the study of the nature and the meaning of life (p. 440)

plague disease that spreads quickly and kills many people (p. 365)

plateau area of high flat land (p. 208)

*policy general rules and procedures of the government (p. 185)

popular sovereignty idea that a government receives its power from the people (p. 537)

porcelain type of ceramic ware that is made of fine clay and baked at high temperatures (p. 262)

*portion a part of the whole (p. 298)

*positive to have a good reaction or ending (p. 504)

predestination belief that no matter what a person does, the outcome of his or her life is already planned by God (p. 431)

*previous to occur earlier or in the past (p. 462)

*primary the first and most important thing or duty (p. 495)

*prime to be of highest quality or importance (p. 213)

*process all the steps one must take to reach a goal (p. 342)

*project a planned large task that has many steps (p. 254)

*publish to release a book or letter for the public to read (p. 388)

*purchase to buy something (p. 146)

quipu rope with knotted cords of different lengths and colors (p. 464)

Quran holy book of Islam (p. 179)

rationalism the belief that reason is the chief source of knowledge (p. 522)

Reconquista ("reconquest") Christian struggle to take back the Iberian peninsula from the Muslims (p. 369)

reform change that tries to bring about an improvement (pp. 147, 255)

Reformation movement to reform the Catholic Church; led to the creation of Protestantism (p. 423)

regent person who acts as a temporary ruler (p. 164)

*release to set free (p. 233)

Renaissance ("rebirth") period of renewed interest in art and learning in Europe (p. 385)

representative government system of government in which people elect leaders to make laws (p. 535)

*resource a reserve of supplies (p. 428)

*reveal to make known or show plainly (p. 310)

*role a specific function in a group (p. 303)

Glossary

S

saint Christian holy person (p. 164)

samurai class of warriors in feudal Japan who pledged loyalty to a noble in return for land (p. 305)

satire a story that pokes fun and shows weakness (p. 140)

scholasticism medieval way of thinking that tried to bring together reason and faith in studies of religion (p. 361)

scientific method orderly way of collecting and analyzing evidence (p. 522)

sect a smaller group with distinct beliefs within a larger religious group (p. 310)

secular interested in worldly rather than religious matters (p. 385)

* **seek** to look for (p. 256)

seminary school for training and educating priests and ministers (p. 436)

separation of powers equal division of power among the branches of government (p. 528)

serf peasant laborer bound by law to the lands of a noble (p. 336)

sheikh leader of an Arab tribe (p. 175)

* **shift** to change place, position, or direction (p. 335)

Shiite Muslim group that accepts only the descendants of Muhammad's son-in-law Ali as rightful rulers of Muslims (p. 185)

shogun military ruler of feudal Japan (p. 306)

shrine holy place (p. 301)

* **significant** to have a lot of importance (p. 325)

sinkhole a place in the ground where the earth has caved in and where water collects (p. 457)

social contract agreement between rulers and the people upon which a government is based (p. 526)

* **source** the place where something begins (p. 457)

* **stable** fixed or constant (p. 145)

steppe wide, rolling, grassy plain (p. 268)

Stoicism philosophy founded by Zeno in Hellenistic Athens; taught that happiness came not from following emotions, but from following reason and doing one's duty (p. 142)

* **stress** special importance given to something (p. 164)

* **style** a particular way something is done or created (p. 189)

sultan military and political leader with absolute authority over a Muslim country (pp. 186, 227)

Sunni Muslim group that accepts descendants of the Umayyads as rightful rulers of Muslims (p. 185)

Swahili refers to the culture and language of East Africa (p. 227)

T

tanka Japan's oldest form of poetry; an unrhymed poem of five lines (p. 312)

* **tension** uncertainty and stress between groups (p. 535)

terror violent actions that are meant to scare people into surrendering (p. 270)

theology the study of religion and God (pp. 361, 431)

theory an explanation of how or why something happens (p. 515)

* **topic** the subject to be discussed (p. 529)

* **transfer** to move to a different place (p. 503)

* **transport** to carry from one place to another (p. 175)

treason disloyalty to the government (pp. 282, 476)

Glossary

trial jury group that decided whether an accused person was innocent or guilty (p. 349)

tribe group of related families (p. 268)

*****utilize** to make use of something (p. 159)

*****vary** to be different (p. 223)

vassal in feudalism, a noble who held land from and served a higher-ranking lord, and in return was given protection (pp. 308, 335)

vault curved structure of stone or concrete forming a ceiling or roof (p. 139)

vernacular everyday language used in a country or region (pp. 363, 398)

warlord military leader who runs a government (p. 253)

***** **widespread** scattered over a large area (p. 192)

Glossary

Spanish Glossary

This glossary includes all the yellow highlighted and boldfaced vocabulary words from your text. Content vocabulary (those words highlighted in yellow in your text) are words that relate to history content. Academic vocabulary (those words **boldfaced** in your text) are words that will help you understand all of your school subjects. Academic vocabulary is shown with an asterisk (*).

A

* **abandon / abandonar** dejar o renunciar completamente (pág. 369)

absolutism / absolutismo sistema de gobierno en que los monarcas tiene poder absoluto y alegan gobernar según decreto divino (pág. 532)

* **accompany / acompañar** ir o unirse a alguien como compañero (pág. 225)

* **advocate / defensor** persona que apoya una teoría o causa (pág. 530)

* **aid/ ayudar** prestar auxilio (pág. 495)

alliance / alianza acuerdo político entre pueblos o países para trabajar conjuntamente (pág. 458)

anatomy / anatomía estudio de la estructura corporal (pág. 141)

animism / animismo creencia de que todas las cosas naturales están vivas y tienen sus propios espíritus (pág. 301)

annul / anular el acto de invalidar (pág. 433)

* **anticipate / prever** esperar que algo suceda de determinada manera (pág. 499)

anti-Semitism / antisemitismo odio hacia los judíos (pág. 359)

* **approach / enfoque** manera particular de manejar las cosas o tratar a las personas (pág. 516)

* **approximate / aproximado** un cálculo que es casi exacto (pág. 366)

aqueduct / acueducto canal construido por el hombre para transportar agua (pág. 141)

astrolabe / astrolabio instrumento usado en el mar para hallar la latitud (pág. 487)

* **available / disponible** fácil de conseguir (pág. 261)

B

barbarian / bárbaro persona incivilizada (pág. 286)

barter / trueque intercambiar bienes sin utilizar dinero (pág. 146)

bazaar / bazar mercado (pág. 192)

* **benefit / beneficio** algo bueno o útil para alguien (pág. 228)

* **bond / lazo** vínculo que une cosas o personas (pág. 231)

bourgeoisie / burguesía la clase media francesa; parte del sistema de clases del Tercer Estado (pág. 538)

C

caliph / califa importante líder político y religioso musulmán (pág. 182)

calligraphy / caligrafía el arte de producir tal hermosa escritura (págs. 265, 312)

capitalism / capitalismo sistema en el que la gente, en lugar de los gobiernos, poseen propiedades y fabrican productos (pág. 499)

caravan / caravana grupo itinerante de mercaderes y animales (pág. 175)

Spanish Glossary

caravel / carabela antigua embarcación portuguesa (pág. 488)

cartography / cartografía ciencia de diseñar mapas (pág. 488)

census / censo conteo del número de personas (pág. 283)

chiaroscuro / claroscuro técnica de pintura que crea bordes suaves por el uso de luz y obscuridad (pág. 410)

clan / clan grupo de familias relacionadas por sangre o casamiento (págs. 228, 298)

*****clarify / aclarar** hacer algo comprensible (pág. 432)

clergy / clero funcionarios religiosos, como los sacerdotes, con autoridad concedida para llevar a cabo servicios religiosos (pág. 350)

codices / códices libros, por lo general hechos de gamuza, tela o corteza, que los aztecas usaban para documentar su historia y religión (pág. 461)

colony / colonia asentamiento en un territorio nuevo que mantiene lazos cercanos con su tierra natal (pág. 497)

Columbian Exchange / Intercambio colombino intercambio global de personas, bienes, tecnología, ideas y enfermedades que comenzó luego de los viajes de Cristóbal Colón (pág. 503)

commerce / comercio compra y venta de bienes en cantidades grandes y a través de largas distancias (pág. 497)

compass / brújula instrumento usado para encontrar la orientación en los viajes (pág. 487)

*****compile / compilar** agrupar en una lista o grupo (pág. 283)

*****conclude / concluir** tomar una decisión sobre algo mediante el razonamiento y la investigación (pág. 425)

concordat / concordato acuerdo entre el Papa y el gobernante de un país (pág. 333)

*****conduct / conducta** manera personal de comportarse (pág. 305)

conquistador / conquistador soldado español en las Américas (pág. 472)

*****consent / consentir** aprobar lo que se ha hecho (pág. 432)

*****consider / considerar** pensar en lago de cierta manera (pág. 152)

constitution / constitución plan de gobierno (págs. 299, 535)

*****contact / contactar** encontrarse o interactuar con otros (pág. 286)

*****contradict / contradecir** decir lo opuesto a lo que otro ha dicho (pág. 436)

*****contribute / contribuir** agregar a algo (pág. 315)

*****convert / convertir** cambiar de una creencia a otra (pág. 429)

*****cooperate /cooperar** trabajar juntos para hacer algo (pág. 457)

*****credit / valorar** reconocer públicamente a alguien por su trabajo o esfuerzo (pág. 399)

crier / almuecín anunciador que llama a los creyentes musulmanes a orar cinco veces al día (pág. 197)

— D —

daimyo / daimyo poderoso señor militar en el Japón feudal (pág. 307) *debate / debatir argumentar las razones a favor y en contra de un tema (pág. 398)

*demonstrate / manifestar expresarse públicamente (pág. 360)

denomination / denominación rama organizada del cristianismo (pág. 425)

*design / diseñar crear algo para un propósito específico (pág. 454)

*devote / dedicarse concentrar el tiempo y la energía en algo en particular (pág. 186)

dhow / dhow velero árabe (pág. 214)

*differentiate / distinguir ver las diferencias entre dos cosas (pág. 409)

*diminish/ disminuir tornarse gradualmente menor o más pequeño (pág. 211)

diplomacy / diplomacia el arte de negociar con otros países (pág. 391)

*distinct / distinto ser muy diferente al resto (pág. 139)

divine right / derecho divino creencia de la antigua Europa de que la autoridad del rey para gobernar era otorgada por Dios y no por el pueblo (pág. 440)

*document / documento papel escrito o impreso que da prueba de algo o información acerca de algo (pág. 349)

doge / dux jefe de estado en Venecia (pág. 390)

*drama / drama historia narrada por actores que simulan ser los personajes de la misma (pág. 283)

Dutch East India Company / Compañía Holandesa de las Indias Orientales imperio comercial holandés en Indonesia (pág. 505)

East India Company / Compañía de las Indias Orientales imperio comercial inglés en India (pág. 505)

economy / economía manera organizada en la que las personas producen, venden y compran bienes y servicios (pág. 254)

*element / elemento cada una de las partes que forman algo (pág. 227)

*eliminate / eliminar deshacerse de algo (pág. 440)

*emphasis / énfasis importancia especial que se le da a algo (pág. 140)

*enable / posibilitar hacer que algo sea posible o fácil de realizar (pág. 326)

*encounter / encontrar hallar inesperadamente (pág. 270)

*energy / energía estar muy activo y motivado (pág. 428)

*environment / medioambiente todos aquellos factores en nuestro entorno que influyen en la capacidad de sobrevivir de una planta, animal o ser humano (pág. 451)

*erode / erosionar desgastar lentamente (pág. 282)

*error / error creencia o aserción falsas (pág. 525)

estate / estado clase social en Francia (pág. 538)

*eventual / posterior más adelante o en el futuro (pág. 270)

*exclude / excluir no admitir en un grupo (pág. 333)

excommunicate / excomulgar declarar que una persona o grupo no pertenece más a la iglesia (págs. 333) *expert / experto persona con habilidades especiales o conocedora de un tema (pág. 389)

export / exportar vender a otro país (pág. 497)

extended family / familia extendida grupo familiar que incluye a varias generaciones así como a otros parientes (pág. 231)

*fee / precio dinero que se paga por un servicio (pág. 210)

feudalism / feudalismo sistema político basado en lazos de lealtad entre señores y vasallos (págs. 308, 335)

fief / feudo bajo el feudalismo, la tierra que un señor otorgaba a un vasallo a cambio de su servicio militar y lealtad (pág. 336)

*finance / financiar dar dinero para algo (pág. 471)

fjord / fiordo valle de paredes abruptas que es una bahía del mar (pág. 330)

fresco / fresco pintura hecha en yeso húmedo con acuarelas (pág. 410)

*fund / fondos dinero disponible para un propósito específico (pág. 488)

*generate / generar crear algo (pág. 473)

glacier / glaciar masa inmensa de hielo (pág. 451)

grand jury / gran jurado grupo que decide si hay suficiente evidencia para acusar a una persona de un delito (pág. 349)

griot / griot narrador en poblados africanos (pág. 211)

*guarantee / garantía promesa de que se cumplirá una condición (pág. 349)

guild / gremio grupo medieval de negocios formado por artesanos y mercaderes (págs. 314, 342)

heresy / herejía creencia que difiere de las enseñanzas aceptadas de una religión o que las contradice (págs. 358, 436)

humanism / humanismo movimiento del renacimiento basado en las ideas y los valores de los antiguos romanos y griegos, de tal manera que los individuos y la sociedad humana eran importantes (pág. 395)

hypothesis / hipótesis explicación que se propone de los hechos (pág. 522)

*image / imagen objeto o estatua hecho a semejanza de una persona o cosa (pág. 161)

*impact / impactar tener un fuerte efecto sobre alguien o algo (pág. 439)

import / importar comprar de otro país (pág. 497)

*impose / imponer forzar a alguien a aceptar o hacer algo (pág. 189)

indulgence / indulgencia perdón de los pecados cometidos por una persona dado por la Iglesia Católica (pág. 423)

inflation / inflación período de incremento rápido de precios (pág. 146)

*innovate / innovar hacer algo de una forma nueva (pág. 194)

Spanish Glossary

*instance / ejemplo** mencionar algo para ilustrar otra cosa (pág. 325)

*intense / intenso** un grado extremo (pág. 175)

invest / invertir** poner dinero en un proyecto (pág. 498)

*investigate / investigar** examinar atentamente los hechos para llegar a la verdad (pág. 515)

*involve / implicar** incluir algo o ser parte de algo (pág. 310)

*job / trabajo** tarea que una persona realiza regularmente a cambio de un pago (pág. 359)

knight / caballero** en la Edad Media, un guerrero noble que peleaba a caballo (pág. 336)

*locate / ubicar** buscar y encontrar un lugar u objeto (pág. 489)

martial arts / artes marciales** deportes, como el judo y el karate, que involucran combate y defensa personal (pág. 310)

mass / misa** servicio de culto Católico (pág. 357)

matrilineal / matrilineal** se refiere a un grupo de personas que busca su ascendencia a través de las madres más que de los padres (pág. 231)

*medical / médico** el tratar con medicina y doctores (pág. 257)

meditation / meditación** práctica de reflexión silenciosa para aclarar la mente y encontrar la paz interior (pág. 310)

mercantilism / mercantilismo** doctrina según la cual un país obtiene poder al amasar un abastecimiento de oro y plata (pág. 497)

*method / método** procedimiento para hacer algo (pág. 263)

minaret / minarete** torre de una mezquita desde donde el almuecín llama a los creyentes a la oración cinco veces al día (pág. 197)

missionary / misionero** persona que viaja para llevar las ideas de una religión a otros (pág. 332)

monastery / monasterio** comunidad religiosa donde los monjes viven y trabajan (pág. 257)

monopoly / monopolio** el control de todo (o casi todo) el comercio o la producción de ciertos bienes (pág. 454)

mosaic / mosaico** figura hecha con muchos trozos de vidrios de colores, azulejo o piedra (pág. 164)

mosque / mezquita** casa de culto musulmana (pág. 192)

natural law / ley natural** ley que se aplica a todos y la cual puede entenderse por razonamiento (pág. 525)

*network / red** sistema de rutas que conecta varias ciudades (pág. 387)

Spanish Glossary

Spanish Glossary

*nonetheless / aun así lograr un objetivo a pesar de las adversidades en contra de su éxito (pág. 351)

novel / novela historia ficticia larga (pág. 283)

oasis / oasis área verde en un desierto, alimentada por agua subterránea (pág. 175)

*obtain / obtener ganar algo, normalmente con planificación y esfuerzo (pág. 361)

*occur / ocurrir suceder (pág. 297)

ode / oda poema que expresa emociones fuertes acerca de la vida (pág. 140)

oral history / historia oral historias transmitidas de generación en generación (pág. 231)

pampas / pampas planicies con pastura (pág. 504)

Pax Romana / Paz Romana era prolongada de paz y seguridad en el Imperio Romano (pág. 137)

*perspective / perspectiva técnica de pintura que representa los objetos de manera que parezcan tener profundidad y distancia (pág. 409)

*philosophy / filosofía estudio de la naturaleza y el significado de la vida (pág. 440)

plague / peste enfermedad que se esparce rápidamente y mata a muchas personas (pág. 365)

plateau / meseta área de tierra alta y plana (pág. 208)

*policy / política normas y procedimientos generales de gobierno (pág. 185)

popular sovereignty / soberanía popular idea de que un gobierno recibe su poder de los ciudadanos (pág. 537)

porcelain / porcelana tipo de artículo de cerámica hecho de arcilla fina y horneado a altas temperaturas (pág. 262)

* portion / porción una parte del todo (pág. 298)

* positive / positivo que tiene una buena reacción o final (pág. 504)

predestination / predestinación creencia de que sea lo que sea que haga una persona, el resultado de su vida ya ha sido planificado por Dios (pág. 431)

* previous / previo que ocurrió antes o en el pasado (pág. 462)

* primary / principal cosa o deber primero o más importante (pág. 495)

* prime / de primera de la más alta calidad o importancia (pág. 213)

* process / proceso cada uno de los pasos que se deben dar para alcanzar un objetivo (pág. 342)

* project / proyecto tarea planificada, de gran proporción y que tiene muchos pasos a seguir (pág. 254)

* publish / publicar divulgar un libro o carta para que sea leído por el público (pág. 388)

* purchase / adquirir comprar algo (pág. 146)

quipu / quipu lazo con cuerdas anudadas de longitudes y colores diferentes (pág. 464)

Quran / Corán libro sagrado del Islam (pág. 179)

rationalism / racionalismo la creencia de que la razón es la fuente principal del conocimiento (pág. 522)

Reconquista ("reconquest") / **Reconquista** lucha cristiana para recuperar la península Ibérica de los musulmanes (pág. 369)

reform / reforma cambio que intenta producir una mejora (págs. 147, 255)

Reformation / Reforma movimiento para reformar la iglesia católica; condujo a la creación del protestantismo (pág. 423)

regent / regente persona que opera como un gobernante temporal (pág. 164)

*__release / liberar__ poner el libertad (pág. 233)

Renaissance / Renacimiento ("nacer de nuevo") período en que se renovó el interés en las artes y el conocimiento en Europa (pág. 385)

representative government / gobierno representativo sistema de gobierno en que los ciudadanos eligen a sus líderes para promulgar leyes (pág. 535)

*__resource / recurso__ reserva de suministros (pág. 428)

*__reveal / revelar__ hacer conocer o evidente (pág. 310)

*__role / papel__ función específica en un grupo (pág. 303)

saint / santo persona cristiana santificada (pág. 164)

samurai / samurai clase de guerreros en el Japón feudal que prometía lealtad a un noble a cambio de tierra (pág. 305)

satire / sátira obra que hace burla y muestra las debilidades (pág. 140)

scholasticism / escolasticismo forma de pensamiento medieval que trató de unir a la razón y a la fe en estudios religiosos (pág. 361)

scientific method / método científico manera organizada de recoger y analizar pruebas (pág. 522)

sect / secta un grupo más pequeño con creencias distintas dentro de un grupo religioso más grande (pág. 310)

secular / secular que se interesa en bienes materiales en lugar de asuntos religiosos (pág. 385)

*__seek / buscar__ procurar (pág. 256)

seminary / seminario escuela en donde se entrenan y se educan a los sacerdotes y los ministros (pág. 436)

separation of powers / separación de poderes división equitativa de los poderes entre las ramas del gobierno (pág. 528)

serf / siervo trabajador campesino atado por ley a las tierras de un noble (pág. 336)

sheikh / jeque líder de una tribu árabe (pág. 175)

*__shift / cambiar__ variar de lugar, posición o dirección (pág. 335)

Shiite / chiíta grupo musulmán que acepta sólo a los descendientes de Ali, el hijo político de Mahoma, como auténticos líderes de los musulmanes (pág. 185)

shogun / shogun gobernante militar del Japón feudal (pág. 306)

shrine / santuario lugar sagrado (pág. 301)

*__significant / significativo__ que tiene mucha importancia (pág. 325)

Spanish Glossary

Spanish Glossary

sinkhole / sumidero; cenote: lugar en el suelo en donde la tierra se ha hundido y se acumula agua (pág. 457)

social contract / contrato social acuerdo entre mandatarios y ciudadanos sobre el cual se basa un gobierno (pág. 526)

*__source / fuente__ el lugar donde algo comienza (pág. 457)

*__stable / estable__ fijo o constante (pág. 145)

steppe / estepa ancha planicie ondeada cubierta de hierba (pág. 268)

Stoicism / estoicismo filosofía fundada por Zeno en la Atenas Helenista; enseñaba que la felicidad provenía no de seguir a las emociones, sino a la razón y de cumplir con nuestro deber (pág. 142)

*__stress / énfasis__ importancia especial que se le da a algo (pág. 164)

*__style / estilo__ manera particular de hacer o crear algo (pág. 189)

sultan / sultán líder político y militar con autoridad absoluta sobre un país musulmán (págs. 186, 227)

Sunni / Sunita grupo musulmán que sólo acepta a descendientes de los omeyas como auténticos gobernantes de los musulmanes (pág. 185)

Swahili / suajili se refiere a la cultura e idioma de África oriental (pág. 227)

tanka / tanka forma más antigua de poesía en Japón; poema sin rima de cinco líneas (pág. 312)

*__tension / tensión__ incertidumbre o estrés entre grupos (pág. 535)

terror / terror acciones violentas para atemorizar personas para que rendirse (pág. 270)

theology / teología el estudio de la religión y de Dios (págs. 361, 431)

theory / teoría explicación de cómo o por qué ocurre algo (pág. 515)

*__topic / tema__ asunto a ser discutido (pág. 529)

*__transfer / transferencia__ mover a un lugar diferente (pág. 503)

*__transport / trasportar__ llevar de un lugar a otro (pág. 175)

treason / traición deslealtad al gobierno (págs. 282, 476)

trial jury / jurado grupo que decide si una persona acusada es inocente o culpable (pág. 349)

tribe / tribu grupo de familias relacionadas (pág. 268)

*__utilize / utilizar__ hacer uso de algo (pág. 159)

*__vary / variar__ ser diferente (pág. 223)

vassal / vasallo en el feudalismo, un noble que ocupaba la tierra de un señor de más alto rango y lo servía, y a cambio le daba protección (págs. 308, 335)

vault / bóveda estructura curva de piedra o cemento que forma un techo (pág. 139)

vernacular / vernáculo idioma cotidiano empleado en un país o región (págs. 363, 398)

warlord / caudillo líder militar que dirige un gobierno (pág. 253)

*__widespread / extendido__ esparcido sobre una gran superficie (pág. 192)

Gazetteer

A Gazetteer (GA•zuh•TIHR) is a geographic index or dictionary. It shows latitude and longitude for cities and certain other places. Latitude and longitude are shown in this way: 48°N 2°E, or 48 degrees north latitude and two degrees east longitude. This Gazetteer lists most of the world's largest independent countries, their capitals, and several important geographic features. The page numbers tell where each entry can be found on a map in this book. As an aid to pronunciation, most entries are spelled phonetically.

A

Aachen [AH•kuhn] City in Germany near the Belgian and Dutch borders; capital of Charlemagne's Frankish empire. 50°N 6°E (pp. 324, 328)

Aden Port city of the Red Sea in southern Yemen. 12°N 45°E (p. 284)

Adrianople [AY•dree•uh•NOH•puhl] Ancient city in northwestern Turkey, now called Edirne. 41°N 26°E (p. 150)

Adriatic [AY•dree•A•tihk] **Sea** Arm of Mediterranean Sea between Italy and the Balkan Peninsula. (pp. 66, 68, 328, 359, 385, 416, 533, 544)

Aegean [ih•JEE•uhn] **Sea** Gulf of the Mediterranean Sea between Greece and Asia Minor, north of Crete. (pp. 69, 359)

Afghanistan [af•GA•nuh•STAN] Central Asian country west of Pakistan. (pp. 63, 71, 74, 76)

Africa Second-largest continent, south of Europe between the Atlantic and Indian Oceans. (pp. 62, 63, 64, 65, 70, 72, 73, 86, 87, 88, 89, 138, 150, 182, 188, 223, 234, 246, 284, 330, 365, 451, 486, 490, 493, 502, 503)

Agincourt [A•juhn•KOHRT] Village in northern France. 52°N 6°E (p. 372)

Ahaggar [uh•HAH•guhr] **Mountains** Arid, rocky, upland region in southern Algeria in the center of the Sahara. (pp. 73, 207)

Alaska Largest state in the United States, located in the extreme northwestern region of North America. (pp. 62, 64, 78, 79, 90)

Albania [al•BAY•nee•uh] Country on the Adriatic Sea, south of Yugoslavia. (p. 66)

Alexandria [A•lihg•ZAN•dree•uh] City and major seaport in northern Egypt in the Nile River delta. 31°N 29°E (pp. 138, 150, 158, 176)

Algeria [al•JIHR•ee•uh] Country in North Africa. (pp. 72, 73)

Algiers [al•JIHRZ] Capital city of Algeria, largest Mediterranean port of north-western Africa. 36°N 2°E (pp. 72, 73, 188)

Alps Mountain system of south central Europe. (pp. 66, 68, 325, 326, 385, 416)

Altay Mountains Mountain range in Asia. (pp. 75, 77)

Altun [al•TOON] **Mountains** Range of mountains that are a part of the Kunlun Shan in China. (pp. 75, 77)

Amazon River River in northern South America, largely in Brazil, second-longest river in the world. (pp. 82, 83, 234, 454)

Amhara [ahm•hahr•uh] **Plateau** Plateau in northern Ethiopia. (p. 207)

Amsterdam Capital of the Netherlands. 52°N 4°E (pp. 66, 359)

Amu Darya [AH•moo•DAHR•yuh] Largest river of central Asia. (p. 76)

Andes [AN•deez] Mountain range along the western edge of South America. (pp. 82, 83, 454)

Angola [ang•GOH•luh] Southern African country north of Namibia. (pp. 72, 73)

Antarctica Fifth-largest of the earth's seven continents; it surrounds the South Pole. (pp. 62, 63, 64, 65, 86, 87, 88, 89, 90)

Antioch [AN•tee•AHK] Ancient capital of Syria, now a city in southern Turkey. 36°N 36°E (p. 353)

Antwerp [ANT•WUHRP] City in northern Belgium. 51°N 4°E (p. 359)

Apennines [A•puh•NYNZ] Mountain range that runs through Italy. (pp. 68, 385)

Appalachian Mountains Mountain system of eastern North America. (pp. 79, 535)

Arabia [ah•RAY•bee•uh] Desert peninsula of southwestern Asia across the Red Sea from Africa. (pp. 63, 65, 71, 74, 76, 138, 158, 182, 188, 269, 284, 365)

Arabian Peninsula Desert peninsula in southwestern Asia. (pp. 63, 65, 71, 74, 76, 176, 207, 209)

Arabian Sea Portion of the Indian Ocean between the Arabian Peninsula and the subcontinent of India. (pp. 176, 182, 245, 253, 269, 365)

Aral [AR•uhl] **Sea** Large saltwater lake, or inland sea, in central Asia. (pp. 71, 182, 185, 200, 268, 269, 365)

Arctic Ocean Smallest of the earth's four oceans. (pp. 74, 75, 78, 79, 88, 89, 90, 451)

Asia Largest of the earth's seven continents. (pp. 65, 75, 77, 84, 86, 87, 89, 245, 247, 253, 268, 290, 330, 451, 490)

Asia Minor Region of the ancient world, roughly corresponding to present-day Turkey. (pp. 65, 75, 77, 84, 86, 87, 89, 138, 150, 156, 158, 176, 182, 188, 353)

Astrakhan [AS•truh•KAN] City in southern European Russia on the Volga River near the Caspian Sea. 46°N 48°E (p. 365)

Athens Capital of Greece. 38°N 23°E (pp. 67, 69, 138)

Atlantic Ocean Second-largest body of water in the world. (pp. 62, 64, 66, 68, 72, 78, 79, 81, 82, 83, 85, 86, 87, 88, 138, 150, 158, 168, 188, 207, 209, 211, 223, 234, 245, 246, 325, 326, 328, 330, 350, 353, 366, 367, 428, 437, 451, 454, 490, 491, 508, 535)

Atlas Mountains Mountain range in northwestern Africa on the northern edge of the Sahara. (pp. 72, 73, 207)

Augsburg [AWGZ•boork] City in southern Germany. 49°N 11°E (p. 437)

Australia Island continent southeast of Asia. (pp. 63, 65, 84, 86, 87, 89, 490)

Austria [AWS•tree•uh] Country in central Europe. (pp. 66, 188, 359, 428, 437, 533, 544)

Azores [AY•ZOHRZ] Group of nine islands in the North Atlantic Ocean. 37°N 29°W (pp. 62, 64)

B

Baghdad [BAG•DAD] Capital city of Iraq. 33°N 44°E (pp. 71, 74, 76, 176, 181, 182, 185, 188, 200, 267, 269, 365)

Bahamas [buh•HAH•muhz] Country made up of islands between Cuba and the

United States. 23°N 74°W (pp. 62, 64, 78, 79, 81, 85, 490)

Balkan [BAWL•kuhn] Peninsula Peninsula in southeastern Europe bounded on the east by the Black and Aegean Seas, on the south by the Mediterranean Sea, and on the west by the Adriatic and Ionian Seas. 42°N 20°E (pp. 67, 69, 70, 156, 158)

Baltic [BAWL•tihk] Sea Sea in northern Europe connected to the North Sea. (pp. 63, 65, 66, 67, 68, 69, 325, 330, 350, 359, 366, 437, 508, 533)

Baltimore City in northern Maryland in the United States. 39°N 77°W (p. 535)

Bangkok [BANG•KAHK] Capital of Thailand. 14°N 100°E (pp. 63, 65, 75, 77, 84, 284)

Bangladesh [BAHNG•gluh•DEHSH] South Asian country bounded by Myanmar and India. 24°N 90°E (pp. 75, 77)

Barcelona City in northeastern Spain. 41°N 2°E (pp. 66, 366)

Bay of Bengal Arm of the Indian Ocean between India and the Malay Peninsula. (pp. 63, 65, 74, 76, 245, 253, 255, 269, 290, 498)

Beijing [BAY•JIHNG] Capital of China. 40°N 116°E (pp. 63, 65, 75, 77, 84, 253, 255, 281, 282, 290, 365)

Belgium [BEHL•juhm] Country in northwestern Europe. (pp. 63, 66, 68)

Belgrade [BEHL•GRAYD] Capital of Yugoslavia. 45°N 21°E (pp. 359, 533, 544)

Belize [buh•LEEZ] Central American country east of Guatemala. (pp. 62, 78, 79, 80)

Benin [beh•NEEN] Southern Nigerian trading city during the 1500s. (p. 211)

Bering Sea Part of the North Pacific Ocean, situated between the Aleutian Islands and the Bering Strait. (pp. 62, 64, 78, 79, 90, 451)

Berlin Germany's capital and largest city. 42°N 14°E (pp. 66, 68, 531, 533)

Bhutan [boo•TAHN] South Asian country northeast of India. (pp. 63, 65, 75, 77)

Black Sea Inland sea between southeastern Europe and Asia Minor. (pp. 63, 65, 67, 69, 70, 74, 76, 138, 150, 158, 176, 182, 185, 188, 200, 245, 269, 325, 330, 350, 353, 359, 365, 366)

Bohemia Historical region and former kingdom in what is now the Czech Republic. (pp. 428, 533, 544)

Bombay Port city in western India, now called Mumbai. 18°N 72°E (pp. 63, 65, 74, 76, 498)

Bordeaux [bawr•DOH] City in southwestern France. 44°N 0°W (pp. 367, 372)

Borneo Third-largest island in the world, located in the Malay Archipelago in southeastern Asia. (pp. 63, 65, 75, 77, 269, 284, 365, 498)

Boston Capital of Massachusetts. 42°N 71°W (p. 535)

Brazil Largest country in South America. (pp. 62, 64, 82, 83, 234)

Britain Largest island in the British Isles. (pp. 62, 64, 66, 68, 136, 138, 144, 150, 324)

Bruges [BROOZH] City in northwestern Belgium. 51°N 3°E (p. 334)

Buda [BOO•duh] Town in Hungary that combined with Pest and Óbuda in 1873 to form Budapest. 47°N 19°E (pp. 533, 544)

Budapest [BOO•duh•PEHST] Capital of Hungary. 47°N 19°E (pp. 66, 68)

Bulgaria [BUHL•GAR•ee•uh] Country in southeastern Europe on the Balkan Peninsula. (pp. 67, 69)

Byzantine [BIH•zuhn•TEEN] Empire Eastern part of the Roman Empire that survived after the breakup of the western part of the empire in the A.D. 400s; Constantinople was its capital. (pp. 185, 200, 330, 350, 353)

Byzantium [buh•ZAN•tee•uhm] Ancient city that became the capital of the Eastern Roman Empire; was later renamed Constantinople and is now called Istanbul. 41°N 29°E (p. 138)

Cairo [KY•roh] Capital of Egypt. 31°N 32°E (pp. 63, 65, 70, 72, 73, 182, 188, 211)

Calcutta City in eastern India, now known as Kolkata. 22°N 88°E (pp. 74, 76, 498)

Calicut Seaport on the Arabian Sea in southwestern India, now called Kozhikode. 11°N 75°E (pp. 490, 498)

California State in the western United States. (pp. 78, 79)

Canada Country in North America north of the United States. (pp. 62, 64, 78, 79)

Canterbury [KAN•tuhr•BEHR•ee] City in Kent in southeastern England; site of an early Christian cathedral. 51°N 1°E (p. 437)

Cape of Good Hope Cape on the southern tip of Africa. 34°S 18°E (pp. 72, 73, 207)

Caribbean [KAR•uh•BEE•uhn] Sea Part of the Atlantic Ocean bordered by the West Indies, South America, and Central America. (pp. 62, 64, 78, 79, 81, 82, 83, 234, 490, 491)

Carthage [KAHR•thihj] Ancient city on the northern coast of Africa. 37°N 10°E (pp. 138, 158, 168, 326)

Caspian [KAS•pee•uhn] Sea Saltwater lake in southeastern Europe and southwestern Asia, the largest inland body of water in the world. (pp. 63, 65, 67, 69, 71, 74, 76, 138, 150, 158, 176, 182, 185, 188, 200, 245, 269, 325, 330, 353, 365)

Caucasus [KAW•kuh•suhs] Mountains Range of mountains between the Caspian and Black Seas. (pp. 76, 176)

Ceylon [sih•LAHN] Country in the Indian Ocean south of India, now called Sri Lanka. 8°N 82°E (pp. 74, 76, 498)

Chang'an [CHAHNG•AHN] Capital of China during the Tang dynasty, now called Xian. 34°N 108°E (pp. 252, 253, 255, 260)

Chang Jiang [CHAHNG JYAHNG] River in China, third-longest in the world; formerly called the Yangtze River. (pp. 77, 253, 268, 269)

Charles Town City in southeastern South Carolina, now called Charleston. 33°N 80°W (p. 535)

Chernigov [chehr•NEE•guhf] Principality in the Kievan Rus. 51°N 31°E (p. 359)

Chichén Itzá [chee•CHEHN eet•SAH] Most important city of the Mayan peoples, located in the northern part of the Yucatán Peninsula. 20°N 88°W (p. 453)

China Country in East Asia, world's largest by population; now called the People's Republic of China. (pp. 63, 65, 75, 77, 84, 245, 253, 255, 268, 284, 365, 486, 490, 493, 498, 502)

Chittagong [CHIH•tuh•GAHNG] Port city in southeastern Bangladesh. 22°N 90°E (p. 365)

Clermont City in central France. 45°N 3°E (pp. 346, 353, 355)

Cologne [KUH•LOHN] City in west central Germany on the Rhine River. 50°N 6°E (p. 353)

Congo Basin Basin draining the Congo River system in east central Africa. (p. 207)

Congo River River in Central Africa. (pp. 72, 73, 207)

Connecticut A state in the northeastern United States. (pp. 78, 535)

Constantinople [KAHN•STAN•tuhn•OH•puhl] City built on the site of Byzantium, now known as Istanbul in present-day Turkey. 41°N 29°E (pp. 136, 144, 150, 156, 158, 168, 176, 181, 182, 269, 330, 366)

Copan Ancient city of the Mayan people, in northwestern Honduras. 14°N 89°W (p. 453)

Córdoba [KAWR•duh•buh] City in southern Spain. 37°N 4°W (pp. 181, 182, 366)

Corsica Island in the Mediterranean Sea. 42°N 8°E (pp. 66, 68, 138, 158, 168, 350, 385, 416)

Costa Rica [KAHS•tuh REE•kuh] Republic in southern Central America. (pp. 62, 64, 78, 79, 81)

Crete [KREET] Greek island southeast of mainland in the southern Aegean Sea. 35°N 24°E (pp. 67, 69, 138, 158, 168, 188, 353, 359, 366)

Crimea Peninsula in southeastern Ukraine. (p. 359)

Cuba Island country in the West Indies. (pp. 62, 64, 78, 79, 81, 490)

Cuzco [KOOS•koh] City in southern Peru. 13°S 71°W (pp. 450, 454, 456, 470)

Cyprus [SY•pruhs] Island country in the eastern Mediterranean Sea, south of Turkey. 35°N 31°E (pp. 67, 69, 138, 158, 188, 353, 366)

Damascus [duh•MAS•kuhs] Capital of Syria. 34°N 36°E (pp. 176, 182, 185, 188, 200)

Danube [DAN•yoob] River Second-longest river in Europe. (pp. 66, 68, 138, 158, 168, 185, 188, 200, 269, 325, 326, 350, 533)

Danzig City in northern Poland. 54°N 18°E (p. 366)

Dead Sea Salt lake in southwestern Asia, bounded by Israel, the West Bank, and Jordan. (pp. 70, 76)

Delaware Second smallest state in the United States located on the east coast south of New Jersey. (pp. 78, 535)

Delhi [DEH•lee] City in northern India. 28°N 76°E (pp. 74, 76, 181)

Denmark Scandinavian country in northwestern Europe. (pp. 66, 68, 428, 437, 533)

Drakensberg Range Mountain range in southeastern Africa. (p. 207)

Dublin [DUHB•lihn] The capital and largest city in the Republic of Ireland. 53°N 6°W (pp. 66, 68, 508)

East China Sea Arm of the northwestern Pacific Ocean between the eastern coast of China and the Ryukyu Islands, bounded by the Yellow Sea and Taiwan. (pp. 75, 77, 253, 255, 269, 290)

Edinburgh [EH•duhn•buh•ruh] Capital city of Scotland. 55°N 3°W (pp. 66, 68)

Egypt Country in North Africa on the Mediterranean Sea. (pp. 63, 65, 70, 72, 73, 136, 138, 144, 150, 156, 176, 182, 185, 188, 200, 211)

Elbe [EL•buh] River River running east through central Europe, emptying into the North Sea in northern Germany. (p. 533)

England Part of the island of Great Britain lying east of Wales and south of Scotland. (pp. 62, 64, 66, 68, 328, 330, 334, 346, 353, 355, 428, 437, 490)

English Channel Narrow sea separating France and Great Britain. 49°N 3°W (pp. 66, 68)

Estonia [eh•STOH•nee•uh] Republic in northeastern Europe, one of the Baltic states. (p. 359)

Ethiopia [EE•thee•OH•pee•uh] Country in East Africa north of Somalia and Kenya. (pp. 63, 65, 72, 73)

Euphrates [yu•FRAY•teez] River River in southwestern Asia that flows through Syria and Iraq and joins the Tigris River near the Persian Gulf. (pp. 74, 76, 138, 158 176, 182, 185, 188, 200)

Europe One of the world's seven continents, sharing a landmass with Asia. (pp. 63, 65, 66, 67, 68, 69, 234, 245, 246, 451, 486, 490, 493, 502, 503)

Finland European country between Russia and Sweden. (pp. 63, 65, 67, 69, 508)

Florence City in the Tuscany region of central Italy at the foot of the Apennines. 43°N 11°E (pp. 384, 385, 416, 428, 514)

Florida State in the southeastern United States bordered by Alabama, Georgia, the Atlantic Ocean, and the Gulf of Mexico. (p. 78)

France Third-largest country in Europe, located south of Great Britain. (pp. 63, 65, 66, 68, 188, 330, 334, 346, 353, 355, 359, 428, 437)

Frankfurt Port city in west central Germany on the Main River. 50°N 8°E (pp. 66, 68, 366, 533)

Ganges [GAN•JEEZ] River River in India that flows from the Himalaya to the Bay of Bengal. (pp. 74, 76, 253, 268, 498)

Gao [GAHO] City in Mali on the Niger River. 16°N 0°E (p. 211)

Gaul Ancient Roman name for the area now known as France. (pp. 136, 138, 144, 150)

Geneva [juh•NEE•vuh] City in western Switzerland. 46°N 6°E (pp. 66, 68, 422, 437)

Genoa City and seaport in northwestern Italy. 44°N 9°E (pp. 353, 359, 384, 385, 416, 428)

Georgia A state on the east coast of the United States south of South Carolina. (pp. 78, 535)

Germany Western European country south of Denmark. (pp. 63, 65, 66, 68, 330, 359)

Ghana [GAH•nuh] Country in West Africa on the Gulf of Guinea. (pp. 62, 64, 72, 73)

Gobi [GOH•bee] Vast desert covering parts of Mongolia and China. 43°N 103°E (pp. 75, 77, 253, 255, 269, 282, 290)

Gomel Port city in southeastern Belarus on the Sozh River. 52°N 31°E (p. 359)

Granada [gruh•NAH•duh] Province on the southern coast of Spain. 37°N 3°W (pp. 182, 364)

Great Rift Valley Depression extending from Syria to Mozambique. 5°S 35°E (p. 207)

Great Wall Wall built in the 200s B.C. to protect China's northern border. 38°N 109°E (pp. 269, 282)

Great Zimbabwe Trading center around A.D. 700 now known as Zimbabwe. (pp. 206, 230)

Greece Country in southeastern Europe on the Balkan Peninsula. (pp. 67, 69, 136, 138, 144, 150, 188)

Greenland The largest island in the world. A province of Denmark located in the north Atlantic. (pp. 62, 64, 90)

Gazetteer

Guangzhou [GWAHNG•JOH] Port city in southern China on the Chang Jiang. 23°N 113°W (pp. 253, 269, 282, 290)

Gulf of Aden Gulf separating eastern Africa from the Saudi Arabian Peninsula (pp. 74, 76, 207)

Gulf of Mexico Gulf on part of the southern coast of the United States. (pp. 62, 64, 78, 79, 80, 453)

Hadrian's Wall Ancient Roman stone wall built to protect the northern boundary of Roman Britain. 55°N 3°W (p. 138)

Hamburg City in north central Germany near the North Sea. 53°N 10°E (p. 359)

Hangzhou [HAHNG•JOH] Port city in southeastern China, capital during the Song dynasty. 30°N 120°E (pp. 252, 253, 260, 268, 269, 290, 365)

Himalaya [HIH•muh•LAY•uh] Mountain system forming a barrier between India and the rest of Asia. (pp. 74, 76, 253, 268, 269, 290)

Hispaniola [HIHS•puh•NYOH•luh] Island in the West Indies. 19°N 72°E (pp. 81, 490)

Hokkaido [hah•KY•doh] Second-largest island of Japan. 43°N 142°E (pp. 63, 65, 75, 77)

Holy Roman Empire Lands in western and central Europe, empire founded by Charlemagne. (pp. 324, 334, 346, 350, 353, 355)

Honshu [HAHN•shoo] Largest island of Japan, called the mainland. 36°N 138°E (pp. 63, 65, 75, 77)

Hormuz [HOR•mooz] Straits separating the Gulf of Oman from the Persian Gulf. 27°N 56°E (p. 284)

Huang He [HWAHNG HUH] Second-longest river in China, formerly called the Yellow River. (pp. 253, 268, 269)

Hudson Bay Large inland sea in Canada. (pp. 62, 64, 78, 79, 90, 490)

Hungary Eastern European country south of Slovakia. (pp. 63, 65, 66, 68, 330, 359, 428, 437, 508, 533)

India South Asian country south of China and Nepal. (pp. 63, 65, 74, 76, 182, 185, 253, 269, 365, 486, 490, 493, 498, 502)

Indian Ocean Third-largest ocean. (pp. 63, 65, 74, 76, 209, 223, 245, 284, 365, 490, 498)

Indonesia [IHN•duh•NEE•zhuh] Island republic in Southeast Asia, consisting of most of the Malay Archipelago. (pp. 63, 65, 75, 77, 84)

Indus [IHN•duhs] **River** River in Asia that begins in Tibet and flows through Pakistan to the Arabian Sea. (pp. 74, 76, 182, 185, 253, 268, 269)

Ionian [eye•OH•nee•uhn] **Sea** Arm of the Mediterranean Sea separating Greece and Albania from Italy and Sicily. (pp. 66, 68)

Iran Southwest Asian country on the eastern shore of the Persian Gulf, formerly called Persia. (pp. 63, 65, 71)

Iraq Country in southwestern Asia at the northern tip of the Persian Gulf. (pp. 63, 65, 71)

Ireland Island west of Great Britain occupied by the Republic of Ireland and Northern Ireland. (pp. 62, 64, 66, 68, 330, 350, 428, 437)

Israel Southwest Asian country south of Lebanon. (pp. 70, 74, 76)

Italy Southern European country south of Switzerland and east of France. (pp. 63, 65, 66, 68, 138, 144, 150, 156, 158, 168, 328, 330, 334, 353, 437, 533, 544)

Jamestown First permanent English settlement in North America, in southeast Virginia. 37°N 77°W (p. 491)

Japan Country occupying a chain of islands in the northern Pacific Ocean. (pp. 63, 65, 75, 77, 84, 245, 253, 269, 490)

Java Island of the Malay Archipelago in southern Indonesia. 8°S 111°E (pp. 63, 65, 75, 77, 84, 269, 284, 365, 498)

Jeddah City in western Saudi Arabia. 21°N 39°E (p. 284)

Jerusalem [juh•ROO•suh•luhm] Capital of Israel and a holy city for Christians, Jews, and Muslims. 31°N 35°E (pp. 70, 74, 76, 158, 182, 188, 200, 346, 353, 355)

Jordan River River flowing from Lebanon and Syria to the Dead Sea. (p. 70)

Kalahari Desert [kah•la•HA•ree] Desert area in eastern Namibia and western Botswana. (pp. 72, 73, 207)

Karakorum [KAR•uh•KOHR•uhm] Capital of the Mongol Empire during most of the 1200s. 47°N 102°E (pp. 267, 268, 269)

Kathmandu [KAT•MAN•DOO] Capital of Nepal. 27°N 85°E (pp. 74, 76)

Khanbaliq [KAHN•buh•LEEK] Capital of Kublai Khan's Mongol Empire, now called Beijing. 40°N 116°E (pp. 267, 269)

Kiev [KEE•EHF] Capital of Ukraine, on the Dnieper River. 50°N 30°E (pp. 67, 69, 269, 330, 346, 359, 366)

Kievan [KEE•EHF•AHN] **Rus** [ROOS] State made of small territories around Kiev, destroyed by Mongols in 1240. (p. 350)

Korea [KOH•REE•uh] Peninsula in eastern Asia, divided into the Democratic People's Republic of Korea (North Korea) and the Republic of Korea. (pp. 63, 65, 75, 77, 84, 253, 255, 290)

Kunlun [KOON•LOON] **Shan** [SHAHN] Major mountain system in western China. (pp. 74, 75, 76, 77)

Kyoto [kee•OH•toh] Ancient capital of Japan, formerly called Heian. 35°N 135°E (pp. 75, 77)

Kyushu [kee•OO•shoo] One of the four major islands of Japan. 33°N 131°E (pp. 75, 77, 84)

Lake Baikal [BY•KAHL] The world's deepest lake located in south central Russia. 47°N 107°E (pp. 75, 77, 268)

Lake Chad A lake in west central Chad. 13°N 14°E (pp. 72, 73, 207, 211)

Lake Malawi A finger lake in east central Africa. 11°S 33°E (pp. 72, 73, 207)

Lake Tanganyika A finger lake in east central Africa. 6°S 30°E (pp. 72, 73, 207)

Lake Texcoco A dry lakebed north east of Mexico City. (p. 453)

Lake Turkana A finger lake in northern Kenya. 3°N 36°E (pp. 72, 73, 207)

Lake Victoria The largest lake in east central Africa. 2°S 33°E (pp. 72, 73, 207, 209)

Lake Volta A lake on the Volta River in Ghana. 7°N 1°E (pp. 72, 73, 207)

Gazetteer

Lebanon [LEH•buh•nahn] Southwest Asian country on the eastern coast of the Mediterranean Sea. (p. 70)

Libya [LIH•bee•uh] North African country west of Egypt. (pp. 70, 72, 73)

Libyan Desert The desert area between the Sahara and the Nile River. (pp. 72, 73, 207)

Lima [LEE•muh] The capital and largest city in Peru. 12°S 73°W (pp. 62, 82, 83, 454)

Lisbon [LIHZ•buhn] Capital of Portugal. 39°N 9°W (p. 366)

London Capital of the United Kingdom, on the Thames River in southeastern England. 52°N 0° (pp. 62, 64, 66, 68, 330, 353, 364, 366, 367, 422, 435, 514, 531)

Luanda [luh•ahn•dah] Atlantic port city in north central Angola. 8°S 13°E (pp. 72, 73, 234)

Luoyang [luh•WOH•YAHNG] City in northern China on the Huang He. 34°N 112°E (pp. 253, 255)

Lyon [lyawn] France's third largest city. 46°N 5°E (p. 508)

Macao [muh•KOW] Region on the southeastern coast of China. (pp. 281, 498)

Machu Picchu [MAH•choo•PEE•choo] Incan settlement in the Andes northwest of Cuzco, Peru. 13°S 72°W (p. 454)

Madagascar [MA•duh•GAS•kuhr] Island in the Indian Ocean off the southeastern coast of Africa. 18°S 43°E (pp. 63, 65, 72, 73, 207)

Madinah [mah•DEE•nuh] Holy Muslim city in western Saudi Arabia. 24°N 39°E (pp. 174, 182, 185, 188, 200)

Madrid [muh•DRIHD] The capital and largest city in Spain. 53°N 7°W (pp. 66, 68, 508)

Maine The northern and eastern most state in the United States. (pp. 78, 535)

Makkah [MAH•kuh] Holy city of Muslims, also known as Mecca, in western Saudi Arabia. 21°N 39°E (pp. 174, 176, 182, 185, 188, 200, 211, 269, 284)

Mali [MAH•lee] Republic in northwestern Africa. (pp. 62, 64, 72, 73)

Malindi [MAH•lin•dee] Kenyan port city on the Indian Ocean. 3°S 40°E (p. 284)

Maryland State in the northeastern United States. (pp. 78, 535)

Massachusetts State in the northeastern United States. (pp. 78, 535)

Massalia [muh•SAH•lee•uh] Ancient Greek colony on the site of present-day Marseille. 44°N 3°E (p. 138)

Mecca [MEH•kuh] Holiest city in Islam, located in western Saudi Arabia. 21°N 39°E (pp. 74, 76, 365)

Mediterranean Sea Inland sea of Europe, Asia, and Africa. (pp. 63, 65, 66, 67, 68, 69, 70, 72, 73, 138, 150, 158, 168, 176, 182, 185, 188, 200, 207, 211, 223, 269, 325, 326, 330, 350, 353, 359, 366, 385, 416, 428, 437, 508)

Mekong [MAY•KAWNG] **River** River in southeastern Asia that begins in Tibet and empties into the South China Sea. (pp. 253, 255, 268, 290, 498)

Mesopotamia [MEH•suh•puh•TAY•mee•uh] Early center of civilization, in the area of modern Iraq and eastern Syria between the Tigris and Euphrates Rivers. (p. 182)

Mexico North American country south of the United States. (pp. 62, 64, 80, 453, 490)

Mexico City Capital of Mexico. 19°N 99°W (pp. 62, 64, 80)

Milan City in northern Italy. 45°N 9°E (pp. 359, 385, 416, 428, 508, 533, 544)

Mississippi River Large river system in the United States that flows southward into the Gulf of Mexico. (pp. 78, 234, 491)

Mogadishu [MAH•guh•DIH•shoo] Capital of Somalia. 2°N 45°E (pp. 72, 73, 222, 284)

Moluccas [muh•LUH•kuhz] Group of islands in Indonesia, formerly called the Spice Islands. 2°S 128°E (pp. 75, 77, 498)

Mombasa City and seaport of Kenya. 4°S 39°E (pp. 72, 73, 284)

Mongolia [mahn•GOH•lee•uh] Country in Asia between Russia and China. (pp. 75, 77, 253, 269, 282)

Montreal [mon•tree•AWL] The second largest city in Canada, located in southern Quebec. 45°N 73°W (pp. 78, 79, 491)

Morocco [muh•RAH•koh] North African country on the Mediterranean Sea and the Atlantic Ocean. (pp. 62, 64, 72, 73, 182)

Moscow [MAHS•koh] Capital of Russia. 55°N 37°E (pp. 63, 65, 67, 69, 269, 346, 531)

Mount Everest Highest mountain in the world, located in the Himalaya

between Nepal and Tibet. 28°N 86°E (p. 76)

Mount Kenya Second highest mountain in Africa at 17,058 ft. 1°S 37°E (p. 207)

Mount Kilimanjaro Highest peak in Africa at 19,331 ft. 3°S 37°E (p. 207)

Mozambique [MOH•zuhm•BEEK] Country on the south east coast of Africa. (pp. 63, 65, 72, 73, 234)

Namib Desert [NAH•mib] Desert area of southern Namibia. (pp. 73, 207)

Nanjing [NAHN•JIHNG] City in eastern China, capital during the Ming dynasty. 32°N 118°E (pp. 281, 284)

Naples City in southern Italy. 40°N 14°E (pp. 366, 416, 428)

Nepal [nuh•PAWL] Mountain country between India and China. (pp. 63, 65, 74, 76)

Netherlands [NEH•thuhr•luhnz] Country in northwestern Europe. (pp. 66, 68, 428, 437, 490)

New Carthage City and seaport in southern Spain on the Mediterranean Sea also called Cartagena. 38°N 1°W (pp. 66, 68)

New Jersey Fifth smallest state in the United States located on the north east coast. (pp. 78, 535)

New York City The largest city in the United States located in New York State. 43°N 74°W (pp. 78, 535)

Nile River World's longest river flowing north from the heart of Africa to the Mediterranean Sea. (pp. 70, 72, 73, 138, 176, 182, 185, 188, 207, 211, 245, 269)

Ningxia [NIHNG•shee•AH] Region in northwestern China. (p. 268)

Norfolk [NAWR•fuhk] Port city on the east coast of the United States. (pp. 78, 535)

Normandy Region and former province of France, bordering the English Channel. (p. 330)

North America Continent in the northern part of the Western Hemisphere between the Atlantic and Pacific Oceans. (pp. 62, 64, 78, 234, 451, 486, 490, 491, 493 502, 503)

North Carolina A state on the east coast of the United States known for growing tobacco and manufacturing furniture. (p. 535)

North Sea Arm of the Atlantic Ocean between Europe and the eastern coast of Great Britain. (pp. 63, 65, 66, 68, 138, 150, 325, 328, 330, 350, 353, 359, 366, 428, 437, 508, 533)

Norway Northern European country on the Scandinavian peninsula. (pp. 63, 65, 66, 68, 428, 437)

Novgorod [NAHV•guh•RAHD] City in western Russia. 58°N 31°E (p. 366)

Oder River River in north central Europe, emptying into the Baltic Sea. (p. 325)

Oman [oh•MAHN] Country on the Arabian Sea and the Gulf of Oman. (pp. 63, 65, 71, 74, 76)

Orange River [oh•RAN•ghee] Major river flowing west from central South Africa to the Atlantic Ocean at the Namibian border. (p. 72, 73, 207)

Orléans [AWR•lay•AHN] City in north central France. 47°N 1°E (p. 364)

Ostia [AHS•tee•uh] Ancient city of Italy in Latium at the mouth of the Tiber River. 44°N 10°E (p. 138)

Ottoman Empire Turkish empire from the late 1200s in Asia Minor, spreading throughout the Middle East. (pp. 428, 437)

Pacific Ocean The largest and deepest of the world's four oceans, covering more than a third of the earth's surface. (pp. 62, 64, 75, 77, 78, 79, 80, 82, 83, 84, 85, 86, 87, 88, 89, 90, 245, 247, 253, 269, 284, 365, 451, 453, 454, 490, 491, 498)

Pakistan [PA•kih•STAN] Officially the Islamic Republic of Pakistan, a republic in South Asia, marking the area where South Asia converges with southwest Asia. (pp. 63, 65, 71, 74, 76)

Palestine A historic region, situated on the eastern coast of the Mediterranean Sea. 31°N 35°E (p. 353)

Papal States A territory in Italy formerly under direct temporal rule of the pope. 43°N 13°E (pp. 350, 428)

Paris Capital of France. 49°N 2°E (pp. 63, 65, 66, 68, 330, 364, 366, 422, 435, 437, 514, 531)

Persepolis Ancient capital of Persian empire, now in ruins. 30°N 53°E (p. 176)

Persia The conventional European designation of the country now known as Iran. 32°N 55°E (pp. 182, 200, 365)

Persian Gulf An arm of the Arabian Sea in southwestern Asia, between the Arabian Peninsula on the southwest and Iran on the northeast. (pp. 71, 74, 76, 176, 182, 188, 245, 284, 365)

Philadelphia City in eastern Pennsylvania on the Delaware River. 40°N 75°W (pp. 78, 535)

Philippines [FIH•luh•PEENZ] Island country in the Pacific Ocean southeast of China. 14°N 125°E (pp. 63, 65, 75, 77, 490, 498)

Pinsk City in southern Belarus. 52°N 26°E (p. 359)

Pisa City in central Italy. 43°N 10°E (pp. 353, 385, 416)

Plymouth Town in eastern Massachusetts, first successful English colony in New England. 42°N 71°W (p. 491)

Poland Country in central Europe. (pp. 63, 65, 66, 68, 428, 437, 533)

Po River River in northern Italy, the longest in the country. (pp. 325, 326, 385, 533)

Portugal A long narrow country on Atlantic Ocean, sharing the Iberian Peninsula with Spain. (pp. 62, 64, 66, 68, 428)

Posen City in western Poland. 52°N 17°E (p. 359)

Puteoli Roman empire city in central Italy 41°N 14°E (p.138)

Pyrenees Mountain range in southwestern Europe, extending from the Bay of Biscay to the Mediterranean Sea. (pp. 68, 325, 326)

Quanzhou [chuh•WAHN•JOH] City in southeastern China. 25°N 111°E (pp. 255, 284)

Quebec [kih•BEHK] Capital city of Quebec Province, Canada, on the St. Lawrence River. 47°N 71°W (pp. 78, 79, 491)

Red Sea Narrow, inland sea, separating the Arabian Peninsula, western Asia, from northeastern Africa. (pp. 63, 65, 70, 72, 73, 74, 76, 138, 158, 182, 185, 188, 200, 207, 211, 245, 269, 284, 365)

Rhine [RYN] **River** One of the principal rivers of Europe, rising in eastern Switzerland. (pp. 138, 325, 326, 328)

Rhode Island The smallest state in the United States, located on the north east coast. (pp. 78, 535)

Rhône River River of southeastern France. (pp. 367, 372)

Rio Grande [REE•oh GRAND] River that forms part of the boundary between the United States and Mexico. (pp. 78, 79, 80)

Rocky Mountains Mountain system in western North America. (pp. 78, 79)

Rome Capital of Italy. 41°N 12°E (pp. 63, 65, 66, 68, 136, 138, 144, 150, 156, 158, 168, 324, 326, 328, 330, 334, 346, 353, 359, 384, 416, 422, 435, 437, 508, 514)

Russia Independent republic in Eastern Europe and northern Asia, the world's largest country by area. (pp. 63, 65, 67, 69, 346, 437)

Sahara [suh•HAR•uh] Desert region in northern Africa that is the largest hot desert in the world. 23°N 1°W (pp. 72, 73, 176, 207, 211)

Saleh [sah•Leh] Trading center in north east Africa. 15°N 9°W (p. 211)

Salonica [sah•LOH•nihkah] City and port in northeastern Greece. 40°N 23°E (p. 359)

Samarkand Capital of Samarqand Oblast, central Uzbekistan. 39°N 67°E (pp. 268, 269, 365)

Santa Fe Capital of New Mexico located in the north central part of the state. 36°N 106°W (p. 491)

Sardinia Island off western Italy, in the Mediterranean Sea. 40°N 9°E (pp. 138, 158, 350, 366, 385, 416)

Saudi Arabia [SOW•dee uh•RAY•bee•uh] Monarchy in southwestern Asia, occupying most of the Arabian Peninsula. (pp. 63, 65, 71, 74, 76)

Savannah [sah•VAN•uh] Chief port city in the Southern United States. 32°N 81°W (p. 535)

Scotland One of the four countries that make up the United Kingdom, the mainland occupies the northern part of Great Britain. (pp. 62, 64, 66, 68, 330, 428, 437)

Sea of Japan Arm of the Pacific Ocean lying between Japan and the Asian mainland; also called the East Sea. (pp. 75, 77, 84)

Seine [SAYN] River River in northern France. (pp. 325, 328, 372)

Shikoku [shih•KOH•koo] One of the four largest islands of Japan. 33°N 133°E (pp. 75, 77, 84)

Siberia Large region consisting of the Asian portion of Russia as well as northern Kazakhstan. (pp. 74, 75, 76, 77, 269)

Sicily [SIH•suh•lee] Largest island in the Mediterranean Sea off the coast of southern Italy. 37°N 13°E (pp. 63, 65, 66, 68)

Sofala [SOH•fah•lah] Slave gathering area on the south east coast of Africa during the 1600s. (p. 234)

South America Continent in the southern part of the Western Hemisphere lying between the Atlantic and Pacific Oceans. (pp. 62, 64, 82, 83, 234, 451, 486, 490, 491, 493, 502)

South Carolina A state on the east coast of the United States between North Carolina and Georgia. (pp. 78, 535)

South China Sea Arm of the Pacific Ocean, located off the eastern and southeastern coasts of Asia. (pp. 75, 77, 245, 253, 255, 269, 284, 290, 365, 498)

Spain Country in southwestern Europe. (pp. 62, 64, 66, 68, 136, 138, 144, 150, 156, 158, 168, 188, 324, 330, 334, 346, 353, 355, 359, 428, 437)

Sri Lanka [sree•LAHNG•kuh] Country in the Indian Ocean south of India, formerly called Ceylon. 8°N 82°E (pp. 63, 65, 74, 76)

Stockholm Capital city and seaport of Sweden. 59°N 18°E (p. 366)

St. Petersburg Second-largest city and largest seaport in Russia, located in the northwestern part of the country. 59°N 30°E (pp. 67, 69, 531)

Strait of Gibraltar Narrow passage connecting the Mediterranean Sea with the Atlantic Ocean. 35°N 5°W (pp. 66, 68, 182, 188, 207)

Strait of Magellan Channel between the Atlantic and Pacific Oceans on the southern tip of South America. 52°S 68°W (pp. 82, 83)

Strasbourg [STRAHZ•bohrg] City in eastern France. 48°N 7°E (p. 359)

Sumatra Island in western Indonesia. 2°N 99°E (pp. 75, 77, 269, 284, 365, 498)

Sweden Northern European country on the eastern side of the Scandinavian peninsula. (pp. 63, 65, 66, 68, 437, 508, 533)

Syria [SIHR•ee•uh] Southwestern Asian country on the east side of the Mediterranean Sea. (pp. 63, 65, 70, 138, 182, 200)

Taiwan [TY•WAHN] Island country off the southeast coast of China, the seat of the Chinese Nationalist government. 23°N 122°E (pp. 63, 65, 75, 77, 84)

Taklimakan [TAH•kluh•muh•KAHN] Desert Desert in northwestern China. (p. 76)

Tenochtitlán [tay•NAWCH•teet•LAHN] Aztec city in the Valley of Mexico. 19°N 99°W (pp. 453, 456, 470, 490, 491)

Teotihuacán [TAY•oh•TEE•wuh•KAHN] Site in central Mexico that in ancient times was one of the largest cities in the world. 19°N 98°W (pp. 450, 453)

Terraco Roman empire city in southeastern Spain. 41°N 0°E (p. 138)

Tian [tee•AHN] Shan Mountain range in central Asia. (pp. 76, 77)

Tibesti [tuh•BEh•stee] Mountains Mountain range in northern Chad. (p. 207)

Tibet [tuh•BEHT] Country in central Asia. (pp. 74, 76, 253, 268, 269, 290, 365)

Tigris River River in southeastern Turkey and Iraq that merges with the Euphrates River. (pp. 74, 76, 138, 158, 182, 185, 188, 200)

Timbuktu [TIHM•BUHK•TOO] Trading city of Muslim learning in West Africa. 16°N 3°W (pp. 72, 73, 206, 211, 222, 230, 234)

Tlaxcala [tlah•SKAH•luh] State in east central Mexico. (pp. 78, 79, 80, 453)

Tokyo Capital of modern Japan, formerly called Edo. 34°N 131°E (pp. 63, 65, 75, 77)

Toledo Historic city in central Spain. 39°N 4°W (p. 366)

Trieste Seaport in northeastern Italy. 45°N 13°E (p. 359)

Tripoli [TRIH•puh•lee] Capital city of Libya. 32°N 13°E (pp. 188, 211)

Tula Aztec city in central Mexco in the 1500s. 20°N 99°W (p. 453)

Tunis Capital city of Tunisia. 36°N 10°E (pp. 72, 73, 188, 211, 366)

Turkey Country in southeastern Europe and western Asia. (pp. 63, 65, 70)

Turkmenistan [tuhrk•MEH•nuh•STAN] Central Asian country on the Caspian Sea. (p. 71)

Tyre [TYR] Town in southern Lebanon on the Mediterranean Sea. 33°N 35°E (p. 353)

Tyrrhenian [tuh•REE•nee•uhn] Sea Arm of the Mediterranean Sea between Italy and the islands of Corsica, Sardinia, and Sicily. (p. 385)

Ukraine [yoo•KRAYN] Eastern European country west of Russia on the Black Sea. (pp. 67, 69, 359)

Ulaanbaatar [OO•lahn•bah•tahr] Capital and largest city in Mongolia. 48°N 107°E (pp. 75, 77, 268)

Ural [yoorahl] Mountains Mountain chain running from northern Russia southward to the Kirgiz Steppe. (pp. 74, 76)

Venice City and seaport in northeastern Italy. 45°N 12°E (pp. 334, 353, 359, 384, 416, 508)

Vienna [vee•EHN•uh] The capital and largest city in Austria. 49°N 17°E (pp. 508, 531, 533, 544)

Virginia State on the central east coast of the United States. (pp. 78, 535)

Vistula River Longest river in Poland. (p. 325)

Volga River River in western Russia, longest in Europe. (pp. 67, 69, 268, 269, 325)

West Indies Islands in the Caribbean Sea between North America and South America. 19°N 79°W (pp. 78, 79, 81)

Williamsburg An historic city in the state of Virginia. 37°N 76°W (p. 535)

Wilmington A port city on the southern coast of North Carolina. 34°N 78°W (p. 535)

Wittenberg [WIH•tuhn•BUHRG] City in east central Germany on the Elbe River. 51°N 12°E (pp. 422, 437)

Worms [vawrms] A river port city in southern Germany. 50°N 8°E (p. 437)

Xian [SHYEHN] Capital of Shaanxi Province in central China. 32°N 116°E (p. 365)

Xi Jiang [SHEE•JYAHNG] River in southern China. (pp. 75, 77)

Yathrib [YA•thruhb] Town in Saudi Arabia, now called Madinah. 24°N 39°E (p. 176)

Yellow Sea Arm of the Pacific Ocean bordered by China, North Korea, and South Korea. (pp. 75, 77, 268, 282)

Yucatán [YOO•Kuh•tan] **Peninsula** Land mass in southern Mexico extending northeast into the Gulf of Mexico. (pp. 79, 80, 453)

Zanzibar [ZAN•zuh•bahr] Island in the Indian Ocean off the Tanzanian coast. 6°S 39°E (p. 234)

Zurich [ZUR•ihk] The largest city in Switzerland, located on Lake Zurich. 48°N 9°E (pp. 66, 68, 437)

Gazetteer

Italicized page numbers refer to illustrations. The following abbreviations are used in the index:
m = map, c = chart, p = photograph or picture, g = graph, crt = cartoon, ptg = painting, q = quote

Index

Index

Index

Index

Index

Index

Index

Index

Index

Index

Acknowledgements

Text

199 Excerpt from *An Interpretation of the Qur'an*, translated by Majid Fakhry, copyright © 2000, 2002 Majid Fakhry and Mahmud Zayid. Reprinted by permission of New York University Press. **215** "Sundiata: The Hungering Lion" from *African Kingdoms of the Past*, by Kenny Mann. Copyright © 1996 by Kenny Mann. Reprinted by permission of the author. **225** "Mali in the Fourteenth Century" from *The African Past: Chronicles from Antiquity to Modern Time*, by Basil Davidson. Copyright © 1964 by Basil Davidson. Reprinted by permission of Curtis Brown Ltd. **264** "Still Night Thoughts" by Li Bo, from *The Columbia Book of Chinese Poetry*, translated by Burton Watson. Copyright © 1984 by Columbia University Press. Reprinted by permission. **265** "Spring Landscape" by Tu Fu, translated by David Hinton, from *The Selected Poems of Tu Fu*, copyright © 1988, 1989 by David Hinton. Reprinted by permission of New Directions Publishing Corp. **317** From *An Introduction to Haiku* by Harold G. Henderson, copyright © 1958 by Harold G. Henderson. Used by permission of Doubleday, a division of Random House, Inc. **401** "A Midsummer Night's Dream" from *The Children's Shakespeare* by E. Nesbit. Copyright © 1938 by Random House, Inc. Reprinted by permission. **465** "The Flood" from *The Emerald Lizard* by Pleasant DeSpain. Copyright © 1999 by Pleasant L. DeSpain. Published by August House Publishers, Inc. and used by permission of Marian Reiner on their behalf. **474 & 478** Excerpt from "Epic Description of the Beseiged City" from *The Broken Spears* by Miguel Leon-Portilla. Copyright © 1962, 1990 by Miguel Leon-Portilla. Expanded and Updated Edition © 1992 by Miguel Leon-Portilla. Reprinted by permission of Beacon Press, Boston.

Glencoe would like to acknowledge the artists and agencies who participated in illustrating this program: American Artists Rep., Inc.; Mapping Specialists, Ltd.; Morgan Cain; QA Digital; Studio Inklink; WildLife Art Ltd.

Photo Credits

Cover: (1)Darama/CORBIS, (r)Robert Harding World Imagery/Getty Images, (bkgd)Mark L. Stephenson/CORBIS; **89** (t)Dallas and John Heaton/CORBIS,(c)Jamie Harron/CORBIS,(b)Owen Franken/CORBIS; **90** Getty Images; **91** Getty Images; **106** (r)Getty Images, (c)AFP Worldwide, (l)Comstock Images; **107** (t)Ron Sheridan/Ancient Art & Architecture Collection, (c)Katie Deits/Index Stock Imagery, (b)James King-Holmes/Photo Researchers; **108** (t)Scala/Art Resource, NY, (b)Nimatallah/Art Resource, NY; **109** (r)Museum of Ethnology, Vienna, (l)Michel Zabe/Museo Templo Mayor; **110** (t) American Museum of Natural History, (tc)Scala/Art Resource, NY, (bc)Chester Beatty Library, Dublin/Bridgeman Art Library, (b)Reunion des Musees Nationaux/Art Resource, NY; **113** Lawrence Manning/CORBIS; **127** Peter Turnley/CORBIS; **128** (t)Victoria & Albert Museum, London/Bridgeman Art Library, (b)Merilyn Thorold/Bridgeman Art Library; **129** (t)Scala/Art Resource, NY, (b)Nik Wheeler; **130-131** ©Worldsat International Inc. 2004, All Rights Reserved; **130** (tl)Sean Sexton Collection/CORBIS, (cl)Brian Lawrence/SuperStock, (br)Earl & Nazima Kowall/CORBIS, (bc)Scala/Art Resource, NY, (bl)Werner Forman/Art Resource, NY; **131** (cw from top)Nabeel Turner/Getty Images, Peter Adams/Getty Images, Brand X Pictures, Courtesy Museum of Maritimo(Barcelona); RamonManent/CORBIS, Bettmann/CORBIS; **132-133** Picture Finders Ltd./eStock; **135** Stapleton Collection, UK/Bridgeman Art Library; **139** Nik Wheeler/CORBIS; **140** Bibliotheque Nationale, Paris, France, Giraudon/Bridgeman Art Library; **145** CORBIS; **146** The Newark Museum/Art Resource, NY; **147** Scala/Art Resource, NY; **148** (t)Hagia Sophia, Istanbul, Turkey/ET Archives, London/SuperStock, (b)C. Boisvieux/Photo Researchers; **149** Scala/Art Resource, NY; **151** Mary Evans Picture Library; **152** (l)Sean Sexton Collection/CORBIS, (r)Donald Dietz/Stock Boston/PictureQuest; **154** Bettmann/CORBIS; **155** Bettmann/CORBIS; **157** Stapleton Collection, UK/Bridgeman Art Library; **159** Scala/Art Resource, NY; **160** Andre Durenceau/National Geographic Society Image Collection; **161** Scala/Art Resource, NY; **162** Scala/Art Resource, NY; **163** (l)Giraudon/Art Resource, NY, (c)Brian Lawrence/SuperStock, (r)Ronald Sheridan/Ancient Art & Architecture Collection; **164** The Art Archive/Haghia Sophia Istanbul/Dagli Orti; **165** Ancient Art & Architecture Collection; **166** (t)The Newark Museum/Art Resource, NY, (b)Pierre Belzeaux/Photo Researchers; **170-171** Nabeel Turner/Getty Images; **173** Richard Bickel/CORBIS; **175** (l)DiMaggio/Kalish/CORBIS, (r)Kevin Fleming/CORBIS; **177** Bibliotheque Nationale, Paris/Bridgeman Art Library; **178** C. Hellier/Ancient Art & Architecture Collection; **179** (l)AFP/CORBIS, (r)ARAMCO; **183** Burstein Collection/CORBIS; **184** The Art Archive/Hazem Palace Damascus/Dagli Orti; **185** Nik Wheeler; **186** Alison Wright/CORBIS; **187** James L. Stanfield/National Geographic Society Image Collection; **188** Bettman/CORBIS; **190** (l)Mary Evans Picture Library, (r)Bettmann/CORBIS; **191** Richard Bickel/CORBIS; **192** Jeff Greenberg/Photo Researchers; **193** (l)Stapleton Collection, UK/ Bridgeman Art Library, (r)David Turnley/CORBIS; **194** (l)R & S Michaud/Woodfin Camp & Assoc, (r)Paul Dupuy Museum, Toulouse, France/Lauros-Giraudon, Paris/SuperStock; **195** Bettmann/CORBIS; **197** Galen Rowell/CORBIS; **198** (t)Giraudon/Art Resource, NY, (b)Bettmann/CORBIS; **202-203** Peter Adams/Getty Images; **205** Lawrence Migdale/Getty Images; **207** (t)Christine Osborne/Lonely Planet Images, (tc)FransLemmens/Getty Images, (bc)Brand XPictures, (b)MichaelDwyer/StockBoston/PictureQuest; **212** Volkmar Kurt Wentzel/National Geographic Image Collection; **221** Laura Sifferlin; **224** Charles & Josette Lenars/CORBIS; **225** Giraudon/Art Resource, NY; **226** (t)Courtesy Museum of Maritimo (Barcelona), Ramon Manent/CORBIS, (b)Steven Rothfeld/Getty Images; **227** (r)Werner Forman/Art Resource, NY, (l)HIP/Scala/Art Resource, NY; **228** Giraudon/Art Resource, NY; **231** Jason Laure; **232** (t)National Maritime Museum, London, (b)Maggie Steber/CORBIS Saba; **233** Art Resource, NY; **234** Michael Holford; **235** Lawrence Migdale/Getty Images; **236** (r)Andy Sacks/Getty Images, (l)Werner Forman/Art Resource, NY; **237** Jason Laure; **242** (l)Smithsonian Institution,(c)Giraudon/Art Resource, NY, (r)The Metropolitan Museum of Art, The Michael C. Rockefeller Memorial Collection, Gift of Nelson A. Rockefeller, 1964 (1978.412.310); **243** (tl)Stock Montage, (tr)Michael Holford, (cl)Scala/Art Resource, NY, (cr)The British Museum, London/Bridgeman Art Library,(bl)Roy Rainford/Robert Harding/Getty Images, (br)Bibliotheque Nationale, Paris/Bridgeman Art Library; **244** (tl)The British Museum/ Topham-HIP/The Image Works, (tr)Angelo Hornak/CORBIS, (bl)Ronald Sheridan/Ancient Art & Architecture Collection (br)Erich Lessing/Art Resource, NY; **245** (t)National Museum of Taipei, (cl)Ron Dahlquist/SuperStock, (cr)Ancient Art & Architecture Collection, (b)akg-images; **246-247** Worldsat International Inc. 2004, All Rights Reserved; **246** (tl)Stock Boston, (cl)Dave Bartruff/The Image Works, (bl)Art Resource, NY, (bc)Ali Meyer/CORBIS, (br)Mary Evans Picture Library; **247** (cw from top) Tom Wagner/Odyssey Productions, Greg Gawlowski/Lonley Planet Images, Jim Zuckerman/CORBIS, Christie's Images/CORBIS, China Stock, Museum of Fine Arts, Houston, Texas, USA/Robert Lee Memorial Collection, gift of Sarah C. Blaffer/Bridgeman Art Library, Kadokawa/Ancient Art & Architecture Collection; **248-249** CORBIS; **251** The Bodleian Library, Oxford, Ms. Bodl. 264, fol.219R; **254** (l)The Art Archive/Bibliothèque Nationale Paris, (r)Christopher Liu/ChinaStock; **256** Ira Kirschenbaum/Stock Boston; **257** Snark/Art Resource, NY; **258** Bettmann/CORBIS; **259** Michael Freeman/CORBIS; **261** (l)Keren Su/CORBIS, (r)Philadelphia Free Library/AKG,Berlin/SuperStock; **263** Werner Forman/Art Resource, NY; **265** (l)The Art Archive/National Peace

Museum Taiwan, (c)Naomi Duguid/Asia Access, (r)Private Collection/Bridgeman Art Library; **266** (l)The British Museum/Topham-HIP/The Image Works, (c)Laurie Platt Winfrey, (r)Seattle Art Museum/CORBIS; **268** (t)National Museum of Taipei, (b)J. Bertrand/Photo Researchers; **269** James L. Stanfield; **270** Werner Forman Archive; **271** (t)Kadokawa/Ancient Art & Architecture Collection, (b)Bibliotheque Nationale, Paris, France/Bridgeman Art Library; **272** The Bodleian Library, Oxford, Ms. Bodl. 264, fol.219R; **280** Laura Sifferlin; **282** Christie's Images/CORBIS; **283** SEF/Art Resource, NY; **284** ChinaStock; **285** ChinaStock; **286** The Art Archive; **287** Bonhams, London, UK/Bridgeman Art Library; **288** The Art Archive/National Peace Museum Taiwan; **289** Bildarchiv Preussischer Kulturbesitz/Art Resource, NY; **292-293** Orion Press/Getty Images; **295** Nicholas Devore III/Photographers/Aspen/PictureQuest; **297** Masao Hayashi/Dunq/Photo Researchers; **298** Sakamoto Photo Research Laboratory/CORBIS; **300** (t)Art Resource, NY, (b)mediacolor's/Alamy Images; **301** Frederic A. Silva/Lonely Planet Images; **303** Angelo Hornak/CORBIS; **304** (t)AFP/CORBIS, (b)Tom Wagner/Odyssey Productions; **306** Ancient Art & Architecture Collection; **307** Bettmann/CORBIS; **308** Dave Bartruff/The Image Works; **310** Nicholas Devore III/Photographers/Aspen/PictureQuest; **311** (l)Private Collection, Paul Freeman/Bridgeman Art Library, (r)Keren Su/CORBIS; **312** (l)T. Iwamiya/Photo Researchers, (r)Werner Forman/Art Resource, NY; **313** (t)Mary Evans Picture Library, (b)Private Collection/Bridgeman Art Library; **314** Erich Lessing/Art Resource, NY; **316** Bettmann/CORBIS; **317** Mary Evans Picture Library; **320-321** Greg Gawlowski/Lonely Planet Images; **323** Erich Lessing/Art Resource, NY; **327** Scala/Art Resource, NY; **328** Giraudon/Art Resource, NY; **329** (t)Ali Meyer/CORBIS, (b)Vanni/Art Resource, NY; **330** Private Collection/Bridgeman Art Library; **331** Hulton/Getty Images; **332** (l)Abbey of Montioliveto Maggiore, Sienna/E.T. Archives, London/SuperStock, (c)Jim Zuckerman/CORBIS, (r)Ronald Sheridan/Ancient Art & Architecture; **338** Scala/Art Resource, NY; **340** (l)Scala/Art Resource, NY, (r)Guildhall Library, Corporation of London, UK/Bridgeman Art Library; **341** (l)akg-images, (r)Ancient Art & Architecture Collection; **342** (l)Archivo Iconografico, S.A./CORBIS, (r)Time Life Pictures/Getty Images; **343** akg-images; **344** Giraudon/Art Resource, NY; **345** Erich Lessing/Art Resource, NY; **347** Tom Lovell/National Geographic Society Image Collection; **348** (l)Bildarchiv Preussischer Kulturbesitz/Art Resource, NY, (r)John Neubauer/PhotoEdit; **349** Ronald Sheridan/Ancient Art & Architecture Collection; **352** (l)Archivo Iconografico, S.A./CORBIS, (r)Robert W. Nicholson/National Geographic Society Image Collection; **353** Scala/Art Resource, NY; **356** Scala/Art Resource, NY; **357** Scala/Art Resource, NY; **358** Borromeo/Art Resource, NY; **360** (l)Ancient Art & Architecture Collection, (tr)akg-images/Schutze/Rodemann, (br)SuperStock; **361** Staatliche Museen, Berlin, Photo ©Bildarchiv Preussicher Kulturbesitz; **362** (t)Museum of Fine Arts, Houston, Texas, Robert Lee Memorial Collection, gift of Sarah C. Blaffer/Bridgeman Art Library, (b)The Art Archive/Dagli Orti; **365** Museo del Prado, Madrid, Spain/Giraudon, Paris/SuperStock; **368** A. Woolfitt/Woodfin Camp & Assoc./PictureQuest; **370** Ronald Sheridan/Ancient Art & Architecture Collection; **374** Laurie Platt Winfrey; **375** (cw from top) Scala/Art Resource, NY, Erich Lessing/Art Resource, NY, Vanni/Art Resource, NY, Private Collection, Paul Freeman/Bridgeman Art Library, Seattle Art Museum/CORBIS, CORBIS; **376** (t)The Pierpont Morgan Library/Art Resource, NY, (tc)The Art Archive/E.T. Archive, (bc)Peabody Essex Museum, Salem, MA, (b)Bettmann/CORBIS; **377** (t)Art Resource, NY, (c)The Oakland Museum, (b)Scala/Art Resource, NY; **378** (tl)SuperStock, (cl)Dave G. Houser/CORBIS, (bl)The Art Archive/Museo Pedro de Osma Lima/Mireille Vautier, (bcl)Timothy McCarthy/Art Resource, NY, (bcr)SuperStock, (br)The Art Archive/National History Museum Mexico City/Dagli Orti; **379** (cw from top) Jeremy Horner/Getty Images, Chinch Gryniewicz; Ecoscene/CORBIS, Buddy Mays/CORBIS, North Wind Picture Archives, National Portrait Gallery, London, Victoria & Albert Museum, London/Art Resource, NY; **380-381** Bill Ross/CORBIS; **383** National Gallery Collection; by kind permission of the Trustees of the National Gallery/CORBIS; **386** akg-images; **387** Palazzo Ducale, Mantua, Italy/M. Magliari/Bridgeman Art Library, London/SuperStock; **389** (l)Scala/Art Resource, NY, (r)Kindra Clineff/Index Stock; **390** Archiv/Photo Researchers; **391** Araldo de Luca/CORBIS; **392** SuperStock; **393** Archivo Iconografico, S.A./CORBIS; **394** (l)Erich Lessing/Art Resource, NY, (c)Mary Evans Picture Library, (r)Art Resource, NY; **395** (l)Maiman Rick/CORBIS Sygma, (r)Giraudon/Bridgeman Art Library; **396** (t)Timothy McCarthy/Art Resource, NY, (b)Musee du Louvre, Paris/Giraudon, Paris/SuperStock; **397** (t)Baldwin H. Ward & Kathryn C. Ward/CORBIS, (c)The Art Archive/Manoir du Clos Luce/Dagli Orti, (b)Alinari Archives/CORBIS; **398** The Pierpont Morgan Library/Art Resource, NY; **407** Laura Sifferlin; **408** (l)Mary Evans Picture Library, (c)Erich Lessing/Art Resouce, NY, (r)Scala/Art Resource, NY; **409** (l)Bettmann/CORBIS, (r)Summerfield Press/CORBIS; **410** (l)Vatican Museums & Galleries, Rome/Fratelli Alinari/SuperStock, (r)Araldo de Luca/CORBIS; **411** (l,r)National Gallery Collection; By kind permission of the Trustees of the National Gallery/CORBIS; **412** Erich Lessing/Art Resource, NY; **413** Snark/Art Resource, NY; **414** (t)Timothy McCarthy/Art Resource, NY, (b)Summerfield Press/CORBIS; **415** (l)Archivo Iconografico, S.A./CORBIS, (r)Vatican Museums & Galleries, Rome/Canali PhotoBank; **418-419** James L. Amos/CORBIS; **421** Giraudon/Art Resource, NY; **423** Scala/Art Resource, NY; **424** (t)Michael Hampshire/National Geographic Society Image Collection, (b)Sammlungen des Stiftes, Klosterneuburg, Austria/Erich Lessing/Art Resource, NY; **425** akg-images; **426** (l)Bildarchiv Preussischer Kulturbesitz/Art Resource, NY, (r)Getty Images; **427** (t)SuperStock, (b)Dave G. Houser/CORBIS; **429** Gianni Dagli Orti/CORBIS; **430** (l)Scala/Art Resource, NY, (c)Erich Lessing/Art Resource, NY, (r)Scala/Art Resource, NY; **431** Erich Lessing/Art Resource, NY; **432** Scala/Art Resource, NY; **433** (t)Scala/Art Resource, NY, (b)Michael Holford; **438** Victoria & Albert Museum, London/Art Resource, NY; **439** (t)Nik Wheeler/CORBIS, (b)CORBIS; **442** akg-images; **443** Mary Evans Picture Library; **446-447** Robert Fried; **449** The Oakland Museum; **451** file photo; **453** Werner Forman/Art Resource, NY; **455** (t)Nathan Benn/CORBIS, (b)Nathan Benn/CORBIS; **457** David Hiser/Getty Images; **459** Charles & Josette Lenars/CORBIS; **460** (inset)Gianni Dagli Orti/CORBIS, **460** (bkgd)Gianni Dagli Orti/CORBIS; **461**(r)The Art Archive/E.T. Archive; (others)Michel Zabe/Museo Templo Mayor; **463** (t)The Art Archive/Museo Pedro de Osma Lima/Mireille Vautier, (b)Jeremy Horner/Getty Images; **469** (cl)Doug Martin, (others)Laura Sifferlin; **471** The City of Plainfield, NJ; **472** (l)Mary Evans Picture Library, (r)Dave Bartruff/CORBIS; **473** (tl)The Oakland Museum, (tcr)Michel Zabe/Museo Templo Mayor, (tr)Museum of Ethnology, Vienna, (tcl, bl, br) Biblioteca Colombina, Sevilla, Spain; **474** HIP/Scala/Art Resource, NY; **475** (t)Archivo Iconografico, S.A./CORBIS, (b)The Art Archive/National History Museum Mexico City/Dagli Orti; **476** Werner Forman/Art Resource, NY; **478** Archivo Iconografico, S.A./CORBIS; **479** Doug Stern & Enrico Ferorelli/National Geographic Society Image Collection; **482-483** Chinch Gryniewicz; Ecoscene/CORBI; **485** Reunion des Musees Nationaux/Art Resource, NY; **487** (t)Peabody Essex Museum, Salem, MA, (c)SuperStock, (b)Michael Holford; **488** Bettmann/CORBIS; **491** (l)The Metropolitan Museum of Art, Gift of J. Pierpont Morgan, 1900(00.18.2), (cl)Stock Montage, (c)Collection of The New-York Historical Society, (cr)Reunion des Musees Nationaux/Art Resource, (r)North Wind Picture Archives; **492** Bob Krist/CORBIS; **495** National Maritime Museum, London; **496** National Portrait Gallery, London/SuperStock; **497** Reunion des Musees Nationaux/Art Resource, NY; **500** Bettmann/CORBIS; **501** Archivo Iconografico, S.A./CORBIS; **506** SuperStock; **507** Stock Montage;

510-511 Buddy Mays/CORBIS; 513 Louvre, Paris/Bridgeman Art Library; 516 Louvre, Paris/Bridgeman Art Library; 517 Bettmann/CORBIS; 518 (l)Scala/Art Resource, NY, (r)Dennis Scott/CORBIS; 519 Jean-Leon Huens/National Geographic Society Image Collection; 521 (t)North Wind Picture Archives, (b)Mike Southern; Eye Ubiquitous/CORBIS; 524 (l)National Portrait Gallery, London, (c)Stefano Bianchetti/CORBIS, (r)Tate Gallery, London/Art Resource, NY; 525 Bettmann/CORBIS; 526 Stefano Bianchetti/CORBIS; 527 (t)National Portrait Gallery, London, copyright Snark/Art Resource, NY, (b)Bettmann/CORBIS; 528 (l) Reunion des Musees Nationaux/Art Resource, NY, (r) Giraudon/Art Resource, NY; 529 Tate Gallery, London/Art Resource, NY; 530 Giraudon/Art Resource, NY; 532 Archivo Iconografico, S.A./CORBIS; 533 (l)Giraudon/Art Resource, NY, (r)Reunion des Musees Nationaux/Art Resource, NY; 534 (l)Michael Holford, (r)Hermitage, St. Petersburg, Russia/Bridgeman Art Library; 536 ©Virginia Historical Society. All Rights Reserved; 537 Frances Tavern Museum, NY; 538 Mozart Museum, Prague, Czech Republic, Giraudon/Bridgeman Art Library; 539 (l)akg-images/SuperStock, (r)The Art Archive/Society Of The Friends Of Music Vienna/Dagli Orti; 540 Giraudon/Art Resource, NY; 542 Giraudon/Art Resource, NY; 543 Reunion des Musees Nationaux/Art Resource, NY; 546 (t)Vatican Museums & Galleries, Rome/Canali PhotoBank, (b)Boltin Picture Library; 547 (tl)Scala/Art Resource, NY, (tc)Werner Forman/Art Resource, NY, (tr)Bettmann/CORBIS, (cl)The Pierpont Morgan Library/Art Resource, NY, (cr)©Virginia Historical Society. All Rights Reserved, (b)Michel Zabe/Art Resource, NY; 548-549 CORBIS; 548 (l)Picture Finders Ltd./eStock, (r)Sylvain Grandadam/Getty Images; 557 Pierre Belzeaux/Photo Researchers; 562 akg-images; 564 Museum of Ethnology, Vienna; 565 Reunion des Musees Nationaux/Art Resource, NY; 566 Tim Flach/Getty Images; 567 Jerry Barnett.

One-Stop Internet Resources This textbook contains one-stop Internet resources for students, teachers and parents. Log on to ca.hss.glencoe.com for more information. Online study tools include Study Central, ePuzzles and Games, Self-Check Quizzes, Vocabulary e-Flashcards, and Multi-Language Glossaries. Online research tools include Student Web Activities, Beyond the Textbook Features, Current Events, Web Resources, and State Resources. The interactive online student edition includes the complete Interactive Student Edition along with textbook updates. Especially for teachers, Glencoe offers an online Teacher Forum and Web Activity Lesson Plans.